FAULT LINES OF INTERNATIONAL LEGITIMACY

Fault Lines of International Legitimacy addresses the following questions: What are the features and functions of legitimacy in the international realm? How does international legitimacy – as exemplified in particular by multilateral norms, organizations, and policies – change over time? What role does the international distribution of power and its evolution have in the establishment and transformation of legitimacy paradigms? To what extent do democratic values account for the growing importance of legitimacy and the increasing difficulty of achieving it at the international and national levels?

One of the central messages of the book is that although the search for international legitimacy is an elusive endeavor, there is no alternative to it if we want to respond to the intertwined demands of justice and security and make them an integral and strategic part of international relations.

Hilary Charlesworth is an Australian Research Council Federation Fellow and Director of the Centre for International Governance and Justice at the Australian National University in Canberra. She has written widely on international law and human-rights law and has held visiting appointments in U.S. and European universities.

Jean-Marc Coicaud is the Director of the United Nations University (UNU) Office at the United Nations in New York. His published books include *L'introuvable démocratie autoritaire; Legitimacy and Politics: A Contribution to the Study of Political Right and Political Responsibility;* and *Beyond the National Interest: The Future of UN Peacekeeping and Multilateralism in an Era of U.S. Primacy.* He is now finishing a new book titled *Kissing War Good-bye.*

Fault Lines of International Legitimacy

Edited by

HILARY CHARLESWORTH
Australian National University

JEAN-MARC COICAUD
United Nations University

CAMBRIDGE
UNIVERSITY PRESS

UNITED NATIONS
UNIVERSITY

CAMBRIDGE UNIVERSITY PRESS
Cambridge, New York, Melbourne, Madrid, Cape Town,
Singapore, São Paulo, Delhi, Tokyo, Mexico City

Cambridge University Press
32 Avenue of the Americas, New York, NY 10013-2473, USA

Published in the United States of America by Cambridge University Press, New York

www.cambridge.org
Information on this title: www.cambridge.org/9781107404557

First published 2010
First paperback edition 2011

A catalogue record for this publication is available from the British Library

Library of Congress Cataloguing in Publication Data

Fault lines of international legitimacy / edited by Hilary Charlesworth, Jean-Marc Coicaud.
p. cm.
Includes bibliographical references and index.
ISBN 978-0-521-76446-9 (hardback)
1. International law. I. Charlesworth, Hilary. II. Coicaud, Jean-Marc. III. Title.
KZ3410.F38 2009
341–dc22 2009022589

ISBN 978-0-521-76446-9 Hardback
ISBN 978-1-107-40455-7 Paperback

Contents

Acknowledgments

This book is the product of a research project conducted within the framework of the Peace and Governance Program of the United Nations University (UNU), headquartered in Tokyo. It follows a first volume published a few years ago under the title *Legitimacy of International Organizations.* The editors and contributing authors wish to thank Yoshie Sawada, Programme Administrative Assistant for the UNU Peace and Governance Program, for her support throughout the duration of the project. They also wish to thank the UNU Institute for Advanced Studies, which hosted a workshop in the course of the book preparation. At various stages of the project, a number of UNU colleagues – mainly Junior Professional Fellows from the UNU Office in New York – improved the language of the chapters, for which we wish to thank them: Anna Chrisp, William Brian Clayton, Delphine Hayim, Jibecke Johnsson, Durlabh Maharishi, Ranita Ragunathan, Ken Stretch, Ibrahim Tahri, and John Tzanos. Thank you also to Celeste Ecuyer and Susan Harris-Rimmer of the Australian National University. Finally, the editors wish to thank the two anonymous peer reviewers from Cambridge University Press, as well as John Berger, Senior Editor at Cambridge University Press, for his trust and support.

Contributors

Nathaniel Berman is Rahel Varnhagen Professor of International Affairs, Law, and Modern Culture at the Institute in Global Governance Research of Brown University. Prior to joining the Institute in 2009, he taught public international law, European Union law, international trade law, and human rights at Brooklyn Law School. Before 2002, he taught at Northeastern University School of Law for twelve years. Professor Berman's scholarship focuses on the relationships among nationalism, colonialism, and international law.

Hilary Charlesworth is an Australian Research Council Federation Fellow and Director of the Centre for International Governance and Justice at the Australian National University in Canberra. She has written widely on international law and human-rights law and has held visiting appointments in U.S. and European universities.

B. S. Chimni is a legal academic and a key figure in the Third World Approaches to International Law (TWAIL) network of scholars. He is a Professor of International Law at the School of International Studies, Jawaharlal Nehru University, New Delhi. His publications include *International Law and World Order: A Critique of Contemporary Approaches* (1993) and the co-edited volume *The Third World and International Order: Law, Politics, and Globalization* (2004).

Jean-Marc Coicaud is Director of the United Nations University (UNU) Office at the United Nations in New York. He also served as a speechwriter in the Executive Office of the UN Secretary General from 1992 to 1996 and taught at the University of Paris I – Sorbonne, Harvard University, and Keio University. Recent books include *Beyond the National Interest* (U.S. Institute of Peace Press, 2007); in Japanese, *Limits of the UN/Future of the UN* (Fujiwara

Shoten, 2007); and, in Chinese, *Toward the International Rule of Law* (SDX Joint Publishing Company, 2008). Dr. Coicaud is currently finishing a new single-authored book, *Kissing War Good-bye.*

Lorraine Elliott holds a Senior Fellowship in the Department of International Relations at the Australian National University. Her most recent books are *The Global Politics of the Environment* (Palgrave Macmillan/New York University Press, 2004) and, co-edited with Graeme Cheeseman, *Forces for Good: Cosmopolitan Militaries in the Twenty-first Century* (Manchester University Press, 2004).

Ian Johnstone is a Professor of International Law at the Fletcher School of Law and Diplomacy, Tufts University. From 1991 to 2000, he held various positions in the United Nations Secretariat, including five years in the Executive Office of the Secretary-General. He also served in the Department of Peacekeeping Operations and the Office of the Legal Counsel. His recent publications include *The United States and Contemporary Peace Operations: A Double-Edged Sword?* (2009), as editor and contributing author; *The Annual Review of Global Peace Operations*, as editor and lead scholar for the 2006 and 2007 volumes; "Legislation and Adjudication in the UN Security Council: Bringing Down the Deliberative Deficit," *American Journal of International Law* (2008); and "The Secretary-General as Norm Entrepreneur" in *Secretary or General? The Role of the UN SG in World Politics* (2007).

Jun Matsukuma has been a Professor of International Law since 2001 at the Faculty of Law of the Seinan Gakuin University. He also held a variety of positions with the Japanese Diplomatic Service in the United Kingdom and the United States.

Vasuki Nesiah teaches International Relations and is Director of International Affairs at Brown University. Before joining Brown, Nesiah was Senior Associate and Head of the Gender Program at the International Center for Transitional Justice and Adjunct Associate Professor at the School of International and Public Affairs at Columbia University.

Dianne Otto is Director of the International Human Rights Law Program of the Institute for International Law and the Humanities (IILAH) at the Melbourne Law School. Recent publications include "Making Sense of Zero Tolerance Policies in Peacekeeping Sexual Economies," in Vanessa Munro and

Carl F. Stychin (editors), *Sexuality and the Law: Feminist Engagements* (2007), and "Lost in Translation: Re-scripting the Sexed Subject of International Human Rights Law," in Anne Orford (editor), *International Law and Its Others* (2006).

Nishkala Suntharalingam is currently Political Affairs Officer in the Office of Operations in the Department of Peacekeeping Operations of the United Nations. She was based in Kinshasa with the UN Organization Mission in the Congo (MONUC) in 2003 and 2004, where she was a Political Officer and later Senior Demobilization Officer. She is the author of "The Cambodian Settlement Agreements," in Doyle, Johnstone, and Orr, *Keeping the Peace* (Cambridge University Press, 1997), and the co-author with Michael Doyle of "The UN in Cambodia: Lessons for Multidimensional Peacekeeping," *International Peacekeeping* 1, 2 (Summer 1994).

Ralph Wilde has been a member of the Law Faculty at University College London, University of London, since July 2002; he is currently Associate Dean for Research. He works in the fields of international relations and international law. His current research focuses on the administration of territory by international organizations and the extraterritorial application of human-rights norms.

JEAN-MARC COICAUD

Introduction

For Samir Kassir, in memoriam[1]

The question of legitimacy has a paradoxical status in international relations. On the one hand, it is a feature of international life. Indeed, as far as a country tries to live in relative harmony with its neighbors, it has to factor in what is right and what is wrong internationally so that peace can be maintained. As such, issues of legitimacy (e.g., legitimate and illegitimate behavior) are part and parcel of international relations, and one of the tasks of international law – a key tool for the regulation of international affairs – is to draw a line between legitimacy and illegitimacy in international life. On the other hand, over time, questions of international legitimacy have received secondary

[1] Samir Kassir (1960–2005) – fellow philosophy student in the middle of the 1980s at the University of Paris I – Sorbonne, journalist, person of passion and integrity, and friend – was assassinated by a car bomb in Beirut on the morning of Thursday, June 2, 2005. His assassination has still to be elucidated. For more on Samir Kassir's assassination and the context in which it took place in Lebanon (including the assassination of former Lebanese Prime Minister Rafik Hariri), see the *Fourth Report of the International Independent Investigation Commission Established Pursuant to Security Council Resolutions 1595 (2005), 1636 (2005), and 1644 (2005)* (Beirut: United Nations, S/2006/375, June 10, 2006). Refer also to the establishment of a special UN tribunal for Lebanon to try those responsible for the terrorist bombing that killed former Lebanese Prime Minister Rafiq Hariri and others, *Report of the Secretary-General on the Establishment of a Special Tribunal for Lebanon* (New York: United Nations, S/2006/893, November 15, 2006), and, more important, Security Council Resolution 1757, adopted on May 30, 2007, which decided that the Special Tribunal for Lebanon would enter into force on June 10, 2007 (New York: United Nations, S/RES/1757(2007), May 30, 2007).

This introduction, as well as Chapters 1, 2, and 3, have benefited from the research assistance of John Tzanos, Delphine Hayim, Ken Stretch, Ibrahim Tahri, Anna Chrisp, and Durlabh Maharishi, whom the author wishes to thank. The author also wishes to particularly thank Anna Chrisp for her help in making these chapters more clear.

attention.[2] It is not surprising because the socialization of individuals have taken place historically first at the national level; it is at this level that legitimacy has been principally addressed. This has been particularly the case in the context of reflecting on whether the organization and functioning of society is just and, therefore, whether its political institutions and leaders are legitimate.

However, in the past twenty years, legitimacy at the international level has been the object of increased attention. The international redistribution of power resulting from the collapse of the Soviet Union; the possibility of and need for multilateral institutions (primarily the United Nations [UN]) to be more involved than in the past in the management of the international system; the use of democratic and human-rights values as benchmarks of legitimate and illegitimate behaviors internationally, especially in connection with the use of force are some of the factors that account for the emergence of legitimacy on the international scene. In this perspective, following the seminal work of Thomas M. Franck,[3] a stream of books and articles dedicated to international legitimacy in the fields of international relations and international law is now being published.[4]

[2] The few publications on international legitimacy before the 1990s include Inis L. Claude, Jr., "Collective Legitimization as a Political Function of the United Nations," in *International Organization* (Vol. 20, No. 3, Summer 1966); and Martin Wight, "International Legitimacy," in *International Relations: Journal of the David Davies Memorial Institute of International Studies* (Vol. 4, No. 1, May 1972).

[3] Thomas M. Franck, *The Power of Legitimacy Among Nations* (Oxford: Oxford University Press, 1990). For an analysis of this book, refer, for example, to José E. Alvarez, "The Quest for Legitimacy: An Examination of *The Power of Legitimacy Among Nations* by Thomas M. Franck," in *New York University Journal of International Law and Politics* (Vol. 24, No. 1, Fall 1991).

[4] In recent years, books that focus essentially on legitimacy at the international level include Brad R. Roth, *Governmental Illegitimacy in International Law* (Oxford: Oxford University Press, 1999); Christopher Gelpi, *The Power of Legitimacy: Assessing the Role of Norms in Crisis Bargaining* (Princeton, NJ: Princeton University Press, 2003); Allen Buchanan, *Justice, Legitimacy, and Self-Determination: Moral Foundations for International Law* (Oxford: Oxford University Press, 2004); Ian Clark, *Legitimacy in International Society* (Oxford: Oxford University Press, 2005) and *International Legitimacy and World Society* (Oxford: Oxford University Press, 2007); and Ian Hurd, *After Anarchy: Legitimacy and Power in the United Nations Security Council* (Princeton, NJ: Princeton University Press, 2007). Journal articles include Dencho Georgiev, "Politics or Rule of Law: Deconstruction and Legitimacy in International Law," in *European Journal of International Law* (Vol. 4, No. 1, 1993); David Dyzenhaus, "The Legitimacy of Legality," in *University of Toronto Law Journal* (Vol. 46, No. 1, Winter 1996); Mattias Kumm, "The Legitimacy of International Law: A Constitutionalist Framework of Analysis," in *European Journal of International Law* (Vol. 15, No. 5, 2004); J. H. H. Weiler, "The Geology of International Law: Governance, Democracy, and Legitimacy," in *Max-Planck-Institut für ausländisches öffentliches Recht und Völkerrecht* (Vol. 64, 2004); David Armstrong and Theo Farrell (2005). Force and Legitimacy in World

The Legitimacy of International Organizations, a book that evolved from a United Nations University (UNU) research project and was published in 2001,[5] was part of this new attention given to legitimacy at the international level. As the title indicates, the book focused on the institutions of global governance, including the UN and the Bretton Woods institutions, and their various policies in the fields of collective security, development, trade, environment, and so on. The book's main objective was to assess the legitimacy of international organizations and their activities in the aftermath of the Cold War. In this regard, the mixed picture that emerged from the book showed that the legitimacy of international organizations – and that of their values, internal mechanisms, and policies – was anything but secure. In retrospect, the first ten years of the twenty-first century have confirmed this state of affairs.

During this period, the insistence of progressive scholars of global governance on the need for international institutions to fulfill the demands of democratic legitimacy, including the need to develop a better sense of accountability,[6] also pointed toward the current difficulty of these organizations in doing so. Moreover, September 11 and the U.S. response to it – particularly the war in Iraq – showed, on both sides of the issue, a radicalization of international politics at odds with the very raison d'être of the UN. In the process, the legitimacy of the international system, as well as that of the international organizations that comprise an integral part, has come under fire. This explains the fact that "talk of crisis is everywhere in contemporary international relations, and crises of legitimacy seem especially widespread."[7]

Does this mean that this book, *Fault Lines of International Legitimacy*, conceived as a sequel to *The Legitimacy of International Organizations*, is itself going as far as arguing that we are now facing a crisis of international legitimacy? A crisis of international legitimacy has been defined recently in the following terms:

Politics: Introduction. *Review of International Studies*, 31, pp. 3–13. Steven Wheatley, "The Security Council, Democratic Legitimacy, and Regime Change in Iraq," in *European Journal of International Law* (Vol. 17, No. 3, 2006); Allen Buchanan & Robert O. Keohane, "The Legitimacy of Global Governance Institutions," in *Ethics and International Affairs* (Vol. 20, No. 4, Winter 2006); Ian Clark & Christian Reus-Smit, guest editors of the special issue of *International Politics, Resolving International Crises of Legitimacy* (Vol. 44, Nos. 2/3, March/May 2007).

5 Jean-Marc Coicaud & Veijo Heiskanen (eds.), *The Legitimacy of International Organizations* (Tokyo: United Nations University Press, 2001).

6 See, for instance, Ruth W. Grant & Robert O. Keohane, "Accountability and Abuses of Power in World Politics," in *American Political Science Review* (Vol. 99, No. 1, February 2005).

7 Ian Clark & Christian Reus-Smit, "Preface," in the special issue of *International Politics, Resolving Crises of International Legitimacy* (ibid.), p. 153.

> . . . we use the term "international" to refer to that amorphous social realm that encompasses the complex array of political relations among states and non-state actors (and the institutions they construct and maintain) that transcend and constitute the territorial boundaries of sovereign states. An international crisis of legitimacy is thus one that afflicts these actors, their institutions, or the political orders they constitute. . . . [C]rises will be defined as critical turning points in which the imperative to adapt is heightened by the imminent possibility of death, collapse, demise, disempowerment, or decline into relevance. What kind of crisis, then, is a crisis of *legitimacy*? When we say that an actor or institution is suffering a crisis of legitimacy, we are saying that the decline in its legitimacy, or its failure to cultivate sufficient legitimacy, has reached a critical turning point. Because legitimacy is but one source of social power, the critical turning point is not necessarily, or immediately, marked by a precipitous decline in an actor's or an institution's political capacity.[8]

The answer is "no." The editors of and contributors to *Fault Lines of International Legitimacy* do not think that international order and its values, mechanisms, and institutions are facing a crisis of the magnitude alluded to in the previous quote. Surely, we do not deny the seriousness of the situation. We see that the current tensions and conflicts at work internationally are the result of competitive and unresolved claims that, for most of them, are based on the disputed interpretation and implementation of key international norms. In addition, we see that these tensions and conflicts have the potential to undermine the international system; however, at the moment, it is simply a potentiality. The stability and legitimacy of the international system are very much under stress but, so far, there is no systemic breakdown; the system is holding up. For example, no member state, much less any major member state, is leaving the UN because of pending disputes – hence, the free use of the expression "fault line," which provides the title to this book, helps describe the areas of friction, analyze their nature, and understand what is at stake in their handling by international actors. In this regard, somewhat like what happens in geology,[9] fault lines of international legitimacy are simultaneously zones of fracture and opportunities for adjustment – opportunities through which, in the midst of adversarial claims, the international system seeks its

8 Christian Reus-Smit, "International Crises of Legitimacy," in *International Politics* (ibid.), pp. 166–167.

9 In geology, the creation and behavior of faults, or fault lines, in both an individual small fault and the greater fault zones that define the tectonic plates, are controlled by the relative motion of rocks on either side of the fault surface. Because of friction and rigidity of the rock, the rocks cannot simply glide or flow past each other. Rather, stress builds up in rocks and when it reaches a level that exceeds the strain threshold, the accumulated energy is released as strain, which is focused onto a plane along which relative motion is accommodated – that is, the fault. See Frank D. Stacey & Paul M. Davies, *Physics of the Earth*, fourth edition (Cambridge: Cambridge University Press, 2008).

preservation. It is only when fault lines of international legitimacy are not kept under check, when they become critical and define the international system essentially by its contradictions, that – in extreme circumstances – there is a risk of an "extinction-level event" (ELE),[10] so to speak, bringing about its unraveling and demise. In the context of the 1930s, the work of Nathaniel Berman shows convincingly how this ELE can occur.[11]

Against this background, *Fault Lines of International Legitimacy* – moving beyond the rather straightforward assessment of the legitimacy of international institutions in the previous UNU project, *The Legitimacy of International Organizations* – focuses on some of the battles of legitimacy occurring within international institutions, especially in the context of the UN Security Council, and examines how they relate to the quest for stability and legitimacy of the international system. This leads the book's editors and contributors to address the following questions, among others: What are the features and functions of legitimacy in the international realm? How does international legitimacy (as exemplified, in particular, by multilateral norms, organizations, and policies) change over time? What role does the international distribution of power (and the position of major actors with regard to this distribution) and its evolution have in the establishment and transformation of a legitimacy paradigm(s)? To what extent do democratic values account for the growing importance of legitimacy and the increasing difficulty of achieving it at the international (as at the national) level, all the while constituting its best recourse?

As such, issues surrounding fault lines of international legitimacy are entry points to analyze the socialization of international life – its limits but also the opportunities that it entails – in connection with the international norms, mechanisms, and institutions, which bring the world and its actors together while also keeping them apart, and how this state of affairs could unfold in the future. In addition, by adopting a critical approach to the discourses and practices of global governance, mainly examined within the field of international law,[12] *Fault Lines of International Legitimacy* aims to identify ways to strengthen international legitimacy and, consequently, the

[10] This is also called "mass extinction." See Vincent Courtillot, *Evolutionary Catastrophes: The Science of Mass Extinction*, translated by Joe McClinton (Cambridge: Cambridge University Press, 1999).

[11] Nathaniel Berman, *Passions et ambivalences: Le colonialisme, le nationalisme et le droit international*, translated under the direction of Nathaniel Berman and Emmanuelle Jouannet by Lucie Delabie, Marie Blocteur, Leila Choukroune, Céline Clerfeuille, & Olivia Harrison (Paris: Editions Pedone, 2008); see especially pp. 317–387.

[12] Most of the contributors to the book are international lawyers.

international rule of law. That is, in a relatively indirect manner, the book pursues a normative agenda; it elucidates how international life could take "right" more seriously.

Ultimately, one of the central messages of the book is that although the search for international legitimacy is an elusive endeavor and one that cannot avoid confrontations and struggles, there is no alternative – at least, not if one wants to respond to the intertwined demands of justice and security and make them all an integral and strategic part of international relations.

The Book at a Glance

The book is organized into four parts. The first part discusses the history of international legitimacy and its structure while setting the stage for the question of fault lines of international legitimacy. It explores the normative and institutional tensions in international order, including fault lines, and how they affect the perception and validity claims of international legitimacy. The second part analyzes the role that the UN Security Council plays in shaping international legitimacy – which is only natural, considering the crucial function of the Security Council as a key organ of global governance, in terms of both interpretation and implementation but also with regard to its limits. The third part of the book focuses on the issue of international humanitarian intervention. It approaches this question as an illustration and a test of matters of international legitimacy in the post–Cold War era, especially pertaining to individuals as international right holders and the question of the rightful conduct of states. The importance that this issue has acquired since the early 1990s and its continued evolution – particularly in connection with the Responsibility to Protect and the unresolved crisis in Darfur – justify this choice. The fourth part of the book identifies the emergence of new forms of international legitimacy based on debates and practices in the UN context and beyond. The ideas explored at this level must be understood relative to the question of balance between status quo and change, which is examined specifically in the first part of the book.

From the History and Structure of International Legitimacy to Fault Lines in Contemporary International Politics. Jean-Marc Coicaud's chapters set the stage for the book regarding the notions of international legitimacy and fault lines of international legitimacy. Chapter 1 offers a general definition of legitimacy and proceeds with the identification of what distinguishes political legitimacy at the national and international levels. It then provides an historical overview of the issue of international legitimacy by examining a number of case studies. The main objective of the overview is to emphasize the fact that the question of international legitimacy has long been significant, although it has acquired a special importance in recent decades. Chapter 2 focuses on the main characteristics of international legitimacy. Considering the complexity of the notion and its relative lack of academic analysis, the editors of and contributors to the book wanted to unpack, in detail, some of the key aspects of international legitimacy. This process entails examining the meaning and mechanisms, at the international level, of the notions of right holders, hierarchy of right holders, and rightful conduct. Chapter 3 moves from a relatively static analysis of international legitimacy to a more dynamic one, exploring the notion of fault lines of international legitimacy per se. From this perspective, it focuses on the need to balance status quo and change internationally and shows how international fault lines of legitimacy tend to be unresolved disputes between them. In the process, the chapter identifies some of the main types of fault lines of international legitimacy, doing so within the framework of resolutions adopted by the UN Security Council since the end of World War II.

Nathaniel Berman's chapter, Chapter 4, "Intervention in a 'Divided World': Axes of Legitimacy," examines some of the ideas discussed in the first three chapters. In this context, he contradicts the idea that the first post–Cold War decade represented the "golden age" of internationalism, in terms of the status and coherence of internationalism. Indeed, Berman rejects any temptation to be nostalgic about the post–Cold War decade as historically inaccurate and theoretically flawed. More fundamentally, he proposes to eliminate the utopian dream of an international community that integrates power and principle. Moreover, the final integration of power and principle is impeded by the fact that internationalist principles and institutions are themselves deeply heterogeneous. According to Berman, the September 11 terrorist attacks are only the most recent example of perennial challenges to international order – challenges that reveal much about the theoretical and practical elements of internationalist legitimacy. Against this background, Berman advocates a focus on the situational, provisional aspect of legitimacy – on the way internationalist actors must continually seek to reaffirm legitimacy relative to a variety of constituencies and in the face of ever-changing developments. He calls for an understanding of legitimacy that is less foundational and more vulnerable, less static and more tentative, less certain and messier. In the process, he also recognizes that the internal tensions of internationalism have been a source of great strength, which allowed the creation of its most audacious experiments. The work-in-progress nature of internationalism is linked to the heterogeneity of its elements and the flexibility that results.

In conclusion, Berman argues that legitimacy, especially the composite of power and idealism that has marked the most robust internationalism of the past century, can and should only ever be a provisional achievement. It is a provisional achievement arrived at through internationalism's wrestling with its doubles, whether ideological adversaries, heterogeneous elements in local conflicts, or specters of its own unsavory past.

In Chapter 5, "From Berlin to Bonn to Baghdad: A Space for Infinite Justice," Vasuki Nesiah studies the fault lines of legitimacy in the relationship between internationalist humanitarian and military intervention. She contends that humanitarianism functions not only in opposition but also as a complement to militarism. She argues that Kosovo marked a great temporal line because, to many, it legitimized the use of militarism for humanitarian purposes and increased states' humanitarian confidence in the ability to use military power for good. In addition, Nesiah deconstructs how the discourse of humanitarianism permeated the military offensive in Afghanistan, discussing in the process the notion of Responsibility to Protect. Here, she emphasizes that proponents of the war in Afghanistan couched much of the normative rationale for intervention in the Responsibility to Protect, not only in the right to intervene. Human rights, particularly women's rights, were strongly emphasized, as were less obvious discourses regarding intercivilizational dialogue, poverty alleviation and economic development, democratization, multiculturalism, cultural authenticity, and peace. These discussions created the space for militarism by giving the Anglo-American coalition the moral authority to challenge the policies and practices of the Taliban government. Ultimately, Nesiah seeks to identify humanitarian principles to produce legitimacy for military intervention. However, she argues that efforts to fortify the ramparts of humanitarianism against the grasp of imperial interventionists may prove futile. Indeed, based on the record of humanitarian militarism since the end of the Cold War, one can see that there is complicity on the part of humanitarians in that they enabled the linkage between humanitarian and militarist arguments, in some contexts, even as they resented the linkage in others. Thus, Nesiah concludes that the intervention in Iraq remains mired in legitimacy fault lines, "connecting the dots" from Berlin 1884 to Baghdad 2003.

The UN Security Council: Expression, Venue, and Promoter of International Legitimacy? In Chapter 6, "Legal Deliberation and Argumentation in International Decision Making," Ian Johnstone draws on the theory of deliberative democracy and, in the context of international organizations and the UN Security Council, analyzes the following question: Can democracy be transposed beyond the level of the nation-state? In this regard, indicating that international law operates largely through a process of justificatory discourse – which is fundamentally an effort to gain assent to value judgments on reasoned rather than idiosyncratic grounds – he stresses that it is possible to apply the deliberative principle at the transnational level. To be sure, one must recognize that international law, like any other type of law, can be used in strategic, instrumental, and hypocritical ways. However, the fact is that once governments accept a legal norm at the international level, they begin to argue about its interpretation and its application to the particular case at hand. This creates a discursive opening for their critics (e.g., "If you say you respect human rights, why then do you violate them?"), which eventually becomes an incentive for governments to match words with deeds. Of course, the constraint this imposes is not absolute, and it is felt more by the weak states than by the strong. Yet, the real or anticipated judgment of the interpretive community is one factor that the most powerful states cannot ignore. Johnstone tests this thesis by considering whether decision making in the UN Security Council is influenced at all by deliberative conventions and constraints. His answer is "yes," especially in light of the fact that the past two decades have heralded some convergence of understanding about the rules of international life. Moreover, he argues that there is evidence in those failed deliberations (e.g., Iraq in early 2003) of a fairly robust normative framework that structured debates and affected the course of events. According to Johnstone, this shows that because there is an interpretive community to guard the normative framework, the law cannot be manipulated infinitely. He concludes his chapter by suggesting avenues for reform that would reduce the deliberative deficit in the UN Security Council, thereby enhancing the legitimacy of its decisions and of the UN as a whole.

In Chapter 7, "The UN Security Council, Regional Arrangements, and Peacekeeping Operations," Nishkala Suntharalingam poses the following questions: What is the scope for involvement of regional arrangements in peace and security issues? How is legitimacy conferred on the actions and interventions of regional organizations in maintaining international peace and security via peace operations? To what extent is the capacity of using force a prerequisite for the effectiveness and legitimacy of these operations? Suntharalingam addresses these issues in the context of recent crises. In this perspective, she argues that there is growing consensus among member states that UN Security Council authorization is necessary to provide legitimacy for intervention regardless of whether the UN is the implementer. Nevertheless, conferring this legitimacy by the UN Security Council comes at a price because it requires the UN to better coordinate and manage the partnerships as and when required, as well as to ensure that the operations authorized are effective in their undertaking. In practice, despite persistent calls for a new division of labor between the UN and regional organizations, this has proved difficult to achieve. However, a broad range of cooperation between the UN and regional organizations has emerged within the realm of peace and security. This includes peacemaking and preventive diplomacy as well as a number of mixed, or "hybrid," peace operations, whereby the regional arrangement and the UN deploy operations in a conflict situation in some form of combination with each other. Suntharalingam concludes her chapter by stating that the reliance on regional arrangements should not lead to a tribalization of peace-operations activities in context such that conflicts in Europe would be viewed as the responsibility of Europeans and conflicts in Africa as the domain of Africans. To some extent, this would mean the end of collective security.

In Chapter 8, "The Security Council's Alliance of Gender Legitimacy: The Symbolic Capital of Resolution 1325," Dianne Otto stresses that there is an urgent need to overcome gendered impediments to thinking about security. This is particularly important in pursuing the idea that security can be fostered through the empowerment of women and other marginalized groups as well as the promotion of human rights and social justice. From this perspective, she views the UN Security Council's post–Cold War movement toward a broader reading of the causes of international peace and security as a double-layered phenomenon. Its enlarged mandates mean that we are faced with the prospect that militarism will be extended into even more aspects of our everyday lives, and it also raises the possibility that more multidimensional understandings of security could emerge. Against this background, for Otto, the challenge for feminism is to forge links between the Security Council's expanded agenda and nonmilitary and emancipatory ideas about international peace and security. This presupposes moving away from the traditionally state-centered, militaristic, and male-dominated conception of collective security. It is all the more important to do so considering that this conception entrenches and normalizes women's inequality. However, Otto also recognizes that in recent years, this conception has left room for progress. In particular, she points to UN Security Council Resolution 1325 on women, peace, and security, which acknowledges the participation of women in decision making related to the prevention, management, and resolution of armed conflict. As such, Resolution 1325 is significant for enhancing the legitimacy of the Security Council. It helps to make the Council more in sync with requirements of justice as well as with the increasing awareness of the devastating consequences for women of the spreading militarization that has followed the Cold War. Ultimately, Otto wonders whether it is possible to use Resolution 1325 to build a gender legitimacy based on an emancipatory discourse of feminist security or whether women's participation will be limited to the traditionally feminized work of reintegrating overmilitarized men.

Legitimacy of International Interventions and Hierarchy of International Rights. In Chapter 9, "Cosmopolitan Militaries and Cosmopolitan Force," Lorraine Elliott begins with the challenge that humanitarian interventions constitute for international order and its legitimacy. They violate the norms of noninterference, maintenance of sovereignty, and the nonuse of force except in self-defense. They also challenge an idea central to international law – that is, that states are its primary legitimate subjects and moral agents. Against this background, Elliot examines the legitimacy of the proposition that military force (and forces) can and should be used for cosmopolitan purposes – that is, the protection of strangers and those who are not co-nationals because of their equal and universally acknowledged individual moral value and right. This question is particularly important considering that in articulating a wider moral community (i.e., ethical cosmopolis), the cosmopolitan project has become intimately associated with the project of transforming, or reimagining, the political community (i.e., political cosmopolis). This leads Elliot to address the following question: What form could, should, or must coercive force take if it is to be a legitimate methodology for achieving cosmopolitan objectives? There is no single answer to this question, especially when militaries asked to undertake such cosmopolitan roles are the product of inherited institutional structures related to war fighting in the interests not of the cosmopolis but rather of the state. For Elliot, the solution to this problem amounts to having cosmopolitan force being cosmopolitan in its ends as well as in its means. This in itself, however, only brings about more questions, among which are the following: Whose interests will cosmopolitan militaries promote (or undermine)? Can militaries serve both cosmopolitan and statist objectives at the same time? Can militaries – traditionally hierarchical, closed, and nondemocratic – be deployed as agents of what is an essentially and inherently democratic, open, and nonhierarchical normative purpose?

In Chapter 10, "Sovereignty, Rights, and Armed Intervention: A Dialectical Perspective," B. S. Chimni suggests that the promotion and protection of human rights hinges less on a critique of the doctrine of sovereignty and more on the elimination of neo-imperial economic policies and practices. This assertion, however, is not to be interpreted as a defense of an absolute doctrine of sovereignty; nor does it imply a necessary support for the practice of armed humanitarian intervention. According to Chimni, although humanitarian intervention can be justified under certain circumstances, there are alternative ways to conceptualize and enforce rapidly evolving international human-rights law. In making these contentions, the chapter examines the "sovereignty as trap" thesis, which insists that the spread of the discourse and doctrine of sovereignty to postcolonial countries only facilitated their continuing domination and legitimized intervention. In addition, the chapter analyzes the more ubiquitous – and, therefore, of greater concern – "sovereignty as anachronism" thesis and claims that the antinomy between the principle of sovereignty and the evolving commitment of the international community to prevent the gross violation of human rights can be resolved. In the end, Chimni argues that what is certainly illegitimate is armed unilateral humanitarian intervention outside the UN system because it is mainly practiced by hegemonic states, selectively exercised, and likely to cause more harm than good. In contrast, subject to certain preconditions being met, collective armed humanitarian intervention through the UN can be seen as a permissible response to prevent genocide or gross violations of human rights. To be sure, the legitimacy of intervention in such situations derives more from the realities on the ground than from the fact that it is authorized by the UN. However, the fact that intervention takes place through the UN framework goes a long way in ensuring that it occurs exclusively when absolutely necessary.

In Search of New Forms of International Legitimacy: Between Power and Principles. In Chapter 11, "Determining How the Legitimacy of Intervention Is Discussed: A Case Study of International Territorial Administration," Ralph Wilde considers some of the different ways in which territorial administration by international organizations – such as the UN missions in Kosovo and East Timor – has been represented in certain academic texts. Wilde discusses the manner in which these representations frame the nature and purposes of the activity in general and certain administration projects in particular, including through associations with more general concepts such as the idea of "state failure." The point of the exercise is to appraise the significance of these representations in mediating how the political character and legitimacy of the missions are understood. Wilde argues that the missions are often presented in a manner that, in this respect, is problematic. He does so by identifying four different "discursive strategies" evident in the literature.

The first discursive strategy situates international territorial administration within a progressivist historical narrative, positioning the Kosovo and

East Timor projects as the pinnacle of an evolutionary process. Misleading in its own terms, this presentation is also damaging on a normative level in that it legitimates recent projects on spurious grounds. The second discursive strategy unifies all the administration projects through a simplified presentation of their purposes, using the "postconflict" and "state-building" labels. Again, this strategy is both misleading in its own terms and unhelpful normatively because it obscures the full range of purposes with which international territorial administration has been associated, many of which are relatively controversial when compared to the postconflict and state-building objectives. The third discursive strategy associates international territorial administration with a concept – the notion of the failed state – that arguably implies a skewed conception of responsibility. Apart from other problems, this legitimizes international territorial administration by portraying the indigenous factors with which it is concerned as the exclusive cause of the problems it seeks to address. It is easier to justify the introduction of international territorial administration with this narrow conception of responsibility than if the causes were presented in a more complex manner. The fourth discursive strategy presents international territorial administration in a wholly or primarily technocratic manner, obscuring and/or downgrading its political aspects, thereby potentially attenuating the range of issues considered in appraisals of the activity in general and individual missions in particular. Through his case study on a particular type of international intervention, Wilde brings to the foreground the importance of critically analyzing what is at stake for questions of legitimacy when commentators characterize and classify international public policy.

In Chapter 12, "The Legitimacy of Economic Sanctions: An Analysis of Humanitarian Exemptions of Sanctions Regimes and the Right to Minimum Sustenance," Jun Matsukuma examines general issues surrounding the legality and legitimacy of economic sanctions. More specifically, the chapter focuses on the oil-for-food program in Iraq, using it as an example of humanitarian exemptions applied when imposing sanctions. In this regard, Matsukuma argues that the concept of the right to minimum sustenance had a direct effect on the legitimacy of economic sanctions in Iraq and, subsequently, the establishment of the oil-for-food program. He also indicates that the legitimacy of sanctions must be explored in connection with the sources of legitimacy for the UN system. This introduces a fundamental question: How is the legitimacy of the UN Security Council resolutions that impose economic sanctions (here, against Iraq) and are allegedly causing humanitarian problems determined? According to Matsukuma, the answer is that the ultimate justification in ruthlessly applying economic sanctions lies in the fact that they are still a desirable alternative to the use of military force. However, this does not eliminate the validity of the criticism that has been formulated in recent years about economic sanctions.

Hilary Charlesworth's conclusion describes the intermittent interest of international lawyers in the concept of legitimacy. She notes that the main context for much discussion of legitimacy is the revival of interest in the doctrine of humanitarian intervention since the end of the Cold War. In this regard, the conclusion contrasts two strands of scholarship on legitimacy – the procedural and the normative – and then attempts to situate the book's chapters within these strands. Charlesworth argues that the common thread among the chapters is their concern with fault lines within the concept of legitimacy weaknesses that threaten to fracture the certainty of its foundations at any moment.

We therefore can see that thinking about the fault lines of international legitimacy entails reflecting on how norms, institutions, and decision making are inhabited and shaped by conflicts. How these conflicts are handled depends on the evolution of international law and legitimacy and their ability to socialize international life (i.e., the interactions of its various actors). Success in this would mean pursuing a healthy relationship between power and legitimacy, in which power would be indexed on legitimacy; as the chapters in this book show, this is anything but an easy undertaking. Whereas it is already difficult at the national level, it is all the more challenging at the global level. The fragmentation of the world makes it difficult to achieve the unity or, at least, the convergence of authority, purpose, and values that is required, in part, by legitimacy. Moreover, integration at the international level often implies one country dominating others and imposing its values and interests, which makes it particularly challenging for law and international law – at least, if law in general and, more specifically international law, are supposed to be connected with the demands and imperatives of justice. Hence, one must realize that an ultimate challenge of international politics is to identify values, mechanisms, and institutions with the ability to engineer a middle ground between too much fragmentation and too much integration – that is, to build a form of international unity dovetailed with pluralism. This is a key condition for strengthening international legitimacy today and tomorrow.

PART I: FROM THE HISTORY AND STRUCTURE OF INTERNATIONAL LEGITIMACY TO FAULT LINES IN CONTEMPORARY INTERNATIONAL POLITICS

JEAN-MARC COICAUD

1. Legitimacy, Across Borders and Over Time

This chapter addresses the question of international legitimacy at the general level and argues that although legitimacy has been an issue of importance at the international level over time, it has become all the more so in recent decades. The chapter proceeds in two parts. First, it analyzes the notion of legitimacy in general and stresses why legitimacy has had more significance nationally than internationally. Second, it describes cases that illustrate how throughout history, questions of legitimacy have always had relevance at the international level.

Political Legitimacy, National and International

Let us start with a brief discussion of political legitimacy and why it has always been more important on the national than on the international plane.

Defining Political Legitimacy. In the political context, *legitimacy* is defined as the governed recognizing the right of the governors to lead and, to a certain extent, their entitlement to the perks of power. It is a process through which both political power and obedience are justified.

Yet, it is not as if the recognition of the right to govern is without constraints on those who govern. Three conditions must be met for the acknowledgment, or the justification, of the right to govern to take place. First, those in power must deliver services to the governed. These services may vary from one society to another and from one period to another, but the benefits that result for the governed comprise a requirement that cannot be overlooked. Second, the services provided must respond to and reasonably satisfy the key needs (of which security is one[1]) of the governed. These key needs are themselves associated with the sense of possibility and the values (and the expectations they create) that are constitutive of the identity of society. As such, key needs are crystallized in the rights of people. Third, in the process, the key needs benchmark the responsibility and accountability of those in the position of command as well as of the political institutions, including the procedures for exercise of power and how they oversee the general arrangements of society.

That is, political legitimacy is perceived as the distribution of power satisfying the demands of justice. It is seen as expressing, defending, and promoting justice, which is understood as the allocation of and access to resources and opportunities (political but also legal, economic, cultural, and others) due to each individual[2] and, therefore, the attribution of rights and duties on which social cooperation rests.[3] Conversely, when political leaders and institutions, as well as the social system they underwrite, are viewed as illegitimate because they allow injustice to take root, it is not surprising that challenging the sense of social injustice and challenging political order become one and the same thing.[4]

Based on the previous statements, one should not infer that political legitimacy is without ambiguity, or pure; nor should we believe that the relationship between power and legitimacy is unilateral, designed to make power essentially positive because it limits it through the services demanded by political legitimacy. Although political legitimacy is about justifying the hierarchy between the governors and the governed based on the rights of the governed that it recognizes, it does not entirely escape the violence inherent in the differentiation of power. In this regard, history shows that regimes of legitimacy – that is, the modalities that paradigms of legitimacy take –

1 See, for example, Jean-Marc Coicaud, "Quest for International Justice: Benefits of Justice versus the Trappings of Paranoia," in Hans Günter Brauch, John Grin, Czeslaw Mesjasz, Pál Dunay, Navnita Chadha Behera, Béchir Chourou, Úrsula Oswald Spring, P. H. Liotta, & Patricia Kameri-Mbote (eds.), *Globalization and Environmental Challenges: Reconceptualising Security in the Twenty-first Century* (Berlin: Springer-Verlag, 2007).

2 On justice as the establishment of the right portion that is to be attributed to each individual, see in particular Aristotle, *Nicomachean Ethics*, translated by Frederick Apthorp Paley (J. Hall, 1872), Book V, Part 9, p. 111.

3 John Rawls argues that the "primary subject" of justice is "the basic structure of society, or more exactly, the way in which the major social institutions distribute fundamental rights and duties and determine the division of advantages from social cooperation," in *A Theory of Justice* (Cambridge, MA: Harvard University Press, 1971), p. 6. Consequently, the central problem for a theory of justice is to identify principles by which the basic structure of society can be appraised.

4 For more on political legitimacy from a theoretical standpoint, see Jean-Marc Coicaud, *Legitimacy and Politics: A Contribution to the Study of Political Right and Political Responsibility*, translated by David Ames Curtis (Cambridge, UK: Cambridge University Press, 2002).

emanate from an acquired position of power by often brutal means, which the winners work on strengthening and perpetuating as much as possible vis-à-vis the losers through legitimization. When they succeed, legitimization (i.e., the process of "naturalization" of social reality) constructs social arrangements into legitimacy.[5] A regime of power and a regime of legitimacy then go hand in hand. The facts that history, to a large extent, is written by those who make it and win it, and that those contesting history's winners frequently need to do so using the categories of the winners (e.g., legal, normative, political, and cultural) constitute a case in point.[6] Obviously, this makes the relations between legitimacy and power, on the one hand, and between legitimacy and justice, on the other, tense and complex. Aiming to keep power under check by factoring in the rights of the governed is the virtue and appeal of political legitimacy. The constant challenge is the association with and proximity to power, which put political legitimacy in danger of being the captive of the self-serving dynamics of power. This is true at both the national and international levels.

Political Legitimacy, from National to International. Historically, it is mainly in the national realm that the issue of political legitimacy has gained preeminence. The reasons for this are fourfold, all interconnected and related to the development of social integration and state authority at the national level.[7] First, particularly in the past four centuries, socialization (i.e., economic, political, and cultural) has taken place principally at the national level, starting with leading European societies.[8] Individually and collectively, people

5 Pierre Bourdieu, *The Logic of Practice,* translated by Richard Nice (Stanford, CA: Stanford University Press, 1990); and *Distinction: A Social Critique of the Judgement of Taste,* translated by Richard Nice (Cambridge, MA: Harvard University Press, 1984). Bourdieu examines how law helps to set in place, via the medium of the *habitus,* a social nature. For him, the *habitus* is at once the generative principle of objectively classifiable practices and the system of classification (*principium divisionis*) of these practices. It is in the relationship between these two characteristics that the social world as represented – what Bourdieu calls "the space of life-styles"– is constituted. Bourdieu states that legal regulation is – *par excellence* – an instrument of naturalization. It is capable, in time, of passing from some kind of orthodoxy or from a belief identified as a duty to an opinion characterized by immediate adherence to what is perceived as both natural and normal. According to Bourdieu, this results in law being rendered legitimate by the exploited themselves.

6 In modern times, the challengers of the status quo often have to use the democratic aspects of law to make their case and defend their rights.

7 See, for instance, A. John Simmons, *Justification and Legitimacy: Essays on Rights and Obligations* (Cambridge: Cambridge University Press, 2001), Chapter 7 in particular.

8 See, for example, Christian Reus-Smit, *The Moral Purpose of the State: Culture, Social Identity, and Institutional Rationality in International Relations* (Princeton, NJ: Princeton University Press, 1999), Chapter 5.

have come to identify primarily with the national realm. Second, the social density generated by the movement of national integration of societies, combined with the fact that societies became increasingly more differentiated (i.e., the more complex the society, the more differentiated), puts pressure on the need to justify the differentiation of power, particularly between the governors and the governed.[9] Third, the monopoly of the use of force had to be accounted for – a monopoly that over time, as national integration deepened, turned more exclusive and lethal. Finally, justification of the differentiation of power became more necessary when democratic values shaped political legitimacy. The double burden that democratic values – making the rights of individuals the cornerstone – put on political legitimacy helps to explain this state of affairs. To begin with, because democratic values imply the involvement of people in the management of society – namely, through mechanisms of participation and representation – individuals' consent is key for legitimizing the political divide. Moreover, democratic values – by assigning major responsibilities to political institutions with accountability, to a large extent, resting on their ability to fulfill them – make institutions the custodians of individual rights, ensuring that access to these rights is as universal and as real as possible.[10]

The counterpart of the historically high level of national integration is the low degree of international integration. With people's sense of belonging engineered first and foremost in the national realm, the international sphere is remote from immediate concerns. Incidentally, this continues to be the case today. Surely, for example, the universality of democratic values calls for and contributes to the mitigation, internationally, of the divisive effects of the national bent of international life.[11] However, even the internationalist commitments of democratic nations – including, or perhaps especially, the most powerful of them – never lead them to lose sight of the priority given to their own citizens over foreigners.[12]

[9] For interesting insights on this issue, see Georg Simmel, *Conflict and the Web of Group Affiliations*, translated by Kurt H. Wolff & Reinhard Bendix (New York: Free Press, 1964).

[10] Democracy, and the form of political legitimacy associated with it, is largely about "de-kinshipisation." Whereas traditional socialization and politics conceive of the "we versus them" divide and access to resources in narrow terms, particularly based on and legitimized by kinship, democratic values are benchmarked on universality and, consequently, (relatively) open membership and access to resources.

[11] Jean-Marc Coicaud, *Beyond the National Interest: Peacekeeping and Multilateralism in the Era of US Primacy* (Washington, DC: U.S. Institute of Peace Press, 2007), Chapter 3.

[12] Nationalism and competition among states express and fuel this reality, as illustrated by their eagerness to use the contradictory forces of globalization – at the same time, bringing people and nations closer and keeping them apart – to their advantage, regardless of the cost for the poorer countries. Consider also the fact that regional integration in the context

Against this background, it is not surprising that political legitimacy has not been a centerpiece of international life. Short of a strong global socialization and sense of community, mechanisms and institutions of international socialization have been somewhat thin,[13] as have been the expectations of actors (states as well as their people) vis-à-vis them. With limited political responsibility and weak demands for accountability, with fewer tasks for and pressure on governance at the global level, political legitimacy has been a lesser issue internationally.

Nevertheless, this does not mean that political legitimacy has had no place – and no place of importance in its own terms – at the international level. To think so would be to assess characteristics of the international realm on the basis of those at the national level, falling into the trappings of domestic analogy.[14] International life may be less integrated than national life; however, it does not follow that questions of political legitimacy are absent internationally. The specific conditions of international life, of international relations, generate major issues of legitimacy, especially in connection with the projection of power internationally.

Legitimacy in the History of International Relations: Historical Examples

Despite its secondary status compared to the national level, political legitimacy – throughout history and across cultures – has been part of the structure and the stakes of international relations. In this regard, the three themes, or clusters of themes, that Chris Brown, Terry Nardin, and Nicholas Rengger convincingly argue constitute the framework in which international life and its "we" and "them" relations unfold and are shaped over time are well suited to introduce the significance of political legitimacy at the international level.[15]

The three themes are as follows: (1) at the most fundamental level, the "inside/outside" theme, which refers to how collective identities and

of the European Union does not eliminate states' competition within Europe. Furthermore, a purpose of the European project is to enhance the global competitiveness of its member states.

13 We refer to the simple meaning of this notion, not to how Michael Walzer uses it in *Thick and Thin: Moral Argument at Home and Abroad* (Notre Dame, IN: University of Notre Dame Press, 1994).

14 On the domestic analogy and its impact on thought about international relations, see Hidemi Suganami, *The Domestic Analogy and World Order Proposals* (Cambridge: Cambridge University Press, 1989).

15 Chris Brown, Terry Nardin, & Nicholas Rengger (eds.), *International Relations in Political Thought: Texts from the Ancient Greeks to the First World War* (Cambridge: Cambridge University Press, 2002).

relations between them are forged and where the "domestic/international" line is to be drawn; (2) the "universalist/particularist" theme, which concerns the normative orientation of actors (collective or individual) toward their collectivity and the wider whole; and (3) the "system/society" theme, which builds on the idea that international relations presume the existence of regular contacts between collectivities and refers to the quality of those contacts, the roles of norms and power, and the possibility that relations can be managed, even governed.[16]

At the international as at the national level, historicity plays a role. The modalities of the relations among collectivities and their members evolve over time,[17] varying among types of international socialization[18] or within a given type of international socialization.[19] As a result, the three themes defined previously and their relationships are not intended to provide the list of all possible historical versions of specific rights and duties among collectivities and their members. However, they certainly can bring light to the generic modicum of international relations and political legitimacy at the international level. Indeed, as the next chapter discusses in more detail, the various aspects of international legitimacy are about figuring out how to rightfully handle the inside/outside, universalist/particularist, and system/society distinctions. For instance, these distinctions help address questions such as who is and what makes a legitimate actor on the international scene. It is in connection with them that the degrees of inclusion and exclusion, the hierarchies of rights and duties, and even authority existing among actors are established. It is in connection with them that the legitimate behaviors of actors toward one another are established. The following examples illustrate this state of affairs.

Consider Ancient Greece. In the context of international relations, the way in which the classical period established and questioned distinctions between insiders and outsiders – as well as how these distinctions were taken

[16] Ibid., p. 6. For further elaboration on each of these themes, see pp. 6–12.

[17] On the notion of change at the international level and the various scopes of change, see Nicholas Greenwood Onuf, *The Republican Legacy in International Thought* (Cambridge: Cambridge University Press, 1998), pp. 188–190.

[18] An example is the influence of the American and French revolutions on the evolution of international legitimacy in modern times. See Mlada Bukovansky, *Legitimacy and Power Politics: The American and French Revolutions in International Political Culture* (Princeton, NJ: Princeton University Press, 2002).

[19] For an analysis of the changes that have taken place in recent years in the international system, see Jean-Marc Coicaud, *Beyond the National Interest: Peacekeeping and Multilateralism in the Era of US Primacy* (op. cit.).

to generate and limit moral obligations between collectivities and between individuals – is indicative of where and how the line between legitimate and illegitimate actors and behaviors was drawn internationally.[20] Philosophical arguments, of course, were part and parcel of the debates that took place around these issues. For example, for Aristotle, the political community has a responsibility to act in accordance with the welfare of its citizens as well as other human beings. This implies a type of cosmopolitanism, and it explains that a common tone in Aristotle's thinking is the criticism of those communities – the Scythians, Persians, Thracians, Celts, and Spartans – that glorified war and praised domination and conquest. For Aristotle, it is not appropriate to conquer and rule other regimes because doing so effectively denies the freedom and status of fellow humans.[21] This led Aristotle to argue that war, when necessary, must serve peace – peace that cannot be dissociated from virtue.[22] From this perspective, defensive war is perfectly permissible; however, the justification of offensive war is limited to two types of cases: (1) when a self-ruled community is under attack and in need of help or outside intervention, and (2) when a community cannot rule itself.[23]

This stance is not foreign to Ancient Chinese views. Indeed, at more or less the same time, Mencius (372–289 BC) also reflected on how leaders should legitimately relate to the outside world, specifically addressing what makes war just. For this, he drew on the general Confucian principles of good governance (or domestic political legitimacy), specifically that which indicates that rulers should strive for peace, referring to government by benevolence – which, at a minimum, entails securing the conditions for people's basic means of subsistence and intellectual and moral development. On this basis, Mencius was critical of rulers who launched bloody wars of conquest simply to increase

20 Brown, Nardin, & Rengger (eds.), *International Relations in Political Thought: Texts from the Ancient Greeks to the First World War* (op. cit.), p. 17. For an overview of international obligation in antiquity, see David J. Bederman, *International Law in Antiquity* (Cambridge: Cambridge University Press, 2001).

21 Aristotle: "how completely unreasonable it would be if the work of a statesman were to be reduced to an ability to work out how to rule and be master over neighboring peoples, with or without their consent. How could that be a part of statecraft or lawgiving, when it is not even lawful in itself? To rule at all costs, not only justly but unjustly, is unlawful, and merely to have the upper hand is not necessarily to have a just title to it" (Book VII, ii, 1324b22, p. 397); and "to say that a state has trained itself in the acquisition of power with a view to ruling its neighbors – that is no ground for calling it happy or applauding its lawgiver" (Book VII, xiv, 1333b26, p. 435), in *The Politics*, translated by Thomas Alan Sinclair & revised by Trevor J. Saunders (London: Penguin Books, 1992).

22 Ibid., Book VII, xv, 1334a11, p. 437.

23 Brown, Nardin, & Rengger (eds.), *International Relations in Political Thought: Texts from the Ancient Greeks to the First World War* (op. cit.), p. 27.

their territory and engage in economic plunder.[24] That said, he recognized that some defensive and offensive wars can be just:

> For Mencius . . . , a defensive war is justified only if an actually or potentially virtuous and capable ruler (one who aims to provide peace and benevolent government), with the support of his people, must resort to violence to protect his territory against would-be conquering hegemons. An offensive war is justified if (and only if) it is led by an actually or potentially virtuous ruler who aims to punish oppressive rulers and bring about global peace. The "conquering" army must be welcomed by the "conquered" people, and if the welcome is not long-lasting, the "conquering" army should appoint a local leader in consultation with the "conquered" people and withdraw as soon as possible. The punitive expedition should only be launched if the conquering ruler can make a plausible claim to have the world's support.[25]

In other words, not everything is legitimate in the international behavior of states and, ultimately, the right line of international action for governments is rooted in a key principle of domestic political legitimacy applied to the international realm: benevolence.[26]

The conquest that followed the European discovery of America at the end of the fifteenth century is another example in the context of which issues of legitimacy in the international realm were much debated. Did Native Americans have rights and, if so, what were those rights? What obligations did the Europeans have toward them? In particular, was it legitimate to seize the lands of native populations and either eliminate or enslave the people? Also, what constituted legitimate relations among the European countries that were competing for territories and riches? These are some of the questions at the center of the debates.[27] Needless to say, although these questions generated

24 Mencius, *Book 1*, Part A, translated by D. C. Lau (London: Penguin Books, 2004), pp. 3–14.

25 Daniel A. Bell, *Beyond Liberal Democracy: Political Thinking for an East Asian Context* (Princeton, NJ: Princeton University Press, 2006), Chapter 2, p. 40. See also the comments of Francois Julien, *Fonder la morale*, Chapters 12 and 13, in *La pensée chinoise dans le miroir de la philosophie* (Paris: Editions du Seuil, 2007).

26 For more on the traditional Chinese view of the world, see John King Fairbank (ed.), *The Chinese World Order: Traditional China's Foreign Relations* (Cambridge, MA: Harvard University Press, 1968).

27 On this question and the debates generated in particular by the positions of Francisco de Vitoria and Bartolomé de la Casas, see Richard Tuck, *The Rights of War and Peace: Political Thought and the International Order from Grotius to Kant* (Oxford: Oxford University Press, 2001), pp. 72–77; and Michel Villey, *La formation de la pensée juridique moderne* (Paris: Editions Montchrestien, 1975), pp. 356–367. In the case of the Aztec and Inca Empires, despite the fact that as highly organized and sophisticated political communities, they could not be deprived of their rights on the grounds that their members were still in a state of nature, precepts were found to clear the way for Spanish rule. See, for instance, Anthony Pagden, *Spanish Imperialism and the Political Imagination: Studies in European and Spanish-American Social and Political Theory 1513–1830* (New Haven, CT: Yale University Press,

concerns of foreign policy for the colonizing powers of the time (beginning with Spain), they were never taken seriously enough to put an end to the conquest. In addition, the concerns lost their practical importance relatively quickly. Regarding Spanish America, this was particularly the case because of the catastrophic decline in the Native American population.[28] Nevertheless, the questions continued to have overall relevance until the beginning of the twentieth century. The Western powers spread over the world kept them on the international agenda.[29] In the process, with the claimed superiority of European civilization over "uncivilized" societies being a crucial part of its toolbox, international law came to serve as a key instrument in the legitimization of the expansion and acquisitions of the West overseas.[30]

The Vienna Settlement, which ended the Napoleonic Wars in 1815, is also a well-known example of how legitimacy came to play a significant role internationally. This settlement aimed at reestablishing both the possibility and legitimacy of international order in a world that had experienced a period of deep instability. The crises of revolutionary upheaval, gradual domination of Europe by Napoleon's France, and resulting violent international conflicts represented major challenges for the old system of international legitimacy.[31] To address these challenges, and because of the perception that

1990), especially Chapter 1. For an overview of the worldwide expansion of the Spanish monarchy during the sixteenth and seventeenth centuries, its foreign policy, and attempts to establish a universal version of international legitimacy, see Serge Gruzinski, *Les quatre parties du monde: Histoire d'une mondialisation* (Paris: Editions de la Martinière, 2004).

28 Also of interest here is the fact that the conquest of North America produced debates in the field of political philosophy concerning property rights, but the conquest itself was more or less taken for granted in the context of international thinking. See, for example, Locke's Chapter V of Book II, *The Second Treatise of Civil Government*, in *Two Treatises of Government* (Cambridge: Cambridge University Press, 1988); Rousseau's Chapter 9 of Book 1 of *The Social Contract, or Principles of Political Right*, translated by Maurice Cranston (London: Penguin Classics, 1968); and Richard Tuck, *The Rights of War and Peace: Political Thought and the International Order from Grotius to Kant* (op. cit.), Chapters 6 and 7. For an analysis of the spirit in which the early phases of the colonization of North America took place, see Bernard Bailyn, with the assistance of Barbara DeWolfe, *Voyagers to the West: A Passage in the Peopling of America on the Eve of the Revolution* (New York: Vintage Books, 1986), Chapters 1 and 2.

29 By the end of the nineteenth century, the partition of Africa was a *fait accompli*. On the Conference of Berlin (November 1884–February 1885) and its implications for Africa, see Henri Wesseling, *Le partage de l'Afrique: 1880–1914*, translated into French by Patrick Grilli (Paris: Gallimard, 2002).

30 Antony Anghie, *Imperialism, Sovereignty, and the Making of International Law* (Cambridge: Cambridge University Press, 2005). See also Martti Koskenniemi, *The Gentle Civilizer of Nations: The Rise and Fall of International Law 1870–1960* (Cambridge: Cambridge University Press, 2002), Chapter 2 in particular.

31 Bukovansky, *Legitimacy and Power Politics: The American and French Revolutions in International Political Culture* (op. cit.). On the system of international legitimacy envisioned by

the changes brought about by the French Revolution in the domestic realm had wide international repercussions,[32] much attention was given to the issue of rightful membership in international society. The goal was to contain if not reverse the tide of popular sovereignty. As a result, an ideological commitment was made to dynasticism. Moreover, the rightful conduct of states was sought on the basis of great-power consensus (i.e., Concert). Such consensus – mindful of inclusion but also a product of the pursuit of self-interest by key European powers – was closely associated with a balance of power among them. Overall, "just equilibrium," the much-favored expression of the age, became a convenient synonym for the idea of international legitimacy. It embraced and replicated two dimensions of legitimacy: "[O]ne strand fastened upon issues of rightful possession and entitlement, the other amounted to an elaboration of the guiding principles of interstate conduct."[33] Eventually, however, the fact that the unity of conservative interests was formed out of a vision of political legitimacy that did not allow for the integration of nationalist forces proved to be a dangerous weakness. As nationalism increasingly reshaped individual and collective identities throughout the continent of Europe, the inability of the Concert to mitigate or bridge the gap between the politics of the balance of power and nationalist values contributed to its demise as well as to the one of the international system that it underwrote.[34]

The Versailles Settlement of 1919 is another illustration of the importance of questions of legitimacy at the international level. Although the Vienna Settlement is seen as having a somewhat iconic status as a success, Versailles is tainted as having produced an order considered highly unstable, mainly due to its illegitimacy. This is, in part, because the Wilsonian principles that shaped the terms of the Versailles Treaty and the League of Nations could not generate consensus or produce an integrated international postwar order. The "principle of public right"[35] – at the core of Wilson's vision – foresaw

Napoleon, see Thierry Lentz, *Nouvelle histoire du premier empire*, Volume I: *Napoléon et la conquête de l'Europe 1804–1810* (Paris: Fayard, 2002), pp. 14–15.

32 Edmund Burke, *Reflections on the Revolution in France* (Oxford: Oxford University Press, 1999), pp. 9–10, for example.

33 Ian Clark, *Legitimacy in International Society* (Oxford: Oxford University Press, 2005), p. 105. For more on the Vienna Settlement of 1815, see G. John Ikenberry, *After Victory: Institutions, Strategic Restraint, and the Rebuilding of Order after Major Wars* (Princeton, NJ: Princeton University Press, 2001), Chapter 4.

34 Jean-Marc Coicaud, "Legitimacy, Socialization, and International Change," in Charles A. Kupchan, Emanuel Adler, Jean-Marc Coicaud, & Yuen Foong Khong (eds.), *Power in Transition: The Peaceful Change of International Order* (Tokyo: United Nations University Press, 2001), pp. 76–80.

35 Woodrow Wilson, in "Address Delivered at the First Annual Assemblage of the League to Enforce Peace: American Principles," Washington, DC, May 27, 1916, quoted in Kalevi J.

a system grounded on shared values meant to encourage and manage an international dialogue on legitimacy. It was to be based not only on the acts of states and governments but also on the will – the goodwill – of the people, to whom governments and states were seen simply as servants. From the import of legitimacy – grounded in the principle of justice for all peoples – to the interstate discourse followed the demand for democratic institutions, both domestic and international. Nevertheless, this conception of legitimacy did not translate into effective political legitimization. An initial problem was the lack of consistency in the interpretation and use of norms at the center of the system. Self-determination was a case in point; it was a principle to be called on in southeastern Europe but not for dismantling the great European empires that bestrode the rest of the globe.[36] Furthermore, the concerns if not the voices of key powers were partly ignored by the Versailles Peace Treaty, which applied not only to vanquished Germany[37] but also to Bolshevik Russia and Japan – the latter whose wish to include a prohibition on racial discrimination was denied (the issue came to be known as "the racial equality clause").[38] It is not surprising that this made the exclusion of certain states and nationalities a critical element of the new world order and left many with little interest in preserving the system – especially because the United States, following the rejection of the Treaty by the U.S. Senate, was among those that ultimately did not participate in the League. Therefore, because the principal powers did not share a common approach to the order of priority among principles of international legitimacy, the required political accommodations between competing powers and principles of international legitimacy were never found.

Holsti, *Peace and War: Armed Conflicts and International Order 1648–1989* (Cambridge: Cambridge University Press, 1991), p. 177.

36 Ian Clark, *Legitimacy in International Society* (op. cit.), p. 117. For an interesting legal and historical analysis of some of the issues associated with this question in the interwar period, see Nathaniel Berman, "The International Law of Nationalism: Group Identity and Legal History," in Robert J. Beck & Thomas Ambrosio (eds.), *International Law and the Rise of Nations: The State System and the Challenge of Ethnic Groups* (Washington, DC: CQ Press, 2001), and "Beyond Colonialism and Nationalism? Ethiopia, Czechoslovakia, and 'Peaceful Change'," in *Nordic Journal of International Law* (Vol. 65, Nos. 3–4, 1996).

37 For a study of German thinking on international affairs and international legitimacy following the Versailles Peace Treaty, see Michel Korinman, *Quand l'Allemagne pensait le monde: Grandeur et décadence d'une géopolitique* (Paris: Fayard, 1990), pp. 208–211.

38 Margaret MacMillan, *Paris 1919: Six Months that Changed the World* (New York: Random House, 2003), p. 321: "The failure to get the racial equality clause was an important factor of the interwar years in turning Japan away from cooperation with the West and towards more aggressively nationalistic policies." See also Walter LaFeber, *The Clash: U.S.–Japanese Relations throughout History* (New York: W.W. Norton, 1998), pp. 120–126; and Frederick R. Dickinson, *War and National Reinvention: Japan in the Great War, 1914–1919* (Cambridge, MA: Harvard University Press, 1999), Chapter 6.

Finally, the UN – and the normative and institutional framework that it comprises – is the most recent regime of international legitimacy. The mandates and tasks set out in this multilateral context constitute the most advanced system of international legitimacy so far. Building on the overall goals of collective security, human rights, development, and, to some extent, democracy referred to in the UN Charter, the international community and its member states have created a complex web of norms and organizations in the past six decades. These norms and organizations are engaging the responsibility of the states and international community in an increasingly comprehensive and detailed manner at both the global and national levels.[39] Along the way, the requirements of legitimacy and accountability have become increasingly demanding.

[39] Once member states ratify international treaties, they are meant to take them into account in their national legislation. On this question, see Paul Reuter, *Introduction au droit des traités* (Paris: Presses Universitaires de France, 1985).

JEAN-MARC COICAUD

2. Deconstructing International Legitimacy

As alluded to in the Introduction and Chapter 1, the post–Cold War era underscored the importance of international legitimacy. Once the danger of Armageddon associated with the East–West confrontation had been removed, initially there was less visceral need – at least, among winners – to pursue security at all costs, whatever the means.[1] Giving greater attention to right (i.e., legitimacy) and not simply might, as well as recognition to the overall benefits that international cooperation and socialization embedded in legitimacy would bring to interstate politics, seemed the best option. The window of opportunity that this created for human rights and democratic values to increasingly shape policies[2] could only contribute to enhancing the visibility and relevance of legitimacy, as it called for more accountability. Tragically, the conflicts that marked the post–Cold War period offered their own openings. By triggering the establishment of international criminal tribunals, the massive human-rights violations and humanitarian crises accompanying wars in collapsing countries sent the message that basic requirements of legitimacy would not be denied with impunity.[3] Here, particularly in the 1990s, the

[1] That being said, it is not as if international legitimacy concerns were absent during the Cold War. Besides the system of international legitimacy represented by the UN, the East–West showdown was itself about legitimacy. It referred to communist and democratic legitimacy fighting for hegemony, domestically and internationally. However, the harsh realities of global struggles and the decades-long competition between the two blocs put might in a commanding position.

[2] Human rights and democratic values could build on the work that had been done in their favor in the previous years within the framework of international law and multilateralism. This shows that describing the Cold War as a time of immobilization is inaccurate and does not do justice to the normative progress achieved during this period.

[3] Consider the establishment of the International Criminal Tribunal for the Former Yugoslavia (ICTY), the International Criminal Tribunal for Rwanda (ICTR), the International Criminal Court (ICC), and the "internationalized criminal courts and tribunals," such as the Special Court for Sierra Leone and the so-called Extraordinary Chambers in the Courts of Cambodia;

sympathetic coverage provided by global media[4] and the involvement of world society (especially nongovernmental organizations [NGOs])[5] in support of civilian victims of conflicts played a positive role. In addition, globalization highlighted international legitimacy. Indeed, whereas it was perceived as affecting millions of people, it was often also seen as affecting them negatively, and many argued that this was happening with the collaboration of international institutions.[6] Making globalization more human, more legitimate, therefore became a top priority of the international agenda.[7]

However, the developments that installed questions of legitimacy at the forefront of international life did not necessarily do so in an atmosphere of consensus. In fact, many of the instances that contributed to putting international legitimacy "on the map" in the past twenty years did so in the midst of controversies. From this perspective, there is a long list of heated debates surrounding key questions of legitimacy during the period, including the following: What are the conditions for a legitimate secession from a country and, for a new entity, for accession to full international community membership (e.g., the Balkans, including Kosovo)? Why and when can force be used legitimately (*jus ad bellum*), either in the context of humanitarian interventions (e.g., the Balkans and Africa) or in the context of the war against terror (e.g., Iraq)? What are the legitimate modalities for the use of force (*jus in bello*) once the conflict is under way?[8] In the aftermath of September 11, is it legitimate to torture prisoners who are suspected to be or confirmed as terrorists?[9] Who is/has the ultimate authority to be a producer and guarantor

on this later point, see Cesare P. R. Romano, André Nollkaemper, & Jann K. Kleffner (eds.), *Internationalized Criminal Courts: Sierra Leone, East Timor, Kosovo, and Cambodia* (Oxford: Oxford University Press, 2004). Refer as well to the notion of Responsibility to Protect, endorsed in the context of the 2005 World Summit (New York: United Nations Headquarters, 2005 World Summit Outcome, UN Document A/RES/60/1, October 24, 2005).

4 In the 1990s, CNN played a significant awareness role concerning humanitarian crises, which it appears to no longer play in the 2000s. In this regard, it still remains to be seen if the Internet will be able to mobilize people at the global level for the protection of human rights.

5 Ian Clark, *International Legitimacy and World Society* (Oxford: Oxford University Press, 2005), pp. 189–197.

6 On the backlash against the Bretton Woods institutions and the World Trade Organization (WTO), see Joseph E. Stiglitz, *Globalization and Its Discontents* (New York: W.W. Norton & Company, 2003).

7 Thomas M. Franck, *Fairness in International Law and Institutions* (Oxford: Oxford University Press, 1995); and Jean-Marc Coicaud, "Can Global Governance Make Globalization more Legitimate?," in Pierre de Senarclens & Ali Kazancigil (eds.), *Regulating Globalization: Critical Approaches to Global Governance* (Tokyo: United Nations University Press, 2007).

8 Jean-Marc Coicaud, *Beyond the National Interest: Peacekeeping and Multilateralism in the Era of US Primacy* (Washington, DC: U.S. Institute of Peace Press, 2007), pp. 102–105.

9 Karen J. Greenberg & Joshua L. Dratel (eds.), *The Torture Papers: The Road to Abu Ghraib* (Cambridge: Cambridge University Press, 2005).

of norms of international legitimacy (i.e., the United Nations [UN] or the United States)?[10] In the end, it is normal that the sensitive and pressing nature of these issues also showed that political legitimacy could not be overlooked in the international realm. As a whole, this demonstrates that Martin Wight's assessment of international legitimacy in the early 1970s loses a significant part of its relevance relative to the international system of today:

> In international society . . . principles of legitimacy remain normative without becoming structural. . . . Conceptions of international legitimacy have had a minor part in shaping international history, except where they have run with the grain of state-consolidation.[11]

Incidentally, the fact that in the past two decades matters of legitimacy have become both a defining element of international life and – considering the geopolitical fluidity of the time – a work in progress may carry some intellectual benefit. Such exposure might facilitate the outlining of a relatively systematic analysis of legitimacy at the international level. If this is the case, it would prove useful because the task is now to examine in greater detail the main characteristics of international legitimacy and the fault lines that can inhabit it.

It is in the context of the three themes referred to in Chapter 1 (i.e., the inside/outside, universalist/particularist, and system/society themes) that political legitimacy plays a socialization role in international relations, which happens at three complementary levels. The first two are the most general and it is on these levels that the other builds and develops. First, international legitimacy contributes to the establishment of international life as a non-zero-sum game. Second, it seeks to provide a rationale for the organization of international relations, especially the inequalities of power it contains. Third, the lines that norms of legitimacy draw between what is right and what is not take place in connection with notions such as community and membership, right holder, hierarchy of right holders, rightful conduct, and authority.

Legitimacy and the Socialization of International Life

In a number of places, Thomas Hobbes invites the comparison of international relations with the unmitigated war of everyman against everyman that is characteristic of the mere state of nature, in which Hobbesian individualism is at its most rampant. From this perspective, nations "live in a condition

[10] Coicaud, *Beyond the National Interest: Peacekeeping and Multilateralism in the Era of US Primacy* (op. cit.), pp. 164–167.

[11] Wight, "International Legitimacy," in *International Relations* (Vol. 4, No. 1, May 1972), p. 28.

of a war one against another . . . having their weapons pointing, and their eyes fixed on one another; that is, their forts, garrisons, and guns upon the frontiers of their kingdoms . . . which is a posture of war."[12] When physical hostilities cease, there is no condition of peace but merely a breathing space during which time preparations are made for the next encounter. Nations, on every visible advantage, will invade one another.[13] This pessimistic view, which has made Hobbes's name synonymous with the doctrine of realism in international relations,[14] presents states' interests as utterly in opposition with one another, with the gain of one necessarily being the loss of another – that is, a zero-sum game.

If this has ever been the reality of the past, the increasingly interdependent and rights-aware environment of today renders this conception of international life neither possible nor desirable for our world. Because the existence as well as the coexistence of international actors, beginning with states, are now largely defined and based on their economic, political, and normative relations, they cannot afford to have conflict ruling the international realm all the time; it would result in collective suicide. Each actor, therefore, must pursue its self-interest without entirely ignoring the interests of others, which makes cooperation a structuring element of international politics. Cooperation implies some type of transaction founded on accommodation and compromise that while constraining and limiting one's interest also aims at enhancing it.[15] Surely, by creating room for others' interests, cooperation leads one to lose the possibility – although always uncertain – of "having it all." However, the benefit of knowing that what is obtained is secured because it rests on accepted give and take is meant to be greater than what is lost. Having cooperation generating more benefits than costs is even more a prospect, considering that it does not focus exclusively on the present; it extends to the future as well. In this regard, cooperation seeks to produce the additional advantage of making results of the interactions reasonably predictable in their secured character. Incidentally, as long as this predictability is perceived as credible, appealing, and durable, it reinforces the incentive and meaning for actors to work together in the present.

12 Thomas Hobbes, *Leviathan* (Oxford: Oxford University Press, 1998), p. 85.

13 Thomas Hobbes, *A Dialogue between a Philosopher and a Student of the Common Laws of England*, edited by Joseph Cropsey (Chicago & London: University of Chicago Press, 1997), p. 17.

14 Martin Wight, *International Theory: The Three Traditions* (New York: Holmes & Meier, 1992), p. 229. There are interpretations of Hobbes's philosophy of international relations that have more nuances. See, for example, David Boucher, *Political Theories of International Relations: From Thucydides to the Present* (Oxford: Oxford University Press, 1998), pp. 145–167.

15 Robert Axelrod, *The Evolution of Cooperation* (New York: Basic Books, Inc., 1984).

Against this background, the task of the regime of norms, institutions, and mechanisms that constitute international legitimacy is to ensure that relations among international actors take the form of a transaction – of a commitment to play by the rules in exchange for the benefits associated with doing so. The task is to ensure that relations are turned into transactions designed to engineer socialized international interactions, which includes having them regulated, mainly pacified, producing a security dividend, self-reinforcing and geared toward sustainability. Needless to say, finding the proper equation that will render the transaction possible is not an easy task. The challenge is to establish the right formula that will lead actors to believe that they are gaining more than they are losing by engaging in and being bound by a dynamic of reciprocity based on mutually acknowledged rights and duties. It entails coming up with the appropriate terms that will lead them to believe that their rights and their implementation render worthwhile their duties at the international level. When this happens, even conditions of war among states, for instance, can be an expression and source of socialization, with certain conducts permitted and others prohibited.

Legitimacy and the Rationale for the Organization of International Inequalities

Turning relations into transactions is particularly difficult considering that the existence of disparities among actors is part and parcel of international life. When international relations are minimally socialized, offering a rationale for inequalities is not really a requirement. The little there is of reciprocity of rights and duties, of exchange or transaction, does not amount to much expectation on the side of the powerless or constraint for the powerful. In this context, the hierarchy gaps tend to be seen as more or less a fact of life, a situation to be benefited from by those in commanding positions and endured by those at the receiving end of power. Conversely, when international socialization is significant, serious attention must be given to disparities of power among actors. Factoring in and accounting for these disparaties becomes a crucial aspect of socialization. This is the case because – at the international level as in the national realm – inequalities of power can be mitigated but not entirely eliminated. There are three reasons for this.

First, all systems of social interaction that enable actors to function as competent members are constructed on complex webs of inclusion and exclusion, which implies the need to satisfy minimum criteria and meet basic conditions before rights of access or participation are conferred.[16] As such, these webs of inclusion and exclusion, which vary according to the levels of social life and the types of culture across space and time, invariably both echo and translate into relations of inequalities. In this connection, utopian or revolutionary national politics – especially the history of communism in the twentieth century – has taught us that attempting to eradicate hierarchies in order to achieve total equality and unity is prone to result in a totalitarian nightmare.[17] With socialized relations conceived in terms of ideality, differences of power – particularly among those in charge and others – rather than disappearing become absolute in all domains of people's life.[18] Although until now this route has been traveled internationally only at the regional level by the Eastern European Soviet bloc,[19] there is no reason to believe that the outcomes would be better if tried at the global level.

Second, international life is still built around the national bent, with most individuals' experience of key elements of socialization (e.g., identification, representation, expectation, and obligation) occurring chiefly in the national realm. This leads national politicians to focus on domestic demands, but it also leads countries to compete with one another and, in conjunction, more often than not to cooperate internationally principally within the limits of their narrowly understood national interest – that is, essentially in ways in which cooperation is part of or second to competition, not the reverse. Instead of combating it, this feeds international inequality. In the process, far from optimizing the probability of rising together, nations increase the risk of falling together.

Third, even a strong level of international socialization is not a guarantee that hierarchy of power among actors will be at a minimum. As alluded to previously,[20] regimes of international legitimacy are related to international

[16] Andrew Linklater, *The Transformation of Political Community: Ethical Foundations of the Post-Westphalian Era* (Columbia: University of South Carolina Press, 1998), pp. 114–117.

[17] Coicaud, *Legitimacy and Politics: A Contribution to the Study of Political Right and Political Responsibility* (op. cit.), pp. 29–30.

[18] Concerning, for instance, the Terror during the French Revolution, see Marc Richir, "Révolution et transparence sociale," introduction to Johann Gottlieb Fichte's *Considérations destinées à rectifier les jugements du public sur la Révolution française* (Paris: Payot, 1974). For Russian communism, see Isaiah Berlin, *The Soviet Mind: Russian Culture under Communism* (Washington, DC: Brookings Institution Press, 2004). More generally on modern national and world revolutionary politics, see Benjamin I. Schwartz, "The Reign of Virtue: Leader and Party in the Cultural Revolution," in *China and Other Matters* (Cambridge, MA: Harvard University Press, 1996), pp. 175–186.

[19] For a literary evocation of this world, see Czeslaw Milosz, *The Captive Mind*, translated by Jane Zielonko (London: Penguin Classic, 2001).

[20] See Chapter 1, this volume.

dominance and hegemony, with much of their purpose being to embed a sense of legitimacy in such dominance. In this regard, hegemonic power is more likely to succeed in ensuring acquiescence from secondary countries when it co-opts some of their members and values in its sphere. The Roman Empire is an illustration of this.[21] As demonstrated by the establishment of systems of alliances and of the UN by the United States in the aftermath of World War II, having a hegemon sharing (although in a restricted fashion), the management of international order is quite effective as well.[22]

Because inequalities of power among actors cannot be entirely eliminated, the responsibility of international legitimacy is to articulate and align them with the requirements of justice in international relations at a given time. Doing so amounts to having a regime of legitimacy able to convey that the organization of international life is the best possible in the period considered, specifically concerning access to and allocation of resources. It comes down to having it viewed as the best possible scenario for the international system in terms of reciprocity of rights and duties. From this perspective, there is legitimacy when the determination of the extent to which disparities are tolerable – including indicating the extent to which they should be reduced – is accepted by international standards. Of course, these standards and how they are institutionalized are not set forever. As part of history, they evolve in connection with the overall socialization of international affairs. For instance, the norms, organizations, and mechanisms in which they crystallize and the types of hierarchies they monitor change over time, as does the judgment passed on them. Consider the current standards of international legitimacy; it is probable that in two hundred years, compared to the present, they will be assessed differently. However, what is essential is that in their time, international standards are perceived as credible enough to be expressions and tools of socialization. When this is the case, their ability to empower international actors gives them a present and a future. In conjunction, the international system and its standards of legitimacy have a future. Conversely, once an atmosphere of alienation settles in, the standards are in danger of becoming a thing of the past.

21 On aspects of this phenomenon in the Roman Empire, see Paul Veyne, *L'empire gréco-romain* (Paris: Seuil, 2005), pp. 163–257; François Julien, *De l'universel, de l'uniforme, du commun et du dialogue entre les cultures* (Paris: Fayard, 2008), pp. 77–83; and Claudia Moatti, *La Raison de Rome* (Paris: Seuil, 1997).

22 G. John Ikenberry, *After Victory: Institutions, Strategic Restraint, and the Rebuilding of Order after Major Wars* (Princeton, NJ: Princeton University Press, 2001), Chapter 6; and G. John Ikenberry & Charles A. Kupchan, "Socialization and Hegemonic Power," in *International Organization* (Vol. 44, No. 3, Summer 1990).

In this respect, the thicker the socialization of international relations, the more challenging it can be to communicate a sense of present and future. Indeed, the thicker the international socialization, the greater the demands on legitimacy and the international system. For example, the larger the number of stakeholders – at both the collective and individual levels – called on to endorse international standards of legitimacy, the stronger is the need for this endorsement to be qualitative, the more urgent is the imperative to tackle inequalities, and the more pressure there is on legitimacy. Also, the more pressure there is on legitimacy, the more the international system is made accountable. Ultimately, this can result in the legitimacy of the international system and the international system itself being questioned more and more. In some ways, the fact that many see contemporary international order and its regime of legitimacy – socially the thickest and encompassing the most democratic values ever – as in crisis is not foreign to this phenomenon. The difficulty they have in reaching their high normative thresholds highlights their shortcomings and generates doubts about their validity.

The previous comments about the task of international legitimacy to justify the international organization of inequalities cover only a few aspects of the issue. There is more to say on this topic, especially regarding the conditions under which the criteria for evaluating the legitimacy of the international system can be trusted, despite their tendency to owe much to the power arrangements of the period. There is also more to say on the adjudication among internationally competing claims regarding what is legitimate, when these claims belong to the same cultural system but also when they are part of different cultural systems. The analysis of the interactions between legitimacy and change in the international realm in the next chapter helps answer these questions. To do so, however, we must first examine the lines of discrimination drawn by legitimacy in its various areas of operation at the international level.

The Construction of Legitimacy in International Order

To use a sports analogy, the determination of what is internationally legitimate and illegitimate contributes to the establishment of the playing field, the rules of the game, and the penalties for breaking them. Its purpose is also to identify the players, the referees, and their position on the field. This occurs in connection with the notions of community and membership, right holder, hierarchy of right holders, rightful conduct, and international authority. As will be evident in the analysis of these issues – entangled in the reality of international life but which we distinguish here for the sake of clarity – each in its own way is about addressing the previously discussed inside/outside, universalist/ particularist, and system/society themes.[23]

International Community Membership. In connection with the notions of community and membership, international legitimacy defines who is and who is not a member of the international community, of the community of legitimacy that the international community constitutes. This determination takes place on the basis of what is conceived of as a legitimate form of collective organization. As such, international legitimacy relies on qualities that a social group must embody to benefit from international recognition. This dimension of international legitimacy is of great importance because the identity of who is a legitimate member of the international system parallels the types of social interactions existing in it, the interests, values, and meanings it favors, and its very structure.[24] An international community in which members are nation-states is different from a community consisting of medieval polities.[25] For instance, the conception and management of territoriality will differ vastly, as will the legal arrangements. Against this background, membership is significant such that Martin Wight presents it as a foundational element for the socialization of international relations and how it unfolds:

> Let us define international legitimacy as the collective judgement of international society about rightful membership of the family of nations; how sovereignty may be transferred; how state succession should be regulated, when large states break up into smaller, or several states combine into one. It concerns the presuppositions of the region of discourse that international lawyers seek to reduce to juridical system when they write about the recognition of states. It is the answer given by each generation to the fundamental, ever-present question, what are the principles (if any) on which international society is founded?[26]

In the Westphalian system of states that emerged in Europe in the middle of the seventeenth century, the criterion of international legitimacy regarding

[23] Clark, *Legitimacy in International Society* (op. cit), and *International Legitimacy and World Society* (op. cit.), were very helpful for this section.

[24] Alexander Wendt, *Social Theory of International Politics* (Cambridge: Cambridge University Press, 1999), pp. 291–296.

[25] John Gerard Ruggie, *Constructing the World Polity: Essays on International Institutionalization* (London: Routledge, 2002), pp. 137–154. On the international system of city-states (Italy) and territorial estates (Germany), see, for example, Martti Koskenniemi, "Not Excepting the Iroquois Themselves . . . : Sociological Thought and International Law," Max Weber Lecture, Florence (EUI), April 2007.

[26] Wight, "International Legitimacy," in *International Relations* (op. cit.), p. 1.

membership was mainly dynastic[27] until the end of the eighteenth century and the changes brought about by the American and French Revolutions. It was primarily concerned with the status and claims of rulers. However, once the popular-rule principle – shaped around the claims and consent of the people – superseded dynasticism at the national level, it was prone to influence international legitimacy. With the sovereignty of an individual prince passing over to the sovereignty of the people he ruled in the national realm, it was only a matter of time before popular rule would play a role in the recognition of a collective entity as a legitimate member of the international community.[28] During the nineteenth century, particularly relative to the rise of democratic values, nationalities, and nationalism, the self-determination of peoples became an eminent aspect of the popular-rule story, both challenging and supporting statehood.

Yet, it was really the peace settlement of 1919 that marked the birth of national self-determination as a principle in international law. This principle was a key recommendation of Woodrow Wilson's Fourteen Points program. Between the two world wars, self-determination was largely implemented in Europe, whereas the opposition of colonial powers – specifically, Great Britain and France – prevented its application overseas. Nonetheless, after World War II, the colonial powers could not stop self-determination from being an engine of decolonization. Understood as the right of cohesive national groups (i.e., "peoples") to choose for themselves a form of political organization and their relation to other groups,[29] it was instrumental in the international recognition of the countries being liberated from Western domination.[30] Along the way, the number of member states of the international community, which had grown from 42 in the League of Nations in 1920[31] to 51 at the establishment of the UN in 1945, reached 159 by the end of the Cold War

[27] Other kinds of states besides dynastic entities included Venice and the United Provinces of the Low Countries, which assumed the status of sovereign republics. For an historical analysis of the United Provinces, see Jonathan I. Israel, *The Dutch Republic: Its Rise, Greatness, and Fall 1477–1806* (Oxford: Clarendon Press, 1998).

[28] Philip Allott, *Eunomia: New Order for a New World* (Oxford: Oxford University Press, 1990), pp. 306–309, offers a critical interpretation of this phenomenon.

[29] Ian Brownlie, *Principles of International Law* (Oxford: Clarendon Press, 1990), p. 595.

[30] Antonio Cassese, *International Law in a Divided World* (Oxford: Clarendon Press, 1994), pp. 131–137. An overview of the principle of self-determination and its recent evolution is in Jan Klabbers, "The Right to Be Taken Seriously: Self-Determination in International Law," in *Human Rights Quarterly* (Vol. 28, No. 1, February 2006).

[31] During the League of Nations' twenty-six-year history, from 1920 to 1946, after which the League was replaced by the United Nations, a total of sixty-three nations were members at one time or another. Twenty-eight countries were members for the entire period.

in 1990.[32] The fact that in 2008 the UN counted 192 members[33] (i.e., 33 more than 18 years previously) demonstrated that the need to determine who is a legitimate member of the international system – with the function that self-determination has in the process – remains high. In addition, the topic remains as much a source of tension and debate as in the past, which is illustrated by the problems of secession and recognition associated with the Balkan wars in the 1990s[34] and, more recently, the unilateral declaration of independence of Kosovo from Serbia in February 2008[35] and the divisions it created in the UN Security Council.[36]

Over time, access to membership has moved toward universality because of the idea – triggered both by pragmatic and democratic considerations – that the goals of the UN would be best served if all the states of the world were members of the international community. This is in contrast with the time when many non-European polities were empirically sovereign but did not organize their authority according to the standards of "civilization"[37] of the period and, therefore, were left out from what constituted – at least, from the Western viewpoint – the international community of legitimacy. From this perspective, the current requirements for becoming a member of the international system appear quite inclusive. For example, it is not necessary for states to have a specific type of political regime or general identity, as was previously the case when Christianity was considered a foundation for legitimacy. A permanent population, a defined territory, a government, and the capacity to enter into relations with other states[38] – regardless of whether the regime of the country is authoritarian, dictatorial, monarchical, religious, or other – are sufficient.

These basic conditions, however, also form somewhat of a paradox. On the one hand, with popular rule at the root of the present process of international

[32] United Nations, *Growth in United Nations Membership, 1945–Present* (UN official Web site, available at www.un.org/members/growth.shtml, 2008).

[33] Ibid.

[34] Marti Koskenniemi, "National Self-Determination Today: Problems of Legal Theory and Practice," in *International and Comparative Law Quarterly* (Vol. 43, No. 2, April 1994).

[35] Dan Bilefsky, "Kosovo Declares Its Independence from Serbia," *New York Times* (February 18, 2008).

[36] United Nations, *Security Council Discusses Secretary-General's Decision to Reconfigure Kosovo* (United Nations Department of Public Information, News and Media Division, New York, available at www.un.org/News/Press/docs/2008/sc9407.doc.htm, July 25, 2008).

[37] Gerrit W. Gong, *The Standard of "Civilization" in International Society* (Oxford: Oxford University Press, 1984). See also Alexander Wendt, *Social Theory of International Politics* (op. cit.), pp. 292–293.

[38] José E. Alvarez, *International Organizations as Law-Makers* (Oxford: Oxford University Press, 2006), p. 148.

recognition and membership, with most of the progressive UN values being democratic and closely linked to the sovereignty of the people, democracies are seen in the UN more favorably than other political regimes; they may even be perceived as more valid. On the other hand, the importance that the political appeal of universal membership has acquired implies that it is not imperative for a nation to be a democracy in order to be a UN member. Furthermore, the practice of the past forty years of access to UN membership demonstrates that it is possible for an entity to ignore troublesome questions such as whether it is "peace-loving"[39] and truly "able and willing to carry out"[40] all of its UN Charter responsibilities and still be a member.[41]

That said, the inclusiveness and pluralism of membership in today's international community should not mislead us. It is selective; for instance, it does not escape the ideological constraints of the time. Member states are required to be increasingly committed to liberal economics and capitalism. Moreover, and more important, the relative openness of access to international membership is limited, or closed, by the fact that the legitimate type of collective organization is restricted to the state, or the "nation"-state.[42] In this context, most types of social organizations heterogeneous to the one shaped by the state have already been eliminated by or absorbed into the state structure.[43]

[39] Article 4, Paragraph 1, *Charter of the United Nations* (New York: United Nations), p. 6.

[40] Ibid.

[41] Alvarez, *International Organizations as Law-Makers* (op. cit.), p. 149.

[42] On this question, in connection with the distinction between state sovereignty and national sovereignty, see Samuel Barkin & Bruce Cronin, "The State and the Nation: Changing Norms and the Rules of Sovereignty in International Relations," in *International Organizations* (Vol. 48, No. 1, Winter 1994).

[43] See, for instance, Maurice Godelier, *Au fondement des sociétés humaines: Ce que nous apprend l'anthropologie* (Paris: Albin Michel, 2007), pp. 203–204. When, in the aftermath of Australian colonization, Papua New Guinea was created as an independent country in 1975, the Baruya, who live in the eastern highlands, did not regain the sovereignty they had enjoyed on their territory prior to colonization. Having become, without having wanted it, members of a new independent state and of a nation in formation, they were not granted the rights they had enjoyed before colonization, such as the right to exercise justice themselves and to attack their neighbors and take over their territory. The Baruya society became a local tribe, subject to the authority of the state, an institution totally foreign to their ways of thinking. See also Marcelo G. Kohen, *Possession contestée et Souveraineté territoriale* (Paris: Presses Universitaires de France, 1997), and the notion of "uti possidetis, ita possidetis" ("as you possess, you continue to possess"), Chapter 6. In Latin America in the early part of the nineteenth century, it allowed Spanish-American states to inherit the territories that had been acquired by the European colonial powers (i.e., Spain and Portugal) in the administrative limits previously established. In the process, the rights of indigenous peoples – that is, the ones who survived colonization – continued to be denied. Later, after World War II, this notion was used in the context of African decolonization. Newly independent

The fate of indigenous peoples is part of this process. In the words of Benedict Kingsbury:

> "History" has often seemed to leave indigenous peoples not so much as participants and subjects but as marginal objects contained within a much broader account of the nation, prominent perhaps as to customs and folk dances but peripheral in national politics and national law.[44]

In addition, the forms of multilateral politics, whether regional or international,[45] build on the nation-state. They incorporate it and are incorporated into it. With the caveat that it unfolds within the framework of democratic and democratizing states (specifically, the former communist countries of Eastern Europe), the contemporary "postnational" politics of the European Union (EU) is no exception. So too is the rise of the individual on the international scene.

Because the will of the people has historically placed increasing importance on the democratic dimension of state sovereignty, popular rule has become one of the benchmarks of international recognition. Statehood thus helped the individual to gradually evolve into a subject of international law. This development principally occurred in normative terms, with international norms outlining what is owed to individuals but not imposing on states the responsibility of ensuring the implementation. In the aftermath of the Cold War, under the leadership – albeit reluctant[46] – of major democratic powers, humanitarian interventions, establishment of the international criminal tribunals and the International Criminal Court, and discussions that these generated worked on filling the gap. They contributed to the linking of the normative international recognition of individuals with political accountability – that is, making the credibility of states and the international community increasingly measured by their ability to look after people wherever they are. In this regard, although there remains a long way to go before individuals

states did not take into account ethnic or other realities. They respected the administrative delimitations set by colonial powers.

44 Benedict Kingsbury, "'Indigenous Peoples' in International Law: A Constructivist Approach to the Asian Controversy," in *American Journal of International Law* (Vol. 92, No. 3, July 1998), pp. 422–423. This phenomenon recalls the abandonment of popular traditional cultures as Western-based societies progressed: these cultures developed into folklore as they disappeared. On this, see Michel de Certeau, *The Writing of History*, translated by Tom Conley (New York: Columbia University Press, 1988), p. 23.

45 Ruggie, *Constructing the World Polity: Essays on International Institutionalization* (op. cit.), Chapter 4.

46 Coicaud, *Beyond the National Interest: The Future of UN Peacekeeping and Multilateralism in an Era of U.S. Primacy* (op. cit.).

become full-fledged members of the international community, more than ever, they now have a foot in the door.[47]

Right Holding. The second point regarding legitimacy at the international level is how the determination concerning membership in the international system introduces the issue of right holding. Indeed, establishing who is and who is not a member of the international community, who is "in" and who is "out," translates into drawing the line between who is and who is not a right holder. From this perspective being excluded from the international realm of legitimacy historically tended to mean having few or no rights at all at both the collective and individual levels.

The fact that not being recognized as a member of the international community turns into being essentially without rights is, for a collective entity, an imprint of modernity. As discussed previously, a defining trait of the West in most of the past four centuries is that by presenting itself as the embodiment of civilization, it has been prone to deny recognition and right of existence to non-Western, heterogeneous forms of social organizations. Considering that the West has managed to emerge as the champion of the culture of rights, particularly because of democratic values, this situation is somewhat ironic. Furthermore, one must not overlook the dual identity of predatory and humanistic orientations and the constant oscillation between them that has characterized Western relations with other international entities. In any case, from the end of the fifteenth century to the early decades of the twentieth, the disqualification of the legitimacy of other (non-Western) types of social organization by the West has been mainly the rule. For them, denial of membership in the international community of legitimacy has resulted in a rejection of their right to be themselves and to be respected as such.

Surely, when "exotic" societies have been too established to be dismissed altogether, this has not been an easy proposition. In the Far East, for example, China was a country that proved difficult to disregard entirely, having received favorable attention in the West in the seventeenth and first half of the eighteenth centuries because of the broad dissemination of books and published correspondence by Catholic (especially Jesuit) missionaries.[48] The negative view of China that developed in the second part of the eighteenth

[47] Mervyn Frost, *Constituting Human Rights: Global Civil Society and the Society of Democratic States* (London: Routledge, 2002), pp. 137–138; and Ian Clark, *International Legitimacy and World Society* (op. cit.), pp. 193–196.

[48] Etiemble, *L'Europe Chinoise*, Volume I: *De L'empire Romain à Leibniz* (Paris: éd. Gallimard, 1988); Volume II: *De la sinophilie à la sinophobie* (Paris: éd. Gallimard, 1989), for example, p. 27.

century[49] and the deepening of China's structural problems throughout the nineteenth century paved the way for a colonial mentality toward it. However, what had been a high-value target for Western powers could not be totally appropriated. The treaty system, initiated by the 1842 Treaty of Nanjing forced on China by Britain, led the Qing dynasty (which would rule until 1912) to lose control of vital elements of Chinese commercial, social, and foreign policies[50] and furthered the internal crisis. As a country and a culture, however, China survived.

This example contrasts with other cases in which – the asymmetry of power being absolutely to the advantage of the West – there was no stopping the dismissal and exploitation of non-Western societies. Once a judgment of illegitimacy had been pronounced on these societies, once they were said to be out of the realm of international legitimacy determined by the West, the floodgates were opened for the European states to pursue aggressive expansion in spheres of influence and territorial appropriation. The fate of Africa from the 1870s onward is as an illustration of this aggression. In 1876, territories under European colonial rule occupied 11 percent of the African Continent; by 1890, it was 90 percent.[51] As Achille Mbembe stated:

> [C]olonial sovereignty... regarded itself as the sole power to judge its laws – whence its one-sidedness, especially as... its supreme right was (by its capacity to assume the act of destroying) simultaneously the supreme denial of right.... Colonial sovereignty... [f]irst... eliminated all distinction between ends and means; depending on circumstances... sovereign violence was its own end and came with its own "instructions for use." Second, it introduced virtually infinite permutations between what was just and what was unjust, between right and not-right. Thus, in regard to colonial sovereignty, right was on *one* side. And it was seized in the very act of occurring. In face of it, there could only be "wrong" and infraction. Anything that did not recognize this

49 Ibid., Volume II, pp. 341–342 and 380–382.

50 Jonathan D. Spence, *The Search for Modern China* (New York: W.W. Norton, & Company, 1999), pp. 160–166. This was illustrated by extensive "concession" areas made available for British, French, and other foreign settlements and the principle of extraterritoriality (i.e., the right to be judged by one's own national law in criminal cases on Chinese soil) adopted for the benefit of Western powers (ibid., pp. 163–164). On the question of extraterritoriality, see Kal Raustiala, *Does the Constitution Follow the Flag?* (Oxford: Oxford University Press, forthcoming). In Chapter 3, Kal Raustiala describes the work of the "United States District Court for China," which was created and commenced operation in 1906. The District Court was a federal court and it answered to the Ninth Circuit and had jurisdiction over the whole of China and Korea, although it was headquartered in Shanghai. The United States District Court for China came to an end with World War II and was formally disbanded in 1943.

51 Yasuaki Onuma, "When Was the Law of International Society Born? An Inquiry of the History of International Law from an Intercivilizational Perspective," in *Journal of the History of International Law* (Vol. 2, 2000), pp. 39–50.

> violence as authority, that contested its protocols, was savage and outlaw.... This is why the colonial state... did not rule out either the exercise of naked force against the native or the destruction of the forms of social organization that existed prior to its arrival – even their "recycling" for ends other than those for which they had once been instituted. The lack of justice of the means, and the lack of legitimacy of the ends, conspired to allow an arbitrariness and intrinsic unconditionality that may be said to have been the distinctive feature of colonial sovereignty.[52]

As the international demarcation of legitimacy and illegitimacy enabled the denial of rights to certain political communities, it followed that members of these communities suffered the same fate. The invalidation of the collective entity, the stripping of the legitimacy it had enjoyed in its own international cultural area, brought about the invalidation of its people. Colonization at its worst in Africa was the epitome of this state of affairs. The specific humanity and rights of the colonized, in the social form of community to which they belonged, were canceled and not replaced by a new type of humanity or rights. Naming or renaming[53] and making an individual a tool at the service of Western greed[54] were part of a process of depersonalization in which the individual self of the colonized person was lost as he or she was lumped into an undifferentiated group. Undoubtedly, this must have been facilitated by the fact that Africans at one time were traded as a commodity – that is, as slaves.[55] Ultimately, the colonized exist but not really, because humans alone exist. To quote Achille Mbembe again:

> In the colonial principle of rationality, the native is... that *thing that is, but only as so far as it is nothing.* And it is at this point where the thingness and its nothingness meet that the native's identity lies. The work of the colonizer will henceforward consist in self-representing that thingness and nothingness, *what* they are and *how* they are. As for the native, it will only be possible to represent him or her within these two categories outside which he/she no longer has constituted form.[56]

The determination of legitimacy and illegitimacy at the international level leading to the distinction between societies and its members who do and

[52] Achille Mbembe, *On the Postcolony* (Berkeley: University of California Press, 2001), pp. 25–26.

[53] Ibid., p. 186. See also Godelier, *Au fondement des sociétés humaines: Ce que l'anthropologie nous apprend* (op. cit.), p. 204, footnote 1.

[54] Adam Hochschild, *King Leopold's Ghost: A Story of Greed, Terror, and Heroism in Colonial Africa* (Boston: Mariner Books/Houghton Mifflin Company, 1999).

[55] On the slave trade, to which African societies were themselves part and parcel, see Olivier Pétré-Grenouilleau, *Les traites négrières: Essai d'histoire globale* (Paris: éd. Gallimard, 2004).

[56] Mbembe, *On the Postcolony* (op. cit.), p. 187.

do not have rights has not taken place exclusively in the situations discussed here. International denial of rights for collectivities and people based on the difference between the civilized (legitimate) and the uncivilized (illegitimate) has happened in other circumstances. During World War II, the treatment of Eastern European countries and their populations by the Nazi regime is one example. Having rejected principles of international law such as universality and equality of states,[57] Hitler saw the ruthless domination of the East and expansion of "living space," or *Lebensraum*,[58] as a self-evident right for Germany. His racism fit this approach. Among the inferior races, he viewed the Slavs as degraded and unable to appreciate Western values; the lowest were the Jews, in great numbers in that part of Europe. The fact that Hitler identified them with Bolshevism, linking old anti-Semitic stereotypes with anti-communism, was another reason for the Jews to be a primary target.[59] Because this meant that Eastern European countries and their people had basically no rights, the conduct of the war on this front differed drastically from that of the Western Front.[60] Humanitarian considerations and the traditional norms of behavior of the professional soldier (including not killing civilian populations and treating captured soldiers as prisoners of war [POWs]) did not apply. In addition, the Third Reich sought to establish a colonial empire,[61] planning to achieve in the East what other European powers had realized overseas.[62] To arrive at this objective, the Third Reich stood ready to impose on the conquered the method of rules and policies of

[57] On international law and Nazism, see John H. Herz, "The National Socialist Doctrine of International Law and the Problems of International Organization," in *Political Science Quarterly* (Vol. 54, No. 4, December 1939); and Detlev F. Vagts, "International Law in the Third Reich," in *American Journal of International Law* (Vol. 84, No. 3, 1990).

[58] On the history and Hitler's conception of *Lebensraum*, see Woodruff D. Smith, *The Ideological Origins of Nazi Imperialism* (Oxford: Oxford University Press, 1986), Chapters 9 and 10.

[59] Christopher R. Browning indicates that "for Hitler, Bolshevism was merely the most recent and nefarious manifestation of the eternal Jewish threat. His anti-Bolshevism was a derivative of his racist anti-Semitism." Christopher R. Browning with contributions by Jürgen Matthäus, *The Origins of the Final Solution: The Evolution of Nazi Jewish Policy, September 1939–March 1942* (Lincoln: University of Nebraska Press, 2004), p. 224.

[60] Omer Bartov, *Hitler's Army: Soldiers, Nazis, and War in the Third Reich* (Oxford: Oxford University Press, 1990).

[61] Götz Aly & Susanne Heim, *The Architects of Annihilation: Auschwitz and the Logic of Destruction*, translated by A. G. Blunden (London: Weidenfeld & Nicolson, 2003), Chapter 12.

[62] For more on the connection between nineteenth-century European imperialism and racism and twentieth-century totalitarianism, see Sven Lindquist, *Exterminate All the Brutes* (New York: New Press, 1996), Part IV; and Annegret Ehman, "From Colonial Racism to Nazi Population Policy: The Role of the So-Called Mischlinge," in Michael Berenbaum & Abraham J. Peck (eds.), *The Holocaust and History: The Known, the Unknown, the Disputed, and the Reexamined* (Bloomington: Indiana University Press, 1998).

population decimation that Western Europeans had hitherto inflicted outside Europe.[63]

Finally, in the war against terror, the designation of the al Qaeda and Taliban prisoners detained by the United States as "unlawful combatants,"[64] following their presentation as "enemy combatants,"[65] has not been foreign either to distinguishing between legitimate and illegitimate political communities and their members, and making the latter rightless.

As Nathaniel Berman noted, the use of this expression in the 2000s by the Bush administration was tantamount to putting many of the detainees beyond the reach of any law at all.[66] This meant that they did not merit the protections of criminal law because of their combatant activities, and they did not merit the protections of *jus in bello* because of the unlawful nature of their combat. Neither criminal suspects nor POWs, and not entitled to *habeas corpus*,[67] they were committed to the caprice of unreviewable state power.[68] This approach was not new; indeed, the issues associated with the

[63] Browning with contributions by Matthäus, *The Origins of the Final Solution: The Evolution of Nazi Jewish Policy, September 1939–March 1942* (op. cit.), p. 14.

[64] "Based on the facts supplied by the Department of Defense and the recommendation of the Department of Justice, I determine that the Taliban detainees are unlawful combatants and, therefore, do not qualify as prisoners of war under Article 4 of Geneva. I note that, because Geneva does not apply to our conflict with al Qaeda, al Qaeda detainees also do not qualify as prisoners of war." George W. Bush, "Memo 11. Human Treatment of al Qaeda and Taliban Detainees," The White House, February 7, 2002, in Karen J. Greenberg & Joshua L. Dratel (eds.), *The Torture Papers: The Road to Abu Ghraib* (Cambridge: Cambridge University Press, 2005), p. 135.

[65] The definition of "enemy combatant" by the Bush administration has evolved over time but, in short, it means anyone who is supporting the Taliban and al Qaeda forces or associated forces engaging in hostilities against the United States and its coalition partners. See Mark Denbeaux, with Joshua Denbeaux, David Gratz, John Gregorek, Matthew Darby, Shana Edwards, Shane Hartman, Daniel Mann, & Helen Skinner, *Report on Guantanamo Detainees: A Profile of 517 Detainees through Analysis of Department of Defense Data* (Newark, NJ: Seton Hall University School of Law, 2006). For the official definitions of "unlawful enemy combatant" and "lawful enemy combatant," see *Military Commissions Act of 2006*, Public Law 109–366, October 17, 2006, Chapter 47A – Military Commissions: Subchapter I – General Provisions: Paragraph 948a, Definitions.

[66] Nathaniel Berman, "Privileging Combat? Contemporary Conflict and the Legal Construction of War," in *Columbia Journal of Transnational Law* (Vol. 43, No. 1, 2004), p. 13.

[67] Habeas corpus is the legal concept according to which a prisoner has a right to challenge the basis of confinement – to demand that the government produce a valid reason for detention. Habeas corpus has been a part of the American legal system since colonial times and it cannot be suspended "unless when in cases of Rebellion and Invasion the public safety may require it" (Article 1, Section 9 of the United States Constitution), www.archives.gov/exhibits/charters/print˙friendly.html?page=constitution˙transcript. Habeas corpus has been suspended a number of times, most notably by Abraham Lincoln during the early days of the Civil War.

[68] Ibid., p. 13. It is interesting that *The National Defense Strategy of the United States* of 2005 mentions "judicial processes" as a "strategy of the weak" under a heading called "our

term *unlawful combatant* (Berman prefers *unprivileged combatant*[69]) and the controversies they generate refer to the inherent fact that war is a legal construction with specific implications. This legal construction defines what is and what is not a legitimate form of violence (i.e., what is a war), as well as who is and who is not a legitimate combatant. Because today this construction remains grounded in the state – in the statist bias that shapes what is seen as a legitimate collective entity – war as a legitimate form of violence is principally understood as an interstate conflict between recognized public entities.[70] In the course of this operation, the rights of some are recognized and those of others are denied. With the Bush administration framing the war against terror in terms of a struggle between what it considered the embodiment of legitimacy (i.e., Western civilization) and the enemies of civilization,[71] it was all the more inclined to use this conception of war and its consequences concerning allocation of rights. The Bush administration was even more inclined to label suspected terrorists unlawful combatants. Being perceived as out of the realm of legitimacy, they did not qualify to benefit from the cardinal principle of the law of war, the "equality of belligerents"; the view was that a civilized handling was not owed to them.[72]

vulnerabilities," *The National Defense Strategy of the United States of America* (Washington, DC: Department of Defense, March 2005), p. 6. Note also George W. Bush: "After the chaos and carnage of September 11th, it is not enough to serve our enemies with legal papers," *State of the Union* (Washington, DC: The White House, January 20, 2004).

69 Ibid., p. 14.

70 For more on the definition of war and its contestation, especially in connection with anti-colonial and anti-colonial struggles, see Berman, "Privileging Combat? Contemporary Conflict and the Legal Construction of War," in *Columbia Journal of Transnational Law* (op. cit.), pp. 15–37.

71 *The National Security Strategy of the United States of America* (Washington, DC: The White House, September 2002), Foreword, p. 2. George W. Bush, *State of the Union* (Washington, DC: The White House, January 28, 2003), p. 7, www.whitehouse.gov/news/releases/2003/01/print/20030128–1.

72 The U.S. Supreme Court rejected, on June 29, 2006, this approach by the Bush administration. A few months later, Congress, then controlled by Republicans, responded by passing, on September 22, 2006, the Military Commissions Act, which stripped the federal courts of jurisdiction to hear habeas corpus petitions filed by detainees challenging the basis of their confinement. Instead, such challenges were to be governed by the December 31, 2005, Detainee Treatment Act, which allowed detainees to appeal decisions of the military tribunals to the District of Columbia Circuit, but only under circumscribed procedures, including a presumption that the evidence before the military tribunal was accurate and complete. However, in June 2008, in a 5-to-4 decision, the Supreme Court ruled this to be unconstitutional, declaring that foreign terrorism suspects held at the Guantánamo Bay naval base in Cuba have the right to challenge their detention there in U.S. federal courts. For an analysis of this latter decision, see James Ross, "Supreme Court to Bush: You're Not Above the Law," *Human Rights Watch*, hrw.org/english/docs/2008/06/13/usint19126˙txt/htm. On this question in connection with the issue of territoriality in American law in general, see Raustiala, *Does the Constitution Follow the Flag?* (op. cit.), Chapter 7.

Hierarchy of Right Holders. When actors, collective and individual, are recognized as part of the community of international legitimacy, it is not implied that as right holders they are equal. Even in the contemporary international system, committed as it is, in principle, to equality, hierarchy applied to right holding is a fact of life.

The political hierarchy among states is an indication of this. Nondemocratic regimes (e.g., dictatorships or de facto governments) have a lower international standing than democracies and, in the process, they tend to debilitate the rights of their country. Eliciting less international respect, they are more likely than a democratic regime, for example, to have their sovereignty challenged by a collective intervention.[73] The war against Iraq illustrates this point. To be sure, the Bush and Blair administrations' arguments concerning violations of human rights by Iraqi leadership as justification for invasion did not appear genuine.[74] Yet, one has to admit that the oppressive nature of Saddam Hussein's regime did not help its case. Although the existence of weapons of mass destruction (WMD) in Iraq could not be proved,[75] a track record of violence against Iraqi people and others, combined with the factor of instability in the region, played into the hands of the American–British push for war. It contributed to weakening Iraq's sovereignty.

Internationally, the power hierarchy that separates states is another fact of life: major states have more international weight than weak states and, therefore, arguably a greater legitimacy. Furthermore, major states do not have to be democratic to have a louder voice. The international community most likely will not stay passive vis-à-vis a small country ignoring international norms, particularly if it is nondemocratic and not supported by a strong power. However, powerful countries are prone to be exonerated as can medium- or small-sized countries when they have the backing of big powers. Consider Russia, which successfully opposed the UN's interference regarding its nonrespect of human rights in the two wars in Chechnya since the early 1990s[76]; or consider Israel and its decades-long policy of nuclear ambiguity.[77] Whereas

[73] Roth, *Governmental Illegitimacy in International Law* (Oxford: Oxford University Press, 1999), pp. 30–33; and Fernando R. Tesón, *A Philosophy of International Law* (Boulder, CO: Westview Press, 1998), Chapter 2.

[74] Bob Woodward, *Plan of Attack* (New York: Simon & Schuster, 2004), p. 291; and John Kampfner, *Blair's Wars* (London: Free Press, 2003), p. 225.

[75] Hans Blix, *Disarming Iraq* (New York: Pantheon Books, 2004), pp. 176–178.

[76] For an overview of post–Cold War Russian foreign policy, see Ekaterina Stepanova, "Cultures of Solidarity and National Interest: Russia's Conflict Management Policies," in Jean-Marc Coicaud & Nicholas J. Wheeler (eds.), *National Interest and International Solidarity: Particular and Universal Ethics in International Life* (Tokyo: United Nations University Press, 2008), pp. 87–119.

[77] Israel has neither officially confirmed nor denied that it possesses nuclear weapons. Because it has never signed the Nuclear Non-proliferation Treaty (NPT), designed to prevent the global

the United States does not make an issue of Israel's weapons program, it insists that other countries – notably prewar Iraq, Iran, and Syria – are a threat to peace because of their alleged WMD. This has led Arab states in the Middle East to accuse the United States of operating a double-standard regional approach.[78]

This hierarchy among actors in the daily reality of the international system has much to do with the norms of socialization of international life and the power structure they establish among right holders. The analysis of the fundamental principles governing international relations – which comprise the apex of the entire body of international legislation – and the hierarchy of right holders they establish are helpful for understanding this situation.

Fundamental Principles and the Hierarchy of Right Holders. The principles are as follows: sovereign equality of states, self-determination of peoples, prohibition of the threat or use of force, peaceful settlement of disputes, nonintervention in the internal or external affairs of other states, respect for human rights, international cooperation, and good faith.[79] Each principle is

spread of nuclear weapons, it is not subject to inspections and the threat of sanctions by the UN watchdog, the International Atomic Energy Agency (IAEA). For an assessment of Israeli nuclear forces, see Shannon N. Kile, Vitaly Fedchenko, & Hans M. Kristensen, "Appendix 8A: World Nuclear Forces, 2008," in *Sipri Yearbook 2008: Armaments, Disarmament, and International Security* (London: Oxford University Press, 2008), pp. 396–397.

78 On the Arab states' concerns about the Israeli nuclear weapons program, see M. Cherif Bassiouni, *Documents on the Arab–Israeli Conflict*, Volume 1: *Emergence of Conflict in Palestine and the Arab–Israeli Wars and Peace Process* (Ardsley, NY: Transnational Publishers Inc., 2005), Chapter V. See also Cecilia Albin, *Justice and Fairness in International Negotiation* (Cambridge: Cambridge University Press, 2001), Chapter 6.

79 See the "Declaration on Principles of International Law Concerning Friendly Relations and Cooperation among States, in Accordance with the Charter of the United Nations," adopted by consensus in the UN General Assembly on October 24, 1970 (New York: United Nations, UN General Assembly Resolution 2625). For a study of the fundamental principles, see Antonio Cassese, *International Law in a Divided World* (Oxford: Clarendon Press, 1994), pp. 126–165. For another perspective, see Hedley Bull, *The Anarchical Society: A Study of Order in World Politics* (New York: Columbia University Press, 1995), pp. 64–68. On the occasion of the World Summit held at the UN in the fall of 2005, the heads of state and government rededicated themselves to the spirit of the basic guidelines for the life of the whole community, *2005 World Summit Outcome: Resolution Adopted by the General Assembly* (New York: United Nations, A/Res/60/1, October 24, 2005), Section 1, Paragraph 5, p. 1: "We are determined to establish a just and lasting peace all over the world in accordance with the purposes and principles of the Charter. We rededicate ourselves to support all efforts to uphold the sovereign equality of all States, respect their territorial integrity and political independence, to refrain in our international relations from the threat or use of force in any manner inconsistent with the purposes and principles of the United Nations, to uphold resolution of disputes by peaceful means and in conformity with the principles of justice and international law, the right to self-determination of peoples which remain

a piece of international legitimacy, of the aggregate of legitimacies that international legitimacy is,[80] working on socializing international affairs. From this perspective, each principle constitutes a value-ideal with which international actors – states and increasingly nonstate actors, including individuals – identify; that is, a value-ideal for which integration in international law is viewed as indispensable for actors to feel that there is room for them to be represented and to participate in the quest for a workable and equitable system of international relations. That is, by empowering international actors, fundamental principles are sources, expressions, and tools of legitimacy at the international level.

The empowerment rests on the closely intertwining and coordinating principles in the sense that actors must comply with all of them but also in the sense that in the application of any of them, all the others must simultaneously be borne in mind.[81] Still, two layers are distinguishable in the empowering mechanism that revolves around, directly or indirectly, both the state and the people. The first layer deals with the elementary but crucial goal of securing the existence and coexistence of states. Sovereign equality of states, prohibition of the threat or use of force, peaceful settlement of disputes, nonintervention in the internal or external affairs of other states, international cooperation, and good faith pursue this objective. The second layer has a more qualified character; it concerns the quality of empowerment within states. Principles concerned with the democratic aspects of international relations, such as self-determination of peoples and respect for human rights, are in this category.

Although these fundamental principles are essential for the framework of international legitimacy that they help establish, they are not on an equal plane. There is hierarchy among the principles, with some prevailing over others. This is especially evident when difficult policy choices must be made in the international realm. This hierarchy among principles parallels the hierarchy among actors that are international right holders. Unpacking the types of relations existing among fundamental principles – that is, compatibility,

under colonial domination and foreign occupation, non-interference in the internal affairs of States, respect for human rights and fundamental freedoms, respect for the equal rights of all without distinction as to race, sex, language or religion, international cooperation in solving international problems of an economic, social, cultural or humanitarian character and the fulfillment in good faith of the obligations assumed in accordance with the Charter."

80 For legitimacy, both national and international, as an aggregate of various legitimacies, see Francois Furet, *The Passing of an Illusion: The Idea of Communism in the Twentieth Century*, translated by Deborah Furet (Chicago: University of Chicago Press, 2000), particularly Chapter 1.

81 Cassese, *International Law in a Divided World* (op. cit.), p. 160.

competition, and hierarchy – brings clarity to these relations. Doing so is all the more important considering that these relations enable the principles at the core of international law and, therefore, international law itself, to participate in the socialization of international life.

The merit of compatibility is to ensure that fundamental principles complement one another and point in the same direction. Short of this, the sustainability if not the possibility of any system of law – international or national – is at risk. There is compatibility among the principles of sovereign equality of states, prohibition of the threat or use of force, peaceful settlements of disputes, and nonintervention in the internal and external affairs of other states. Self-determination of peoples and respect for human rights are compatible as well,[82] as are the principles of good faith and cooperation. Good faith conveys the idea that states must not take advantage of their rights or discharge their obligations so as to thwart the purpose and object of international legal rules. They must not betray the expectations created in other states by international rules; neither must they ridicule by their behavior the confidence that relevant international norms have given to their fellow states.[83] In other words, without good faith, trust and consequently cooperation are not conceivable.

Competitive relationships among fundamental principles are problematic but essential. They are problematic because they cause tensions. However, competitive principles cannot be omitted; like compatible principles, they are ideal-values that are strategic, part of international legitimacy. Furthermore, as long as mobilizing these principles does not upset the international legal framework, they provide alternative views from within the system. As such, they offer flexibility and maneuvering space in the handling of international demands that, more than a rigid total convergence of principles, helps preserve the overall architecture of the international system. Competition among fundamental principles tends to be found between sovereign equality of states and nonintervention in the internal and external affairs of other states, on the one hand, and self-determination of peoples and respect for human rights on the other. The former reflects the traditional Westphalian model of international relations and refers to the most basic requirements of

[82] Self-determination of peoples does not necessarily serve respect for human rights. As part of the dynamics of nationalism and the mixture of inclusive solidarity and exclusive particularism that it is, it can play a contradictory role: asking for rights of people to be respected but also, with nationalist forces clashing, being a source of violations of human rights. See Koskenniemi, "National Self-Determination Today: Problems of Legal Theory and Practice" (op. cit.); and Berman, *Passions et ambivalences: Le colonialisme, le nationalisme et le droit international* (op. cit.), pp. 393–401.

[83] Cassese, *International Law in a Divided World* (op. cit.), pp. 152–153.

states' coexistence. The latter, indicative of the post-Westphalian pattern, is the product of new trends that emerged in the world community after World War I and particularly after World War II, partly deriving from Third World advocacy and partly from the universalization of Western democratic values.

Against this background, hierarchy is crucial. Its function is to organize the relations among principles according to priorities, with some predominating without overlooking those that come in second. The focus and the difficulty of the task of hierarchy consist in ranking the principles in competition and ordering their coexistence. It is a balancing act that amounts to not only identifying prevailing principles but also the commanding international right holder.

International Actors and the Hierarchy of Right Holders. The principles firmly rooted in the Westphalian model – that is, sovereign equality of states and nonintervention in the internal and external affairs of other states – are those that have benefited from greater consideration in the international system. This is epitomized by the respect commanded by the principle of sovereign equality of states; indeed, this principle has always been construed by all states along the same lines and has not generated major differences in its interpretation. This has led the state to be the primary international right holder, from which other right holders depend and around which they revolve. As the primary beneficiary of the hierarchy among fundamental principles, the state has been the cornerstone of a system of law, both internationally and nationally, designed to make it the main agency and secure this status.

From this privileged standing follows the fact that the possibility, defense, and evolution of the international system, to a large extent, cannot be dissociated from the state. This applies as well to the rise of principles belonging to the new pattern, the post-Westphalian model. Without the help of the state, even if at times it had to be pressured to go along, the principles of self-determination of peoples, peaceful settlement of disputes, respect for human rights, and cooperation would not have officially become part of international law.[84] In this regard, because state agency entails looking after people, the state has been involved with the individual becoming an increasingly significant right holder at the international level.

It is also in this context of the "old" participating in its own transformation in the emergence of the "new" that the norms and institutions of international

[84] Cassese argues that good faith, although it has been revitalized in recent debates and now enjoys wide support among developing countries, is strongly embedded in the Westphalian pattern of international relations; ibid., p. 159.

and regional governance may be understood. They have been established with the involvement of the state and they continue to rely on it. In this perspective, powerful states can be a cause of weakness for international and regional organizations – for instance, forcing them to live in their shadow or to become instruments of their interest. Ultimately, however, international and regional organizations are prone to be as strong as their supporting states, including in the pursuit of their global and regional public-good mandates and goals. The North Atlantic Treaty Organization (NATO) is an aspect of this phenomenon, as is the disparity of capability between the European Union (EU) and the Southern Cone Common Market (MERCOSUR).[85]

This also shows that if the state is the primary international right holder, there are other international actors. Other international actors exist whose development was facilitated by the state and who remain closely connected to it; however, those actors with a growing right-holding status are also increasingly challenging the state. This introduces a sense of fluidity in the hierarchy among fundamental principles and international right holders that makes it impossible to continue viewing the primacy of the state as a given. This brings about changes in the sources and benchmarks of legitimacy as well, both nationally and internationally.

The rise and impact of the individual as a right holder in international life, contradicting the Westphalian characteristics of international order, are testimony to this change, as are the push for more democratization in politics in the national and international realms and the pressure that the defense of human rights is putting on national sovereignty in the aftermath of the Cold War. In this regard, with the humanitarian interventions of the 1990s and the seal of approval that the notion of "Responsibility to Protect"[86] received in 2005, the state is being asked to embrace further the idea that people, not

[85] On how going beyond the state at the regional level requires a well-institutionalized state, see Philippe de Lombaerde (ed.), *Multilateralism, Regionalism, and Bilateralism in Trade and Investment* (Dordrecht, The Netherlands: Springer, 2007), pp. 99–125.

[86] The *2005 World Summit Outcome*, A/RES/60/1 (New York: United Nations, 24 October 2005) recognized, under the notion of "responsibility to protect," the possibility for the international community to use appropriate diplomatic, humanitarian, and other peaceful means, in accordance with Chapters VI and VIII of the Charter, but also, if necessary, to take collective action, in a timely and decisive fashion, through the Security Council, in accordance with the Charter, including Chapter VII, on a case-by-case basis and in cooperation with relevant regional organizations as appropriate, should peaceful means be inadequate and national authorities are manifestly failing to protect their population from genocide, war crimes, ethnic cleansing, and crimes against humanity (p. 30, paragraphs 138 and 139). See also *A More Secure World: Our Shared Responsibility: Report of the High-Level Panel on Threats, Challenges, and Change*, A/59/565 (New York: United Nations, 2 December 2004), p. 66, paragraph 203.

states, are the ultimate beneficiary. The state is being asked to come to terms with the fact that its legitimacy at the national and international levels should rest primarily on being responsible and accountable to individuals.

The challenge that international and regional organizations constitute for the state on the institutional front may help it to "step up to the plate," so to speak.

International organizations are transforming the rules of the game. They have and continue to transform the international sources of law; their substantive content; the actors that make them, including states; and the ways states are compelling, persuading, or otherwise enticing relevant actors (no longer just fellow nation-states) to comply with international standards.[87] They do so while, despite their general entitlement to international legal personality, they are denied the power all nation-states inherently have as international legal persons (e.g., the plenary power to conclude treaties on any topic) and are not fully "supranational."[88] At the same time, notwithstanding their darker edge and the risks they carry,[89] international organizations have the broad mandate of serving people in the fields of international security, development, and others.

This role at the service of individuals is that of regional organizations as well. With them, arguably, the strain on the state can be even greater, as the EU illustrates. In the dynamics of mutual influence between national and European law, the latter has an increasing impact on the former.[90] For instance, EU directives can have direct effect and treaty obligations on member states of the Council of Europe to change domestic law in conformity with rulings issued by the European Court of Human Rights (ECHR).[91] However, this is also an expression of the commitment of the European project to regional public policy. It demonstrates that regardless of the "democratic deficit" that afflicts it, its ambition concerning public service is serious.

Likewise, international nongovernmental organizations (INGOs), an integral part of the process of "destatization" or decentralization, can support the state in achieving more accountability vis-à-vis individuals because they have mandated themselves to make the world better. Particularly, without being

[87] Alvarez, *International Organizations as Law-makers* (op. cit.), pp. 588–627.

[88] Ibid., pp. 15–16.

[89] Ibid., pp. 627–645.

[90] Mireille Delmas-Marty, *Les forces imaginantes du droit. II: Le pluralisme ordonné* (Paris: éd. Du Seuil, 2006), pp. 71–77 and 156–159.

[91] Alvarez, *International Organizations as Law-makers* (op. cit.), p. 16 and pp. 474–480. For an analysis of the evolution of law in the EU environment, see Francois Ost & Michel van de Kerchove, *De la pyramide au réseau? Pour une théorie dialectique du droit* (Brussels: Publications des Facultés Universitaires Saint-Louis, 2002), pp. 65–78.

necessarily a pure good in this area,[92] they are playing a positive function for human rights.[93]

Nevertheless, there are domains in which the state is relinquishing control where it is less clear that the trend is aiming at and reconcilable with the welfare of people. Accompanying if not fueling globalization, the internationalized corporate sector is one of these domains. Because the state borrows from national, international, and transnational sources to establish rules and regulations fitting its needs, the state is more often than not left with little choice but to align itself, whatever the cost to individuals.[94]

The rearrangement of hierarchy among international right holders, however, must not lead us to lose sight of the fact that the state remains the building block of the international system. After all, the global accountability of political institutions that is emerging in favor of people continues to be more of an ideal than a reality. Although progress is being made, at the international level, victims of major crimes still cannot be certain that action will be taken to bring perpetrators to justice.

To be sure, the state is far from perfect. Its agency, having at the same time positive and negative effects, can generate conflict and anomie internationally as much as socialize international life – or, it can as much violate human rights as protect individuals. However, until other international actors can replace the positive role of the state and prove to be better at it, the state will remain indispensable. The negative use of state power will not be sufficient to displace the state from its current relevance. Indeed, one lesson to draw from fragile, much less failed states – where lack of reliable institutions renders the protection of people's basic human rights impossible – is that a world without states is not an enviable situation.[95]

Furthermore, it is telling that the development of new international right holders is principally taking place under the leadership of the West, where the state – beyond its various ideological leanings – is highly institutionalized. It is

[92] Daniel A. Bell & Jean-Marc Coicaud (eds.) *Ethics in Action: The Ethical Challenges of International Human Rights Non-governmental Organizations* (Cambridge: Cambridge University Press, 2007), for example, Chapter 1.

[93] Jean-Marc Coicaud, "Conclusion: INGOs as Collective Mobilization of Transnational Solidarity: Implications for Human Rights Work at the United Nations," in Bell & Coicaud (eds.), *Ethics in Action: The Ethical Challenges of International Human Rights Non-governmental Organizations* (op. cit.), pp. 279–301.

[94] Mireille Delmas-Marty, *Les forces imaginantes du droit: Le relatif et l'universel* (Paris: éd. du Seuil, 2004), pp. 96–103.

[95] Sandra Eugène, "Droits fondamentaux et critères de fragilité des Etats," in Jean-Marc Châtaigner & Hervé Magro, *Etats et sociétés fragiles: Entre conflits, reconstruction et développement* (Paris: éd. Karthala, 2007), pp. 41–54.

as if destatization requires not only vibrant non-state actors but also relatively well-functioning institutions allowing non-state actors to be vibrant.

Rather than marking its ultimate demise, the state's current loss of ground due to increased competition from other international actors is probably therefore the latest instance of interactions between the state and other right holders in the evolving history of post-Westphalian society.[96] There is no doubt that this time, it is an exceptionally dramatic interaction. It is therefore eroding the previously mentioned distinctions that comprise the framework in which international relations and international legitimacy evolve – that is, the inside/outside, universalist/particularist, system/society distinctions. It is even more so the case considering that this is part of a larger movement that tends to threaten classical legal and political thought and order as a whole by diluting the main dichotomies on which it was founded: public/private, autonomy/heteronomy, and others.[97] Yet, the present moment does not completely erase the formative distinctions of the international system; neither is it eliminating the need for them.[98] If anything, it is an indication that with the plurality of international right holders and the legitimacy to which each aspires and endeavors to convey, international legitimacy has become more complex, more of a hybrid. As discussed in the next two sections, this complicates the task of determining appropriate international conduct – namely, with the resulting dilemmas – and identifying the legitimate international authority and its role. However, it does not suspend the imperative of pursuing it; on the contrary, it underlines the importance of taking this task at hand for the construction of legitimacy in international order.

International Rightful Conduct. It is logical that the hierarchy among international right holders, itself associated with the hierarchy among fundamental principles, translates primarily into the issue of determining the rightful conduct for the state internationally. There are three main reasons for this. First, when an actor is ranked as a top international right holder, which happens to be the case with the state, its preservation is important. This entails defining the international conduct that will make this preservation possible. Second, allocating the state the highest position as an international right

[96] By focusing on the interlocking relations between international society (for the most part, the realm of the governmental and the official [p. 6]) and world society (the realm of the individual, of the nonofficial group or movement, and of the transnational network of nongovernmental agents [p. 6]), Clark's book, *International Legitimacy and World Society* (op. cit.), studies an aspect of this history; pp. 209–214 are especially illuminating.

[97] Ost & van de Kerchove, *De la pyramide au réseau? Pour une théorie dialectique du droit* (op. cit.), pp. 125–182.

[98] Ibid., pp. 179–182.

holder amounts to recognizing and constructing it as a key international agency, essential for the maintenance of the international system. Entirely denying the rights of the state as a top right holder would mean dismantling its power as an agent, rendering it unable to perform a useful function in support of the international system, and signaling that the overall stability and legitimacy of the system is in question. Third, conservation of the state and the international order in which it exists demand protection of each state from other states. This structures the identification of rightful conduct in the international realm principally around the rights and, more crucially, the duties or obligations of states toward one another.

However, as actors other than the state emerge as significant international right holders, rightful conduct cannot be limited to these elements. It must factor in what type of behavior, notably from the state, is required vis-à-vis the other actors to ensure respect of their rights. A crucial part of this story is how this has come to include the state's attitude concerning the individual, both within and across borders. Ultimately, because rightful conduct does not flow naturally, the need to engineer it, in a variety of ways, introduces the issue of international authority.

Rightful Conduct and Interstate Relations. Regarding the rightful conduct of states relative to other states, the following consideration helps to clarify the topic: the more that states are recognized as top international right holders, the more their power must be constrained. The rights of each state must be protected from other states' power – that is, the level of duties imposed on a state vis-à-vis others is an indicator of the level of right each state is enjoying. The more that states have duties toward one another and the more stringent rightful conduct there is among states, the greater are their rights. Historically, the track record shows that states' rights are taken more seriously when they are embedded in a dynamic of reciprocity of rights and duties among states. From this perspective, the Westphalian system was weak. Although it was instrumental for the emergence of the society of states and their rights, it had a low degree of commitment to their protection and, consequently, a low degree of states' rights.

More specifically, on the one hand, the Peace of Westphalia, signed in October 1648, is generally regarded as a decisive watershed for the foundations of the system of states and their rights.[99] Although it did not institute a fully

[99] For a dissenting interpretation, see Clark, *Legitimacy in International Society* (op. cit.), pp. 68–70.

formed system of demarcated states,[100] it played a key role in determining the scope of territorial rule, in making each state sovereign within its territory, and in acknowledging one organizing principle: the will of states.[101] This explains the acquisition by the state of several other monopolies, including the right to monopolize control over the means of violence, the sole right to tax citizens, and the prerogative of ordering the political allegiances of citizens and enlisting their support in war. They also entailed the sovereign right to adjudicate in disputes between citizens and the exclusive right of representation in international society that is linked with the authority to bind the whole community in international law.[102]

On the other hand, the level of security and, therefore, of rights from which states benefited in this system was anything but high. The set of Christian and dynastic values that contributed to the definition of legitimate statehood and rightful state action could not stop expediency and pursuit of self-interest from running their course. In a world in which social hierarchy was the norm and enhancing and preserving the state's international standing was a central objective of diplomacy – with increases in stature representing a significant foreign-policy achievement and decreases a humiliating failure – power struggles were prone to shape relations among states.[103] This was even more the case because states, including in the context of the Congress of Vienna,[104] were more concerned with the resolution of particular conflicts and crises than with the negotiation of generalized, reciprocally binding rules of international conduct.[105] Westphalian states, as Alexander Wendt stated, "do not appreciate the ways in which they depend on each other... being instead 'jealous' of their sovereignty and eager to make their

[100] Reus-Smit, *The Moral Purpose of the State: Culture, Social Identity, and Institutional Rationality in International Relations* (op. cit.), pp. 112–114.

[101] Ruggie, *Constructing the World Polity: Essays on International Institutionalization* (op. cit.), p. 47.

[102] Linklater, *The Transformation of Political Community: Ethical Foundations of the Post-Westphalian Era* (op. cit), p. 28.

[103] James R. Sofka argues that the eighteenth century, for instance, in contrast to the assumption that it was evocative of and dictated by balance of power and the acceptance of the status quo, was in fact a period during which "monarchs and statesmen displayed ingenious and ruthless attempts to dismember, depopulate, demilitarize, and destroy rivals without regard to fidelity to a doctrinal set of rules," in "The Eighteenth-Century International System: Parity or Primacy?," Michael Cox, Tim Dunne, & Ken Booth (eds.), *Empires, Systems, and States: Great Transformations in International Politics* (Cambridge: Cambridge University Press, 2001), p. 151.

[104] Reus-Smit, *The Moral Purpose of the State: Culture, Social Identity, and Institutional Rationality in International Relations* (op. cit.), pp. 139–140.

[105] Ibid., p. 107.

own way in the world."[106] As a result, rightful conduct was not an absolute imperative.

The fragility of states' rights, in addition to the lack of an international system of interlocking rights and duties and of effective guidelines of reciprocity for rightful conduct of states, was even more evident after the collapse of the Concert of Europe[107] in the second half of the nineteenth century. In the context of rising nationalisms, heightened rivalries, and the rush to build empires, the intensified competition between major European powers demonstrated how matters of rightful conduct and respecting other states' rights had become secondary concerns. In this regard, Max Weber's views on foreign policy were typical of the epoch; he never pursued the idea of international understanding. He belonged to the circle of liberal imperialists who saw participation in great-power politics as the historical duty of the German nation. From this perspective, he hoped that other great powers would concede to Germany its "fair" share of the still-free regions of the globe by means of a policy of increased armament. Weber was of the opinion that

> we cannot carry on a policy of national *comfort* but must seek one of national greatness and therefore [willy nilly] take this risk upon our shoulders, provided that we want a national existence different from that of Switzerland.[108]

In this atmosphere, it would take two world wars to realize that relations among states had to change, to realize that the rights of states would be stronger if the conduct of external affairs was, to a certain extent, similar to internal affairs, determining rightful conduct within the framework of a reciprocal system of rights and duties.

To achieve this, the multilateral construction of the post–World War II world built on previous developments. Its foundations were laid by the Hague peace conferences: the first in 1899, focusing on disarmament, regulations of warfare, and arbitration concerning the peaceful settlement of international disputes; and the second in1907, seeking to refine and strengthen what had been accomplished in 1899 in the area of arbitration.[109] The Versailles Settlement, the League of Nations, and – above all, perhaps – the lessons of their shortcomings contributed as well. In addition, and from a more general standpoint, the move toward multilateralism benefited from and elaborated

[106] Wendt, *Social Theory of International Politics* (op. cit.), p. 295.

[107] Coicaud, "Legitimacy, Socialization, and International Change," in Kupchan, Adler, Coicaud, & Khong (eds.), *Power in Transition: The Peaceful Change of International Order* (Tokyo: United Nations University Press, 2001), pp. 78–80.

[108] Max Weber, quoted in Wolfgang J. Mommsen, *Max Weber and German Politics 1890–1920,* translated by Michael S. Steinberg (Chicago: University of Chicago Press, 1990), p. 72.

[109] Clark, *International Legitimacy and World Society* (op. cit.), Chapter 3.

on the democratic evolution of domestic politics and its exportation in the international realm. The ideas that social rules should be authored by the people subject to them and that rules should be equally applicable to all were particularly important:

> By the middle of the nineteenth century... legitimate statehood and rightful state action were... increasingly tied to the augmentation of individuals' purposes and potentialities. As a consequence, the authoritative norm of procedural justice was supplanted by a new principle that prescribed the legislative codification of formal, reciprocally binding rules of conduct. The ascendance of these new constitutional values marks the birth of modern international society, and the rise of this new "standard of civilization" provided the crucial catalyst for the development of the fundamental institutions of contractual international law and multilateralism.[110]

Hence, after 1945, rightful conduct of states became an essential element of the UN system of collective security. The UN Charter, the fundamental principles governing international relations, and the various legal instruments and multilateral institutions that have been put in place in connection with questions of war and peace all reflect this commitment. Theoretically, with the strengthening of the rights of states paralleling the strengthening of their duties toward other states, each state is made an "obligé" of UN collective security for the advantages it obtains. The state is also made a support for the system – as well as a potential target if the state acts in wrongful ways.

However, the multiplicity of crises and conflicts and the repeated need for international and multilateral involvement in conflict resolution since the end of World War II shows that rightful conduct of states vis-à-vis one another remains an uphill battle.

Rightful Conduct and the Rise of the Individual. Moreover, in recent decades and distinctively in the post–Cold War era, the issue of rightful conduct has become more challenging with the international rise of individuals. Rather than simply geared toward other states, rightful conduct of states encompasses actions in favor of people; this has been a long time coming.

In modern times, with the democratization of politics initiated in the late eighteenth century, pressure has been exercised on the state to make the individual its moral and political purpose, to make it "morally and practically prior to the state."[111] Throughout the nineteenth and twentieth centuries, this has been one if not *the* principal cause of profound normative, political,

[110] Reus-Smit, *The Moral Purpose of the State: Culture, Social Identity, and Institutional Rationality in International Relations* (op. cit.), pp. 122–123.
[111] Ibid., p. 128.

economic, and cultural transformations in the internal affairs of countries and at the international level. After the rights of people became a key principle of political legitimacy domestically, the fact that a significant part of the international legal instruments adopted since the creation of the UN deals, in one way or another, with human rights allowed the rights of individuals to take off externally.[112] Respect for human rights was integrated in the guidelines of rightful conduct of states. If this attention given to human rights did not translate into a determinant political factor in the foreign-policy deliberations and decisions of states during the Cold War, the post–Cold War period brought some progress in this domain. The rightful conduct of states continued to be focused on how a state behaved toward other states, but less exclusively. How they act vis-à-vis individuals, within and among borders, became increasingly important. The increased amenability of the Western permanent members of the UN Security Council – that is, the United States, the United Kingdom, and France – to be implicated in the handling of humanitarian and human-rights crises in the 1990s illustrates this state of affairs.

In the UN Security Council in the immediate aftermath of the Cold War, Russia and China favored diplomatic channels and mediation for resolving conflicts. They were wary of the combination of peacekeeping and peace enforcement, in particular, to uphold human rights. It was not so much the confusion that this mixture introduced and the operational difficulties it generated that made them uneasy. It was the breach of national sovereignty and the possibility of the use of force in support of humanitarian and human-rights concerns. The fact that enforcement was becoming an almost routine option as a means to address humanitarian crises contradicted China's and Russia's views of international relations and some of their vested interests.[113] In this context, they took more or less a back seat in the multilateral management of the wars of the 1990s and their devastating human-rights consequences.

Unlike them, the Western permanent members of the UN Security Council simply could not let the conflicts, mainly in the Balkans and Africa, unfold totally unchallenged. Having a bystander attitude would have undermined

[112] On the international protection of human rights after World War II, see Cassese, *International Law in a Divided World* (op. cit.), 287–316. The database of the UN Treaty Section shows that on the more than 100 conventions adopted in the framework of the UN, the number of those explicitly tackling human rights (not counting the conventions on refugees and stateless persons, traffic in persons, declaration of death of missing persons, status of women, and penal matters) is the highest: thirteen. UN Treaty Collection, Chapter 4: *Human Rights* (UN, available at treaties.un.org/Pages/CTCTrea&ties.aspx?id=4&subid=0&lang=en, 2008).

[113] For more on China's and Russia's positions, see Coicaud, *Beyond the National Interest: Peacekeeping and Multilateralism in the Era of US Primacy* (op. cit.), pp. 55–60.

their credibility. In their own way, they each identified with a sense of international solidarity, of helping people beyond national borders. This sense of solidarity was rooted in the values and rights at the heart of their domestic democratic culture. Furthermore, they had played a critical role after World War II in the metamorphosis of the idea of constitutional rights into international human rights by contributing to the establishment of international legal instruments. Also, as the menace of Armageddon associated with the Cold War had been lifted, there was more room for internationalist considerations.[114] As a result, for the United States, the United Kingdom, and France, ignoring humanitarian and human-rights questions in the UN Security Council and calling on their national interest conceived narrowly as the only compass of their foreign policy would have been at odds with their claimed beliefs. Therefore, these permanent members took the initiative to lead and get involved – in the UN Security Council and other diplomatic settings as well as on the ground – in the search for solutions to the wars and humanitarian crises of the period.

When necessary, they pushed for authorization of the use of force, on the basis of Chapter VII of the UN Charter. By following this course of action, the Western permanent members of the UN Security Council recognized that the nation-state was not the sole actor and right holder that counted in political terms internationally. They recognized that the international community had growing obligations to individuals beyond borders, whoever and wherever they are, and that there was increasing legitimacy in a transnational moral community centered on people and human rights. In other words, they acknowledged that the global moral community of human beings beyond the national moral community had become strong enough for decision makers to not dismiss international solidarity or to evade their responsibility to it.

Yet, because the rise of the individual in international life did not radically alter the hierarchy of fundamental principles and international right holders, the rightful conduct of states – although broadened to factor in human rights – has not been revolutionized. Surely, we are witnessing a normative inclination demanding the respect of human rights internationally, such that it has become an aspect of international legitimacy and of the rightful conduct of states. Nonetheless, on the political front, there is resistance. Regardless of the declared commitments to human rights, democratic regimes (much less nondemocratic regimes) are averse to making human rights a top priority of their foreign policy, with which they would align rightful conduct. This is even more the case because their lack of unbridled enthusiasm in favor

[114] Ibid., pp. 87–89.

of human rights echoes the absence of an international legal obligation to act decisively to stop massive human-rights violations in other countries. Yes, democratic values have been a cultural pressure that led human rights to be incorporated into international law; however, this pressure has not made international law and its institutions the primary guardians of human rights.

International legal instruments stipulate that states primarily look after their own human rights, that human rights are mainly exercised domestically. In addition, there are no legal provisions in international law to oblige the international community and its member states to take action when a state does not respect its obligations to human rights. When human-rights transgressions hamper the development of friendly relations among states, the coupling of human-rights problems with crises of international peace and security can constitute an incentive and a possible justification for UN intervention. Here, Article 39 of Chapter VII of the UN Charter and a flexible interpretation of the definition of a "threat to the peace" by the UN Security Council proved useful in the 1990s. The Council stretched the definition to allow UN intervention in internal conflicts and humanitarian crises that previously had been considered matters of domestic jurisdiction under Article 2 (7) of the UN Charter.[115] However, international law per se neither envisions nor organizes an international right to intervene to end human-rights violations. The fact that a state is required to consent to the deployment of international troops on its territory where there is a situation of humanitarian emergency shows that an intervention from the outside in the name of human rights, while superseding the state's sovereign right, is no right in itself.[116] The obligation or duty of humanitarian intervention is even less of a possibility.

[115] Article 2 (7) of the UN Charter states: "Nothing contained in the present Charter shall authorize the United Nations to intervene in matters which are essentially within the domestic jurisdiction of any state or shall require the Members to submit such matters to settlement under the present Charter; but this principle shall not prejudice the application of enforcement measures under Chapter VII." Article 39 of Chapter VII stipulates: "The Security Council shall determine the existence of any threat to the peace, breach of the peace, or act of aggression and shall make recommendations, or decide what measures shall be taken in accordance with Articles 41 and 42, to maintain or restore international peace and security." See Coicaud, *Beyond the National Interest: Peacekeeping and Multilateralism in the Era of US Primacy* (op. cit.), pp. 96 and 235; Tarcisio Gazzini, *The Changing Rules on the Use of Force in International Law* (Manchester: Manchester University Press, 2006), Chapter 1; and Tetsuo Sato, "The Legitimacy of Security Council Activities under Chapter VII of the UN Charter after the End of the Cold War," in Coicaud & Heiskanen, *The Legitimacy of International Organizations* (op. cit.), pp. 309–352.

[116] On this question in the context of Darfur, see Ademola Abass, "The United Nations, the African Union, and the Darfur Crisis: Of Apology and Utopia," in *Netherlands International*

In a case as extreme as that of genocide, there is no legal imperative to become involved. The Convention on the Prevention and Punishment of the Crime of Genocide does not clearly express an obligation for states to intervene.[117] From this perspective, if the notion of "Responsibility to Protect" points in the direction of greater human-rights protection, it does not create a legally binding obligation. By framing the need to get involved in terms of responsibility, it basically relies on the sense of decency of states. It admits that when it comes to "saving strangers,"[118] the best that can be done is counting on the goodwill of member states, appealing to their ethical conscience. This is better than nothing but, notwithstanding the merits of acting internationally on moral grounds, it is a more uncertain path than action grounded in and backed by law and its institutions.[119] When its occurrence is voluntary, doing the "right thing" amounts to having expectations that generally exceed the reality of international affairs.

Considering this noncommittal context of international human rights, it is not surprising that the Western permanent members of the UN Security Council addressed the conflicts of the 1990s in a half-hearted manner. The goal of ending the crises and saving people was valued but not above everything else. When acting in support of humanitarian and human-rights concerns, they kept in mind their national interest or the interest of their citizens, constantly balancing the pros and cons of the imperative to defend human rights versus the demands of national interest. This was prone to producing dilemmas that complicated the deliberations, negotiations, drafting,

Law Review (No. 54, 2007); and *UNAMID Deployment on the Brink: The Road to Security in Darfur Blocked by Government Obstructions* (Joint NGO Report, December 2007).

[117] William A. Schabas, *Genocide in International Law* (New York: Cambridge University Press, 2000), pp. 545–546: "Perhaps the greatest unresolved question in the Convention is the meaning of the enigmatic word 'Prevent.' The title of the Convention indicates that its scope involves prevention of the crime and, in article I, State parties undertake to prevent genocide. Aside from article VIII, which entitles State parties to apply to the relevant organs of the United Nations for the prevention of genocide, the Convention has little specific to say on the question. The obligation to prevent genocide is a blank sheet awaiting the inscriptions of State practice and case law. A conservative interpretation of the provision requires States only to enact appropriate legislation and to take other measures to ensure that genocide does not occur. A more progressive view requires States to take action not just within their own borders but outside them, activity that may go as far as the use of force in order to prevent the crime being committed. The debate of this is unresolved, and is likely to remain so, at least until the next episode of genocide, if there is no insistence that the subject be clarified."

[118] Nicholas J. Wheeler, *Saving Strangers: Humanitarian Intervention in International Society* (Oxford: Oxford University Press, 2000).

[119] Coicaud, *Beyond the National Interest: Peacekeeping and Multilateralism in the Era of US Primacy* (op. cit), pp. 94–96.

and implementation of the UN Security Council resolutions.[120] In addition, it certainly did not facilitate the task of these countries in making the case, nationally and internationally, for involvement in humanitarian crises.

Indeed, to combine as they did, the importance of protecting human rights with the need to reframe traditional threats to international peace, so that humanitarian crises would touch more directly on the national interest of member states (by far, the strongest rationale for triggering international action), introduced a quandary. Because in the United States, the United Kingdom, and France, the perception was that the defense of human rights was not sufficiently strategic to justify a decisive international engagement,[121] at the national level, the protection of human rights was not a compelling argument. On the international plane, Russia and China were uncomfortable with this type of justification and the policies it motivated. Moreover, most developing countries were also uneasy about going down this path – not simply because of self-serving factors (at times, their human-rights track record) but for understandable motives as well (e.g., respect for national sovereignty). The rationale of the threat to international peace and security and the demands of national interest were equally problematic. Nationally, in the West, the feeling that humanitarian crises were not vital for the future of the world diluted the national-interest justification. In the United States, especially, this situation contributed to making the commitment to international solidarity tentative. Internationally, justifying a humanitarian intervention for reasons of national interest aggravated the opposition of non-Western and developing nations. It invited them to conclude that the West was launching the interventions for self-centered purposes. The fact that the national-interest justification was a significant aspect of the American rhetoric only increased their suspicions.

In any event, the middle-course approach that the UN Security Council adopted under the leadership of its Western permanent members – that is, trying to satisfy both the national and internationalist requests – was biased.

[120] On dilemmas and the social context in which they take place, see ibid., pp. 97–98. For a detailed analysis of some of the dilemmas and trade-offs faced by the international community in the 1990s in connection with humanitarian crises, see ibid., pp. 99–105.

[121] The following is to some extent at the core of the international role of the United States, the United Kingdom, and France: on the one hand, internationally they have done and continue to do much for the development of democratic ideals. On the other hand, they have made and continue to make the pursuit of national interest the defining element of their foreign policy. The fact that they are permanent members of the UN Security Council gives to this hybrid identity a significant impact, in particular when it comes to the United States. Ibid., pp. 107–109.

As member states remained accountable primarily in the national realm (i.e., there is no election at the global level to vote in or vote out international policies), their involvement in favor of the universality of human rights never overrode their ethics of national particularism.[122] Especially in the Balkans and in Africa, this made their actions hesitant if not reluctant. At times, the indifference was so deep that no action was taken to end the carnage, as in Rwanda in the spring of 1994. For when difficult choices had to be made between internationalist and national-interest concerns, the latter prevailed. In this regard, for the intervening powers (notably the United States), their eagerness to avoid casualties among their armed forces was understandable; however, making it the key objective was more questionable. It was a telling example of the "national preference" – and one that did not leave a positive impression. Because of the dubious message, it undercut the moral and political value of the humanitarian intervention and the sincerity of its promotion. To intervening forces – primarily Western soldiers and, more specifically, American soldiers – the message was that they were good enough to use force and even to kill others but too good to be killed themselves. To victims of war, the message was that they were worth helping but were not worth the sacrifice of Western citizens, with the caveat that upholding this limited commitment to them depended on their cultural, geographical, or strategic proximity to the West.[123] More generally, it appeared as if the unwillingness of powerful member states to act swiftly in matters of international solidarity was matched only by their propensity to mobilize military power when their national interest was at risk.

In the multilateral policies of the 1990s deployed to address humanitarian crises, saving lives and restoring peace were at stake. However, there was more to these policies, which charted a course between conservative and progressive approaches to international human rights, between universal and particular ethics, and between the fundamental principles that serve as the sources of legitimacy entering into the fabric of international legitimacy. At stake also was how these policies would influence the evolution of the

[122] This restricted commitment to human rights beyond borders is not specific to humanitarian crises. The same applies to the field of development. Economic rights, although declared universal by the International Covenant on Economic, Social, and Cultural Rights, are still enjoyed in reality by a minority of individuals around the world, and the policies of rich countries are not foreign to this. Thomas Pogge, *World Poverty and Human Rights: Cosmopolitan Responsibilities and Reforms* (Cambridge: Polity Press, 2002), for instance, Chapter 4. See also *The Millennium Development Goals Report* (New York: United Nations, 2007).

[123] Michael Walzer, *Arguing about War* (New Haven, CT: Yale University Press, 2004), pp. 16–18 and 99–103.

defining characteristics of the international system, including the actors, distribution of power, socialization of international relations, and values on which it is based. As shown in this discussion, states – predominantly those in positions of power – played a crucial role. Nevertheless, it was not a role they were performing on their own, in their name and for their exclusive benefit. Rather, they did it as part of an institution embodying the sense of international legitimacy – the UN; hence, this shows the importance of the issue of authority for legitimacy in the international realm.

International Authority. One reason why legitimacy has not been examined much internationally is that the ways in which authority has unfolded at the international level have been at odds with the traditional assumption concerning authority and the understanding of its connection with legitimacy. Indeed, the belief has been that authority must be centralized and that the task of legitimacy is to account for rights and obligations, first among the governors and the governed, within the framework of "centralism." It is obvious that this assumption not only owes a great deal to the emergence of the state as a political model, but it also is an intellectual translation of this model – so much so that over time, it has become more or less a given in political studies. In this context, the lack of a similar centralized feature in international life has been an invitation to overlook legitimacy internationally.

Max Weber, who is such an emblematic figure in the analysis of legitimacy, especially with his thesis regarding the charismatic, traditional, and rational ideal-types of political legitimacy, is certainly a chief example. His conception of legitimacy cannot be separated from the fact that according to him, the "state is the highest and ultimate principle in the world.... The state is the highest organization of power in the world."[124] In other words, there is nothing beyond or above the state. The idea of an international authority, therefore, is neither thinkable nor – if it were thinkable – would it have a positive value. This is true because he was of the opinion that competitive systems of values could not be differentiated on a rational basis.[125] This de facto excluded the possibility of international norms and institutions, allowing states to transcend their differences and to achieve durable reconciliation.[126]

[124] Weber, August 1, 1916, quoted in Mommsen, *Max Weber and German Politics 1890–1920* (op. cit.), p. 238.

[125] Coicaud, *Legitimacy and Politics: A Contribution to the Study of Political Right and Political Responsibility* (op. cit.), pp. 155–161.

[126] "He (Weber) totally rejected the efforts of the early twenties to break the diabolical cycle of European power politics of the imperialistic era and to seek new forms for political relations between nations," Mommsen, *Max Weber and German Politics 1890–1920* (op. cit.), p. 330.

This explains Weber's vision of international relations as a juxtaposition of state national monopolies of power, among which competition and struggle have an ontological character and are part of both the being of the state and state interactions.[127]

Yet, as discussed in the opening chapters of this book, matters of legitimacy at the international level are of utmost importance – that is, if we accept that mitigating tensions and conflicts internationally is an absolute necessity; also, if we accept that the way to achieve this is to work at drawing the line between right and wrong and to do so not in the service of power, as it so often happens, but rather keeping in mind the imperative to mobilize power in the quest for justice.

Whereas accepting this means acknowledging that there is a place for legitimacy in international life, it also means recognizing that this does not occur on its own. It must be engineered and nurtured, which calls for an international authority, and one that is in need of legitimacy as much as its national counterpart – or, rather, an international authority that is, due to the specificity of the challenges it faces, arguably more in need of legitimacy than national authority. For being not as institutionalized, centralized, unified, and hierarchical as national authority and having to deal with a greater autonomy and plurality of actors and a system of values, the nature and function of international authority is all the more in question. Such uncertainty is problematic if not tragic, considering the costs associated with not trying to behave humanly and avoid conflicts internationally, with not trying to pursue international peace as a serious endeavor – not as a war in the waiting but as a fair balance of rights and obligations.

Against this background, unpacking authority at the international level should help stress its significance. This can be done by analyzing international authority, especially in connection with the UN, relative to the international distribution of power, its institutionalization, its role, its third-party status, and its decentralized constitution. This latter issue entails addressing the gap between the UN and the United States and the difficulties generated by the increasingly diffused aspect of the regulation of international interactions.

International Authority and the Distribution of Power. Authority in international life – its norms, institutions, and mechanisms – echoes the hierarchy of

[127] Michael Joseph Smith, *Realist Thought from Weber to Kissinger* (Baton Rouge: Louisiana State University Press, 1986), pp. 23–33.

right holders, which itself echoes the international distribution of power. This is not surprising; because legitimacy is closely linked to power dominance internationally as it is nationally, it is logical that international authority tends to be an outgrowth and part and parcel of this dominance. Historically, it can be suggested that there are types of imperial rule[128] that have operated as a form of international authority and have been an extreme version of this state of affairs.

In this perspective, empire as a political system projected in its sphere a sense of international authority that was the direct embodiment of the central power. International authority was organizing relations by incorporating – while leaving them somewhat independent – previously standalone collectivities in a continuum of hierarchical relationships between the center and the periphery. The range of imperial power may have occupied a middle ground, wider than international power but narrower than domestic power.[129] However, by combining dimensions of domestic and international politics, it made international political authority a strict extension of the domestic imperial authority within its zone of control.

Consider the Chinese Empire. In East Asia – which now encompasses approximately China, the Korean peninsula, Japan, Taiwan, and Vietnam – there was a civilization with China at its core. Although collective political entities in this civilization differed greatly from one another in size, culture, and structure, they shared common features originating from China, including a normative framework that regulated interactions between the countries. In accordance with its egocentric and universalistic world image and feeling of superiority, Sino-centrism stipulated (connecting the cosmos to mankind) that the emperor, as the Son of Heaven, had the mandate of Heaven to rule *Tianxia* (i.e., all-under-heaven). Not only domestic local rulers in China but also rulers beyond the immediate pale of China (not necessarily its territory in the modern sense) were supposed to obey the emperor, the sole supreme authority. All relations in the imperial region had to be regulated by Chinese rules, customs, and rituals, not by "treaties" between the parties. Foreign rulers were expected to send a mission to the emperor and pay a tribute to him. In return, the emperor conferred official ranks and titles that were generally the same as those applied to domestic local rulers – that is, the normative framework of regional relations was an expansion of the domestic setting of the central power (i.e., China). In a way, the separation between the

[128] This excludes those that either denied rights or some sort of independence status to the communities that fell under imperial rule.

[129] Michael W. Doyle, *Empires* (Ithaca, NY: Cornell University Press, 1986), p. 41.

"international" and the "domestic" in modern international relations and international law did not exist.[130]

Today, the empire structure is no longer an option. To be sure, when countries are weak, they must learn to live with the relatively informal modes of international influence, such as the hegemony and/or imperialism[131] of the powerful. However, the idea of a formalized hierarchy among collectivities within a system of empire has become unacceptable, regardless of how tempting it may seem to some of the most self-centered characters of the post–September 11 American foreign policy scenario.[132] The principles of sovereign equality of states and self-determination of peoples have too much influence on our contemporary national and international political cultures to make imperial rule a viable official policy. If, as discussed previously,[133] the present evolution of international relations tends to dilute the distinction between the internal and the external, it is not because of an embrace of the empire model. It is more due to the fact that the primary international actor of the time – the state – is being challenged, yet remaining the point of reference from which international authority currently emanates first and foremost. This is demonstrated by the relationship between the UN and member states.

The UN is meant to transcend the particular interest of states. In addition, the scope of its legal activities – international and regional institutions in general – is increasingly constraining the state. However, this does not eliminate the fact that the UN, created by states, remains heavily dependent on them to function politically, financially, and in other aspects. Furthermore, major powers have had and continue to have a large impact on the fate of the UN. The U.S. role in its establishment – without which the UN

[130] Onuma, "When Was the Law of International Society Born? An Inquiry of the History of International Law from an Intercivilizational Perspective," in *Journal of the History of International Law* (op. cit.), pp. 11–18; Yongjin Zhang, "System, Empire, and State in Chinese International Relations," in Cox, Dunne, & Booth (eds.), *Empires, Systems and States: Great Transformations in International Politics* (op. cit.), p. 43–63; and, in more general terms, Fairbank (ed.), *The Chinese World Order: Traditional China's Foreign Relations* (op. cit.).

[131] To Doyle's definition of imperialism in his book *Empires* (op. cit.), p. 45, "imperialism is simply the process or policy of establishing or maintaining an empire," we could add another element: the notion of imperialism started to gain intellectual currency in the early decades of the twentieth century and then flourished in the 1960s as the exercise of our attempt to exercise effective control over other polities at a time when the emergence and later recognition of the principles of sovereign equality of states and of self-determination of peoples gradually rendered empire illegitimate as a political system. Imperialism was a second best when empire was not a possibility anymore.

[132] Pierre Hassner, "Etats-Unis: l'empire de la force ou la force de l'empire?," in *La terreur et l'empire: La violence et la paix II* (Paris: éd. du Seuil, 2003), pp. 160–206.

[133] In this chapter.

would not have been created – and its policies over the years illustrates this situation. In this regard, international authority deriving from the state and being secondary to and seconded by it can have both positive and negative effects. Concerning positive effects, the intertwining of the UN and member states has potential benefits for both. The power-backing that the state can provide the UN, as well as the production of and access to global public goods that the latter can facilitate for the former, is one effect. The fact that the UN and member states are stakeholders for one another is an additional advantage. The representation and participation of states in the UN give them a vested interest in its success, and it is an incentive for the UN to serve them.

Nevertheless, the dovetailing of states and international authority is prone to negative effects as well. Having the states as the principal carriers and enforcers of international rights and duties for which the UN, as the international authority, is the custodian results in two sets of difficulties.

Although this responsibility is delegated to states on the basis of, as an expression of, and overseen by UN legitimacy, in a variety of ways it makes dependency and heteronomy permanent characteristics of the UN. States, small and large, rarely hesitate to use this for their profit whenever needed. Moreover, if these characteristics allow the UN to be a normative global-security contributor, with international legal instruments adopted in the context of the UN as a result of the cooperation of member states, it certainly does not make it an operational global-security provider. When they have a choice, states prefer to rely on more concrete security alliances – regional (e.g., NATO) or bilateral (e.g., the United States–Japan alliance) – or on their own means to preserve their safety. This has not helped the credibility of the UN, which is often perceived as a "talking shop," not capable of much action. Finally, the dependency and heteronomy of the UN further underline the risk of a credibility deficit considering the role that they play in the lack of unity of the UN as an international authority, an element that is not conducive to decisiveness.

The second set of difficulties is that in the UN, states tend to be judge and party. In a multilateral environment, this can be a source of self-serving policies. Indeed, permanent members of the UN Security Council are frequently suspected of putting items on the agenda that primarily suit their own concerns or to frame and handle international issues in a manner that favors them.[134] Having states as judge and party also can be a strong impediment

[134] José E. Alvarez, "Hegemonic International Law," in *American Journal of International Law* (Vol. 97, No. 4, October 2003).

to change; it is an attribute that is likely to encourage the status quo. Because states are sovereign entities, they have latitude and they are inclined to call on it when their interest is at stake. The uphill battle of trying to improve the UN politically is a case in point. In the most recent attempt to reform the Security Council, in 2005, some developing countries – fearing the admission of regional competitors as permanent members – calculated that it was better for them to torpedo the enlargement of the Security Council.[135] In effect, this permitted the persistence of the imbalance of power in the Security Council and the UN as a whole.

The Institutionalization of International Authority. The forms of international authority have varied over the course of history. However, except for certain types of empires and of transnational religious norms and institutions and their contribution to guidelines of international legitimacy (e.g., Christianity in feudal Europe[136]), international authority tended to be ad hoc and incidental until the twentieth century. The notion of continuous politico-diplomatic organizations used to address long-term international questions held little attraction. The preference was to engage in diplomatic interaction when circumstances demanded – for instance, when unilateral claims and the use of force failed to achieve their objectives or to tackle and resolve specific

[135] Jean-Marc Coicaud, *Kokuren no Genkai/Kokuren no Mirai* (Limits of the UN/Future of the UN) (Tokyo: Fujuwara Shoten, 2007), Chapter 7.

[136] Michael Mann, *The Sources of Social Power*, Volume 1: *A History of Power from the Beginning to A.D. 1760* (Cambridge: Cambridge University Press, 1986). Mann argues, pp. 382–383, that the transcendent nature of the church's extensive identity was obvious at four levels: "First at the regional level, bishops and priests coordinated campaigns to rid a neighborhood of bandits and predatory lords.... Although the success of these movements was limited, both lay rulers and the papacy were later able to build on top of them. They gave rise to medieval distinctions between "just" and "unjust" wars and to the rules governing treatment of noncombatants and the vanquished. None of these norms and rules was universally accepted.... But the moralizing and the admonitions were felt to have some potential force, and they emanated not from within the state but from Europe as a whole. Second, at the political level, the bishops and abbots assisted the ruler to control his domains, providing both sacral authority and literate clerics for his chancellery, backing his judicial authority with legitimacy and efficiency.... Third, at the continental level, the papacy was the main arbiter of interstate politics, preserving a balance of power, restraining overweening monarchs in their conflicts with lesser rulers. Excommunication could release vassals of a monarch from their oath of fealty. Anyone was then entitled to grab his land. The church guaranteed continental order but could unleash chaos.... And, fourth, in intercontinental politics, the papacy coordinated the defense of Christendom and the first counterattacks, the Crusades in the Holy Land, which, although they were transitory, indicated that western Christendom would not fall to Islam.... The greatness of Latin Christendom and its papacy was not merely spiritual. In a secular, diplomatic sense the church was superior – without directly commanding a single army."

problems after major conflagrations. More than anticipatory and preventive, this approach was reactive. This was true of the Peace of Westphalia and of the Utrecht Settlement – signed in the period 1713–1714 and indicating that the reach of dynastic entitlements could legitimately be curtailed to preserve European peace and security[137] – and of the Congress of Vienna.

In contrast, the institutionalization of international authority that followed World War I provided relatively stable institutional tools, including a professional international bureaucracy, to oversee international affairs. In addition, the institutionalization of international authority had the advantage of paralleling that of international politics, allowing international relations to be monitored along general principles with the support of established mechanisms and institutions:

> Over time, postwar settlements have moved in the direction of an institutionalized order, and have begun to take on constitutional characteristics. Power is exercised – at least to some extent – through agreed-upon institutional rules and practices, thereby limiting the capacities of states to exercise power in arbitrary and indiscriminate ways or use their power advantages to gain a permanent advantage over weaker states. This model of postwar institution building is an ideal type. None of the major postwar settlements fully conform to its ideal logic. The model allows, however, for the identification of a logic of order building that is more or less present in the settlements of 1815, 1919, and 1945, and that is most fully evident in the 1945 settlement among the industrial democracies.[138]

The League of Nations and the UN, even more so, marked the institutionalization of the notion of international authority. In the years following the creation of the UN, the sense of international authority widened and deepened with the establishment of new entities as part of the UN. Corresponding to arising needs and awareness in emerging areas, this led to the development of the UN in a system of global governance. In the process, the UN, member states, and international institutions in general became involved in the regulation of international interactions among states, regional organizations, civil society, the private sector, and individuals in a multitude of domains.[139]

This growth made room for NGOs such that the relationship between the UN and NGOs has come to illustrate how authority at the international level, like at the national, can no longer be limited to a one-way, command, and vertical arrangement. It must be more horizontal and interactive – for

[137] Clark, *Legitimacy in International Society* (op. cit.), Chapter 4.

[138] Ikenberry, *After Victory: Institutions, Strategic Restraint, and the Rebuilding of Order after Major Wars* (op. cit.), p. 19.

[139] Alvarez, *International Organizations as Law-makers* (op. cit.), pp. 264–267; see also Table of Conventions, pp. xxxiii-xlii.

example, by factoring in the expertise and opinion of civil-society actors. In this, there is risk of undermining the formal character of the UN as an international authority and of making its mechanisms for coordinating decisions and policies more complicated than they already are.[140] However, the gain is greater than the risk, if only because resisting the pressure of being more open would weaken the credibility of the UN.

The Role of the UN as an International Authority. Regarding the role of the UN as an international authority, it has a task no others can do. This is rooted in its unique normative, moral, and political identity that no other international actor can match. This authority and the function associated with it have the overall purpose of determining, communicating, and fulfilling, where possible, the various facets of international legitimacy in service of the socialization of the international realm. This is what makes the UN valued as an instrument of collective legitimization.[141]

The role that the UN performs as an international political authority notably entails seven principal aspects: expression, identification, negotiation, officialization, interpretation, implementation, and validation. These aspects apply to the normative guidelines and policies of the UN relative to membership, right holding, the hierarchy of right holders, rightful conduct, and rightful international authority. Although some aspects overlap with or are not entirely distinguishable from one another in the mandates and practice of the UN, we disaggregate them herein for the sake of analysis.

Expression is international actors putting forward concerns they perceive as having global relevance, and having these heard in the multilateral arena. These concerns, when they generate sufficient support, can lead to claims that the UN may have to consider in the future.

Identification is focusing on concerns that are important enough to be placed on the UN agenda, at the very least as an object of discussion, with the possibility of further action required later.

Negotiation is deliberation among UN actors about how matters recognized as meaningful should be integrated into the UN body of norms and policies. Deciding by which organ or organization, in which manner (e.g., normative, operational), and to what extent this should occur is part of the negotiation process.

Officialization is endorsing – putting a seal of approval on – what has been, after deliberation, agreed on so that it becomes UN policy. This can happen

[140] Ibid., p. 265.
[141] Claude, "Collective Legitimization as a Political Function of the United Nations," in *International Organization* (Vol. 3, No. 3, Summer 1966).

in a variety of ways and through a plurality of UN entities. The significance of the General Assembly in the development and codification of international law illustrates this.[142]

Interpretation is a crucial dimension of the UN function as an international authority. Its strategic character derives particularly from what can be the low level – itself complicated by the divergent orientations it contains – of determinacy of the international norms of the UN. This low level of determinacy involves the need for norms to embrace specific situations. However, more often than not, it results from the fact that achieving common ground in the UN environment is a demanding exercise, considering that the positions of member states on the questions at hand can diverge significantly. From this perspective, glossing over the differences between points of view can be helpful in moving forward by permitting the rapprochement necessary for adoption of a UN text. However, the trade-off of this approach is that it leaves the precise signification of the text open to interpretation on usage. This can be problematic because there is no guarantee that disagreements will not resurface on the eve of action, when a meaning has to be chosen and pushed in one direction. Several resolutions voted on in the 1990s and 2000s by the UN Security Council in connection with authorization of the use of force under Chapter VII are an example of this state of affairs.[143] However, it is also the lack of a strict obligation for states to act internationally that explains the low level of determinacy of international norms and the importance of it to interpretation. Short of being told expressly what must be done, it is up to member states – especially those with a decisive impact on decision making and action (i.e., permanent members of the Council) – to fill in the blanks with their interpretations and the subsequent policies.

That is, the moment of truth for interpretation frequently proves to be *implementation*. Indeed, implementation, the manner in which states decide to act, determines within the possible range[144] which interpretation, for example, of a norm, implicitly understood in its relations with others, is the right one – at least, at a given time. By translating and projecting norms and decisions into the concrete reality of international politics, implementation – or, implementation and interpretation – shapes how history unfolds. However,

[142] Alvarez, *International Organizations as Law-makers* (op. cit.), pp. 304–310.

[143] Coicaud, *Beyond the National Interest: Peacekeeping and Multilateralism in the Era of US Primacy* (op. cit), pp. 62–65 for the 1990s and p. 156 concerning UN Security Council Resolution 1441 of November 8, 2002, stressing, among other things, the imperative that Iraq disarm totally or face "serious consequences."

[144] For more on this, see Coicaud, "International Organizations, the Evolution of International Politics, and Legitimacy," in Coicaud & Heiskanen (eds.), *The Legitimacy of International Organizations* (op. cit), p. 542.

it also sets the tone, unveiling where member states stand on issues of international legitimacy. This happens in a reactive way, with the objective of resolving crises, or as an application of general rules pursuing anticipatory or preventive goals.

Validation, as a twofold operation, is the overall goal of the various efforts of the UN as an international authority. First, where necessary, validation is transforming concerns into rights and, by implementing these, showing that their validity is taken seriously. Second, it is the validation of the UN as an international authority that is also at stake. Whether this validation is successful, whether the credibility and legitimacy of the UN is diminished, maintained, or enhanced, depends on whether and to what extent it fulfills its responsibilities, specifically outlined by the UN Charter and international norms. In this context, the demands of validation do not stop with the UN. Because member states influence the workings of the UN, its mandates, and its ability to deliver, and because the UN complements and supplements state action, validation also engages member states. In some measure, the member states are evaluated on the UN's capacity to obtain results, particularly for major powers. For, in the words of Churchill, "the price of greatness is responsibility."[145] In the multilateral setting as in others, this puts the United States – the sole democratic global power – on the front line of international responsibility. At times, this introduces a game of cat and mouse in terms of trying to avoid accountability for policies that go wrong. The situation during the 1990s, when peacekeeping operations went badly in the Balkans, Somalia, and Rwanda, is a case in point of this game-playing at the international level.[146]

The function of the UN as an international authority in these different dimensions is exercised by a diversity of organs and organizations, including the General Assembly, the Security Council, the International Court of Justice, and others. It is with regard to their respective mandates and specific issues they tackle that their particular roles and importance are assigned. In the completion of their tasks, the relationships among the UN entities include the division of labor, complementarity, and convergence. Because the UN system is not perfectly coordinated, to say the least, it suffers from overlaps and gaps. Furthermore, considering its normative and political pluralism and the occasional lack of homogeneity of its mandates and purposes, these relations also entail competition and divergence. This certainly constitutes a "mixed bag" for the status and effectiveness of the UN as an international authority.

[145] Winston Churchill, Address delivered at Harvard University, September 6, 1943.

[146] Coicaud, *Beyond the National Interest: Peacekeeping and Multilateralism in the Era of US Primacy* (op. cit), pp. 73 and 170–172.

The institutional hierarchy existing within the UN – with some organs and organizations and their agendas and constituencies prevailing over others – accentuates this state of affairs. For example, in the area of development, the UN Development Programme (UNDP) has, for good and bad reasons, greater weight than the Department of Economic and Social Affairs of the UN Secretariat (UN DESA) in policy terms and even more so from an operational point of view. The fact that the function of UN entities as components of the UN does not take place in a self-contained or closed fashion is another challenge; however, it is unavoidable: the UN and its role, like that of other institutions, are the products of an interactive dialogue with history, of history being made – and they continue to be so. This implies that the authority of the UN increasingly factors in inputs from the "outside" world and what constitutes it, giving much weight to the international distribution of power and its evolution.

In this regard, since the early 1990s, the UN Security Council, always a key organ of the UN,[147] has gained more significance as an element of the UN international authority. It has come to occupy a central role in the seven aspects of international authority. It is especially its management of the humanitarian crises of the period and involvement in peacekeeping operations envisioning the use of force that have been occasions for the Security Council to widen its domains of competence and to become a crucial contributor to the most consequential recent evolutions of international law. In this perspective, compared to its legal character, the political character of the UN as an international authority has been emphasized. Throughout the Cold War, the UN General Assembly was an important entity in international law, being more or less *the* place for progressive legal transformation. For instance, UN-sponsored conferences relying on the work of the International Law Commission and of the sixth (legal) committee of the General Assembly resulted in the adoption of the most significant and broadly ratified founding documents of the international legal order.[148] More precisely, a number of General Assembly declarations were ultimately followed by human-rights treaties, which was the case for the Universal Declaration of Human Rights; the Declaration on the Elimination of All Forms of Racial Discrimination; the Declaration on the Rights of the Child; and the Declaration on the Protection of All Persons from Being Subjected to Torture and Other Cruel, Inhuman, or Degrading Treatment or Punishment. This prominence of the General

[147] Bruce Cronin & Ian Hurd (eds.), *The UN Security Council and the Politics of International Authority* (London: Routledge, 2008); and Hurd, *After Anarchy: Legitimacy and Power in the United Nations Security Council* (op. cit.).

[148] Alvarez, *International Organizations as Law-makers* (op. cit.), pp. 304–309.

Assembly has been altered in the post–Cold War era.[149] It has been eclipsed by the political powers of the Security Council, which now tends to be in a situation of predominance as a norm entrepreneur vis-à-vis the more judicial organs of the UN.[150] With geopolitical fluidity and conflicts rendering it front and center, the Security Council has been forcing international law to evolve, to the extent that it may not be exaggerated to affirm that in the fields of international security and humanitarian crises, international law and the UN Charter mean more than ever what the Security Council determines they signify.

With such acquired preeminence, it is not wrong to state that the UN Security Council is one of the prime locations of what Ian Hurd evokes as "international sovereignty."[151] It is not wrong to say that the Council is operating as a governing authority in the international system with a power over states. This leads Hurd to formulate the following thesis: "The presence of sovereign authority in the Council means that [this] system cannot be described as an anarchy."[152] Yet, this orientation that favors the Security Council, which could be difficult to reverse, has generated questions and raised doubts, in substantive and procedural terms, on the legitimacy of the Council as a key actor of the UN international authority.

Some of these doubts concern the lack of control of constitutionality of the Security Council's decisions because its areas of competence are expanded seemingly without any check,[153] the absence of "due process" in the

[149] Martti Koskenniemi, "The Police in the Temple: Order, Justice, and the UN: A Dialectical View," in *European Journal of International Law* (Vol. 6, No. 1, 1995), Section 6.

[150] Concerning the judicial interpretation of international law, Claude indicates that the scope of the International Court of Justice (ICJ) is limited because it can only assume jurisdiction in a case with the consent of both sides. In "Collective Legitimization as a Political Function of the United Nations," in *International Organization* (op. cit.), p. 371. See also Heiskanen, "The Rationality of the Use of Force and the Evolution of International Organization," in Coicaud & Heiskanen (eds.), *The Legitimacy of International Organizations* (op. cit). He argues, p. 169, that the role that the ICJ and other international legal institutions "have had in the peaceful settlement of serious international crises suggests that the expectations that were placed on legal procedures by the policy of peace was somewhat misplaced.... [L]egal means of resolving international disputes... tend to prove inadequate in instances where substantial political interests and concerns are at stake and, consequently, in instances that must be seen in terms of a 'crisis' rather than a 'dispute' or 'difference'; that is to say, in situations where armed force is being used, or where recourse to armed force is being contemplated, between the parties. Consequently, such legal means fail precisely when a policy of peace would be most urgently needed."

[151] Hurd, *After Anarchy: Legitimacy and Power in the United Nations Security Council* (op. cit.), p. 187.

[152] Ibid., p. 187.

[153] Mohammed Bedjaoui, *The New World Order and the Security Council: Testing the Legality of Its Acts* (The Hague: Kluwer Law International, 1995).

Council,[154] and its exclusive membership. The doubts are also related to the fact that only a few countries (primarily, the Western permanent members, especially the United States) are "calling the shots" and, arguably, imposing their agenda on others. In addition, there are criticisms of American hegemony. Its eagerness to cater to its own interests in the Security Council – for example, regarding international terrorism[155] – and to go ahead despite its opposition when the Council is not pliable enough, as the launching of the war against Iraq in March 2003 demonstrated, is drawing little support.

It is therefore not surprising that the few member states with the power to counter these features are tempted to do so. It is partly in this context that one must understand the Russian unilateral recognition of South Ossetia and Abkhazia on August 26, 2008. Although a permanent member of the UN Security Council, Russia – already frustrated if not alienated in the early years of the post–Cold War period with the policies of the Security Council, particularly in connection with Kosovo – decided that it was time to draw the line.[156] The deterioration of its relations with Georgia was an occasion not to be missed. Specifically, Russia was determined to send the signal that if previously it had been unable to stop the enlargement of NATO, it was now no longer willing to tolerate encirclement.

The International Authority as a Third Party. One of the important conditions for an international authority (here, the UN) to have authority, so to speak, or legitimacy, is to serve as a third party. Indeed, the notion of third party is a crucial component of the sense of justice. Applied to the multilateral environment, it is a credibility benchmark for the UN as an international authority. It entails acting in a non-self-serving manner, with impartiality vis-à-vis parties in conflict when it is unclear of who is right and who is wrong, but also taking a stance in defense of the victim when there is no ambiguity about who has been harmed. In the domains in which the UN Charter gives a mandate – that is, authority – to the UN to act, it is with those

[154] Koskenniemi, "The Police in the Temple: Order, Justice, and the UN: A Dialectical View," in *European Journal of International Law* (op. cit.), Section 6.

[155] Alvarez, "Hegemonic International Law Revisited," in *American Journal of International Law* (op. cit.), pp. 874–878.

[156] Statement by the president of Russia, Dmitri A. Medvedev, of August 26, 2008, on South Ossetia and Abkhazia: "Russia continually displayed calm and patience. We repeatedly called for returning to the negotiating table and did not deviate from this position of ours even after the unilateral proclamation of Kosovo's independence. However, our persistent proposals to the Georgian side to conclude agreements with Abkhazia and South Ossetia on the non-use of force remained unanswered. Regrettably, they were ignored also by NATO and even at the United Nations," in *New York Times*, August 28, 2008, www.nytimes.com/2008/08/27/world/europe/27medvedev.html.

demands in mind that the UN is supposed to be involved. This has at least three implications. First, the UN is not meant to be the captive of its own interests as an actor, as an international bureaucracy. Second, it is has to be more than the sum of its parts and reach beyond the particular interest of each of its member states. Third, in general terms, it has to be geared toward the global public good.

These goals, from which the UN specifically derives its moral authority, are not easy to achieve. Like any bureaucracy, national[157] or international,[158] the UN has its own limiting pathologies, including the difficulty of ensuring that the international civil servants working at the UN have and keep a sense of mission and do not exclusively use the UN as a platform for their benefit and career, especially at the senior-management level.[159] Having the UN avoid being the prisoner of the interests of its member states is an even greater challenge.[160] The UN may be the closest we have and the most authoritative institution for the expression of a global version of some sort of "General Will"[161] in the context of which the good of the entire international community is pursued. Yet, much more than an organization that is ruled by and for the people worldwide, by and for a global constituency, the UN is an intergovernmental entity. This makes it difficult for the UN to overcome the trappings of national power. For, if the power of the UN as an idea springs from its claimed commitment to the ideal of transcending the narrow point of view of each state, its resources come from the support it receives from states, particularly the most powerful among them.

Considering this, it is tempting for member states and, consequently, for a UN partly controlled by them to overlook the requirements of third-party

[157] Michael Herzfeld, *The Social Production of Indifference: Exploring the Symbolic Roots of Western Bureaucracy* (Chicago: University of Chicago Press, 1993).

[158] Michael Barnett & Martha Finnemore, *Rules for the World: International Organizations in Global Politics* (Ithaca, NY: Cornell University Press, 2004), Chapter 2, specifically pp. 34–41.

[159] On human resources at the UN, Jean-Marc Coicaud, "International Organizations as a Profession: Professional Mobility and Power Distribution," in Andrés Solimano (ed.), *The International Mobility of Talent: Types, Causes, and Development Impact* (Oxford: Oxford University Press, 2008), pp. 263–297. For a more detailed version of this text, see Jean-Marc Coicaud, "International Organizations as a Profession: Professional Mobility and Power Distribution" (Helsinki: UNU-WIDER, Research Paper No 2006/109), www.wider.unu.edu/publications/working-papers/research-papers/2006/en˙GB/rp2006–109.

[160] Jean-Marc Coicaud, "International Organizations, the Evolution of International Politics, and Legitimacy," in Coicaud & Heiskanen (eds.), *The Legitimacy of International Organizations* (op. cit), for example, pp. 525–527.

[161] Jean-Jacques Rousseau, *The Social Contract or Principles of Political Right* (Whitefish, MT: Kessinger Publishing, 2004); and Boucher, *Political Theories of International Relations: From Thucydides to the Present* (op. cit.), pp. 302–306.

philosophy and to be both judge and party. It is even more tempting due to the fact that the national bent of international life fuels competition among states and leads them to focus on their interest to the exclusion of others. Democratic countries are not immune; despite their engagement in favor of the rule of law at home and abroad – which makes them, in principle, more attuned than others with international authority as a third party – they have trouble living by this standard. They have trouble relating to the UN in a non-self-serving fashion. From this perspective, the tension between the UN and member states tends to bring about a rather counterproductive lack of unity in the international authority. The gap between the UN and the United States and the disjunction it creates regarding international authority epitomize this situation.

The Unity of International Authority in Question. The relationship between the UN and the United States was not necessarily supposed to go sour. After all, the United States has been and continues in many ways to be a fundamental underwriter of the UN as an international authority. Among other things, the UN would not have been established without the idealist and internationalist leadership of America and, to this day, without it, it would lose its meaning and ability to function. As such, the United States is the country to which the UN owes the most. Nevertheless, there are also features of American political culture and foreign policy that are prone to generate divisions within and to undermine the UN.

From the origin of the UN, the United States has not perceived the organization exclusively in idealist and internationalist terms; rather, it has approached it from a realist standpoint, as a venue for the pursuit of its national interest. To be sure, this is not specific to the United States; all countries do so. However, the United States is a power unlike any other: it is the main superpower and the sole democratic superpower. This gives America an impact on the UN and the international system that is incomparable to that of other nations. In addition, to a certain extent, the United States identifies its moral values with its political interests. In this context, it conceives the diffusion of its moral beliefs in the world at large as an intrinsic part of the realization of its national interest. With America, moral nationalism coincides with political universalism, and moral universalism with political nationalism. Over time, as America's power increased, this state of affairs has had two results. It has encouraged America to be blind to other points of view, to consider its national interest as more or less the only legitimate one. Furthermore, to defend its national interest, the United States has put forward a foreign policy in the field of security that, although described as defensive, has amounted to a constant quest for expansion of power.[162] It has reached the point of oscillating between what could be called "defensive imperialism" and "expansionist imperialism," to use expressions that were applied to the Roman Empire's modalities of power projection.[163] During the Bush administration, the 2000s have not simply confirmed these characteristics, they also have radicalized them.[164]

In light of these features, after America realized that the UN was not going to be a one-way street and that other countries were eager to mobilize it to make their case, tensions were unavoidable. The situation quickly came to a head during the Cold War. In that period, if much was accomplished in the domain of international norms, less was accomplished in practical terms on the ground. Later, with the end of the East–West confrontation, the 1990s initially brought hope that the relationship between the UN and the United States would improve; however, this was not to be. President Clinton's attitude toward multilateralism and the UN fell into old patterns after a few months in power, with the Somalia debacle of October 1993 triggering his change of heart.[165]

Moreover, as the UN was assuming more responsibilities in the post–Cold War era, especially in the area of peacekeeping operations, it was also getting weaker. It was growing more dependent on member states, particularly the United States, for financial, political, military, logistic, and other types of support. UN–U.S. relations reached rock bottom in the 2000s. In the aftermath of the terrorist attacks of September 11, the "à la carte multilateralism"[166] that the Bush administration had previously presented as its policy vis-à-vis the UN deteriorated rapidly into the dismissal of the UN as an international authority. In this regard, the war against Iraq provided the occasion for the following four core assumptions of the most conservative foreign-policy aspects of the Republican administration to win the day: (1) national security prevails absolutely over considerations of international democratic solidarity (including humanitarian and human-rights issues); (2) the United States has the right to define legitimate American foreign policy on its own; (3) it has the power to influence if not determine international legitimacy, the international law and norms, and the values of which it is constituted

[162] Andrew J. Bacevich, *The Limits of Power: The End of American Exceptionalism* (New York: Metropolitan Books, 2008), p. 3.

[163] Veyne, *L'empire gréco-romain* (op. cit.), pp. 176–177.

[164] Bacevich, *The Limits of Power: The End of American Exceptionalism* (op. cit.), pp. 175–176.

[165] Coicaud, *Beyond the National Interest: Peacekeeping and Multilateralism in the Era of US Primacy* (op. cit.), pp. 116–120.

[166] Richard Haass, quoted in Coicaud, ibid., pp. 149 and 247, note 37.

and (4) American foreign policy is basically accountable to nothing but itself.[167]

However, the way in which the war unfolded on the ground in Iraq and diplomatically at the international level proved these premises to be largely mistaken. At this writing (in the fall of 2008), at best, the jury is still out on the war and its geopolitical consequences; at worst, it is believed to have been a disaster. However, what is hardly in doubt is that the setbacks encountered by the United States demonstrated that it does not enjoy a free hand. Certainly, the United States was able to act unilaterally, without the international community being in a position to stop it. Nevertheless, the United States neither has the capacity to single-handedly reengineer international legality and legitimacy, the key characteristics of it, nor is it answerable only to itself. If anything, the failures of the Bush administration's foreign policy in Iraq recall and emphasize the importance of the social dimension of international legitimacy – that is, legitimacy in the international realm, as in the national, is not a self-declared phenomenon. At the very least, it requires the recognition and consent of others. In addition, as a component of international legitimacy, this social dimension shapes the legitimacy of the foreign policy of countries. They cannot decide alone what will be legitimate in their projection of power; they must consider the interests and rights of others. From this perspective, considering its global reach and democratic claims, such a requirement is of special relevance for the United States. Assuming that it wants to be seen as embodying a sense of international legitimacy, its status as a democratic superpower is as much a source of constraint as it is of opportunities. In fact, unless the United States is aware of the constraints that weigh on its power and act on the responsibilities they entail, it cannot rightfully benefit from these opportunities.

By being inclined to overlook the social character of international legitimacy, the United States not only becomes a structural impediment for the UN as an international authority, it also undermines its own international authority. Indeed, it puts both the UN and the United States in competition with one another. Yet, neither can exercise international authority nor fulfill its specific role (compared to the other) of having international authority on its own; it is by mobilizing some of the assets of the other that each can project international authority. The UN needs to have on board the power, internationalism, and leadership of the United States in order to have its multilateral principles of socialization taken seriously. Conversely, to maximize its international acceptance (i.e., appearing to act at the service of the

[167] Ibid., p. 164.

international interest as well as its own), the United States has to channel part of its power through the multilateral framework and principles of the UN.[168]

Short of this, the gap between power and principles becomes unmanageable internationally. This situation is good for neither the UN nor the United States, or for international stability and international authority. As its principles of socialization find themselves lacking the necessary backing of power, the UN emerges more like a paper tiger, with even less chance to succeed in translating its international norms into reality. For the United States, putting itself above the rules of multilateralism while insisting that they bind others does not work. It reinforces the suspicions of those countries that already have misgivings and deepens its nonreliable reputation. The United States grows isolated and, therefore, its security – far from being strengthened – is weakened. In the process, by undermining the dynamics of reciprocity of rights and duties at the center of the multilateral relations and the predictability, and therefore stability, that these two bring about, the United States heightens international insecurity. Ultimately, it is the possibility of international authority itself that comes under threat, being perceived as increasingly less feasible or even being questioned as an option.

This state of affairs is even more unsettling because today the disjunction of the international authority does not stop here. International nongovernmental organizations (INGOs) and professional networks from the "disaggregated state" and the "disaggregated world order"[169] are another way in which international authority is being challenged. Their decentralized and deterritorialized quality and their dynamism and activism contrast with the modalities and substance of intergovernmental production and control of international norms and practices of governance.

On the other hand, we should not infer that this marks the termination of a relatively centralized authority at the international level or even of the idea of international authority. If the world is ever going to be kept together, international authority is a *must*, if only to negotiate and coordinate cooperation. Furthermore, as alluded to previously, these tendencies are not foreign to the established governing structures; rather, they are an outgrowth of and contribute to them. They spring from and rest on them whether at the level of the state, first with Western democratic states, or of multilateralism, and they participate in them. These tendencies are products of their evolution and they assist this evolution. Moreover, there is no social science or political

[168] Christian Reus-Smit, *American Power and World Order* (Cambridge: Polity Press, 2004), pp. 126–128.

[169] Anne-Marie Slaughter, *A New World Order* (Princeton, NJ: Princeton University Press, 2005), pp. 12–18.

science law indicating that authority always has to follow the pyramid model, with straight and formal lines of super/subordinate relations; alternatives can exist.[170] In fact, alternatives are presently at work, moving away from the either/or logic and creating hybrids in which old and new characteristics are combined.[171] To a certain extent, this is the case in the EU[172] and in the system of global governance, consisting of heterogeneous actors such as states, international institutions, NGOs, private actors, and others, that is constantly evolving.

In other words, the changes underway are an invitation to stretch the limits of imagination about what international as well as domestic authority can be. In expanding the imagination and in understanding and assessing the current transformations, it is essential to identify the conditions under which they will continue to unfold while also looking after the needs for articulation, mutual obligation, and accountability. This all depends on adapting to the vital role that the various aspects of legitimacy play in the evolving socialization of international life.

Adaptation is crucial because the credibility of the authority that determines what is and what is not internationally legitimate, the push for action to follow this determination, and the credibility of the determinations of legitimacy and illegitimacy issued are linked. The appraisal of the validity of the international authority is closely related to the assessment of the validity of what it asserts is and is not internationally legitimate. In this regard, while the questioning of authority leads to questioning the determinations it provides, in time, a high level of questioning of these determinations brings about the questioning of the authority itself.

That is, the fate of the sense of international authority and its determinations of legitimacy and illegitimacy revolves around the negotiations and disputes happening among actors and their respective claims concerning their interests and rights. At stake in these negotiations and disputes is whether the status quo will be upheld or change introduced and to what extent. At stake also is the definition of the just and unjust. In this context, power is frequently on the side of the status quo and justice on the side of change. This is the case for power because once they have acquired a position of dominance, actors all too often tend to focus primarily on consolidating their gains; what they

[170] Ruggie, *Constructing the World Polity: Essays on International Institutionalization* (op. cit.), pp. 59–61.

[171] Ost & van de Kerchove, *De la pyramide au réseau? Pour une théorie dialectique du droit* (op. cit.), p. 539; Delmas-Marty, *Les forces imaginantes du droit: Le relatif et l'universel* (op. cit.), pp. 19–20.

[172] Mireille Delmas-Marty, *Pour un droit commun* (Paris: Seuil, 1994), for example, p. 225.

owe to people is prone to become a sideshow, whatever their political rhetoric may be. It is partly to minimize this tendency that mechanisms of checks and balances exist in democratic regimes. Conversely, when conservative forces stubbornly cling to their advantages, the demands of justice to widen and deepen their impact on reality find themselves in the position of challengers, asking for change.

However, change is not necessarily on the side of justice; it can be driven by negative agendas as well, including agendas of hatred. Consider the example of Adolf Hitler. In January 1933, when he became Chancellor, the transformations he envisioned for Germany and the European landscape certainly did not fit the requirements of national and international justice. Consequently, the interactions that decide the outcome of the confrontation between forces favoring the status quo and those calling for change are not to be taken lightly. This issue is addressed in the next chapter.

JEAN-MARC COICAUD

3. The Evolution of International Order and Fault Lines of International Legitimacy

The interactions that decide the outcome of the confrontation between forces favoring the status quo and those calling for change are not to be taken lightly. This issue is examined in this chapter, moving the study from what has been primarily a static approach to international legitimacy to a more dynamic approach. The objective is simply to offer indirect normative and political clues on what could be the right answers to present controversies and conflicts of international legitimacy. First, we explore how international legitimacy is about socializing international life by trying to find the right balance between status quo and change. Second, the chapter analyzes the main ideal types of fault lines of international legitimacy, specifically through the work of the United Nations (UN) Security Council.

Legitimacy and the Stability and Change of the International System

Legitimacy plays an important role in the stability of international order, and there are at least three reasons for this. First, legitimacy provides a rationale to account for the ways in which the international system is organized, including the inequalities that it never fails to encompass. Second, legitimacy provides tools (e.g., the rationale) to manage the challenges that may be mounted against the international system and the possible changes associated with them. Third, because of the premium that democratic culture puts on the consent,[1] participation, and representation of state and nonstate actors, the stability function of legitimacy has recentlly become even more significant

[1] For a discussion of the question of consent in modern international politics, see Lea Brilmayer, *American Hegemony: Political Morality in a One-Superpower World* (New Haven, CT: Yale University Press, 1994), Chapters 4–6 and 10.

as international order is increasingly influenced by democratic values. That said, it is not an easy task for legitimacy to contribute to the stability of the international system, because of two factors in particular.

Legitimacy and the Challenge of International Stability. First, the scope of a challenge and associated changes faced by international order and its supporting paradigm of legitimacy can be overwhelming. Of course, if the challenge and the change are minimal, if they simply require local adjustments, they can be handled and integrated relatively effortlessly. Not calling for an overall transformation of the international system, they can become part of it without producing a massive commotion. However, the situation is quite different when challenging international order implies profound change. From this perspective, results of the challenge and the related change are likely to generate a redistribution of power, a redistribution of which there are winners and losers. This is even more the case considering that systemic change – because that is what is being alluded to here – does not happen internationally without also happening nationally. For although these two layers are not entirely connected and enjoy some independence from one another, the fact is that a relationship of mutual influence exists between them. On the one hand, the composition of political regimes – especially when they are part and parcel of countries that dominate the international realm and have done so for a long time – help to shape the international system, its values, institutions, and how power is exercised. On the other hand, the international system puts pressure on polities so that they align with the key elements that enter into its composition. The interplay between dynastic and democratic principles following the revolutionary events in America and France at the end of the eighteenth century illustrates this phenomenon of mutual influence.

Consider how the resilience of the dynastic principle of legitimacy in Europe and its contribution to the structuring of international order led the Napoleonic regime to rely on it in part for domestic and foreign-policy purposes.[2] After Napoleon's defeat, this resilience also facilitated the return of the old political system: at the international level, in the context of the Concert of Europe; and, at the national level, with the restoration of the monarchy in France. Furthermore, consider how democratic principles promoted by the American and French Revolutions gradually introduced internationally a transformation of the sense of legitimacy that, in time, affected the fabric of

[2] Thierry Lentz, *Nouvelle histoire du premier empire*, Volume I: *Napoléon et la conquête de l'Europe 1804–1810* (Paris: Fayard, 2002), for example, Chapter 3 (pp. 98–101) and Chapter 20.

domestic legitimacy in the countries on the European Continent and around the world.[3]

The other difficulty for legitimacy in helping to stabilize international order is related to the fact that the gravity of a challenge and the change it may bring do not necessarily reside in the nature of the challenge per se. It is also the arrangement of the international system – its political type, so to speak – and how it is prone to address challenges and changes that determine the danger they constitute. In other words, the type of international system and its regime of legitimacy condition the opposition to them and, in large part, their fate. In the process, we can see whether the international order and its legitimacy are structurally strong or weak and the extent to which this is the case.

For instance, when an international system leaves no room for challenge and change, as can occur under authoritarian or totalitarian rule, any form of challenge – even one that seems small – acquires a strategic character. As such, it can stress the entire system, if not put it at stake. This is reinforced by the fact that in this environment, any confrontation between the system and its opponents is radicalized. Whereas the system in place tends to use force in some way to eliminate the challenge and prevent change, the opponents' defiance – amounting to a call for systematic change – tries to eliminate the established order. Ultimately, this type of international system proves to be weak in structural terms. Because it renounces the social benefits associated with factoring in the demands of legitimacy (i.e., having actors endorsing the distribution of power) and relies crucially on coercion, its collapse seems inevitable. For, if it can take time for an order based primarily on violence to disintegrate, such disintegration does eventually happen. Living by the sword, such a system ends up being the victim of its own rule. It dies, and it dies by the sword.

The high death rate of authoritarian and totalitarian regimes in the twentieth century, much higher than in democratic regimes, is testimony to this. Certainly, the mortality of authoritarian and totalitarian regimes can be slowed by self-contained and isolationist policies. The "hermit" existence of North Korea and its longevity of several decades exemplify this state of affairs. However, their extinction rate tends to accelerate when the regimes seek to expand beyond borders. Had Nazism limited itself to Germany, it is possible (unfortunately) that other major states would have "tolerated" or overlooked its lethal domestic policies. Yet, once international expansion and waging war

[3] Mlada Bukovansky, *Legitimacy and Power Politics: The American and French Revolutions in International Political Culture* (Princeton, NJ: Princeton University Press, 2002), pp. 212–215.

against other countries emerged as a central aspect of Hitler's agenda – with the objectives of achieving absolute security for Nazi Germany and absolute insecurity for others – a fight to the death was inevitable: essentially, kill or be killed. Within five years, Allied forces had defeated a Third Reich that Hitler had vowed would be eternal.[4]

International Legitimacy and the Quest for Socialized Instability. The difficulty of legitimacy contributing to international stability demonstrates that by excluding the idea that the international system can be challenged and changed from the very structure of the system is not the best way to achieve stability. In fact, legitimacy is more likely to be successful in helping stabilize international order when it is part of a socialization of instability.[5] In this context, the goal is not to deny on principle the possibility of contesting and changing the understanding and management of the main elements of international legitimacy, such as right holding, hierarchy of right holders, rightful conduct, and international authority. Rather, the objective is to have the dynamic and the narrative of the international system supporting these elements while integrating as much as possible the eventuality of modifying them, if necessary. It is the aim for stability through a socialized instability that allows for flexibility and plasticity. Because it is better to include than exclude the forces that have the power to contest the status quo, a judicious structure of international order is one that is capable of internalizing these forces. When this occurs, the stability and legitimacy of the international system are displayed when the following four characteristics become defining components of international order and how it is perceived by actors.

First, there is a sense of empowerment among both state and nonstate actors. This sense of empowerment has the actors feeling that the international system not only recognizes and respects their rights but also gives them the means to develop according to the expectations created by these rights. Second, actors have a positive perception of time. They see the international order as offering a present and a future, which permit them to flourish. Third, the mechanisms through which interactions among actors are regulated are viewed as expressions and tools of legitimacy and, therefore,

[4] There was no planning of a Fourth Reich. The Third Reich was supposed to be forever. See Victor Klemperer, *The Language of the Third Reich: LTI – Lingua Tertii Imperii: A Philologist's Notebook*, translated by Martin Brady (London: Continuum Press, 2006), Chapter 18.

[5] Jean-Marc Coicaud, "Legitimacy, Socialization, and International Change," in Charles A. Kupchan, Emanuel Adler, Jean-Marc Coicaud, & Yuen Foong Khong, *Power in Transition: The Peaceful Change of International Order* (Tokyo: United Nations University Press, 2001), p. 70.

are legitimate themselves. Crucially, this applies to legal arrangements. In this regard, whereas law can be challenged in specific situations as needing improvement, as a whole, it is perceived as satisfactory. The fact that the existing shortcomings are interpreted as fixable and that improving the system is considered possible illustrates this state of affairs. Moreover, in the best circumstances, the endorsement of legal arrangements and of the social regulations they oversee is not passive but rather active – actors are engaged. Because of the benefits of international order, they view themselves and act as stakeholders; that is, they have a vested interest in the sustainability and growth of the international system. Their commitment to optimize its performance through their participation and actions is a logical consequence. From this perspective, the pursuit of each actor's interest and that of all actors are convergent and mutually reinforcing. Fourth, when actors feel empowered, temporally satisfied, and consider themselves stakeholders, it is the international system in its entirety that gains from these characteristics. What it gives to actors, it offers to itself; its success and the success of its members go together.

Nevertheless, the appraisal of international order should never be so positive that it becomes naturalized such that the possibility of challenging and changing it totally disappears. The belief that the socialization of life can be perfect is as illusory and dangerous at the international level as it is at the national level. When this belief prevails, it indicates that sound assessment of reality has been replaced by an extreme ideological approach. This is particularly problematic because by removing from the equation the notion that challenge and change are key devices for the preservation of stability, this orientation tends to have the opposite effect than the one desired: it increases the probability of instability. Indeed, it encourages the complacency of those in power; as they become less accountable, their attention to the demands of actors decreases, with the result that the ability of the international system to deliver also decreases. This runs even more the risk of stressing the stability of international order because it leads to the deepening of the "we-versus-them" divide between regular actors and those in commanding positions. This divide acquires a confrontational dimension that is prone to fueling unrest and labeling powerful actors and the international order they underwrite as targets of the discontent.

This scenario is especially lethal when the international system puts a premium on rights of actors, rendering expectations even more pressing. For a rich culture of rights and expectations goes along with a high level of identification and participation of actors, which then have a high level of material and psychological involvement in and reliance on the system.

However, it also renders the international system and its legitimacy heavily dependent on them. Hence, once actors are disappointed and feel that the international environment is an obstacle to their welfare, it pays a price. What was previously its strength – making actors stakeholders – becomes a weakness. When disenchantment settles in, actors – frustrated with what they consider a denial of their rights – become strangers to a sense of duty and responsibility toward others and the system. The spirit of entitlement, resentment, and expediency takes over. Their actions are primarily motivated by self-interest conceived of and sought after in ways at odds with and detrimental to the collective good.

This disenchantment primarily concerns law, which is perceived as an impediment if not a source of alienation. With its legitimacy undermined, including its claim to be at the service of justice, the regulatory power of the law is questioned and its effectiveness wounded. Stability gives way to instability and integration to disintegration. The structural deficiencies of the League of Nations and the penchant for a number of states in the 1920s and 1930s to join and then leave it out of convenience can be analyzed along these lines.[6]

The impact on the collapse of international order demonstrated what occurs when self-centered strategies, functioning also as exit strategies, set the tone.[7] As such, systemic crisis has been reached once it is not simply the institutions, their regulations of the international system, and the international system itself that are emptied of legitimacy and unravel, but their foundational ideals and principles as well. One step further – or, the worst of the worst – occurs when it is believed that there is no substitute to this predicament. This happens when the imagination for and vision of change have been eliminated and the socialization of international life is perceived as neither an option nor desirable; more than cynicism, nihilism and values of death have won the day.[8]

[6] Japan began as a permanent member of the Council of the League of Nations but withdrew in March 1933 after the League voiced opposition to its invasion of the Chinese territory of Manchuria. Italy also began as a permanent member of the Council but withdrew in 1937. The League had accepted Germany as a member in 1926, deeming it a "peace-loving country," but Adolf Hitler, after he came to power, pulled Germany out in September 1933. Other countries withdrew from the League: Costa Rica in January 1925, Brazil in June 1926, Haiti in April 1942, and Luxembourg in August 1942. George Gill, *The League of Nations: From 1929 to 1946* (Garden City Park, NY: Avery Publishing, 1996).

[7] Albert O. Hirschman, *Exit, Voice, and Loyalty: Responses to Decline in Firms, Organizations and States* (Cambridge, MA: Harvard University Press, 1978).

[8] See Carl Schmitt and his views on international politics and international law, *Nomos of the Earth in the International Law of Jus Publicum,* translated by G. L. Ulmen (New York: Telos Press Publishing, 2003).

The Current System of International Legitimacy and Its Internalization of Change. International order and the type of legitimacy supporting it must factor in challenge and change in order to evolve without being destabilized as a whole. However, not all forms of international system and legitimacy fit the requirement. In fact, historically, most have been based on only a few stakeholders and, consequently, have been quite rigid, leaning toward a zero-sum gain structure with little capacity to engineer and endure alterations. This explains their tendency toward fragility.

This is apparently in contrast with the current international order and the associated regime of legitimacy. In the past sixty years, this international order and its regime of legitimacy encountered serious challenges and have significantly changed; for example, they have coped with a variety of wars, including the Cold War. The number of member states increased from 51 in 1945 to 192 in 2008. Following the collapse of the Soviet Union, the United States remained the sole global power, soon replaced in the 2000s – with the rise of China and the laborious progress of the European Union (EU) – by the emergence of a new version of multipolarity. Yet, despite such transformations, the international system and its legitimacy have persisted, demonstrating much resilience in the process – a resilience associated with the power of accommodation made possible by the multilateral dimension of international order and the willingness of states to buy into it.

Unlike with the League of Nations in the 1920s and 1930s, states perceive the international system, including multilateralism and the UN created in the aftermath of World War II, as an important aspect of the socialization of international life. Surely, in the past six decades, Western and non-Western countries have more often than not relied on big-power politics to address and resolve their differences and the resulting crises, therefore being prone to consider multilateralism and the UN as a sideshow. On the other hand, multilateralism and the UN have also made a crucial contribution to the stabilization of international order. For example, the work done by the UN in the field of international law, although frequently overlooked, has been instrumental in making the international system accommodating and, as a result, resilient. The added value that the adoption of international legal norms produced over time for international order helps explain this point.

First, it has kept open the channels of communication among competing powers despite tensions and conflicts. In addition, through negotiating and drafting, it has to some extent generated among countries a sense of give and take that, reflected in the organization of the international system, supports its legitimacy. This is true because international norms have been largely built on recognizing strategic demands and translating them as much as possible into political terms, an approach that aims to widen and deepen the participation and representation of actors. Moreover, even if it has proved difficult to shape daily realities along the requirements of norms, they have served as a basis for action whenever a window of opportunity is presented. The gradual implementation of human rights is indicative of this. During the Cold War, human rights were both institutionalized and restricted from becoming policy priorities. The geopolitical respite brought about by the 1990s partly changed this situation by allowing for human-rights norms to increasingly influence and benchmark the international community's initiatives.

More generally, the resilience of the international system also results from the fact that the multilateral and UN contribution to the socialization of international life is a work in progress and an inclusive one.

Concerning the work-in-progress aspect, rather than being complete, the multilateralization of international relations is relatively open, in two main ways: process and content. It is in terms of process in the sense that multilateralism in the UN context, as a device of accommodation, is designed more than any previous mechanism to ensure that countries, at best, come together or, at least, are not constantly in conflict; needless to say, this is a never-ending task. Second, it is a work in progress from the viewpoint of content because the ideals and goals in the name of which it is conducted (e.g., peace and development) are half-scripted. Yes, they offer normative and political guidance and direction; however, they are uncertain enough to provide room to maneuver, internationally and nationally. This is shown by the fact that member states and the international community have latitude regarding the interpretation and implementation of these ideals and goals. Obviously, this latitude is not only a positive element; it also illustrates the limitations of contemporary global governance, its difficulty to deliver policy convergence, and its compliance based on international norms.[9] It is also a double-edged sword in that it can provide opportunities for states and the international community to not seriously consider multilateral ideals and goals and, ultimately, to avoid responsibility and accountability.

[9] Consider the latitude that the members of the UN Security Council have in their interpretation and implementation of the Charter. Or consider the lack or problematic sense of policy coherence, with the differences of analysis and recommendations this entails among international organizations. For example, in the field of development, see José Antonio Ocampo & K. S. Jomo (eds.), *Towards Full and Decent Employment* (New York: Zed Books and the United Nations, 2007), pp. 38–47.

However, because the world is still normatively and politically quite pluralist, to proceed otherwise is hardly an option. In addition, not allowing for maneuvering room could lead one vision of the good (e.g., the Western one) to prevail at the international and national levels more than already is the case, which would arguably accentuate the tensions between the West and the non-West.

From this perspective, we can see that the work-in-progress character of the multilateral dimension of the international system and that of being inclusive become the same thing. The premium that multilateralism and the UN put on universality of membership, on including as many states as possible, echoes the open-ended aim of having countries working together and being socialized despite their differences. To be sure, disagreements concerning international norms and policies, their interpretation and implementation, and their dilution as a way to diminish them and fulfill the need for common ground are the costs of heterogeneity of membership. It is the price for accepting that a country does not have to be a democracy in order to be part of UN and multilateral arrangements. Nevertheless, the international system has been willing to bear this cost because it comes with greater benefits. After all, one of the crucial benefits is the ability of multilateralism and the UN to cast a wide net, permitting the internalization of divergences, with the help of an approach to normative multilateral priorities that is somewhat flexible. Compared to the dangers associated with having dissenters being made outsiders, and who could, as such, be inclined to radicalize their claims, having them framed and controlled within the international system is not a small gain.

That said, the pluralism of multilateralism and of the UN does not exclude the possibility of a strong endorsement of inclusiveness understood in democratic terms, which is another factor accounting for the resilience of the current international order. This endorsement and its positive impact are at work in various ways. Consider, for instance, the emphasis on the consent of states. Although it is frequently labeled as more theoretical than real, there are many occasions for which consent is required (e.g., the ratification of international legal instruments). Therefore, consent plays a notable role in making states the stakeholders of the international system. Human-rights norms, their inspirational quality with their commitment to improve the living conditions of people worldwide, and their appeal as a consequence comprise another aspect of how the democratic inclusiveness of multilateralism serves international order. Furthermore, there is the support that the international system obtains from the capacity of democratic values inhabiting multilateralism to shape discontent as an internal challenge. The power to criticize offered by the language of democratic rights and duties makes it possible not only to call for change but also to engineer change from within.[10]

As a result, the international system has the resources to be challenged and even to challenge itself – and to learn and evolve – without unraveling altogether. For this to happen presupposes that democratic values do not fall into the trap of becoming dogma. It presupposes that they do not become unreflective and do not identify with a sense of entitlement and righteousness. It presupposes that the values draw the line between right and wrong and defend what is right by being as open as possible to others' positions.

Provided that this condition is met, democratic values, more than anything else, have the ability to demonstrate the political strength and, ultimately, the legitimacy of international order deriving from embedding in itself the capacity to be challenged – if not the need to challenge itself. They have the power to show that the resilience of the current international system can be enhanced by providing the possibility to seek to be right by constantly aiming to improve itself. This includes envisioning that it could be wrong and that, if so, it should change – out of its own volition, so to speak – out of being true to the democratic components of its principles of legitimacy.

The Distinction between Law and Legitimacy. The importance of having law and legitimacy distinct while being locked in an intertwined and interactive relationship is a central feature of the inclusive work-in-progress and democratic dimensions of multilateralism and of its contribution to the resilience of international order. The distance provided by the distinction – the difference between law and legitimacy – is not always easy to pinpoint. This is especially true in periods of stability when, unlike in times of flux or transition, taking for granted the way things are can lead to law and legitimacy being perceived as more or less interchangeable.[11] Yet, law and legitimacy are distinct and ought to remain so, for two related reasons.

The first reason is associated with the fact that short of being aware of what differentiates them, it is the ability to criticize law that is undermined. This situation is risky when it comes to fighting for justice, for if law and legitimacy are merged, from which viewpoint is it possible to challenge law?

[10] Philip Allott, *Eunomia: New Order for a New World* (Oxford: Oxford University Press, 1990), pp. 216–217.

[11] On this question, see, for instance, Pierre Bourdieu's sociology, including his sociology of law, which is to a large extent an effort to unveil and explain how relations of domination can be socially naturalized via legal norms and mechanisms. See his article, "The Force of Law: Toward a Sociology of the Juridical Field," translated by Richard Terdiman, in *Hastings Law Journal* (Vol. 38, 1986); and *Pascalian Meditations*, translated by Richard Nice (Stanford, CA: Stanford University Press, 2000), pp. 164–205.

This question reveals that if law can appear to be more than legitimacy because of its power to elevate and institutionalize values into rights and to interpret and implement them – and, therefore, to indicate and enforce what is legitimate – in the end, legitimacy is more than law. It is more than law because although the power of law can be partly self-generated by the compelling qualities of law and its capacity to deliver, the power mainly derives from legitimacy giving legitimacy to law. Indeed, the values of which legitimacy is made and with which actors identify are the foundation and the horizon on the basis on which law, political institutions, and the system they express and underwrite are evaluated and deemed valid or not.

The second reason for maintaining the distance between law and legitimacy is that it is essential to finding the right balance between status quo and change and to ascertain what is right in this balance. At stake here is to know what needs to be changed and what needs to be preserved in law faced with changing reality, but also what needs to be kept and what needs to be changed in reality faced with changing law. That is, at the center of this exercise of double interpretation (i.e., the interpretations of reality by law and law by reality) is legitimacy. Legitimacy that, with its constitutive values, is at the same time part of reality (otherwise, it would not make sense to actors) and, as an ideal extension of reality, more than simply what is. Hence, the fact that in the best of circumstances, legitimacy is not primarily about defending the status quo; it is not about standing still. It is geared toward positive change, toward a better political community, making it possible for its members to be better.

The International System under Stress. The tensions existing among actors in the international realm demonstrate how far we are from accomplishing this goal. The current international system may have been able to evolve without breaking down; it does not mean that it is in good shape. In fact, it is very much under stress and so is its legitimacy. One could argue that it is as disintegrated and disintegrating as it is integrated and integrating. Two principal factors explain this state of affairs: (1) the high expectations associated with the culture of human rights; and (2) more decisively, the reluctance of powerful actors to truly take international human rights seriously.

The culture of human rights that partly inhabits and structures international order is ambitious from a normative viewpoint, considering that these rights and their fulfillment are presented as universal. As such, they constitute an important aspect of the benchmarks of international legitimacy. However, it is an aspect of the benchmarks of legitimacy that the international system does not seem capable of satisfying – at least, if we focus on the fact that, for instance, worldwide inequalities are staggering – to the point that global poverty is a structural problem. In a lecture delivered in December 2008 at UN Headquarters in New York in the context of the United Nations University Lecture Series, *Emerging Thinking on Global Issues*, Thomas Pogge called the following statistics to the attention of the audience: among the 6.8 billion people alive today, 1 billion are undernourished, 2 billion lack access to essential drugs, 1.085 billion lack access to safe drinking water, and 2.6 billion lack adequate sanitation. He also stressed the fact that between 1990 and 2008, worldwide poverty caused 300 million deaths, compared to 55 million during World War II between 1939 and 1945.[12]

In other words, despite the enunciation of international norms of human rights, the call for justice is not being answered. It is even more the case because, far from being the product of fatality, this situation is largely the responsibility of the powerful actors. In developed as in developing countries, those in ruling positions – rather than adopting the policies and allocating the resources necessary for achieving human rights – too often turn their back on them for short-term gains. This influences the work of international organizations.[13] In these conditions, it is not surprising that for those discovering themselves on the disenfranchised side of history, the international system does not have much legitimacy. Another irony is that because international order is widely perceived as shaped by Western powers, the lack of trust among the West and the rest of the world is deepened.

This leads to the paradox of the current international system likely being more legitimate than any other before and still probably less than any other; it has significant legitimacy while also having very little. The fact that the democratic values and claims to take legitimacy seriously that it entails, in principle, should have the system looking after the weak more than the strong,[14] and that to the contrary it is hardly happening, reinforces this point. That is, sorting out what is right and wrong and implementing what is right – and, by doing so, generating effective support for a more integrated and just world order – remains an uphill battle. It continues to be the object of unresolved and pending problems in the multilateral management of crises. This can be seen in the fault lines at the core of the most difficult questions

[12] Thomas Pogge, "Human Rights: The Second Sixty Years," *UNU Lecture Series Emerging Thinking on Global Issues* (New York: United Nations Headquarters, December 11, 2008), available at www.ony.unu.edu/events-forums/events/2008/unu-lecture-series-emerging-th.html.

[13] Thomas Pogge, "Recognized and Violated by International Law: The Human Rights of the Global Poor," in *Leiden Journal of International Law* (Vol. 18, No. 4, December 18, 2005).

[14] This echoes the fact that a social system that recognizes a central place for justice focuses on the powerless.

that the UN and, more specifically, the Security Council have been handling over the years.

Fault Lines of International Legitimacy

In Chapter 2, in unpacking legitimacy at the international level, we argued that if international politics considers the demands of legitimacy, it has to pay attention to three complementary considerations. First, it must work hard to not be limited to a zero-sum game. Second, inequalities in the international distribution of power must be balanced by an exchange of rights and duties that is mindful of the interest of the various actors; this is especially important in a democratic environment. Third, agreement must be sought after regarding community membership, the identity of right holders, the hierarchy among them, what it means in terms of rightful conduct, and international authority. Also, as described previously, socializing instability has to be a constant concern.

It is principally when disagreement prevails on these matters that fault lines of international legitimacy can develop. The fault lines must be understood in connection with five characteristics. First, they encompass areas of tension that even when they are geographically localized, have significance for the international system as a whole because of the issues with which they are associated. Second, because these issues involve struggles about competing right claims, fault lines are about contested visions of order and justice. Third, fault lines of international legitimacy entail the inability to find common ground between actors (whether states or nonstate) that are part of the dispute, including groups of individuals. Fourth, the points of contention tend to be a mixture, or hybrid, of normative and material considerations. The normative-political disagreements – that is, turning around what is right and what is wrong or access to and respect of rights – frequently project or are incarnated in disputes concerning territories. Fifth, the challenge of resolving the disputes is linked to the reluctance of the international authority to adopt a decisive stance.

The way we conceive the notion of "fault line" is quite distinct from Samuel P. Huntington. In his book, *The Clash of Civilizations and the Remaking of World Order,*[15] he identifies fault lines with conflicts among communities of different civilizations and, more specifically, different religions:

> Fault line conflicts are communal conflicts between states or groups from different civilizations. Fault line wars are conflicts that have become violent. . . . While

[15] Samuel P. Huntington, *The Clash of Civilizations and the Remaking of World Order* (New York: Simon & Schuster, 2003).

> fault line wars share the prolonged duration, high levels of violence, and ideological ambivalence of other communal wars, they also differ from them in two ways. First, communal wars may occur between ethnic, religious, racial or linguistic groups. Since religion, however, is the principal defining characteristic of civilizations, fault line wars are almost always between people of different religions.... Second, other communal wars tend to be particularistic, and hence are relatively unlikely to spread and involve additional participants. Fault line wars, in contrast, are by definition between groups which are part of larger cultural entities.[16]

In contrast to this conception, the fault lines referred to herein may encompass cultural and religious dimensions, but these do not comprise a central aspect of them. Rather, what is important in understanding fault lines of international legitimacy are the competing right claims put forward by actors in the language of norms of the multilateral system, of the UN, on which no resolution or agreement is being found. Therefore, they become pending problems, open wounds. Also, although having relevance for the entire international system because they display struggles around visions of order and justice, they do not amount to a crisis of the international system per se. Although they are a significant source of instability, it does not reach a systemic level. They generate stress for international order yet not to the point that the order is in danger of being invalidated altogether. That is, the tensions and contradictions they point to are not as bad as those that crippled and led to the demise of the League of Nations and the international system in the 1930s.[17] Despite the divergences and conflicts that exist internationally between actors – including in the UN context between members of the General Assembly and the Security Council, or between the permanent members of the Council – international cooperation is primarily the preferred *modus operandi.* "Going rogue," perceived as an attitude carrying too high of a price, remains the exception.

Ideal Types of Fault Lines of International Legitimacy

Fault lines of international legitimacy can be organized into four clusters, or ideal types,[18] each representing a specific version of fault lines and, as a whole, covering some of their main characteristics. Of course, the reality of international relations tends not to espouse the clear-cut qualities of the

[16] Ibid., pp. 252–254.

[17] Berman, *Passions et ambivalences: Le colonialisme, le nationalisme et le droit international* (Paris: Editions Pedone, 2008), Chapter 6, particularly pp. 323, 333, and 384–387.

[18] On ideal-types, see Max Weber, *The Methodology of the Social Sciences,* translated by Edward A. Shils & Henry A. Finch (New York: Free Press, 1949), pp. 90–104.

clusters. In daily international life, fault lines typically overlap if not merge with one another; however, for the sake of analytical clarity, it is helpful to fall back on these distinctions.

The first type concerns normative fault lines. It is about competitive right claims that actors have, as well as about the debates regarding how the international community should address and solve the tensions that spring from them. Arguably, this is the most important type of fault lines. However, the other types should not be overlooked; they are significant because they are the historical incarnations or translations of normative disputes. From this perspective, the second cluster of fault lines – geopolitical fault lines – is concerned with how struggles around right claims unfold on the ground, in the geography of the areas where conflicts take place. The third type – temporal fault lines – is concerned with the duration of hostilities, whether they are long-standing or recent, whether they drag on or are resolved relatively quickly. The fourth type is concerned with the extent of the challenge that a fault line constitutes; specifically, does it encompass a local or global, tactical or strategic, internal or external call for change of the international system?

Because the UN is a key venue in which international crises are negotiated and managed, it is destined to be a forum and a vehicle for fault lines of international legitimacy when there is severe disagreement on major questions. As a result, it makes sense to focus on the UN in order to reflect on these fault lines. In this regard, it is more in the Security Council than the General Assembly that we find them at work institutionally. Therefore, the overview of fault lines provided herein is in connection with the number and content of resolutions that the Council has adopted since the end of World War II.

Normative Fault Lines. Normative fault lines and the conflicts they embody emerge against the background of two types of elements. First, they appear in the context of the three themes discussed previously that comprise the framework of international life and its "we-versus-them" relations: the inside/outside, universalist/particularist, and system/society themes.[19] Second, they are zones of dispute concerning how these themes are constructed through the main dimensions of international legitimacy unpacked previously, such as international community membership, right holder, hierarchy of right holders, rightful conduct, and international authority. From this perspective, normative fault lines are prone to be disagreements in crucial

[19] See Chapter 1 of this book.

domains of the philosophy of international rights, concerning the interpretation and implementation of these rights.

Normative fault lines generated relative to the issue of international community membership – that is, who is and who is not recognized as a legitimate member – in the post–World War II era have been principally on display in connection with collective entities. Indeed, the question of what makes a group legitimate internationally has been a major cause of tension in the past sixty years. At the individual level, however, it has been less of a problem. Universality and equality of rights have made it difficult to refuse recognition to people as (legitimate) members of the human community and deny them, from a principle viewpoint, the rights associated with it. Yet, there are cases when this happens, which never fail to become a source of normative and political controversy, as demonstrated by recent debates about the treatment of those suspected of terrorism by the United States post–September 11. For many, the willingness of the Bush administration to torture terrorists and refuse them due process, on the basis that terrorism is uncivilized, is a grave shortcoming – at least, if the idea of rule of law is to be taken seriously at home and abroad.

Conflicts among actors about right holding – about who is the "right right holder," so to speak – are another aspect of normative fault lines in the international realm. Classically, this type of conflict unfolds in the context of violence resulting from claims at odds regarding rights, preeminently the exercise of the principle of national sovereignty over territories and their people and resources.[20] However, this violence is not necessarily happening in a clear-cut international situation, involving interstate actors and relations. In fact, the violence frequently arises in an environment of historical grievances encompassing disagreements on why and how to draw the line within and among territories, between "us" and "them." In the process, the distinction between the internal and external, or international, in terms of right holding is a key element at stake. This issue plays at the collective level, as with secession, from empires (e.g., decolonization) or from states (e.g., partition); however, it also entails an individual dimension. Territorial-rights disputes are often caused when people who feel mistreated by a dominant power perceive the establishment of their own system of government, of state, as a way to end the violation of their rights. From this perspective, the principle of self-determination, as well as the redesigning of political communities it requires, tends to be marshaled by subjugated groups in order to have their rights better respected. The movement of decolonization in the

[20] Kohen, *Possession contestée et souveraineté territoriale* (Paris: Presses Universitaires de France, 1997), Part III.

1950s and 1960s and the Balkan Wars, including Kosovo, throughout the 1990s are part of this story. And, to some extent, so is the Israeli–Palestinian conflict.

Hierarchy among right holders is an additional source of normative fault lines. This can be explained best by using the example of the fundamental principles that govern international relations: sovereign equality of states, self-determination of peoples, prohibition of the threat or use of force, peaceful settlement of disputes, nonintervention in the internal or external affairs of other states, respect for human rights, international cooperation, and good faith. As discussed previously, these principles are essential to the sense of international legitimacy and outline what is both commendable and condemnable in the conduct of states. They also contribute to the identification of international right holders and their relationships.[21] That is, the three types of relations existing among fundamental principles – compatibility, competition, and hierarchy – apply also to international right holders, including participation in their construction.

In this context, relations of compatibility are not problematic because compatibility makes accommodation possible. However, competitive relations tend to be a cause of tension, considering that they imply that a choice has to be made and that hierarchy relations – meant to help establish this selection – do not always offer decisive support. In fact, the somewhat contested and evolving character of hierarchy among right holders (and principles), especially following the end of the Cold War, has been a factor in making it a point of friction, an aspect of normative fault lines.[22] The heated debates on humanitarian interventions of the past fifteen years, at the UN and beyond, are testimonies to this. Between those who favor international interventions for human rights and humanitarian reasons – and, therefore, assume that individuals across borders have rights that cannot be overlooked for the benefit of the state – and those who think that state rights should prevail, it has been a challenge to find common ground.[23]

[21] See Chapter 2 of this book.

[22] Jean-Marc Coicaud and Nicholas J. Wheeler, "The Changing Ethics of Power beyond Borders," in Jean-Marc Coicaud & Nicholas J. Wheeler (eds.), *National Interest and International Solidarity: Particular and Universal Ethics in International Life* (Tokyo: United Nations University Press, 2008), pp. 1–24.

[23] Non-Western countries tend to advocate a territorial understanding of sovereignty, basically associated with the view that nations are independent realms within which national political institutions are entitled to exercise power without being challenged by external actors. The principle of nonintervention in the affairs of other states is dovetailed with this interpretation of sovereignty. As for Western powers, they put forward a conception of sovereignty that emphasizes its democratic dimension, insisting on the importance of individual and human rights. From this perspective, the principle of respect for human rights opens the possibility of a "droit de regard" and even intervention from the outside world. Nevertheless, Western

The conflicts that result from the question of hierarchy of right holders lead directly to those concerning the rightful conduct of states and the international community. To be sure, not all areas of international conduct are equally prone to be a source of normative dispute. For instance, some of the principles of socialization of international life geared toward indicating what is required from states to coexist with one another (e.g., prohibition of the threat or use of force, peaceful settlement of disputes, international cooperation, and good faith) result in straightforward recommendations about how states are supposed to behave. Consequently, they are widely endorsed, which explains why violations of the recommendations – although not necessarily fought against, particularly when committed by a powerful state – are heavily criticized. The American war against Iraq from 2003 onward – broadly perceived around the world as illegal and illegitimate because it was launched with false motives and without UN Security Council authorization – illustrates this point.

That said, it is in connection with the hierarchy of right holders, especially when there are disagreements on the correct hierarchy of right holders, that conflicts about rightful conduct are the most likely to emerge. These disputes, which usually unfold within the framework of the "state-versus-individual" tension, can hardly be avoided. Indeed, conflicts associated with a contested hierarchy of right holders rarely fail to translate into conflicts about the rightful conduct of states and/or the international community. When a choice must be made about the prime beneficiary of an action, it is logical that divergent views about the hierarchy of right holders lead to dissonant views on the rightful conduct, about who is in the prime position to profit from the action.

It is the task of the UN Security Council, in its international authority role, to handle and attempt to overcome the tensions linked to normative fault lines. It must try to align international legal norms and legitimacy, as well as power and legitimacy, so that an acceptable balance is found between stability and change. This entails negotiating and prioritizing the various legitimacies that enter into international legitimacy and what is owed to the

democratic nations, starting with the most powerful, rein in their advocacy for democratic sovereignty whenever its effects infringe on their own autonomy of decision making. This is shown by U.S reservations vis-à-vis the International Criminal Court. On the issues linking national sovereignty, human rights, and humanitarian interventions, see Allen Buchanan, *Justice, Legitimacy, and Self-Determination: Moral Foundations for International Law* (Oxford: Oxford University Press, 2004); and Robert E. Keohane and J. L. Holzgrefe (eds.), *Humanitarian Intervention: Ethical, Legal and Political Dilemmas* (Cambridge: Cambridge University Press, 2003), particularly Parts III and IV.

constituencies attached to them. Contrary to what positivist[24] and absolutist conceptions of international law believe, this exercise is not self-contained (i.e., internal) or exclusively legal.[25] It is an intertwined and back-and-forth effort of interpretation of international norms and reality.

The UN Security Council assesses reality (e.g., conflicts), qualifies it, and decides what to do about it within the framework of international norms, such as the UN Charter, previous Security Council resolutions, and other sources of international law. However, it also interprets international norms based on reality and its transformations at the national and international levels, which includes the foundational values of norms – that is, the core norms with which actors identify and that comprise their identity. This interpretative interaction of norms and reality is even more important considering that it is through this interaction that change in and of international legal norms and change in and of reality happen over time. Aiming to match one another while evolving, they gradually adjust to their respective changes.

Yet, the criticism leveled at the UN Security Council reveals that it does not accomplish its task in the best way possible. As an organ that has, within limits, the responsibility through its work to preserve or change international legal norms and reality whenever necessary in order to make each of them and their relations as legitimate as possible, it tends to be a target for attacks. This is to the point that the Security Council can be perceived as an institutional producer of normative international fault lines.

From this perspective, four arguments are commonly expressed. First, because its policies are insufficient in one way or another, the UN Security Council has difficulty satisfying all its international clients. Second, it suffers from a representation deficit. As the result of the vision of the World War II victors and big-power politics, the Security Council does not respond to the requirements of fair access to and repartition of power internationally. The self-centered attitude of its permanent members, which are frequently more focused on their interests than on those of other member states, does not help. Hence, members of the UN General Assembly may resent the five permanent members of the Security Council, including the most powerful among them, the United States. Also, the issue of possible enlargement of

[24] Pierre-Marie Dupuy, *L'unité de l'ordre juridique international: Cours général de droit international public (2000)* (Leiden: Hague Academy of International Law, 2003), Vol. 297, pp. 29 and 403–412.

[25] Allen Buchanan, *Justice, Legitimacy, and Self-Determination: Moral Foundations for International Law* (op. cit.), pp. 8–9 and 298–308; and Martti Koskenniemi, "Perceptions of Justice: Of Walls and Bridges between Europe and the United States" (lecture delivered at Heidelberg, Germany, on February 10, 2004).

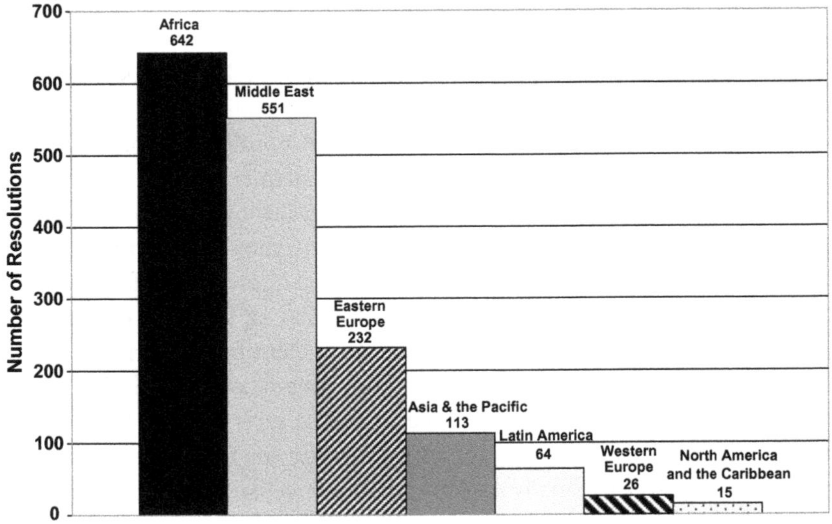

Figure 3.1. Number of UN Security Council Resolutions by Major Geographical Region, 1946–2007.

the Security Council remains a constant item on the UN agenda for reform, without ever being realized. Third, the lack of transparency of the Security Council is an issue; namely, the opaque character of its deliberations and decisions echoes its inability to put the disenfranchised front and center. Fourth, the Security Council is part of an international authority system that is disunited and contradictory, with actors and policies – within and outside the UN – often pursuing divergent objectives.[26]

Geopolitical Fault Lines. As discussed previously, normative fault lines are translated in the geography of the regions where actors are at odds. In other words, geopolitical fault lines are the projection and incarnation of normative disagreements on the ground. The zones where they take place, located between relatively stable and well-established areas, are recurrent regions of conflict, which is reflected in the geographical breakdown of Security Council resolutions (Figure 3.1). Among the 1,794 resolutions between 1946 and 2007, 1,643 can be analyzed and ranked by region, as follows: concerning Africa, 642 resolutions were adopted: the Middle East, 551; Eastern Europe,

[26] On the legitimacy deficit of the UN and on what could help to reduce it, see Allen Buchanan & Robert O. Keohane, "The Legitimacy of Global Governance Institutions," in *Ethics and International Affairs* (Vol. 20, No. 4, 2006).

232; Asia and the Pacific, 113; Latin America, 64; Western Europe, 26; and North America and the Caribbean, 15.[27]

In these regions, tensions and conflicts have occurred within or among countries, eventually triggering UN involvement. El Salvador in the 1980s and Somalia in the early 1990s were in the first category of conflicts within countries. Disputes among states tend to take place along three scenarios: first, among already existing countries (e.g., the UN Security Council resolutions adopted in the context of the invasion of Kuwait by Iraq); second, as the product of territory partition or aspirations to partition; and, third, as a combination of the two previous scenarios. The third scenario has proven to be especially toxic. The wars between Israel and Egypt and between Israel and Lebanon can be understood in connection with the creation of the State of Israel and the rights of Palestinians. The wars in the former Yugoslavia during the 1990s are also in this category.

Long-standing and New Fault Lines. Long-standing and recent fault lines, and the time dimension they entail, are another aspect of fault lines of international legitimacy, linked with the normative and geopolitical fault lines referred to previously.

Long-standing fault lines are defined as decades-long conflicts that the UN has been unable to resolve but continues to monitor at the diplomatic level through the Security Council and on the ground via peacekeeping operations principally involving troop interposition. This is the case in the Arab–Israeli conflict, where the first UN peacekeeping operation, deployed in 1948, remains present under the name of the UN Truce Supervision Organization. This is also the case in Kashmir, where the UN has been involved since 1948 with the UN Military Observer Group in India and Pakistan. New fault lines are mainly those dealing with disputes that followed the end of the Cold War, primarily in the Balkans and Africa (i.e., the Horn of Africa, Central Africa, and Western Africa).

Three elements are noticeable about these types of fault lines. The first element entails how they are inserted into the specific timelines of the UN presence region by region and how those timelines vary significantly.

In Africa, the area of the world in which the UN has been the most engaged, the Security Council began its involvement in the early 1960s, in the context of decolonization and the associated tensions. From 1960 to 1991, the number

[27] The major regions are derived from the report of the Secretary-General, "Composition of the Secretariat" (New York: United Nations Headquarters, 1998, UN Document A/53/375), pp. 94–96. The figures and tables were created by John Tzanos and Ken Stretch.

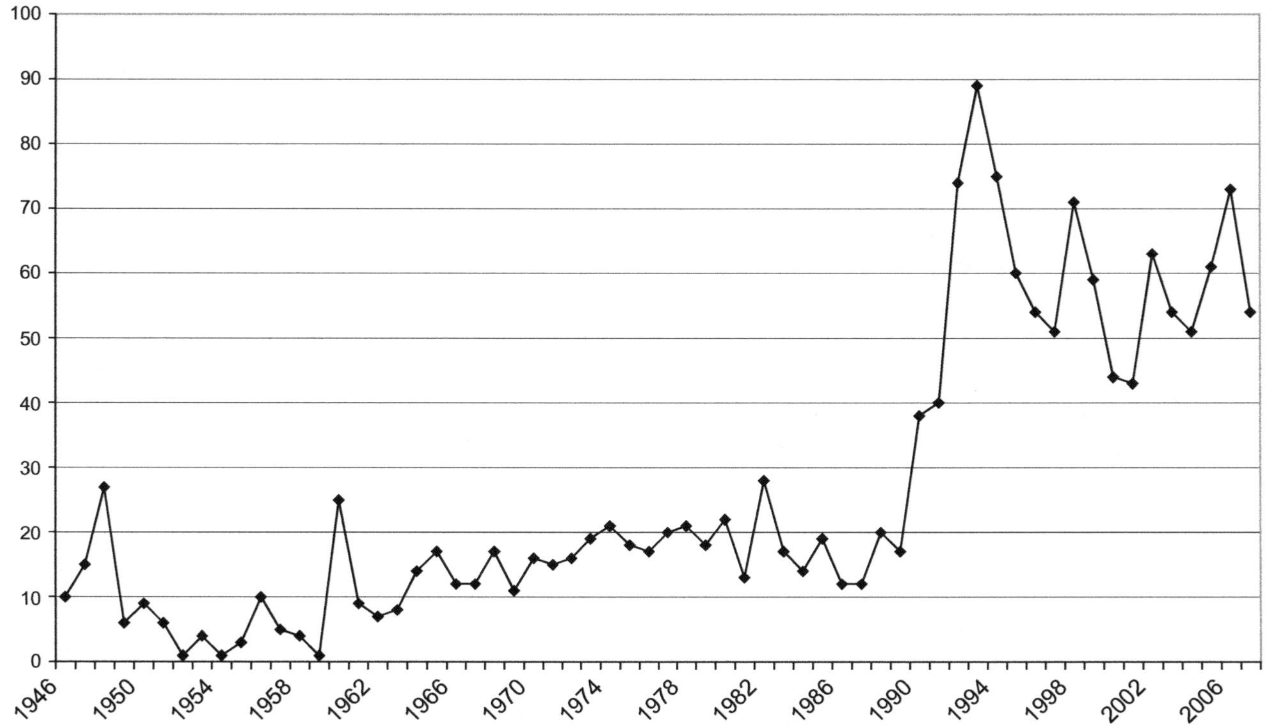

Figure 3.2. Number of UN Security Council Resolutions, 1946–2007.

of resolutions per year oscillated from one (1981) to twenty-two (1960). Since 1992, the activities of the Security Council on the African continent have increased, with a minimum of sixteen resolutions (1992 and 1997) and a maximum of forty-three (2006).

In the Middle East, involvement of the UN Security Council has been more evenly distributed. There was much activity in the late 1940s, particularly with the declaration of independence by Israel in 1948 and the strain that it generated, as indicated by the sixteen resolutions adopted in that year. In subsequent decades, the flow of resolutions has been rather steady: between 1967 and 2007, the number ranged from a minimum of five (1972 and 1976) to a maximum of twenty-seven (1990). In Eastern Europe, the third most active region in terms of the number of Security Council resolutions, most of the 226 resolutions were in the 1990s due to the Balkan Wars.

In Asia and the Pacific, after the decolonization-related activity of the late 1940s and early 1950s, the situation was relatively quiet until the post–Cold War era, when there was an increase in UN involvement, mainly due to events unfolding in Cambodia. In Latin America, it is essentially in the 1990s that the Security Council became involved, with the UN playing a major role in the resolution of conflicts in Central America.

The second characteristic regarding long-standing and new fault lines is how the time framework in which they unfold has changed drastically. More specifically, compared to the past, the last twenty years marked an intensification of the Security Council work, as shown in Figure 3.2.

That is, the end of the Cold War truly constituted a "game change" for the activities of the UN Security Council in areas of conflict. The increase in crises and the geopolitical relaxation of the period both led to greater needs and opportunities for the Security Council to become engaged.

It is not surprising that this increase is reflected in the surge of region-specific resolutions since the early 1990s, as shown in Table 3.1.

These figures allow us to visualize the following evolution (Figure 3.3): Analyzing the content of these UN Security Council resolutions also demonstrates how the UN mandates concerning the handling of the conflicts have grown not only quantitatively but also qualitatively, reaching a high level of complexity.

The third element is concerned with the similarities and differences existing between long-standing and newly established fault lines. Long-standing and new fault lines tend to share three similarities. First, they occur in zones that are at the interstices of great powers' influence, which can be geographical areas caught between zones of influence (e.g., the Balkans) or areas previously

Table 3.1. *Number of Security Council Resolutions by Major Geographical Region, 1945–2007 (a) (e)*

Year	The Middle East (b)	Africa	Latin America (c)	North America and the Caribbean	Asia and the Pacific (d)	Western Europe	Eastern Europe	Total
2007	12	33	0	2	1	0	6	54
2006	17	43	2	0	6	0	5	73
2005	14	40	2	0	1	1	3	61
2004	13	28	3	0	2	1	4	51
2003	17	30	1	0	2	1	3	54
2002	23	24	0	0	4	1	11	63
2001	13	19	0	2	1	0	8	43
2000	11	25	0	0	2	0	6	44
1999	14	25	1	0	9	0	10	59
1998	17	37	1	0	1	0	15	71
1997	12	16	3	0	0	0	20	51
1996	12	22	5	0	0	0	15	54
1995	7	21	3	0	0	0	29	60
1994	13	34	9	0	2	0	17	75
1993	9	28	8	0	7	2	35	89
1992	13	16	4	0	5	1	35	74
1991	22	3	4	0	5	0	6	40
1990	27	2	5	0	3	1	0	38
1989	10	5	2	0	0	0	0	17
1988	15	5	0	0	0	0	0	20
1987	8	3	0	0	1	0	0	12
1986	10	2	0	0	0	0	0	12
1985	8	10	1	0	0	0	0	19
1984	8	5	0	0	1	0	0	14
1983	10	5	1	1	0	0	0	17
1982	21	5	2	0	0	0	0	28
1981	9	1	0	2	1	0	0	13
1980	16	5	0	1	0	0	0	22
1979	11	6	0	1	0	0	0	18
1978	11	8	0	1	1	0	0	21
1977	6	13	0	0	1	0	0	20
1976	5	9	0	0	2	1	0	17
1975	8	7	1	0	2	0	0	18
1974	17	2	0	1	1	0	0	21
1973	10	6	1	1	0	1	0	19
1972	5	11	0	0	0	0	0	16
1971	7	5	0	0	3	0	0	15
1970	7	8	0	0	1	0	0	16

Year	The Middle East (b)	Africa	Latin America (c)	North America and the Caribbean	Asia and the Pacific (d)	Western Europe	Eastern Europe	Total
1969	6	5	0	0	0	0	0	11
1968	11	6	0	0	0	0	0	17
1967	10	2	0	0	0	0	0	12
1966	4	5	0	1	2	0	0	12
1965	4	6	2	0	5	0	0	17
1964	7	5	0	0	1	1	0	14
1963	1	7	0	0	0	0	0	8
1962	1	4	0	2	0	0	0	7
1961	1	7	0	0	1	0	0	9
1960	1	22	2	0	0	0	0	25
1959	0	0	0	0	1	0	0	1
1958	3	1	0	0	0	0	0	4
1957	0	1	0	0	4	0	0	5
1956	3	4	0	0	1	1	1	10
1955	3	0	0	0	0	0	0	3
1954	0	0	1	0	0	0	0	1
1953	2	0	0	0	1	1	0	4
1952	0	0	0	0	1	0	0	1
1951	3	0	0	0	3	0	0	6
1950	1	0	0	0	8	0	0	9
1949	3	0	0	0	2	1	0	6
1948	16	0	0	0	11	0	0	27
1947	0	0	0	0	6	6	3	15
1946	3	0	0	0	1	6	0	10
Totals	**551**	**642**	**64**	**15**	**113**	**26**	**232**	**1,643**

(a) The major regions are derived from the report of the Secretary General (1998), "Composition of the Secretariat," A/53/375, pp. 94–96.
(b) This category includes resolutions on Palestine and issues concerning Palestinians.
(c) This category includes resolutions on the Falkland Islands.
(d) The category "Asia and the Pacific" includes resolutions on Timor Leste.
(e) The number of UN Security Council resolutions that appear here is less than the total number of resolutions adopted throughout the period 1946–2007. The resolutions that have no specific focus or address multiple regions, and those that do not apparently address issues of fault lines of international legitimacy (e.g., resolutions on admittances of judges to tribunals), have been omitted.

under influence that, since this state of affairs disappeared, face instability (e.g., Africa during decolonization and the post–Cold War era). Second, the disputes are over territorial possessions. Third, they are fault lines in the context of which self-determination and human-rights principles are prone to be used by the challengers of the established order to make their case.

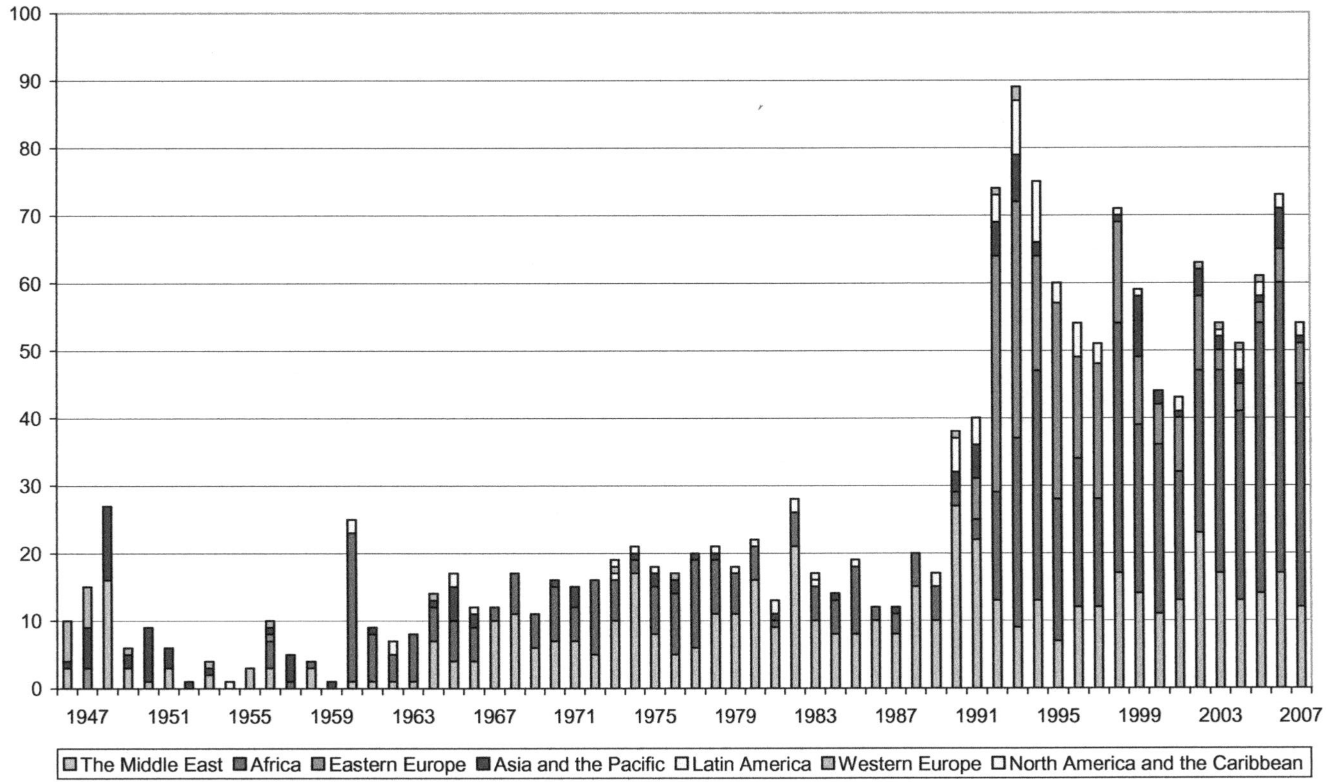

Figure 3.3. Number of Security Council Resolutions, by Year and Region.

However, there are also differences between old and new fault lines. One difference is linked to the question of the legitimacy of use of force beyond borders. Between the end of World War II and the 1990s, this issue mainly referred to interstate conflicts, which continued in the post–Cold War years, as indicated by the debates regarding the launching of the war against Iraq in March 2003. Yet, as mentioned previously, during the 1990s, the Security Council innovated by putting on the agenda the use of force in connection with intrastate conflicts for humanitarian reasons.

Fault Lines as Scopes of Challenge. The final type of fault lines relates to the scope of the challenge mounted by actors that believe the organization of the international system does not fulfill their rights. From this perspective, the scope that the challenge represents depends on whether it unfolds within the framework of the existing norms of international legitimacy. When it does, although this situation may bring about serious changes – as shown by the normative and political evolution of past decades in the environment of multilateralism – it is contained because it is internal to and internalized by the international system.

However, it is another story when international order and its legitimacy are contested as a whole and when challengers do not accept containment and accommodation as a possibility. Here, the challenge is systemic, which can come from within or from outside. Coming from within arises when contradictions within the international system are so deep and the contesting actors are so radicalized and powerful that the situation leads to overall collapse. As discussed previously, the bankruptcy of international order in the 1930s can be understood in these terms. In their own way, Marxist forces counting on and exacerbating the contradictions of the liberal international system to get rid of it could also have generated – had their goals been met – a systemic change from within. However, a systemic collapse also can come from outside or external actors. In Chapter 4, Nathaniel Berman refers to Osama Bin Laden justifying September 11 by the lack of legitimacy of the current international order. That said, external systemic attacks, of course, are not the exclusivity of non-Westerners. After all, for the West to impose its seal globally, it had to first function – starting in about the sixteenth century – as an outside systemic threat vis-à-vis non-Western arrangements of international order, in the Americas, Asia, Africa, and elsewhere.

Fault lines of international legitimacy indicate how challenging it is to socialize international life. They display disputes that are a factor of insecurity on the ground for a time and to an extent that varies with the difficulty of reconciling competing right claims. For the future of international relations, the fault lines point to three possible scenarios.

First, the international system could continue to live with the fault lines remaining more or less the same, meaning that international order would persist the way it is but would not improve. The level of distrust and a sense of false peace would be key features of international culture.

Second, fault lines of international legitimacy could develop into pathologies greater than they already are. They could contribute to putting international life on an ever more conflictive course, affecting more than before the actual zones of tension but also affecting powerful countries.

Third, modalities could be found to overcome the fault lines presently at work. For most international actors, this would presuppose changing their ways, first their conception of "us versus them," of how they relate to others. This scenario would call for coming to terms, more so than has been the case until recently, with the fact that achieving security requires a constant quest for mutual accommodation.

Reviewing the intellectual and political underpinnings of these three scenarios and encouraging the likelihood of the optimal scenario (i.e., the third option) indicates the need for further research on issues of international legitimacy.

NATHANIEL BERMAN

4. Intervention in a "Divided World": Axes of Legitimacy

Following World War I, which ended more than eighty-three years ago, the whole Islamic world fell under the crusader banner – under the British, French, and Italian governments. They divided the whole world.... Those who refer things to the international legitimacy have disavowed the legitimacy of the Holy Book...

– Osama bin Laden, November 2001[1]

[The UN must] prove to the world whether it's going to be relevant or whether it's going to be a League of Nations, irrelevant.

– George W. Bush, September 2002[2]

And while it is difficult to see the world body go down the drain like its predecessor the League of Nations... it is equally difficult to see how the United Nations will regain the **status and relative coherence** it enjoyed before Operation Iraqi Freedom.

– *The Independent* (Banjul), March 2003[3]

Status and Coherence

The Internationalist Dream. It would be tempting to look back at the long post–Cold War decade as an era of the more or less steadily growing legitimacy of an activist internationalism – an era that began with 1989 and

[1] Translation of Osama bin Laden speech, broadcast on Al Jazeera television network on November 3, 2001; available at news.bbc.co.uk/2/hi/world/monitoring/media_reports/1636782.stm.

[2] Remarks by President George W. Bush, available at www.whitehouse.gov/news/releases/2002/09/20020919-7.html.

[3] Baba Galleh Jallow, "Of Iraqi Freedom, Democratic Contagion, and Giant Mistakes," *The Independent* (Banjul), March 24, 2003.

ended somewhere between "9/11" and the U.S. invasion of Iraq. A representative example of this perspective was provided by a writer in a Gambian newspaper shortly after the beginning of the Iraq invasion (the third of the three epigraphs to this chapter).[4] The writer declared that the U.S. attack would probably signal the demise of the "status and relative coherence" previously enjoyed by the United Nations, condemning it to the fate of its predecessor, the League of Nations. This writer's views characterized much of pro-internationalist world opinion at the time of the American action.

If internationalism seems to such observers to have suffered a severe blow, the post–Cold War decade often appears to them by contrast as something of a golden age, in which internationalism had "status" and "coherence." This contrast between the deep fractures of the present with a more harmonious recent past reflects the persistent dream of an international community with the status of a legitimate identity and the coherence of integrated ideals and practices. Above all, this dream is that of a community that would thoroughly integrate state power into internationalist principle – hence, the gravity of the U.S. invasion of Iraq. This internationalist dream has usually been articulated in the mode of absence – as a nostalgic lament for the loss of the community or a millenarian hope for its construction. It is a dream that particularly appeals to legal internationalists – and may account for the fact that writings addressed to the problem of "The Disintegration of International Society"[5] and "International Law in a Divided World"[6] have come to constitute a genre favored by some of the leading international lawyers over the past century. It may also account for the fact that a dichotomy between an international law founded on the principle of equality and one founded on the power of "hegemonism" has seemed a useful analytical axis to widely divergent observers in the past several decades.[7]

It would not be difficult, however, to argue that remembering the long post–Cold War decade as a time of steadily – even if unevenly – growing internationalist legitimacy is a retrospective illusion. Words like *Srebrenica*

[4] Ibid.

[5] Georg Schwarzenberger, The Rule of Law and the Disintegration of the International Society, 33 *American Journal of International Law* 56 (1939).

[6] See, e.g., Antonio Cassese, *International Law in a Divided World* (1986); Rosalyn Higgins, *Conflicts of Interest: International Law in a Divided World* (1965); Oliver Lissitzyn, International Law in a Divided World, 542 *International Conciliation* 1 (1963).

[7] See, e.g., Detlev F. Vagts, Hegemonic International Law, 95 *American Journal of International Law* 843 (2001); UN General Assembly Resolution 103, A/Res/34/103 (December 14, 1979). The 1979 GA Resolution 103, entitled "Inadmissibility of Hegemonism in International Relations," is probably something of a high-water mark of seventies' Third Worldism in international fora.

and *Rwanda* should be enough to remind us of internationalism's *incoherence* during that period, due to the selectivity of its attentions; words like *Kosovo* should remind us of its uncertain *status,* due to the intermittence of respect shown by states for the need to subordinate their action to the authority of the formally constituted international community.

To be sure, many who share the nostalgia for the long post–Cold War decade may readily acknowledge that it was a time of numerous swings in internationalist prestige. Yet, criticism of post–Cold War internationalism is usually presented in the ameliorative mode. Challenges to the selectiveness of internationalists' attentions or the lack of inclusiveness of participation in their decision-making councils are usually intended to lead the international community to make good on its universal claims rather than attack its foundation. Such criticisms, therefore, are not incompatible with treating the failures and disappointments of the long decade as the inevitable travails of a universal international community struggling to be born – however regrettable and even tragic those travails may have been.

Since the end of the long post–Cold War decade, however, the very ideal of the gradual transformation of the world into a community governed by widely accepted internationalist principles and institutions has been subjected to a series of high-profile attacks. Perhaps the best known of these attacks issued from the very different quarters of Osama bin Laden and George W. Bush (see the first and second epigraphs to this chapter). As we shall see, whereas bin Laden primarily attacked the *status* of internationalism due to its putatively illegitimate identity, Bush primarily attacked its *coherence* due to the putative gap between its principles and its institutions. Like the internationalist writer in the Gambian newspaper, both of these challengers cited the League of Nations as an important reference, although each did so with a very different intent. As a result of such attacks, the prospect of the ideological redivision of the world into competing "legitimacies" has begun to appear to some internationalists as a grave danger, provoking a variety of discursive and practical strategies. Strategies designed to meet other challenges to internationalism in the past, such as those of Fascism in the 1930s, Communism during the Cold War, and the United States during the Vietnam era, have begun to play a visible role.

In this chapter, I propose that we reject the nostalgia for the long post–Cold War decade as both historically inaccurate and theoretically flawed. It would be easy, for example, to show that current challenges to internationalism – and the counterattacks on them – were in full play throughout the long decade. More fundamentally, I propose that we reject the utopian dream of an international community that finally would have integrated power and principle.

Activist internationalism will always appear to some as mere power for at least two reasons. First, ideological divisions in the world are not a product of a fall from grace but rather of the human condition – periodic announcements of the "end of ideology" notwithstanding. "Status" challenges – that is, attacking the putatively universal community as ideologically partisan – therefore will be a persistent feature of international debate. Second, the final integration of power and principle is impeded by the fact that internationalist principles and institutions are themselves deeply heterogeneous – rendering the achievement of "coherence," even "relative coherence," a provisional and contested affair. Internationalism, especially in its legal dimension, consists of a body of rules and institutions in which "self-determination" must always confront "sovereignty," "minority protection" must always face "individual rights," "free trade" must always confront the "right to development," the equality principle that governs the UN General Assembly must always face the power principle that governs the UN Security Council, and so on. Attempts at effecting "coordination"[8] among these elements will never achieve more than a temporary consensus. The bin Laden–style attacks on internationalism's status and the Bush-style assaults on its coherence are not exceptional, but only the latest instances of perennial challenges. Indeed, such challenges reveal much about the theoretical and practical elements of internationalist legitimacy – a legitimacy found not in a golden past or future but rather provisionally wrested out of the divisions of the present, particularly out of the crucibles of the types of local conflicts whose pacification our era has implicitly identified as a central task for any internationalism.

Taking the legitimacy of international intervention in local conflicts as my focal point, I argue that we reject the quest for an international community that finally would have achieved status and coherence. Rather, I advocate focusing on the situational, provisional aspect of legitimacy, on the way internationalist actors must continually seek to re-achieve legitimacy in relation to a variety of constituencies and in the face of ever-changing developments. In brief, I argue for an understanding of internationalist legitimacy that is less foundational and more vulnerable, less static and more tentative, less certain and messier.

Axes of Challenge, Axes of Competition. Those who challenge the legitimacy of dominant internationalist ideals and institutions usually present bids to legitimate competing alternatives. Those who attack the *status* of internationalism present an external critique of its identity as a whole, an identity they perceive as both specifiable and pernicious ("Crusader," "Capitalist,"

[8] Cassese, *supra* note 6, pp. 160–163.

"Imperialist," "American," and so on). In keeping with the nature of their challenge, they usually propose a competing internationalism embodying a different identity ("Islamic," "Communist," "Third Worldist," "multilateralist," and so on). Bin Laden provides an example of this type of critique and competing bid.

By contrast, those who attack the *coherence* of internationalism problematize the specifiability of its identity by highlighting the heterogeneity of its internal elements. They allege that these elements – discursive, practical, and institutional – have been wrongfully or irrationally articulated, wrongfully or irrationally assembled, or wrongfully or irrationally implemented. They may make a bid to establish a competing alternative structure by presenting a competing configuration of these elements – for example, by giving some element, such as self-determination or sovereignty, more weight relative to the other elements than it possesses in the prevailing regime, while still seeking to achieve coherence, although a new kind of coherence, between their favorite element and the others. Alternatively, they may reject the search for coherence and seek legitimacy for their perspective by defying the demand for satisfying the claims of all the elements. In opposition to the legitimacy of coherence, they may thus make a bid for a "legitimacy through defiance" – a legitimacy that derives its power by overtly privileging certain elements and denigrating others.[9] George W. Bush provides an example of this type of legitimacy bid.

I argue that external critiques of internationalism's *status* – that is, the ideological rejection of the legal system *as a whole* – do not alone account for the most serious challenges to internationalism in the past century. Rather, the strength of these challenges stemmed from their ability to link this external opposition with an internal critique of internationalism's incoherence. In the past, for example, Nazi and Communist publicists sought to undermine the prevailing international legal order both by attacking its identity (for example, as "Jewish" or "Capitalist") *and* by heightening the tensions between heterogeneous principles as they related to particular local conflicts. The challengers' external critique – their attempt to delegitimate the system as a whole – weakened internationalists' authority to produce persuasive new configurations of these disparate concepts in response to new developments in local conflicts. At times, the challengers made bids for a competing legitimacy of coherence; at other times, they sought a legitimacy of defiance by fiercely denigrating previously hallowed principles and exorbitantly privileging others. This type of linkage between external and internal critique, and

[9] I explored this phenomenon in detail in Legitimacy through Defiance: From Goa to Iraq, 23 *Wisconsin Journal of International Law* 93 (2005).

between critique and competing legitimacy bids, has played a powerful role at various junctures in the past century.

Such double challenges enable us to see, by contrast, the double source of internationalism's legitimacy. In periods of internationalist self-confidence, its internal tensions have been a great resource. It has been precisely international law's ability to marshal a range of seemingly conflicting ideas about personal and collective identity and about local and international political order that has enabled it to create its most audacious experiments. The boldest of these experiments include the international regimes to settle nationalist conflicts ranging from Upper Silesia in 1923 to Kosovo in 1999. A close study of such cases shows internationalists' efforts to dynamically achieve and re-achieve legitimacy – through continually persuading relevant publics that the internationally sponsored regime was producing an evolving and coherent whole out of its heterogeneous elements in response to the changing exigencies of the local situation. These types of local, provisional successes established the identity of internationalism as a whole, not as that of a system with a fixed ideology but rather as a work in progress, subject to constant revision through situational engagement. The revisability of these experiments was made possible precisely by the heterogeneity of their elements, by the fact that no one configuration was logically inevitable. This revisability also meant that power could never be finally integrated into principle because principle was in the process of constant, and contestable, permutation.

A feature of such situational attempts to achieve legitimacy is a third type of legitimacy problem, beyond status and coherence. Precisely at the moment of its successes, internationalism has been haunted by the specters of its discredited past – exercises of internationalist power that have been more or less thoroughly delegitimated. During the long post-1989 decade, this kind of legitimacy problem took the form of the resurgence in public debate of nearly forgotten historical terms: terms like *trusteeship, protectorate, proconsul*, even *recolonization*. These terms were deployed by both detached observers and committed partisans of the post-1989 experiments in bold internationalism: at times with the knowing wink of the ironist, at times with the high tones of the pedant, at times with the angry polemics of the militant.

Although lacking the overtness of systematic opposition and the shrewdness of internal critique, the resurgence of these historical references insidiously gnaws away at internationalist legitimacy. It tarnishes the cutting-edge ventures of internationalist idealism by pairing them with delegitimated forms of outdated power. Indeed, the long post–Cold War decade seems to have forced us to confront frankly the relationship between international law's two famously contradictory talents: making the world safe for the exercise of power and making the world safe for the highest ideals of humanity. At least after Kosovo, no one engaged in internationalist theory or practice could deny that power and idealism were thoroughly intertwined, that pure idealism and pure *realpolitik* had become equally quixotic aspirations. Talk about the enforcement of human rights seemed inevitably to evoke talk about proconsuls and protectorates; talk about strategic projection of power seemed inevitably to evoke talk about international legality and cross-cultural understanding. What once seemed like international law's past (colonial or quasi-colonial institutions and doctrines) and what seemed like its future (human rights and community) now seemed destined to haunt each other.

This third challenge to internationalist legitimacy is a salutary element in the dynamics of legitimacy that I am emphasizing. The inevitable haunting of internationalism by the specters of its unsavory past makes any final achievement of legitimacy impossible and forces internationalists to seek continually to prove their differentiation from those specters. Rather than dream of a final integration of power by principle, I propose that we continually goad powerholders by comparing them to those in the past who are now viewed as unprincipled. Depriving those with power of any secure legitimacy should spur them on to avoid words and deeds deserving of the most ignominious illegitimacy.

This chapter seeks to understand international law's attempts to achieve legitimacy in response to three types of challenges: attacks on the status of its identity, critiques of the coherence of its words as well as its deeds, and attempts to associate it with specters from its unsavory past.

Status

In one of his video pronouncements not long after September 11, 2001, Osama bin Laden made a bid to be the theorist of a new attack on the status of internationalism. In this speech, he opposed "international legitimacy" to an incompatible and superior legitimacy.

> Those who claim that they are the leaders of the Arabs and continue to appeal to the United Nations have disavowed what was revealed to Prophet Muhammad, God's peace and blessings be upon him.
>
> Those who refer things to the international legitimacy have disavowed the legitimacy of the Holy Book and the tradition of Prophet Muhammad, God's peace and blessings be upon him.[10]

[10] Bin Laden, *supra* note 1.

To be sure, this seems a weak bid at a theoretical level – relying on a set of clichéd oppositions between secular law and religion, between international institutions and those of a particular tradition, between self-proclaimed leaders and their authentic counterparts, and so on. Nevertheless, the challenge made up in obsessive comprehensiveness what it lacked in theoretical subtlety. In this rather lengthy manifesto, bin Laden gave an overarching interpretation of the far-flung events of the long post–Cold War decade under the single theme of the oppression of "Islam" by the "West." Somalia, Palestine, Iraq, Bosnia, Chechnya, Kashmir, even poor East Timor: bin Laden cited all these disparate conflicts only to subsume them under his one grand theme. The manifesto sought to delegitimate activist internationalism in all its forms – describing actions undertaken in the name of internationalist principles, such as the interventions in Somalia and East Timor, as mere acts of power by "Crusader forces."

Even leaving aside this last, atavistic, reference, bin Laden's narrative was ambitious in historical scope. Reaching beyond the 1990s to the twentieth century as a whole, he declared: "Following World War I, which ended more than eighty-three years ago, the whole Islamic world fell under the crusader banner."[11] With this quite specific historical frame, bin Laden proposed nothing less than a systematic challenge to the entirety of modern internationalism: for the origins of internationalism's proudest achievements – including human rights, self-determination, and international institutions – lie precisely in its renewal at the end of World War I, exactly eighty-three years prior to bin Laden's speech.

In considering current responses to this latest attack on the status of internationalism, it is useful to compare them with responses to the two other most prominent attacks of this type: the Fascist/Nazi challenge and the Communist/Soviet challenge. These three challenges were radically different in political intent and historical context. Nevertheless, they share a set of formal similarities, among them a broad contempt for the legitimacy of the prevailing form of internationalism, a desire to unmask the self-proclaimed universal as particular, and a bid to establish an alternative international political identity with global aspirations, such as the German *Reich* or the Communist International.

The Fascist and Communist challenges prompted a variety of responses from legal internationalists, responses that may be divided into three broad categories: the *purist responses*, the *alternative community responses*, and the *higher law responses*. Each of these responses has had its counterparts in recent

[11] Ibid.

years, coming into prominence with Kosovo, but accelerating after 9/11 and the invasion of Iraq.

The *purist responses* consisted simply in the reassertion of the dignity and validity of international law and internationalist principles in the face of attacks and distortions by their enemies. Purism came in many political stripes, from mainstream treatises to Popular Front manifestoes. For example, after the Italian invasion of Ethiopia, a group of right-wing French intellectuals issued a pro-Italian "Manifesto in Defense of the West," mocking the League of Nations' "false juridical universalism."[12] In response, a group of leftist and liberal intellectuals responded, not with an equally politicized diatribe, but rather, with a "Manifesto for the Respect of International Law."[13] Among other things, this manifesto defended the League of Nations, which at that "very hour" was "justifying its existence in the eyes of all men of goodwill" – surely a formalist assertion in 1935 if ever there was one. The "falseness" of the League's universality in 1935, like that of the UN in the first half of 2003, was undeniable as an empirical matter – whether or not that universalism could be defended as a matter of normative purism.

The *alternative community responses* were more complex and took various forms. In the face of undeniable ideological division, they accepted that internationalist norms and institutions could not simply claim universal status. Rather, they frankly made a claim to the creation of partial international communities to replace the fractured universal community. Often, this type of effort involved favorably contrasting the antiformalist stance of the alternative community with the legal formalism of the prevailing system.

For example, some justified Munich 1938 as the site of a concrete grappling with real problems, bypassing the formalistic impasses of the League of Nations. Such commentators argued that an international conclave embodying the "spirit of Geneva"[14] had transpired in Munich, whereas only international law's dead letter remained in Switzerland. A similar discourse had begun to develop in 1935 to justify Franco–British plans to make a deal with Italy on Ethiopia.[15] In both cases, the alternative international

[12] "Manifesto for the Defense of the West," *Le Temps*, October 4, 1935, at p. 1 (all translations mine unless otherwise noted).

[13] "Manifesto for the Respect of International Law," *Le Populaire*, October 5, 1935, p. 1.

[14] "An Overshadowed Assembly," Editorial, *Times of London*, October 3, 1938, p. 5.

[15] For some versions of these plans, see Summary of the Franco–British Suggestions, 16 *League of Nations O. J.* 1620 (August 1935). Note of the Committee of Five to the Ethiopian and Italian Representatives, September 1935, in Canadian Secretary of State for External Affairs (ed.), *Documents Relating to the Italo-Ethiopian Conflict* 54 (1936); *Text of the Suggestions for an Agreed Settlement of the Conflict*, December 1935; ibid., p. 173. See also the ambivalent response of leading international lawyers to the proposals; for example, Georges Scelle,

community, although partial, united ideological allies and adversaries: the French, British, and Germans in Munich, the French, British, and Italians in the Ethiopia negotiations.

A different variant of the *alternative community response* focuses not on an informal coalition between ideological adversaries, but rather on an overt presentation of an ideological alliance as the true internationalist community, even if non-universal. This strategy was most fully deployed during the Cold War. The Soviets and the Americans each presented their respective partisan alliances as embodying true internationalism, at the expense of a UN viewed as either paralyzed or under the sway of the ideological adversary.[16] In these cases, the alternative community was a select group of states united by substantive values, as opposed to the merely formally grounded – and merely numerically universal – UN. A somewhat weaker form of this variant developed in the aftermath of Munich, in which some in France sought to forsake the irremediable fractures of Europe in favor a "*repli impérial*" – not so much an assertion that the French empire represented the interests of the entire world, but rather that the empire, not Europe, constituted the center of gravity of the French world.[17]

These *alternative community responses* were elaborate precursors to the "illegal-yet-legitimate" school of international lawyers in response to the Kosovo intervention[18] – and the far smaller "illegal-yet-legitimate" school in response to the invasion of Iraq.[19] In fact, one can divide the recent

La Politique extérieure française et la S.D.N., 10 *Année politique française et étrangère*, pp. 292–293 (1935); Charles Rousseau, Le Conflit Italo-Ethiopien (ch. III), 45 *Revue Générale de droit international public*, 61–62 (1938).

16 Compare the U.S. justification of the 1965 invasion of the Dominican Republic with the Soviet justification of the 1968 invasion of Czechoslovakia. See Leonard Meeker, The Dominican Situation in International Law, 53 *Department of State Bulletin* 60 (1965); Pravda article on Czechoslovakia, 7 *International Legal Matters* 1323 (1968). The U.S. justification relied heavily on the OAS as an international community based on the substantive value of anticommunism; the Soviet justification relied heavily on the Warsaw Pact, as a community based on the substantive value of Marxism-Leninism. Both at least implicitly acknowledged the formal illegality of their actions under the UN Charter. It should perhaps be noted here that the "United Nations" originated as such a partial international community: the coalition of forces arrayed against the Axis Powers.

17 See, e.g., an editorial in *La République*, published a short time after Munich. Under the title "From Munich to Our Colonial Empire," the editorial declared: "Our own Central Europe is the African continent. Our country is too great for quarrels between Germans and Slavs ever-resurgent in the Balkans." Quoted in Charles-Robert Ageron, A propos d'une prétendu politique de 'repli impérial' dans la France des années 1938–1939, 12 *Revue d'histoire maghrebine* 225 (1978).

18 See, e.g., The Independent International Commission on Kosovo, *The Kosovo Report* 186 (2000).

19 See, e.g., Anne-Marie Slaughter, "Good Reasons for Going Around the UN," *International Herald Tribune*, March 19, 2003, available at www.iht.com/articles/90176.html.

"illegal-yet-legitimate" responses into three groups, each with analogies to their historical precursors. Some versions resembled the Munich/Ethiopia method of constructing a pragmatic community of ideologically disparate states, a community that claims to embody the spirit of the formally legal institutions, while bypassing their procedures. Other versions resembled the Cold War Warsaw Pact/NATO method of constructing a partial community grounded in particular substantive values, designed to oppose an ideological adversary. In the case of Kosovo, the question of what type of alternative community should replace the UN partly depended on individual publicists' attitudes toward Russia: a state seen by some as amenable to pragmatic cooperation, whereas viewed by others as the potential leader of some vaguely perceived pan-Slavic ideology. Finally, the valorizations of an "American empire" heard in some U.S. policy-making quarters as the long decade ended, particularly after September 11, may be viewed as an assertion that the United States is the true embodiment of internationalism in our time, however few its allies – or as simply a *repli impérial* in the French style. "Illegal-yet-legitimate" justifications of the U.S. invasion have thus sometimes taken the form of presenting the United States as the only effective agency of the true internationalist interest, an interest impeded and betrayed by the majority of the UN, and have sometimes taken the form of presenting U.S. policy as a *repli Américain*, directed at safeguarding primarily the ideals of an American sphere of influence.

A third type of response to the Fascist and Communist challenges, the *higher law responses*, entailed attempts to surmount ideological division by hoisting law ever-farther upward to achieve a legitimate position above the fray. One can distinguish two strands in these responses: the principled and the functionalist. The principled variant seeks a set of principles, such as peace or minimal distributive fairness among relevant states, that their proponents portray as transcending deep ideological divides. This variant played an important role in the discussions of "peaceful change" in the 1930s, in reaction to the Fascist/Nazi challenge. Of course, the transcendental principles put forward were historically contingent, to put it mildly. Among the principles of minimal distributive fairness at play in these discussions were notions about a fair distribution of colonial possessions between the colonial "haves," France and Britain, and the colonial "have-nots," Germany and Italy.[20]

[20] See, e.g., F. H. Leitner, Les problèmes généraux du 'Peaceful Change', in *Fédération universitaire internationale, Problèmes du "Peaceful Change"* 78 (1936); Joseph L. Kunz, The Problem of Revision in International Law, 33 *American Journal of International Law* 54 (1939).

The second strand, the functionalist, seeks to ground the legitimacy of international law in interests that states share by virtue of their common condition *as states.*[21] Functionalist higher-law responses often argue for a long-term perspective. Although acknowledging that ideological differences may fracture the international community for a while, they assert that the deeper interests that all states share will ultimately assert themselves. The two strands of the higher-law responses, the principled and the functionalist, are often interwoven in the work of a single author, together bolstering the claim that a legitimate international law can be established despite the appearance of a "divided world."[22]

To summarize these three responses to attacks on internationalism's status: whereas the *purist responses* reassert a pristine, universal international law against a deceitful double, and the *alternative community responses* accept the challenge of a divided world by constructing a partial alternative to the formally universal community, the *higher law responses* seek to raise international law above the divided world and establish a relegitimated, if thinner, internationalism, beyond the superficial fractures of a given historical moment.

I argue that none of these responses has been particularly persuasive in the past. The danger that their weakness posed to international law did not lie in their supposed need for an unassailable theoretical foundation. Rather, the danger lay in the damage that the ideological challenges posed to international law's ability to present itself as a unitary and legitimate authority able to persuasively and dynamically reconfigure its heterogeneous internal elements to meet new local crises. The Fascist and Communist challenges coupled their systematic opposition with a kind of challenge that the bin Laden–type opposition has not yet pursued – that of internal critique.

Coherence

One of the secrets of international law's resilience over the past century has resided in its productive use of the tension between the heterogeneous elements of its doctrinal and institutional toolbox for responding to local conflicts. The elements of this toolbox – sovereignty and self-determination, minority protection and individual rights, local democracy and international tutelage, local and international tribunals, and so on – have different and often incompatible historical and conceptual foundations. Yet, it is precisely the fact

[21] See, e.g., Lissitzyn, *supra* note 6, pp. 68–69.
[22] See, e.g., Cassese *supra* note 6, pp. 123–164.

that these legal tools do not cohere in any logically necessary fashion that has permitted the best legal innovators to distribute them differently in individual legal regimes – regimes that present themselves as custom-designed for the unique exigencies of particular local conflicts. As such situations evolve, it is precisely the tensions between the legal tools that make possible the flexibility to redistribute their relative weight to meet changing needs – to re-achieve legitimacy through a new and different coherence of the elements. International law's strength in approaching local conflicts thus does not depend on the provision of "clear mandates."[23] On the contrary, it depends on complex, heterogeneously composed mandates – and on the presence of an agile and legitimate implementer of those mandates, able to use the conflicts between the elements of the international regime as a resource for responding to changing or previously misunderstood features of the situation.

The secret of international law's resilience is also its Achilles' heel. The relative stability of the contents of this toolbox over the past century represents a potential source of blindness for internationalism insofar as it leads decision makers to place very different conflicts in similar conceptual frames. Equally dangerously, the heterogeneity of the tools has served the goals of those who seek to subvert both the local internationalist experiments and the system as a whole. The two major historical challenges to legal internationalism, Fascism and Communism, drew much of their strength from internally subverting the prevailing internationalism in particular cases – exploiting the tensions between the elements in local internationalist experiments to destroy the legitimacy of the prevailing internationalism as a whole.

Alongside their broad contempt for the system as a whole, these challenges thus drew many of their resources in particular cases from that very system. They combined external and internal critique: attacks on internationalism's status and attacks on its coherence. For example, the Italian claim to Ethiopia and the German claim to the Sudetenland were justified in terms of some of the core (albeit heterogeneous) concepts of the Versailles settlement: self-determination for some groups, international tutelage for other ("backward") groups, and minority rights for still other groups.[24] As a result, elite opinion makers in Western Europe, including international lawyers, often found it difficult to respond to these claims without conceding considerable conceptual and even political ground – or, in the words of one contemporary observer, they found it difficult to do so "without belying

[23] See *Contra Report of the Panel on United Nations Peace Operations ("the Brahimi Report")* (2000), available at www.un.org/peace/reports/peace_operations.

[24] I discuss this at length in Beyond Colonialism and Nationalism? Ethiopia, Czechoslovakia, and 'Peaceful Change', 6 *Nordic Journal of International Law* 421 (1996).

themselves."[25] Thus, the Italians criticized the sovereignty of Ethiopia on the grounds that it was just as "backward" and deserving of tutelage as territories under League of Nations Mandate or the colonial rule of the British and French; they claimed that the structure of the Ethiopian state flew in the face of the self-determination or minority rights of the country's non-Amharic peoples; and they claimed that Italian rule would embody the principle of internationalist tutelage. Some prominent liberal international lawyers found it difficult to defend the sovereignty of Ethiopia in light of these other principles. Having conceded much on the terrain of coherence, they responded on the terrain of status – contending that Fascist Italy could not properly represent the international community in the otherwise justified task of placing the country under trusteeship. However, the ideological divisions of the 1930s, and the accompanying external attacks on the international system, meant that it was no longer possible to achieve consensus on the identity of the true agents of the international community.

Similar examples can be drawn from the history of Communist challenges to legal internationalism, including the early anticolonialism of left-wing Communists in the 1920s, which coupled an internal attack on the *prima facie* racism of the unequal application of self-determination with an external attack on the League of Nations as an "association of imperialist pirates."[26] Later examples include Soviet defenses of their various unilateral interventions. These defenses, which mirrored U.S. justifications of analogous interventions, exploited the tensions between prevailing international norms and linked this coherence challenge to an assertion about the status of the Warsaw Pact as an alternative international community.[27] Thus, during the course of nearly a century, legal internationalists have been confounded not by totalizing rejections of their system standing alone, but rather by the ability of the challengers to couple their ideological rejection with internal critique.

The strength of such challenges was thus due to the fact that internationalism's resilience has not resided in purist obliviousness, Manichaean divisions between competing international communities, or Herculean attainments of a higher law above partisan conflict. Rather, it has consisted in Legal Realist–style exploitation of contradictoriness and inconsistency as resources that facilitate case-specific complexity and flexibility. The significance of past ideological attacks on the status of internationalism as a whole stemmed from the

[25] P. Teissonière, Faut-il résister aux violents? 49 *La Paix par le Droit* 13 (1938).
[26] Quoted in Alan Rose, *Surrealism and Communism*, p. 132 (Peter Lang, 1991).
[27] See Meeker and Pravda articles, *supra* note 16.

damage they inflicted on internationalists' authority to persuasively reconfigure their disparate legal concepts in response to changing local conflicts – that is, to establish new legitimacies of coherence. The challengers attacked the particular configuration of international legal elements laid down for particular conflicts by the prevailing international authorities; their external attacks crippled the ability of those authorities to establish new configurations.

Panicked responses to the current crisis in internationalist legitimacy – to the extent that they are provoked solely by the prospect of a new totalizing rejection of the system – are thus misplaced. Current status challenges, such as the Islamicist and U.S. challenges, are likely to have a significant effect on activist internationalism only if the challengers attempt to undermine the system from within as well as from without. Consider, for example, the U.S. administration of Iraq, which lacks status legitimacy in the eyes of most of the world. One could imagine a U.S. occupation authority that was able to overcome its status illegitimacy and achieve a legitimacy of coherence through skillful deployment of the various elements in the international toolbox for local conflicts. Of course, whether the actual U.S. administration of Iraq will ever be able to achieve legitimacy in this way, as of this writing (2006), is highly questionable.

Beyond the skill and intent of the American administrators, there are two key obstacles. First, the high degree of status illegitimacy of the U.S. occupation makes the actions of the American administrators suspect both locally and internationally. Second, the U.S. justification of the invasion of Iraq involved not only an attack on the status of internationalism embodied in the UN, but also – at least in some official pronouncements – a *defiant attack on the coherence* of international norms. The pronouncements I have in mind are those that suggest that the United States was rejecting the legitimacy of coherence by denigrating some principles at the expense of others, rather than merely seeking a reconfiguration of their relative weights – in other words, making a bid to achieve *legitimacy through defiance.* Bids for legitimacy through defiance frankly seek approval for the boldness of their actions precisely by virtue of the fact that they defy some prevailing norms. Such bids thus may be viewed as seeking a *surplus legitimacy* – that is, attempting to use the very legitimacy-deficit of their actions as a basis for a higher legitimacy.

A brief comparison between justifications of the use of force in Kosovo in 1999 and Iraq in 2003 can illuminate the distinctiveness of bids for legitimacy through defiance. Both uses of force were justified through exploiting the tensions between international legal principles. The principles restricting the use of force stated in the UN Charter were juxtaposed to principles permitting unilateral uses of force, such as humanitarian intervention and expansive notions of self-defense, purportedly grounded in customary law; the substantive obligations that the UN Security Council imposed on particular states, Yugoslavia and Iraq, were juxtaposed to the Council's refusal to grant enforcement authority to other states. Both Kosovo and Iraq thus implicated conflicts among substantive principles, between treaty and custom, and between substance and procedure.

However, whereas the Kosovo justifications tended to make the effort to present a competing configuration of the prevailing international requirements, some of the U.S. pronouncements on Iraq tended to denigrate, rather than reconfigure, the elements disfavoring the intervention. NATO pronouncements on Kosovo, for example, tried to show that the intervention represented a legitimate – even if novel – form of cooperation between the UN and NATO. In Bruno Simma's words:

> Indeed, one is immediately struck by the degree to which the efforts of NATO and its member states follow the "logic" of, and have been expressly linked to, the treatment of the Kosovo crisis by the Security Council. In an address delivered in Bonn on 4 February 1999, US Deputy Secretary of State Strobe Talbott referred to an "unprecedented and promising degree of synergy" in the sense that the UN and NATO, among other institutions, had "pooled their energies and strengths on behalf of an urgent common cause"; as to the specific contribution of the UN, he saw this in the fact that "the UN has lent its political and moral authority to the Kosovo effort."[28]

Despite the seeming violation of formal legal norms in their accepted configuration, NATO officials attempted to make their actions appear to conform to the logic of the principles as a whole, once their relative authority had been reconfigured. In other words, they tried to present an alternative legitimacy of coherence.

By contrast, many U.S. pronouncements prior to the invasion of Iraq frankly declared American intentions to defy the prevailing international legal system. The most overt example of this stance was provided by George W. Bush in declaring that it was the UN that had to "prove to the world whether it's going to be relevant or whether it's going to be a League of Nations, irrelevant."[29] Bush thus openly challenged the status of the UN, attacking the legitimacy of its identity.

However, his challenge was not limited to its status aspect. Rather, it also focused on the coherence of the system's internal normative elements, rejecting any obligation to accommodate them all. This aspect of the challenge

[28] Bruno Simma, NATO, the UN, and the Use of Force: Legal Aspects, 10 *European Journal of International Law* 11 (1999). Simma rejects the legal soundness of this position.

[29] Bush, *supra* note 2.

declared American intentions to ignore some prevailing norms, rather than to reconfigure the normative system. In particular, Bush attacked the UN's purported unwillingness to enforce the substantive obligations it had imposed on Iraq and stressed the importance of the substantive obligations at the expense of the procedural norms for enforcement:

> We will work with the U.N. Security Council for the necessary resolutions. But the purposes of the United States should not be doubted. The Security Council resolutions will be enforced – the just demands of peace and security will be met – or action will be unavoidable.[30]

Bush was thus asserting that the United States would not be engaged in a simple act of flouting the UN, as he might have if he were only attacking the status of the UN. Rather, he announced that the United States would be upholding some of its norms at the expense of others – linking his attack on the *status* of the UN, its identity as an "irrelevant League of Nations," with an attack on the legitimacy of the *coherence* of its norms. Indeed, he sought legitimacy for the U.S. action precisely by virtue of its bold willingness to violate certain norms, particularly procedural norms, to support others. This was a bid for a surplus legitimacy for brash, taboo-breaking behavior by means of an attack on both the status and coherence of the international system.

To be sure, this bid for legitimacy through defiance generally failed outside the United States, and the substantive case for the invasion was based on a mass of false factual assertions. Nevertheless, it offers a clear example of such a bid. It is also important to note that bids for legitimacy through defiance have come from across the political spectrum at various times. There are few people who would not view them sympathetically in at least some circumstances – except perhaps for formalists of the "*pereat mundus, fiat jus!*" school.

In the particular situation of the United States in Iraq, however, this bid for legitimacy through defiance has presented serious difficulties for its protagonist. As I have noted, the United States lacks international status legitimacy in Iraq due to the failure of its bid to secure support for the invasion through defying the international system. In the years since the invasion, the United States has tried to achieve a legitimacy of coherence by attempting to show the implementation of widely shared international values in its conduct of the occupation. Yet, the prewar U S. attack on the coherence of international norms, as well as on the status of international institutions, rendered its bids for a new legitimacy of coherence very fragile. Having sought a surplus legitimacy for its coherence-defying action in invading Iraq, the United States has

[30] Ibid.

been ill-equipped to seek the legitimacy of coherence in its self-proclaimed role as internationalist administrator of that country. Nor has the actual conduct of the American occupation of Iraq come close to providing the factual basis for such a legitimacy bid.

"Our Law": Producing Unity through Heterogeneity

I have argued that the secret of internationalism's resilience over the past century has resided in its productive use of the tension between the heterogeneous elements of its doctrinal and institutional toolbox for responding to local conflicts. To portray a successful example of the production of legitimacy out of disparate concepts, I turn to an incident from the early days of the UN Mission in Kosovo (UNMIK). It is in such attempts to manage local crises that the alchemy of international coordination of heterogeneous concepts can be seen in action. Yet it is precisely here, when the alchemy has worked its unifying magic, that international law rediscovers its unsettling historical doubles – internationalist regimes doubled by the word "*protectorate*," internationalist administrators doubled by the word "*proconsul*."

The incident presents a striking allegory of the dynamics of situational legitimacy: the provisional construction of internationalism in a particular context out of heterogeneous conceptions and practices. This incident was widely reported in the elite Western press, exemplified by this symptomatic account in *Le Monde*:

> "A new Kosovo is beginning; we have changed the law," declared Mr. Kouchner to the judges and journalists who surrounded him at the meeting. It had been convened, they explain at UNMIK, after a cascade of resignation threats by those who formed the nucleus of the new "independent and multiethnic" judicial system of Kosovo. A week ago, three judges from Prizren launched the movement. They rejected Section 3 of "Regulation 1" (signed by Mr. Kouchner on July 25th to define his own powers), which declared that "The laws applicable in the territory of Kosovo prior to 24 March 1999 shall continue to apply in Kosovo insofar as they do not conflict with [internationally recognized human-rights standards]." A campaign was then launched by the KLA against what it interpreted as the maintenance in Kosovo of Yugoslav laws which were, in fact if not always in the text, an instrument of Serb repression in the province. Judges were then subjected to pressures to resign. Nipping this offensive in the bud, Bernard Kouchner apologized before fifty of the judges for having "insufficiently consulted them, especially before publishing Regulation 1." Assuring them that his mission is to "permit the emergence of an autonomous administration," he promised not to take any further decisions without "involving the people of Kosovo." A working group, joined by international experts, will draft the law of Kosovo – "*our law, which is neither Serb nor Yugoslav*," he emphasized. This

> work will be coordinated with the Council of Europe, which is supposed to present a first "purge" of existing laws at the end of September.... The great majority of judges declared themselves satisfied with the statements of the UN "proconsul" and promised to get to work to rapidly fill the legal void that has prevented the trials – but not the detention – of hundreds of people already arrested by KFOR in Kosovo.[31]

One would have had to invent this story if it had not been conveniently reported in the press. This real-life allegory contains all the quandaries of the robust internationalism of the long post-1989 decade. A UN administration established itself in a territory on the basis of a use of force of controversial legality. The appointment of a famous humanitarian as the head of the territorial administration symbolized the internationalist desire to transmute this questionable force into legitimate law, to absorb power into principle. In accordance with this desire, Kouchner's first act was to attempt this transmutation by establishing a *legal* framework "to define his own *powers*." This act was particularly urgent because KFOR, itself already an internationalist transmutation of NATO, had arrested hundreds of people outside of a legal framework. The "new beginning of Kosovo," declared Kouchner, was not the NATO intervention but rather the fact that "we have changed the law" – a pronouncement that was not an observation of fact but rather a bid for the construction of legitimacy.

Yet, the question of what constituted legitimate legal change turned out to be a highly contestable matter. Kouchner appears to have first conceived of his task as a matter of legal technique, the establishment of a neutral legal framework to permit the work of his administration to begin. He sought to achieve this goal by declaring that "law" would now prevail over military force and by subjecting domestic law to the test of international human-rights standards. In defining the meaning of *law* as the law in effect before the start of the exercise of NATO power,[32] he chose the seemingly neutral approach of legal continuity, the protection of acquired rights. The Kosovo Liberation Army (KLA) and its allied judges, in response, challenged the notion that the question of a rule of "law" was simply a technical matter. By asserting that *this* "law" had a partisan identity – that of Serbian supremacy – they rejected the neutrality of legal continuity. Nor were they satisfied with

[31] "Vers une 'loi du Kosovo,' ni serbe ni yougoslave," *Le Monde*, August 17, 1999 (emphasis in the original).

[32] The relevant portion of Regulation 1 reads: "The laws applicable in the territory of Kosovo prior to 24 March 1999 shall continue to apply in Kosovo insofar as they do not conflict with [internationally recognized human-rights standards], the fulfilment of the mandate given to UNMIK under United Nations Security Council Resolution 1244 (1999), or the present or any other regulation issued by UNMIK." UNMIK/REG/1999/1 Section 3 (July 25, 1999).

the purging filter of international standards, seeking, instead, a total rejection of the illegitimate Yugoslav legal source. Indeed, Kouchner's law, which pretended to the neutral identity of impartial technique, became for them a mere tributary of this partisan source.

This type of attack on internationalist legitimacy may be interpreted as proceeding from an internal critique of the *coherence* of the elements of the Kosovo regime to an external critique of its *identity*. The internal critique was aimed at Kouchner's initial configuration of the famously conflicting elements in the UNMIK mandate, embodied in Resolution 1244's call for (1) "the *sovereignty* . . . of Yugoslavia"; (2) "*autonomy* and . . . *self-administration* for Kosovo"; and (3) administration by "*international* civil and security presences."[33] Given the many tensions latent in this multiple mandate, Regulation 1's provision banning legal rules incompatible with Resolution 1244 (in addition to those that conflicted with international human-rights standards) provided ample room for internal critique from almost any perspective. The Albanian opposition rejected the version of coherence among Resolution 1244's elements embodied in Regulation 1's stance of technical legal neutrality. It accompanied this critique of Regulation's 1 bid for a legitimacy of coherence with an alternative bid for a legitimacy of defiance – rejecting the notion that the principle of Yugoslav sovereignty should play any role at all. Finally, it implicitly delegitimated Kouchner's internationalist status as a whole, accusing it of partiality, and demoted him from his identity above the fray to that of merely one player in the conflict.

Although one may only imagine his private frustration, Kouchner's admirable public recovery from this *faux pas* shows that he understood precisely what was involved. Without internationalist status legitimacy, the delicate work of coordination among conflicting groups – let alone among legal concepts – would be impossible. He immediately set about, therefore, to ground his authority in a different concept of legitimacy than the one with which he began his tenure. By reshaping his internationalist identity, he sought to relegitimate his status, thus making it possible for him to proceed with the work of reconfiguring the elements of the internationalist regime for Kosovo and to make a new bid for a legitimacy of coherence.

Gathering the Albanian judges, Kouchner made an explicit appeal for an alliance with them. This appeal involved a different identity for international authority – no longer that of neutral technocracy but rather that of an ally, however asymmetrical, with a deserving population. He apologized for his failure to consult and promised henceforth to "involve the people" – hardly

[33] UN Security Council Resolution 1244, S/RES/1244 (1999).

necessary measures when he had conceived the matter at hand as merely technical. He encapsulated his new stance in his declaration that the law to be drafted would be "*our law, which is neither Serb nor Yugoslav.*"

A thought-provoking and ambivalent phrase. For if the "our" in "our law" referred to the pure universality of internationalism (the royal "our"), one would have rather expected the rest of the phrase to read "neither Serb nor Albanian" – that is, it would be a neutral law, not ethnically marked. By contrast, "neither Serb nor Yugoslav" might imply that it would be Albanian – suggesting that Kouchner was abandoning a bid for a universalist internationalism in favor of a partial community that frankly acknowledged its partiality. Yet, if Kouchner were purporting to be speaking solely as the representative of the Albanians, then the "our" would have been sufficient – the "neither . . . nor" phrase would seem a bit like protesting too much. In fact, the very structure of the phrase "neither . . . nor" evoked impartiality, even though the terms that followed those conjunctions partly confounded that evocation.

The ambivalences of his phrase, I argue, suggest that Kouchner sought to achieve his legitimacy by doing something other than asserting *either* neutrality *or* partisan identity. Rather, Kouchner's "our" strove to effect a complex alliance of two seemingly conflicting sources of legitimacy: overarching international authority and Albanian nationalism. He sought to achieve his legitimacy through a paradoxical alliance between the two – an internationalism that wagers its legitimacy on its ability to respond to the deepest needs of nationalist partisans.[34]

At least in this crisis, Kouchner apparently succeeded. By reshaping the identity of his internationalism, he made credible his pledge to reconfigure the conflicting internal elements of the legal regime called for by Resolution 1244. The mass resignation of the judges was averted.

Kouchner eventually repealed Regulation 1, replacing it with Regulation 24. The new Regulation provided that Kosovo would be governed by the law in effect before March 22, 1989 – that is, the law that prevailed during the period of Kosovo's autonomy within Serbia. This 1989 law cannot be said to be "neither Serb nor Yugoslav" in a pure sense. Regulation 24, however, can be seen as a reconfiguration of the internally heterogeneous mandate of Resolution 1244. "Our law," as embodied in Regulation 24, would be neither solely Yugoslav nor solely Albanian – nor solely international. Rather, it would

[34] I have explored this "alliance" in detail elsewhere. See, e.g., 'But the Alternative Is Despair': European Nationalism and the Modernist Renewal of International Law, 106 *Harvard Law Review* 1792 (1993).

be a new configuration of conflicting elements, a new appeal for legitimacy made to the relevant publics.

To be sure, as Kouchner discovered, identifying the relevant publics may be a tricky matter to achieve in advance. Kouchner may have thought his public was a community of lawyers – perhaps international, perhaps Yugoslav, perhaps Kosovar. He may have thought his public was the UNMIK staff or the non-governmental organization (NGO) world. He discovered, through its resistance, that a key relevant public was the organized sphere of Kosovar nationalism.

Conversely, as this example shows, the relevant public may discover itself only through finding itself addressed by an act of internationalist power. One might imagine that some of the Albanian judges may have shared a technocratic idea about the rule of law until finding themselves jolted by the reinstatement of Yugoslav law – or by finding themselves jolted by pressure from the KLA. Finally, internationalist actors themselves may discover their full identity only through this dynamic. Kouchner was undoubtedly more surprised than anyone to discover his identity as a Serb puppet (that is, in the eyes of the KLA) and to be obliged to reconstruct his identity as an ally (however provisional and asymmetrical) of Albanian nationalism.

Internationalist actors like Kouchner, therefore, must necessarily take the risk of appealing for legitimacy without a guarantee of success or even certainty about the addressees of their appeals. With each new fragile configuration of conflicting elements, the cycle can always begin again, as new challenges unsettle the provisional equilibrium among the regime's elements. Legitimacy must be continually re-achieved – and each new achievement will be a new configuration of those elements.

Finally, at the very hour of his success, Kouchner managed to evoke a different type of legitimacy-trouble. In reporting the result of this speech, *Le Monde* declared that the "great majority of judges declared themselves satisfied with the statements of the UN 'proconsul'." Try as he might to ally himself with the Albanians, Kouchner could not shake off another doubling of his role as legitimate international authority: this time, not by the image of him as a Yugoslav proxy but rather as an imperial "proconsul." The term "*proconsul*" may be one the Albanians would have used or it may reflect *Le Monde*'s elite irony about internationalist idealism. Nonetheless, it suggests the impossibility of any definitive achievement of internationalist legitimacy. International humanitarian, Albanian ally, or imperial "proconsul"? Kouchner's variable ability to govern Kosovo, the changing measure of his legitimacy, depended on his ability to recognize these doublings of legitimacy and to shift among their attendant roles.

The "Our Law" allegory presents the construction of legitimacy out of the shifts between its conflicting identities and elements diachronically, in terms of a dynamic unfolding. The UNMIK-promulgated Constitution of Kosovo (2001),[35] by contrast, presents this type of construction in the form of a synchronic legal structure. This Constitution follows in the great tradition of internationalist attempts to resolve nationalist conflict through complex legal experiments, a tradition whose illustrious precursors include the inter-war regimes for Upper Silesia, Danzig, and the Saar; the Palestine Partition Resolution of 1947; and the Washington and Dayton Accords for Bosnia in the 1990s – composite regimes, at once local and international, designed for the pacification of seemingly intractable conflict.

Among the features shared by these experiments, I designate two here. First, they create a legal space for themselves by bracketing the question of sovereignty, either by explicitly deferring the question to a later time (the Saar and Kosovo); superimposing a unified, experimental regime on top of sovereign divisions (Upper Silesia and Palestine); or creating a novel a-sovereign entity (Danzig).[36] Second, they seek to achieve their goals of resolving nationalist conflict by juxtaposing, in a single legal regime, elements that seem to be incompatible – or, at least, that stand in tension with each other. The competing elements may include partition (between sovereigns or ethnic units) and unity (economic or political), minority rights and individual rights, universal suffrage and representation based on ethnic identity, local judiciary, and on-site international or mixed courts.

The tension among the elements that compose such regimes arises from the implicit reference each makes to distinct notions of personal and collective identity, as well as distinct ideas about political organization. At least since the end of World War I, such regimes have wagered their legitimacy on the notion that a high level of legal complexity is needed to match the level of complexity of the local conflict. Legitimacy would be attained when such complex and heterogeneous constructions could prove their ability to both pacify nationalist conflict and provide all nationalist factions with a sense that their deepest longings have been satisfied. The legitimacy of any particular such regime, their proponents have contended, would emerge from a suitable configuration of the conflicting concepts and institutions in the international toolbox. Thus, paradoxically, the advocates of such regimes have believed that *only a configuration of conflicting legal elements can achieve legitimacy*

35 "Constitutional Framework for Provisional Self-Government," UNMIK/REG/2001/9 (May 15, 2001), available at www.unmikonline.org/constframework.htm.

36 See 'But the Alternative Is Despair': European Nationalism and the Modernist Renewal of International Law, *supra* note 34, pp. 1874–1897.

in such conflicts. In my studies of the interwar period,[37] I use the phrase "Modernist faith" to describe this paradoxical set of beliefs – a faith, now more than eighty-three years old, rightly perceived by challengers such as bin Laden as a rival to their own faith. The structure of Modernist faith shows the importance of the two dimensions of legitimacy that I have highlighted thus far: (1) a situational legitimacy of coherence – that is, recognition by relevant publics that regimes embodying particular configurations of the conflicting elements in the international toolbox constitute a good response to local exigencies; and (2) status legitimacy – that is, recognition by relevant publics of the good title to "internationalism" of the authority constructing and administering such regimes.

Following in this tradition, the Kosovo Constitution rests on the suspension of the question of sovereignty. It combines a variety of heterogeneous elements, which implicitly refer to distinct, and potentially conflicting, ideas of identity. Such elements include individual human rights and a variety of institutionalizations of the rights of "Communities" defined by ethnic, religious, or linguistic identity.[38] Such "Community" rights include robust versions of the types of rights originally developed to protect "minorities" in a variety of international instruments since 1919. In relation to the long historical debate about whether minority rights should focus more on groups or individuals,[39] the Kosovo Constitution opts in several specific ways for group-centered provisions for the region's "Communities." For example, rather than simply providing for non-interference with group-educational institutions, it mandates public funding of "Community" schools. More strikingly, the Constitution reserves seats for non-Albanians in the Assembly.[40] It also provides for a complicated procedure, related to provisions in the Bosnia accords, whereby members of a "Community" in the Assembly may temporarily block legislation that they declare violates the "vital interests of the Community."[41] The Constitution declares membership in a Community to be a wholly

[37] Ibid. See also Nathaniel Berman, "Modernism, Nationalism, and the Rhetoric of Reconstruction," in Cecilia Lynch & Michael Loriaux (eds.), *Law and Moral Action in World Politics* (University of Minnesota Press, 1999).

[38] Compare Chapters 3 and 4 of the Kosovo "Constitutional Framework," *supra* note 35.

[39] See, e.g., Oscar Janowsky, *The Jews and Minority Rights, 1898–1919* (Columbia University Press, 1933). For more recent examples of such divergent views on minority rights, compare the relatively individual-rights focus of the European Framework Convention on National Minorities, reprinted in 34 *International Law Matters* 351 (1995), with the more group-focused approach of the prior Council of Europe's Parliamentary Assembly, Recommendation 1201, on an Additional Protocol on the Rights of National Minorities to the European Convention on Human Rights, reprinted in 14 *Human Rights Law Journal* 144 (1993).

[40] See "Constitutional Framework," *supra* note 35, Chapter 9.1.3.

[41] Ibid., Chapter 9.1.39.

voluntary matter and non-membership to bring no "disadvantage."[42] Yet, it is clear from these provisions that non-participation in Communities could "disadvantage" a Kosovar in the distribution of economic and political power – just one example of how the individualist and "Community" strands in the document stand in very concrete tension.

The Constitution's judicial framework also juxtaposes ethnic-based and internationalist conceptions of a proper judiciary. The Consitution provides for both international and local judges.[43] The identity of the local judges should "reflect the diversity of the people of Kosovo."[44] The Constitution leaves latitude in the hands of the Special Representative of the Secretary General to determine the number of international judges and the criteria for their appointment.[45] The balance among the competing elements in these provisions leaves room for reconfiguration aimed at achieving legitimacy among the various relevant constituencies. Such reconfiguration has occurred a number of times, including the incident with the Albanian judges described previously. In a very different vein, a November 2001 Yugoslav–UNMIK agreement[46] provided for increasing the number of international judges (especially for "inter-ethnic" cases) and ethnic Serb judges.

In the history of such local, yet international, regimes, the unity of the complex legal construction may have an on-site human or institutional embodiment, such as the Governing Commission of the Saar. In other regimes, such as Upper Silesia, the unity may simply be intended to emerge from the relation between the elements, often ultimately placed under the distant authority of the Councils of the League of Nations or the UN. In either case, the unity of the regime as a whole may stand in tension with the constitutive parts. In Kosovo, supreme authority is vested in the Special Representative of the Secretary General, whose authority is not "affect[ed] or diminish[ed]"[47] by the constitutionally established institutions – which are nonetheless intended to be precisely those of "*self*-government."

Despite this ultimate tension, the entire document, with all its heterogeneities, expresses the classic Modernist faith: the composite regime seeks to respond to "the legitimate aspirations of the people of Kosovo to live in

[42] Ibid., Chapter 4.2.

[43] Ibid., Chapter 9.4.7.

[44] Ibid.

[45] Ibid. The criteria were adumbrated in provisions such as Regulation No. 2001/2 Amending UNMIK Regulation No. 2000/6, "On the Appointment and Removal from Office of International Judges and International Prosecutors," January 12, 2001, available at www.unmikonline.org/regulations/2001/reg02–01.html.

[46] See "UNMIK – Fry Common Document," November 5, 2001, available at www.serbia.sr.gov.yu/video/UNMIK-FRY.doc.

[47] "Constitutional Framework," *supra* note 35, Chapter 12.

freedom, in peace, and in friendly relations with other people in the region."[48] The legitimacy of any particular regime of this type depends on its ability to persuade others – both the conflicting local populations and the international community – of the validity of Modernist faith in its particular configuration of conflicting principles and on its ability to emulate Kouchner in a flexible willingness to reconfigure them if necessary. This ability depends on the agility of the embodiment of international authority in the particular situation, as well as on the status legitimacy of internationalism in the world generally.

Nevertheless, as shown in the "Our Law" allegory, even at the hour of the success of such endeavors, the entire complex structure remains haunted by the specter of those disconcerting words: *protectorate, proconsul.* The shrewd role shifts of Kouchner, the skillful balancing of the Constitution – all this hard-won legitimacy is unable to shake off its disconcerting double, to which I now turn.

Coming to Terms with the Past: The Specter of Fez

On March 30, 1912, the French Republic and the Moroccan Sultan concluded the Treaty of Fez, with the goal of "establishing a well-regulated regime" in Morocco.[49] The treaty provided for the military occupation of Morocco by France.[50] The "new regime" envisioned by the treaty would include "administrative, judicial, educational, economic, financial, and military reforms which the French Government shall judge useful to introduce on Moroccan territory."[51] This regime would "safeguard the religious situation, the traditional respect and prestige of the Sultan, and the exercise of the Muslim religion and religious institutions."[52] France also agreed "to provide constant support to his Cherifian Majesty against any danger which might threaten his person or his throne or which might compromise the tranquility of his State."[53] Finally, the treaty provided that France would "be represented before his Cherifian Majesty by a Resident General Commissioner, in whom shall be vested all the powers of the Republic in Morocco, and who shall safeguard the execution of the present agreement."[54] In short: France established a protectorate over Morocco.

[48] Ibid., Preamble.

[49] "Traité de Protectorat du 30 Mars 1912," Préamble, reprinted in *Nationality Decrees Case*, Permanent Court of International Justice, Series C, Annex 8, at 343 (1923).

[50] Ibid., Article 2.

[51] Ibid., Article 1.

[52] Ibid.

[53] Ibid., Article 3.

[54] Ibid., Article 5.

On June 10, 1999, the UN Security Council passed Resolution 1244 relating to Kosovo.[55] In the resolution, the Security Council "b[ore] in mind the purposes and principles of the Charter of the United Nations, and the primary responsibility of the Security Council for the maintenance of international peace and security."[56] It declared itself "[d]etermined to resolve the grave humanitarian situation in Kosovo, Federal Republic of Yugoslavia, and to provide for the safe and free return of all refugees and displaced persons to their homes."[57] The resolution provided for an international military presence and civil administration in Kosovo.[58] The goals of this international presence in Kosovo would be overseeing and reestablishing basic governmental functions, humanitarian assistance, democratization, institution-building, and economic reconstruction. Finally, the resolution provided for the appointment of "a Special Representative to control the implementation of the international civil presence, and further request[ed] the Secretary-General to instruct his Special Representative to coordinate closely with the international security presence."[59] One could easily say that, in short, the resolution provided for the establishment of a protectorate over Kosovo. Indeed, the irony and quotation marks that attended the use of the word *protectorate* in the first year of debate about UNMIK gradually disappeared with time.

What is the relationship between these two documents? We could list their similarities. These would include (1) *recitation of international ideals* – in Fez, that of a "well-regulated regime"; in Resolution 1244, that of international peace and security; (2) *military occupation* – in Fez, by France; in Resolution 1244, by the international security presence; (3) *bracketing of sovereignty* – in Fez, by maintaining the nominal sovereignty of the Moroccan Sultan; in Resolution 1244, that of Yugoslavia; (4) *far-reaching internal reforms undertaken by the Protector* – in Fez, administrative, educational, and economic; in Resolution 1244, administrative, economic, political, and civil; (5) *explicit provisions for human rights* – in Fez, in the form of Muslim religious liberty; in Resolution 1244, in the form of broad human rights; (6) *ambiguity about the ultimate goal of the protectorate* – in Fez, between annexation by France and ultimate independence for a modernized Moroccan state; in Resolution 1244, between the restoration of Yugoslav sovereignty and ultimate independence for Kosovo; and (7) *vesting of supreme power in a representative of the Protector* – in Fez, the French

[55] UN Security Council Resolution 1244, S/RES/1244 (1999).
[56] Ibid., Preamble.
[57] Ibid.
[58] Ibid., paragraphs 7–11.
[59] Ibid., paragraph 6.

Resident-General; in Resolution 1244, the Special Representative of the Secretary-General.[60]

However, we could also list their differences. Such differences would reside in part in the source of the legitimacy of the documents – in particular, their relative position on the axes of sovereign consent and international community authority. The protectorate instrument is in the form of a treaty, a nominally consensual document, whereas the UN Security Council resolution is in the form of a mandatory resolution under Chapter VII. Yet, it is important not to overstate the starkness of this contrast. Although Resolution 1244 is in the form of a Chapter VII resolution, it also recites the consent by Yugoslavia to the principles contained in the G-8 document of May 1999 and in the EU document of June 2, 1999.[61] Conversely, although the protectorate document is in the form of a treaty, it was the culmination of steady military and political encroachment by France.

Moreover, both documents seek to ground the legitimacy of their entire structure in a set of substantive international values. The French protectorate treaty recites the principles of what we would today call "good governance" as the goal of the treaty. Moreover, the French elsewhere described the "lofty aims of the protectorate... [as] above all a work of civilization... a matter in which all [nations] have an equal interest"[62] – the functional historical equivalent to the more familiar recitation in Resolution 1244 of "the purposes and principles of the Charter of the United Nations, and the primary responsibility of the Security Council for the maintenance of international peace and security."

If we cannot read unequivocal differences between the two regimes off the text of their founding documents, we probably need to look elsewhere. That elsewhere would include the political intent and historical context in which the two regimes were established. We would need to compare the political and economic motivations for the French occupation of Morocco with those animating the NATO and UN occupation of Kosovo. We would need to compare the substantive merit of the respective claims of France and the UN Security Council to represent the international community. We would need to look at the broader geopolitical context, particularly the outside powers that France and NATO were trying to ward off from the two regions. And we

60 Just as regimes like UNMIK found themselves doubled by the comparison to protectorates, protectorates also found themselves doubled by comparisons to colonies.

61 Resolution 1244, *supra* note 54, Preamble.

62 "Final Conclusions of the French Government," *Nationality Decrees Case*, Permanent Court of International Justice, Series C, No. 2, p. 242 (1923).

might, in the inevitably messy results of such multiple inquiries, arrive at a persuasive judgment of relative legitimacy.

However, this judgment would not reside in a clear characterization of UNMIK as purely law and the French Protectorate as purely politics – a judgment that could only be anachronistic. France justified its action on legal grounds that were relatively plausible in 1912, just as the UN justified its actions on legal grounds that were relatively plausible in 1999. This is not to say that their relative legal plausibility, even in their respective contexts, was equivalent. However, neither could we confidently assert *a priori*, without detailed comparative analysis, that one regime would come out ahead.

Bracketing momentarily the formal legal issues, normative judgment of international regimes should depend on an evaluation of the conception of the affected population that animates them. In the interwar context, I have argued that international lawyers viewed the nationalism to which their legal innovations responded as a "primitive" force to be celebrated on account of its energy, and to be domesticated on account of its dangerousness.[63] This international legal "primitivism," I argued, embodied the same type of fear and fascination exerted on many contemporaneous cultural innovators by fantasies of racial, cultural, geographical, and sexual "Others." Much of Modernist creativity, across a range of domains – including art, music, literature, architecture, and law – emerged from attempts to link these "primitives" with the most advanced technical innovations of the day.

The Modernists' "primitivist" fantasies, of course, had only the most dubious relationship with reality – except, perhaps, when these fantasies were internalized or performed by the Modernists' "Others." Still, these fantasies were often an improvement on colonial conceptions of the "native" – often, although not always. In any case, although this topic would require another chapter, a comparative evaluation of regimes such as UNMIK would have to look carefully at the conception of the affected populations animating them – how they are imagined politically, economically, culturally, and sexually, and how that imagination may be embedded in the details of the legal regime.

Legitimation Effects: Four Hypotheses

I conclude with four hypotheses about the effect on legitimacy of the seemingly unavoidable evocation by regimes such as UNMIK of the specters of protectorates and colonies: the *delegitimizing-effects hypothesis*, the

[63] See, e.g., 'But the Alternative Is Despair', *supra* note 34.

legitimizing-effects hypothesis, the *cautionary-effects hypothesis*, and the *strategic-effects hypothesis*.

The *delegitimizing-effects hypothesis* is that evocation of the colonial past has the effect of an unmasking. In this view, audacious experiments like UNMIK purport to implement the most advanced internationalist principles, but actually represent the continuation or resurrection of colonial power in contemporary form. The claim of such regimes to have thoroughly pressed power into the service of humanitarianism would simply be an ideological cover for the reverse process. This type of effect on legitimacy would primarily concern the status of the international regime.

By contrast, the *legitimizing-effects hypothesis* is that this evocation actually bolsters the claims of these legal regimes. In this view, it is precisely their ability to evoke the colonial past and *to demonstrate their difference from it* that gives these regimes their distinctive legitimacy. To the extent that similarities exist, the regimes' advocates could contend, they stem from structural exigencies arising from any administration of territory by the power of an outside authority. However, the advocates would contend, it is the humanitarian manner in which such power is exercised and the goals for which it is exercised that demonstrate the radical difference of such regimes from their colonial counterparts – a demonstration of difference whose persuasive "edge" depends precisely on the structural similarities. The evocation of colonialism would pose a high-stakes challenge to the regime to persuasively establish this differentiation. The achievement of such a legitimizing effect would depend on the ability of the particular international regime to demonstrate that the coherence of its elements prove its status legitimacy as a whole – in other words, that its actual practices work in such a way as to demonstrate that the regime as a whole is really "internationalist" and not "colonialist."

The *cautionary-effects hypothesis* views the association with colonialism as a useful tool in the hands of friendly critics of these regimes – for example, sympathetic, but wary, human-rights NGOs. The association with colonialism would be a readily available and widely comprehensible criticism that can be made every time the regime threatens to exceed the legitimate bounds of its powers. Such critics would be strategically deploying the critique of status legitimacy as a pressuring device to lobby for a reconfiguration of the coherence of the regime's elements.

The *strategic-effects hypothesis* combines the first three. Like the *cautionary-effects hypothesis*, it views the association with colonialism as a useful tool. However, this hypothesis would extend the range of players in whose hands the tool might be useful. There might be occasions, for example, when the affected population may wish to deploy the colonial association's delegitimizing effect – not because they wish to terminate the regime but rather because they are engaged in a particular struggle over a particular issue. There might even be times when the international authority might wish to affirm the association with colonialism in a threatening manner in order to command respect from a variety of bad actors in the region that may be impervious to gentler, more legitimate arguments about the common good. (After all, if military force can sometimes be appropriate, psychological force also might be.) And so on.

From the perspective of the situational, political-historical approach to legitimacy taken in this chapter, each of these uses of the evocation of the colonial past might be appropriate depending on the particularities of a given international regime and its relation to the local conflict on which it is deployed. Some regimes, in fact, might be illegitimate exercises of power; others might be noble ventures; still others might need to be kept on their toes by a range of vigilant actors. The legitimacy of neither the status nor the coherence of prevailing forms of internationalism should ever be taken for granted. Legitimacy, especially of the purported composites of power and idealism that have marked the most robust internationalism of the past century, can and should only ever be a provisional achievement – an achievement arrived at through internationalism's wrestling with its doubles, be they ideological adversaries, heterogeneous elements in local conflicts, or specters of its own unsavory past.

VASUKI NESIAH

5. From Berlin to Bonn to Baghdad: A Space for Infinite Justice

In 1884, after their respective military expeditions had laid claim to different parts of Africa, colonial powers convened in Berlin to pore over maps, argue boundary lines, and divvy up the continent among themselves.[1] The Berlin conference explicitly concerned the contours of European sovereignty over different parcels of Africa. No Africans were present at the gathering. More than 100 years later, in 2001, Bonn was the venue for another conference convened by the great "Western" powers; this time, the maps were of Afghanistan. Yet, in the twenty-first century, with the ghost of Berlin hovering over the current discourse of intervention, the Bonn conference ostensibly addressed the contours of Afghan sovereignty. The UN searched across the world, from the hills of Rome to the beaches of Cyprus, to find Afghans to attend. Fewer than two years later, in the 2003 "liberation" of Iraq, Baghdad became yet another venue for "recognizing" sovereignty – in an effort that

[1] German Chancellor Otto von Bismarck convened this conference in 1884–1885 – an event that turned out to be a critical milestone in the consolidation and expansion of European imperialism in Africa, as well as in the closely imbricated history of the slave trade. See, e.g., Barbara Harlow & Mia Carter, *Archives of Empire, Vol. 2: The Scramble for Africa* (Duke University Press, 2003); and Adam Horschild, *King Leopold's Ghost* (Houghton Mifflin, 1999).

This chapter has undergone many iterations, acquiring many debts along the way. Most immediately, thanks to Hilary Charlesworth, Jean-Marc Coicaud, my fellow authors in this volume, and the anonymous reviewers for reading and commenting on the analysis of humanitarian intervention. Thanks to Jerry Frug and David Kennedy for shepherding an early engagement with the work of Richard Falk through my doctoral dissertation; to S. Nanthikesan and Ahilan Kadirgamar for feedback on the humanitarianism/militarism analysis in the review of the movie *Three Kings* in *lines magazine*; and finally, to Suzanne Katzenstein and Susan Farbstein for comments and editing advice in the course of preparing an earlier version of the manuscript for the 17 *Harvard Human Rights Journal* 75–98 (Spring 2004).

George W. Bush claimed (and apparently with little intentional irony) is focused on Iraqis choosing their own regime.[2]

Even as the specific rationale for the U.S. intervention in Iraq confronted an ever-growing legitimacy crisis, the normative terrain of legitimacy that was invoked by the Bush administration (whose touchstones of protection and internationalist solidarity are discussed herein) has gained further traction in the realm of humanitarian law and policy. Concepts such as "humanitarian intervention," "cosmopolitan humanitarianism," and "the responsibility to protect" have been expanded and detailed by liberal internationalists in an effort to fortify the normative rationale for the use of military force to address humanitarian concerns.[3] In the normative universe of international law, the production of legitimacy through the concept of humanitarian intervention depends on its contrast with the imperial interventions epitomized by Bismarck's Berlin conference.[4] However, coming of age foreshadowed in the language of protection and cosmopolitan solidarity that undergirded some of the stated rationale for Iraq, the legitimacy norms harnessed by humanitarianism emerge as troubled co-travelers with the logic of empire. Thus, the legitimacy crisis is "not simply local" to Baghdad. Rather, in the interstices of the production of legitimacy for humanitarian intervention on the one hand and imperial intervention on the other, we may find what Coicaud describes in Chapter 3 as "systemic" fault lines that haunt humanitarian law and policy more fundamentally.

This chapter examines the responses to this legitimacy crisis proposed by liberal internationalists. As noted previously, recent proposals regarding the principles that should reinvigorate and fortify the normative terrain of humanitarian intervention may have gained more traction in the international community precisely at the moment when these principles were already "occupied" by the effort to legitimate the U.S. invasion of Iraq.[5] Indeed, the

[2] George W. Bush argued that the Coalition Forces' intervention in Iraq was to "midwife" the democratic will of the Iraqi people: "We're working closely with Iraqi citizens as they prepare a constitution, as they move toward free elections and take increasing responsibility for their own affairs.... The establishment of a free Iraq at the heart of the Middle East will be a watershed event in the global democratic revolution.... America has put our power at the service of this principle." George W. Bush, Remarks at the Twentieth Anniversary of the National Endowment for Democracy (November 2003); available at www.whitehouse.gov/news/releases/2003/11/20031106–2.html).

[3] See International Commission on Intervention and State Sovereignty, "The Responsibility to Protect: Report of the International Commission on Intervention and State Sovereignty," 2001; available at www.dfait-maeci gc.ca/iciss-ciise/report-en.asp (accessed February 9, 2004).

[4] See Footnote 1.

[5] See Nesiah, "Resistance in the Age of Empire: Occupied Discourse Pending Investigation," in 27 *Third World Quarterly* 903–922 (July 2006).

legitimation discourses of humanitarianism and Iraq may prove to have had a symbiotic trajectory. Perhaps in recognition of this intertwined trajectory, Ian Williams warned, "we should not let" Bush's "misappropriation of humanitarian intervention alienate the concept from its natural owners, the left."[6] However, is it possible for us to preserve a "clean" space for humanitarianism? Do we come to terms with a tainted field, confront its complicities head on, and decide whether we should move on in each case? Does the effort to demarcate the field of humanitarian intervention as being in contradistinction to that of imperial intervention mask these complicities? Lamenting the Bush–Blair duet regarding the humanitarian goals that guided their policies in the Second Gulf War, proponents of humanitarian internationalism are anxiously seeking to formulate universal principles to distinguish illegitimate from legitimate intervention, conquest from protection, and militarism from humanitarianism.[7]

Exploring one window into the fault lines in international legitimacy that preoccupy this volume, this chapter examines how legitimacy has been sought in contemporary approaches to international intervention through the proposed legal and normative distinctions between imperial military offensives and humanitarian military interventions. It contends that humanitarianism functions not only in opposition but also as a complement to empire. Ironically, the foundation for the widespread invocation of humanitarian intervention by Anglo-American policy makers supporting the 2003 conquest and occupation of Iraq was generated precisely by the principles of multilateral humanitarianism: protection of the vulnerable and internationalist solidarity. In fact, these same principles were previously invoked relative to the bombing of Kosovo, the genocide in Rwanda, and the plight of the Kurdish community in the First Gulf War. By 2001, the world's superpowers buttressed their military aspirations in Afghanistan with the language of humanitarianism and human rights and succeeded in gaining UN support. As conveyed by the U.S. Defense Department's original title of the intervention, "Infinite Justice," advocates of a humanitarian entry point for military intervention relied on a favorable normative algebra to help legitimate the massive bombing campaign in Afghanistan.[8]

The first part of this chapter examines the fault lines of legitimacy in the relationship between internationalist humanitarian intervention and

[6] Ian Williams, "Intervene with Caution," *These Times*, August 11, 2003, pp. 23 & 24.

[7] For instance, Michael Smith noted, "We still have to maintain and even raise barriers to illegitimate intervention" while also ensuring that we "define the areas, conditions and procedures for legitimate ones." Michael Smith, "Humanitarian Intervention: An Overview of the Ethical Issues," 12 *Ethics and International Affairs* 1, 77 (1998).

[8] Arundhati Roy, "The Algebra of Infinite Justice," *The Guardian*, September 29, 2001, p. 1.

imperial intervention. It explores both the larger context in which this humanitarian discourse has taken shape and internal debates within the humanitarian intervention field, as they have evolved in the past decade. The second part includes a case study of how the discourse of humanitarianism permeated the military offensive in Afghanistan. It discusses "The Responsibility to Protect," a report prepared by the International Commission on Intervention and State Sovereignty.[9] The report proposes a framework shift from the "right to intervene" to the "responsibility to protect" in developing guidelines for distinguishing legitimate humanitarian intervention from illegitimate militarism. This report and the ensuing discussion led to the April 2006 adoption of UN Security Council Resolution 1674 on "Protection of Civilians in Armed Conflict."[10] Drawing from the analysis of "The Responsibility to Protect" report, the chapter concludes by engaging with the legacies of the two Gulf wars relative to the internationalist allegiance to humanitarian principles to produce legitimacy for military intervention. The chapter argues that efforts to fortify the ramparts of humanitarianism against the grasp of interventions grounded in the politics of empire may have proved futile. Indeed, looking back on the rise of humanitarian militarism in the past decade, important questions emerge about humanitarianism's own complicity in enabling the linkage between humanitarian principles and empire in some contexts (e.g., criticism of military inaction to Rwanda in 1993), even as that linkage is resisted in others (e.g., criticism of the invasion of Iraq in 2003).[11]

Debates in the Field: Securing the Legitimacy of Cosmopolitan Humanitarianism

The end of the twentieth century and the beginning of the twenty-first marked a moment when the founding assumptions about large-scale humanitarian intervention underwent a tectonic shift. This transformation simultaneously unnerved and emboldened cosmopolitan humanitarians. The erosion of old assumptions about nonintervention meant that the ground on which they

[9] International Commission on Intervention and State Sovereignty, *supra* note 3, p. VII.

[10] Available at domino.un.org/UNISPAl.NSF/361eea1cc08301c485256cf600606959/e529762befa456f8852571610045ebef!OpenDocument.

[11] A considerable segment of the cosmopolitan humanitarian community sought unsuccessfully to assert a restrictive hand on intervention in the case of Iraq in 2003. Some opposed military intervention (often using the argument that the intervention was not guided by "right intentions"). Others called for alternative routes of engagement, including giving more time to the weapons-inspection team (often using the argument that war should be the choice of last resort, or that war did not constitute "proportionate" and "effective" means to the desired ends). Yet, others supported the war but urged respect for international humanitarian law in the conduct of war.

stood became less secure. At the same time, this less secure ground allowed for a more expansive terrain for humanitarian action and catalyzed an earnest quest for firm principles to determine the contours of legitimate intervention.

To some extent, Kosovo marked a great temporal dividing line. For vast sectors of the international law and policy community, it legitimized the use of militarism for humanitarian purposes and increased states' humanitarian confidence in the ability to use military power for good. As David Chandler noted, "Humanitarian militarism, widely advocated during the 1999 Kosovo war, would have been an oxymoron before the 1990s; today, it has become a tautology."[12] The decision to intervene in Kosovo without UN authorization emphasized the humanitarian–military dichotomy and overlap; it signaled a new era in which the ground for intervention became more fertile while concerns about the legitimacy of intervention became increasingly intense. As David Wippman noted:

> . . . in the aftermath of NATO's military intervention in Kosovo, international lawyers, diplomats, and others vigorously debated the use of force as a means to terminate gross human rights abuses, whether actual or threatened. . . . Scholars advanced and debated legal and moral justifications for such intervention. Distinguished international commissions issued reports on particular cases and the subject as a whole. Governments proposed criteria for identifying conflicts warranting intervention, and for circumscribing the use of the veto to block humanitarian intervention in cases satisfying the relevant criteria. Conferences were held, and books were published.[13]

This tectonic shift forms the backdrop to the current discourse of humanitarian intervention.

Although Kosovo serves as a central moment in the development of a new discourse, the shift should be situated in a broader context that expanded the ground for humanitarian intervention. There are two important elements to this context: (1) the global political backdrop within which the discourse of cosmopolitan humanitarianism is situated; and (2) the discourse's internal dynamics and debates.

The Context of Cosmopolitan Humanitarianism

Changes in the international context influenced development of the humanitarian discourse and extended its reach in the global public sphere. Three

[12] David Chandler, "The Road to Military Humanitarianism: How the Human Rights NGOs Shaped a New Humanitarian Agenda," 23 *Human Rights Quarterly* 678, 698 (2001).

[13] David Wippman, Book Review, 97 *American Journal of International Law* 457 (2003) (reviewing Brian D. Lepard, "Rethinking Humanitarian Intervention: A Fresh Legal Approach Based on Fundamental Ethical Principles in International Law and World Religions" [2002]).

elements of the international context warrant mention. First, struggles in many postcolonial countries led to disillusionment with the defense of sovereignty as a guarantor of democratic rights.[14] Second, developments linked to the new contours of post–Cold War global politics gave rise to an emboldened liberalism on the world stage.[15] Third, the daily operational challenges of humanitarian work led to both increasing dependence on donor agendas for funding and direction and a concomitant questioning of political neutrality as the foundation for international engagement.[16]

Each development enabled the creation of the cosmopolitan humanitarian discourse on legitimate intervention. The disillusionment with sovereignty meant that intervention was no longer automatically equated with imperialism. In many contexts, sovereignty has been rendered passé and deemed an ineffective tool complicit with repressive structures, even when touted as the shield to resist imperial repression.[17] The new world order is fraught with injustice and inequity in ways that have required ongoing struggles against neo-colonial structures and discourses. Thus, although colonialism remains a current preoccupation, it is understood in a manner fundamentally different than conceptions that were dominant even fifty years ago. Today, colonialism is increasingly viewed as a relationship of economic exploitation and political marginalization that is not necessarily captured by tracking the fate of territorial sovereignty.[18]

Second, in addition to a transformative understanding of colonialism, the narrowing ideological terrain of the post–Cold War era (marked by the hegemonic reach of global liberalism) created a climate in which even many of those critical of the new world order were infused with an uncritical

[14] See, generally, Steve Pile & Michael Keith (eds.), *Geographies of Resistance* (Routledge, 1997), for a wide-ranging analysis of such struggles in many countries. See Partha Chatterjee, *Nationalist Thought and the Colonial World: A Derivative Discourse?* (University of Minnesota, 1993), for an India-focused interrogation of postcolonial nationalism's appropriation of subaltern struggles in the name of anticolonialism.

[15] See, e.g., Francis Fukayama. *End of History and the Last Man* (Free Press, 1992); and Samuel Huntington, *Clash of Civilizations and the Remaking of World Order* (Simon & Schuster, 1998).

[16] See Thomas Weiss, "Principles, Politics, and Humanitarian Action," 13 *Ethics and International Affairs* 1, 2 (1999).

[17] The debate regarding intervention is often understood as one between the "values of sovereignty" and the "values of human rights." This is a misleading dichotomy on many counts. For instance, in many early anticolonial struggles, these values were conjoined, with sovereignty asserted in efforts to advance rights for democratic participation. However, it is equally true that in the past few decades, claims to territorial integrity have often been deployed to defeat the democratic aspirations of minorities and dissenters.

[18] See Chatterjee, *supra* note 14. See also Ranajit Guha & Gayatri Spivak (eds.), *Selected Subaltern Studies* (Oxford University Press, 1988).

missionary zeal for human rights and humanitarianism as global public goods. With the end of the Cold War, the Washington consensus consolidated around a particularly self-satisfied brand of liberal internationalism.

Third, as the agendas and self-conceptions of human-rights and humanitarian non-governmental organizations (NGOs) were influenced by the new world order, NGOs engaged more openly with the political nature of their work but largely within the terms of liberal internationalism. Humanitarian work in the field was shaped by a complex interplay of changes in how human-rights and humanitarian institutions were funded and how their projects were defined. As international institutions linked aid to rule-of-law programs that absorbed human-rights agencies and reduced state structures, more of these sectors worked intimately with donor countries, aid agencies, and the United Nations (UN). As David Reiff noted:

> ... by the time the war in Afghanistan began, it was increasingly difficult to distinguish between the rhetoric or even the policies of humanitarian NGOs, the UN system and Western governments. The difficulty was compounded by the fact that few agencies today either choose to or are in a position to refuse contracts from donors or the UN. And this trend toward seeing themselves as, in effect, subcontractors for major donors has only increased since human rights considerations began to be incorporated more and more systematically into the plans and programs of the mainline NGOs.[19]

Not only was human-rights and humanitarian work intertwined with the structural contexts of the field, intimacy with donor constituencies also changed the NGOs' understanding of the political impact of their work. Earlier ideological vagueness was shed, and many human-rights and humanitarian NGO workers were driven by liberal idealism and a cosmopolitan calling,[20] which led to a greater willingness to accept intervention as an option to be considered and perhaps embraced.

Debates in the Field

The evolving environment of humanitarian and human-rights work rendered sovereignty a potentially ineffective tool and made Cold War "neutrality" anachronistic as humanitarian NGOs' increased donor dependence produced tensions and concerns about their role in the political-military agendas of donor countries. Even humanitarian workers began to unpack the myth of political neutrality that had been the mainstay of their work in the past. It is not

[19] David Rieff, "Humanitarianism in Crisis," 81 *Foreign Affairs* 111, 117 (2002).

[20] For instance, see the work of Freedom House; available at www.freedomhouse.org (accessed February 8, 2004).

that the field itself became more complex but rather that humanitarians saw the inherent complexities as connected to the core normative foundation that guided the mandate of their work. If humanitarianism means an apolitical approach to doing good, there was a "new conventional wisdom that there are no humanitarian solutions to humanitarian problems."[21]

As Thomas Weiss argues, this identity crisis was fueled by "severe criticism of the aid establishment."[22] The work of analysts such as Mary Anderson spoke to the complexities of relief efforts in the context of war. The books that now inform the U.S. State Department's optimism about compassionate militarism[23] in Afghanistan and Iraq prompted considerable soul-searching among aid workers concerned that relief programs could do more harm than good. Michael Ignatieff anguishes that "almost everyone who tries . . . has a bad conscience; no one is quite sure whether our engagement makes things better or worse."[24]

These concerns extend to the defining principles of humanitarian action – neutrality between different sides of a political conflict and impartiality in the distribution of aid. In the context of ongoing civil wars, ethnic cleansing, and genocide, humanitarian agencies find it difficult to operate according to the principles of neutrality and impartiality. "Humanitarian principles," Weiss stated, "are no longer sacrosanct."[25] In the past decade, in a day-to-day operational sense, practitioners engaged in humanitarian relief developed a widespread sense of disillusionment about the possibility of neutral engagement, and many even urge that the aspiration to neutrality is moral hypocrisy.

This shift has not gone unchallenged. Some in the field lament the move away from a "nonpolitical approach," arguing that this has provoked an unfortunate "retreat from the principles of neutrality and universalism, and the development of military humanitarianism . . . legitimizing the politics of international condemnation, sanctions, and bombing."[26] Chandler longs to return to a demilitarized and impartial ethos of "relying on empathy with suffering victims."[27] Rieff similarly argues that the "core assumptions" of humanitarianism – "solidarity, a fundamental sympathy for victims, and an antipathy for oppressors and exploiters" – are distinct from political goals.[28] Although "Western military intervention in a case such as Bosnia is

[21] Rieff, *supra* note 19, p. 111.
[22] Weiss, *supra* note 16, p. 2.
[23] See the section on poverty alleviation for the U.S. State Department's articulation of its optimism.
[24] Ibid., p. 7.
[25] Ibid., p. 2.
[26] Chandler, *supra* note 12, p. 700.
[27] Ibid.
[28] Rieff, *supra* note 19, p. 121.

justified," we should not confuse arguments "for military intervention on political grounds" with promoting "military intervention on humanitarian grounds."[29] In fact, Rieff asserts that "to promote military intervention on humanitarian grounds . . . will always be a contradiction in terms. It is a perversion of humanitarianism, which must be either neutral or nothing."[30] This is the position adopted by Médecins Sans Frontières (MSF), which Rieff describes as the only humanitarian NGO that has resisted politicization. Eric Dachy of MSF is quoted as saying that discussions about humanitarian intervention and peacekeeping operations "accompany, or mask, a deliberate political choice with gestures of generosity and compassion."[31]

While Chandler, Rieff, and MSF long to retreat to principles of neutrality and universalism, others in the field have accepted military humanitarianism. Weiss situates military humanitarianism in a more strategic and pragmatic approach that he believes is merited by the contemporary context. Arguing that the classical humanitarian approach of "neutrality" is no longer available given that "humanitarian tragedies have become 'normal'" and "belligerents . . . undisciplined," he advocates an "instrumental humanitarianism" that is more engaged with the particularities of context, cognizant of the complexities of political choices, and more pragmatic about balancing different goals.[32] Weiss calls for a recognition that the "goals of humanitarian action often conflict; good intentions can have catastrophic consequences; there are alternative ways to achieve ends; and even if none of the choices are ideal, victims still require decisions about outside help."[33] This is partly an allusion to the fact that humanitarian action often works in tandem with military intervention. In contrast, Tony Blair abandoned any residual diffidence in his own demand for military intervention in such contexts: "It's right for the international community to use military force to prevent genocide and protect human rights, even if it entails a clear violation of sovereignty."[34]

Blair's unqualified confidence in humanitarian intervention is not universal. Others are concerned that more work must be done to clarify the conditions for the legitimate use of force. Referring to Blair as the shrillest supporter of "humanitarian" war, Daniele Archibugi argued that there is no coherent philosophy that guides politicians and political commentators who advocated military intervention in Kosovo and elsewhere. For Archibugi

[29] Ibid., p. 120.
[30] Ibid.
[31] Quoted in ibid., pp. 116–117.
[32] Weiss, *supra* note 16, p. 2.
[33] Ibid.
[34] Quoted in Daniele Archibugi, "Cosmopolitics," 4 *New Left Review* 147 (July–August 2000).

and other supporters of cosmopolitan democracy, the lack of a coherent philosophy fundamentally undermines the legitimacy of intervention. Thus, "a decade after the fall of the Berlin Wall, the seventeenth-century notion of state sovereignty is threatened by something older still: the law of the jungle."[35]

Seeking, however, to arrest that regression and return to the path of progress, authors of the International Commission on Intervention and State Sovereignty report, "The Responsibility to Protect," are keen to articulate a vision aimed at precisely the legitimacy questions that tax Archibugi. Chaired by Gareth Evans and Mohamed Sahnoun and convened by the Canadian government, the report strives to establish guidelines for legitimate humanitarian interventions that violate state sovereignty. The Commission was formed to address the legitimacy crisis provoked by the past decade's history of intervention and nonintervention: "External military intervention for human protection purposes has been controversial both when it has happened – as in Somalia, Bosnia, and Kosovo – and when it has failed to happen, as in Rwanda."[36] Kofi Annan argued that responses to this crisis must be developed: "If humanitarian intervention is, indeed, an unacceptable assault on sovereignty, how should we respond to a Rwanda, to a Srebrenica – to gross and systematic violations of human rights that affect every precept of our common humanity?"[37]

The next section examines how the Commission sought to answer this question by developing a humanitarian framework for the use of force in a way that is grounded in principles of protection and internationalist solidarities rather than geopolitical ambitions and priorities of empire. The 2006 passage of UN Security Council Resolution 1674 on "The Responsibility to Protect" just five years after its publication in 2001 marks the meteoric success that has met the Commission's recommendations in the highest echelons of the international community. However, taking a step back from the standpoint that gained the imprimatur of the UN's highest body, the following section explores whether humanitarian arguments served to prevent or to legitimize an imperial militarism – with particular attention to the 2001 intervention in Afghanistan. In fact, examining both the organizations that worked on human-rights and humanitarian issues in Afghanistan and the governments that argued for intervention in Afghanistan, the section highlights how the discourse regarding protection, identified with the former, was also key to the rationale for intervention advanced by the latter.

35 Ibid., p. 148.
36 International Commission on Intervention and State Sovereignty, *supra* note 3, p. VII.
37 Ibid.

From "The Right to Intervene" to "The Responsibility to Protect": The Military Offensive in Afghanistan

Cosmopolitan Humanitarianism and the Illusory Compass for Intervention. The work of the International Commission on Intervention and State Sovereignty is instructive in demonstrating both the impetus for identifying principles that will define legitimate intervention and the inability of those principles to provide a secure compass for distinguishing legitimate from illegitimate action. In fact, the same principles are used to defend intervention by some and protest intervention by others. In many cases, the doves and the hawks may be flying in the same skies of cosmopolitan humanitarianism. As is argued herein in the case of Afghanistan, although principles of cosmopolitan humanitarianism may have constrained the use of force to follow the rules of war, cosmopolitan humanitarianism also fundamentally legitimized the intervention.

Constituted by a range of prominent international actors with state and civil society affiliations, the International Commission on Intervention and State Sovereignty outlines four principles for the legitimate use of military action: right intention, last resort, proportional means, and reasonable prospects.[38] The Commission notes that to some extent, its proposals also require a fundamentally different nomenclature to capture its vision – the "the duty to protect" rather than "the right to humanitarian intervention."[39] It argues that the debate regarding humanitarian intervention (particularly within the UN General Assembly) has been mired in a fundamentally misguided conversation about the right to intervene on the one hand and territorial sovereignty on the other. Instead, the Commission argues for focusing on the notion of sovereignty as responsibility, which includes both the responsibility that states owe to their own people and the responsibility the international community owes to all peoples:

> The most compelling task now is to work to ensure that when the call goes out to the community of states for action, that call will be answered. There must never again be mass killing or ethnic cleansing. There must be no more Rwandas. . . . The Commission has sought to give clear articulation to this consensus, and calls on all members of the community of nations, together with non-governmental actors and citizens of states, to embrace the idea of the responsibility to protect as a basic element in the code of global citizenship, for states and peoples, in the twenty-first century.[40]

[38] Ibid., p. IX.

[39] Ibid., p. 11.

[40] Ibid., pp. 70, 75.

Accordingly, "The Responsibility to Protect" is offered as the new guiding normative and legal framework for transnational cosmopolitan engagement. Because people will sometimes require protection through intervention, the Commission views its report to be about "compelling human need, about populations at risk of slaughter, ethnic cleansing and starvation. It has been about the responsibility of sovereign states to protect their own people from such harm – and about the need for the larger international community to exercise their responsibility if states are unwilling or unable to do so themselves."[41]

The Commission's discussion of "protection" and related humanitarian imperatives for the use of force are hardly isolated. For instance, expressing concern about the lack of a coherent philosophy to distinguish legitimate from illegitimate intervention, Archibugi sought to address this problem by developing his own basic legitimacy guidelines. As he wrote in the pages of the *New Left Review*, these guidelines reflect a left-liberal project shaped by a resolute internationalism as well as an anti-imperialist ethos concerned with illegitimate "military adventures." In his words, the principles informing a "cosmopolitical perspective on humanitarian intervention" are tolerance, legitimacy, and effectiveness.[42] Arguing that racism and prejudice were constitutive of colonial brutality, Archibugi sought to ensure that tolerance is built into a commitment to cosmopolitan democracy, which in turn provides the foundation for humanitarian intervention. Similarly, international legal legitimacy and legitimacy with key actors in international civil society comprise a necessary condition for humanitarian intervention. Thus, norms linked with international law – such as the use of force as a last resort and the conduct of military intervention in accordance with the laws of war – are crucial for securing legitimacy.

The principles articulated in "The Responsibility to Protect" are echoed in Archibugi's principles for "cosmopolitical responsibility." The "duty to protect" closely mirrors Archibugi's vision of cosmopolitical responsibility: the principle of right intention is similar to the "tolerance" test; the principles of last resort and proportional means are contained in legal legitimacy; and the principle of reasonable prospects is close to the notion of "effectiveness."

The Commission's work is also echoed in the work of another liberal internationalist, Richard Falk, who articulated a vision for transnational engagement. Carrying strong normative resonance with the vision of the "responsibility to protect" – yet, arguably with even more sensitivity to the weight of colonial and neo-colonial militarism – Falk's guidelines for

41 Ibid., p. 69.

42 Archibugi, *supra* note 34, pp. 147–148.

legitimate transnational engagement are captured in "On Humane Governance."[43] Particularly in his work with the World Orders Project, Falk has been one of the most influential voices articulating a transnational idealism in international law and policy.[44] His approach provides an "instance of discourse" that informs the normative vision of humanitarian intervention.[45]

Paralleling the shift from the "right to intervene" to the "responsibility to protect," Falk characterized his normative vision for transnational engagement as a shift from "geopolitics" to "humane governance."[46] Three overarching dichotomies form the basis of legitimacy in Falk's vision of humane governance: internationalist solidarities over state interests, an effective peace over an anarchic state of war,[47] and international law over arbitrary power.[48] Whereas the latter two resonate with the Commission's criteria on when and how the responsibility to protect triggers intervention, Falk's first

[43] "On Humane Governance: Toward a New Global Politics" (The World Order Models Project Report of the Global Civilization Initiative, 1995).

[44] See, e.g., ibid., p. 149. I take Falk's oeuvre as indicative of one slice of the current debate on humanitarian cosmopolitanism. I focus on Falk and the text "Humane Governance" not only because Falk has long been one of the most prominent and prolific international lawyers of the past few decades but also because the specific context of the book's emergence in the transnational conversations of a nongovernmental collective, the World Order's Project, is itself exemplary of internationalist engagement. This paradigm of engagement sees itself as enabling agency in new locations – not in the nation-state or in global capital, but in transnational democratic tendencies. Ibid., p. 3.

[45] I borrow the phrase "instances of a discourse" from Foucault. The discourses of humanitarian cosmopolitanism are internally heterogeneous and contested. To this extent, my effort here is not to provide a comprehensive discussion of humanitarian cosmopolitanism but rather to focus on one influential instance of it and to explore its internal tensions and heterogeneity.

[46] Here, I am reminded of Anthony Appiah, who describes his project in similar terms but also warns against conflating cosmopolitanism and humanism, arguing that liberal cosmopolitanism values diversity, as humanism may or may not always do. See Anthony Appiah & Henry Louis Gates (eds.), *The Dictionary of Global Culture* (Knopf, 1997). Falk's vision would also highlight pluralism as an important characteristic of his cosmopolitanism and his conception of humanist values.

[47] Arguing that "military means can destroy, but cannot create," Falk asserts that "[t]he more fundamental struggle, at the very center of the normative project, is to challenge war itself, the social and political process of mass international killing in the name of the state . . . allegedly on behalf of security in self-defense." *Supra* note 44, pp. 15, 244.

[48] Falk speaks of "many stages of institutionalization" in the international sphere "that seem to be on the path to human governance. . . . These include the strengthening of international law in relation to the foreign policy of major states, the expansion of international law to the activities of the global market place, the expansion of the authority of the world court, the establishment of peace forces under U.N. command, and, many others." *Supra* note 44, p. 7. The importance of law and legal institutions in Falk's project is underscored when contrasted with the geopolitical worldview that he characterizes as resorting to war rather than law in its participation in the international public sphere.

theme resonates most closely with the focus on the core normative aims of intervention – that is, the "right intentions" captured by Falk's call for a focus on internationalist solidarities over statist interests.

Against the geopolitical model's reduction of "security" to "the well-being of the territorial state in relation to its foreign enemies,"[49] Falk is keen to advance a cosmopolitan humanitarianism premised on "a global civil society"[50] and "human rights for all the peoples of the earth."[51] Using the intervention in Afghanistan as a test case, I interrogate the contrast between geopolitics and humane governance; between the right to intervention and the responsibility to protect; and, particularly, the claim that humanitarian principles will provide a secure shield against deterring militarism. It was these issues – not merely those of geopolitical security and self-defense – that laid the groundwork for intervention in Afghanistan.

The Responsibility to Protect Afghanistan. Proponents of the war in Afghanistan couched much of the normative rationale for intervention on the responsibility to protect, not only the right to intervene. Although legal briefs submitted to the UN supporting intervention in Afghanistan were based on the right to self-defense, this rationale proved less critical than expected in legitimizing the intervention. Moreover, efforts by liberal internationalists to keep self-defense and humanitarian rationales distinct also proved less than successful. For instance, the Commission on Intervention and State Sovereignty presented self-defense and the protection of peoples as two distinct and contrasting imperatives for intervention, and it argued that intervention in Afghanistan was based on self-defense and not the imperatives of humanitarian protection.[52] However, we soon find that these were overlapping and mutually reinforcing rationales. Thus, although the co-chairs of the Commission explicitly stated that interventions like Afghanistan concern the "scope and limit of a country's right to self-defense – not their right or obligation, to intervene elsewhere to protect peoples other than their own,"[53] in fact, humanitarian imperatives were invoked with vigor by advocates of the intervention. Moreover, those advocates follow the Commission's own

49 Falk, *supra* note 44, p. 149

50 Ibid., p. 3. See also Falk (ed.), *Law in an Emerging Global Village: A Post-Westphalian Perspective* (Transnational Publishers, 1998).

51 Falk, *supra* note 44, p. 3.

52 Instead, the Commission locates the relevance of its report in relation to cases such as Somalia, Bosnia, Rwanda, and Kosovo. It is in relation to such cases that the Commission's Foreword describes the policy challenges to which the report seeks to respond.

53 International Commission on Intervention and State Sovereignty, *supra* note 3, pp. 99–100.

proposed shift in the appropriate nomenclature for humanitarian intervention. The Commission argued that what had previously been termed "humanitarian intervention" – meaning "coercive action against a state to protect people within its borders from suffering grave harm" – should be reclassified in terms of the "Responsibility to Protect."[54] It is striking that the American and British arguments favoring intervention in Afghanistan also recast a self-defense issue in terms of the responsibility to protect.[55]

International law scholars note that the American government's *jus ad bellum* rationale for the attack on Afghanistan was based on a rather unconvincing legal premise: If a state is attacked by militant groups such as al-Qaeda, the right to self-defense extends to retaliating against states that harbor such groups. Falk asserts that this rationale "stretched traditional notions of self-defense by attributing to a government ultimate legal accountability for operations emanating from its territory regardless of whether it favored such terrorists' activities or had the capacity to suppress them."[56] Steven Ratner argued that "on the issue of state responsibility," none of the legal tests set forth by the "ICJ, the ICTY, or the ILC supports the harboring theory of the United States . . . normally states would not hold another state responsible per se for the actions of non-state actors on its territory absent proof of a connection closer than harboring, and certainly not to justify the use of force."[57] That said, Ratner noted that notwithstanding the contestable legal rationales, the military intervention in Afghanistan did not draw widespread condemnation from other states and major NGOs. Clearly, much criticism was muted because other states were bullied or self-regulated into compliance by the "either you are with us or against us" political terrain of geopolitics. However, what puzzles Ratner is that even human-rights–focused states, particularly the European Union and NGOs like Human Rights Watch that strongly condemned America's conduct of the war in Afghanistan, failed to challenge the American rationale for the war. For instance, even those "[m]ainstream human rights NGOs" that "were harshly critical of aspects of the treatment of detainees, claiming violations of the Geneva conventions"

54 Ibid., p. 99.

55 See, e.g., pp. 33–46 for a discussion on the prominent role accorded to women's rights, multiculturalism, and poverty alleviation in the U.S. and U.K. governments' discussion of the rationale for intervention. See also Falk, *Appraising the War against Afghanistan*, Social Science Research Council; available at www.ssrc.org/sept11/essays/falk.htm (noting the shift in emphasis from self-defense to humanitarian goals in the Bush administration's discussion of the rationale for the war) (accessed February 9, 2004).

56 Falk, *supra* note, p. 57.

57 Steven R. Ratner, Note and Comment, "*Jus ad Bellum* and *Jus in Bello* after September 11," 96 *American Journal of International Law*, 905, 908–909 (2002).

were "silent or cautious on the decision to use force."[58] Thus, the actions of the international community suggest considerable leniency regarding *jus ad bellum,* even when there was harsher scrutiny than *jus in bello* accord with international humanitarian law and norms.

Part of the explanation for this phenomenon is that the legalistic elaboration of self-defense arguments was not crucial to legitimizing U.S. military actions. In fact, the international legitimacy accorded to U.S. actions would appear less puzzling if considered in the context of the normative rationale for military intervention and, specifically, how the "need-to-protect" rationales complemented and advanced those of the "right-to-defend." Rather than scrutinize the hermeneutics of legal terminology in self-defense doctrine, it may prove more useful to trace the development of humanitarian intervention norms with respect to Afghanistan in the past decade.

Employing normative arguments to support a military campaign is not a new feature of militarism. What was remarkable about the military assault against Afghanistan, however, was the conspicuous role of humanitarian arguments and the uncanny resonance with the guidelines proposed in "The Responsibility to Protect" framework. Although, as noted previously, the Commission on Intervention and State Sovereignty views Afghanistan as more appropriately discussed in terms of a self-defense–based right to intervene, the war's biggest proponents, including George W. Bush, underscored "The Responsibility to Protect" as a rationale supporting war. Granted, the American and British government reports outlining their evidence against Osama bin Ladin for the events of September 11, 2001, constituted the formal briefs supporting the case for a military attack.[59] Yet, in many ways, the evidence cited in those reports and, indeed, the international law of self-defense were largely irrelevant to the ongoing legitimation of the offensive. The past decade's post–Cold War dialogue on humanitarian intervention in furtherance of international norms proved much more crucial. It is not surprising that human rights, particularly women's rights, were heavily emphasized, as were less obvious discourses regarding intercivilizational dialogue, poverty alleviation and economic development, democratization, multiculturalism, cultural authenticity, and peace. These discussions created the space

[58] Ibid., p. 913.

[59] See press release, British Government, "Responsibility for the Terrorist Atrocities in the United States" (October 4, 2001); available at news.bbc.co.uk/2/hi/uk_news/politics/1579043.stm (accessed February 9, 2004). (The British dossier concluded that "Osama bin Laden and al-Qaeda were able to commit these atrocities because of their close alliance with the Taliban regime, which allowed them to operate with impunity in pursuing their terrorist activity.")

for militarism by giving the Anglo-American coalition the moral authority to challenge the policies and practices of the Taliban government. They also enabled movement in the reverse direction – from the coalition's military rout of the Taliban government to the Bonn processes of the UN – to be seamless.

The Commission on Intervention and State Sovereignty argues that a major advantage of the shift from the right to intervene to the language of responsibility is that "it implies evaluating the issues from the point of view of those seeking or needing support, rather than those who may be considering intervention."[60] Ironically, America's sense of its role in the world and its attendant moral responsibilities "to those seeking and needing support" may be one of the enabling conditions of its military offensives. To the extent that critics of the Bush administration's military attacks on Afghanistan and Iraq fashion their arguments against a militaristic world power selfishly focused on its domestic goals, they may be missing the mark entirely. Rather, such interventions legitimated by human-rights and humanitarian discourse, in fact, may represent a particularly Anglo-American voice speaking about "the responsibility of sovereign states to protect their own people from such harm – and about the need for the larger international community to exercise their responsibility if states are unwilling or unable to do so themselves."[61]

Right Intentions. Against the backdrop of calls for intervention based on responsibility and protection, the dubious character of arguments based on national interest and self-defense (that comprised the ostensible legal foundation for the Afghanistan intervention) was less than worrisome to many commentators in the human-rights and humanitarian field. Afghanistan had been under international scrutiny long before September 11. As Franck points out, "In October 1999, the UN Security Council duly censured the Taliban by a unanimous resolution. The General Assembly, too, has shown its disapproval by refusing to accept the credentials of the Taliban's delegation."[62] Falk described pre–September 11 Afghanistan as an "outlaw state" and cited the Special Rappoteur's annual reports on the "severe human rights abuses and crimes against humanity that were taking place routinely in Afghanistan."[63] With specific reference to genocide and "female apartheid" in Afghanistan, the Institute for the Study of Genocide has "for the past fourteen years" berated

[60] International Commission on Intervention and State Sovereignty, *supra* note 3, Section 2.29.
[61] Ibid., Section 8.1.
[62] Thomas M. Franck, "Are Human Rights Universal?" *Foreign Affairs* 191 (January–February 2001).
[63] Falk, *supra* note 56.

foreign policy on intervention for being so narrow that it has not taken into account such atrocities. They "regularly . . . questioned U.S. and international responsibility for tolerating these and encouraged reflection on humanitarian intervention."[64] Thus, commentators like Falk merely expressed regret that Bush initially promoted self-defense as the rationale for intervention in the fall of 2001 "when the case against the Taliban was relatively easy and could have been made stronger had it been linked to a case of humanitarian intervention."[65] In fact, Falk approvingly emphasized a change in the rhetoric from that initial focus on self-defense. In particular, he noted the attention given in the State of the Union address to "the emancipatory impact of the American-led victory on the peoples of Afghanistan, particularly its women."[66] Human-rights and humanitarian concerns were offered to limit and target the use of force. However, these same human-rights concerns simultaneously facilitated the use of force and enabled a military offensive that self-defense arguments failed to fully legitimize.

Women's Rights. Women's rights have emerged as the centerpiece of aspirations for post-Taliban Afghanistan.[67] "Because of our recent military gains in Afghanistan," Laura Bush told the American people, "women are no longer imprisoned in their homes."[68] Echoing her optimism, the Northern Alliance Interior Minister, Younis Qanooni, expressed his hope that a new climate will enable an enlightened law including "rules to ensure women are not disadvantaged."[69] In fact, he claimed "the rights of women in Afghanistan" have been "one of the aims of our resistance."[70] Laura Bush urged that the American government's military offensive is motivated by similar principles. "The fight against terrorism" is, she said, "a fight for the rights and dignity of women."[71]

This marriage of feminists and military hawks is not merely a post facto appropriation of Afghan women to launder a dirty war. Many feminists had

[64] Helen Fein, "Intervention and Responsibility: Afghanistan and Iraq Reconsidered" (Editorial), Institute for the Study of Genocide, International Association of Genocide Scholars; available at www.isg-iags.org/newsletter/28/Fein.html (accessed February 9, 2004).

[65] Falk, *supra* note 56.

[66] Ibid.

[67] For example, the Feminist Majority Foundation urges that "[t]he defeat of the Taliban means the liberation of women from the regime's draconian decrees." See Feminist Majority Foundation, "The Taliban and Afghan Women: Background"; available at www.feminist.org/afghan/facts.html (accessed February 1, 2004).

[68] Laura Bush, Radio Address by Laura Bush to the Nation (November 16, 2001); available at www.whitehouse.gov/new/releases/2001/11/20011117.html (accessed February 1, 2004).

[69] *Afghan Women to Attend Talks*, BBC (November 22, 2001); available at news.bbc.co.uk/2/hi/south_asia/1671186.stm (accessed February 1, 2004).

[70] Ibid.

[71] Bush, *supra* note 70.

long been critical of the international community's inaction to protect Afghan women. For example, British filmmaker Sairah Shah traveled to Afghanistan to shoot *Behind the Burqa* in 2000. Against the backdrop of the Kosovo intervention, this film revealed "scenes of massacres to match anything in Kosovo or Bosnia."[72] Guglielmo Verdirame's article in the August 2001 issue of *Human Rights Quarterly* condemned the UN Security Council "for failing to adopt more pressing measures against sexual apartheid in Afghanistan."[73] The Feminist Majority Foundation had been campaigning to pressure the American government and the UN "to do everything in their power to restore the human rights of Afghan women and girls."[74] Many argued that failure to intervene was equivalent to denying that Afghans were eligible for the same rights enjoyed in the "West." Invoking Shah's film and female apartheid in Afghanistan in her contribution to *The Guardian*'s special report, "Attack on Afghanistan," Polly Toynbee accused the anti-interventionists (i.e., the "peace party") of "a coy form of cultural imperialism" in lacking "the will to spread the same freedoms to others for fear of trespassing on cultural sensitivities... as if these rights are only for us, not for 'them.'"[75] Thus, failing to ensure "human rights for all the people of the earth" may constitute what Toynbee described as a fundamental "moral dereliction" that is "imperialist" in its own way.[76] For Falk, this may be, in fact, a dereliction of the responsibilities of humane governance. Rather than romanticizing global civil society in resisting imperial states, human governance suggests a responsibility to recognize that "[f]rom civil society flow destructive and nihilistic responses as well as compassionate and reconstructive initiatives.... Who is free and who is not free to act democratically at the grassroots is itself a dimension of the liberating concerns of adherents of humane governance.... Regressive tendencies... must be neutralized if the positive prospects of humane governance are to be realized."[77] In such contexts, Toynbee noted, reluctance to intervene may be akin to "wincing at a surgeon's curing knife."[78]

Multiculturalism. Even before September 11, there was considerable pressure for a strong response against religious intolerance in Afghanistan. A year earlier, the U.S. government listed the Taliban as a particularly severe violator of

[72] Polly Toynbee, "There Is Blood on Our Hands but the Taliban Are Worse," *The Guardian*, October 31, 2001, p. 20.

[73] Guglielmo Verdirame, "Human Rights in the Arab World: A Regional Perspective," 23.3 *Human Rights Quarterly* 733, 750 (2001).

[74] Feminist Majority Foundation, "The Taliban and Afghan Women: Background"; available at www.feminist.org/afghan/facts.html (accessed February 1, 2004).

[75] Toynbee, *supra* note 72.

[76] Falk, *supra* note 56.

[77] Falk, *supra* note 44, p. 4.

[78] Toynbee, *supra* note 72, p. 20.

religious freedom, as it undoubtedly was. In March 2001, the Taliban implemented its edict against worshipping idols by destroying the famous Buddha statues in Bamiyan. *The Washington Post* noted that despite widespread condemnation of this act, the international community "found no leverage" to dissuade the Taliban.[79] In May 2001, denouncing the Taliban's plans "to require non-Moslems to wear identifying clothing and yellow badges," there were calls for "the United Nations, international human rights organizations, and other world bodies to protest this gross violation of human and religious rights and to take firm action."[80] As far back as Spring 1998, the Institute for the Study of Genocide made "a legal case based on the UN Genocide Convention" against the treatment of the Bahai in Afganistan.[81] Helen Fein lamented that the realists who make foreign policy believe that "national interests alone should motivate intervention" while "genocide, potential genocide and terrible violations of human rights cry out for international attention."[82]

Multiculturalism created a backdrop to military decisions throughout the Afghan war. Thus, Tony Blair urged that "especially at this time . . . we celebrate the diversity in our country, get strength from the cultures and races that go to make up Britain today."[83] Linking domestic multiculturalism and foreign policy, George W. Bush also situated the military attack as a "crusade" for a multicultural world bringing together "the Christian faith . . . Judiasm . . . the Hindu faith and . . . Islamic tradition."[84] Prioritizing this normative commitment over military goals, "our coalition," Bush said, "is more than just one to rout terrorism out of the world. It's one to bind together, to knit those traditions in a way that helps people in need."[85] Situating September 11 in narratives about the clash of civilizations, the multilateral coalition underscored the importance of dialogue and intercivilizational discourse.

[79] Molly Moore, "Taliban: Most Statutes Destroyed," *The Washington Post*, March 4, 2001, p. A22.

[80] Betty Ehrenberg, Director of International and Communal Affairs of the Orthodox Union, analogized this call to the racial classification policies of Nazi Germany. *Orthodox Union*, "Orthodox Union Condemns Outrageous Taliban Repression" (May 31, 2001); available at www.ou.org/public/statements/2001/betty9.htm (accessed February 4, 2004).

[81] Helen Fein, Editorial: "Intervention and Responsibility: Afghanistan and Iraq Reconsidered," 28 *Institute for the Study of Genocide Newsletter* 1, 2 (Spring 2002); available at www.isg-iags.org/newsletters/28/Fein.html (accessed February 4, 2004).

[82] Ibid., p. 1.

[83] Tony Blair, Labour Party Conference (October 2, 2001), *The Guardian*, October 2, 2001; available at politics.guardian.co.uk/labour2001/story/0%2C1414%2C562006%2C00.html (accessed February 4, 2004).

[84] President George W. Bush, Remarks to the U.S. State Department Employees (October 4, 2001); available at usinfo.state.gov/topical/pol/terror/01100415.htm (accessed February 9, 2004).

[85] Ibid.

In a fortuitous coincidence, the UN designated 2001 the International Year of Dialogue among Civilizations. Underscoring these sentiments, Secretary-General Kofi Annan stated, "Indeed, the perception of diversity as a threat is the very seed of war. Diversity is not only the basis for the dialogue among civilizations, but also the reality that makes dialogue necessary."[86] Thus, in shaping the Bonn agenda, Lakhdar Brahimi followed the urging of the "Six Plus Two" group[87] that there should be the "establishment in Afghanistan of a broad based, multi-ethnic, politically balanced, freely chosen Afghan administration."[88] In fact, reconstruction assistance was explicitly tied to this vision of representative government.[89]

Poverty Alleviation. Reconstruction assistance also has been linked to a deeper normative vision of poverty alleviation and economic development. Assistance to refugees was pressed as a key motivation accompanying the military offensive. In the speech first declaring that British troops would be deployed in Afghanistan, Blair announced "a coalition of support for refugees which is as vital as the military coalition."[90] Thus, the political and geographic access created by the Taliban's defeat transformed the war into a humanitarian-relief operation.

Notwithstanding the claim of commentators such as Falk that his guidelines for cosmopolitan engagement distinguish him from more militaristic interests and imperatives, his rationales for intervention are not dissimilar from those of the American government. "What does seem clear," Falk stated, "is that the appalling economic incompetence and record of human rights abuse during the period of Taliban rule is likely to be superceded by a much improved quality of Afghan governance resulting in material and political

86 General-Secretary Kofi Annan, Welcoming Remarks at the UNESCO Round Table: Dialogue among Civilizations (September 5, 2000); available at www.unesco.org/dialogue2001/en/annan.htm.

87 China, Iran, Pakistan, Tajikistan, Turkmenistan, Uzbekistan, United States, and Russia.

88 Judy Aita, "Afghanistan's Neighbors Call for Broad-Based Government: 'Six Plus Two' Ministers Meet at UN" (November 12, 2001); available at usinfo.state.gov/topical/pol/terror/01111208.htm (accessed February 9, 2004).

89 "Until there is a government that is broadly representative and recognized by us, there's not going to be any reconstruction assistance," a senior U.S. official close to the talks said. This comment by a U.S. official came even as the talks were proceeding near Bonn in a "luxury hotel overlooking the Rhine River" and "overseen," as it were, by a U.S. policy statement that said that aid "is contingent on a broad-based, inclusive government." Available at www.pbs.org/newshour/updates/november01/govttalks_11–27.html.

90 Prime Minister Tony Blair, statement announcing deployment of British troops in Afghanistan (October 7, 2001); available at www.number-10.gov.uk/output/Page1615.asp# (accessed February 7, 2004).

benefits for a large majority of citizens."[91] On October 4, 2001, the eve of the U.S. attack, American officials urged that "you can initiate . . . development programs in the middle of a civil war and a famine."[92] Encouraging reporters to become familiar with the literature on opportunities to pursue humanitarian goals in the context of military engagement, officials cited books such as *Rising from the Ashes* and *Disasters and Development* to promote a learned optimism about compassionate militarism. Similarly, a U.S. State Department fact sheet summarizing the U.S. government's "humanitarian funding" for Afghanistan in the first six weeks of the war announced more than $246 million of aid that had already been contributed.[93]

Gender, pluralism, and development relief are three powerful markers in a complex and multifaceted normative space interpolating the war in Afghanistan. Without doubt, a more militaristic discourse was also a prominent part of the Anglo-American coalition's approach. By drawing attention to the prominence accorded to issues such as women's rights and multiculturalism, I do not suggest that self-defense, racism, machismo, and other factors were irrelevant to the discourse surrounding the attack. However, although the traditionalist discourse of military "muscle" remained potent, it did not dominate public debate as it did even as recently as the First Gulf War. In fact, the conflict in Afghanistan marked an extraordinary moment in the international public sphere when, against the backdrop of a decade-long tussle with humanitarian engagement, the normative force of the "Responsibility to Protect" constituted a different space for war.

Indeed, some of the most established human-rights organizations criticized the military intervention in Afghanistan for not going far enough. Concerned with the Brahimi approach, Human Rights Watch argued in November 2002 that

> A light footprint has failed to protect human rights in western Afghanistan. It is now time to make a larger imprint on the ground in Herat and other parts of Afghanistan experiencing serious human rights violations. . . . Western

[91] Falk, *supra* note 56.

[92] Administrator of the U.S. Agency for International Development, Andrew Natsios, Remarks in U.S. State Department Briefing on U.S. Assistance to Afghan Refugees (October 4, 2001); available at usinfo.state.gov/topical/pol/terror/01100417.htm (accessed February 9, 2004).

[93] This money came from three sources: the U.S. Agency for International Development (USAID); the State Department's Bureau of Population, Refugees, and Migration (PRM); and the Department of Defense. Of these, the Department of Defense was by far the biggest donor, accounting for about 50 percent of the U.S. government's humanitarian funding. These figures are boundary markers in the normative map for the positioning of bombers and troops. See 23 November 2001 Fact Sheet: U.S. Assistance to Afghan People Since October 1, 2001; available at usinfo.state.gov/topical/pol/terror/01112305.htm.

Afghanistan, like other areas of Afghanistan, would greatly benefit from the presence of international peacekeepers. Currently, the International Security Assistance Force (ISAF) is only stationed in Kabul. It is vital that ISAF be expanded as soon as possible. In the absence of an expanded ISAF force (or even in addition to one), U.S. troops stationed around Herat could make a valuable contribution to the security of the region. U.S. forces should take on a greater role in peacekeeping activities, patrolling Herat and other sensitive areas in the west, and using civil and political affairs officers to identify and assist vulnerable persons.[94]

The call for a larger military presence was based not on self-defense rationales but rather "The Responsibility to Protect." This is not the familiar voice of empire as conquest and occupation arguing for expanding territorial ambitions but rather a human-rights voice calling for assistance to the vulnerable. This distinction was underscored by the NGOs themselves. Thus, in November 2001, even as the Bonn process was moving forward, CARE called for a "military presence to protect the delivery of aid" to demonstrate that the intervention was not a military presence of a "conqueror or occupying power" but rather was intended to "assist Afghans."[95] Two years later, in October 2003, CARE continued to call for an expansion of the ISAF in Afghanistan, with a stronger mandate to better enable the ISAF to take military action for the "protection" of Afghans.[96]

In the Cold War and pre–Cold War era, neutrality and impartiality were the constitutive myths of humanitarian intervention. Today, the new context that is said to require "military humanitarianism" carries its own mythologies and misconceptions about its role in the proliferation of spaces for violence. As Doris Lessing noted, "The hearts of innumerable men and women responded with idealistic fervor to [Cecil Rhode's] clarion, because it went without saying that it would be good for Africa, or for anywhere else, to be made British. At this point it might be useful to wonder which of the idealisms that make our heart beat faster (today) will seem wrongheaded to people a hundred years from now."[97]

The Commission on Intervention and State Sovereignty situated its work in an idealistic commitment to addressing human need rather than the right

[94] Human Rights Watch, *All Our Hopes Are Crushed: Violence and Repression in Western Afghanistan,* November 5, 2002; available at www.reliefweb.int/w/rwb.nsf/0/3145e3df5e5451e249256c69002bf304?OpenDocument (accessed February 7, 2004).

[95] Press release, CARE, "CARE Outlines the Role of International Forces to Protect and Assist Afghan People" (November 30, 2001); available at www.careusa.org/newsroom/pressreleases/2001/nov/11302001_afghanistan.asp (accessed February 20, 2004).

[96] Ibid.

[97] Quoted in Pheng Cheah & Bruce Robbins (eds.), *Cosmopolitics: Thinking and Feeling Beyond the Nation* (1998), p. 345.

of intervention. Thus, it said that its "report has been about compelling human need, about populations at risk of slaughter, ethnic cleansing and starvation."[98] In fact, Falk argued that this type of focus on humanitarianism and law as the guiding lights of intervention will be important in not creating conditions that unleash "the dogs of war."[99] However, Afghanistan may have been available for a military offensive before September 11. The ideological ground was laid not by the "dogs of war" or by macho bombastic talk of the "axis of evil" and military conquest. Rather, it was established by the soft promise of the intervention's reluctant advocates, in the name of religious tolerance, women's freedom, human rights, and liberal modernity.

From Berlin to Bonn to Baghdad: Connecting the Dots

An Iraqi soldier presses down an American soldier that he has taken captive, asking what the war was about – and then proceeds to answer his own question by trying to pour oil down the prisoner's throat. No, this was not another news item on CNN from the Gulf but rather from Hollywood – more specifically, a scene in the 1999 movie, *Three Kings.*[100] In the movie, which is set in the wake of the First Gulf War, four American soldiers seek to do some bounty hunting before returning to the United States at the end of Operation Desert Storm. Cynical and war-weary, their goal is to track down and steel a stash of Kuwaiti gold hidden in Iraq. *Three Kings* presents – with, at times, brilliant satirical verve – the political economy suppporting the war at many levels: the oil revenues that fuel American militarism as well as the tough economic conditions of the American working poor that feed military recruitment. The movie also tests the gravitational pull of economic motivations against the humanitarian demands of those who were perhaps Operation Desert Storm's biggest losers, the Kurds. By the movie's end – disillusioned and critical of American policy, the quest for gold both thwarted and abandoned – the four soldiers flout all rules and work in solidarity with a Kurdish community to enable their escape. In so doing, the soldiers maneuver and fight against the

[98] The International Commission on Intervention and State Sovereignty, Canadian Department of Foreign Affairs and International Trade, "The Responsibility to Protect" (2001), available at www.dfait-maeci.gc.ca/iciss-ciise/report-en.asp (accessed February 4, 2004).

[99] Falk, *supra* note 56.

[100] In fact, against the backdrop of the First Gulf War making its appearance in our living rooms via CNN's tele-drama of smart bombs, one of the interventions made by the movie is stylistic experiments with technical stunts about the theater of militarism. It speaks to the production of news as popular culture, while itself being a newsworthy product for popular cultural consumption.

charge of their superiors and, indeed, the policy advanced by the American government itself.

Thus, one principal narrative thread of the movie is the shift from an imperial militarism to military humanitarianism. How do we understand the politics of this shift: Is military humanitarianism an alternative to imperial militarism, or is it part of the same project? The argument is not that humanitarianism is used conspiratorially to launch a stealth attack, but rather that humanitarian discourse and practice has both advanced and curtailed the space for militarism.[101] By placing humanitarian and imperial impulses for intervention side by side, *Three Kings* draws attention to how the legitimacy afforded by arguments for humanitarian intervention and arguments for "imperial" intervention simultaneously compete with and complement each other. It even suggests that humanitarian rationales for intervention fundamentally support and legitimize so effectively more imperial claims for intervention precisely because in discrepant "local" battles, humanitarianism also competes with and may restrain militarism's excesses.

Howard Zinn called on the United States to "pull back from being a military superpower, and become a humanitarian superpower."[102] The question is whether there is a clear line of distinction between these roles. Efforts by the left-liberal intelligentsia to provide normative signposts for legitimate humanitarian action by the international community do not seem to travel in the expected direction. A discourse aimed at situations for protection, like Kosovo, appears indistinguishable from a discourse used in situations described as self-defense, like Afghanistan. Whereas the Commission on Intervention and State Sovereignty sought to distinguish between rights and responsibilities, self-defense, and protection of the other, it is less than clear that their distinctions provide reliable guides. International lawyers and policy makers advocate a transnational idealism to define internationalist norms as opposed to statist norms, pacifist from militaristic goals, efforts grounded in international law against those that are not. Yet, it appears

[101] From Walter Benjamin to Jacques Derrida, many scholars have explored the ways in which the normative assumptions of law have been constitutive of the very violence against which law defines itself. In the context of international law, the darker "underside" of law has been visited from many angles by a range of legal scholars including Illeana Porres, David Kennedy, and Tony Anghie. In registering a related conversation regarding violence in a different disciplinary home, this chapter is also in conversation with the work of Pradeep Jeganathan's essay, "A Space for Violence." Jeganathan is occupied with negotiations with the categories, conventions, and performative spaces for "violence" relative to anthropological technologies for reading "Community, Gender and Violence, Subaltern Studies XI," Partha Chatterjee & Pradeep Jegnanathan (eds.) (2001).

[102] Howard Zinn, "A Just Cause, Not a Just War," *The Progressive*, December 2001, p. 6.

that these polarities fail to provide a reliable compass for humanitarian action.

Today, after the Second Gulf War, liberal internationalists lament that "one of the worst misdeeds that George W. Bush committed, in collaboration with Tony Blair, was to bring humanitarian intervention into disrepute" by appropriating its rhetoric to justify the war.[103] The Institute for the Study of Genocide regrets the fact that the question of humanitarian intervention in Iraq emerged only when self-defense was at stake and not in response, for example, to violations of the Genocide Convention. From 1988 to 1991, the Institute convened discussions on genocide and potential genocide in Iraq and the need for humanitarian intervention. The treatment of the Kurds and Marsh Arabs, in particular, constituted violations of the Genocide Convention that warranted intervention. However, these facts were ignored at the time by policy makers. Yet, if humanitarian discourse regarding issues such as the violation of the Genocide Convention had gained more traction in the international community, would it have made it just that much easier to legitimize the Second Gulf War? Is the widespread international opposition to the Second Gulf War partly explained by the fact that many of the atrocities of the Iraqi regime were partly crowded out by the atrocities of sanctions, oil interests, and other issues that clouded and complicated humanitarian discourse? Or, is there space now for humanitarian operations to be mobilized to offer post facto legitimation of Anglo-American military adventures?

"The Responsibility to Protect" has been criticized precisely because it could be appealed to with equal vigor by both supporters and critics of the war. Ramesh Thakur reported that the Canadian Prime Minister, Jean Chrétien, tried valiantly to promote the Commission's report at a Progressive Governance Summit in England. He encountered difficulty because some at the conference feared that the concept of "responsibility to protect" could be appropriated to justify war in Iraq.[104] As noted previously, the concept has gone on to gain greater support, partly because of arguments made by Thakur and others that the Iraq war would have failed the tests laid out by the report for justified intervention: "We argued that all military intervention must be subject to four precautionary principles: right intention, last resort, proportionate means, and reasonable prospects. Iraq would likely have failed on all four principles." Yet, it is also true that some of Ramesh Thakur's fellow commissioners, including Michael Ignatieff, in fact defended the war. Thus, the

[103] Williams, *supra* note 6, p. 23.

[104] Ramesh Thakur, "It's Time to Redefine a 'Just War'," *UNU Update* 27 (September–October 2003); available at update/unu.edu/archive/issue27.htm (accessed February 20, 2004).

compass for legitimate humanitarian intervention has been lost even within the pages of the report.

Concluding Thoughts

The crisis of cosmopolitan humanitarianism in its quest for a secure compass for legitimate transnational engagement has arrived at a critical point with the Second Gulf War. Because both critics and advocates of the intervention base their arguments on humanitarian goals, cosmopolitan humanitarianism is constituted by trajectories that both advance and constrain intervention. It is in this context that we must grapple with the question of whether humanitarian initiatives for the "reconstruction of Iraq" will fill in the legitimacy gaps that the war has left behind.

The discourse of humanitarianism is not always easy to adapt and assimilate to legitimize military intervention. Notwithstanding humanitarian arguments from Ignatieff to the U.S. State Department – to the extent that the Iraq war was not only about cruise missiles that "shock and awe" but also about ideological discourses that legitimize and rationalize – the Anglo-American coalition faced real skepticism as well as defeat.

The movie *Three Kings* exhibited a shift from a narrative of imperial intervention to one of humanitarian intervention, as well as the evolution of its protagonists in the aftermath of the First Gulf war. In the wake of the Second Gulf War, aspirations toward such a shift inhere in efforts to generate post facto legitimacy for the military intervention through the mobilization of humanitarianism. The strength of the antiwar movement that rallied against the intervention ensured that "coalition" forces were unsuccessful in their invocation of the humanitarian discourse to legitimize intervention for the "liberation" of Iraq. By critically examining the structure of global power and its distributive consequences; unpacking the political economy of oil; by asserting democratic claims for accountability regarding the misuse of political, economic, and military power; and by coalition-building across multiple frontiers, the dominant reference point of the intervention in Iraq was conquest rather than humanitarianism. Moreover, legacies of conquest infuse the legitimacy discourses mobilized by humanitarianism. With the Iraq intervention characterized by the marginalization of humanitarian concerns and the mobilization of humanitarian discourse, humanitarianism haunts both the frontline of imperial brutality and the rearguard of imperial ambition. Thus, international humanitarian intervention stands mired in a legitimacy crisis – fault lines connecting the dots from Berlin 1844 to Baghdad today.

PART II: THE UN SECURITY COUNCIL: EXPRESSION, VENUE, AND PROMOTER OF INTERNATIONAL LEGITIMACY?

IAN JOHNSTONE

6. Legal Deliberation and Argumentation in International Decision Making

Questions about the legitimacy of international decision making have arisen in proportion to the growing autonomy of international organizations. If these organizations are able to wield influence not directly traceable to the consent of member governments, what is the source of their legitimacy? In the context of the European Union (EU), the concern is typically framed in terms of the democratic deficit, characterized by the increasing remoteness of those who make decisions from those who are affected by them. Proposals on how to bring down that deficit bump up against a larger question: Can democracy be transposed beyond the level of the nation-state? This chapter explores that question by drawing on the theory of deliberative democracy. My central claim is that voting arrangements are not the only gauge of legitimacy in international organizations; one must also look at the quality of deliberations that precede and follow decisions taken. I support that claim first by identifying a core principle of the theory of deliberative democracy: any decision must be backed by good arguments. What counts as a "good argument" varies from setting to setting, depending on the normative framework within which the deliberation occurs. I then consider whether, as a matter of theory, there are grounds for applying the deliberative principle at the transnational level. I argue that particular conventions of argument and discourse operate in any deliberative enterprise, the parameters of which are set by an interpretive community associated with the enterprise. I test that proposition at the international level by considering whether decision making in the United Nations (UN) Security Council is influenced at all by deliberative conventions and constraints. A close reading of debates about two difficult cases – Kosovo (1999) and Iraq (2003) – supports the argument that meaningful argumentation is possible even in that setting because there is tacit understanding of the purpose of the enterprise and acceptance of the normative framework within which the deliberations occur. In the conclusion, I suggest avenues for reform that would help reduce the "deliberative deficit" in the Security Council and thereby enhance the legitimacy of its decisions.

Legal Deliberation at the International Level[1]

The theory of deliberative democracy holds that voting alone cannot legitimate collective decisions – the decisions must be *justified* in terms that those who are subject to them can accept. A deliberative democracy is "an association whose affairs are governed by the public deliberation of its members"[2]; the legitimacy of democratic institutions "must be thought to result from the free and unconstrained public deliberation of all about matters of common concern."[3] John Elster usefully distinguishes deliberation from voting, defined as the aggregation of fixed preferences, and bargaining, which involves the making of offers and counteroffers by actors seeking to achieve fixed interests.[4] Deliberation is a third mode or element of decision making, which entails appeals to "impartial values" or "reciprocal reasons" that reach beyond narrow self-interest.[5] Elster and others claim that "presuppositions of rational discourse" steer the course of public debates in a democratic society.[6] Disagreements are (and should be) settled through deliberation, characterized by appeals to reasons that are shared or can be shared by all who are bound by the decisions taken. Reciprocity regulates the types of reasons officials and citizens use to justify their claims to one another: "You make your

1 This section of the chapter draws on Johnstone, Ian (2008). "Legislation and Adjudication in the UN Security Council: Bringing Down the Deliberative Deficit," *American Journal of International Law,* 102, July.

2 Cohen, Joshua (1997). "Deliberation and Democratic Legitimacy," in James Bohman & William Rehg (eds.), *Essays on Reason and Politics: Deliberative Democracy* (Cambridge, MA: The MIT Press), p. 67.

3 Benhabib, Seyla (1996). "Toward a Deliberative Model of Democratic Legitimacy," in Seyla Benhabib (ed.), *Democracy and Difference: Testing the Boundaries of the Political* (Princeton, NJ: Princeton University Press), p. 68.

4 Elster, John (1998). "Introduction," in John Elster (ed.), *Deliberative Democracy* (Cambridge, UK: Cambridge University Press), p. 6.

5 John Elster uses the term *impartial values*; ibid., p. 12. See also Elster (1997). "The Market and the Forum: Three Varieties of Political Theory," in Bohman & Rehg (eds.), see note 2, p. 12. Amy Gutmann and Dennis Thompson use the term *reciprocal reasons.* Gutmann & Thompson (2004). *Why Deliberative Democracy?* (Princeton, NJ: Princeton University Press), pp. 98–102. For a discussion of the role of different types of arguments in world politics, see Neta Crawford (2002). *Argument and Change in World Politics: Ethics, Decolonization, and Humanitarian Intervention* (Cambridge, UK: Cambridge University Press).

6 Elster, ibid., p. 12, quoting Jürgen Habermas (1996). *Between Facts and Norms: Contributions to a Discourse Theory of Law and Democracy,* translated by William Rehg (Cambridge, MA: MIT Press), p. 540.

claims on terms that I can accept in principle . . . I make my claims on terms that you can accept in principle."[7] Deliberative democrats acknowledge that consensus is not always possible, which is why votes are held and votes are often traded in a bargaining process; however, the bargains struck and the outcome of votes are (and should be) shaped by engagement in public debate, argument, and reason giving.[8]

Deliberative democracy owes much to Jurgen Habermas's theory of communicative action and marks a turn away from the constitutional liberalism of John Rawls and others.[9] Habermas imagined an "ideal speech situation" within which discourse occurs unaffected by relationships of power and coercion or any other factors extraneous to "the force of the better argument."[10] Sincere (as opposed to strategic) communicative action occurs when actors seek a reasoned consensus on the basis of shared understandings, in which each actor not only tries to persuade others but is also prepared to be persuaded. This ideal is not meant to describe an actual state of affairs, but its basic principles are presupposed in any linguistic communication.[11] Communicative rationality involves arguing in terms of "*intersubjective* standards of truth, rightness, and sincerity" (emphasis added).[12] Like Rawls, deliberative democrats stress the importance of "public reason" but offer a more inclusive and pluralistic conception of what counts as a good reason.[13] They insist that deliberation is not a communicative free-for-all, in which any argument is as good as any other. The felt need to offer reasons others can

[7] Gutmann, Amy, & Thompson, Denis (1996). *Democracy and Disagreement* (Cambridge, MA: Harvard University Press), p. 55. See also Gutmann (1999), "Deliberative Democracy and Majority Rule: Reply to Waldron," in Harold Koh & Ronald Slye (eds.), *Deliberative Democracy and Human Rights* (New Haven, CT: Yale University Press), p. 234.

[8] Deliberative democracy, it should be stressed, is not "a theory in search of practice" but rather a theory that claims to elucidate some aspects of existing democratic practice. Benhabib (1996), see note 3, p. 84.

[9] Macedo, Stephen (1999). "Introduction," in Stephen Macedo (ed.), *Deliberative Politics: Essays on Democracy and Disagreement* (Oxford, UK: Oxford University Press), p. 4.

[10] Habermas, Jürgen (2001). "Why Europe Needs a Constitution," *New Left Review*, 11, September–October.

[11] Cunningham, Frank (2002). *Theories of Democracy: A Critical Introduction* (London, UK: Routledge), p. 176. See also Lose, Lars (2001). "Communicative Action and the World of Diplomacy," in K. Fierke & K. E. Jorgensen (eds.), *Constructing International Relations: The Next Generation* (Armonk, NY: M. E. Sharpe, Inc.)

[12] Eriksen, Erik Oddvar (2000). "Deliberative Supranationalism in the EU," in Erik Eriksen & John Erik Fossum (eds.), *Democracy in the European Union: Integration through Deliberation?* (London, UK: Routledge).

[13] Benhabib (1996), see note 3, pp. 73–75; Bohman, James (1999). "Citizenship and Norms of Publicity: Wide Public Reason in Cosmopolitan Societies," *Political Theory* 27(2), 180; Young, Iris Marion (1997). "Difference as a Resource for Democratic Communication," in Bohman & Rehg (eds.), see note 2.

accept as relevant – even if they do not agree with the conclusions drawn – sets the parameters of discourse.

If the standards are intersubjective, then what counts as a "good argument" depends in part on the class of people to whom reasons are owed. Amy Gutmann and Dennis Thompson claim that decisions must be justified "to all who are bound by them and some who are affected by them."[14] In a national democratic polity, presumably this would include at least all citizens. However, many noncitizens are also affected by decisions taken at the national level. Are democratic leaders expected to provide reasons that these affected noncitizens can accept? Asked another way, do expectations about democratic deliberation extend to the transnational level? To most democracy theorists and students of international affairs, the notion of majority rule (based on population) beyond the level of the nation-state is deeply problematic, but at least some deliberative democrats see the possibility of meaningful "reason giving" across borders.[15] Following Habermas, they see evidence of multiple "public spheres," in which a range of opinions is developed and exchanged on matters of common concern: "a highly complex network that branches out into a multitude of overlapping *international*, national, regional, local, and subcultural arenas"[emphasis added].[16] Public reasoning and justification occurs in the institutions of government and intergovernmental bodies, as well as political parties, nongovernmental organizations (NGOs), social movements, and other elements of civil society, whose activities are not confined by national borders.[17]

These theorists tend to focus on Europe and the "no-demos" thesis of the German Constitutional Court. In a famous decision on the Maastricht Treaty, the Court stated that

> A democratic polity depends on a sense of social cohesion, shared destiny and collective self-identity . . . [which, in turn] is conditioned on some though not

[14] Gutmann & Thompson (1996), see note 7, p. 8 and Chapter 4 generally.

[15] Eriksen, Erik Oddvar (2000), see note 12, p. 49; Bohman, James (1999). "International Regimes and Democratic Governance: Political Equality and Influence in Global Institutions," *International Affairs*, 75(3), 499; and Dryzek, John (2000). *Deliberative Democracy and Beyond: Liberals, Critics, Contestations* (Oxford, UK: Oxford University Press), p. 115. On the role of argumentation in world politics generally, see Crawford (2002), note 5; and Harald Muller (2004). "Arguing, Bargaining, and All That: Communicative Action, Rationalist Theory, and the Logic of Appropriateness in International Relations," *European Journal of International Relations*, 10(3), 395–435.

[16] Habermas quoted in Schlesinger, Philip, & Kevin, Deirdre (2000). "Can the European Union Become a Sphere of Publics?," in Eriksen & Fossum (eds.), see note 12, p. 211. See also Jennifer Mitzen (2005). "Reading Habermas in Anarchy: Multilateral Diplomacy and Global Public Spheres," *American Political Science Review*, 99(3), 401.

[17] Benhabib (1996), see note 3, p. 74.

> necessarily all of the following elements: common language, common history, common cultural habits and sensibilities, common ethnic origin, common religion.[18]

These elements, the Court held, are lacking at the European level and, therefore, the chances of a Europe-wide democratic polity ever emerging are slim. Habermas, Michael Zurn, Joseph Weiler, and others reject the no-demos thesis and posit a notion of European citizenship that rests on a civic conception of "the nation" or people.[19] A group can be full political and civic members of a polity without all being from the same national/ethnic background, as long as they are committed to a shared set of values. Various developments in the EU are cited to support the proposition that a European "public sphere" and sense of citizenship is emerging, based in part on deliberative principles.[20]

The most enthusiastic advocates have even found some evidence of democratic deliberation at the global level, exemplified by the growing influence of nonstate actors.[21] John Dryzek, for example, saw "discursive sources of governance and order" in the power of transnational civil society to question, criticize, and shed the light of publicity on governmental action.[22] Similarly, James Bohman pointed to the increasing importance of informal transnational networks, which "by fostering communicative interaction . . . have produced self-regulating forms of cooperation among those affected by global processes."[23] Deliberation within these decentralized and overlapping spheres of governance does seem to occur, especially in areas such as the environment, where nongovernmental actors have been active.[24]

18 Quoted in Bodansky, Daniel (1999). "The Legitimacy of International Governance: A Coming Challenge for International Environmental Law," *American Journal of International Law*, 93(3), 616.

19 Habermas (2001), see note 10, p. 8; Zürn, Michael (2000). "Democratic Governance beyond the Nation-State: The EU and Other International Institutions," *European Journal of International Relations*, 6(2); Weiler, Joseph (1999). *The Constitution of Europe: "Do the New Clothes Have an Emperor?" and Other Essays on European Integration* (Cambridge, UK: Cambridge University Press).

20 The drafting of an EU constitution, the practice of seeking consensus in the Council of Ministers, the authority of the European Court of Justice, the growing power of the European Parliament, "interparliamentary discourse," the committee system, and the emergence of an EU-oriented media are among the developments identified by the various contributors to Eriksen & Fossum (see note 12).

21 See generally, Bohman, James (2007). *Democracy across Borders: From Demois to Demoi*; Dryzek (2000), see note 15; Bohman (1999), see note 13.

22 Dryzek (2000), see note 15, p. 131.

23 Bohman (1999), see note 15, pp. 500, 506.

24 Barber, Walter, & Bartlett, Robert (2005). *Deliberative Environmental Politics: Democracy and Ecological Rationality* (Cambridge, MA: MIT Press).

Yet, if the sphere of deliberation is opened up to the entire globe, is it possible to imagine a discursive process that is bounded in any way? Deliberative democrats see it as a virtue of their theory that it resists tying political prescriptions to foundational theory; the aim is to justify collective decisions without resorting to metaphysical truths about human nature, human rights, or self-evident reason.[25] They do not necessarily reject foundationalism but rather argue that reasoning about public policy and values is possible without some transcendent, prepolitical understanding of what those values mean and how to prioritize among them when they conflict. However, is such reasoning possible in a heterogeneous, pluralistic international system? It is, and I turn now to a discussion of international legal deliberations to make that case.

Legal Deliberation and Interpretive Communities[26]

International law operates largely through a process of justificatory discourse, which is fundamentally "an effort to gain assent to value judgments on reasoned rather than idiosyncratic grounds."[27] As Abram Chayes and Antonia Handler Chayes stated, international relations are conducted in large part through "diplomatic conversation – explanation and justification, persuasion and dissuasion, approval and condemnation. . . . In this discourse, the role of legal norms is large."[28] Governments typically seek to claim that their actions are consistent with international law, and the felt need to make a legal case imposes limits on the style of argument.[29] Although deeply influenced by power and calculations of interest, the law affects how decision makers frame the choices available to them and how they explain and justify those choices to relevant domestic and international audiences.

[25] Gutmann & Thompson (1996), see note 7, p. 5; Cunningham (2002), see note 11, p. 170.

[26] This section summarizes a longer argument in Johnstone (2003). "Security Council Deliberations: The Power of the Better Argument," *European Journal of International Law*, 14(3). See also Johnstone (2005). "The Power of Interpretive Communities," in Barnett & Duvall (eds.), *Power in Global Governance* (Cambridge, UK: Cambridge University Press), p. 185.

[27] Kratochwil, Friedrich (1989). *Rules, Norms, and Decisions: On the Conditions of Practical and Legal Reasoning in International Affairs* (Cambridge UK: Cambridge University Press), p. 214.

[28] Chayes, Abraham, & Chayes, Antonia Handler (1995). *The New Sovereignty: Compliance with International Regulatory Agreements* (Cambridge, MA: Harvard University Press), p. 119. See also Franck, Thomas (1995). *Fairness in International Law and Institutions* (Oxford, UK: Clarendon Press); Koh, Harold (1997). "Why Do Nations Obey International Law?," *Yale Law Journal*, 106(8).

[29] Kratochwil (1989), see note 27, p. 214. See also Kratochwil, Friedrich (2000). "How Do Norms Matter?," in Michael Byers (ed.), *The Role of Law in International Politics* (Oxford, UK: Oxford University Press), p. 51; Sunstein, Cass (1996). *Legal Reasoning and Political Conflict* (New York: Oxford University Press), p. 13.

An objection may be raised that legal or any other form of justificatory discourse is at best strategic and at worst insincere: government officials pay lip service to the law and a legal justification can be found for any action. Because there is no authoritative, impartial arbiter of many interpretive disputes, the law cannot impose any constraint. Yet, as Quentin Skinner observed, there is a limit to which any legitimating language, including the language of the law, plausibly can be stretched.[30] If it can be stretched only so far, whether the speaker is sincere does not matter; once he or she has accepted the need to offer justifications on grounds other than self-interest, he or she is impelled to behave in a way that is not transparently hypocritical. Elster called this the "civilizing force of hypocrisy." Even "strategic" appeals to collective interests and generalizable principles moderate behavior because if positions change rapidly to suit self-interests, it will be seen as opportunistic and greeted with suspicion.[31] "Hypocrisy is the homage vice pays to virtue," as Elster put it.[32] Having to pay lip service to the collective interest and shared principles does not necessarily make speakers more public-spirited but can lead to what Thomas Risse called "argumentative self-entrapment." Once governments rhetorically accept a legal norm, they begin to argue about its interpretation and its application to the particular case at hand rather than the validity of the law itself. This creates a "discursive opening" for their critics – "If you say you accept human rights, then why do you systematically violate them?" – that eventually induces governments to match deeds with words.[33]

30 Skinner, Quentin (2002). *Visions of Politics: Regarding Method* (Cambridge, UK: Cambridge University Press), p. 156. For an instructive application of Skinner's theory to debates about humanitarian intervention, see Wheeler, Nicholas J. (2002). *Saving Strangers: Humanitarian Intervention in International Society* (Oxford, UK: Oxford University Press), p. 7. International lawyers have long recognized that in any interpretive dispute, the range of possible legal arguments is not infinite. See Schachter, Oscar (1991). *International Law in Theory and Practice* (Dordrecht: Martinus Nijhoff), p. 46; Koskienniemi, Marti (1989). *From Apology to Utopia* (Helsinki: Lakimiesliiton Kustunnus), p. 48; Toope, Stephen (2000). "Emerging Patterns of Global Governance," in Byers (ed.), see note 29, p. 98.

31 Elster, John (1995). "The Strategic Uses of Argument," in K. Arrow, R. Mnookin, L. Ross, A. Tversky, & R. Wilson (eds.), *Barriers to Conflict Resolution* (New York: W.W. Norton and Company), pp. 236, 249. See also Fearon, James (1998). "Deliberation as Discussion," in Elster (ed.), see note 4, p. 53.

32 Elster (1998), in Elster (ed.), see note 4, p. 111.

33 Risse, Thomas (2000). "'Let's Argue': Communicative Action in World Politics," *International Organizations*, 54(1), 32–33. Quentin Skinner argues that because speakers seeking to legitimate action "cannot hope to stretch the application of existing terms indefinitely... they can only hope to legitimize, and hence to perform, a correspondingly restricted range of actions. To study the principles they invoke will thus be to study one of the key determinants of their behavior." Skinner (2002), see note 30, p. 156.

That is not the end of the story, however, because it implies that good legal arguments can somehow be distinguished from bad. How is this possible at the transnational level, where most interpretive disputes are not settled in court? It is possible if one understands deliberation as intersubjective, constrained by the conventions of argument, persuasion, and justification associated with the particular enterprise in which the deliberations occur. Participants in the international legal enterprise are part of or influenced by what Stanley Fish labeled an "interpretive community."[34] Fish never defined the concept precisely but rather explained it in terms of its function in any type of interpretive practice: legal, literary, or religious. It is best understood as a way of speaking about the power of institutional settings or disciplines, within which assumptions and modes of arguments are deeply entrenched. The interpretive community constrains interpretation and gives meaning to texts by providing the categories of understanding – that is, stipulations of relevance and irrelevance – that are embedded in legal practice. All professional interpreters are situated within an institutional context, and interpretive activity makes sense only in terms of the purposes of the enterprise in which the interpreter is participating. Marrying this insight with the claims of deliberative democracy, rational discourse, or deliberation is possible as long as there is an understanding – largely tacit – of the enterprise's general purpose.[35] To be persuasive, one must offer arguments that are consistent with the conventions of its practitioners. As Friedrich Kratochwil stated:

> [M]y interpretation of a rule as well as my uses of words are monitored and reinforced by a group of competent speakers. Thus, while there are likely to be disagreements about the proper use of a term or the interpretation of a rule, purely idiosyncratic uses are excluded even if the use of the concepts remains contestable and contested.[36]

Who are the practitioners? The notion of a legal interpretive community is not meant to describe a well-defined collection of people, but it is useful to imagine two concentric circles: an inner circle composed of officials directly or indirectly responsible for the formulation, negotiation, and implementation of a particular legal norm; and an outer circle of lawyers, experts,

[34] Fish, Stanley (1990). *Is There a Text in This Class? The Authority of Interpretive Communities* (Cambridge, MA: Harvard University Press). See also Abraham, Kenneth (1988). "Statutory Interpretation and Literary Theory: Some Common Concerns of an Unlikely Pair," in S. Levinson & S. Mailloux (eds.), *Interpreting Law and Literature: A Hermeneutic Reader* (Evanston, IL: Northwestern University Press), pp. 115, 122–124.

[35] Fish, Stanley (1989). *Doing What Comes Naturally: Change, Rhetoric, and the Practice of Theory in Literary and Legal Studies* (Durham, NC: Duke University Press), p. 116.

[36] Kratochwil (2000), in Byers (ed.), see note 29, p. 52.

knowledgeable observers, and others engaged in the professional activities associated with the practice or issue area regulated by the norm. Analogous to but broader than Oscar Schachter's "invisible college of international lawyers,"[37] it includes political leaders, diplomats, judges, national and international bureaucrats, legal academics, and nongovernmental actors who participate directly or indirectly in the international legal process. The members of a legal interpretive community may hail from different political and cultural settings, but they share a perspective and style of argument. By arguing with each other and reasoning together, the interpretive community becomes, in a sense, the arbiter of what constitutes a good legal argument. A political cost is paid for exceeding its conventions and defying its judgment. The constraint that this imposes is not absolute, of course, and it is felt more by weak than strong states. However, the real or anticipated judgment of the interpretive community is one factor even the most powerful states consider in whether to proceed with a course of action. Moreover, interaction within an international regime generates a sense of being in a relationship, the meaning of which has been constructed collectively by the participants. The networks that emerge from this interaction are – in deliberative democracy terms – multiple public spheres interpenetrating one another and giving concrete form to the notion of transnational deliberation. These networks, which may find a home in and around international organizations, do not represent "global democracy" but rather serve, by opening up "the possibility of public accountability and accessibility to the political influence of all those affected,"[38] as venues for nascent forms of democratic deliberation.

The UN Security Council as a Deliberative Setting

Deliberative democrats call into question the contrast that lawyers often make between the "principled decision making of courts" and "the prudential lawmaking of legislators," between the notion of courts as forums for deliberation and legislatures as brokers of interests.[39] They argue that all makers of public policy should and do give principled reasons for their decisions and add that legislators should be required to do that more often.[40] The same logic applies to international institutions: courts and quasijudicial tribunals are

[37] Schachter, Oscar (2005). "The Invisible College of International Lawyers," *Northwestern University Law Review*, 72, 217.

[38] Bohman (1999), see note 15, p. 505; Mitzen (2005), see note 16.

[39] Gutmann & Thompson (1996). "Democracy and Disagreement," see note 7, pp. 45–46, 358; Johnstone (2008). "Legislation and Adjudication in the UN Security Council," see note 1.

[40] Gutmann & Thompson, ibid., p. 46.

seen erroneously as the exclusive domain for deliberation based on rules and principles when, in fact, international legal discourse takes place in a variety of settings. It occurs through diplomatic correspondence; the speeches and statements of government officials; meetings within and between governments; and in public, press, and academic commentary. It is especially intense in international organizations, even the UN Security Council.

According to Habermas, Cohen, and others, the ideal of deliberation requires that participants have equal standing and equal voice in public debates.[41] The "rules of discourse" presuppose that "no speaker may be prevented, by internal or external coercion," from joining the debate.[42] Moreover, if the speakers are to speak to rather than at or past one another, they must share some experiences, assumptions, and understandings of the world.[43] On the surface, it would seem that none of these preconditions are met in the UN Security Council: members do not share values, a history, or even a language; the participants are anything but equal; and the proceedings are hardly public. Indeed, the Security Council is designed to be as heterogeneous as possible, with balanced representation from each geographical region and ten of its fifteen members rotating every two years. Five of its members have permanent status and the veto power, which gives some members disproportionate influence in the deliberations even when they do not use the veto. The ability to participate meaningfully varies among members based on access to intelligence and information and even on mundane matters like mission size and time zones. More to the point, the Security Council is composed of only a small fraction of the total UN membership and participation by nonmembers is severely restricted. The outcomes of deliberations – that is, the resolutions and statements adopted or defeated – are public and are usually accompanied by explanations of votes; however, the debates themselves increasingly take place in semiprivate informal consultations. The ideal of deliberation free from "relationships of power, force, and coercion" would seem to be so removed from reality that it offers no help in understanding how decisions are actually made.

On closer inspection, however, the situation is more complex. First, perfect consensus on values and definitions of interest is not a precondition for meaningful discourse (i.e., if such consensus existed, there would be no need to deliberate). All that is necessary is a sense of being in a relationship of some duration, from which common meanings and expectations have emerged, and of being engaged in an enterprise the general purpose of

[41] Cohen (1997) in Bohman & Rehg (eds.), see note 2, p. 74.
[42] Habermas, cited in Cunningham (2002), see note 11, p. 176.
[43] Risse (2000), see note 33, p. 10–11.

which all understand in roughly the same way. The Security Council meets that condition. Its mission is to "maintain international peace and security," and debates are structured by a normative framework embodied in the UN Charter. That normative framework has been supplemented by the Security Council's own decisions and operational activities, as well as treaty law, opinions of the International Court of Justice, and other judicial bodies; "soft law" in the form of General Assembly resolutions; and decisions of other intergovernmental bodies such as the Human Rights Commission (now Council). There are standard forms of argument used to appraise and ultimately accept or reject competing claims, a legal discourse that is fundamentally about the limitations imposed by the UN Charter and the relative weight to be assigned to the UN's overarching purposes. These normative considerations and constraints were notoriously weak during the Cold War, but there is evidence that the last eighteen years have heralded some convergence of understandings about the rules of international life. The five permanent members (P5) of the Security Council interacted with each other on an almost daily basis in those years – in effect, debating the shape of the post–Cold War world while responding (or not responding) to particular crises. In a sense, the P5 have become an exclusive club with a common history, set of experiences, and shared understandings about the meaning of the UN Charter. The immediate response to the events of September 11, 2001, reinforced this image of convergence. A resolution strongly condemning the terrorist attacks and implicitly endorsing the U.S. position that a military response in self-defense was justified was followed by an unprecedented resolution that outlaws a long list of activities relating to terrorism.[44] The breakdown over Iraq in early 2003 might suggest a reversal of this post–Cold War trend, but as I argue herein, there is evidence even in those failed deliberations of a fairly robust normative framework that structured debates and affected the course of events.

Moreover, there are elements of Security Council practice to suggest that the notion of equal status in and access to the discourse is not entirely fanciful. The Security Council can be conceived of as a four-tier deliberative setting.[45] The top tier is the P5 of the Council, who have equal voting power and engage in deliberations on relatively free and equal terms. Differences in material power have a profound impact on the ability of each of the P5 to

[44] United Nations (2001). S/RES/1368, New York: Security Council, 12 September; and United Nations (2001). S/RES/1373, New York: Security Council, 28 September.

[45] See Johnstone, Ian (2008). "The Security Council as Legislature," in Bruce Cronin & Ian Hurd (eds.), *The UN Security Council and the Politics of International Authority* (New York: Routledge).

influence deliberations; however, to the extent that political struggle among them takes place on the basis of deliberations, it is more evenly matched.[46] Deliberation reduces without eliminating disparities in material power.

The second tier is the Security Council as a whole. Nonpermanent members are formally equal in the sense that sovereign equality is a basic principle of the UN Charter and each has one vote, but their votes count for less because they lack veto power. The voting power of members at this tier resides largely in the fact that any member of the P5 who wants to pass a resolution must solicit their support, sometimes competing with other P5 members soliciting votes for a differently worded resolution. The competition is often crass, as it is in any lawmaking body, but it is typically characterized by appeals to reason, principles, and collective interests. Moreover, UN Charter Article 24 stipulates that the Security Council acts on behalf of the entire UN membership. Thus, even the smallest members count equally as representatives of the international community and – at least, notionally – are expected to speak for all in the collective interest. Whether sincere or strategic, many of the nonpermanent members do "speak in the common interest," whose arguments must be met by responses "in the common interest." They contribute to the deliberative process by setting the parameters of the more equal deliberations among the P5. Although the debates occur against a backdrop of bargaining and with a view to voting (and in full consciousness of which Security Council members wield the most material and bargaining power), outcomes that cannot be justified in principled terms are more difficult to push through.

The third tier is the remaining UN members, who do not have votes in the Security Council. In multiparty democracies, majority-party claims are "examined, challenged, tested, criticized, and rearticulated" by the opposition.[47] There is no functional equivalent of a parliamentary opposition in the Security Council, but nonmembers do have opportunities to wield influence. They can speak in public meetings and, although they do not participate in informal consultations (where most of the real business of the Council is now done), they are often invited to "private meetings," in which official records are kept but the public and media are excluded. In so-called Arria-formula gatherings, visiting dignitaries of nonmembers or representatives of nonstate parties to a dispute address the Security Council in an informal and confidential setting. Troop contributors to peace

[46] Gutmann and Thompson make this point in response to criticism that deliberation at the national level is elitist, and disadvantages certain groups and points of view. Gutmann & Thompson (1996), see note 7, p. 133.

[47] Benhabib (1996), see note 3, p. 72.

operations regularly meet with the Security Council president. More often than in the recent past, open debates are held before the day of a vote to give others a chance to weigh in on an issue and to gain insight into what members of the Security Council are thinking. Groups of countries may get together in the General Assembly to lead initiatives that relate to the Council's work, operating as a sort of "shadow Council."

The fourth tier is the constellation of engaged representatives of NGOs – that is, organs of international public opinion and other citizens who have a stake in and keep a close watch on what is happening in the Security Council. One need not invoke a mythical "international community" to make the case that the members of the Security Council feel compelled to appeal to networks of actors and citizens beyond governmental chambers. This network is part of the broader interpretive community described previously, whose judgment – real or anticipated – matters to governmental decision makers. The Security Council is not a sealed chamber, deaf to voices and immune to pressure from beyond its walls. Most of the effort at persuasion (as opposed to after-the-fact justification) takes place behind closed doors, where one would suppose reason and legal arguments count for less. However, the effort at persuasion is influenced by the subsequent need to justify. If a Council member states in a private meeting, "We will push this to a vote," then other members must consider whether their positions and explanations will pass muster with the outside world. Debates in private are animated by arguments that will be used later to justify positions in public. In fact, informal consultations of the Security Council are not treated by participants as completely private. With fifteen representatives, plus aides and Secretariat staff present, rarely is a word uttered that the speaker would not want to be known publicly. Because there are no official records of the meeting, the utterances can always be denied – a not-insignificant point – but the glare of publicity does find its way into even informal consultations of the Security Council, if only through the cracks in the chamber windows.

Kosovo and Iraq

Debates about the NATO intervention in Kosovo in 1999 and the U.S.-led intervention in Iraq in 2003 support the argument that legal considerations do animate debates in and around the Security Council and affect the positions governments take. I do not try to prove that the law greatly affected the initial decision to intervene in either case (and in fact both interventions were widely seen as illegal), but rather that the legal discourse had an impact on the degree of support for the interventions, subsequent developments, and the evolution of international law.

Kosovo. The North Atlantic Treaty Organization (NATO) intervention in Kosovo provoked sharp debate on a fairly well-defined although far-reaching issue – namely, the legality of humanitarian intervention without explicit Security Council authorization. The weight of official and scholarly opinion was against the legality of intervention; yet, NATO went ahead anyway, which might be read as suggesting that legal considerations were either ignored or irrelevant. Yet, legal arguments were prevalent in deliberations in and around the Security Council. Was the legal discourse mere window dressing, or does it suggest that deliberation and appeals to impartial values matter even if they do not impose an absolute constraint on action?

Various legal justifications for the use of force in Kosovo were put forward, each of which was met with compelling counterarguments. It is not my purpose to enter the debate but rather to illustrate how the interpretive community shapes Security Council deliberations.[48] I highlight five features of the deliberations and then draw a number of conclusions. First, the range of legal arguments made in the Security Council is significant. In the 1999 debates of March 24 (i.e., the day the airstrikes began) and March 26 (i.e., the date of a failed resolution to condemn the bombing), every permanent member of the Security Council (and most others) invoked legal norms and principles. Legal arguments on both sides were pressed with varying degrees of vigor, with some speakers (e.g., the United Kingdom, the Netherlands, Russia, and China) passing direct judgment on the legality or illegality of the intervention, whereas others (e.g., the United States, Canada, Argentina, and Slovenia) commented more generally on the legal context in which it took place.[49]

Second, the opposition (real and anticipated) that greeted efforts to justify the intervention on legal grounds caused some NATO governments to refrain from pushing the strongest versions of the legal claim. This is certainly true of the United States, which consistently asserted the legality of its position but ultimately relied on a "laundry list" of factors and a general claim of

[48] For a fuller analysis of the official debates and scholarly commentary, see Johnstone (2003). "Security Council Deliberations,"see note 26. For a similar analysis, see Corneliu Bjola (2005). "Legitimating the Use of Force in International Politics: A Communicative Action Perspective," *European Journal of International Relations*, 11(2), 266.

[49] For records of the debates, see United Nations (1999). S/PV.3988, Meeting Records, New York: Security Council, 24 March, S/PV.3988; and United Nations (1999). S/PV.3989, Meeting Records, New York: Security Council, 26 March.

legitimacy, rather than a single legal justification.[50] One important – perhaps overriding – reason is that the United States was concerned about the precedent that could be set by acceptance of a customary-law doctrine of humanitarian intervention. NATO allies, such as the United Kingdom and the Netherlands, were more explicit about the legal basis for the claim, but they did not push it with the same vigor at the end of discussions as they had at the start, and many turned to emphasizing the exceptional nature of the intervention.[51] Thus, opinions in NATO ranged from countries that had real doubts about the legality of the action, to those that had no such doubts but were reluctant to push the legal case because of the precedent it might establish, to those who neither had doubts nor were concerned about pushing the claim. The net result was a collective decision (or nondecision) to emphasize the legitimacy of the action, without denying its legality, while putting forward a range of factors – both legal and nonlegal – to justify it.[52]

Third, the positions of non-NATO states were varied and nuanced. Russia and China were deeply opposed, not because they feared "humanitarian intervention" directed against them (given the extreme unlikelihood of that), but rather because they were disturbed by the notion of a norm- or value-driven intervention, which could shake the foundations of non-Western regimes elsewhere and alter the global balance of power.[53] The Islamic world was not unambiguously supportive of NATO,[54] and not even Bosnia and

[50] Thus, in the Security Council debates of 24 and 26 March 1999, the U.S. representative referred to the earlier resolutions in vague terms and simply asserted that "we believe that action by NATO is justified and necessary to stop the violence and prevent an even greater humanitarian disaster." Ambassador Peter Burleigh, S/PV.3988, see note 46, p. 5. See also S/PV.3989, note 46, pp. 4–5. On that same day, the U.S. mission to the UN circulated a list of ten factors supporting NATO action in Kosovo without specifying the precise legal justification. "Factors Supporting NATO Action in Kosovo," confidential document on file with author.

[51] For thorough analyses of debates within NATO and other countries, see various chapters in Schnabel, Albrecht, & Thakur, Ramesh (eds.) (2000). *Kosovo and the Challenge of Humanitarian Intervention* (New York: United Nations University Press).

[52] As the Acting Legal Advisor to the U.S. State Department later explained, NATO came up with a "pragmatic basis for moving forward without establishing new doctrines or precedents that might trouble individual NATO members or later haunt the alliance if misused by others." Matheson, Michael (2000). "Justification for the NATO Air Campaign in Kosovo," in *Proceedings of the Ninety-fourth Annual Conference of the American Society of International Law*, p. 301.

[53] Baranovsky, Vladimir (2001). "Humanitarian Intervention: Russian Perspectives," in Pugwash Study Group Occasional Papers, *Intervention, Sovereignty, and International Security*, 2(1), 12, 17–18; Zhang, Yunling (2000). "China: Whither the World Order after Kosovo?," in Schnabel & Thakur (eds.), see note 51, p. 121.

[54] Karawan, Ibrahim (2000). "The Muslim World: Uneasy Ambivalence," in Schnabel & Thakur (eds.), see note 51, pp. 215–216.

Albania were explicit about the legality of the intervention in their statements in the Security Council (as nonmembers).[55] Among countries in the Middle East, there was sympathy for the suffering of fellow Muslims and some stated concern about human rights, but they also feared that NATO interference, if unchecked, would extend to their part of the world – to combat terrorism, for example.[56] This ambivalence is telling; if the legal discourse were meaningless, Islamic leaders would have had fewer qualms about giving in to natural (and politically beneficial) sympathy for the Kosovar Albanians by offering their wholehearted support to the intervention. They would have had no reason to fear that doing so would make intervention against them any more likely unless they believed that the precedent would have legal significance. (I subsequently return to this point.)

Fourth, the debates within NATO suggest that the legal discourse over Kosovo may have had an impact on the enunciation of NATO's new strategic concept. As the Washington Summit of April 1999 to celebrate NATO's Fiftieth Anniversary approached, there were debates and differences of opinion among NATO countries about whether the alliance could intervene out-of-area (i.e., not in self-defense) without Security Council authorization. Previously, it had been assumed that NATO would only act in such cases in support of and under the authority of the UN.[57] The United States (supported by the United Kingdom), however, was pushing for a revision of this doctrine – a position that was resisted by a number of NATO countries, including France and Germany. Although all NATO countries supported the Kosovo action in the end, they were divided on the justification, and the experience was sufficiently disturbing to many that, surprisingly, the new strategic concept reinforced the role of the UN.[58]

Fifth, a broader circle of actors who did not represent governments weighed in on the legal issues. Prominent among them was UN Secretary-General

[55] Statement of the representative of Bosnia to the Security Council, United Nations (1999). S/PV.3988, Meeting Records, New York: Security Council, 24 March, p. 19. Statement of the representative of Albania to the Security Council (1999). S/PV.3988, 24 March, p. 18.

[56] Karawan (2000), see note 54, citing by way of example an article in the semiofficial Egyptian publication *Al-Ahram*.

[57] Butler, Nicole (2000). "NATO: From Collective Defense to Peace Enforcement," in Schnabel & Thakur (eds.), see note 51, p. 276.

[58] Paragraph 31 of the Alliance's Strategic Concept reads: "NATO recalls its offer, made in Brussels in 1994, to support on a case-by-case basis in accordance with its own procedures, peacekeeping and other operations under the authority of the UN Security Council or responsibility of the OSCE.... In this context, NATO recalls its subsequent decisions with respect to crisis response operations in the Balkans." North Atlantic Treaty Organization (1999). "The Alliance's Strategic Concept," NAC-S(99)65, NATO Press Release (Washington, DC: NATO), 24 April.

Kofi Annan. He contributed to the discourse before the intervention by speaking often and eloquently about the Serb campaign against the Kosovars, never calling directly for forcible intervention but rather suggesting that the use of force ultimately may be necessary.[59] On the day that the NATO bombing started, the Secretary-General issued a carefully worded statement regretting the failure of diplomacy and stating that "there are times when the use of force may be legitimate in the pursuit of peace" but adding that "the Council should be involved in any decision to resort to force."[60] After the campaign and the adoption of Resolution 1244 establishing the United Nations Mission in Kosovo (UNMIK) and Kosovo Force (KFOR), he put the issue of humanitarian intervention squarely on the international agenda by means of his statement at the opening of the general debate in the General Assembly, in which he said that "the core challenge to the Security Council and the United Nations as a whole in the next century is to forge unity behind the principle that massive and systematic violations of human rights – wherever they take place – cannot be allowed to stand."[61] International legal scholars also weighed in, mainly after the fact, and although opinions were varied, they leaned in the direction of illegality.[62] In reviewing the scholarly comment, José Alvarez noted that even commentators who supported the objectives of the intervention found NATO's action to be inconsistent with the UN Charter, and he pointed to a significant degree of uniformity among them about the range of tools they could use in interpreting it.[63] At the risk of overstating the case, one can infer from the relative weight of opinion against legality that this was the judgment the U.S. government anticipated facing.

59 See, for example, statement of the UN Secretary-General, United Nations (1999). "Secretary-General Calls for Unconditional Respect for Human Rights of Kosovo Citizens, in Statement to North Atlantic Treaty Organization," SG/SM/6878, UN Press Release, New York: United Nations, 28 January.

60 UN Wire (1999). "Annan Offers Qualified Endorsment of NATO Bombing," 25 March. www.unwire.org/unwire/19990325/1668_story.asp.

61 Annan, Kofi (1999). "Presentation of the Secretary-General's Annual Report to the United Nations General Assembly" (20 September), reprinted in UN Press Release SG/SM/7136, GA/9596, New York: United Nations.

62 In a series of editorial comments by seven leading legal scholars (all but one American) in the *American Journal of International Law* of October 1999, only one concludes unequivocally that the intervention was lawful (i.e., Michael Riesman) and one other found a measure of legitimacy (i.e., Ruth Wedgewood). See Henkin, Louis; Wedgewood, Ruth; Charney, Jonathan; Chinkin, Christine; Falk, Richard; Franck, Thomas; & Riesman, W. Michael (1999). "Editorial Comments: NATO's Kosovo Intervention," *American Journal of International Law*, 93(4), 83.

63 Alvarez, José (2001). "Constitutional Interpretation in International Organizations," in Jean-Marc Coicaud & Veijo Heiskanen (eds.), *The Legitimacy of International Organizations* (New York: UNU Press), pp. 134, 136.

Legal advisors would have been conscious of the difficulty in making a case that differed substantially from the conclusions legal scholars would be likely to draw after the fact.

What can be inferred from this discussion? First, the variegated nature of the legal argumentation is circumstantial evidence of a functioning interpretive community associated with Security Council practice. Legal arguments are advanced in anticipation of the judgment of that community. Its impact in part will depend on the degree of unity within it. Clearly, the international community was not unified on the norm of humanitarian intervention at the time of the Kosovo crisis, which is why arguments in the Security Council ranged from clear statements of legality or illegality to more tentative statements about the legal context in which the intervention took place. However, the mere fact that legal arguments were advanced by all members of the Security Council, including the most powerful, suggests that the normative framework provided by the UN Charter and other instruments is sufficiently robust to warrant an effort to justify positions on legal grounds. Also, because there is an interpretive community to "guard" that normative framework, the law is not infinitely malleable. If it were, either legal arguments would not have been made or they all would have been more straightforward claims of (il)legality because there would be no concern about the test of credibility. (Who would administer that test?)

Second, concerns about precedent are only intelligible if something like an interpretive community is at work. As noted previously, many states that supported the action either refrained from pushing the claim of legality or did so with less vigor than might be expected. The United States, Germany, Brazil, and various Islamic countries were all concerned about the implications of endorsing a doctrine of humanitarian intervention. One can imagine that the Islamic countries were concerned about such humanitarian intervention being directed against them (and the United States was concerned about Israel), but the Kosovo "precedent" would not render that any more likely unless one assumes some mechanism for issuing credible judgments that it really is a precedent – that is, some way of evaluating whether like cases are being treated alike. In a decentralized legal system, that mechanism can only be the interpretive community – it is what gives the whole notion of precedent its "bite."

Third, concerns about plausibility – and the reputational costs associated with advancing implausible arguments – are further evidence of rational discourse within an interpretive community. Ultimately, it is the interpretive community – and not just those at whom the arguments are directed – that determines plausibility. The interpretive community, in effect, says the following about far-fetched claims: "Your legal position is untenable; your arguments are not only patently self-serving, they are wrong." In the Kosovo case, reputational concerns cut both ways: on the one hand, some states may have been reluctant to put forward implausible legal arguments for fear they would be seen as far-fetched and hypocritical; on the other hand, once it was clear that the intervention would go forward, no NATO country wanted to cast doubt publicly on the legality of the action because all have a stake in maintaining a reputation for good-faith compliance with the law. Either way, the interpretive community has done its work because it is the entity that extracts reputational costs.

Fourth, although the legal discourse did not affect the decision to intervene, it did affect subsequent developments. The debate about the legality of the action caused such unease among NATO countries that many believed it was important to highlight the exceptional nature of the event rather than set a new policy. NATO enunciated a new strategic concept within a few weeks of the start of the bombing campaign, which reaffirmed the role of the Security Council in authorizing interventions and implicitly treated the Kosovo case as an exception. Similarly, the felt need to return to the Security Council for a long-term solution (i.e., "whereas NATO made war, it still needed the UN to help secure the peace"[64]) is revealing. Legal boundaries may be pushed by norm entrepreneurs[65]; however, to be generally accepted internationally, those pushing the limits must work to some extent within what are regarded as the legitimate venues for discourse. U.S. leadership was followed and the norm of humanitarian intervention may have received a boost (despite U.S. concerns about the precedent),[66] but the event also provoked a reaction on the broader legal and institutional questions it raised, including among NATO allies. Returning to the UN via Resolution 1244 alleviated the "morning-after" regrets by diluting the threat to legal order that the NATO intervention was seen as presenting. It reinforced the sense that institutions are an important check on the unilateral exercise of power in the name of collective values.[67]

[64] Schnabel, Albrecht, & Thakur, Ramesh (2000). "Kosovo and the Challenge of World Order," in Schnabel & Thakur (eds.), see note 51, p. 14.

[65] Johnstone, Ian (2007). "The Secretary-General as Norm Entrepreneur," in Simon Chesterman (ed.), *Secretary or General? The UN Secretary-General in World Politics* (Cambridge: Cambridge University Press), p. 123.

[66] The international debate provoked by the Kosovo intervention led to the establishment of the International Commission on Intervention and State Sovereignty, whose report, "The Responsibility to Protect," was instrumental in leading to the endorsement of the concept at the World Summit in September 2005. The language of the declaration is more tepid than the most enthusiastic proponents of the responsibility to protect would have liked, but it is significant that the concept has been endorsed in a consensus document adopted at a global summit.

[67] Ikenberry, John (2000). "The Costs of Victory," in Schnabel & Thakur (eds.), see note 51, p. 96.

Iraq. Debates about the U.S.-led military action against Iraq in March 2003 also illustrate how deliberative principles infuse international decision making. Again, it is not my purpose to enter the debate about the legality of military action but rather to identify features of the discourse from which conclusions may be drawn about the nature of Security Council deliberations.[68] First, it is significant that President Bush even went to the UN with his speech to the General Assembly on September 12, 2002. In so doing, he launched an extended and highly public deliberative process from which the United States certainly had something to gain – or lose. Explicit Security Council authority for military action would translate into greater international and domestic support. Something less than explicit authorization also would have been desirable from the Washington point of view, given its position that it already had the authority to take military action on the basis of existing resolutions.[69] Even if (especially if!) the decision to go to war had been made before September 12, 2002 (i.e., there is evidence that President Bush himself had not made the final decision at that time[70]) and the timetable was set by military rather than diplomatic considerations, to suggest that the United States had nothing to lose by going to the UN requires an extraordinarily narrow reading of how the United States defines its interests. Among other factors, the American electorate cares about international opinion – as polls throughout the period between September 2002 and March 2003 showed[71] – and with midterm Congressional elections approaching, the Bush administration was cognizant of the political cost of publicly seeking and not obtaining international support. Some may regret having made the effort; however, that supports rather than undermines the argument that the outcome of those deliberations indeed did matter.

Second, the ambiguous commitments in Resolution 1441 to "assess" (i.e., paragraph 4) and "consider the situation" (i.e., paragraph 12) if Iraq failed to

68 For an analysis of the normative framework in which the debates about the military action in Iraq took place, see Johnstone, Ian (2004). "US–UN Relations after Iraq: The End of the World (Order) As We Know It?," *European Journal of International Law,* 15(3), 813, 830–835. On the legal debates themselves, see the collection of opinions in Fisler Damrosch, Lori, & Oxman, Bernard (eds.) (2003). "Agora: Future Implications of the Iraq Conflict," *American Journal of International Law,* (97)3, 553–642.

69 Taft, William H., IV, & Buchwald, Todd F. (2003). "Preemption, Iraq, and International Law," in Damrosch & Oxman, ibid., pp. 557–563.

70 In a carefully researched three-part series, the *Financial Times* reports that the "internal moment" when the U.S. president and his closest aides decided that military action was inevitable came in mid-December 2002 after reviewing Iraq's 12,000-page declaration in response to Resolution 1441. *Financial Times* (2003). "War in Iraq: How the Die Was Cast before Transatlantic Diplomacy Failed," 27 May, p. 15.

71 Kull, S.; Ramsey, M.; & Lewis, C. (2003–2004). "Misperceptions, the Media, and the Iraq War," *Political Science Quarterly,* 118, 569.

comply with its obligations are revealing. The United States and the United Kingdom made it clear in voting for the resolution that they would feel obliged to engage in further deliberations but not to submit the decision to take military action to a new vote. France and Russia were prepared to vote for the resolution (indeed, it was thanks to the French that the resolution passed unanimously[72]) knowing the U.S.–UK position and, thus, tacitly accepted it, even if they wanted to reserve the right to read it differently "when push came to shove." A second set of Security Council deliberations meant that those who were resisting precipitous military action could tell their domestic constituents that there was "no automaticity" in Resolution 1441. The United States, meanwhile, opened itself to another round of public persuasion, explanation, criticism, and justification, giving the "interpretive community" the opportunity to pass judgment on its legal stance. Thus, the second round of deliberations was not a mere gimmick to "paper over" different interpretations of the core legal question; rather, from the perspective of both sides, it had real consequences.

Third, the relative emphasis that the United States placed on the two principal legal justifications for the military action – that is, self-defense against terrorism and enforcement of Security Council resolutions to rid Iraq of weapons of mass destruction (WMD) (Saddam Hussein's human-rights record was a distant third in the official discourse) – is telling.[73] In his briefing to the Security Council on February 5, 2003, Secretary Colin Powell sought to present forensic evidence to support the case on both counts, and he clearly failed on the terrorism-based claim. There is ample evidence that the international community was prepared to accept the legality of military action against Al Qaeda and the Taliban in Afghanistan – including preambular paragraphs in two Security Council resolutions as well as widespread tangible and rhetorical support for the intervention[74] – but it was not prepared to

[72] Baker, Gerard; Blitz, James; Dempsey, Judy; Graham, Robert; Peel, Quentin; & Turner, Mark (2003). "Blair's Mission Impossible: The Doomed Effort to Win a Second Resolution," *Financial Times*, 29 May, p. 4.

[73] For an account of developments relating to Iraq in and around the Security Council from 8 November 2002 (when Resolution 1441 was adopted) until the end of April 2003, see Murphy, Sean D. (2003). "Use of Military Force to Disarm Iraq," *American Journal of International Law*, 97(2), 419.

[74] Johnstone, Ian (2005). "The Plea of 'Necessity' in International Legal Discourse: Humanitarian Intervention and Counter-terrorism," *Columbia Journal of Transnational Law*, 43(2), 338, 370–372. See also Johnstone, "US–UN Relations after Iraq," see note 66, pp. 828–829. Evidence in support of that conclusion includes preambular paragraphs in Security Council Resolutions 1368 and 1373, which reaffirm the "inherent right of self-defense," signaling the Security Council's judgment that the 11 September attacks constituted an "armed attack within the meaning of Article 51, justifying a response in self-defense." See also the largely supportive responses to the U.S. letter of 7 October 2001, that the President of the Security

stretch the argument to Iraq seventeen months later. The debate was waged intensely in and around the UN in the months between September 2002 and March 2003 and, in the end, the "interpretive community" was not persuaded that the links between Iraq and the events of September 11 were sufficiently tight to justify military action on that basis.[75] When that became obvious, the Bush administration largely gave up trying to make the case in those terms – at least, to international audiences. There is no better evidence than the letter of March 20, 2003, from the United States to the President of the Security Council setting out the legal justification for the war.[76] The letter contains only a cryptic reference to the need "to defend the United States and the international community" and not a word about terrorism or preemption.[77] The legal case is based almost entirely on the enforcement of existing Security Council resolutions relating to Iraq's WMD.

Moreover, the decision to withdraw the famous second resolution in March 2003 is evidence that legal arguments carry weight. That draft, deemed essential by Prime Minister Tony Blair and supported reluctantly by the United States, was first floated on February 24 and debated outside Security Council chambers for five weeks. The resolution would have had the Council decide that "Iraq has failed to take the final opportunity afforded to it in Resolution 1441 (2002),"[78] which would have been understood by all concerned as the trigger for military action. The draft sparked a frantic scramble for votes, which the United States ultimately lost. In a press conference on March 11, President Bush said he would put the resolution to a vote, "win or lose,"[79] presumably because he believed the weight of international and domestic opinion would see matters as the United States did, regardless of the outcome

Council (S/2001/946, 7 October 2001) cited in Murphy, Sean (2002). "Terrorist Attacks on the World Trade Center and Pentagon," *American Journal of International Law*, 96(1), 244–249; Ratner, Stephen (2002). "Jus Ad Bellum and Jus in Bell after September 11," *American Journal of International Law*, 96(4), 909–910.

75 *The New Republic* reported that even the U.S. intelligence community was sharply divided on whether there was such a link. Ackerman, Spencer, & Judis, John B. (2003). "The First Casualty," *New Republic*, 30 June, p. 14.

76 United Nations (2003). "Letter dated 20 March 2003 from the Permanent Representative of the United States of America to the United Nations Addressed to the President of the Security Council," S/2003/351, New York: Security Council, 21 March.

77 I argued in "Discursive Power in the UN Security Council," *Journal of International Law and International Relations*, 2(1) (2006), 76, footnote 9, that the reference to defense "of the United States and international community" is more plausibly read as a claim that in enforcing Security Council resolutions, the United States is defending collective interests rather than as a claim of self-defense.

78 Quoted by Murphy (2003), see note 71, p. 423.

79 Sanger, David (2003). "Canvassing the Votes to Gain Legitimacy," *New York Times*, 13 March, p. A12.

of the vote. Yet, on March 18, the United States decided not to table the draft, knowing it would not get even a majority. It is interesting that both Spain (a supporter of the United States) and France (an opponent) urged the Bush administration to withdraw the draft because both believed that a failed vote would do more diplomatic harm than no vote at all.[80] This "deliberative move" by Spain and France helped to salvage some credibility for the Security Council and international law. The decision to go to war having been made, it was better to do so on the basis of existing resolutions than to push the doomed draft to a vote, rendering it all but impossible to claim that the military action was being taken to enforce Security Council demands. The fact that the United States agreed, despite the desire of some to use the Iraq crisis as an opportunity to permanently damage the Security Council (i.e., what better way than to lose the vote and declare the Council irrelevant!) is evidence that "the better legal argument" mattered to both sides.[81] Richard Haass, director of policy planning in the U.S. State Department at the time, said that by avoiding a vote on the second resolution, "[n]ow we can argue that we are acting pursuant to the UN, in 1441. This is a way, I believe, quite honestly, of preserving the UN's potential viability in the future. We've not destroyed it. We've just admitted, though, that it can't do everything when the great powers of the day disagree."[82]

Fourth, the deliberations on Iraq highlight the role of nonpermanent members. The main protagonists were the United States and France; however, the debates were conducted in large part with a view to persuading nonpermanent members. After what has been called the "diplomatic ambush" of Powell by French Foreign Minister de Villepin on January 20, the United States and the United Kingdom largely gave up trying to win France's support directly and instead focused on the nonpermanent members, thinking that if six or seven could be convinced to vote yes, France and Russia would be under pressure to abstain. Even if France or Russia were to vote no, the United States and the United Kingdom could claim majority support and argue that they had been blocked – in Prime Minister Blair's words – by an "unreasonable veto,"[83] giving the military action a veneer of legitimacy. Of the nonpermanent members, Spain and Bulgaria were supportive of the United States from

80 Baker, et al. (2003), see note 70.

81 Among those who anticipated the end of the UN with pleasure were Richard Perle, who at the time of writing the article was Chairman of the Defense Policy Board, an advisory panel to the Pentagon (2003), "Thank God for the Death of the UN," *Guardian*, 21 March, and Charles Krauthammer (2003). "UN: RIP," *Washington Post*, 31 January.

82 Quoted in Lehman, Nicholas (2003). "How It Came to War," *New Yorker*, 31 March.

83 Baker et al. (2003), see note 70, p. 4.

the start, whereas Germany and Syria were opposed. That left six "swing votes" – Pakistan, Cameroon, Angola, Guinea, Chile, and Mexico – that came under intense pressure. The U.S. failure to secure their support suggests that material power is not all that matters. Despite the threats made and incentives offered, the presidents of Chile and Mexico made clear in private meetings with Bush administration officials that they could not vote with the United States, and the African members had not indicated their support.[84] If the United States had hammered away in the deliberations on the issue that had preoccupied the Security Council since 1991 – namely, the need to rid Iraq of its WMD – the result may well have been different. As Joseph Nye reported, "a number of close observers – such as British Ambassador to the UN Sir Jeremy Greenstock – believe that with a little more patience and diplomacy, the administration could have obtained another resolution that would have focused on the sins of Saddam Hussein rather than allowing France and Russia to turn the problem into one of American power."[85] By speaking at diplomatically inopportune moments about tenuous linkages to acts of terrorism, a doctrine of preemption that was difficult to square with existing international law and the desire to transform the entire Middle East, Bush administration officials made it more difficult for leaders of most of the six swing-vote countries to sign on to a war that appeared to their constituents to be the first step in a U.S. effort to remake the world in a manner that served only U.S. interests.[86]

Fifth, there were serious costs associated with not being able to get an explicit authorization for the war. Despite U.S. offers of billions of dollars in new assistance, for example, the Turkish government could not get parliamentary support to allow American troops to move into Iraq from Turkish bases, which complicated U.S. military strategy. The criticisms that the U.S. and UK governments faced for exaggerating evidence relating to Iraq's WMD programs would have had much less sting if the Security Council had authorized the military action. Unlike the alleged connection with Al Qaeda, U.S. and UK beliefs about the status of Iraq's WMD programs were broadly shared

[84] Ibid., p. 4. See also Rubin, James (2003). "Stumbling into War," *Foreign Affairs*, 82(5), 55.

[85] Nye, Joseph (2003). "American Power and Strategy," *Foreign Affairs*, July/August, p. 63. As late as early March, not even France had ruled out signing on to a resolution authorizing force following a thirty-day deadline with tough benchmarks. Baker et al. (2003), see note 70.

[86] Johnstone, "US–UN Relations after Iraq," see note 66, p. 833. As Fareed Zakaria said about Bush administration policy more generally, the United States suffers from "a deep and widening mistrust and resentment of American foreign policy around the world. . . . What worries people above all is living in a world shaped and dominated by one country – the U.S. And they have come to be deeply suspicious and fearful of us." Zakaria, Fareed (2003). "The Arrogant Empire," *Newsweek*, 24 March.

in the runup to the war. The UN weapons inspectors never declared Iraq to be free of WMD programs. No member of the Security Council claimed that Iraq was fulfilling all of its obligations, and none doubted that Iraq remained a WMD threat. Differences of opinion concerned the magnitude of the threat and the urgency of the need for military action to address it. The case for war looks weaker in hindsight – having discovered that Iraq had no WMD and little capacity to restart its WMD programs while under sanctions and the inspection regime[87] – than it did at the time military action was taken.

When the United States began seeking international help in reconstructing Iraq, in terms of both financial aid and troop contributors, it came up against considerable resentment bred of the "go-it-alone" approach during the war. In July 2003, for example, India decided not to contribute the seventeen thousand soldiers it had planned to dispatch, despite the obvious benefits a closer relationship with the United States would bring. India made this decision because the war in Iraq was extremely unpopular domestically, and military participation in the aftermath would be seen as joining an occupation.[88] The calculation would have been different if the war had been explicitly authorized and, in fact, the Indian government stated that it would participate in peacekeeping in Iraq if there were "an explicit UN mandate for the purpose."[89] Pakistan, Bangladesh, Russia, and Turkey all concurred.[90] In the end, none contributed even after the Security Council adopted resolutions authorizing the multinational presence, which may be read as suggesting that the earlier offers were "cheap talk."[91] Nevertheless, the absence of a clear legal basis for the intervention made it easier (i.e., less costly in political terms) for those countries to avoid doing what they did not want to do as a matter of policy. "The India effect" apparently had an impact on the United States and led to serious discussion about a new Security Council resolution, first in July and then in September 2003 following the attack in Baghdad

87 Final Report of the Iraq Survey Group; available at www.cia.gov/cia/reports/iraq_wmd_2004.

88 Kifner, John (2003). "India Decides Not to Send Troops to Iraq Now," *New York Times*, 13 July, p. A13.

89 Quoted in Kifner, ibid.

90 Pakistan's position was stated by Foreign Minister Khurshid Mahmood Kasuri, as quoted by the BBC (2003). "Pakistan Troops Only under UN," 13 October; available at news.bbc.co.uk/2/hi/south_asia/3187946.stm. A Bangladeshi official is quoted as saying, "We will be willing to take part in the peacekeeping in Iraq only after a clear UN mandate," Hossain, Farid (2003). "Bangladesh against Sending Troops to Iraq," *Guardian*, 27 September; available at www.guardian.co.uk/worldlatest/story/0,1280,-3198501,00.html. On the Russian position, see "Putin: Russia Won't Rule Out Sending Troops to Iraq," in an AP report published in 2003, *USA Today*, 20 September; available at www.usatoday.com/news/world/iraq/2003–09-20-russia-iraq_x.htm. On Turkey, see Fisher, Ian (2003). "Iraqi Leaders Condemn Plan for Troops from Turkey," *New York Times*, 9 October, p. A14.

91 Security Council Resolutions 1511 (2003) and 1546 (2004).

that took the life of Special Representative of the Secretary-General, Sergio Vieira de Mello, and culminating in Resolution 1511 of October 16. Ad hoc coalition-building may result in fewer entanglements than working through established multilateral institutions, but it is not cost-free. The adoption of Security Council Resolutions 1483, 1500, 1511, and 1546 on postwar Iraq reflects an effort to minimize the risks and costs. Ultimately, it was not until Kofi Annan was replaced by Ban Ki Moon in 2007 that the Secretary-General's office became more receptive to a greater role for the UN in Iraq; even then, the approach was cautious, focusing on purely political rather than security-related functions.

Three conclusions must be highlighted. First, justificatory discourse does matter to the weaker states in the Security Council. At least some of the members who did not support the United States in March 2003 likely would have done so if the diplomacy surrounding the deliberations had been conducted more adroitly. The Security Council had agreed unanimously on Resolution 1441, which papered over differences, but papering over differences is an inherent part of diplomacy. By March 2003, even members that may have been inclined to support the United States in the Security Council could not do so, given the difficulties that they would have in explaining and justifying that support to their own constituents. Moreover, conceivably even those who had doubts about the wisdom of military intervention as a matter of policy would have been more supportive if its legal basis was more certain. They had much to lose by opposing the United States; some may have found it convenient to maintain good relations with the United States despite misgivings about the policy by claiming that they were simply falling in line with the collective will of the Security Council.

Second, even the United States was influenced by "the force of the better argument." The Bush administration probably decided to go to war prior to September 12, 2002, regardless of what would happen in the Security Council, but that reinforces the point. If the United States felt unilateral action was no more risky or costly than multilateral action, why engage so strenuously in diplomatic efforts to obtain multilateral support? If the entire diplomatic game between September 2002 and March 2003 was a charade, why bother? Clearly, some in the Bush administration thought it was worth the effort and worked hard to build a factual and legal case that could be supported by others. There was something to gain (and lose) by the argumentation; it cannot be dismissed as inconsequential "cheap talk."

Third, the different reactions to the Kosovo and Iraq interventions can be explained in part by the differing normative contexts.[92] NATO's action

[92] Johnstone, "US–UN Relations after Iraq," see note 66.

in Kosovo, although widely viewed as unlawful, built on an evolving legal framework and may well have contributed to an emerging consensus on humanitarian intervention. The Iraq intervention, conversely, was perceived as a sharp break from the existing normative and institutional framework, for which the United States has paid a price economically, politically, and in other ways. The Bush administration calculated that the price was worth paying, although it underestimated the difficulty of winning the peace in Iraq. It is too early to state conclusively that efforts to curb terrorism and the proliferation of WMD have been set back by the Iraq misadventure, but some knowledgeable observers already see evidence of that.[93] It is difficult to quantify what portion of the costs can be attributed to the decision to act outside of the legal and Security Council framework; any risky policy entails costs. In a rough calculation in 2003, Lael Brainard and Michael O'Hanlon estimated that maintaining security in and rebuilding Iraq between 2003 and 2007 would cost the United States $100 billion more than what it would pay for a multilateral reconstruction effort in Iraq along the lines of Bosnia or Kosovo. Thus, they concluded, "unilateralism has a price: about $1,000 for each American household."[94] That was a rough estimate and impossible to prove empirically because there is no way of definitely knowing whether a more multilateral operation would have had more early success in winning the peace (and, therefore, be less costly) or what portion of the overall costs would be borne by others. However, the fact that the total cost to the United States of the Iraq war and reconstruction had reached more than $500 billion by February 2008 suggests that the American taxpayers are paying a high price indeed.[95] A hardheaded empiricist would surely have more trouble making the case that there are no costs associated with the lack of clear legal authority.

Conclusion

In this chapter, I argued that the legitimacy and effectiveness of international decision making is tied in part to the quality of deliberations that go into it. Drawing insights from the theory of deliberative democracy, I argued that

[93] Cirincione, Joseph (2007). *Bomb Scare: The History and Future of Nuclear Weapons* (New York: Columbia University Press), pp. 118–120; Albright, Madeleine (2003). "Bridges, Bombs, or Bluster?," *Foreign Affairs*, 82(5), 4; Rubin (2003), see note 82, p. 64.

[94] Brainard, Lael, & O'Hanlon, Michael (2003). "The Heavy Price of America's Going It Alone," *Financial Times*, 6 August, p. 17.

[95] Amy Belasco, "Congressional Research Service Report for Congress on the Cost of Iraq, Afghanistan, and Other Global War on Terror Operations since 9/11," updated 8 February 2008; available at www.fas.org/sgp/crs/natsec/RL33110.pdf. For a running total of the figure, based on CRS calculations, see zfacts.com/p/447.html.

reasoned discourse is possible even in the UN Security Council, where material power and calculations of national-security interest dominate. An interpretive community sets the parameters of those deliberations, constraining the range of arguments that are likely to be offered and accepted. In both the Kosovo and Iraq cases, a body of law shaped the discourse, and fairly robust deliberations occurred. History has judged the so-called humanitarian intervention in Kosovo relatively kindly – a judgment that is not undermined by the lack of agreement on the final status that led to Kosovo's unilateral declaration of independence in early 2008. History has been less kind to the intervention in Iraq, in part because the enterprise was cast by the United States in a way that marked too sharp a break from accepted norms. The lesson for those who seek to change international law is that they are more likely to succeed by building on the existing normative and institutional framework than by tearing it down and trying to rebuild from scratch.

This is not to suggest that the Security Council is an ideal deliberative setting or that it is the only institution capable of conferring legitimacy. However, for the time being, it is the best institution the world has to serve that function; even the United States continues to benefit from working through the Security Council in advancing human rights (e.g., in Darfur), fighting terrorism (e.g., through Resolution 1373), and countering WMD proliferation (e.g., in Iran and elsewhere). If it is a valued institution and deliberation in it is consequential, then reflection on Security Council reform should include consideration of how the "deliberative deficit" might be reduced.[96] Indeed, debates about Security Council reform that preceded the World Summit of 2005 demonstrate a keen awareness of that principle.[97] Consider, for example, the call by the High-Level Panel on Threats, Challenges, and Change (HLP) for a system of "indicative voting" as a way of increasing the "accountability" of the veto function.[98] The rationale seems to be that governments that are required to announce their positions publicly prior to an actual vote will be less likely to cast a veto if the reasons for it are unlikely to pass muster in the court of international public opinion. Although the debate among member states focused on expansion of the permanent membership, the resolution tabled by the G-4 – Brazil, Germany, India, and Japan – included detailed proposals for improving working methods in the Security Council

[96] Johnstone, "Legislation and Adjudication in the UN Security Council," see note 1.

[97] Summaries of the debates and the various proposals put forward in the lead-up to the summit are available at www.reformtheun.org.

[98] Report of the Secretary-General's High-Level Panel on Threats, Challenges, and Change, "A More Secure World: Our Shared Responsibility," UN GAOR, Fifty-ninth Session, Supp. No. 565, UN Doc. A/59 (2004); available at www.un.org/secureworld/report.pdf, para. 257.

to enhance its "transparency, inclusiveness, and legitimacy." Moreover, one of the strongest criticisms of the G-4 proposal for six new permanent members was that if eleven of the world's "great powers" had permanent seats at the table, there would be less incentive to consult more broadly. Following the logic of "deliberative democracy," the legitimacy of the Security Council can be enhanced by greater accountability and transparency, within the limits imposed by the need for efficient decision making. Recent procedural innovations that the Security Council has taken are steps in that direction.[99] Other measures might include setting out criteria or guidelines for intervention – as the Secretary-General called for in the report he prepared for the 2005 World Summit.[100] Premised on the idea that the legitimacy of Security Council decision making is tied to voting arrangements alone, such criteria would compel members to justify action (or inaction) publicly on the basis of agreed standards. The Kosovo and Iraq cases demonstrate that deliberative principles already inform Security Council working methods and that more can be done to improve the quality of the Council's deliberations.

[99] See United Nations (1999). "Note by the President of the Security Council," S/1999/1291, New York: Security Council, 30 December, and the documents referred to therein; United Nations (2001). "Note by the President of the Security Council," S/2001/640, New York: Security Council, 29 June; United Nations (2001). S/RES/1353, New York: Security Council, 13 June, and the documents referred to therein.

[100] Report of the Secretary-General (2005). "In Larger Freedom: Towards Development, Security, and Human Rights for All," March. Available at www.un.org/largerfreedom. The notion of criteria for intervention as also put forward in the Report of the Secretary-General's High Level Panel on Threats, Challenges, and Change (2004), available at www.un.org/secureworld.

NISHKALA SUNTHARALINGAM

7. The UN Security Council, Regional Arrangements, and Peacekeeping Operations

Since the end of the Cold War, there has been an escalation of demands for United Nations (UN) intervention, mostly in situations of convoluted internal conflict that require complex and novel peacekeeping operations. Such internal conflicts are not limited to their boundaries but also affect entire regions through the displacement of persons as well as the flow of arms and resources. This generally requires both a regional and an international response. The international legitimacy of a UN peacekeeping operation is usually derived from obtaining a mandate from the UN Security Council. The uniquely broad representation of member states that contribute personnel and funding to UN operations strengthens this international legitimacy. So, too, does the fact that UN peacekeeping operations are directed by the UN Secretary-General, an impartial and well-respected international figure who is committed to upholding the principles and purposes of the UN Charter.

Since 1989, the UN has established more than thirty new peacekeeping operations, which contrasts with the fifteen instituted in the previous forty-one years. These growing commitments have stretched to the limit the capacity of the UN for effective response. The surge in UN peacekeeping activity has come at a cost. Few current UN peacekeeping missions enjoy a full degree of support and attention from member states and the UN, particularly in terms of reflection and review of strategy, policy, and effective public communications. In the first generation of peacekeeping surge in activity immediately following the end of the Cold War, "successful" peacekeeping operations deployed to Namibia, Cambodia, El Salvador, and Mozambique with a comprehensive peace settlement in place. The belligerents were limited in number, easily identifiable, and relatively cohesive; international troops

The views here are entirely those of the author and should not be attributed in any manner to the UN.

were largely self-sustaining, and the areas of deployment were small. At the beginning of the twenty-first century, the "honeymoon" effects of the end of the Cold War have been replaced with strains on the international system exacerbated by divisions over the Iraq war, responses to the "Global War on Terror," and increased competition for scarce energy resources and global markets. Developments in Iraq and the broader Middle East make it more difficult to attract sustained political attention and resources to conflicts in Africa and elsewhere, unless such countries offer significant political or economic opportunities – in which case the potential for a united international effort is limited.

The potential for regional arrangements has become increasingly relevant as part of that burden-sharing for peace and security issues. They have the advantage of proximity to conflict and interest in reaching settlement for the maintenance of peace and security in the region. They also have critical disadvantages: the possibility of hegemonic tendencies, lack of impartiality to the actors in the conflict as a result of historic ties and interests, and (in most cases, except for the European arrangements) a lack of resources. The issue of legitimacy has become somewhat blurred in regional contexts, not least because authorization from the Security Council for collective action is often provided after the fact or not even sought. In the particular cases of U.S. air strikes over Afghanistan in 2001–2002 and military operations in Iraq from 2003 by a "coalition of the willing," the legitimacy and authority of the Security Council was severely compromised. This erosion of legitimacy is based on the interpretation that "the claim to use force is only potentially legitimate if there can be made a *prior* demonstration of defensive necessity based on the imminence, plausibility and severity of a security threat, with these conditions normally to be determined by a *multilateral* process, preferably by the Security Council."[1] However, even for these states, legal sanction by the Security Council for military action is important, increasingly at the political level, not least to appease the concerns of their own local electorates.

This chapter answers the following questions: What is the scope for involvement of regional arrangements in peace and security issues? How is legitimacy conferred on the actions and interventions of regional organizations vis-à-vis the UN in maintaining international peace and security and peacekeeping operations? To what extent is the capability of using force a prerequisite for the "effectiveness" and "legitimacy" of these operations? Other issues increasingly associated with the legitimacy of these operations include

[1] Falk, Richard (2005). "Legality and Legitimacy: The Quest for Principled Flexibility and Restraint." *Review of International Studies*, 31, 33–50, 43.

credibility and the promotion of national and local ownership. To address these issues, this chapter reviews the framework and scope of regional arrangements as well as the operational record of such arrangements in West Africa, the former Yugoslavia, and Eastern and Central Africa.[2] It argues that in recent years there has been a shift among member states such that Security Council authorization is necessary for legitimizing intervention by a coalition of states or by an individual state, regardless of whether the UN has a role as the implementer. Nevertheless, the conferring of this legitimacy by the Security Council comes at a price because it also requires the UN to better monitor and coordinate the partnerships as and when required, as well as to ensure that the operations authorized are effective in their undertaking.

Classification of Regional Organizations and Arrangements. Although the UN Charter provides no definition of regional arrangements,[3] three broad categories of regional organizations are recognizable:[4] (1) the classic regional organizations; (2) collective self-defense organizations with potential for peacekeeping; and (3) regional groups that have been created for more general functions other than foreign- and security-policy issues. A fourth category is emerging as increasingly significant to certain aspects of peace and security matters, especially in Africa.

The classic regional organization fits within the framework of Chapter VIII of the UN Charter – that is, organizations encompassing a defined geographic region to which all members of the region are entitled to belong.

[2] The author notes that in identifying these studies other important regional arrangements have been overlooked, despite the various internal mechanisms that have been set up by each organization to address peacekeeping and security issues in the Americas and in Africa, respectively.

[3] United Nations (1992). "Agenda for Peace," A/47/277-S/24111, New York: General Assembly, Security Council, June 17, provides at paragraph 61:

> The Charter deliberately provides no precise definition of regional arrangements and agencies, thus allowing useful flexibility for undertakings by a group of states to deal with a matter appropriate for regional action, which could contribute to the maintenance of international peace and security. Such associations or entities could include treaty-based organizations, whether created before or after the founding of the United Nations, regional organizations for mutual security defense, organizations for general regional development or for cooperation on a particular economic topic or function, and groups created to deal with a specific political, economic or social issues of current concern.

[4] This classification of regional arrangements draws on Roper, John (1999). "The Contribution of Regional Organizations in Europe," in Olara A. Otunnu & Michael W. Doyle (eds.), *Peacemaking and Peacekeeping for the New Century* (Oxford, MD: Rowman & Littlefield Publishers), pp. 255–271.

The prototype seems to be the Organization of American States (OAS), which was discussed at length at the San Francisco Conference in 1945. Others include the African Union (AU) (formerly the Organization for African Unity [OAU]); the Organization for Security and Cooperation in Europe (OSCE) (formerly the Conference for Security and Cooperation in Europe [CSCE]); and, to a lesser extent, the Arab League.[5] These organizations, in a sense, are all mini-UNs with structures parallel to the UN; however, none has the power or decision-making capacity that exists in the Security Council. Although the regional character lends slightly more homogeneity to the membership of these organizations, there remains a broad range of political and social structures in their member states. Membership in these organizations has not significantly affected the sovereignty of these states.

At its creation in 1963, the OAU placed a premium on sovereignty, territorial integrity, and noninterference in the internal affairs of member states.[6] This legacy of nonintervention largely persisted for the first three decades of the organization's existence. The end of the Cold War provided the impetus for the OAU to revitalize itself, not least because of the escalation of intrastate conflicts on the African Continent and the increasing need for greater responsiveness to these issues at the subregional and regional levels. The adoption of the Mechanism for Conflict Prevention, Management, and Resolution in 1993 at the Summit in Cairo was an important step in the process of the OAU redefining itself,[7] which culminated in the AU succeeding the OAU in 2002. Whereas the primary purpose of the AU is the promotion of accelerated socioeconomic integration of the continent, which will lead to greater unity and solidarity among African countries and peoples, its constitutive documents also stress that the promotion of peace, security, and stability on the African continent is a prerequisite for the implementation of the development and integration agenda of the AU.[8]

The second group of organizations includes those whose primary purpose had been for collective self-defense but which have potential for peacekeeping

[5] At the time of recognition of the Arab League as a regional body, a resolution was passed by the General Assembly (A/RES/477, 1950) that gave broad interpretation to the term *regional*. This interpretation considered not only geographic dimensions but also the community and affinity of traditions and interests of the members of regional organizations: United Nations (1950). A/RES/477(V), New York: General Assembly.

[6] Articles II and III, Charter of the Organization of African Unity, 25 May 1963, reprinted in *International Legal Materials*, 2(4), 1963, 767–778. See also www.africa-union.org.

[7] Berman, Eric, & Sams, Katie (2000). *Peacekeeping in Africa: Capabilities and Culpabilities* (New York: United Nations Institute for Disarmament Research [UNIDIR]), pp. 61–74.

[8] African Union – Constitutive Act 2000; see Article 3; available at www.africa-union.org/root/au/AboutAU/Constitutive_Act_en.htm.

in the post–Cold War world. Of these organizations, the North Atlantic Treaty Organization (NATO) and the Western European Union (WEU) existed during the Cold War; additionally, there is the Commonwealth of Independent States (CIS), particularly those members who agreed to the Tashkent Agreement.[9] At the time of their establishment, there was a debate about how far both the WEU and NATO were to be seen as regional organizations or solely as organizations for collective self-defense. For the WEU, this issue was raised when the Brussels Treaty was ratified in 1948, with the prevailing view being that the WEU should be based primarily on the collective-defense provision of Article 51 of the UN Charter rather than Article 52 as a regional organization.[10] Similarly, it was agreed that the primary purpose of NATO was to ensure the collective self-defense of its member states, as countries having common interests in the North Atlantic area, while also reaffirming their existing obligations for the maintenance of peace and the settlement of disputes among them.[11]

The third group of organizations encompasses regional and subregional groups and regional arrangements that were developed initially for facilitating greater economic cooperation but which have since developed varying degrees of operational capability in the peace and security area. These include *inter alia* the European Union (EU), Economic Community of West African States (ECOWAS), Inter-governmental Authority on Development (IGAD), and Southern African Development Community (SADC).

The fourth category refers to localized groupings, or "neighborhoods," that are emerging with regard to a particular conflict or dispute – for example, the Mano River Union, the Economic Community for the Great Lakes (CEPGL), and the Great Lakes Conference. These neighborhoods have been encouraged and legitimized by Security Council resolutions[12] to play a more active role in conflict prevention within their locales. Although these neighborhoods have yet to be institutionalized, they provide the possibility of an important forum for discussion on a number of cross-border issues, including arms-trafficking

9 "Agreement on the Principles and Procedures for the Implementation of the Treaty on Conventional Armed Forces in Europe," Tashkent, 15 May 1992. The parties were the Republics of Azerbaijan, Armenia, Belarus, Kazakhstan, Georgia, and Moldova; the Russian Federation; and Ukraine, as states successors of the USSR in regard to the Treaty on Conventional Armed Forces in Europe.

10 Roper, *The Contribution of Regional Organizations*, see note 5, p. 257.

11 Ibid., p. 258, citing Escott, Reid (1977). *Time of Fear and Hope: The Making of the North Atlantic Treaty 1947–1949* (Toronto: McClelland & Stewart).

12 With regard to the Great Lakes Conference, see *inter alia* United Nations (2001). S/RES/1341, OP 26 (New York: Security Council), which calls for the holding of a Great Lakes Conference.

and exploitation of natural resources, which have an impact on the escalation of conflicts.

Evolving Roles and Responsibilities. There is growing consensus that regional action as a matter of decentralization, delegation, and cooperation with UN efforts would not only lighten the burden of the Security Council but also contribute to a deeper sense of participation, consensus, and democratization in international affairs. This is the case even though under the UN Charter, the Security Council has primary responsibility for maintaining international peace and security.[13] The UN Charter recognizes in Chapter VIII that regional arrangements play an important role in maintaining peace and security, provided that their activities are in keeping with the purposes and principles of the UN Charter and that the Security Council is kept fully appraised of activities contemplated or undertaken. Article 52 of the UN Charter allows states to achieve the peaceful settlement of "local disputes" through regional arrangements or agencies before referring them to the Security Council. It has been an early and persistent belief that disputes and threats to peace involving states within a region should be addressed initially by regional bodies.[14] The framers of the UN Charter envisaged that the Security Council should be a forum of last resort when states were unable to resolve local conflicts among them through the peaceful means listed in Chapter VI or through regional arrangements.[15] The authority of regional arrangements and agencies under Chapter VIII is limited to the peaceful settlement of local disputes. The Security Council, however, is encouraged in Article 53(1) "where appropriate [to] utilize regional arrangements or agencies for enforcement action under its authority."[16] At the same time, however, "no enforcement action shall be taken under regional arrangements or by regional agencies without the authorization of the Security Council."[17]

The geopolitical reality concerning relations and coordination between the UN and regional arrangements have rarely followed the parameters set forth in the UN Charter. The UN Charter envisages a hierarchy such that the Security Council has primary responsibility for maintaining international

[13] See, generally, United Nations (1992). "Agenda for Peace," A/47/277-S/24111 (New York: General Assembly, Security Council), June 17.

[14] Schacter, Oscar (1991). "Authorized Uses of Force by the United Nations and Regional Organizations," in Damrosh & Scheffer (eds.) (1992), *Law and Force in the New International Order* (Boulder, CO: Westview Press), pp. 65–110.

[15] Goodrich, E. Hambro, & A. Simons (1969). *Charter of the United Nations* (New York: Columbia University Press), pp. 360–364.

[16] Article 53 of the UN Charter.

[17] Ibid.

peace and security and regional arrangements serve global interests as set forth by the Security Council. During the Cold War, American- and Soviet-led alliances generally circumvented the UN. At the beginning of the twenty-first century, although the UN is still not a critical player where the national security interests and concerns of the permanent five members of the Security Council are at stake, the quest for legitimacy by regional arrangements has required deference – sometimes belated – to the Security Council, particularly by the major powers that participate in such arrangements.

Following a series of high-level meetings between the UN and regional and other intergovernmental organizations from 1994 to 2005, there was a more concerted effort to clarify the division of responsibilities between the UN and regional arrangements and thus to establish more clearly defined partnerships.[18] The establishment of a partnership depends on the establishment of closer cooperation with the Security Council and regional organizations that reflects the comparative advantage of each organization. At the same time, what has become particularly relevant to legitimacy is that the Security Council has the primary responsibility for maintaining international peace and security.

Operational Record of Regional Arrangements: Scope of Involvement

The section below reviews the experience of regional arrangements in West Africa, the former Yugoslavia, and East and Central Africa.

Role of the ECOWAS: Liberia and Sierra Leone. In the West Africa subregion, the ECOWAS has taken the lead both diplomatically and militarily in responding to crises. Implicit in this development was the recognition that neither the OAU nor the wider international community could summon the political will to respond meaningfully to armed conflict in West Africa. Seeking to fill the void, the ECOWAS has deployed several sizeable peacekeeping operations – first in Liberia (1990), then in Sierra Leone (1997), Guinea-Bissau (1998), and more recently in Cote D'Ivoire (2002). In the process of fulfilling its new responsibilities, the ECOWAS underwent a significant transformation from its inception as an arrangement established in 1975 with primarily economic functions.[19]

[18] See Report of the Secretary-General (2006). "A Regional–Global Security Partnership: Challenges and Opportunities," S/2006/590, July 28.

[19] Berman, Eric, & Sams, Katie (2000). *Peacekeeping in Africa: Capabilities and Culpabilities* (New York: UN Institute for Disarmament Research [UNIDIR]).

The ECOWAS heads of state agreed at their 1978 summit to modify the organization's treaty to incorporate collective security provisions, based on the understanding that economic integration could no longer be detached from larger political and security concerns.[20] However, the Protocol on Non-aggression did not address aggression coming from states outside the region or the problem of civil conflicts taking place wholly within signatory states.[21] Consequently, in 1981, another protocol on mutual defense was adopted, under which member states agreed to provide support and mutual defense in case of *inter alia* "internal armed conflict within any Member State engineered and supported actively from outside likely to endanger the security and peace in the entire Community."[22] Despite the existence of this framework, the defense pact was not made operational at the military level until 1990 when the ECOWAS Ceasefire Monitoring Group (ECOMOG) intervened in Liberia.

Following the incursion into Liberia of rebel forces led by Charles Taylor in 1989 and the military stalemate that transpired between rebel forces and remnants of President Doe's military forces thereafter, regional actors from West Africa made unsuccessful attempts to place the Liberian crisis on the international agenda. Despite its historical links with Liberia, the United States refused to intervene on the basis that the disintegration of Liberia was an internal matter and counseled against armed intervention undertaken without the consent of the parties.[23] The UN Security Council also declined to have the matter set on its agenda, in part because many of its members shared the U.S. position that Africans should solve the problem. Moreover, the two African members of the Security Council, Ethiopia and Zaire, resisted

[20] Sesay, Max Ahmadu (1995). "Collective Security or Collective Disaster? Regional Peacekeeping in West Africa," *Security Dialogue*, 26(2), 205–222; see also Wippman, David (1993). "Enforcing the Peace: ECOWAS and the Liberian Civil War," in Lori Damrosh (ed.), *Enforcing Restraint: Collective Intervention in Internal Conflicts* (Washington, DC: Brookings Institution Press), pp. 157–203; Vogt, Margaret (ed.) (1993). *The Liberian Crisis and ECOMOG: A Bold Attempt at Regional Peacekeeping* (Lagos: Gabumo Press); Berman, Eric, & Sams, Katie (2000). *Peacekeeping in Africa: Capabilities and Culpabilities* (New York: UNIDIR); Olonisakin, Funmi (2000). *Reinventing Peacekeeping in Africa: Conceptual and Legal Issues in ECOMOG Operations* (Leiden, the Netherlands: Kluwer Law International).

[21] Economic Community of West African States (1978). "Protocol of Non-aggression," done at Lagos, April 22; available at www.ecowas.int.

[22] Economic Community of West African States (1991). "Protocol Relating to Mutual Assistance in Defence," done at Freetown, May 29; available at www.ecowas.int.

[23] The United States also had strong reservations about the warring factions and the leadership that was claiming power: Charles Taylor (NPFL) and Prince Johnson (INPFL). Moreover, the United States had in the late 1980s been increasingly concerned by the human-rights record and the corruption of President Doe's regime.

Security Council involvement in Liberia because they wished to avoid creating a precedent that might someday apply to them.[24]

As civil war engulfed the whole of Liberia and it became apparent that neither the United States nor the UN was willing to intervene directly to stop the fighting, the ECOWAS heads of state took action to halt the rapid disintegration of one of their number. Initial involvement was limited to a mediation role; however, it was soon apparent that more forcible action was required to prevent the continuing massacre of civilians, including women and children; to protect foreign nationals; and to maintain international peace and security in the region. The ECOWAS therefore established ECOMOG, the aim of which was to maintain peace, restore law and order, and ensure respect for the ceasefire.[25] The initial deployment from five ECOWAS countries consisted of approximately three thousand troops. Within days of their arrival in Monrovia, ECOMOG was on the offensive against the rebel faction led by Charles Taylor. However, Taylor's refusal to accept ECOMOG's peacekeeping role and his continued attacks on the regional force led to (1) a change in the force's mandate from peacekeeping to peace enforcement, and (2) the force adopting a "defensive offensive posture."[26] ECOMOG's combative posture continued in varying degrees throughout its seven-year mission in Liberia.[27]

The ECOWAS experience in Liberia suggests that if regional organizations can muster the necessary political will – spurred perhaps by massive cross-border refugee flows or threats to regional stability – then the obstacles to regional action are surmountable. Like many other regional organizations, ECOWAS had no history of collective military action, and its institutions and decision-making procedures were not designed for such action. However, on a more or less ad hoc basis, ECOWAS adapted itself to the needs of the moment.[28] Significantly, its ability to mount and sustain a large-scale military operation contributed to ECOWAS's credibility as an effective regional–subregional organization, despite criticisms about human-rights abuses.[29]

[24] See Wippman (1993), see note 20, p. 165.

[25] Economic Community of West African States (1990). "Final Communique of the First Session of the Community Standing Mediation Committee," Banjul, Republic of Gambia: ECOWAS, August 6–7.

[26] Berman & Sams (2000), see note 19, pp. 75–124.

[27] The Liberian civil war ended in 1997, following the holding of elections and the selection of Charles Taylor as President of the Republic.

[28] Wippman (1993), see note 20.

[29] See "Assessment of ECOMOG's Liberia Intervention," in *Human Rights Watch World Reports*, 5(6), 1993; see "Sierra Leone Getting Away with Murder, Mutilation, Rape: New Testimony from Sierra Leone," *Human Rights Watch World Reports*, 11(3A), 1999.

The ECOWAS experience in Sierra Leone, especially in the aftermath of the coup in 1997, built upon its experience from Liberia.. West African involvement in Sierra Leone in 1997, in support of restoring the elected Kabbah government, was initiated by Nigeria. In the absence of an institutionalised mechanism in ECOWAS, Nigeria took military action first and sought approval afterwards. ECOWAS authorization was given three months after the Nigerian intervention. Even then it was limited to extending the scope of ECOMOG's activity to Sierra Leone to assist in creating the conducive atmosphere that would ensure the early reinstatement of the legitimate Government of Sierra Leone.[30]

ECOWAS actions in Sierra Leone, to a large extent, were aimed at forestalling what were perceived as Nigeria's hegemonic aspirations. However, it soon became clear that rebel groups in Sierra Leone were not negotiating in good faith, requiring ECOMOG to take necessary military actions to help restore the Kabbah government with substantial external assistance. This proved to be an extremely protracted process, especially in the face of ECOMOG's operational difficulties and financial constraints, as well as the lack of a clear ECOWAS strategy.[31]

At the international level, the Security Council's response in October 1997 to the unfolding crisis in Sierra Leone was to impose an embargo on the sale or supply of petroleum products and arms, as well as related materiel, to Sierra Leone and to authorize the ECOWAS to ensure its implementation.[32] A small observer mission was established in Sierra Leone in June 1998 under UN auspices.[33] In view of logistical and financial constraints, ECOMOG forces were re-hatted as UN "blue helmets," and the UN mission in Sierra Leone took on a more comprehensive mandate to cooperate with the government of Sierra Leone and other parties in the implementation of the Peace Agreement in June 1999.[34]

Although much of the ECOWAS's intervention in Liberia and Sierra Leone was conducted in the absence of an institutionalized framework, it propelled the ECOWAS to set up a mechanism to address crisis prevention,

[30] See Economic Community of West African States (1997). "Final Communique, Meeting of Ministers of Foreign Affairs of ECOWAS," Abuja: ECOWAS, August 28. See also United Nations (1997). S/1997/695, New York: Security Council, Annex 1, paragraph 25.

[31] Berman & Sams (2000), see note 19, pp. 125–128.

[32] United Nations (1997). S/RES/1132, New York: Security Council.

[33] UN Observer Mission in Sierra Leone (UNOMSIL), United Nations (1998). S/RES/1181, New York: Security Council, July 13.

[34] See United Nations (1999). "Eighth Report of the Secretary-General on the United Nations Observer Mission in Sierra Leone," S/1999/1003, New York: Security Council, September 28; United Nations (1999). S/RES/1270, New York: Security Council, October.

management, and resolution within the subregion. The purpose was to try and overcome a number of the problems concerning the ECOWAS's mode of deployment, force composition, command structure, and lack of involvement by all of the ECOWAS member states. Consensus among member states to have the ECOWAS develop "appropriate mechanisms for the timely prevention and resolution of intra- and inter-state conflicts" was apparent as early as 1993[35]; however, it was only discussed at the level of the ECOWAS authority in 1997. The proposed mechanism was adopted by the ECOWAS in 1999 in response to the unfolding developments in Sierra Leone and the need at the subregional level to address other such crises, including Guinea-Bissau, within a more structured framework.

European Security Arrangements: Responses in the Former Yugoslavia and Central Africa. The initial reluctance of the UN to take decisive action in response to the unravelling of the former Yugoslavia[36] was due as much to the prevailing view that it was a European problem and therefore should be handled by European institutions as to the principle of noninterference in the "internal matters" of a member state.[37] There also remained within the UN a Cold War attitude that it should not become entangled in European conflicts, for no other reason than that one side or the other would use its Security Council veto. Within Europe, there was paralysis and basic disagreement about the course of action to be pursued and the amount that European states were willing to pay to bring about an end to the fighting and reach a political settlement in the former Yugoslavia. Historical, cultural, ethnic, and religious ties, as well as contemporary disagreements about Western Europe's interest in Eastern and Southeastern Europe, produced these divergent perspectives.[38]

[35] Berman & Sams (2000), see note 19, p. 138.

[36] The former Socialist Federalist Republic of Yugoslavia was composed of six republics – Slovenia, Croatia, Serbia, Bosnia-Herzegovina, Montenegro, and Macedonia – and the two autonomous regions of Kosovo and Vojvodina. After the collapse of communism, secessionist tendencies became stronger and hostilities commenced when, in June 1991, Croatia and Slovenia declared their independence from Yugoslavia. The Serb-controlled federal government and the Yugoslav People's Army opposed the move and supported the Serbian militia in their struggle against Croatian and Slovenian authorities. The conflict was further aggravated when Bosnia-Herzegovina declared its independence in March 1992, an act supported by Bosnian Croats and Bosnian Muslims but violently opposed by Bosnian Serbs.

[37] Steinberg, James (1993). "International Involvement in the Yugoslavia Conflict," in Lori Damrosh (ed.), see note 20, pp. 27–75. See also Steinberg, James (1992). *The Role of European Institutions in Security after the Cold War: Some Lessons from Yugoslavia* (Santa Monica, CA: RAND), Note N-3445-FF.

[38] For a discussion of the historical roots of the conflict, see *inter alia* Malcolm, Noel (1994). *Bosnia: A Short History* (New York: Macmillan); Kaplan, Robert (1993). *Balkan Ghosts* (New York: St. Martin's Press).

The operational record of European regional arrangements in the Balkan crisis remains mixed. This is due in part to problems stemming from institutional weaknesses in each of the organizations that were all in the early stages of adapting to the post–Cold War era and the demands being placed on them. The CSCE in November 1990, seven months before fighting broke out, was at the beginning of a transformation process. CSCE members had agreed in the Charter of Paris[39] to establish permanent institutions for the organization, which had hitherto not existed. The focus of these bodies was human rights and democratization. Prior to the outbreak of fighting in Slovenia, the CSCE membership finally agreed to a crisis-response procedure that would allow for an emergency meeting of its members. CSCE's early involvement was limited to action supported by a consensus of all members, including Yugoslavia.[40] As a result of the Yugoslavian experience, the concept was elaborated to "consensus minus one."[41] In the face of Yugoslavia/Serbia's continued intransigence, the CSCE acted for the first time to suspend a member's participation.

The European Community (EC) and the CSCE were unable to resolve the Yugoslavia crisis within the framework of the Conference on Yugoslavia, chaired by Lord Carrington in 1991–1992. The UN Security Council remained inactive for three months despite the massive scale of bloodshed. In September 1991, the Security Council unanimously adopted Resolution 713, which expressed concern about the armed conflict in Yugoslavia and its consequences for neighboring countries and stated that "the continuation of this situation constitutes a threat to international peace and security." In its operative paragraph, Resolution 713 expressed support for the efforts of the EC and the CSCE and invited the UN Secretary-General to offer assistance. The majority of delegations in the Security Council still viewed the conflict in Yugoslavia as an internal one, except for its consequences for neighboring states.

The Yugoslavia crisis enhanced the CSCE's ability to respond to internal conflicts. Whereas the Moscow Declaration strengthened the tools available to the CSCE for human-rights enforcement,[42] at the Helsinki follow-up conference in July 1992, CSCE members took a number of steps mainly

[39] "Consensus minus one" decision making requires all delegates but one to support the decision. The individual dissenter – in this case, Yugoslavia – could not block the decision.

[40] Austria initiated the emergency mechanism on June 28, 1991, which provided for the holding of a special meeting of the CSCE at the request of one member, if that request received the support from twelve other member states. The purpose was to have Yugoslavia clarify its military intentions.

[41] Charter of Paris; available at www.osce.org/item/4047.html.

[42] In the Moscow Declaration (October 1991), CSCE leaders suggested that they were prepared to intervene to enforce a member nation's obligations to respect human rights, at least to

motivated by the Balkan crisis. The CSCE created the post of High Commissioner for National Minorities, which was charged with providing early warning of potential conflicts and early action to prevent the outbreak of conflicts; established a more extensive range of possibilities for conflict prevention and crisis management, including fact-finding and rapporteur missions and CSCE peacekeeping that could draw on the EC, NATO, and WEU and the peacekeeping mechanism of the Commonwealth of Independent States; and agreed to explore other ideas for conciliation and arbitration mechanisms.[43]

Despite the formalizing of the Maastricht Treaty in 1992 enshrining the principle of a common foreign and security policy for the EC states,[44] European security arrangements continued to be hampered in finding a solution to the Yugoslavia crisis. This was primarily because European actors remained largely paralyzed by fundamental disagreements over which course of action to pursue and what price they were prepared to pay to bring about an end to the fighting and a political settlement. The problem was exacerbated because serious domestic political problems with ethnic, religious, and national minorities colored some but not all of the European states' approach to the Yugoslavia crisis.[45]

Developments in Yugoslavia during this period also accelerated the evolution of two self-defense organizations: the WEU[46] and NATO; the WEU, however, remains very much on paper. The self-denying limitation against out-of-area actions and the military orientation of NATO forces toward defense of members' territory, rather than peacekeeping, had constrained NATO's initial ability to respond. Under the 1949 Washington treaty, the only formal

the extent of sending rapporteurs without the target government's consent. Commission on Security and Cooperation in Europe (1991); available at www.osce.org.

43 Commission on Security and Cooperation in Europe (1992). "Helsinki Document 1992: The Challenges of Change, Helsinki Summit Declaration"; available at www.osce.org.

44 The Maastricht Treaty is available at www.eurotreaties.com/maastrichtext.html.

45 France, Italy, Spain, and the United Kingdom all had, to varying degrees, problems with ethnic groups seeking greater autonomy or independence. In addressing the problem of Yugoslavia, the United Kingdom was mindful of the situation in Northern Ireland, which made it wary of other countries' intervening in internal ethnic or religious conflicts and also sensitized the government to the difficulty of imposing a solution through the use of military force. Steinberg, James (1993). "International Involvement in the Yugoslavia Conflict," in Lori Damrosh (ed.), see note 20.

46 Despite several innovations to operationalize, the WEU remains largely an organization on paper with no forces under its direct command. This is due in part to the division among its member states that the use of force through a European-only institution would contribute over the long run to decoupling the United States from Western European security. See Roper, John (1993). "A Wider Range of Tasks," in John Roper, Masashi Nishihara, Olara Otunnu, & Enid Schoettle (eds.), *Keeping the Peace in the Post–Cold War Era: Strengthening Multilateral Institutions*, Report to the Trilateral Commission, No. 43.

constraint on NATO members is the commitment to refrain from using force "in any manner inconsistent with the purposes of the United Nations."[47] The principal affirmative obligation of the NATO members to come to each others' assistance in the event of "an armed attack against one or more of them in Europe or North America"[48] was interpreted as restricting NATO involvement to matters concerning the territorial security of member states. Consequently, during the first year of the conflict, NATO allies consulted but took no action because the crisis did not appear to affect directly the security of its member states.

In the June 1992 Oslo Declaration, NATO leaders began to enlarge the scope of potential NATO action by noting that the "Alliance has the capacity to contribute to effective actions by the CSCE in line with its new and increased responsibilities for crisis management" and stating that "we are prepared to support, on a case by case basis in accordance with our own procedures, peacekeeping activities under the responsibility of the CSCE including by making available Alliance resources and expertise."[49] This NATO decision led almost immediately to the greater involvement of NATO in the Yugoslavia crisis. In July 1992, NATO agreed to send naval forces to the Adriatic to monitor compliance with trade sanctions against Serbia and Montenegro; that mission was expanded after the adoption of Security Council Resolution 787 on November 16 to include enforcing the arms embargo. At the request of the UN Secretary-General, NATO also contributed aircraft with built-in airborne early warning and control systems (AWACS) to monitor the no-fly zone established by Security Council Resolution 781. These initial measures by NATO were part of its evolution from a traditional posture of collective defense toward the broader scope of collective security. This embraces crisis management and peacekeeping operations under UN auspices, whether or not under NATO command. NATO's willingness to contribute to peacekeeping had been expressed on several occasions: to support on a case-by-case basis, in accordance with its own procedures, peacekeeping and other operations under the authority of the UN Security Council or the responsibility of the CSCE.[50] However, the 1994 and 1995 NATO air strikes were sporadic and did not have the effect of protecting the safe havens of Srebrenica or Zepa

47 North Atlantic Treaty Organization (1949). *North Atlantic Treaty*, Washington, DC: NATO, Article 1; available at www.nato.org.

48 Ibid., Article 5.

49 North Atlantic Treaty Organization (1992). "Final Communiqué," Ministerial Meeting of the North Atlantic Council in Oslo, June 4, paragraph 11; available at www.nato.org.

50 See Kriendler, John (1993). "NATO'S Changing Role: Opportunities and Constraints for Peacekeeping NATO Review," 41(3), 16–21; available at www.nato.int/docu/review/1993/9303–4.htm.

set up by the Security Council or of deterring Serbian aggression. It was only after concerted U.S. intervention and involvement in the Balkans after 1994, culminating in the signing of the Dayton Agreement in 1995, that the war in Bosnia and Herzegovina was brought to an end, marking a turning point in the Balkan crisis.[51]

Increasing involvement of European actors – France, Germany, and Austria – in the Balkans and specifically with regard to the situation in Kosovo became more evident in 1998. Following the refusal of Yugoslav President Slobodan Milosevic to accept the proposals negotiated in Rambouillet and to abide by the limitations agreed on by the Serb army and the Special Police Forces in Kosovo, NATO launched air strikes over the Federal Republic of Yugoslavia at the end of March 1999. NATO Secretary-General Javier Solana and many of the NATO member heads of state said that the air strikes were necessary "to prevent more human suffering and more repression and violence against the civilian population of Kosovo."[52] Despite the failure to seek Security Council sanctions due to the possibility of veto by Russia and China, the NATO action was largely defended by its member states on political and moral grounds. Following the suspension of NATO air strikes against the former Yugoslavia, the Security Council adopted Resolution 1244, which entrusted to the UN Secretary-General the task of establishing an international civilian administration in Kosovo, under which the people of Kosovo could enjoy substantial autonomy. The lack of clear mechanisms and institutions stymied European arrangements in resolving the crisis in the former Yugoslavia, and historical allegiances and ties of European actors to the Balkan players exacerbated matters. However, the role of the United States, as a player outside the European framework and as the remaining superpower, was critical in negotiating the Dayton Agreement and in providing a turning point in the cycle of violence that had continued largely unabated for four years. Moreover, although European security arrangements played a direct role in controlling and managing the process toward the Rambouillet agreement, especially with the development of a common European Security and Defense Policy (ESDP) within the framework of the EU, it nevertheless was limited

[51] The 1995 Dayton Agreement designated a High Representative (OHR) to oversee the implementation of civilian aspects of the Peace Agreement in Bosnia and Herzegovina on behalf of the International Community. OHR is also tasked with coordinating the activities of civilian organizations operating in the country, including the OSCE (to coordinate elections), the EU (reconstruction and development), the UN (civilian police), and the UN High Commissioner for Refugees (refugees); NATO was to provide ceasefire implementation and supervision.

[52] Press statement of Dr. Solana, March 23, 1999. Available at www.nato.int/ ocu/pr/1999/p99–040e.htm.

in its role to negotiations and political pressure in the absence of an accepted operational framework. Consequently, there was still a need to resort to NATO for peace support.

As a result of the Kosovo conflict, the Cologne European Council placed the "Petersberg tasks," referring to a range of crisis-management activities including peace-enforcement,[53] at the core of the common ESDP.[54] Whereas such action was aimed at enabling the EU to make decisions on the full range of conflict-prevention and crisis-management tasks, it ensured that the EU had "the capacity for autonomous action backed up by credible military forces, the means to decide to use them and a readiness to do so, in order to respond to international crises without prejudice to actions by NATO."[55] Moreover, under the Helsinki Headline Goal, the EU was to be "able by 2003, to deploy within sixty days and sustain for at least one year military forces of up to sixty thousand persons capable of the full range of Petersberg tasks." Simultaneously, a political-military structure was established in Brussels, composed of a Peace and Security Committee (PSC), a Military Committee, and a Military Staff. The purpose of this political-military structure is to enable the EU to plan at the strategic level and conduct Petersberg tasks. In the meantime, following an agreement in December 2002 between the EU and NATO, EU-led operations could be characterized by two types: EU-led operations with and without recourse to NATO assets and capabilities. Regarding the relationship with the UN, the Council of the EU has reiterated that "the efforts made [in the ESDP field] will enable Europeans to respond more effectively and more coherently to requests from leading organizations such as the UN."[56] In this regard, there is a growing sense within the EU that an increased role for it in crisis-management activities will contribute to the maintenance of international peace and security, which is still considered the primary purpose of the UN.

53 The Petersberg tasks include humanitarian and rescue operations, peacekeeping, and tasks of combat forces in crisis management, including peace enforcement. See EU (1997). "Amsterdam Treaty," Amsterdam: European Union, June, Article 17.2.

54 See European Council (1999). "Presidency Conclusion," Cologne: Cologne European Council, June 3 and 4; available at www.eurounion.org/legislat/Defense/esdpweb.htm or www.europarl.europa.eu/summits/kol1en.htm.

55 Ibid.

56 European Council (2000). "Presidency Conclusions," Nice: Nice European Council, December; General Affairs Council of the EU (2001). "EU-UN Cooperation in Conflict Prevention and Crisis Management," June 11. See also Council of the European Union (2003). "Agreement between the European Union and the United Nations Establishing a Framework for Cooperation in the Field of Crisis Management," Council of the European Union, September 11. See Tardy, Thierry (2003). "Limits and Opportunities of UN–EU Relations in Peace Operations: Implications for DPKO," External UN Study, Geneva Center for Security Policy, for a discussion of these issues.

During the course of 2003, the EU launched its first three operations: (1) the EU Police Mission (EUPM) in Bosnia and Herzegovina, which took over from the UN mission (UNMIBH) on January 1, 2003; (2) Operation Concordia in Macedonia, which took over from NATO operation Allied Harmony on March 31, 2003; and (3) Operation Artemis in the Democratic Republic of Congo (DRC), which was deployed from June 2003 to September 1, 2003, with France as the lead nation. Whereas EUPM and Operation Concordia were deployed on the basis of an invitation by the respective hosts and without a formal UN mandate, Operation Artemis was created following Security Council Resolution 1484 (2003).

The Security Council established the UN Operation in the Congo (MONUC) in 1999 to provide assistance to the various parties in implementing political agreements for the withdrawal of foreign forces. MONUC deployed to a number of sectors in the DRC. This led to a call for the expansion of MONUC's presence into northeastern DRC, particularly the Ituri region. The province had suffered years of conflict because fighting among ethnic militias had been exacerbated by the intervention of the neighboring states, Rwanda and Uganda. In April 2003, the long-awaited Ituri Interim Administration (IIA) was established, facilitating the withdrawal of Ugandan forces from the province. However, their departure on May 6 created a security vacuum that MONUC was unable to fill despite reinforcement of the UN presence in Bunia by the MONUC reserve of seven hundred Uruguayan troops.[57] In view of MONUC's light military capacity (i.e., primarily an observer presence at this stage), an enhanced military capacity was believed necessary to facilitate the restoration of security to Bunia and its environs until MONUC was in a position to deploy troops to the area. On May 15, 2003, in a letter addressed to the President of the Security Council, the UN Secretary-General called for "the rapid deployment to Bunia of a highly trained and well-equipped multinational force, under the lead of a Member State, to provide security at the airport as well as to other vital installations in the town and to protect the civilian population."[58] Subsequently, the UN Secretary-General directly approached President Jacques Chirac to request French support. This resulted in the deployment of an EU-led Interim Emergency Multinational Force (IEMF) under French operational command, following the adoption of a Joint Action by the Council of the EU on June 5.[59]

[57] Second special report of the Secretary-General (2003). S/2003/566, May 27.

[58] S/2003/574, May 28, 2003.

[59] Joint Action on EU military operation in DRC: 2003/423/CFSP, June 5, 2003; available at www.consilium.eu.int.

The mandate of Operation Artemis derived from UN Security Council Resolution 1484 of May 30, which authorized the IEMF "to contribute to the stabilization of security conditions and the improvement of the humanitarian situation in Bunia, to ensure the protection of the airport, internally displaced persons in the camps in Bunia, and if the situation requires it, to contribute to the safety of the civilian population, UN personnel and the humanitarian presence in the town."[60] Because the resolution was passed under Chapter VII of the UN Charter, Operation Artemis was authorized to use force in carrying out its mandate. Operation Artemis deployed to Bunia in June 2003 and reached its full strength of 1,400 troops on July 6. Through its robust presence, it brought a measure of security to the area and facilitated a cessation of hostilities among many of the Ituri armed groups. In September 2003, Operation Artemis withdrew and was replaced by an expanded MONUC presence.[61] As a short-term bridging operation and the first EU peacekeeping mission in Africa, Artemis was a success. It restored order in Bunia town, secured its airport, and facilitated the deployment of a full brigade by MONUC to take over the situation.

Unlike Operation Concordia, which made use of a Supreme Headquarters for Allied Forces in Europe (SHAPE) planning and command capabilities, Operation Artemis was conducted without recourse to NATO assets and was the first "autonomous" EU military operation. It also reflected a strengthened interinstitutional operational relationship between the EU and the UN, particularly because the EU was able to rapidly deploy forces to an area of Central Africa on an emergency basis. Significantly, the process for the authorization and deployment of Operation Artemis required a Security Council resolution/mandate prior to any action being taken by the Council of the EU.

A similar hierarchy of actions ensued for the deployment of the European Union Force (EUFOR) to the DRC in 2006 to support MONUC with a rapid-reaction reinforcement capability for the presidential elections in the DRC. The deployment of EUFOR in Kinshasa in support of MONUC took place at a critical juncture in the transitional process, which had been underway in the country since the signing of the Global and All-Inclusive Peace Agreement in 2002. As the polling approached, MONUC's seventeen thousand troops – deployed across a country the size of Western Europe – faced the risk of being overstretched as they strove to support the Congolese authorities' efforts to ensure secure conditions for the elections. With this in mind, the UN initiated

60 United Nations (2003). SC/Res/1484 OP 1.

61 United Nations (2003). SC/Res/1493 increased MONUC's military strength to 10,800 personnel, as requested in the report of the Secretary-General, and approved the concept of operations for the Ituri brigade.

informal discussions with EU counterparts on the possible deployment of a force to support MONUC in November 2005. Subsequently, on December 27, 2005, the UN formally requested the EU to consider deploying a force to provide MONUC with a rapid-reaction capability for the electoral period. The EU formally conveyed its agreement to the request on March 28, 2006.[62] The Security Council authorized the deployment of EUFOR DRC in Resolution 1671(2006) on April 25. Following the adoption of the Joint Action by the European Council[63] in August 2006, a 1,200-strong EUFOR was deployed as a temporary reinforcement to MONUC until December and played a significant role in securing the historic electoral process.

During its deployment, EUFOR complemented the efforts of MONUC by adding extra capacity and flexibility in addressing security challenges and any potential escalation of violence. With a robust posture and visible presence, including air assets, EUFOR was also an essential element in the overall deterrence provided by MONUC's military and police forces on the ground. Its deployment was an important additional demonstration of the EU's commitment to ensuring the successful conduct of the elections. Joint MONUC–EUFOR actions were particularly effective when tensions arose in Kinshasa shortly before the announcement of the provisional results of the presidential election on August 20, 2006. Clashes occurred between the security guards of President Kabila and then–Vice President Jean-Pierre Bemba, who were contesting the second presidential round scheduled for October. In response, EUFOR personnel, closely coordinated with MONUC, were swiftly dispatched, while UN, EU, and EU member-state officials worked closely at headquarters level and in Kinshasa, intervening with the Congolese parties to obtain an immediate resolution of the situation. As a result, order was restored and the electoral process remained on track.[64]

The AU Role in Sudan. In 2004 and 2005, while progress was being made in the north–south conflict in Sudan, a violent conflict and humanitarian crisis that had been unfolding since February 2003 took a turn for the worse as a group called the Darfur Liberation Front took up arms against the Sudanese

[62] S/2006/219. Letter dated April 12, 2006 from the Secretary-General addressed to the President of the Security Council enclosing the December 27, 2005 (Annex 1) and the response of March 28, 2006 (Annex 2).

[63] Joint Action on EU military operation in DRC: 2006/319/CFSP, April 27, 2006; available at www.consilium.eu.int.

[64] See "Twenty-Second Report of the Secretary-General on the United Nations Organization Mission in the Democratic Republic of the Congo" (2006). S/2006/759, September 21. See also "Twenty-Third Report of the Secretary-General on the United Nations Organization Mission in the Democratic Republic of the Congo" (2007). S/2007/156, March 20.

government to protest many years of political and economic marginalization. In March 2003, as the Sudan Liberation Movement Army, the Darfur Liberation Front announced the launch of an armed rebellion against the Sudanese government and was soon joined by other groups, including the Justice and Equality Movement and the National Movement for Reform and Development. The government of Sudan reacted by mobilizing the Arab militia known as the "Janjaweed." Disputes over access and distribution to resources (i.e., land and/or livestock) contributed to the escalation of the conflict, and tens of thousands were killed in fighting or died from hunger and disease in Darfur. Negotiations led by the AU produced the N'djamena Humanitarian Ceasefire Agreement on April 8, 2004, between the government of Sudan and the two rebel movements.[65] This was followed on May 28, 2004, by the Addis Ababa Agreement that paved the way for the AU to play a specific role in Darfur. The first step was to deploy military observers to the field to monitor the ceasefire agreement, accompanied and supported by a small protection force. Alleged violations were reported to a Ceasefire Monitoring Commission consisting of representatives of the parties and international support staff and observers. The first contingents of the African Mission in Sudan (AMIS) arrived in the region in early June 2004 and, by October, it included 465 personnel from ten African countries. The UN Security Council adopted a number of resolutions on the situation in Darfur, including Resolution 1556 in July 2004, which welcomed a joint communiqué between the government of Sudan and UN Secretary-General Kofi Annan. In September 2004, the Security Council established an International Commission of Inquiry to determine whether genocide was being committed in Darfur. In its January 2005 report, the Commission concluded that the government had not pursued a policy of genocide, although "in some instances individuals . . . may commit acts with genocidal intent. Whether this was the case in Darfur, however, is a determination that only a competent court can make on a case-by-case basis."[66] The report added that the crimes against humanity and war crimes that were committed may be "no less serious or heinous than genocide."

Following reports of continuing attacks on civilians and restrictions on the movement of humanitarian workers, it soon became clear that the monitors, troops, and humanitarian components on the ground were facing a worsening situation, which prompted the AU PSC on October 20, 2004, to expand the AMIS force to 3,320, including a civilian-police component of

[65] Available at www.amis-sudan.org/agreements.html.

[66] International Commission of Inquiry (2005). "Report of Then International Commission of Inquiry on Darfur to the United Nations, Secretary-General," January 5, paragraph 641.

815, and to give it a stronger mandate.[67] The largest troop-contributing countries were Rwanda, Nigeria, and South Africa, with additional contributions by Senegal, Gambia, and Kenya. The expanded AMIS was based on plans drawn up in August with extensive assistance from the UN. Its new mandate included help to create "a secure environment for the delivery of humanitarian relief and beyond that, the return of IDPs [internally displaced persons] and refugees to their homes." The mission was also tasked with protecting civilians "under imminent threat and in the immediate vicinity" within the limits of its resources and capabilities. It was authorized to deploy proactively to areas where trouble was expected, "to deter armed groups from committing hostile acts against the population," and not just in response to reports of violations. The option of a mixed UN–AU protection force was considered at the time, but AU determination to score a success in Darfur dovetailed with the government of Sudan's opposition to non-African troops and the unwillingness of Western countries to make the necessary material and political commitments. In September 2004, the UN Security Council passed Resolution 1564, which gave Sudan the ultimatum of accepting an expanded AU force or facing sanctions on its oil industry. The resolution also authorized AMIS to "closely and continuously liaise and coordinate . . . at all levels" its work with the UN Mission in Sudan (UNMIS). Although the AU had hoped to have three thousand additional troops in place in the region in November, it was unable to do so because of continuing difficulties with a lack of money and necessary logistics.

By October 2005, there was an alarming deterioration in the security situation of all three Darfur states. The high level of banditry and violence seemed to take on a more overtly political character. Attacks and counterattacks by government forces, government-aligned militias, and the armed rebel groups led to numerous deaths, human-rights violations, sexual violence, abducted children, and newly created internally displaced persons (IDPs). As disturbing were the attacks by the Janjaweed against government forces and the growing split within the Sudan Liberation Movement. The continuation of this trend was particularly worrisome; the UN Secretary-General reported in November 2005 that "the looming threat of complete lawlessness and anarchy draws nearer, particularly in western Darfur, as warlords, bandits and militia groups grow aggressive."[68]

In the meantime, although AMIS pursued its mandate in 2005 to act robustly to provide security and protect civilians, it continued to have

[67] This larger force became what is now known as AMIS II and, on April 28, 2005, was further expanded to a total of 6,171 with the proportion of Civilian Police raised to 1,560.

[68] United Nations, Monthly Report of the Secretary-General on Darfur, Sudan S/2005/719, November 16, 2005.

difficulties and was itself the target of attacks during the year. In September–October, five AU peacekeepers were killed, three were wounded, and forty were taken hostage. As hostilities toward AU peacekeepers became more common, humanitarian-aid agencies began to refuse to travel with AU personnel, stating that the mere presence of the peacekeepers could draw fire. This resulted in another partial suspension of aid to the region by the UN. Maximizing the capabilities and capacity of AMIS to respond to the widespread and systematic violence continued to be an important preoccupation, as the EU, the UN, and bilateral donors tried to address the equipment shortages combined with intelligence and communication problems that were an obstacle to AMIS's operational efficiency.

Progress in the AU-led mediation efforts on a Darfur political process continued at a halting pace, although the efforts of South African President Mbeki and former Nigerian President Obasanjo were critical to ensuring that Sudanese President Bashir and the Darfur rebel groups remained engaged in the process. In the meantime, the UNMIS continued to provide assistance to promote a settlement to the conflict by providing good offices, substantive expertise, and logistical support to the AU mediation and the participants attending the talks in Abuja in Nigeria. In July 2005, the Abuja Declaration of Principles was signed to shape future negotiations on unity, religion, power-sharing, wealth-sharing, security arrangements, and land use and ownership. However, the follow-up rounds of Abuja talks were stymied by splits and internal power struggles within participating rebel groups. Nevertheless, the talks culminated in the signing of the Darfur Peace Agreement (DPA) in Abuja on May 5, 2006. It soon became apparent that serious problems existed not only with the Sudanese government's vision for implementation of the agreement but also among Darfur's other rebel groups, which were given a grace period until May 31 to sign the DPA but failed to do so.

On January 10, 2006, the AU PSC decided, in principle, to hand over the operation to the UN. The Security Council generally welcomed the decision and requested that the Secretary-General embark on contingency planning in consultation with the AU, the Government of National Unity, and other stakeholders.[69] The AU PSC reiterated its position in March and extended the AMIS mandate until September 30, 2006, while stressing that the transition would require the consent of the Sudanese government and the continued African character of the mission. A Security Council mission visited Sudan and Chad in June to boost efforts to implement the DPA and pave the way

[69] See Statement by the President of the UN Security Council on the situation in Sudan S/PRST/2006/5, February 3, 2006.

for the transition. The Security Council visit was followed by a joint UN–AU technical-assessment team led by the UN/DPKO Under-Secretary-General Jean Marie Guéhenno and AU Commissioner Said Djinnit. The Security Council and the assessment team concluded that AMIS should hand over to a larger, more robust multidimensional UN operation and that AMIS should be strengthened in the interim.[70] Sudanese President Omar al-Bashir rejected the proposed transition, arguing that the AU had no right to hand over its mission, especially because the DPA had deliberately omitted such a reference.

Nevertheless, based on recommendations presented by the UN Secretary-General on August 31, 2006, the Security Council adopted Resolution 1706, expanding the mandate of UNMIS to include support for implementation of the DPA and the N'djamena Agreement and to use all necessary means to protect civilians. The resolution also called for the UN to support AMIS, pending the transition to a UN force. The government of Sudan forcefully rejected the deployment, reiterated its threats to wage a holy jihad on any UN troops deployed to Darfur, and demanded that the AU leave Darfur at the expiration of its mandate on September 30, 2006. This failure by the Security Council to adopt a resolution on the proposed UN peacekeeping force of twenty thousand for Darfur resulted in the AU extending AMIS's mandate until December 31, 2006, and then again until June 30, 2007.

In view of the reservations of the Sudanese government to a UN-led mission in Darfur, the UN embarked on an alternative approach to begin stabilizing the region through the phased strengthening of AMIS. The first phase of UN augmentation – the Light Support Package – assisted AMIS during the second half of 2006 in establishing an integral command-and-control structure and increased the effectiveness of AU operations. The second phase – the Heavy Support Package – was designed not only to add to military and police personnel but also to support AMIS in more substantive areas such as humanitarian liaison, public information, and civil affairs, as well as to assist in the Darfur peacekeeping process.

In the meantime, in mid-November 2006, a meeting convened by the UN Secretary-General in Addis Ababa led to an agreement "in principle" on a hybrid UN–AU force. This was confirmed at an AU PSC meeting in December, as part of a three-phase process: UN light support to AMIS, followed by a larger support package, and eventual transition to a hybrid force.

[70] See United Nations (2006). "Report of the Security Council Mission to the Sudan and Chad, June 4–10, 2006," of June 22, S/2006/433; and United Nations (2006). "Report of the Secretary-General to the Security Council on Darfur," July 28, S/2006/591.

At the end of December 2006, the Sudanese government finally agreed to the hybrid force but with continuing reservations about size and command-and-control arrangements. The official plan for joint UN–AU peacekeeping operations in the region was officially sanctioned on July 31, 2007, when the Security Council unanimously adopted Resolution 1769, authorizing the establishment of the UN–AU hybrid peacekeeping mission in Darfur (UNAMID) under Chapter VII of the UN Charter for an initial period of twelve months. Establishing a peacekeeping operation under joint UN–AU command translated into the following basic elements: joint decision making by the UN Secretary-General and the AU chairperson about the appointment of the special representative and force commander, operational command at the field level by the force commander, and joint reporting to the AU PSC and the UN Security Council. By identifying troop contributors for UNAMID, the UN and AU focused on ensuring that they had the required capabilities to perform the mandated tasks and can deploy in a timely manner. The two organizations also sought to assemble a balanced force that would unquestionably meet the "African character" criterion referred to in Resolution 1769, whose impartiality would be beyond reproach. Additionally, the AU and the UN agreed on the appointment of Rudolphe Adada and General Martin Luther Agwai as the joint special representative and force commander, respectively, of the hybrid UN–AU peacekeeping force.

Serious difficulties with the swift and effective deployment of peacekeepers emerged in the second half of 2007, not least concerning the Sudanese government's objection to certain non-African units planned for the force, raising obstacles concerning the identification of the land that UNAMID could use, paralyzing custom clearances, and continuing to withhold permission for the mission to conduct night flights, which is a fundamental prerequisite to the effective functioning of UNAMID. These challenges, along with others, persisted until the end of 2007. By the time of transfer of authority on December 31, 2007, UNAMID was short of its full capacity with slightly more than 9,000 personnel in uniform on the ground in Darfur, including approximately 6,800 contingent military personnel, more than 650 staff officers or military observers, and more than 1,500 law-enforcement personnel, including units from Bangladesh, China, Gambia, Kenya, Nigeria, Rwanda, and South Africa.

Legitimacy, Cooperation, and Effectiveness

The escalation of intrastate conflicts and their increasing complexity in the aftermath of the Cold War have often resulted in the devolution of the UN

Security Council's responsibility, whether officially or unofficially, to regional arrangements. More often than not, regional arrangements – because of their proximity to the conflict – have become more active in developing solutions to address a situation. Enhancing strategic partnerships with multilateral and regional organizations also has become an important priority for the burden-sharing of peacekeeping. These regional arrangements, although reinforcing the validity of Chapter VIII of the UN Charter, undermine the primacy of the UN Security Council in international security and peacekeeping operations.

There is growing consensus among member states that Security Council authorization is necessary to provide legitimacy for military intervention whether or not the UN is actually engaged in the task. Consequently, there is a growing trend among some nations to disassociate from military interventions that do not have the endorsement of the Security Council, such as actions taken by member states that may constitute a "coalition of the willing." The conferral of legitimacy by the Security Council comes at a price, however, because it requires the UN to better coordinate and manage partnerships with regional organizations.

Effective collaboration and task-sharing between the UN and regional arrangements require an understanding of the possibilities and limitations of each, as well as the development of principles, rules, and procedures to govern such partnerships.[71] In practice, despite persistent calls for a new division of labor between the UN and regional organizations – under which the regional arrangement carries the main burden while a small UN operation supports and verifies that it is functioning in a manner consistent with positions adopted by the Security Council – it has been difficult to develop and adhere to a criterion that would be applicable to every occasion. The legitimacy of a regional organization in undertaking peacekeeping and security actions also depends on whether it has the capacity to implement it. Among the factors to be considered are the institutional capacity of regional arrangements to make

[71] Among those identified in United Nations (1995). "Supplement to an Agenda for Peace," A/50/60-S/1995/1, New York: General Assembly, Security Council, paragraph 88, are (a) Agreed mechanisms for consultation should be established, but need not be formal; (b) The primacy of the United Nations, as set out in the UN Charter, must be respected. In particular, regional organizations should not enter into arrangements that assume a level of United Nations support not yet submitted to or approved by its member states. This is an area where close and early consultation is of great importance; (c) The division of labor must be clearly defined and agreed in order to avoid overlap and institutional rivalry where the United Nations and a regional organization are both working on the same conflict. In such cases, it is also particularly important to avoid a multiplicity of mediators; (d) Consistency by members of regional organizations who are also member states of the United Nations is needed in dealing with a common problem of interest to both organizations; for example, standards for peacekeeping operations.

decisions and implement them; whether the arrangements can harness the necessary financial, human, and military resources to effectively conduct the operation; and the acceptability of regional arrangements by the parties to the conflict or the impartiality and vested interests of the members of the regional arrangement with regard to the conflict. Consequently, a broad range of mechanisms for cooperation between the UN and regional organizations has emerged within the realm of peace and security, including peacemaking and preventive diplomacy, as well as mixed missions or hybrid peace operations whereby the regional arrangements and the UN deploy operations in a conflict situation in combination with each other.[72]

Preventive Diplomacy and Peacemaking: The Need for Coordination. Before the end of the Cold War, preventive diplomacy[73] and peacemaking[74] were generally viewed as prerogatives of regional arrangements. Article 52 of the UN Charter provides that "local disputes" are to be addressed in the first instance by regional organizations, if at all possible; however, it does not elaborate on which of the measures provided for in Chapter VI can be taken. With the proliferation and increasing intensity of internal conflicts, the primacy of regional arrangements in this area is no longer clear.

The difficulties encountered by the CSCE/OSCE and the EU in addressing the unravelling of the former Yugoslavia were due as much to the lack of an institutional framework as to the geopolitical situation. Because many states in the region had historical alliances or adversarial relations with the parties to the Yugoslav conflict, their impartiality as mediators was questionable. Russia, France, and – to a lesser extent – the United Kingdom were viewed as sympathetic to Serbia, whereas Germany's support for and early recognition of Croatia and Slovenia were attributed to historical, political, cultural, and religious ties.

Similarly, with the conflict in Liberia, Cote d'Ivoire and Burkina Faso were sympathetic to and provided support for Charles Taylor, whereas Nigeria was

[72] Jones, Bruce, & Cherif, Feryal (2003). "Evolving Models of Peacekeeping: Policy Implications and Responses 2003," UN Department of Peacekeeping Operations, Best Practice Unit; available at www.un.org/Depts/dpko/lessons.

[73] "Preventive action to prevent disputes from arising between parties, to prevent existing disputes from escalating into conflicts, and to limit the spread of the latter when they occur": United Nations (1992). "Agenda for Peace," A/47/277-S/24111, New York: General Assembly, Security Council, paragraph 20.

[74] Peacemaking or "action to bring hostile parties to agreement, essentially through such peaceful means as those foreseen in Chapter VI of the UN Charter": United Nations (1992). "Agenda for Peace," A/47/277-S/24111, New York: General Assembly, Security Council, paragraph 20.

in favor of President Samuel Doe and, on his death, the interim government of Liberia that it helped establish. The West African situation was further complicated by the perceived hegemonic aspirations of Nigeria. The UN should take a more active role with regard to ongoing peacemaking initiatives so that in these processes, collective interests and international standards are maintained and not merely the national imperatives or preferences of the regional actors.[75] For example, the Security Council could prohibit amnesty clauses for perpetrators of massive human-rights violations in particular cases.

Despite the problems of partiality, the comparative advantage of these regional arrangements lies, in part, in their flexibility and informality and the quality of relations and affinities that tend to characterize their internal rapport with conflicting parties that can be present only through regional and local players.[76] This quality is especially evident with the fourth category of regional arrangements: neighborhood initiatives, such as the CEPGL and the Mano River Union. The support required from the Security Council is generally recognition and sanctioning for the initiatives proposed by these ad hoc groups, especially with regard to addressing cross-border violations.

In Sudan, efforts to revitalize the Darfur peace process in 2007 were led by Salim Ahmed Salim and Jan Eliasson of the Joint UN–AU Mediation Support team. The team undertook intensive shuttle diplomacy throughout the year in pursuit of a political settlement to the Darfur crisis through negotiations aimed at achieving a peace agreement between the Sudanese government and the various Darfurian movements. The peace process entered a new phase on October 27 with the start of peace talks in Sirte, Libya. This was followed by high-level contacts with the Darfur movements aimed at consolidating their positions and representation before the face-to-face negotiations expected in early 2008. Despite the various setbacks to the Darfur peace process, the involvement of regional mediators in the shuttle diplomacy is critical for any progress to be achieved among the Darfur movements.

Enforcement Operations. Difficulties faced by the UN in conducting enforcement operations were apparent with the UN operations in Somalia

[75] Alagappa, Muthiah. "Introduction in Regional Institutions, the United Nations and International Security," p. 290, citing Chopra & Weiss (1999). *The United Nations and the Former Second World: Coping with Conflicts*, in Alagappa & Inoguchi, *International Security Management and the United Nations* (New York: UNU Press), p. 259.

[76] A similar mechanism was set up by the OAU in 1994 to address the preventive diplomacy and peacemaking aspects of conflict resolution in Africa. This mechanism has now been transformed and is an intrinsic part of the African Union.

and the former Yugoslavia. These problems were due as much to the UN's traditional notions of peacekeeping – which were largely consensual and impartial operations – as to the lack of resources and capabilities for rapid deployment in robust peacekeeping. Consequently, the UN has increasingly tried to "farm out" the enforcement aspect of peace operations to regional arrangements or individual states; UN operations in East Timor and Kosovo are two cases in point.[77]

The inconsistent application and policing of the UN Charter provision requiring regional organizations undertaking enforcement action to address threats to international peace and security and to seek Security Council authorization for such action is for geopolitical rather than legal reasons. Whereas the UN Charter did not provide clear guidelines as to what constitutes "enforcement action" or when or how it should be exercised, the International Court of Justice in the *Expenses* case equated "coercive acts" with "enforcement measures" and indicated that those under the UN Charter were only for the Security Council to direct.[78]

During the Cold War, regional organizations were sometimes viewed as a means to circumvent the veto-blocked Security Council. Most interventions were justified internationally by demonstrating that a regional organization or group of countries "requested" the intervention to solve a problem.[79] Cases in point include the establishment in 1965 of an Inter-American Force to cooperate with the establishment of normal conditions in the Dominican Republic, under the auspices of the OAS,[80] and the 1983 U.S. intervention in Grenada, together with troops from several Caribbean countries claiming *inter alia* that they were authorized to do so by the Organization of Eastern Caribbean States (OECS) to bring peace and order to a country in a condition of anarchy.[81] Although the Security Council was unable to condemn the

77 In the case of Kosovo, the arrangement with NATO was after the fact, in that UNMIK was set up after the NATO air strikes.

78 International Court of Justice (1962). "Certain Expenses of the United Nations," *ICJ Reports*, 151, 171–172.

79 Gamba, Virginia (1993). "Justified Intervention? A View from the South," in Laura W. Reed & Carl Kaysen (eds.), *Emerging Norms of Justified Intervention: A Collection of Essays from a Project of the American Academy of Arts and Sciences* (Cambridge, MA: Committee on International Security Studies, American Academy of Arts and Sciences), pp. 115–125.

80 During discussions in the Security Council, the Soviet representative took the position that this constituted enforcement action in violation of Article 53; the U.S. representative held the view that the action being taken in the Dominican Republic was "most certainly not enforcement action" any more than action taken by the UN in Cyprus, Congo, or the Middle East. See Goodrich & Simons (1969), see note 16.

81 See statement of Mr. Robinson, Legal Advisor of the U.S. Department of State, in *American Journal of International Law* 78 (1984), 664, and also the statement by Ambassador Motley,

intervention in Grenada because of the exercise of veto power by the United States, the General Assembly described it as a violation of the UN Charter.[82]

In the case of the ECOWAS intervention in Liberia without Security Council approval, the Security Council remained silent for geopolitical reasons. Although Liberia had once shared a "special relationship" with the United States, in the post–Cold War era, it was apparent that no U.S. strategic interest would be served by intervention. Moreover, the UN was at this time overwhelmed by competing concerns and demands from Somalia, the former Yugoslavia, and Iraq; consequently, the crisis in Liberia was consigned to a regional solution. Arguably, the initial intervention in 1990 had the consent of the *de jure* government, President Samuel Doe, and one of the rebel group leaders, and it was characterized by ECOWAS ministers as a peacekeeping operation. However, the impartiality of the ECOMOG troops did not last because they were soon involved in combat with the rebel groups. ECOMOG's use of force to maintain control of its operation in Liberia was largely unheeded by the Security Council, despite increasing reports of coercion, human-rights violations, and other atrocities committed by ECOMOG forces.

Regional military intervention by the ECOWAS in Liberia and, to a lesser extent, in Sierra Leone had the effect of deepening and widening the conflict across the region. In West Africa, the ECOWAS failed to limit the conflict to the boundaries of Liberia. Despite a relatively early deployment, ECOMOG watched as the conflict spread into Sierra Leone in 1991, resulting in the overthrow of the government of Joseph Momoh. Moreover, the illegal exploitation of natural resources, including diamonds, gold, and timber – in which members of some of the contingents of ECOMOG were implicated – also contributed to prolonging the conflict. In this regard, it was only after the establishment of a UN special investigation panel that some of this exploitation was checked because it rendered such behaviors criminal and embarrassing to national authorities.[83]

For its part, the Security Council only formally addressed the Liberian crisis in November 1992 in connection with a request from the ECOWAS for the imposition of an embargo against one of the factions. Even during

Assistant Secretary for Inter-American Affairs, *Department of State Bulletin* 84 (1984), 70 et seq.

82 United Nations (1983). A/RES/38/7, New York: General Assembly; United Nations (1983). A/38/L.8, New York: General Assembly.

83 Adibe, Clement (2003). "Do Regional Organizations Matter? Comparing Conflict Management Mechanisms in West Africa and the Great Lakes Region," in Jane Boulden (ed.), *Dealing with Conflict in Africa: The United Nations and Regional Organizations* (Palgrave: MacMillan), p. 99.

that session, however, ECOMOG's decision to use force was not addressed. The discussion in the Security Council, however, would seem to indicate that there was implicit approval by Council members concerning the use of force.[84] David Wippman observed that the "willingness of the international community to acquiesce in but not overtly approve forcible intervention as in Liberia suggests that, as in the past, states or groups of states willing to undertake interventions perceived as genuinely humanitarian will not incur condemnation or international sanction, especially when the decision to intervene stems from a multilateral decision-making process."[85]

In view of the precedent set by the ECOMOG case, NATO air strikes over the former Yugoslavia in March 1999 – even in the absence of Security Council authorization – would seem to be allowable under the rubric of "humanitarian intervention" if the specific rules for such a principle could be formulated and agreed on. At the root of the notion of humanitarian intervention is the recognition that populations in danger of starvation, massacre, or other forms of massive suffering have the right to receive assistance. That principle, set out in UN General Assembly resolutions,[86] has been confirmed by many subsequent Security Council resolutions.[87] The combined right of victims to assistance and of the Security Council to authorize humanitarian intervention by military means, however, does not amount to a right of humanitarian intervention by states, individually or collectively.[88] The "hypocrisy" of this matter in international law[89] was captured by UN Secretary-General Kofi Annan in his opening statement to the General Assembly in 1999:

> While the genocide in Rwanda will define for our generation the consequences of inaction in the face of mass murder, the more recent conflict in Kosovo has prompted important questions about the consequences of action in the absence of complete unity on the part of the international community. It has cast in stark relief what has been called *humanitarian intervention* on the one side, and the question of UN mandate on the other; the universally recognized imperative of effectively halting gross and systematic violations of human rights with grave

[84] Wippman (1993), see note 20, p. 185. [85] Ibid., p. 193.

[86] For example, United Nations (1988). A/RES/43/131, New York: General Assembly, re-affirmed and specified in United Nations (1990). A/RES 45/100, New York: General Assembly.

[87] United Nations (1991). S/RES/688, New York: Security Council (protection of Iraq/Kurds); United Nations (1992). S/RES/770, New York: Security Council (all necessary measures to facilitate humanitarian relief to embattled Bosnians); United Nations (1992). S/RES 794, New York: Security Council (intervention in Somalia for humanitarian objectives); United Nations (2003). S/RES 1484 (authorizing deployment of a EU-led force to Ituri in the DRC to stabilize the security situation and improve the humanitarian situation).

[88] See Guicherd, Catherine (1999). "International Law and the War in Kosovo," *Survival* 41(2), 19–34.

[89] Ibid., citing French lawyer, Mario Bettati, and a study conducted in 1996.

humanitarian consequences. The inability of the international community in the case of Kosovo to reconcile these two equally compelling interests – universal legitimacy and effectiveness in defense of human rights – can only be viewed as a tragedy.

NATO's decision to conduct action not against a member or within its area of membership but rather against a nonmember was controversial. However, NATO maintained that the conflict in Kosovo had potential spillover effects on the borders of NATO member states, was a potential cause for severe disruption, and was therefore a matter of direct concern. Other regional and subregional organizations that have mounted military operations have generally acted within their geographical boundaries against member states.

Even in those cases in which UN operations have had a clear Chapter VII mandate to protect civilian populations and vulnerable groups, there have been problems in implementing this mandate. A case in point includes the difficulties that the UN faced in protecting the safe havens in the former Yugoslavia.[90] At the same time, the difficulties that UN operations face in exercising the use of force are due in part to the persistence of traditional notions of peacekeeping as much as to the need to be accountable to troop-contributing countries and to minimize casualties.

The involvement of regional arrangements in peacekeeping operations is critical because it allows the UN to do what it does best: provide legitimacy for collective actions in the service of international peace and security. In West Africa, as in Kosovo in later years, the UN did not have to get involved with uncooperative factional militias, the containment of which is a *sine qua non* for any meaningful effort toward a political solution. That task fell to a regional arrangement/collective-defense organization, while the UN maintained, to a large extent, the moral high ground by insisting on strict adherence to humanitarian principles and international humanitarian law. Where such regional arrangements are absent or have difficulty acting as a UN partner, as is the case in the Great Lakes region in Africa, the UN faces the dilemma of having to assume responsibility for maintaining the peace by default, with all its attendant risks and criticisms.[91]

[90] See United Nations (1999). "Report of the Secretary-General Pursuant to General Assembly Resolution 53/35 – Srebrenica Report A/54/549; available at www.un.org/peace/srebrenica.pdf. See also Li, Daryl (2000)." "Anatomy of a Balkan Massacre: The Failure on International Peacekeeping at Srebrenica," *Harvard International Law Review*, 22(3); Sudetic, Chuck (1994). Conflict in the Balkans: The Overview; Gorazde in Panic as Serbian Forces Enter "Safe" Area. *The New York Times*, April 18.

[91] Adibe (2003), see note 83, p. 101. This was also the case in the DRC with the UN peace-operation (MONUC), where in May 2004, despite the Chapter VII mandate and the presence

The intervention of the AU in Darfur and Sudan opened new horizons both politically and operationally for the AU and the UN. The AU PSC's decision to deploy forces to Darfur was politically significant because it was the first major operational decision undertaken by the new council under its new charter, which recognized internal conflict as an issue for regional attention and possible intervention.[92] It is even more significant because intervention in Darfur involved a "fractioned" rather than a "failed" state and, as such, required a significant degree of continuing deference and consultation with the "national" authorities in Khartoum first by the AU and now by the UN. These protracted consultations with the Sudanese authorities in Khartoum also raised a number of fundamental issues, including the question of whether the requirement of host-country cooperation for the legitimacy of an operation jeopardizes the international legitimacy of a UN peacekeeping operation when the host authorities place too many conditions preceding intervention by a UN operation.

The requirement to maintain the African character of the UNAMID has been a unique challenge. Although AU member states have demonstrated a willingness to participate in peacekeeping missions in their backyards, their overall capacity to mount and sustain them is less clear. In particular, most potential African troop contributors lack the equipment (e.g., attack helicopters and armored personnel carriers) that are essential for UNAMID's effectiveness. Attempts to overcome these difficulties through the provision of equipment from Sweden, Norway, and other countries were stymied by the Sudanese authorities.

The potential effectiveness of UNAMID also seems to be compromised by the complex command-and-control arrangements that were another requirement of the Sudanese authorities. Although Security Council Resolution 1769 emphasizes that the mission will adhere to the unity of command and control, there is no guarantee against rifts that may appear at the strategic level, particularly in terms of the necessary operational support required for the mission from the UN and the AU. Moreover, a formal mechanism has still to be established for resolution of potential disagreements between the AU and the UN. In the past, UN and regional actors typically maintained ad hoc communication and coordination arrangements. Such processes, as illustrated in the negotiation of logistics arrangements between MONUC and

of seven thousand blue helmets, MONUC continued to face difficulties in exercising its mandate to protect civilian populations and to support the transitional government.

92 See Jones, Bruce D. (2008). "Looking to the Future: Peace Operations in 2015," a commissioned paper for the International Forum for the Challenges of Peace Operations (unpublished paper), paragraphs 39–44.

EUFOR DRC or for UNAMID, are often laborious and time-intensive.[93] These cumbersome arrangements also can lead to serious operational problems and delays, particularly in situations requiring rapid response, and can contribute to compromising the effectiveness of the operation on the ground.

Observations

The uniqueness of the UN lies in its universal legitimacy and its responsibility for maintaining peace and security worldwide. To maintain this legitimacy, it has become increasingly important that the UN is perceived to be effective and to be fulfilling its mandate in the peacekeeping operations that it undertakes. In the past decade, the escalation of internal conflicts that impact international peace and security has stretched the UN's capacity to the limits, requiring an increasing reliance on regional arrangements to take a more active role in either conducting the peacekeeping operations or participating with the UN in the conduct of them. UN authorization is required not least to ensure that a mission subcontracted by the international community to a powerful state (or regional institution) reflects the collective interests and norms, not merely of the national imperatives and preferences of the regional arrangement. At the same time, it has become apparent that these common and coordinated efforts undertaken by the UN and regional organizations in matters of peacekeeping and security should be based on their complementary capacities and comparative advantages and make full use of their

[93] In the case of the AU–UN operations and particularly in view of the operational exigencies for the deployment of the Mission to Darfur, the UN Security Council in Resolution 1809 (2008) authorized an expert panel to be set up to review and make recommendations on enhancing the predictability, sustainability, and flexibility of financing UN-mandated operations undertaken by the AU, with a focus on the expeditious and effective deployment of well-equipped troops and effective mission-support arrangements. In its report to the Security Council in December 2008 (S/2008/813), the panel recommended *interalia* that funding mechanisms to support capacity-building in the African Union should be focused at the continental level and that United Nations assessed contributions to Security Council–mandated African Union operations should be on a "case-by-case basis"; the panel also recommended that long-term capacity-building be financed by a multi-donor trust fund governed by an eleven-member board made up of perhaps five African Union representatives, five main donors, and one Secretariat official, so as to be "broadly representative." The report of the Panel emphasised that while ownership of the process must belong to Africa, all Member States must be committed to supporting the process. The report also stressed that the process would require detailed follow-up to assess both the practicality and implications of the recommendations.

experience, in accordance with the UN Charter and relevant statutes of the regional organizations.[94]

The UN and regional organizations are made up of the same member states and grapple with the same conflicts. However, instead of promoting consistency across institutions, this has led occasionally to divergence of approach. The same member states sometimes employ different criteria and considerations for blue helmets than for regional peacekeeping: from scope of mandates to the composition and duration of missions, from rules of engagement to relations with host states and populations. EU missions in DRC and Chad – unlike typical UN deployments – deployed with a preestablished end date that, in turn, has significant impact for the UN. AU, EU, and NATO missions, meanwhile, deployed with mandates far more robust than typical UN peacekeeping operations.

Consequently, the legitimacy of such interventions by UN and/or regional organizations needs to be seen in terms of the effectiveness, cooperation, and participation of the larger international community. Increasingly, the effectiveness of these operations also is being measured by their ability to use force. However, a regional arrangement's ability to effectively use force is usually resource-dependent, whereby arrangements from the south generally fare worse than their northern counterparts. Western nations have tried to address this gap through support in terms of logistics and other technical resources, which has become particularly evident in the development of African peacekeeping capacity in recent years. Western assistance to ECOMOG during the operation in Liberia and Sierra Leone included airlift capability and other logistical assets. Such assistance contributed to the effectiveness of ECOMOG's operations in West Africa and also provided a basis for a division of labor between the UN and the ECOWAS. Similarly, the hybrid UN–AU operation in Darfur continues to face such challenges while also having to grapple with the dictates of Sudanese authorities.

Once a peacekeeping mandate is authorized by the Security Council, the burden for implementation shifts to the UN Secretariat, even though the obligation is mutually reinforcing on member states and the UN Secretariat. These mandates require, at least, the sustained political, diplomatic, financial, and in-kind support of the international community because the Secretariat is only as capable as the support given to it. Whereas the use of targeted political

[94] Statement by the President of the Security Council at the 5649th meeting of the Security Council (March 28, 2007). "Relationship between the United Nations and Regional Organizations, in Particular the African Union, in the Maintenance of International Peace and Security," S/PRST/2007/7.

leverage and the unanimity of the international community in this regard are critical, just as significant are the resources that need to be obtained to facilitate timely deployment. The obligation and mobilizing role of the international community, particularly the Security Council, is critical in this regard. This has raised a number of other questions concerning the limits of such assistance, including whether the UN Security Council should pay for such an action if it authorizes an intervention by a regional arrangement. This issue has taken on particular significance in the context of peacekeeping operations in Africa.[95]

Nevertheless, this increasing reliance on regional arrangements should not lead to a "tribalization" of peacekeeping operations,[96] whereby conflicts in Europe are viewed as the responsibility of Europeans and conflicts in Africa as the domain of Africans. The UN–AU hybrid operation in Darfur and the European-led Artemis and EUFOR DRC operations are important cases in point. Such cooperation between regional arrangements and the UN should be encouraged because it not only lends credence to the UN's assertion of universal legitimacy, it also creates a situation whereby effective military action can be taken, thus fulfilling mandate expectations.

[95] Report of the Secretary-General (April 1, 2008). "Relationship between the United Nations and Regional Organizations, in Particular the African Union, in the Maintenance of International Peace and Security," S/2008/186.

[96] Otunnu, Olara (1999). "The Peace and Security Agenda of the United Nations," in Olara A. Otunnu & Michael W. Doyle (eds.), *Peacemaking and Peacekeeping for the New Century* (Oxford, MD: Rowman & Littlefield Publishers).

DIANNE OTTO

8. The Security Council's Alliance of Gender Legitimacy: The Symbolic Capital of Resolution 1325

> The Security Council recognizes that peace is inextricably linked with equality between women and men . . . [and] that the equal access and full participation of women in power structures and their full involvement in all efforts for the prevention and resolution of conflicts are essential for the maintenance and promotion of peace and security.
>
> – Ambassador Anwarul Karim Chowdury (2000)[1]
> President, UN Security Council

Recent feminist efforts to engage with the United Nations (UN) Security Council could be dismissed as a futile attempt to employ the "master's tools" to dismantle the "master's house."[2] There is a long history of lip service by international institutions to the antimilitaristic ways of thinking that have been at the heart of women's peace movements for centuries.[3] However unlikely it was, these efforts have borne fruit as evidenced by the Statement of the Council's President, Bangladeshi Ambassador Chowdury, on International Women's Day in 2000, linking gender equality "inextricably"

[1] Chowdury, Anwarul Karim (2000). "Peace Inextricably Linked with Equality Between Women and Men Says Security Council, in International Women's Day Statement," UN Security Council, Press Release SC/6816, March 8.

[2] Lorde, Audre (1993). "The Master's Tools Will Never Dismantle the Master's House," in *Zami, Sister Outsider, Undersong* (New York: Quality Paperback Book Club), pp. 110–113; see also Ashworth, Georgina (1999). "The Silencing of Women," in Tim Dunne & Nicholas J. Wheeler (eds.), *Human Rights in Global Politics* (Cambridge: Cambridge University Press), p. 259.

[3] Otto, Dianne (2006). "A Sign of 'Weakness'? Disrupting Gender Certainties in the Implementation of Security Council Resolution 1325," *Michigan Journal of Gender and Law*, Vol. 13, no. 1, 113. See also Wiltsher, Anne (1985). *Most Dangerous Women: Feminist Peace Campaigners of the Great War* (London: Pandora); Rupp, Leila (1997). *Worlds of Women: The Making of an International Women's Movement* (Princeton, NJ: Princeton University Press), pp. 19, 51–81.

with peace,[4] the core project of the UN. The Statement was followed several months later, on October 31, by the Council's unanimous adoption of Resolution 1325 on Women, Peace, and Security.[5] The resolution calls for *inter alia* the increased participation of women in decision making related to the prevention, management, and resolution of armed conflict.[6] Although it is nonbinding, the resolution has been enormously productive. Not only has it provided the basis for strengthening institutional commitment to gender mainstreaming and continuing annual dialogue between women's peace advocates and the Security Council in New York, it has also supplied leverage for many grassroots women's groups to claim a role in peace negotiations and postconflict decision making.

The Security Council's endorsement of women's formal participation in decision making, aimed at preventing and resolving disputes that threaten international peace and security, potentially takes its work into uncharted waters. Equally, the aspiration that the Security Council might act as a conduit for feminist ideas introduces, for women's peace advocacy, a new strategy of engagement with power from within rather than from outside the military and diplomatic establishment – an opportunity that Virginia Woolf so famously declined many years ago.[7] In this chapter, I explore these developments as an "alliance of gender legitimacy" between the Security Council and international women's peace advocates as represented by the Women's International League for Peace and Freedom's Office in New York (WILPF-UN). The WILPF-UN has taken a leading role in the Non-governmental Organization Working Group on Women, Peace, and Security (NGO Working Group),[8] which formed in the wake of Chowdury's Statement, initially to convince the Security Council to adopt such a resolution and, since its adoption, to promote its implementation.[9] On the one hand, I suggest that Resolution 1325 formed a plank in the Council's efforts to enhance its flagging legitimacy at the end of the twentieth century. On the other hand, from

[4] Chowdury (2000), see n. 1.

[5] United Nations (2000). "Women, Peace and Security," S/RES/1325 (New York: Security Council), October 31.

[6] Ibid., paragraph 1.

[7] Woolf, Virginia (1938). *Three Guineas* (London: Hogarth).

[8] Five NGOs were initially involved in the NGO Working Group: the Women's International League for Peace and Freedom (WILPF), International Alert, Amnesty International, Women's Commission for Refugee Women and Children, and the Hague Appeal for Peace. Some of the founding NGOs have since left the working group and others have joined it. In April 2008, there were thirteen member NGOs. Available at www.womenpeacesecurity.org/about/.

[9] Cohn, Carol, Kinsella, Helen, & Gibbings, Sheri (2004). "Women, Peace and Security: Resolution 1325," *International Feminist Journal of Politics*, Vol. 6, no. 1, 130, 131.

the point of view of women's peace activists, engagement with the Security Council was an effort to enhance the legitimacy of their own agenda through association with the Council. I examine the fault lines produced by this seemingly unlikely alliance to expose the tensions and the synchronicities of the struggle over gender legitimacy.

As I argue in the next section, the Security Council's legitimacy problems mounted precipitously during the 1990s, as it adopted an expanded mandate that took its work into new and often controversial areas. I describe the increasingly insistent calls for reform of the Security Council and the convergence of many feminist concerns with these reform efforts. Building on Ian Hurd's compelling analysis of legitimacy and power in the context of the Council,[10] I draw parallels between the issues raised in the recent debates and those that were of concern to smaller states in San Francisco in 1945, when they were consulted about the shape of the new institutions to be created by the UN Charter. The Security Council responded by seeking to "manage" the recent reform proposals in a way that is similar to the reaction of the Great Powers to the anxieties expressed in 1945, which was to represent the Council as committed to "procedural correctness" and produce a "discourse of assurance" to mitigate fears that it would be driven by self-interest rather than act in the collective good.[11] I suggest that the Security Council's response to its waning legitimacy has been to rebuild its "symbolic capital"[12] by employing similar techniques. In the process, the Council has developed a new means of assurance in the form of thematic resolutions, which demonstrate its concern for the well-being of civilians, including children and refugees, who may be affected by its interventions.

In the second section, I suggest that the Security Council's emerging discourse of gender remained deeply troubling for feminists, leading to the adoption of a bold new strategy for women's peace advocates. Despite having traditionally worked from "outside" institutions of power, it was decided to appropriate one of the Security Council's new techniques of assurance for feminist ends by seeking the adoption of a thematic resolution on women, peace, and security. I examine the contests over the text of Resolution 1325 in the processes that led to its adoption, highlighting the concessions made by WILPF-UN and other members of the NGO Working Group in their efforts to be "taken seriously" by Security Council members. I suggest that it was also a concession by the Security Council to add so-called women's issues to its agenda. I go on to examine the final text of Resolution 1325 as constituting

[10] Hurd, Ian (2007). *After Anarchy: Legitimacy and Power at the United Nations* (Princeton, NJ: Princeton University Press).

[11] Ibid., pp. 98–105.

[12] Ibid., p. 59.

the Council's means of managing doubts about its gender legitimacy. My textual analysis highlights the precariousness of the alliance that has been struck between the Security Council and its newfound allies and suggests that the reliance of the resolution on the Council's legitimacy presents a conundrum for feminists.

In the final section, I examine some of the purposes to which Resolution 1325 – as symbolic capital of the Security Council – has since been put in order to explore the production of gender legitimacy that is emerging from its implementation. To this end, I draw on the examples of Afghanistan, East Timor, and Iraq. In particular, I am interested in whether Resolution 1325 is providing a means of increasing the gender legitimacy of the Security Council in a feminist sense, which must involve delegitimizing at least some of the aspects of the Council's *modus operandi* that are inconsistent with feminist ideas. I also question whether this new engagement, and the compromises it necessitates, has enhanced the institutional legitimacy of feminist peace activism at the price of its popular legitimacy. My goal is to examine the extent to which the alliance of gender legitimacy between the Security Council and women's peace advocates provides yet another lesson in the futility of engaging the master's tools and the extent to which it may have opened new possibilities for feminist peace activism as it "comes to power."[13]

In critically examining Resolution 1325, my intention is not to undermine any of the efforts to work for peace that are associated with it. The issues are urgent: every day, many women's lives, families, neighborhoods, and communities are being destroyed by the brutalities and humiliations of armed conflict.[14] There is no doubt that the expanding mandate of the Security Council, which continues to expand in the "war on terror" and an impending "environmental crisis," presents new challenges for women's peace advocates to creatively utilize opportunities to influence those who make the decisions that have such far-reaching consequences. My goal is not to generate "tensions between activist and academic approaches to thinking about 1325"[15] but rather to make a contribution to the activist endeavor in a climate of spreading militarization and the hostility to women's equality that accompanies it.[16]

[13] Halley, Janet; Kotiswaran, Prabha; Shamir, Hila; & Thomas, Chantal (2006). "From the International to the Local in Feminist Legal Responses to Rape, Prostitution/Sex Work, and Sex Trafficking: Four Studies in Contemporary Governance Feminism," *Harvard Journal of Law and Gender*, Vol. 29: 335.

[14] Rehn, Elisabeth, & Sirleaf, Ellen Johnson (2002). *Women, War, and Peace: The Independent Experts' Assessment on the Impact of Armed Conflict on Women and Women's Role in Peacebuilding* (New York: United Nations Development Fund for Women).

[15] Cohn et al. (2004), see n. 9, p. 139.

[16] Centre for Women's Global Leadership (2003). *No CSW Agreed Conclusions on Women's Human Rights and Elimination of All Forms of Violence Against Women and Girls* blames the

The Security Council's "Management" of Its Legitimacy Quotient

The Security Council relies on ideas to legitimate its decisions and practices. It needs to discursively persuade states – and, increasingly, civil society – that it can be trusted to identify threats to international peace and security and respond in a way that ultimately serves the collective interests of the international community, despite being dominated by the Great Powers. This persuasive power relies on social processes, producing (and contesting) shared beliefs and stories about the Security Council, in order to establish and maintain its legitimacy. In the context of international institutions like the Council, which rely on "soft power" to persuade, Hurd provided a definition of the concept of legitimacy that I have found useful in thinking through the fault lines produced by the adoption of Resolution 1325. He described legitimacy as follows:

> ... the subjective condition in which actors internalize rules given by institutions ... [which then] changes the relationship between the rule and the actor, redefining the actor's sense of its own interests, and gives the actor an internal orientation that is biased towards following rules.[17]

Hurd's reference to "rules" includes the expansive discursive tools utilized by international institutions in the process of governing, in their efforts to influence the decision-making calculus of states and other actors in the international community. In the interaction between "internalization" of rules and the changed behavior of international actors that results, "symbolic resources" are generated, which are empowered by association with the legitimized institution.

The Security Council, as Hurd argued, has many such symbolic resources that are often highly sought after not only by small states but also by the Great Powers. For example, many states devote great energy to having an issue of importance to them placed on the agenda of the Security Council, even when they expect no substantive response from the Council. If not acted on, the issue is listed, by default, in the Security Council's Summary Statement, from where it is unlikely to be raised again; yet, states have vociferously resisted attempts to prune the list.[18] In Hurd's view, holding a place on the list has become a kind of "prestige resource" – quite independent from any concrete action taken on the matter – whereby the formal recognition of problems

failure of the Forty-seventh Commission on the Status of Women (CSW) to reach consensus on the agreed conclusions on women's human rights and the elimination of all forms of violence against women and girls on the breakdown of efforts in the Security Council to reach agreement about the pending war in Iraq.

17 Hurd (2007), see n. 10, pp. 64–65.

18 Ibid., pp. 113–116.

by the international community has become a resource that derives its value from the legitimacy of the Security Council. Powerful states also have sought to use the symbolic capital of the Council to enhance the legitimacy of their actions. For example, the United States sought Security Council authorization for both of its armed interventions in Iraq in 1990 and 2003, and Russia appropriated the "blue helmets and white trucks" associated with UN peacekeeping missions to legitimize its interventions in Georgia, Moldova, and Tajikistan during the 1990s – despite adhering to none of the basic principles that characterize the Security Council's peacekeeping efforts.[19] These examples illustrate the power that association with the Security Council has "by virtue of beliefs in its legitimacy"[20] and help to explain why feminist peace advocates might also see some advantage in association with the Council. This analysis also accounts for the widespread concern about the Security Council's waning legitimacy during the 1990s, which was presenting a threat to the usefulness of its symbols for other actors.

Because the processes by which international actors internalize and act on such rules are subjective, the Security Council cannot exert complete control over its symbolic capital. Therefore, although the internalization of its rules putatively strengthens the legitimacy of the Council – and, thus, the power of the strong states within it – it also leaves the rules open to contestation and reinterpretation, which can in turn place constraints on the states that produced the rules in the first place. In this sense, the use of the Security Council's symbols is not limited to maintaining power relationships that benefit the Council but also can be utilized to transform them.[21] Drawing from the work of French linguistic theorist, Pierre Bourdieu, Hurd argued that "once constituted, a symbol is a form of power . . . which allows a person or object to do things that could not be done before."[22] The flexibility of symbols makes it possible for the legitimacy of the Security Council to be contested by redefining whose interests it serves, such as when Libya challenged the Council's sanctions imposed pursuant to the Lockerbie bombing.[23] By questioning the Security Council's procedural fairness and accusing the United States and the United Kingdom of using the Council to serve their individual interests, Libya was effective in impugning the Council's own sanctions as presenting a threat to international peace and security, instead of Libya's refusal to hand over the

[19] Ibid., pp. 125–129.

[20] Ibid., p. 112.

[21] Ibid., p. 52.

[22] Ibid. See also Bourdieu, Pierre (1991). *Language and Symbolic Power*, Gino Raymond & Matthew Adamson (trans.) (Cambridge: Polity Press).

[23] United Nations (1992). S/RES/748 (New York: Security Council), March 31, imposes selective sanctions under Article 41.

bombing suspects for trial.[24] I am interested in examining how Resolution 1325 – as part of the Security Council's store of symbols – in a similar way might be used to serve feminist interests by challenging the Council's exclusionary procedures and its well-worn militarist assumptions that depend on women's inequality for their efficacy.

The legitimacy of the Security Council has always provided a ready point of contention,[25] and it is not difficult to understand why. The "serious" power of the UN – to authorize and mandate enforcement measures including the collective use of force – is located within the Security Council, which was designed by the United States, United Kingdom, and Union of Soviet Socialist Republics, later joined by China and eventually also France, to ensure their "legalized hegemony" in the realm of international security.[26] To this end, the design awarded the five "great" powers permanent membership in the Security Council and the power to veto any nonprocedural "decisions" of the Council, which was to have "primary responsibility" for international peace and security.[27] Nonpermanent rotating membership was to be enjoyed by six states, which was later increased to ten.[28]

The design of the Security Council was the subject of great controversy at the San Francisco Conference in 1945. The Great Powers that had drafted the UN Charter invited other states to participate in its finalization, thereby creating an opportunity for the UN Charter – including the design of the Security Council – to be accepted and internalized as serving the collective interests of all states. The major points of contention were the voting privileges of the Great Powers, especially the wide range of matters over which the veto could be exercised, the criteria for both permanent and rotating membership, and the absence of limits to the Council's powers.[29] Hurd described how the opposition of the smaller states was "managed" procedurally by the Great Powers through a deliberative process that allowed all participants to express their views and, substantively, through reassurances that the veto would not be used capriciously.[30] These legitimizing strategies resulted in smaller states

[24] Hurd (2007), see n. 10, p. 156.

[25] Hurd (2007), see n. 10, p. 83.

[26] Simpson, Gerry (2003). *Great Powers and Outlaw States: Unequal Sovereigns in the International Legal Order* (New York: Cambridge University Press), pp. 167–179.

[27] See *Charter of the United Nations* (1945), Articles 23–27.

[28] The UN Charter was amended in 1965 to increase the number of nonpermanent members from six to ten, allowing for three seats for African states and two for Asian states. Even so, efforts by postcolonial states to further "democratize" the Security Council continued through the 1970s and 1980s. See also Geiger, Rudolph (2002). "The Security Council," in Bruno Simma (ed.), *The Charter of the United Nations: A Commentary* (Oxford: Oxford University Press), Vol. I, second edition, pp. 437–442.

[29] Simpson (2003), see n. 26, pp. 180–188.

[30] Hurd (2007), see n. 10, pp. 95–105.

eventually embracing the proposed structure of the Security Council without change. Having voiced their concerns and exhausted the available avenues to oppose the veto, small states were won over by the sense of "procedural correctness" and the "discourse of reassurance" that the Security Council would act only in the collective welfare,[31] internalizing a commitment to the Council that turned their relationship with the new institution from contestation to cooperation. It was these same two "rules" that Libya used in its attempts to delegitimize the Security Council five decades later.

Indeed, opportunities to test these rules took a long time to emerge. Misuse of the veto, in the way that was feared by small states in San Francisco, did not materialize for many years because of the Cold War. During this period, the Security Council suffered a paralysis that, although assisted by the veto, was not an abuse of power in the sense that had been anticipated in San Francisco. However, the end of the Cold War brought an immediate change to the Security Council's state of inaction. Commencing in 1991 with its united response to Iraq's invasion of Kuwait, there was a period of unprecedented cooperation among the Great Powers. The apparent success of the collective enforcement action in Kuwait saw a sharp upturn in the Security Council's legitimacy quotient, and many commentators happily predicted that the Council was finally poised to assume fully its UN Charter responsibilities by acting decisively in the event of threats to the peace.[32]

However, as the Security Council's confidence grew, its interpretation of its Chapter VII powers of enforcement became rapidly more expansive,[33] and concerns about its legitimacy – similar to those that had been expressed in San Francisco – started to emerge. The Council's expansiveness included interventions into what were essentially domestic disputes in Somalia,[34] Haiti,[35]

31 Ibid., pp. 109–110.

32 Evans, Gareth (1993). *Cooperating for Peace: The Global Agenda for the 1990s and Beyond* (Sydney: Allen & Unwin); Chayes, Abram (1991). "The Use of Force in the Persian Gulf," in Lori F. Damrosch & David J. Scheffer (eds.), *Law and Force in the New International Order* (Boulder, CO: Westview Press), p. 3.

33 Security Council Summit Meeting at the level of Heads of State adopted a Statement, S/23500, January 31, 1992, which declared that the absence of military conflict does not of itself ensure international peace and security, and that problems of an economic, social, or ecological kind also may become threats to international peace and security.

34 United Nations (1992). S/RES/733 (New York: Security Council), January 23, imposing an arms embargo; and United Nations (1992). S/RES/794 (New York: Security Council), December 3, authorizing the Secretary-General and member states "to use all necessary means" to create a secure environment for humanitarian relief operations.

35 United Nations (1993). S/RES/841 (New York: Security Council), June 16, imposing economic sanctions; and United Nations (1994). S/RES/940 (New York: Security Council),

and Angola[36]; the adoption of quasijudicial powers in delineating the border between Kuwait and Iraq[37]; and the assumption of unprecedented legislative powers in the establishment of the Iraqi Compensation Commission[38] and the ad hoc international criminal tribunals for the former Yugoslavia and Rwanda.[39] Before long, the Security Council's measure of legitimacy "took a dive" as the enthusiasm for the revitalized Council gave way to growing concern, creating an environment that made many international actors more responsive to the Libyan strategy to delegitimize the Council than might otherwise have been possible.

The post–Cold War concerns about the legitimacy of the Security Council fueled a burgeoning of proposals for its reform,[40] coming from two main camps: (1) those who focused on the "democratic deficit" of the Council's procedural arrangements, and (2) those who were concerned about the substantive injustice that was resulting from its operations in peacekeeping and, increasingly, enforcement. The proposals were generally sympathetic to the Security Council rather than presenting a fundamental challenge to its increased activism. Whereas the calls for reform are a measure of unease about the Council's assumption of expanded powers, they also indicate a widespread desire for reassurance in the form of new "rules," which can be internalized.

July 31, authorizing a multinational force "to use all necessary means" to ensure the return of democratically elected President Aristede.

[36] United Nations (1993). S/RES/864 (New York: Security Council), September 15, imposing an embargo on the supply of arms and petroleum products to the UNITA rebel forces.

[37] United Nations (1991). S/RES/687 (New York: Security Council), April 3.

[38] Ibid.

[39] United Nations (1993). S/RES/827 (New York: Security Council), May 25, establishes the International Criminal Tribunal for the Former Yugoslavia (ICTY); and United Nations (1994). S/RES/955 (New York: Security Council), November 8, establishes the International Criminal Tribunal for Rwanda (ICTR).

[40] Weston, Burns H. (1991). "Security Council Resolution 678 and Persian Gulf Decision Making: Precarious Legitimacy," *American Journal of International Law*, Vol. 85: 516; Caron, David D. (1993). "The Legitimacy of the Collective Authority of the Security Council," *American Journal of International Law*, Vol. 87: 552; Murphy, Sean D. (1994). "The Security Council, Legitimacy, and the Concept of Collective Security After the Cold War," *Columbia Journal of Transnational Law*, Vol. 32: 201; Koskenniemi, Martti (1995). "The Police in the Temple: Order, Justice, and the UN: A Dialectical View," *European Journal of International Law*, Vol. 6/3: 325. In 1992, the General Assembly initiated a process of seeking the views of member states on Security Council Reform in General Assembly Resolution 48/26 (1993); United Nations (1992). A/RES/47/62 (New York: General Assembly), December 11, Article 1. The following year it established an open-ended Working Group on Security Council Reform to consider these submissions and develop reform proposals in General Assembly Resolution 48/26, United Nations (1993). A/RES/48/26, Articles 1 and 2. The Working Group reported annually from 1994 to 2004. Available at globalpolicy.igc.org/security/reform/reports.htm.

"Democratizing" the Security Council by addressing perceptions of procedural unfairness has been urged primarily by states.[41] As in San Francisco, the "un-representativeness" of the Council's permanent and nonpermanent membership has emerged as a central issue[42] but with a heightened awareness of the northern bias of its veto arrangements and a concern that its membership should reflect contemporary geopolitical realities.[43] Anxieties about the lack of transparency of the Security Council's decision making have also mounted.[44] Since the end of the Cold War, the Council has become considerably more secretive, to the point that its public sessions are little more than a "rubber-stamping" of decisions negotiated earlier in private, including decisions under Chapter VII.[45] Combined with the absence of institutional checks on the Security Council's powers,[46] this secrecy has made transparency a pressing concern. As Michael Reisman observed, "[d]ecisions that appear to go further than at any time in the history of the United Nations are now ultimately being taken, it seems, by a small group of states separately meeting in secret."[47] Nonstate actors also have raised concerns about the Council's lack of openness to international civil society.[48] All these proposals are aimed at rebuilding confidence in the Council's "procedural correctness."

[41] Malone, David M. (2000). "The Security Council in the 1990s: Inconsistent, Improvisational, Indispensable?," in Ramesh Thakur & Edward Newman (eds.), *New Millennium, New Perspectives: The United Nations, Security, and Governance* (Toronto: United Nations University Press), p. 21.

[42] Working Group on Security Council Reform, see n. 40.

[43] Ibid.; Boutros Boutros-Ghali (1996). *An Agenda for Democratization* (New York: United Nations), p. 49; Smith, M. (1994). "Expanding the Permanent Membership in the UN Security Council: Opening a Pandora's Box of Needed Change?," *Dickenson Journal of International Law*, Vol. 12: 173; *contra*, Commission on Global Governance (1995). *Our Global Neighborhood*, Co-Chairs Ingvar Carlsson & Shridath Ramphal (New York: Oxford University Press), pp. 240–241, who propose phasing out the veto.

[44] Working Group on Security Council Reform, see n. 42. See also Russett, Bruce (ed.) (1997). *The Once and Future Security Council* (New York: St. Martin's Press).

[45] Kirgis, Frederic L. (1995). "The Security Council's First Fifty Years," *American Journal of International Law*, Vol. 89: 506, 518–519.

[46] International Court of Justice (1992). "Questions of the Interpretation and Application of the 1971 Montreal Convention Arising from the Aerial Incident at Lockerbie" (Libya v. UK; Libya v. US), where the International Court of Justice declined to decide whether and in what ways it might be competent to review Security Council actions taken under Chapter VII. See also Franck, Thomas M. (1992). "The 'Powers of Appreciation': Who Is the Ultimate Guardian of UN Legality?," *American Journal of International Law*, Vol. 86: 519.

[47] Reisman, Michael (1993). "The Constitutional Crisis in the United Nations," *American Journal of International Law*, Vol. 87: 83, 86.

[48] The Hague Appeal for Peace (2000). *The Hague Agenda for Peace and Justice for the Twenty-first Century*, Part I, "endorses reform and democratization of the United Nations, including... extending consultative rights to civil society representatives, nongovernmental organizations and parliamentarians at all levels of the UN"; available at www.haguepeace.org/index.php?name=agenda_english. See also United Nations (2004).

Addressing perceptions that the Security Council may be abusing its power in a substantive sense has been urged primarily by NGOs,[49] bringing this constituency more into the purview of the Council. Reform proposals from this camp are concerned with the impact of the Council's decision making on the ground in terms of economic justice, human rights, and sustainable peace. Proponents of "human security," for instance, have challenged the Security Council's state-centered approach, especially in light of its expanding mandate.[50] Whereas Thomas Franck argued that issues of justice or fairness are separate from the notion of legitimacy – at least, in the international community of states where order must receive priority over justice[51] – I believe that the legitimacy of international institutions is increasingly measured by the extent to which outcomes are consistent with contemporary notions of justice and human rights.[52] These reforms highlight the need for a new discourse of assurance, which will allay concerns about the Security Council's apparent lack of concern for the effects of its actions on ordinary people.

During the same period as the Security Council's renaissance, women's international peace movements also were enjoying resurgence. One impetus was widespread awareness of the brutalities directed at women during the

"We the Peoples: Civil Society, the United Nations, and Global Governance, Report of the Panel of Eminent Persons on United Nations–Civil Society Relations," A/58/817 (New York: General Assembly), June 11, pp. 45–46, recommending that the Security Council strengthen its dialogue with civil society in order to improve its effectiveness.

49 Ibid.; The Hague Appeal for Peace (2000). "Root Causes of War/Culture of Peace," Part I, "[i]t is time to redefine security in terms of human and ecological needs instead of national sovereignty and national borders"; Commission on Global Governance (1995), see n. 43, ch. 4, suggests the establishment of an Economic Security Council that would complement the work of a reformed Security Council; Alston, Philip (1992). "The Security Council and Human Rights: Lessons to be Learned from the Iraq–Kuwait Crisis and Its Aftermath," *Australian Yearbook on International Law*, Vol. 13: 107.

50 Newman, Dwight (1999–2000). "A Human Security Council? Applying a 'Human Security' Agenda to Security Council Reform," *Ottawa Law Review/Revue de droit d'Ottawa*, Vol. 31: 213, 219, proposing that "security *should* be measured in terms of the security of human people [rather than the security of states], in terms of their safety and their ability to access basic human needs without disruption."

51 Franck, Thomas M. (1989). "Is Justice Relevant to the International Legal System?," *Notre Dame Law Review*, Vol. 64: 945; Franck, Thomas M., & Hawkins, Steven W. (1989). "Justice in the International System," *Michigan Journal of International Law*, Vol. 10: 127; *contra*, Georgiev, Dencho (1989). "Letter," *American Journal of International Law*, Vol. 83: 554. See also Franck, Thomas M. (1990). *The Power of Legitimacy Among Nations* (New York: Oxford University Press). For discussion, see Alvarez, José (1991). "The Quest for Legitimacy: An Examination of *The Power of Legitimacy Among Nations* by Thomas M. Franck," *New York University Journal of International Law and Policy*, Vol. 24: 199 (book review essay).

52 Mertus, Julie (2000). "Reconsidering the Legality of Humanitarian Intervention: Lessons from Kosovo," *William and Mary Law Review*, Vol. 41: 1743, 1751; Commission on Global Governance (1995), see n. 43, p. 237.

conflict in the former Yugoslavia, which was generating a "sea change" in the way that such violence had previously been understood.[53] Military institutions were finding it less tenable to dismiss sexual violence as an unavoidable side effect of war[54] as people came to understand that it served, in many instances, as an organized tool of armed conflict.[55] At about the same time, women who had been forced into sexual servitude by the Japanese army during World War II were coming forward to speak of their experiences, despite the humiliation and shame that had kept them silent for so long.[56] In light of these revelations, an increasingly confident international women's peace lobby was calling for action that would bring an end to the impunity that attended these crimes.[57]

It did not take long for the feminist agenda to overlap with that of Security Council reform as reports alleging rape and sexual exploitation by peacekeepers in Cambodia, Mozambique, and Bosnia – as well as by forces involved in the Council's apparently successful enforcement action in Kuwait – suggested that militaries acting under the imprimatur of the UN were no different.[58] Anne Orford noted that these and other negative consequences for women that have flowed from the Security Council's operations, including its sanctions regimes, have been totally ignored by mainstream analyses of these events. In her view, the apparent efficacy of the international security system relies on the silences of women and other marginalized groups, whose security and social status deteriorate as a result of Council interventions.[59] Thus, feminist proposals for reform of the Security Council emerged, seeking to enhance its gender legitimacy through both procedural and substantive innovation.

[53] See, generally, Stiglmayer, Alexandra (ed.) (1994). *Mass Rape: The War Against Women in Bosnia-Herzegovenia* (Lincoln: University of Nebraska Press).

[54] Copelon, Rhonda (1994). "Surfacing Gender: Reconceptualizing Crimes Against Women in Time of War," ibid., pp. 197–198.

[55] Brownmiller, Susan (1975). *Against Our Will: Men, Women, and Rape* (New York: Simon & Schuster), pp. 40–86, reporting evidence of sexual abuse during the two world wars and the conflicts in East Pakistan and Vietnam; Chang, Iris (1997). *The Rape of Nanking: The Forgotten Holocaust of World War II* (New York: Basic Books).

[56] Chinkin, Christine (2001). "Women's International Tribunal on Japanese Military Sexual Slavery," *American Journal of International Law*, Vol. 95/2: 335.

[57] Gardam, Judith (1998). "Women, Human Rights, and International Humanitarian Law," *International Review of the Red Cross*, Vol. 324: 421.

[58] Orford, Anne (1996). "The Politics of Collective Security," *Michigan Journal of International Law*, Vol. 17: 373, pp. 378–380; Gardam, Judith, & Jarvis, Michelle (2000). "Women and Armed Conflict: The International Response to the Beijing Platform for Action," *Columbia Human Rights Law Review*, Vol. 32: 1, p. 18.

[59] Ibid., p. 386.

Procedurally, feminists drew attention to the male-dominated membership of the Security Council, linking this to its militaristic approach and poor record of addressing "women's issues."[60] They insisted that democratization must also include women's participation in decision making, within the Security Council as well as in peace negotiations and peacebuilding processes.[61] Feminists were also concerned about the Council's lack of transparency, urging the establishment of mechanisms for it to consult with local communities whose "security" is directly affected by its actions and to allow people to seek redress for Council actions that adversely impact them. The creation of bodies to monitor complaints of sexual abuse by peacekeepers[62] and investigate allegations of trafficking by UN peacekeeping personnel[63] was among the proposals.

Substantively, feminists questioned the Security Council's "impoverished" understanding of international peace and security that "focuses on militarism and power supported by force"[64] rather than on the substance or "justice" of its determinations and actions.[65] They argued that the Council's militaristic and state-centered notions of peace and collective security reproduce hierarchical ideas about gender, which explains why many of its actions lead to an increase in the insecurity of women and other nonelite groups.[66] They criticized the Security Council for not including women's security in its official calculus of military security,[67] for failing to take into account the impact that Council-sponsored sanctions might have on civilian women,[68] and for not factoring women's security and rights into the design and

[60] Women's International League for Peace and Freedom (2003). "Lists as Sentences," p. 1 (handout), records that only two of the eighty-eight ambassadors who have sat on the Security Council have been women; Enloe, Cynthia (1993). *The Morning After: Sexual Politics at the End of the Cold War* (Berkley: University of California Press), p. 259.

[61] Orford (1996), see n. 58, p. 392.

[62] Ibid., pp. 393–394. Orford suggests that the World Bank Inspection Panel may provide a useful model.

[63] Murray, Jennifer (2003). "Note: Who Will Police the Peacebuilders? The Failure to Establish Accountability of United Nations Civilian Police in the Trafficking of Women in Postconflict Bosnia and Herzegovina," *Columbia Human Rights Law Review*, Vol. 34: 475, 528.

[64] Chinkin, Christine (2003). "Gender, Human Rights, and Peace Agreements," *Ohio State Journal on Dispute Resolution*, Vol. 18: 867, 874.

[65] Tickner, J. Anne (1992). *Gender in International Relations: Feminist Perspectives on Achieving Global Security* (New York: Columbia University Press), pp. 54–66.

[66] Orford (1996), see n. 58, pp. 383, 395.

[67] Charlesworth, Hilary, & Chinkin, Christine (2000). *The Boundaries of International Law: A Feminist Analysis* (Manchester: Manchester University Press), pp. 275–276.

[68] Bahdi, Reem (2002). "Iraq, Sanctions, and Security: A Critique," *Duke Journal of Gender, Law, and Policy*, Vol. 9: 237.

implementation of postconflict reconstruction.[69] They argued the corollary to Ambassador Chowdury's recognition that peace is "inextricably linked" with gender equality,[70] that military solutions to international disputes cannot bring peace until they no longer rely fundamentally on gender inequality for their effectiveness.

In response, the Security Council followed the same course of management that was successful in San Francisco. Procedurally, although agreement about altering its composition remains elusive, some members of the Council have taken the initiative and sponsored several new practices designed to improve its democratic credentials. In 1992, during the crisis in the Balkans, Venezuelan Ambassador Diego Arria invited Security Council members to an informal gathering to hear the testimony of a Bosnian priest.[71] The practice was continued and Arria Formula Meetings now take place nearly every month and are organized as part of the regular Security Council schedule.[72] Another informal dialogue, between Council members and the NGO Working Group on the Security Council, was initiated in 1996 by the Global Policy Forum, involving about thirty NGOs.[73] These briefings now occur almost every week with at least one of the ambassadors on the Security Council.[74] Field visits by Council members to areas of conflict is another new practice, which has had the effect of sensitizing individual members to many of the realities of everyday civilian experiences of armed conflict.[75] Although all of these exchanges are informal, they are tightly controlled by the Security Council, which issues invitations, approves the agenda, and requires the exchanges to be largely scripted.[76] Even so, the innovations send positive signals about the Security Council's amenability to more open procedures. That the Council is acutely aware of the need to maintain perceptions of "procedural correctness" was evident in the President's 2000–2001 Annual Report to the General Assembly, when he reported the many public meetings

[69] Charlesworth & Chinkin (2000), see n. 67, p. 262.
[70] Chowdury (2000), see n. 1.
[71] Paul, James (2003). "The Arria Formula," www.globalpolicy.org/security/mtgsetc/arria.htm.
[72] Ibid.
[73] Paul, James (2001). "A Short History of the NGO Working Group on the Security Council," www.globalpolicy.org/security/ngowkgrp/history.htm. Members are listed at www.globalpolicy.org/security/ngowkgrp/members.htm.
[74] NGO Working Group on the Security Council (2008). "Information Statement," www.globalpolicy.org/security/ngowkgrp/statements/current.htm.
[75] Interview with Felicity Hill, former Executive Officer of Women's International League for Peace and Freedom (WILPF), working at the time of the interview for UN Development Fund for Women (UNIFEM), New York, May 3, 2002, p. 6.
[76] Ibid., p. 30.

that had been held to improve the Council's transparency and facilitate the participation of a wider group of UN members.[77]

The Security Council also has made efforts to address some of the substantive issues raised by reformers. Significantly, it has departed from its usual practice of discussing international peace and security only in a specific context by holding open thematic debates about what might be defined broadly as "human-security" issues. Initiated by Canada during its presidency in 1999, with an Open Debate on the subject of civilians caught in armed conflict[78] (followed soon after by another on the protection, rights, and welfare of war-affected children), thematic Open Debates have become a regular feature of the Security Council's work. The debates have led to the adoption of a number of thematic resolutions that set out a type of social agenda for the Council. The resolutions seek to address some of the problems faced by civilians,[79] especially children,[80] in the context of armed conflict and its aftermath.[81] These efforts have produced a new discourse of reassurance for the Security Council, expressing its concern to protect the most vulnerable victims of war.

In summary, the Security Council responded to anxieties about its legitimacy – precipitated by its rapid assumption of expanded powers following the end of the Cold War – by producing new rules that would rebuild its symbolic capital. To this end, it adopted procedural innovations aimed at resuscitating confidence in its procedural correctness and a new discourse of reassurance designed to rebuild trust in the Council's commitment to acting for the common good. However, from a feminist perspective, these new developments did not come close to addressing the problem that the Security Council's enlarged mandate presented the prospect that militarism will be extended into even more aspects of our everyday lives.[82] Yet, as philosopher

[77] Hill, Felicity (2002). "NGOs and the Security Council," *Disarmament Forum*, Vol. 1: 27.

[78] Malone (2000), see n. 41, p. 28.

[79] United Nations (1999). S/RES/1265 (New York: Security Council), September 17; United Nations (2000). S/RES/1296 (New York: Security Council), April 19; United Nations (2006). S/RES/1674 (New York: Security Council), April 28; United Nations (2006). S/RES/1738 (New York: Security Council), December 23.

[80] United Nations (1999). S/RES/1261 (New York: Security Council), August 30; United Nations (2000). S/RES/1314 (New York: Security Council), August 11; United Nations (2001). S/RES/1379 (New York: Security Council), November 20; United Nations (2003). S/RES/1460 (New York: Security Council), January 30; United Nations (2004). S/RES/1539 (New York: Security Council), April 22; United Nations (2005). S/RES/1612 (New York: Security Council), July 26.

[81] True-Frost, Cora C. (2007). "The Security Council and Norm Consumption," *New York University Journal of International Law and Policy*, Vol. 40: 115.

[82] Otto, Dianne (1999). "Whose Security? Re-imagining Post–Cold War Peacekeeping from a Feminist Perspective," in Robert G. Patman (ed.), *Security in a Post–Cold War World* (London: Macmillan Press), pp. 81–85.

Michel Foucault once observed, whereas certain ways of thinking can have hegemonic effects, they also have within them the possibility of resistance and transformation.[83] Foucault's observation links with Hurd's view that the Security Council can never fully control the purposes to which its rules might be put. The challenge that faced feminists was to forge links between the Council's expanded agenda and their own antimilitary, transformative ideas about international peace and security.[84]

Creating the Security Council's Symbolic Capital in Gender Legitimacy

Although the Security Council was responsive to many of the proposals aimed at improving its legitimacy, its emerging discourse on gender remained untouched by feminism, at least until Chowdury's International Women's Day Statement in 2000. The Council's thematic resolutions on civilians were couched in language that conflated women and children into an undifferentiated "vulnerable group."[85] Although the resolutions break the silence about sexual violence during armed conflict, the lack of references to women's rights and equality confirms traditional gender stereotypes. Women are represented as dependent and defenseless victims needing military protection rather than as equal partners in dispute resolution, which exposes the gender conservatism of the Security Council's emerging social agenda. Together with the rare references to women in previous resolutions, which were all concerned

[83] Foucault, Michel (1986). "Space, Knowledge, and Power," in Paul Rabinow (ed.), *The Foucault Reader*, p. 245, cited in Gordon, Colin (1991). "Governmental Rationality: An Introduction," in Graham Burchell, Colin Gordon, & Peter Miller (eds.), *The Foucault Effect: Studies in Governmentality* (Chicago: University of Chicago Press), pp. 1, 46.

[84] Feminist conceptions of international peace and security are diverse but generally involve a comprehensive approach that is concerned with addressing the many insecurities experienced by women and other marginalized groups, not only those associated directly with armed conflict but also the connected insecurities, in private and public life, that result from structural inequalities. Further, feminist conceptions are usually antimilitarist, drawing on the pacifist strategies, often developed by grassroots women, to organize against violence and conflict in their communities. See also Pettman, Jan Jindy (1996). *Worlding Women: A Feminist International Politics* (St. Leonards, Australia: Allen & Unwin), pp. 105–106; Enloe, Cynthia (2000). *Maneuvers: The International Politics of Militarizing Women's Lives* (Berkley: University of California Press), pp. 3–4; Petersen, V. Spike, & Runyan, Anne Sisson (1999). *Global Gender Issues* (Boulder, CO: Westview Press), pp. 115–116.

[85] United Nations (1999). S/RES/1265 (New York: Security Council), September 17, preamble paragraph 4; United Nations (2000). S/RES/1296 (New York: Security Council), April 19, preamble paragraph 4 and paragraphs 9 and 10; United Nations (2001). S/RES/1379 (New York: Security Council), November 20, paragraph 4. These provisions refer to "women, children and other vulnerable groups." See also United Nations (1999). S/RES/1265 (New York: Security Council), September 17, paragraph 13.

with their suffering as victims of sexual violence,[86] the possibility that the Council might also recognize women's agency in their own "protection" and in the resolution of armed conflicts would seem to be foreclosed – that is, until the adoption of Resolution 1325. In this section, I examine how Resolution 1325 emerged from a new strategy adopted by WILPF-UN and the coalition of NGOs that it facilitated, which was to engage directly with the Security Council by seeking a thematic resolution on women, peace, and security. I outline the contours of the alliance between the Council and feminist peace activists, suggesting that the engagement poses dilemmas for both parties, particularly for feminists.

In deciding to seek a Security Council thematic resolution, WILPF-UN faced some immediate problems. The organization has a long history of antimilitarism that dates back to World War I, when the first international women's committee devoted exclusively to advocacy for peace was established (renamed WILPF in 1919).[87] Since then, WILPF has tirelessly promoted a reduction in military expenditure, ending the arms trade, and bringing about general disarmament. Yet, not all members of the NGO Working Group agreed with these aims, and WILPF-UN was also aware that its antimilitarist goals were not taken seriously in the UN system.[88] Therefore, WILPF-UN made the strategic decision to repackage its approach to make it more palatable to its NGO partners and to those it wanted to persuade within the UN.[89] The decision was to promote the gender mainstreaming of the work of the Security Council, given that this policy already enjoyed systemwide support.[90] As Sherri Gibbings suggested, "[t]he route to peace and ending war in this approach was no longer a reduction in military spending but the integration of women and a gender perspective."[91] By making this decision, WILPF-UN chose to pay a high price to gain access to the Security Council's symbols, conceding substantial power to the Council before the real negotiations had even begun.

Although the idea of persuading the Security Council to adopt a resolution had been discussed informally by NGOs two years earlier at the 1998

86 See, for example, United Nations (1993). S/RES/827 (New York: Security Council), May 25 (expressing concern about "massive, organized and systematic detention and rape of women" in the former Yugoslavia).

87 Rupp (1997), see n. 3, p. 29. The Committee was originally called the International Committee of Women for Permanent Peace.

88 Gibbings, Sheri (2004). *Governing Women, Governing Security: Governmentality, Gender Mainstreaming, and Women's Activism at the UN*, unpublished thesis, Graduate Program in Social Anthropology (Toronto: York University), pp. 60–61.

89 Ibid., p. 59.

90 Ibid.

91 Ibid., p. 60.

Commission on the Status of Women (CSW),[92] it was Chowdury's Statement that served to mobilize them. Their resolve stiffened with the release of the Brahimi Report in June 2000, which made only two references to gender in its "comprehensive" review of the Security Council's peacekeeping operations.[93] Incensed, the NGO Working Group drafted the initial version of the resolution,[94] which gave them the power to shape its core content. The NGOs agreed that their primary aspiration was to focus attention on women's positive contributions to peace, aiming to shift the Council's gender discourse from casting women exclusively as victims of armed conflict to also recognizing their role as peacemakers.[95] The NGOs took the course of devoting "equal time" to issues associated with women as victims of armed conflict and as agents in peacebuilding. More specifically, the NGOs had three goals in mind: (1) to have gender issues routinely considered in the Security Council's work; (2) to reinforce protections provided by existing international instruments and extend them into new areas such as Disarmament, Demobilization, and Reintegration (DDR) programs; and (3) to raise the profile of women's local and national peacebuilding activities.[96] After drafting the resolution, the NGO Working Group produced "talking points" and lists of "ideas and arguments" that they used to lobby UN agencies, Security Council members, other NGOs, and anyone else they thought could help.[97] It is a testament to their remarkable lobbying efforts that the final text still reflected their general goals.

After the NGO Working Group had persuaded the Namibian Mission to take the lead in bringing the issue to the Security Council during its turn in the rotating presidency,[98] others within the UN – including the UN Development Fund for Women (UNIFEM) and some key individuals – provided substantial support.[99] It fell to the Namibian Mission to undertake the hard work of persuading other Security Council members that the resolution was worth supporting. As the Mission's responsible desk officer observed later in an interview with Gibbings, this process was often more about diplomatic

92 Cohn et al. (2004), see n. 9, p. 131.

93 Ambassador Lakhdar Brahimi (2000). *Report of the Panel on United Nations Peace Operations*, UN Doc. S/2000/809, A/55/305, August 21.

94 Cohn et al. (2004), see n. 9, p. 130; Gibbings (2004), see n. 88, p. 51.

95 Gibbings (2004), see n. 88, p. 52.

96 Cohn et al. (2004), see n. 9, pp. 131–132.

97 Gibbings (2004), see n. 88, p. 56.

98 Namibia had supported gender mainstreaming in peace-support operations in the past, hosting a UN Department of Peacekeeping Operations (DPKO) seminar on "Mainstreaming a Gender Perspective in Multidimensional Peace Support Operations" in Windhoek, May 2000, which produced the *Windhoek Declaration and Namibia Plan of Action*, UN Doc. S/2000/693, A/55/138, July 14, 2000.

99 Gibbings (2004), see n. 88, p. 53.

socializing and bartering than support for the content of the resolution.[100] Another of Gibbings's interviewees described the process as "politics over gin and cigars."[101] Despite this performance, many Security Council members had strong views on the issue. Some were firmly of the opinion that the Council was not the place for discussion of women's issues. As Gibbings argued, they were afraid that the Council's association with women would weaken its symbolic power as a "masculine" institution, concerned with the "muscular" issues of military diplomacy and not with "soft" humanitarian issues, which belonged elsewhere.[102] Fortunately for the NGO Working Group, there was a coincidence of supportive Security Council members who formed a critical mass and helped to persuade those who were reluctant.[103] In the view of Felicity Hill, who was Executive Director of WILPF-UN at the time, the Security Council's new practice of field visits also helped to make members more sympathetic to the concerns of the NGO Working Group.[104]

Other new procedures adopted by the Security Council also came to the rescue of Resolution 1325. On October 23, 2000, an Arria Formula Meeting was convened, bringing Council members together with NGO representatives and women's peace activists from several areas of armed conflict.[105] At this meeting, the NGO Working Group urged the Security Council "to draw, *to the utmost*, on the insights, experience, indeed expertise, of women and civil society in matters of daily human security, conflict prevention, resolution, reconciliation, and reconstruction."[106] Having secured agreement from the other NGOs, WILPF-UN made an organizational statement that implored the Security Council to address the root causes of war, including regulating and reducing armaments, although this point was not linked to women's

[100] Ibid., pp. 54–55.
[101] Ibid., p. 56.
[102] Ibid., pp. 40–42.
[103] Hill (2002) interview, see n. 75, p. 3. In addition to Ambassador Chowdury, Patricia Durrant, the Jamaican Ambassador and a tireless supporter of women's human rights, played a key role, as did Theo-Ben Gurirab from Namibia, who held the rotating presidency when the Open Session was held. The delegations from Canada, the United Kingdom, and the Netherlands were also supportive from the start.
[104] Ibid., p. 6.
[105] Statements were made by Isha Dyfan (Women's International League for Peace and Freedom, Sierra Leone), Luz Mendez (Union National de Mujeres Guatemaltecas), Faiza Jama Mohamed (Equality Now), Ininge Mbikusita Mohamed (Federation of African Women's Peace Movements), and the NGO Working Group on Women and International Peace and Security. Available at www.international-alert.org/women/.
[106] NGO Statement (2000). "The Role of Women in Achieving Peace and Maintaining International Security," presented at the Arria Formula Meeting of the UN Security Council, October 23, pp. 4–5 (oral statement).

equality.[107] Anticipation was palpable. The next day, the Council held an Open Debate on Women, Peace, and Security at which more than forty governments made statements in support of a resolution promoting the incorporation of a gender perspective into much of the work of the Council. Although every statement referred to women's suffering as victims of war, the emerging consensus was that women's contributions to peace also needed recognition, as evident in Canada's statement:

> We must also ensure that our focus is not restricted to issues of the victimization of women – vital as it is to grapple with them. We must also address ourselves to the positive contribution that women . . . can and do make to conflict prevention and postconflict peacebuilding.[108]

Namibia's official statement, undeterred by qualms about emasculation, proclaimed that the "mindset, especially of men, must change and give way to new thinking and a new beginning for the UN in the field of conflict resolution and peacekeeping."[109] Also bringing new life to the Security Council was the applause from the spectators in the Council's gallery when Resolution 1325 was unanimously adopted a week later.[110] It would seem that feminist activism had indeed moved from the margins of military diplomacy to its internal chambers.

Resolution 1325 not only responds to some of the concerns about the Security Council's legitimacy raised earlier by feminists but also bears many marks of the long-standing objectives of women's peace movements.[111] Its starting point is the need for the increased participation of women in decision making related to the prevention, management, and resolution of disputes – in international negotiations as well as in field-based operations[112] – reflecting the primary aspiration of the NGO Working Group. Attributing political agency to women in the realm of military affairs had received rhetorical

[107] Gibbings (2004), see n. 88, p. 62.

[108] Statement by Ambassador Paul Heinbecker, Permanent Representative of Canada to the United Nations, to the UN Security Council on Women, Peace, and Security, New York, October 24, 2000.

[109] Statement by Honorable Dr. Theo-Ben Girirab, MP, Namibia Minister for Foreign Affairs, Information, and Broadcasting, during the Security Council Open Debate on Women, Peace, and Security, United Nations, New York, October 24, 2000.

[110] Statement by U.S. Ambassador Nancy Soderberg, U.S. Special Representative to the United Nations for Political Affairs, in the Security Council, on the issue of Women, Peace, and Security, October 24, 2000 (revised – as delivered).

[111] Rupp (1997), see n. 3, p. 207. The "first wave" of women's international opposition to war was strongly influenced by the suffragettes, many of whom hoped that women's political participation would make armed conflict impossible.

[112] United Nations (2000), see n. 5, paragraphs 1–4.

endorsement in earlier soft-law instruments[113] but was yet to be realized in UN practice.[114] By embracing women as political actors, the Security Council marks a break in its previous tradition of treating "women and children" as an object of protection in the context of armed conflict. For the first time, the Security Council formally recognizes women not merely as participants but also as *indispensable* participants in conflict resolution and peace negotiations, opening new opportunities for women's entry into these traditionally "male" spaces.

In a limited way, Resolution 1325 also responds to some of the substantive concerns raised by feminists by acknowledging the need for the Security Council to be attentive to the gender-differentiated consequences of its decisions. To this end, under Article 41, the Council affirms its "readiness" to "consider" the potential impact on the civilian population, "especially women and girls," of measures taken short of the use of force.[115] Significantly, however, there is no expression of "readiness" to extend such considerations to the adoption of forceful measures taken under Article 42. This silence preserves well-worn gendered assumptions about what is considered in the calculus of military decision making[116] and in official assessments of military "success."[117] The only reference to "disarmament" is in the limited context of postconflict reintegration of former combatants.[118] With the Security Council's military enforcement powers located firmly outside the Resolution 1325 sphere of influence, the Council is insulated from feminist critiques of militarism.

Would the outcome have been different if WILPF-UN had taken a different course and insisted on drawing links between gender inequality and militarism in the first draft of Resolution 1325? It is telling that even the Security Council's own responsibilities under Article 26 of the UN

[113] See, for example, the "Spanish Resolution" adopted by the Twelfth Assembly of the League of Nations on September 24, 1931; "Women's Participation in the Strengthening of International Peace and Security," United Nations (1975). A/RES/3519 (New York: General Assembly), December 15; United Nations (1982). "Declaration on the Participation of Women in Promoting International Peace and Cooperation," A/RES/37/63 (New York: General Assembly), December 3; *Beijing Declaration and Platform for Action*, A/CONF.177/20, Strategic Objectives E.1 and E.4, 1995.

[114] Otto (2006), see n. 3.

[115] United Nations (2000), see n. 5, paragraph 14. Measures employed under Article 41, to give effect to Security Council decisions, are those that do not involve the use of armed force, including economic sanctions, the curtailment of communications, and the severance of diplomatic relations.

[116] Cohn, Carol (1993). "Wars, Wimps, and Women," in Miriam Cooke & Angela Woollacott (eds.), *Gendering War Talk* (Princeton, NJ: Princeton University Press), p. 227.

[117] Orford (1996), see n. 58, p. 385.

[118] United Nations (2000), see n. 5, paragraph 13.

Charter to establish systems to "regulate" armaments do not rate a mention in Resolution 1325. This omission is conspicuous when compared with the commitments made by states in Beijing at the 1995 Fourth World Conference on Women to reduce excessive military expenditure and control the availability of arms.[119] Neither does the resolution give any indication that the Security Council might be ready to rethink its approach to security in other ways that were endorsed in Beijing – for example, by highlighting the importance of nonviolent forms of conflict resolution and fostering a culture of peace.[120] The preemptive WILPF-UN concession may have given away more than was necessary.

Even so, Resolution 1325 opens important new opportunities for exposing the Security Council to alternative conceptions of security by acknowledging its "willingness" to ensure that its missions consider gender issues, including through "consultation" with local and international women's groups,[121] and to urge that peace agreements adopt a "gender perspective,"[122] including measures that "support local women's peace initiatives and indigenous processes for conflict resolution."[123] These commitments provide leverage for local and national women's peace advocates to claim a role in mainstream political processes concerned with negotiating and implementing peace agreements and facilitating peacebuilding. If successful, the inclusion of women produces multigendered spaces that are likely to be more hospitable to perspectives that are normally excluded from the calculus of military decision making because they are marked as "feminine" or "wimpish."[124] Valuing women's political participation at the local level may help communities to embrace alternative forms of dispute resolution that, in turn, may destabilize the foundational assumptions that have informed the Security Council's approach to international peace and security. The diverse representations of women in Resolution 1325 – as leaders, combatants, and human-rights defenders – also unsettle the gender dualities that sustain militarism, challenging the "bright line" between the public world of military and political affairs and the private world of home and family, where "feminine" values are said to belong. Disturbing the sense of permanency that is attached to dichotomous

[119] Beijing Declaration and Platform for Action (1995), see n. 113, Strategic Objective E.2. See also paragraph 143(f)(i), in which governments undertake to "work actively towards general and complete disarmament under strict and effective international control."

[120] Ibid., Strategic Objective E.4.

[121] United Nations (2000), see n. 5, paragraph 15.

[122] Ibid., paragraph 8.

[123] Ibid., paragraph 8(b).

[124] See also Gardam, Judith G., & Jarvis, Michelle J. (2001). *Women, Armed Conflict, and International Law* (The Hague: Kluwer), ch. 2; Cohn (1993), see n. 116.

conceptions of gender is a necessary precondition for the "new thinking" and "new beginning" anticipated by the Namibian Ambassador in the Open Debate.

From the viewpoint of the NGO Working Group, Resolution 1325 promotes a gender-mainstreaming agenda, as it had hoped. In addition to urging the participation of women in decision making at all levels, the resolution expresses the Security Council's "willingness" to incorporate a "gender perspective" into peacekeeping operations[125] and urges "gender-sensitive" training for peacekeeping personnel.[126] The Secretary-General is requested "where appropriate" to include information about progress toward gender mainstreaming throughout peacekeeping missions in his reports to the Security Council.[127] Also in keeping with the strategy of the NGO Working Group, Resolution 1325 gives "equal time" to women's protection as victims of armed conflict and their contributions as active participants in peacemaking. The language of "protection"[128] is offset by the language of "women's rights."[129] However, although women's "equality" may be implicit in the notion of women's rights, it is significant that there is only one explicit reference to "equality," which is in the resolution's preamble.[130] Chowdury's recognition that women's equality is "inextricably linked" to peace is absent.

Accountability mechanisms that could monitor its overall implementation are absent from Resolution 1325, as are bodies that could address complaints by civilians who are adversely impacted by the Security Council's operations. Although the NGO Working Group's draft envisaged that the Secretary-General would set up an expert panel to work with UN agencies and departments to implement the resolution, this was missing from the final text.[131] Also lost was a recommendation that the Security Council commit itself to further discussions with NGOs over the course of the resolution's implementation.[132] In place of the missing proposals, the Secretary-General is requested to carry out a study on "the impact of armed conflict on women and girls, the role of women in peacebuilding and the gender dimensions of peace processes and conflict resolution."[133] Formal responsibility for follow-up was to be an internal matter, ignoring the need for independent monitoring.

[125] United Nations (2000), see n. 5, paragraph 4. See also preamble paragraph 8.
[126] Ibid., paragraphs 6–7.
[127] Ibid., paragraph 17.
[128] Ibid., paragraphs 9–11. See also preamble paragraphs 4, 9, and 10.
[129] Ibid., paragraphs 6, 8, 9, and 15. See also preamble paragraphs 6 and 9.
[130] Ibid., preamble paragraph 5.
[131] Gibbings (2004), see n. 88, pp. 57–58.
[132] Ibid., p. 58.
[133] United Nations (2000), see n. 5, para. 16.

From the viewpoint of the Security Council, Resolution 1325 was designed to "manage" the concerns that had been expressed about its gender legitimacy, using the same techniques that had been successful in San Francisco. Having accepted an initial draft – conveniently drawn up by a group of international NGOs who had modified their views so they would be more palatable to the Council – and consulted widely about its content, the Council could be assured that the resolution would be well received by states, UN agencies and departments, and civil society. By expressing the Security Council's desire to ensure women's inclusion in decision making related to international peace and security, Resolution 1325 enhances perceptions of its procedural correctness. By communicating the Council's appreciation of the contributions made by women as peacemakers and its concern about the many ways that women may be adversely affected by armed conflict, the resolution strengthens the Council's discourse of reassurance. The Security Council's control over the final wording of Resolution 1325 ensured the erasure of text that might disrupt its *modus operandi* and dampened expectations that the Council might internalize its own new "rule" by failing to establish a means of accountability. Gender mainstreaming was something that the Security Council – as part of the UN system – was expected to implement, and Resolution 1325 provided a means for the Council to engage with women on its own terms. Although it was a risk that a resolution on "women's" issues would be perceived as a "sign of weakness," thereby delegitimizing the Council's standing as the guardian of international peace and security, members were persuaded that the risk was outweighed by the benefits that would flow from the symbolic enhancement of its gender legitimacy.

Still, the alliance between the Security Council and the NGO Working Group, brought into being by Resolution 1325, is not totally within the Council's control. There is no doubt that WILPF-UN paid a substantial price for access to the Council's symbols, as did many of the other NGOs involved.[134] Also, the Council has significant power as gatekeeper of the resolution because it can set the formal conditions under which it is used.[135] However, as I have argued, the resolution also creates leverage that can be utilized by women's peace activists to insist on their participation in conflict resolution and peacebuilding, and it opens new opportunities for promoting women's equality and challenging militarist orchestrations of international

[134] Another member of the NGO Working Group, The Hague Appeal for Peace, wanted the resolution to promote a "culture of peace" and "peace education" and, like WILPF-UN, also wanted to press its critique of militarism. Gibbings (2004), see n. 88, p. 61.

[135] Hurd (2007), see n. 10, p. 59.

peace and security. Resolution 1325 has this power because on becoming part of the Security Council's store of symbolic capital, it attained special political significance, even without the Council acting on it. Simply being coupled with the Council gives the resolution power, which opens the potential that it will be internalized by other international actors, enabling new practices in the name of gender mainstreaming.[136] As a valuable resource – a "currency of power"[137] – it may be possible for the NGO Working Group to use Resolution 1325 to challenge hierarchical gender relations and perhaps even militarism. Although this power creates some risks for the Security Council, the greater risk has been assumed by WILPF-UN and other members of the NGO Working Group who face the prospect that Resolution 1325 will help to legitimize the Council's military projects rather than their own transformative feminist agendas. Crucial to understanding this struggle, and how it might unfold, is appreciating that Resolution 1325 is reliant on the legitimacy of the Security Council for its credibility. Therefore, the power of the resolution depends on its being used "within the boundaries of meaning" set by the Council.[138] This produces a puzzle for the NGO Working Group: how to utilize this new power for feminist ends without undermining the Council's legitimacy.

Negotiating the Alliance of Gender Legitimacy between the Security Council and Feminists

Once adopted, the value of Resolution 1325 as symbolic capital – for the Security Council on the one hand and the NGO Working Group on the other – remained heavily dependent on the political struggle between them over its meaning and application. Unlike resolutions adopted under Chapter VII of the UN Charter, Resolution 1325 is not binding. Without formal mechanisms for monitoring and implementation, it is likely that many Council members expected it to simply gather dust in the UN archives. However, having succeeded in creating a new and potentially powerful symbol of women's agency in the cause of peace, the NGO Working Group was not about to allow that to happen. In this final section, using the examples of Afghanistan, Timor-Leste, and Iraq, I explore some of the struggles that have taken place in the implementation of the resolution and the challenges they have presented for the NGO Working Group.

Immediately following its adoption, Resolution 1325 became a site of concerted feminist activity with far-reaching effects within the UN system and

[136] Ibid., p. 52.
[137] Ibid., p. 54.
[138] Ibid., p. 57.

outside it in peace negotiations and postconflict reconstruction.[139] The NGO Working Group worked tirelessly to publicize the resolution, presenting it as a women's manifesto that was "binding" on the Security Council.[140] It made a particular effort to ensure that women in conflict zones were aware of the resolution by translating it into dozens of languages[141] and distributing thousands of print copies. The WILPF-UN divided its operations into two projects, marking a separation that would enable it to continue its work with the Council as well as move forward with its antimilitarist agenda. Fostering the implementation of Resolution 1325 became the task of its "PeaceWomen" project, whereas "Reaching Critical Will" was aimed at enhancing NGO participation in UN disarmament forums.[142] PeaceWomen focused on raising awareness and exchanging information about Resolution 1325 by launching a Web site[143] and producing a regular e-mail newsletter.[144] To foster innovative thinking about how the resolution could be used, many consultations and workshops with women's peace advocates were organized. Local women's groups, in the midst of conflicts and postconflict reconstruction, proved more than eager to embrace the resolution and exploit the possibilities it offered. The PeaceWomen portal records use of the resolution by women's groups in more than fifty-eight situations of conflict.[145] Many creative projects have based their rationale on Resolution 1325, such as building a women's support network spanning Kosovo, Macedonia, and Albania and establishing women's community media in Melanesia.[146] Transnational women's peace and human-rights networks have been strengthened, often serving to bolster local efforts to promote feminist approaches to peace and security. As

[139] See NGO Working Group (2001). *Resolution 1325: One Year On*, October, available at www.peacewomen.org/un/UN1325/since1325.html; NGO Working Group (2002). *Resolution 1325: Two Years On*, October 31, available at www.peacewomen.org/un/UN1325/NGOreport.html; NGO Working Group (2005). *From Local to Global: Making Peace Work for Women: Security Council Resolution 1325 – Five Years on Report*, available at www.womenpeacesecurity.org/publications/NGOWG_5_Years_On_Report_ENG.pdf.

[140] Cohn et al. (2004), see n. 9, p. 132.

[141] The resolution was available online in eighty-four languages, with a further eight translations pending, April 28, 2008, available at www.peacewomen.org/1325inTranslation/index.html.

[142] See home page of the WILPF-UN Office, www.wilpf.org/International.

[143] See www.peacewomen.org. UNIFEM also established a Women, Peace, and Security Portal in 2003, www.womenwarpeace.org.

[144] The newsletter commenced in May 2002. See *1325 PeaceWomen E-News*, www.peacewomen.org/news/1325News/1325ENewsindex.html.

[145] See *Women, Peace, and Security Initiatives: Country Index*; available at www.peacewomen.org/campaigns/countriesindex.html.

[146] Cohn, Carol (2004). "Feminist Peacemaking," *Women's Review of Books*, Vol. 21/5: 8–9.

observed by the authors of an independent study commissioned by UNIFEM to complement the Secretary-General's study requested by Resolution 1325, the resolution has given a new "political legitimacy" to the long history of women's peace activism.[147]

Within the UN, the Inter-agency Network on Women and Gender Equality established a Task Force on Women, Peace, and Security – including nearly all UN agencies – to promote the integration of gender perspectives into all the peace and security work of the UN bureaucracy.[148] Supportive states organized into an intergovernmental group – called the Friends of Women, Peace, and Security – to support the resolution's implementation. As a result of an intensive lobbying campaign by NGOs, the Department of Peacekeeping Operations finally created the position of Gender Advisor in 2003, whose role is to support gender initiatives in peacekeeping missions. These and many other developments meant that pressure continued to build for a mechanism that would review and evaluate implementation of Resolution 1325. Finally, following a request from the Security Council, a UN Systemwide Action Plan was adopted in 2005.[149] The work of the Inter-agency Task Force, the ambitious plan is organized into twelve areas of action and identifies objectives, strategies, timelines, and resources for each area. However, although the Secretary-General's 2006 review of the plan's implementation confirmed that significant institutional activity had been generated by the resolution, there was little evidence of overall coordination or coherence.[150] The review concluded that the role of women in peace processes generally is still considered a "side issue" rather than fundamental to sustainable peace.[151]

Two years after Resolution 1325 was adopted, the Secretary-General's study was presented to the Security Council[152] along with the study commissioned by UNIFEM.[153] Affirming the approach of the resolution, both studies found

147 Rehn & Sirleaf (2002), see n. 14, p. 3.

148 "Friends of Women, Peace, and Security," *1325 PeaceWomen E-News*, Vol. 3, June 28, 2002, p. 4.

149 Secretary-General (2005). *Report of the Secretary-General on Women, Peace, and Security*, S/2005/636, 10 October, Annex: "Systemwide action plan for the implementation of Security Council Resolution 1325 (2000)."

150 Secretary-General (2006). *Report of the Secretary-General on Women, Peace, and Security*, S/2006/770, September 27.

151 Ibid., paragraph 47.

152 Secretary-General (2002). *Women, Peace and Security: Study Submitted by the Secretary-General Pursuant to Security Council Resolution S/RES/1325 (2000)* (New York: United Nations). This report is supplemented by a summary of its major findings and recommendations; United Nations (2002). "Report of the Secretary-General on Women, Peace, and Security," S/2002/1154 (New York: Security Council), October 16.

153 Rehn & Sirleaf (2002), see n. 14.

that armed conflict was having devastating consequences for women and that UN peacemaking and peacebuilding practices needed to be more inclusive of women and more responsive to their needs and concerns. However, striking differences between the two studies emerge because of their different methodologies. Whereas the Secretary-General's report – which reviews the activities of the UN and its specialized agencies in light of Resolution 1325 – conveys a strong message about the urgent need for substantial change in the UN's peacekeeping work, its diplomatic language mutes feminist analysis and points to technical solutions to the problems identified. In contrast, the UNIFEM study bases its analysis on interviews with women victims and survivors of armed conflict,[154] which results in forthright criticism of present practices and concreteness in describing their harmful consequences for women. Its conclusions are informed by a feminist awareness of the entrenched nature of gender inequality and the need for careful strategizing if change is to occur.

Follow-up efforts by the Security Council have been erratic, at best, despite the store of information provided by these studies, which could inform its implementation of Resolution 1325. In contrast to the increased activism of women's peace movements and the impressive array of institutional developments, actions by the Security Council in the spirit of the resolution have been rare. Increased women's participation in formal decision-making processes has been uneven, as the case studies of Afghanistan and East Timor demonstrate, despite the resolution's clear injunction that it is a priority. Indeed, NGOs have had to work hard just to keep Resolution 1325 on the Council's agenda. Largely as a result of their perseverance, the resolution has been reaffirmed by the Security Council in annual activities, including follow-up Arria Formula Meetings,[155] Open Debates,[156] and Presidential

[154] Charlesworth, Hilary (1999). "Feminist Methods in International Law," *American Journal of International Law* 93/2: 379; Mertus, Julie (2000). "Feminist Curiosity Unravels Militarism: Why Method Matters," *Berkley Women's Law Journal*, p. 338; Enloe, Cynthia (2000). *Maneuvers: The International Politics of Militarizing Women's Lives* (Berkley: University of California Press) (book review).

[155] The second Arria Formula Meeting was held on October 30, 2001, at which Security Council members heard testimonies from women from East Timor, Kosovo, and Afghanistan and a statement from the NGO Working Group. At the third Arria Formula Meeting, October 23, 2002, it was planned that women from Uganda, Burundi, India, and Israel would make presentations. In the end, only Angelina Atyam from Uganda was able to officially address the Security Council because two of the other women were unable to get to New York for the occasion. Gila Svirsky, from Women in Black in Israel, was only allowed to say a few words due to the "sensitivity of Middle East politics." See "Statements by Women from War-Torn Countries," *1325 PeaceWomen E-News*, Vol. 12, November 1, 2002, p. 6.

[156] Security Council Open Debates on Women, Peace, and Security were held on October 28–29, 2002, October 29, 2003, and annually since then.

Statements.[157] Although, as Hill observed, input to the Security Council by these means primarily has been in the form of individual testimonies from women affected by armed conflict rather than critical debates about strategy and implementation.[158] Many of the official statements at the Open Debate marking the resolution's third anniversary in October 2003 expressed deep dissatisfaction with the pace of implementation.[159] In 2006, the Secretary-General reported that since the adoption of Resolution 1325, only 55 of the Security Council's 211 country-specific resolutions (i.e., 26.07 percent) made any reference to "women" or "gender."[160] The dismal record of the Council's substantive engagement with gender mainstreaming demonstrates that it has not internalized its own new "rule."

Lack of internalization is also evident in the Secretary-General's work. In the study prepared for the Security Council pursuant to Resolution 1325, he observed that "[o]ne of the greatest challenges is harnessing the energy and activism that many women exhibit in informal activities and translating that into their participation and influence in formal activities."[161] However, the insight that women have a crucial contribution to make to conflict resolution and peacebuilding was nowhere apparent in his detailed proposals for major UN reform in March 2005.[162] Only five months earlier, in a follow-up report on the resolution to the Security Council, he had expressed his intention to "analyze the obstacles and missed opportunities for women's full participation in peace negotiations and develop strategies accordingly."[163] To the extent that women's informal peacemaking activities have translated into direct participation in formal processes of postconflict decision making, it

[157] United Nations (2001). "Security Council Reaffirms Support for Enhanced Women's Role in Conflict Prevention, Resolution: Statement by the President of the Security Council," S/PRST/2001/31 (New York: Security Council), October 31; United Nations (2002). "Statement by the President of the Security Council," S/PRST/2002/32 (New York: Security Council), October 31; United Nations (2003). "Press Release from the President of the Security Council, Summary of the Open Debate on the Implementation of Resolution 1325," USUN Press Release 213(03), October 31.

[158] Cohn et al. (2004), above n. 9, p. 133 (comment by Hill).

[159] A summary of the debate is available at www.peacewomen.org/un/SCOpenDebate2003/OpenDebate2003index.html.

[160] Report of the Secretary-General (2006), see n. 150, para. 28. The PeaceWomen Project continues to monitor Council resolutions. Updated to June 29, 2007, they report that 77 of 272 country-specific resolutions (28.31 percent) passed since the adoption of Resolution 1325 contained language on women or gender.

[161] Secretary-General (2002), see n. 152, para. 212.

[162] United Nations (2005). *In Larger Freedom: Towards Development, Security, and Human Rights for All*, UN Doc. A/59/2005, March 21, paragraphs 12–17.

[163] United Nations (2004). *Report of the Secretary-General on Women, Peace, and Security*, UN Doc. S/2004/814, October 13, paragraph 55.

has been due more to the new political legitimacy of women's peace activism than to the efforts of the Security Council or the Secretary-General.

Afghanistan, the first major testing ground for Resolution 1325, provides a good example. Although the Security Council made no reference to Resolution 1325 in any of its resolutions on rebuilding Afghanistan following the U.S. occupation in November 2001,[164] it was used to rally a coalition of women – including Hollywood celebrities, women's-rights activists, politicians, and UN ambassadors – to demand that women be included in political negotiations following the occupation.[165] As a direct result, four women[166] were included in the Bonn Conference held in December 2001, where the first stage of these negotiations took place, despite the initial plan to include women only at a later stage.[167] The Bonn Agreement included a commitment to the eventual establishment of a "broad-based, gender-sensitive, multiethnic, and fully representative government,"[168] and two women were appointed to the thirty-member Interim Administration.[169] The Bonn Agreement also called for women's participation in the Emergency Loya Jirga (i.e., Tribal Council) to elect the transitional government, which led to the involvement of about two hundred women from all regions in this crucial meeting.[170]

Yet, at the same time as women's increased participation in formal decision-making processes was being celebrated, the majority of women in Afghanistan continued to feel powerless and insecure.[171] As the Secretary-General's study observes, women's inequality can persist and even deepen in postconflict societies.[172] In Afghanistan, particularly outside Kabul, warlords were

[164] United Nations (2001). S/RES/1378 (New York: Security Council), November 14; United Nations (2001). S/RES/1383 (New York: Security Council), December 6; United Nations (2001). S/RES/1386 (New York: Security Council), December 19. Neither has there been any reference to Resolution 1325 in any Security Council resolutions on Afghanistan since 2001.

[165] Neuwirth, Jessica (2002). "Women and Peace and Security: The Implementation of UN Security Council Resolution 1325," *Duke Journal of Gender Law and Policy*, Vol. 9: 253, 255.

[166] Secretary-General (2002), see n. 152, paragraph 195, noting that two of the women were delegates and two were observers. *Contra* Neuwirth, ibid., p. 256, who claims that six women attended, three of them as delegates and three as observers.

[167] Brahimi, Lakhdar (2001). Briefing to the Security Council for Afghanistan, November 14, cited in Neuwirth (2002), see n. 165, p. 255.

[168] "Agreement on Provisional Arrangements in Afghanistan Pending the Re-establishment of Permanent Government Institutions," December 5, 2001, preamble paragraph 7.

[169] Ibid., Annex IV. They were Dr. Sima Samar (Vice-Chair and Minister for Women's Affairs) and Dr. Suhaila Seddiqi (Minister for Public Health).

[170] United Nations (2002), see n. 152, paragraph 195.

[171] Rehn & Sirleaf (2002), see n. 14, p. 2.

[172] Secretary-General (2002), see n. 152, paragraph 338; Gardam & Jarvis (2001), see n. 124, p. 21.

reentrenching themselves[173] and violence against women was increasing at a dramatic rate[174] – not only violating women's and girls' rights to bodily integrity but also denying them access to education, political participation, health care, and employment.[175] In March 2004, two and a half years after the U.S. occupation, the *New York Times* reported that increasing numbers of young Afghan women were committing suicide in order to escape the cruelties of traditional family practices and conservative Islamic beliefs, which countenance forced marriages and domestic violence.[176] Nearly seven years after the initial U.S. occupation, there are reports that Afghanistan's Parliament, at the behest of fundamentalist religious elites, is considering laws that will formally reimpose many of the Taliban-era restrictions on women's freedom.[177] The measured increase in women's participation in formal politics was not stemming the tide of militarism or improving women's status more generally as the NGO Working Group had hoped; on the contrary, in some respects, life was worse for women.

A similar picture emerged in Timor-Leste. Although the Security Council established the UN Transitional Authority in East Timor (UNTAET) twelve months before the adoption of Resolution 1325, it was the first Council mandate to refer to the importance of including personnel who had "training" in the gender-related provisions of international law.[178] At the first National Congress of Women in June 2000,[179] a statement was adopted that called for UNTAET to "fulfill the United Nations commitment to gender equity."[180] The women's lobby succeeded in having thirteen women included in the thirty-three–member National Council, which was established in July 2000 to advise the Transitional Administrator on legislative

[173] Human Rights Watch (2002). *"We Want to Live as Humans": Repression of Women and Girls in Western Afghanistan* (New York: Human Rights Watch), December; Amnesty International (2003). *Afghanistan: "No One Listens to Us and No One Treats Us as Human Beings": Justice Denied to Women* (London: Amnesty International), October; Abdela, Lesley (2003). "No Place for a Woman," *London Times*, Op-Ed, April 29.

[174] Editorial (2003). "Afghan Women's Rights," *New York Times*, September 24.

[175] Human Rights Watch (2003). *"Killing You Is a Very Easy Thing for Us": Human Rights Abuses in Southeast Afghanistan* (New York: Human Rights Watch), July, pp. 24–28, 70–88.

[176] Gall, Carlotta (2004). "For More Afghan Women, Immolation Is Escape," *New York Times*, March 8.

[177] Heikkila, Pia (2008). "Afghanistan Weighs Ban on Jeans and Make-up," *Age* (Melbourne), April 25–26.

[178] United Nations (1999). S/RES/1272 (New York: Security Council), October 25, paragraph 15. Charlesworth, Hilary, & Wood, Mary (2002). "Women and Human Rights in the Rebuilding of East Timor," *Nordic Journal of International Law*, Vol. 71: 325, 329. Observe that this was the first time that such a reference was made in the mandate of a comparable body.

[179] Charlesworth & Wood (2002), ibid.

[180] Ibid., p. 333.

matters.[181] After its adoption, Resolution 1325 was used by women in Timor-Leste to reinforce their insistence on formal participation in decision-making processes.[182] As in Afghanistan, the resolution helped local women to argue for their political inclusion, despite subsequent Security Council resolutions making no reference to it.[183] A national campaign was organized in support of the election of women candidates to the Constituent Assembly, which was to draft the new constitution. As a result, twenty-four women were elected to the eighty-eight–member Assembly in August 2001, three of whom were given ministerial or vice-ministerial responsibilities in the transitional government.[184] Despite these promising political developments, violence against women soared in the postconflict environment of Timor-Leste, as it had in Afghanistan. Crimes perpetrated against women constituted 40 percent of officially reported offenses in December 2001,[185] and the majority of complaints made to the Vulnerable Persons Unit of the fledgling police force concerned domestic violence.[186] The landmark increase in women's political participation was having few if any positive effects on their everyday lives.

The experiences in Afghanistan and Timor-Leste suggest that the presence of women in decision making is not in itself enough to bring about substantive change in the "mindset" of postconflict reconstruction, heavily influenced by military and diplomatic agendas focused on state-building. In the rush to establish transitional governance, adopt new constitutions, and hold elections, the worsening security of women was ignored, despite "gender mainstreaming." In interviews with women in Timor-Leste, Hilary Charlesworth and Mary Wood found many who felt frustrated by the

[181] Kent, Lia. "Sweet Flowers, Bitter Flowers: Women, Self-Determination, and the Reconstruction of East Timor," unpublished manuscript, on file with author, p. 13.

[182] See www.peacewomen.org/campaigns/Timor-Leste/TimorLeste.html. On October 30, 2001, Natercia Godinho-Adams presented a statement to the Security Council in New York on behalf of East Timorese women at an Arria Formula Meeting. See n. 155.

[183] United Nations (2001). S/RES/1338 (New York: Security Council), January 31, and United Nations (2002). S/RES/1392 (New York: Security Council), January 31 (both extending the mandate of UNTAET); United Nations (2002). S/RES/1410 (New York: Security Council), May 17; United Nations (2003). S/RES/1473 (New York: Security Council), April 4; and United Nations (2003). S/RES/1480, (New York: Security Council), May 19 (concerning UNMISET).

[184] UNTAET Press Office (2002). "Fact Sheet 11," April.

[185] UNTAET Press Office (2002). Fact Sheet 11, April. Charlesworth & Wood (2002), see n. 178, p. 331, referring to O'Kane, Maggie (2001). "Return of the Revolutionaries," *Guardian*, January 15.

[186] UN Commission on Human Rights (2004). "Report of the United Nations High Commissioner for Human Rights on the Situation of Human Rights in Timor-Leste," E/CN.4/2004/107 (New York: Economic and Social Council), January 19, paragraph 52.

preoccupation with counting the *number* of women in the various UNTAET bodies because this conceived of women's empowerment in "excessively narrow terms."[187] Such frustrations highlight the dangers of mainstreaming a feminist agenda, which can lose its substantive political content in the conversion to bureaucratic goals. Sally Baden and Anne-Marie Goetz described this process in the context of development programs, showing how gender analysis can be reinterpreted as an "interesting statistical variable" to suit institutional needs, stripping it of feminist goals like realizing human rights and social justice.[188] In the same way, the statistics showing an increase in women's political participation, pursuant to Resolution 1325, may serve institutional needs by enhancing the gender legitimacy of the UN's efforts at postconflict state-building in a procedural sense while failing to address women's daily insecurities in the postconflict period.

The use of Resolution 1325 in Iraq, following the invasion in March 2003 by the United States, the United Kingdom, and their "coalition of the willing," presented further dilemmas for the NGOs in alliance with the Security Council. In contrast to Afghanistan and Timor-Leste, where the Council's missions were widely supported, the war in Iraq was intensely controversial, and WILPF-UN and others in the NGO Working Group had lobbied in an effort to prevent it. Even so, they pressed the Security Council to ensure that gender mainstreaming took place in Iraq's reconstruction.[189] In this case, it suited the United States and the United Kingdom to be seen as supporting women's participation in Iraq, to bolster the claim that they were bringing "freedom" and "democracy" to an Islamic population. When Paula Dobriansky, U.S. Under-secretary of State for Global Affairs, addressed women participating in a day of workshops in Baghdad, she conveyed a "personal message" from President Bush commending them on their commitment to creating a free and inclusive Iraq.[190] The Security Council's resolution on Iraq, which "permitted" the ongoing occupation and gave the UN a role in providing humanitarian assistance, recalled Resolution 1325 in its preamble in the

[187] Charlesworth & Wood (2002), see n. 178, p. 339.

[188] Baden, Sally, & Goetz, Anne Marie (1998). "Who Needs [Sex] When You Can Have [Gender]? Conflicting Discourses on Gender at Beijing," in Cecile Jackson & Ruth Pearson (eds.), *Feminist Visions of Development: Gender Analysis and Policy* (New York: Routledge), pp. 19, 22.

[189] Gibbings (2004), see n. 88, pp. 84–85.

[190] Ibid., p. 91. The workshop entitled "The Voice of Women in Iraq" was held July 9, 2003. Gibbings quoted this example from Permanent Mission of the United States to the United Nations (2003). "Statement by Ambassador John D. Negroponte, U.S. Representative to the United Nations, Remarks to the United Nations Security Council, New York, October 29, 2003." Available at www.state.gov/g/wi/25782.htm.

context of encouraging the establishment of a representative government.[191] This move implicated the NGO Working Group in the Council's legitimation of the Iraqi occupation, clearly compromising many of its constituents and the broader antiwar efforts of women's peace advocates. Furthermore, as Gibbings pointed out, the advocacy of the NGO Working Group assumed that Iraqi women, who had suffered for many years under the Security Council's sanctions regime, would welcome the Council's endorsement of their participation in reconstruction.[192] Here, as in Afghanistan, where women had been heralded by the U.S. State Department as the "new democracy leaders,"[193] the invocation of Resolution 1325 was used to justify military occupation in the name of "liberating" women.

The political struggle between the Security Council and the NGO Working Group over the interpretation and application of Resolution 1325 has had mixed results for both members of the alliance. On the NGO Working Group's side of the ledger, the symbol of the resolution has legitimated one of the long-standing demands of feminist peace advocates: women must be included in decision making about international peace and security. There is no doubt that Resolution 1325 provides powerful leverage toward this goal and, in the process, it has helped to focus and strengthen local and international networks of women's peace activists. However, women's new political inclusion is not translating into the paradigm shift in thinking about security and postconflict reconstruction that was the hope of many in the NGO Working Group. Instead, the increased presence of women is being harnessed to facilitate the existing projects of the Security Council[194] by legitimating military intervention and occupation in the name of women's rights and supporting "business-as-usual" state-building in postconflict reconstruction. In this way, the resolution poses a threat to the legitimacy of the international women's peace movement to the extent that it provides a smokescreen for the Council's military and imperial projects.

On the Security Council's side of the ledger, its legitimacy is also enhanced by the increased participation of women in postconflict decision making, which strengthens perceptions of its commitment to procedural correctness – one of the cornerstones of its store of symbolic capital. In addition,

[191] United Nations (2003). S/RES/1483 (New York: Security Council), May 22.

[192] Gibbings (2004), see n. 88, pp. 87–88.

[193] Otto (2006), see n. 3, pp. 162–163, quoting from Brinkley, Joel, & Gall, Carlotta (2005). "Afghans Delay Vote a Third Time: Assembly Elections Moved to September," *International Herald Tribune*, March 18, p. 5.

[194] Orford, Anne (2002). "Feminism, Imperialism, and the Mission of International Law," *Nordic Journal of International Law*, Vol. 71: 275, p. 286.

Resolution 1325 has boosted the Council's substantive legitimacy by providing a ready store of gender capital that can be used to reassure skeptics about its commitment to gender mainstreaming. The extensive institutional support systems that have been established to "implement" the resolution provide ample evidence of this commitment, even if the Security Council's own practice is wanting. However, it must be of concern to the Council that women's *informal* participation in peacebuilding processes has drawn great sustenance from the resolution and is flourishing in its wake. Women are continuing to explore how Resolution 1325, as a form of power, might be used to transform the relationship between the Council and feminist ideas so that the paradigm shift in security thinking might yet occur. This development potentially poses a great threat to the legitimacy of the Security Council's military mindset if – as Audre Lorde, Virginia Woolf, and so many others might have counseled – the best position to push international actors toward internalization of the resolution is from "outside" the "master's house."

Indeed, many nonstate actors have employed the symbolic capital of international institutions to legitimize their local struggles for change by infusing those symbols with new meaning. Hurd used as one example the strategic choice by Chiapas protesters in Mexico to launch their rebellion on January 1, 1994, the same day that the North American Free Trade Agreement came into operation.[195] Two other examples are the use of UN General Assembly Declarations by movements of indigenous peoples to promote their rights[196] and the use of symbols from international conferences by feminists to advance women's rights.[197] Clearly, a resolution of the Security Council lends itself to similar appropriation. Hurd's concept of "legitimacy" does not consider the potential for nonstate actors to take the "rules" given to them by international institutions and promote their internalization from "outside" those institutions, forcing the institutions and their member states to act consistently with their own rules in ways that they never intended. Yet this is the hope of PeaceWomen and others in the NGO Working Group.

Conclusion

The product of a new alliance between the Security Council and feminists, Resolution 1325 is a new "rule" of the Council that opens a space for struggle

[195] Hurd (2007), see n. 10, p. 57.

[196] Ibid., p. 56, relying on Brysk, Alison (2000). *From Tribal Village to Global Village: Indian Rights and International Relations in Latin America* (Stanford, CA: Stanford University Press).

[197] Ibid., relying on Keck, Margaret E., & Sikkink, Kathryn (1998). *Activists Beyond Borders: Advocacy Networks in International Politics* (Ithaca, NY: Cornell University Press).

over women's equality and the gender relations that attend militarism. For the Council, the resolution symbolizes its commitment to including women in decision making and addressing the gendered effects of armed conflict, designed to manage post–Cold War concerns about its gender legitimacy. For the feminists in the NGO Working Group, Resolution 1325 provides a conduit for feminist ideas to enter the "master's house" of the military and diplomatic establishment, intended to enhance the legitimacy of women's peace advocacy by association with the Security Council.

Many fault lines have emerged from this new alliance. Resolution 1325 has leveraged small increases in women's political participation in postconflict decision making, which both allies have claimed to their advantage. However, the inclusion of women does not necessarily challenge militarism, as the women's peace activists of the early twentieth century found when women's suffrage did not make armed conflict impossible, as they had hoped.[198] Although the resolution opens important new opportunities for feminists to promote women's equality in ways that delegitimize militarism, it also presents them with the conundrum that women's increased participation may be used to advance military and institutional agendas that maintain the marginality of women and other disenfranchised groups, while enacting the formal performance of inclusivity. Such a result would engage women as "peacemakers" in yet another disciplinary project that increases the Security Council's store of gender legitimacy, while diminishing the legitimacy of feminist critiques of militarism.

At the heart of the struggle over the interpretation and application of Resolution 1325 is the question of its internalization by other international actors, which leads to conduct that is biased toward following the new rule. The struggle over the implementation of Resolution 1325 shows that its power to change the conduct of other actors is not solely dependent on the meaning attributed to it by the Security Council, despite being the institution that produced it. Instead, the experience of implementing the resolution – which has been driven largely by the NGO Working Group and local women in their peacebuilding efforts – demonstrates that nonstate actors can play a significant role in encouraging internalization of the rules of an international institution – in this case, even in the absence of internalization by the institution. Despite the decision of WILPF-UN and the NGO Working Group to embark on a bold new strategy of engagement with the Security Council from within, on the Council's own terms, the result has been to reconfirm the importance of outside movements for change. Indeed, the experience

[198] Rupp (1997), see n. 3, p. 207.

of the resolution suggests that feminist movements that escape institutional capture are in the best position to use the symbolic capital of Resolution 1325 to transform the gendered moorings of the Security Council, opening the real possibility of achieving a world in which succeeding generations will be saved from the scourge of war.

As "coalitions of the willing" threaten the newfound activism of the Security Council, I have a lingering concern that the small advances toward gender legitimacy, represented by the adoption of Resolution 1325 and the struggle over its implementation, already may have rendered the Council too feminized for militarism's devotees. Francis Fukuyama's provocative warning that the feminization of the West endangers its survival in a world of "undemocratic" (i.e., non-European) states[199] seems to have resonated with the world's superpower and its coalition allies, who seem intent on pursuing an even more intensely militarized global order outside the auspices of the Security Council. These events portend a more dangerous time for women and for nonmilitary narratives of international peace and security. Despite this, Resolution 1325 continues to create bridges between countless women's groups and peace advocates, who remain focused on reminding the Council that its deficit in gender legitimacy remains.

[199] Fukuyama, Francis (1998). "Women and the Evolution of World Politics," *Foreign Affairs* Vol. 77/5: 24, 36. *Contra* responses from Ehrenreich, Barbara; Pollitt, Katha; Ferguson, R. Brian; & Jaquette, Jane S. (1999). "Fukuyama's Follies: So What If Women Ruled the World?," *Foreign Affairs* Vol. 78/1: 118–129.

PART III: LEGITIMACY OF INTERNATIONAL INTERVENTIONS AND HIERARCHY OF INTERNATIONAL RIGHTS

LORRAINE ELLIOTT

9. Cosmopolitan Militaries and Cosmopolitan Force

The contemporary system of international law and international political practice has come to be characterized by two patterns that now "live side by side."[1] Together, they provide an apparently settled understanding about the legal and legitimate deployment of force in international relations. The legal and political norms of the Westphalian order proscribe the use of force between states except in self-defense. Since the period immediately following World War II, another pattern – the so-called United Nations (UN) Charter model – has been superimposed on this older model. The collective security provisions of the UN Charter legitimate the use of multilateral force but only in defense of any member state under attack or, under Chapter VII, when the Security Council determines that there is a threat to or breach of international peace and security. Although it is not specifically stated in the UN Charter, such threats have been assumed to arise from military attack. All other "external" uses of military force and forces, therefore, are deemed illegal under both Westphalian and the UN Charter models of international law. A number of international-relations scholars, whose orientation falls within a broadly cosmopolitan framework, argue that military institutions now have a new role in the management of security crises through what has been variously described as "cosmopolitan law enforcement"[2] and the "new

[1] Cassese, Antonio (1986). *International Law in a Divided World* (Oxford: Clarendon Press), p. 30.

[2] See Kaldor, Mary (1999). *New and Old Wars: Organised Violence in A Global Era* (Cambridge: Polity Press).

The questions addressed in this chapter constitute part of a broader research project on cosmopolitan militaries. Some of the material here draws on collaborative work with Dr. Graeme Cheeseman. I am grateful to Balliol College, Oxford, for electing me to a Visiting Fellowship during Hilary and Trinity Terms, 2002, which supported further work on the theoretical aspects of this project, and to the Department of International Relations at the Australian National University for supporting sabbatical leave.

military humanism."[3] Since at least the beginning of the 1990s, multilateral military force has increasingly been deployed to intervene in states to protect and defend those who are victims of complex emergencies and gross abuse of human rights, or what Axel Honneth called "morally uncurbed aggression."[4] The challenge is a real one: contemporary accounts suggest that in the twentieth century, four times as many people were killed by their own governments than those who died in international and civil wars in the same period.[5]

The challenges for legitimacy are clear. First, cosmopolitanism in this form violates the norms of noninterference, maintenance of sovereignty, and nonuse of force except in self-defense.[6] Second, it challenges the principles of international law that the primary legitimate subjects and moral agents are states. Third, the means of delivery of cosmopolitan peace and democracy is via force – which whispers of normative inconsistency even as a means of last resort – and, for the most part, via structures such as the Security Council or coalitions of national militaries, which are discursively and materially communitarian and statist.

This chapter examines the legitimacy of the proposition that military force (and forces) can and should be used for cosmopolitan purposes – that is, the protection of strangers and those who are not co-nationals because of their equal and universally acknowledged individual moral value and right. In articulating the moral community (i.e., the ethical cosmopolis), the cosmopolitan project has become intimately associated with the project of transforming[7] or re-imagining[8] political community (i.e., the political cosmopolis). We must understand both to investigate further claims to the legitimacy of cosmopolitan force. The context for this chapter is the practice of international relations rather than the specific content of international law. It explores two fundamental questions about normative legitimacy and

[3] Beck, Ulrich, cited in Noam Chomsky (2002). *The New Military Humanism: Lessons from Kosovo* (London: Pluto Press), p. 4.

[4] Honneth, Axel (1997). "Is Universalism a Moral Trap? The Presuppositions and Limits of Human Rights," in James Bohman & Matthias Lutz-Bachmann (eds.), *Perpetual Peace: Essays on Kant's Cosmopolitanism* (Cambridge, MA: MIT Press), p. 159.

[5] Murphy, Sean D. (1996). *Humanitarian Intervention: The United Nations in an Evolving World Order* (Philadelphia: University of Pennsylvania Press), p. 291.

[6] Reisman suggested that the legal "right to self-defense" is, in fact, a new norm articulated as such only in the UN Charter of 1945. See Reisman, W. Michael (2000). "Unilateral Action and the Transformations of the World Constitutive Process: The Special Problem of Humanitarian Intervention," *European Journal of International Law* 11(1): 3–18, 9.

[7] Linklater, Andrew (1998). *The Transformation of Political Community: Ethical Foundations of the Post-Westphalian Era* (Cambridge: Polity Press).

[8] Archibugi, Daniele; Held, David; & Köhler, Martin (eds.). (1998). *Re-imagining Political Community: Studies in Cosmopolitan Democracy* (Cambridge: Polity Press).

political legitimacy. First, can force legitimately be used for international purposes other than self-defense and collective security and, if so, what is the normative basis for such a claim? Second, what form could or should (or must) coercive force take if it is to be a legitimate "methodology" for achieving cosmopolitan objectives? This is not simply an issue of policy choices about military deployment; it is also about something more than humanitarian intervention, although that is clearly a component of this discussion. Rather, it problematizes the moral imperative for the use of force and destabilizes assumed truths about the contours of the moral and political community. It suggests, in effect, that Westphalian and UN Charter legitimacies are vulnerable, a position Ulrich Beck characterized as the "cosmopolitan paradigm of the second age of modernity."[9]

The issue of how to define and measure legitimacy is contentious, particularly when it is conventionally measured against the prevailing rules and body of practice. Mark Suchman defined legitimacy as a "generalized perception or assumption that the actions of an entity are desirable, proper or appropriate within some socially constructed set of norms, values, beliefs and definitions."[10] Legitimacy then is not fixed or given; rather, it is a product of shifting norms about who should do what and how. This understanding weaves sociological approaches to legitimacy that focus on popular attitudes and beliefs about whether institutions, rules, and practices are to be accepted with normative ones about the sources of and justifications for the right to rule and claims to authority. Legitimacy also must be distinguished from legality – that is, strict and formal accordance with international law.[11] As an ethical vocabulary, legitimacy is bound up as much with concepts of justice and acceptability as it is with authority and legality. In the international system, force has been construed historically as a "primary source of legitimation" for states.[12] In contemporary terms, it is now incumbent on states to demonstrate that their deployment of force is legitimate. Public announcements reveal tensions between legalism and morality but would also seem to suggest that the latter can take priority over the former in

[9] Beck, Ulrich (2000). "The Cosmopolitan Perspective: Sociology of the Second Age of Modernity," *British Journal of Sociology* 51(1): 79–105, 83.

[10] Suchman, Mark C. (1995). "Managing Legitimacy: Strategic and Institutional Approaches," *Academy of Management Review* 20(3): 571–610, 574.

[11] The distinction between legitimacy and legality has been particularly pronounced in debates about intervention in Kosovo. For a discussion, see Orford, Anne (1999). "Muscular Humanitarianism: Reading the Narratives of the New Interventionism," *European Journal of International Law* 10(4): 679–711; and Pellet, Alain (2000). "Brief Remarks on the Unilateral Use of Force," *European Journal of International Law* 11(2): 385–392.

[12] Cassese (1986), see note 1, p. 31.

international political practice. The Independent International Commission on Kosovo concluded that the 1999 North Atlantic Treaty Organization (NATO) campaign was illegal yet legitimate.[13] The Foreign Affairs Committee of the British House of Commons, also examining NATO's campaign in Kosovo, concluded that even if NATO's action was of "dubious legality in the current state of international law, [it] was justified on moral grounds."[14] Disputes about legality, legitimacy, and morality have been a central theme in assessments of the U.S. invasion of Iraq in 2003 and the continued occupation of Iraq by forces from the "coalition of the willing." Whereas many argue against both the legality and legitimacy of the war, others have claimed that morality stands independent of legality and legitimacy. Thus, David Mellow argued that "failings in regard to legitimate authority and right intention do not undermine the morality of th[e] resort [to force]."[15]

From the perspective of moral philosophy and political theory, legitimacy has been embedded in disputes about natural law and objective reason and about moral agents and subjects. For the purposes of political practice, conversely, legitimacy rests on normative consistency, legal argument, precedent, and "in important part [as] a product of performance."[16] Nicholas Wheeler argued that "state actions will be constrained if they cannot be justified in terms of a plausible legitimating reason."[17] This chapter begins with an outline of the key propositions that underpin claims for cosmopolitanism as just such a plausible legitimating reason for the deployment of force to manage security crises in a multilateral setting. It then explores some of the key issues for cosmopolitan legitimacy and the use of force that derive from the fault lines that Jean-Marc Coicaud identifies in Chapters 1 through 3 of this volume. Those that are of particular relevance are the normative fault lines over contested visions of justice, community, right claims, and right holders and the fault lines that derive from tensions over stability and change. To have political legitimacy, the cosmopolitan commitment to humanity must

[13] Cited in Weiss, Thomas G. (2002). "Instrumental Humanitarianism and the Kosovo Report," *Journal of Human Rights* 1(1): 121–127, 121.

[14] Cited in Reichberg, Gregory (2002). "Just War or Perpetual Peace?," *Journal of Military Ethics* 1(1): 16–35, 17.

[15] Mellow, David (2006). "Iraq: A Morally Justified Resort to War," *Journal of Applied Philosophy* 23(3): 293–310, 293.

[16] Prins, Gwyn, & Sellwood, Elizabeth (1998). "Global Security Problems and the Challenge of the Democractic Process," in Daniele Archibugi, David Held, & Martin Köhler (eds.), *Re-imagining Political Community: Studies in Cosmopolitan Democracy* (Cambridge: Polity Press), p. 256.

[17] Wheeler, Nicholas (2000). *Saving Strangers: Humanitarian Intervention in International Society* (Oxford: Oxford University Press), p. 4.

be more than a regulative ideal; it has to generate specific political and institutional actions that can meet the test of "rightful conduct." It is therefore reasonable to ask whether or how militaries can be made legitimately cosmopolitan in their structure, deployment, and discourse, thereby providing the focus for the third section of the chapter.

Cosmopolitan Thought

The prefiguring of the complex body of work that comprises cosmopolitan thought is frequently traced to the Cynics and the Stoics (spanning the period 445 BC to approximately 180 AD).[18] In its influential Enlightenment form, scholars give particular attention to the works of Immanuel Kant.[19] Kant postulated a form of cosmopolitanism based on a world order of states but in which cosmopolitan rights took precedence over sovereign rights. Peace was to be achieved through an international order of republican forms of government, based on individual autonomy, rights, and consent. For Kant, this was part of the progress of humanity from a state of nature not through the Hobbesian social contract (based on the trade-off of "freedom" for security) but rather through the "acquisition of honor and esteem."[20] This Kantian tradition also rested on natural-law claims, albeit a form of law known through rationality and reason rather than as the result of divine injunction.

Contemporary interpreters of cosmopolitan theory tie the political project of cosmopolitan democracy more firmly to demands for a "rights-based system of global governance"[21] and the development of alternative and transformative models for the practice of world politics. This is presented as a

18 It is beyond the scope of this chapter to explore the relationship between cosmopolitan ideas and the political contexts in which they arose. For a brief introduction to the varieties of cosmopolitan thought, see Van den Anker, Christien (2000). "Introduction: The Need for an Integrated Cosmopolitan Agenda," *Global Society* 14(4): 479–485; Erskine, Toni (2000). "Embedded Cosmopolitanism and the Case of War: Restraint, Discrimination, and Overlapping Communities," *Global Society* 14(4): 569–590; and Jones, Charles (1999). *Global Justice: Defending Cosmopolitanism* (Oxford: Oxford University Press), especially Chapters 2–4.

19 International-relations scholars are also often inclined to acknowledge the influence of Hugo Grotius. Wheeler (2000), see note 17, p. 45, observes that Grotius "considered that the rights of the sovereign could be limited by the principle of humanity." For more on the relationship with the Stoics, see Heater, Derek (1997). "Cosmopolis, the Way to Peace?," *Peace Review* 9(3): 315–320.

20 See Pagden, Anthony (1998). "The Genesis of 'Governance' and Enlightenment Conceptions of the Cosmopolitan World Order," *International Social Science Journal* 50(1): 7–15, 9.

21 Kaldor, Mary (2000). "Cosmopolitanism and Organised Violence," paper prepared for a conference on Conceiving Cosmopolitanism, University of Warwick, 27–29 April, unpublished, p. 7.

necessary response to various forms of transnational harm and to the need to limit and overcome violence within states and between peoples. The goal is to reconstruct democratic legitimacy in a globalizing world characterized by intensified spatial and temporal interconnectedness and increasing exclusion and marginalization. In general, the cosmopolitan political project anticipates an emerging post-Westphalian order in which "sovereign statehood and territoriality are loosening their grip on modern political life."[22] Statist approaches, associated with particularist and exclusivist values, are judged to be counterproductive in the search for just and equitable responses to these contemporary challenges. This is not simply an intellectual account of the good political community. Rather, as Anthony McGrew pointed out, it "identifies the political possibilities inherent in the present"[23] and, as Graeme Cheeseman observed, "seeks to put in place the means to translate these into future actualities."[24]

In the contemporary cosmpolitan literature, normative arguments for the legitimate deployment of cosmopolitan force have proceeded as follows. First, humankind is bound together as a single moral community with shared rights and obligations that "transcend the morally parochial world of the sovereign state."[25] The consequence of such a world is (as Kant avowed) that "a violation of rights in one part of the world is felt everywhere."[26] In turn, such a community generates a moral commitment to those who are not our conationals. Richard Falk referred to this as an "ethos of responsibility and solidarity."[27] Second, this compassion to "outsiders" goes beyond Kant's cosmopolitan right of hospitality to include a powerful normative commitment to the creation of democratic or humane forms of global governance.[28] This

[22] McGrew, Anthony (1997). "Globalisation and Territorial Democracy: An Introduction," in Anthony McGrew (ed.), *The Transformation of Democracy?* (Milton Keynes, England: Open University Press), p. 19.

[23] McGrew, Anthony (1997). "Democracy Beyond Borders? Globalisation and the Reconstruction of Democratic Theory and Practice," in Anthony McGrew (ed.), *The Transformation of Democracy?* (Milton Keynes, England: Open University Press), p. 252.

[24] Cheeseman, Graeme (2001). "Defending the 'Other': Military Force(s) and the Cosmopolitan Project," paper presented to the Chief of Army Land Warfare Conference, Future Armies, Future Challenges: Land Warfare in the Information Age, Australian Defence Force Academy, Canberra, 9–11 October, unpublished, p. 13.

[25] Linklater, Andrew (1998). "Cosmopolitan Citizenship," *Citizenship Studies* 2(1): 23–41, 26.

[26] Heater, Derek (1996). *World Citizenship and Government: Cosmopolitan Ideas in the History of Western Political Thought* (London: Macmillan), p. 84.

[27] Falk, Richard (1996). "The Complexities of Humanitarian Intervention: A New World Order Challenge," *Michigan Journal of International Law* 17(2): 491–513, 499.

[28] McGrew, Anthony (1997), see note 22; and Falk, Richard (1995). *On Humane Governance: Towards a New Global Politics* (Cambridge: Polity Press).

cosmopolitan democratic imperative requires new forms of global political community in which the sources of legitimacy are based on dialogue and consent rather than power and force, articulated through the construction of universal frameworks of communication.[29] The intended consequence is that those who are most vulnerable, powerless, and marginalized are empowered to refuse, renegotiate, and contest.[30] For the most part, this is not a plea for world government. As Daniele Archibugi observed, "cosmopolitan democracy does not argue – as the federalist tradition does – that existing states must be dissolved to create a world state."[31] Rather, humanity is argued to form a democratic political community in which centers of power are diverse and overlapping and in which structures of governance are (or should be) representative, accountable, and equitable. The state is thus decentered as a political actor and as a moral agent.

Third, according to this line of argument, these political arrangements are embedded in a growing body of international law that embodies both democratic[32] and humanitarian[33] principles, including those of international humanitarian law and the laws of warfare. *Inter alia*, this cosmopolitan law, as a subset of international law, is argued to permit and facilitate (and perhaps require) intervention "in the internal affairs of each state in order to protect certain rights."[34] Finally, cosmopolitan scholars argue that cosmopolitan law and the *pax cosmopolitica* ultimately may require the backing of coercive force, provoking a rather awkward reinterpretation of the realist mantra, *si vis pacem, para bellum* (i.e., if you want peace, prepare for war). This deployment of cosmopolitan force is to be advanced through the reform of existing transnational military structures,[35] the "creation of new internationalized and accountable military structures,"[36] or even the creation of a "new" kind of soldier whose loyalties are to "abstract cosmopolitan ideals in place of patriotism."[37]

29 Linklater (1998), see note 8.
30 O'Neill, Onora, cited in Linklater, Andrew (1998). "Citizenship and Sovereignty in the Post-Westphalian European State," in Daniele Archibugi, David Held, & Martin Köhler (eds.), *Re-imagining Political Community: Studies in Cosmopolitan Democracy* (Cambridge: Polity Press), p. 28.
31 Archibugi, Daniele (2000). "Cosmopolitical Democracy," *New Left Review* 4, July/August: 144.
32 Held, David (1995). *Democracy and the Global Order: From the Modern State to Cosmopolitan Governance* (Stanford, CA: Stanford University Press).
33 Kaldor (1999), see note 2.
34 Archibugi, Daniele (1995). "Immanuel Kant, Cosmopolitan Law, and Peace," *European Journal of International Relations* 1(4): 430.
35 Held (1995), see note 32.
36 McGrew (1997), see note 23, pp. 251–252.
37 Kaldor, Mary et al. (2000). "Conclusion by the Authors," in Mary Kaldor (ed.), *Global Insecurity* (London: Pinter), p. 185.

Normative Legitimacy

The legitimacy or moral acceptability of cosmopolitan intervention and the use of cosmopolitan force as a technique for managing security crises require confirmation that there is – normatively even if not yet in practice – a singular community of moral persons that encompasses all humanity. As suggested previously, legitimacy relies in part on normative consistency. Challenges to the legitimacy of the cosmopolitan argument rest on a combination of moral relativism and political realism. There are two themes in this: (1) a moral-philosophy concern that in the absence of objective moral truths, moral values can be known only in a bounded social context that relies on shared experience and identity; and (2) focusing more on the political project, cosmopolitanism has become a vehicle for the export or imposition of liberal democratic values and the particularistic interests of the most powerful states. First, it is therefore incumbent on cosmopolitan thinkers to demonstrate that there can be universal moral truths on which a single moral community is based, whether or not those values are located as preexisting and objective foundations in natural law. Legitimacy, as Gustav Däniker observed, must be "derived from universal human values."[38] Second, normative legitimacy rests on the strength of arguments that such values or truths do reconfigure the boundaries of the moral and political community. Third, this value-universalism must not (as Fiona Robertson-Snape stated) "smother difference."[39]

Social Identity, Globalization, and the State. Critics of cosmopolitan thought argue that it discounts the "crucial humanizing role played by identity politics."[40] Neither moral obligation nor citizenship, according to this position, can be separated from the state for a number of reasons. Mervyn Frost proposed, for example, that individuals are "fully actualized as free moral persons *only* by state membership."[41] In the absence of moral truths, according to this form of communitarian thought, we can know the just and the good only in the context of the values and norms that are shared by the members of the same political community (in this case, the state). It is this shared

[38] Däniker, Gustav (1995). *The Guardian Soldier: On the Nature and the Use of Armed Forces*, Research Paper No. 36 (New York: UN Institute for Disarmament Research), p. 11.

[39] Robertson-Snape, Fiona (2000). "Moral Complexity and the International Society," *Global Society* 14(4): 507–524, 512.

[40] Barber, Benjamin R. (1996). "Constitutional Faith," in Joshua Cohen (ed.), *For Love of Country: Debating the Limits of Patriotism* (Boston: Beacon Press), pp. 30–31.

[41] Robertson-Snape (2002), see note 39, p. 515; emphasis added.

identity as citizens within the state that defines the boundary of maximalist or thick moral commitment. The moral community is thus constructed or imagined as bounded and particularist. The concept of "world citizenship" (on which claims for legitimating the exercise of force are based) is argued to have little meaning in the absence of authorizing political structures. David Miller argued that "citizenship is a particular kind of identity . . . rooted in the solidarity of a particular political culture."[42] Thus, in this view, intervention for the purposes of protection is either what Onora O'Neill described as an "optional act of charity"[43] or cast in terms of states' interests rather than deriving its legitimacy from universal values of justice.

If state membership, as the critics of cosmopolitanism maintain, is crucial to an individual's sense of moral being and identity – indeed, that it constitutes individuality – then it follows that state sovereignty must provide the normative basis for the international political order. States therefore are understood to be the subjects of international law, the constitutive "individuals" of international society, and the bearers of rights and duties. A political and moral community and an international order, based on bounded states, therefore preclude a moral community coterminous with humanity. At best, then, action can be taken against states because they – or political regimes – default on legitimate statehood by virtue of their antidemocratic or nonliberal behavior; in so doing, they undermine the ethic of coexistence that sustains the society of states. This may demonstrate that sovereignty is conditional on "domestic arrangements which promote individual well-being."[44] One cannot apply a test of legitimacy to states and then argue that there is no normative ground on which to take action against illegitimate behavior. However, it is normatively and possibly operationally distinct from positive action taken to protect individuals because they possess (or we believe that they possess) equal moral value and therefore are deserving of and requiring protection.

Cosmopolitan legitimacy in the exercise of force also relies on claims that the social bond between the citizen and the state, on which citizenship and moral obligation are (allegedly) based, has been ruptured by globalization. David Held argued, for example, that the political authority of the state and its relationship with self-determining collectivities is being

[42] Hutchings, Kimberly (1999). "Political Theory and Cosmopolitan Citizenship," in Kimberly Hutchings & Roland Dannreuther (eds.), *Cosmopolitan Citizenship* (London: Macmillan), p. 28; see also Miller, David (1994). "The Nation-State: A Modest Defence," in Chris Brown (ed.), *Political Restructuring in Europe: Ethical Perspectives* (London: Routledge).

[43] Cited in Jones (1999), see note 18, p. 92.

[44] Robertson-Snape (2002), see note 39, p. 518.

fractured.[45] It can no longer be assumed that the state is the only or primary locus of political power or the only legitimate source of public policy and, therefore, the only agent constitutive of individual identity or moral community. The transnationalizing of "threat" through such problems as environmental degradation, pandemics, drug trafficking, and small-arms trafficking – along with the development of a transnational public sphere of civil society – creates overlapping communities of fate. Held observed that the "quality of lives of others is [now] shaped and determined in near or far-off lands without their participation, agreement or consent."[46] This is a "community of shared risks."[47] The displacement of cause and effect, both spatially and temporally, extends the bounds of those to whom we owe obligations or against whom we might claim rights.

It is in such a world, Held argued, that "citizens must come to enjoy multiple citizenships."[48] In response to those who claim that citizenship is meaningless without formal structure, cosmopolitan thinkers argue that there is no necessary requirement that the concept of world or global citizenship requires an institutional and a moral foundation to be legitimate. Neff argued that the moral position that is cosmopolitanism does not "need to be directly instantiated in a trans-state sovereign power."[49] This is because in the cosmopolitan view, citizenship presents as a "system of moral duties rather than legal rights"[50] and one that draws "attention to the higher ethical aspirations, have yet to be embedded in political life."[51] This follows Thomas Pogge's distinction between legal and moral cosmopolitanism.[52]

[45] Held, David (1998). "Democracy and Globalisation," in Daniele Archibugi, David Held, & Martin Köhler (eds.), *Re-imagining Political Community: Studies in Cosmopolitan Democracy* (Cambridge: Polity Press). See also Köhler, Martin (1997). "Towards a Cosmopolitan Public Sphere," *Peace Review* 9(3): 385–391, who suggested that globalization has unsettled the fit between the agency of the individual as citizen in the public sphere and "bourgeois" in the private.

[46] Held, David (1997). "Cosmopolitan Democracy and the Global Order: A New Agenda," in James Bohman & Matthias Lutz-Backmann (eds.), *Perpetual Peace: Essays on Kant's Cosmopolitan Ideal* (Cambridge, MA: MIT Press), p. 244.

[47] Habermas, Jürgen (1997). "Kant's Idea of Perpetual Peace, with the Benefit of Two Hundred Years Hindsight," in James Bohman & Matthias Lutz-Bachmann (eds.), *Perpetual Peace: Essays on Kant's Cosmopolitan* Ideal (Cambridge, MA: MIT Press), p. 131.

[48] Held, David (1997). "Globalisation and Cosmopolitan Democracy," *Peace Review* 9(3): 309–314, 310. Martin Shaw anticipated a form of "post-military citizenship" in which the duty to defend the state and co-nationals gives way to a broader duty to the disadvantaged and, he suggested, to the environment. See Shaw, Martin (1991). *Post-military Society: Militarism, Demilitarization, and War at the End of the Twentieth Century* (Philadelphia, PA: Temple University Press), p. 187.

[49] Hutchings (1999), see note 42, p. 30.

[50] Linklater (1998), see note 25, p. 26.

[51] Linklater, Andrew (1999). "Cosmopolitan Citizenship," in Kimberly Hutchings & Roland Dannreuther (eds.), *Cosmopolitan Citizenship* (London: Macmillan), p. 36.

[52] Pogge, Thomas (1992). "Cosmopolitanism and Sovereignty," *Ethics* 103(1): 48–75.

Constructing Universal Values. Cosmopolitan thought continues to struggle with the balance between universality and difference, and scholars have been keen to deflect claims that their universalizing project is a hierarchical one in which the claims to moral and normative legitimacy are effectively based on Western liberal values and interests, or what Beck referred to as "some version of Western petit-bourgeois morality inflated to megalomania."[53] One of the most persuasive defenses to the challenges of universalism is that the recognition of "others" as "moral co-equals" and, therefore, worthy of and requiring protection does not necessarily imply sameness beyond this moral claim. The universality of moral laws and the moral "equal-ness" of all people(s) do not necessarily undermine recognition of the diversity of lived experiences.[54] Neither does valuing individual life equally as a universal principle necessarily implicate other forms of universality. The universalism of the contemporary cosmopolitan project is as much a claim about those to whom legitimate obligations are owed as it is about the content of those obligations or the moral purpose that informs them. In seeking to be fundamentally inclusive of those "beyond" or "outside" the state – that is, those who are "other" than co-nationals – the cosmopolitan project destabilizes the definitions of "beyond" and "outside" and "other." However, it does not assume the replacement of local and national forms of political organization.[55]

Historically, cosmopolitan values regarding the oneness of humankind and the moral equality of all humans have relied on natural law.[56] This natural-law tradition, however, is not the only basis on which universal values can be based. To argue, as some do, that because morality is neither innate nor natural there can be no moral absolutes is to ignore the ways in which claims about what is good and what is just are not simply socially contingent within the confines of the state but rather can be produced globally through dialogue, consensus, and practice. Cosmopolitan scholars therefore have sought to understand and explain how the cosmopolitan community is constructed intersubjectively, rather than in accordance with objective truths and natural law, thus allowing what Richard Shapcott called "justice to difference."[57] The

53 Beck, Ulrich (1999). "Democracy Beyond the State: A Cosmopolitical Manifesto," *Dissent* (Winter): 53–55, 54.

54 Beck likened this to the difference between a "melting pot" and a "salad bowl" in which "cultural identities coexist with and against one another in a colorful... way." Beck (1999), see note 53, p. 55.

55 See Nussbaum, Martha (1996). "Patriotism and Cosmpolitanism," in Joshua Cohen (ed.), *For Love of Country: Debating the Limits of Patriotism* (Boston: Beacon Press).

56 Heater (1997), see note 19.

57 Shapcott, Richard (2001). "Cosmopolitan Conversations: Justice, Dialogue, and the Cosmopolitan Project," unpublished draft paper, p. 2.

cosmopolitan community is articulated through dialogue and communication, and it is this process that establishes by unforced force of the better argument those norms that are acceptable and that acquire legitimacy and "universal" status by consent. Consent and consensus thus are central to a legitimate ethics and to an ethics of legitimacy. The universality of cosmopolitanism lies first and foremost in inclusiveness in the dialogic community, the ambit of those who can and must be included in the processes by which consent on norms and moral values is reached and by which such moral and political arrangements gain legitimacy. Norms and values that are intersubjectively created nevertheless can be held universally. Indeed, norms and values – or moral conditions – do not have to be externally referenced to natural law or objective "truths" to make them legitimate or universal. As Wheeler observed, just because norms are socially constructed "does not make them any less real."[58] This is an important issue for the legitimacy of the deployment of cosmopolitan force in multilateral security crises. If morality and the social practice that flows from it can be said to be based on universal, dialogic principles of justice, then "no [other] external justification is required."[59]

Critics of the cosmopolitan argument are concerned that the promotion of individuals rather than states as moral subjects and, indeed, as equal moral subjects across the boundaries of the state also has consequences for international order. They argue that absent a consensus on moral community and, therefore, on the right to intervene (or, in this case, to deploy cosmopolitan force), such intervention or use of force will reflect the cultural and particularist values or political interests of the most powerful. This, in turn, will weaken or undermine the principles on which international order is maintained (i.e., sovereignty, noninterference, and nonuse of force). Reisman stated it another way, drawing attention to the "fear that any erosion of the principle of sovereignty can only increase the vulnerability of weaker states to more powerful states."[60]

Yet, as an organizing principle of international relations, sovereignty is increasingly contingent. Post–Cold War, there is a "greater expression of doubt about the sanctity of the sovereign right of states to govern their internal affairs."[61] International law also has become increasingly

58 Wheeler (2000), see note 17, p. 22.

59 Robertson-Snape (2002), see note 39, p. 510.

60 Reisman (2000), see note 7, p. 6.

61 Dandeker, Christopher (1994). "A Farewell to Arms? The Military and the Nation-State in a Changing World," in James Burk (ed.), *The Military in New Times: Adapting Armed Forces to a Turbulent World* (Boulder, CO: Westview Press), p. 124.

attendant to individual rights. Scholars including Michael Reisman and Fernando Tesón argued that international law is based on individual rights and popular sovereignty.[62] As well as a defining principle of legitimate statehood (discussed previously), the protection of human sanctity or dignity through human-rights law and international humanitarian law has become a peremptory norm from which no derogation is permitted. The International Law Commission's draft articles on state responsibility, adopted by the UN General Assembly at its fifty-sixth session in December 2001, include in the definition of "wrongful acts" a breach of an obligation arising under a peremptory norm of general international law. The articles provide that obligations may be owed to the international community as a whole and that responsibility may be so invoked by the international community.[63] The international protection of human rights, Reisman suggested, has been elevated "to an imperative level of international law"[64] partly in response to the expansion of the international constitutive process to include nongovernmental participation. International humanitarian and human-rights law is a process based increasingly – although by no means perfectly – on dialogue, consent, and consensus that, as explored previously, are key features of legitimacy. The "development of human-rights law [has also] had a natural effect on the international community's expectations of what constitutes a threat to the peace"[65] and, therefore, which actions legitimately can be taken to protect such rights.

Obligation and Force. Emmerich de Vattel suggested in his *Law of Nations* (1758) that even when people are "united in civil society and form a separate state or nation . . . their duties towards the rest of the human race remain unchanged."[66] Cosmopolitan thinkers have differed in their conclusions about the legitimate extent of those duties. The Roman scholar Cicero (106–43 BC) argued that because all were subject to a single law of nature, each was bound not to harm the other.[67] Enlightenment thinking, in general, viewed humans as possessing natural rights that states could not infringe. For Kant, however, obligations to protect those rights were expressed

[62] Reisman (2000), see note 7; and Tesón, Fernando R. (1996), "Collective Humanitarian Intervention," *Michigan Journal of International Law* 17(2): 323–372.

[63] United Nations (2002). "Responsibility of States for Internationally Wrongful Acts," A/RES/56/83 (New York: General Assembly), January 28.

[64] Reisman (2000), see note 7, p. 15.

[65] Murphy (1996), see note 5, p. 284.

[66] Heater (1996), see note 26, p. 75.

[67] Cited in Nussbaum, Martha (1997). "Kant and Cosmopolitanism," in James Bohman & Matthias Lutz-Bachmann (eds.), *Perpetual Peace: Essays on Kant's Cosmopolitan Ideal* (Cambridge, MA: MIT Press), p. 3.

in the right of "outsiders" to equal hospitality. These are, in effect, minimally protective obligations – that is, we have a duty to avoid depriving individuals in the cosmopolitan community of their rights or the conditions under which they can exercise those rights. Contemporary arguments have given greater attention to more activist obligations motivated partly by the political influence of postcolonial, gender, and indigenous movements.[68] Henry Shue contended, for example, that we also have a duty actively to protect individuals from being deprived of their rights and to aid them when protection has failed.[69]

This tells us little, however, about whether the use of force is a legitimate cosmopolitan means to achieve the goal of rescuing or protecting those who are the victims of aggression and abuse. We might turn first to historical texts for some insight into this question. In *De Justitia et Jure* (published in 1593), Luis de Molina argued that "warfare against barbarians" (or *tyrants*, in modern terms) was permitted if its purpose is to protect innocent victims of barbarian aggression.[70] He did make it clear, however, that the purpose of such warfare must be to liberate victims, not to occupy their lands; otherwise, it was neither an act of rescue nor legitimate.[71] Emeric de Crucé proposed in the early seventeenth century that his cosmopolitan federation of states would have the right to enforce peace if arbitration between states failed. In his tract on England's declaration of war on Spain in 1655, Milton argued that such deployment of force was justified because "all great and extraordinary wrongs done to particular persons ought to be considered in a manner done to all the rest of the human race."[72] Kant, however, was opposed to intervention; he took the view that if states did not voluntarily recognize the principle of cosmopolitan right, there was little that other states could do to compel them. Kant did not approve, however, of patriotism or group sentiment, defending rather a politics based on reason. Coercive public law, for Kant, was expressed

[68] It is notable that in articulating his concept of cosmopolitan right, Kant offered a "striking rejection of colonialism"; Held (1997), see note 46, p. 228.

[69] Cited in Jones (1999), see note 18, p. 65.

[70] In Tuck, Richard (1999). *The Rights of War and Peace: Political Thought and the International Order From Grotius to Kant* (Oxford: Oxford University Press), p. 52. See also Jean-Marc Coicaud's discussion of the Chinese philosopher Mencius in the introduction to this volume.

[71] See, for example, Fernando R. Tesón (2006). "Eight Principles for Humanitarian Intervention," *Journal of Military Ethics* 5(2): 93–113, 98–102.

[72] Cited in Coker, Christopher (2001). *Humane Warfare* (London: Routledge), p. 143. In this case, it was Spain's treatment of "New World" Indians that invoked Milton's concern (or at least provided him with a rhetoric of cosmopolitan claims). One is mindful, of course, of the fact that the Spanish imperial invasion of South America was justified in part as an intervention to protect innocents against the barbaric practices of human sacrifice.

through influence rather than force and through the exposure of violations of rights to the verdict of world public opinion.[73]

Contemporary thought is more explicit on the deployment of force and its connection to a rights-based view of cosmopolitan claims. If human rights are to be juridical rather than simply moral, Habermas claimed, they require "an order of positive and coercive law in which claims to individual rights are enforceable."[74] Such enforcement, he proposed, should be legitimized through the constitutional power of an international court that understands violations of human rights as crimes against cosmopolitan law. Even Michael Walzer, who, on the whole, objected to what he called the moral maximalism of the cosmopolitan project, accepted that there are universal principles that prohibit brutal oppression of minorities and majorities in both democratic and nondemocratic states[75] and that there are times when "it is morally justified to send armed men and women across a border" to defend life as an "act of solidarity."[76] The 2003 invasion of Iraq also has illuminated the need to interrogate both intent and motive in setting a benchmark test for cosmopolitan legitimacy. Whereas Mellow asserted that one can commit the right acts (i.e., intent) even if for the wrong motives,[77] a cosmopolitan legitimacy demands both right intent and right motive. As Johnson argued, to be legitimate, right intent must meet two tests: the negative test of "avoiding evil motivations" and the positive test of "aiming to create or restore peace."[78]

Operational Legitimacy

As well as contemplating the normative dimensions of the debates about cosmopolitan force, it is essential that in examining how intervention on cosmopolitan grounds is to be assessed as legitimate, we grapple with the question of what such force actually "looks like." That is, as suggested previously in this chapter, legitimacy also rests on practice and precedent. This is especially so because of the dangers that cosmopolitan ideas and values can be used to justify the use of force for self-regarding rather than other-regarding purposes. In practice, legitimacy and demands for action are predicated as

[73] Bohman, James, & Lutz-Bachmann, Matthias (1997). "Introduction," in James Bohman & Matthias Lutz-Bachmann (eds.), *Perpetual Peace: Essays on Kant's Cosmopolitan Ideal* (Cambridge, MA: MIT Press), p. 12.

[74] Habermas (1997), see note 47, p. 140.

[75] Walzer, Michael (1994). *Thick and Thin: Moral Argument at Home and Abroad* (Notre Dame, IN: University of Notre Dame Press), p. x.

[76] Ibid., p. 16.

[77] Mellow (2006), see note 15, p. 299.

[78] Johnson, James Turner (2006). "Humanitarian Intervention After Iraq: Just War and International Law Perspectives," *Journal of Military Ethics* 5(2): 114–27, p. 116.

much on the "concrete other" of moral choice as on the "generalized other" of moral philosophy. Gross inhumanity and extreme suffering is real, as the introduction to this chapter explained.

The apparently settled practices associated with the state's monopoly on legitimate violence raise a series of questions about the nature of cosmopolitan law enforcement and intervention. To what extent, for example, is it possible for militaries to undertake such cosmopolitan roles and prefigure this cognitive shift when they remain the product of inherited institutional structures related to war fighting in the interests not of the cosmopolis but of the state? Can a traditional military – constituted by the Weberian state as the agent of its legitimate monopoly on violence and Clausewitzian war making, and imbued with particularist and exclusivist (to say nothing of masculinist) images of the moral and political community – be restructured materially and normatively in the goals of nonstatist and universal moral values? Whose interests will cosmopolitan militaries promote (or undermine)? Should the command-and-control structures remain tied to the UN Security Council and, therefore, the exercise of the veto? Can militaries serve both cosmopolitan and statist objectives at the same time? Can militaries – traditionally hierarchical, closed, and nondemocratic – be deployed as agents of what is an essentially and inherently democratic, open, and nonhierarchical normative purpose? These questions identify practical as well as normative challenges for the legitimate deployment of cosmopolitan force and forces. This chapter makes no claim to providing definitive answers. We can, however, begin to think about these challenges through a reexamination of the mission, force structure, and value-orientation of contemporary militaries.

The Cosmopolitan Mission. The traditional organizing principle of military force is war fighting – that is, the "systematic and extensive use of violence as a means of policy."[79] As David Segal and Robert Waldman pointed out, problems "internal" to other states have generally been considered a diversion from this purpose.[80] Yet, the missions of cosmopolitan forces are expected to be interventionist or protective on humanitarian terms, part of the process of defending the "other" rather than defending *against* the "other." The tenets of traditional peacekeeping have specified neutrality and the nonuse of force. For these reasons, peacekeepers have been either not armed or only lightly armed for the purposes of self-defense. For scholars such as Mary Kaldor,

[79] Shaw (1991), see note 48, p. 10.

[80] Segal, David R., & Waldman, Robert J. (1994). "Multinational Peacekeeping Operations: Background and Effectiveness," in James Burk (ed.), *The Military in New Times: Adapting Armed Forces to a Turbulent World* (Boulder, CO: Westview Press), p. 163.

peacekeeping of this type is not enough; cosmopolitan intervention also should be understood as cosmopolitan law enforcement, which means that cosmopolitan forces might become involved as an actual party to the conflict guided by impartiality but not necessarily neutrality.[81]

The cosmopolitan mission, Kaldor argued, is to defend citizens and save lives rather than to engage the enemy or destroy infrastructure.[82] Mission success is measured in lives saved and individuals protected rather than enemies killed or the minimization of casualties among one's own troops (i.e., force protection). More specific mission tasks therefore might be anticipated in the pursuit of cosmopolitan law enforcement, including protecting civilians, enforcing safe havens and humanitarian corridors, arresting war criminals, implementing ceasefires, controlling weapons and overseeing demilitarization, and ensuring public security.[83] This is global policing rather than war fighting. Furthermore, rather than just "ending" conflict (or other forms of violence), cosmopolitan intervention also must engage in rebuilding local legitimacy and pluralist democratic practices.[84]

Cosmopolitan Deployment and the Rules of Engagement. The actual deployment of force for cosmopolitan purposes goes to the heart of the rules of engagement and legitimacy. If cosmopolitan force is to avoid being decried as the cosmopolitan *imperium* or the modern-day equivalent of the *mission civilatrice*, such deployment must be cosmopolitan in its means as well as its ends. One of the more difficult normative and operational challenges is whether cosmopolitan force can be legitimate if its deployment results in the death not just of those who would obstruct or oppose military intervention (whether civilian or military) but also, directly or indirectly, the deaths of noncombatants.[85] The rules of engagement of any cosmopolitan military must conform to the laws of warfare and the customary norms of international humanitarian law as they apply to any party to armed conflict. As Sidney Axinn argued, a "moral military" has to be loyal to moral principles if it is to succeed.[86] This operates at two levels: the conduct of individual (i.e., cosmopolitan) soldiers and the doctrine that informs the rules of

[81] Kaldor (1999), see note 2, p. 128.

[82] Kaldor (2000), see note 21, p. 8.

[83] Kaldor et al. (2000), see note 37, p. 184.

[84] See Shaw, Martin (2000). "The Contemporary Mode of Warfare?," *Review of International Political Economy* 7(1): 171–180.

[85] On this issue as it relates more generally to humanitarian action in war, see Roberts, Adam (1996). *Humanitarian Action in War: Aid, Protection, and Impartiality in a Policy Vacuum*, Adelphi Paper No. 305 (Oxford: Oxford University Press for the International Institute of Strategic Studies).

[86] Axinn, Sidney (1989). *A Moral Military* (Philadelphia: Temple University Press), p. xiii.

engagement. The just-war tradition provides a foundation for interpreting what counts as legitimate cosmopolitan force in practice. The cause for which cosmopolitan force is exercised must be just. Cosmopolitan force must be a last resort; however, in the face of gross abuse of human rights, including murder and genocide, difficult questions arise as to what other actions could or should be taken and for how long. It must meet the test of proportionality. Cosmopolitan militaries must be committed to a minimum use of force and must not themselves abuse the human or legal rights of civilians or combatants. Cosmopolitan law enforcement has to "minimize casualties on all sides."[87] As Richard Glick stated:

> ...wholly unrestricted UN action [or any other such action for that matter]...cannot be justified as effectively maximizing human rights if [it is] inconsistent with the principles of humanity.[88]

Finally, there must be high probability for a cosmopolitan outcome. The use of force for cosmopolitan purposes must, as Falk advised, "benefit the peoples of the target society."[89] The outcomes themselves must enhance – or, at least, not undermine – cosmopolitan values of common or shared humanity.

This redeployment of militaries for cosmopolitan purposes and tasks, it is assumed, will require at a minimum some restructuring of armed forces and introduction of new training methods and regimes. As Däniker, himself a former serving officer, asked, can new tasks be performed with old methods?[90] These debates are taking place against a background of sociological change in the militaries – the transition to a postmodern military, from a "force in being" to a professionalized "cadre-reserve" system, a more "civilianized military" (in a number of senses) that is being made more accountable to publics and that (in liberal democracies, at least) no longer has a monopoly over its "product."[91]

87 Kaldor (1999), see note 2, p. 130.

88 Glick, Richard D. (1995). "Lip Service to the Laws of War: Humanitarian Law and United Nations Armed Forces," *Michigan Journal of International Law* 17(1): 53–107, 62. Glick's particular concern is that the UN itself has sought to minimize the applicability of IHL to troops under Security Council auspices.

89 Falk (1996), see note 27, p. 492.

90 Däniker (1995), see note 38, p. 9.

91 For a summary, see Dandeker, Christopher (1994). "A Farewell to Arms?"; and Moskos, Charles C., & Burk, James (1994). "The Post-modern Military," in James Burk (ed.), *The Military in New Times: Adapting Armed Forces to a Turbulent World* (Boulder, CO: Westview Press). They take place also in the context of a broader critique of militarism, which can be understood as what Mann calls the "persistent use of organized military violence in pursuit of social goals"; as the cultural and social institutionalization of assumptions about the world, in particular that it is conflictive, hierarchical, and uncertain; and as an often "boundless reverence" for military status symbols (including the "warriors" themselves), or what Shaw also calls "nostalgia militarism"; see Mann, Michael (1996). "Authoritarian

The literature provides some guidance on what we might expect cosmopolitan militaries to look like as operational units: they will be continuously prepared, rapidly deployable, and professional; they should be trained for contact as well as combat roles;[92] and their command-and-control structures are to be democratic, transnational, and accountable. The question is how this might be achieved. Held suggested that

> [A] proportion of a nation-state's military (perhaps a growing proportion over time) could be "seconded" to the new international authorities and, once moulded into coherent units placed at their disposal on a routine basis. Or, preferably, these authorities could increase enforcement capabilities by creating a permanent independent force, recruited directly from among individuals who volunteer from all countries.[93]

Such a transnationalization is proposed as a means of overcoming state concern about any "deep or enduring military involvement."[94]

The issue of democratic authorization is central in any assessment of cosmopolitan legitimacy. Charlotte Ku and Harold Jacobson suggested that international authorization through democratic and consultative processes is crucial to establishing legitimacy, partly because it helps gather "domestic support for the deployment of military forces."[95] In the absence of actual transnational military structures, the UN has become the operational focus, first, for the authorization of cosmopolitan intervention and, second, for the actual deployment of cosmopolitan force.[96]

Security Council action is not enough to bestow legitimacy on cosmopolitan claims for intervention or the practices that accompany it. The

and Liberal Militarism: A Contribution from Comparative and Historical Sociology," in Steve Smith, Ken Booth, & Marysia Zalewski (eds.), *International Theory: Positivism and Beyond* (Cambridge: Cambridge University Press), p. 224; Shaw, Martin (1994). "Theses on a Post-military Europa: Conscription, Citizenship, and Militarism After the Cold War," in Chris Rootes & Howard Davies (eds.), *Social Change and Political Transformation* (London: UCL Press), p. 65.

92 Druckman, Daniel; Wall, James A.; & Diehl, Paul F. (1999). "Conflict Resolution Roles in International Peacekeeping Missions," in Ho-Won Jeong (ed.), *The New Agenda for Peace Research* (Aldershot: Ashgate).

93 Held (1997), see note 46, p. 276.

94 Roberts (1996), see note 85, p. 8. See also Murray, Alistair J. H. (1997). *Reconstructing Realism: Between Power Politics and Cosmopolitan Ethics* (Edinburgh: Keele University Press), p. 151.

95 Ku, Charlotte, & Jacobson, Harold K. (2000). "Using Military Force Under International Auspices and Democratic Accountability," *International Relations of the Asia Pacific* 1(1): 21–50, 38.

96 There is also a heated debate within international law and international relations about the legality and legitimacy of *unilateral* intervention on humanitarian grounds. See Krisch, Nico (2002). "Legality, Morality, and the Dilemma of Humanitarian Intervention After Kosovo," *European Journal of International Law* 13(1): 323–335, for a review.

domination of the major powers, as Sean Murphy observed, "raises serious questions about the legitimacy of the process by which the Security Council authorizes humanitarian intervention"[97] – or, for our purposes, cosmopolitan force. The Security Council, in its present formulation, is not a democratic body. It remains "largely off limits for public influence,"[98] yet it is anticipated as a key agent in the democratic deployment of cosmopolitan force. Can states within the UN system or the Security Council whose own domestic structures do not guarantee or protect the fundamental freedoms of their own citizens act as agents of the wider moral good? At a minimum, if cosmopolitan force is to be legitimate, then it is closely bound up with the practical debates about UN reform in general and Security Council reform in particular. Whereas Danilo Zolo characterized reform to reinforce the UN's "authority and power to coerce" along with the establishment of a permanent military force as "autocratic cosmopolitanism,"[99] cosmopolitan scholars tend to take the approach that although the UN might have flaws, it is still the best institution on offer. Held suggested that "we must consider how the UN can be effectively transformed to better reflect the challenges of the new millennium."[100] In a similar vein, Archibugi argued that despite the flaws of the UN, "it is unrealistic to look for a more finely tuned vehicle to achieve a democratic world order and that we must mobilize forces to reform the [UN] democratically."[101] His suggestions for reform include the possibility that cosmopolitan intervention should be authorized not by the Security Council as the agent of states but rather by an independent judicial authority.[102]

Whereas most cosmopolitan scholars seek to find ways to "neutralize" the impact of the major powers and their interests, most also accept that the UN, albeit a reformed one, remains the best place for some form of international or transnational cosmopolitan force. Habermas, for example, argued that it is crucial that the UN has a "military force under its own command" and is able to "exercise its own policing functions."[103] Mel Gurtov anticipated an international peace force acting under UN command

[97] Murphy (1996), see note 5, p. 3.

[98] Köhler (1997), see note 45, p. 389.

[99] Zolo, Danilo (1997). *Cosmopolis: Prospects for World Government* (trans. David McKie) (Cambridge: Polity Press), p. 40.

[100] Held (1997), note 48, p. 311.

[101] Archibugi, Daniele (1998). "Principles of Cosmopolitan Democracy," in Daniele Archibugi, David Held, & Martin Köhler (eds.), *Re-imagining Political Community: Studies in Cosmopolitan Democracy* (Cambridge, MA: Polity Press), p. 211.

[102] Archibugi, Daniele (2000). "Cosmopolitical Democracy," *New Left Review* 4 (July/August): 137–150.

[103] Habermas (1997), see note 47, p. 135.

to "prevent or minimize large-scale threats to human life."[104] Such recommendations are not the province of academic speculation alone. The Report of the Panel on United Nations Peace Operations (i.e., the Brahimi Report) recommended that the Secretariat would require one or a combination of "standing reserves of military, civilian police and civilian expertise, materiel and financing . . . extremely reliable standby capacities . . . or a sufficient lead time" to strengthen the UN's capacity to deploy peacekeeping and peacemaking field operations "rapidly and effectively."[105]

Cosmopolitan Patriots? Militaries, of course, have always performed tasks other than war fighting or preparation for such. Their activities have always been constrained – in theory, at least – by the normative laws of war and the injunctions of the Geneva Conventions. Militaries in Western liberal democracies, in the wake of the end of the Cold War, also seem to be recasting their roles and purposes in ways that resonate – although rarely in explicit terms – with cosmopolitan values. This includes deployment for international-security objectives and the often-contentious issues of force restructuring and training for peacekeeping and operations other than war. Furthermore, in the debates about whether the UN standing army should now be commissioned, or in the debates about establishing a European reaction force, or in the role of NATO troops in Kosovo, we seem to be witnessing a gradual (albeit piecemeal and ad hoc) move toward the transnationalization of military capacity in support of cosmopolitan goals.

It seems reasonable to argue that we have begun to see some small degree of "cosmopolitanization" of militaries, at least in a thin operational or material sense. The UK Ministry of Defense now styles itself as a "force for good in the world."[106] The New Zealand Army has used the slogan "kiwis armed to make a difference" to convey its purpose and ethos. At a declamatory level, political leaders have felt compelled to deploy cosmopolitan values to explain or legitimate the use of force, suggesting that other justifications based on national self-interest have diminished legitimacy. Former U.S. Ambassador to the UN, Thomas Pickering, characterized intervention to protect the Kurds in Iraq, in accordance with Security Council Resolution 688, as a "rebalancing of claims of sovereignty and those of extreme humanitarian

[104] Gurtov, Mel (1999). *Global Politics in the Human Interest*, 4th edition (Boulder, CO: Lynne Rienner), pp. 268–269.

[105] United Nations (2000). "Report of the Panel on United Nations Peace Operations," A/55/305-S/2000/809 (New York: General Assembly, Security Council), p. 15.

[106] Ministry of Defence, The Defence Vision, www.mod.uk/DefenceInternet/AboutDefence/Organisation/DefenceVision; accessed April 2, 2008.

need."[107] British Prime Minister Tony Blair, speaking on NATO action in the Balkans, claimed that "it is right for the international community to use military force to prevent genocide and protect human rights even if it entails a violation of national sovereignty."[108] The UN's 1999 report on Srebrenica stated that "a deliberate and systematic attempt to terrorize, expel or murder an entire people must be met decisively with all means."[109] U.S. President George W. Bush emphasized the importance of liberating the people of Iraq from the tyranny of Saddam Hussein's rule – particularly when it became clear that the justifications for war on the basis of weapons of mass destruction would no longer stand scrutiny. Although caution about the normative commitment inherent in such pronouncements is required, one should also be mindful of Wheeler's observation that "legitimacy is constitutive of state action."[110]

At the same time, there is no doubt that we do not yet have anything like the full-fledged cosmopolitan forces of the type anticipated by Kaldor, Held, Martha Nussbaum, and others. In particular, changes in mission and rules of engagement have not been accompanied by a normative shift. The ideational structures of military forces remain profoundly statist, and the experience of the NATO forces in Kosovo demonstrates that neither militaries nor governments are yet prepared to sacrifice their soldiers' lives to protect strangers. War and the deployment of force are increasingly risk-averse. Coker observed that in 1998, for example, more civilians from NGOs working in disrupted states died than did peacekeepers.[111] There remains strong resistance within military establishments in Western liberal democracies to any suggestion that their "core business" (as opposed to, perhaps, their "adjunct business") should be redirected away from war fighting and defense of the state toward cosmopolitan law enforcement or peacemaking purposes.[112]

This suggests that operational changes are a necessary but not sufficient condition in the transition to cosmopolitan forces. Something more than redeployment and restructuring of conventional forces may be required for the achievement of cosmopolitan objectives. Kaldor and her colleagues

[107] Cited in Dunne, Tim; Hill, Cameron; & Hanson, Marianne (2001). "The New Humanitarian Interventionism," in Marianne Hanson & William T. Tow (eds.), *International Relations in the New Century: An Australian Perspective* (Melbourne: Oxford University Press), p. 100.

[108] Cited in Archibugi (2000), see note 101, p. 147.

[109] Cited in Dunne, Hill, & Hanson (2001), see note 107, p. 103.

[110] Wheeler (2000), see note 17, p. 4.

[111] Coker (2001), see note 72, p. 108.

[112] Cheeseman, Graeme (1998). "Structuring the ADF for UN Operations: Change and Resistance," in Tom Woodhouse, Robert Bruce, & Malcolm Dando (eds.), *Peacekeeping and Peacemaking: Towards Effective Intervention in Post–Cold War Conflicts* (London: Macmillan).

argued, for example, that cosmopolitan militaries also require a "profound cognitive shift concerning what it means to be a soldier."[113] The international or cosmopolitan soldier is now expected to risk her or his life for humanity rather than for country. "The new peacekeepers [are expected to] represent, in person, the new citizens of the emerging global community" rather than the particularistic interests of the nation-state or their co-nationals.[114] These are the "humanitarian warriors"[115] or the "cosmopolitan patriots"[116] or the "guardian warriors."[117]

Concluding Thoughts

The normative and operational legitimacy of the deployment of military force and forces for cosmopolitan purposes is bound up in what Robertson-Snape called the unresolved difficulty of the "practical application of ideal standards in a flawed world."[118] In the international-relations context explored in this chapter, cosmopolitan political thought supported by a growing body of international law and international practice provides a sufficiently robust normative argument to legitimize – with a number of caveats and warnings – the deployment of force to protect "others." This has at least two key consequences. First, it helps to authorize a legitimacy based on justice and consent that competes with the sovereign orthodoxies of the international system. Governments can no longer rely on the norm of nonintervention to explain why they will not act to protect against extreme aggression and violence. Second, the "transnationalization" of cosmopolitan force is a process of transnationalizing legitimate violence.[119] It brings into question the state's legitimate monopoly of organized violence. Held viewed this as part of a longer-term shift to the transfer of coercive capability away from nation-states to regional and global institutions and then the "demilitarization and the transcendence of the war system."[120]

113 Kaldor et al. (2000), see note 37, p. 185.
114 Ibid.
115 Wheeler (2000), see note 17, p. 37.
116 Appiah, Kwame Anthony (1996). "Cosmopolitan Patriots," in Joshua Cohen (ed.), *For Love of Country: Debating the Limits of Patriotism* (Boston: Beacon Press). Appiah is not actually talking about military activities when he uses the term, but I find it a useful phrase in this discussion.
117 Däniker (1995), see note 38.
118 Robertson-Snape (2000), see note 39, p. 507.
119 See Kaldor, Mary (1998). "Reconceptualising Organised Violence," in Daniele Archibugi, David Held, & Martin Köhler (eds.), *Re-imagining Political Community: Studies in Cosmopolitan Democracy* (Cambridge: Polity Press), p. 103.
120 Held, David (1995). "Democracy and the New International Order," in Daniele Archibugi & David Held (eds.), *Cosmopolitan Democracy: An Agenda for a New World Order* (Cambridge: Polity Press), p. 111.

Humanitarian interventions became more familiar to the performance of international politics in the 1990s. However, governments also remain cautious about sacrificing soldiers' lives to save strangers. Such interventions also have been compromised by geopolitical interests. As Beck pointed out, the justification of intervention on human-rights grounds is often connected – sometimes quite explicitly – to interests of national security rather than the moral imperatives of humanity.[121] Robert Cooper's latest contribution, calling for a "new kind of imperialism" – albeit one "acceptable to a world of human rights and cosmopolitan values"[122] – has simply muddied the waters.

However, caution about committing soldiers' lives in the interests of strangers or the existence of a range of motivations does not undermine the broader cosmopolitan project or the normative legitimacy of the claims for the deployment of cosmopolitan force. Shaw argued that "history grants us progress not in the form of inevitability but in the form of possibility."[123] The possibilities lie in the types of normative and institutional transformations that are required to support cosmopolitan action. Two final points, therefore, are worth making. To be legitimate, the deployment of cosmopolitan force (and forces) first must be detached as much as possible from statist and Great-Power purposes and based on democratic and accountable international processes. The second point reinforces this; it suggests that military forces used in support of cosmopolitan force must be qualitatively as well as materially different from traditional militaries in their identity and value structures.

[121] Beck (2000), see note 10, p. 82.

[122] Cooper, Robert (2002). "The Postmodern State," in Mark Leonard (ed.), *Re-ordering the World: The Long Term Implications of September Eleventh* (London: Foreign Policy Centre), March, available at fpc.org.uk (accessed April 17, 2002).

[123] Shaw (1991), see note 48, p. 186.

B. S. CHIMNI

10. Sovereignty, Rights, and Armed Intervention: A Dialectical Perspective

Sovereignty as a normative conception is a "distinctive ideal." It is "about the rights and duties of states and their citizens with respect to the rest of the world."[1] Historically, the ideal translated from the principle of non-intervention into the internal and external affairs of other states. Today, this principle is in tension with the doctrine of human rights. In the past two decades, ever since the end of the Cold War, "constituted governments [have] unsuccessfully protested that their national sovereignty should shield their abuse of human rights."[2] Yet, a clear normative consensus is yet to emerge on when sovereignty can be set aside, particularly in favor of armed humanitarian intervention. Indeed, in the case of armed humanitarian intervention, "the normative scene is still rather cloudy, and the extent to which we have moved beyond traditional norms is dubious."[3] However, the consequences of armed humanitarian intervention are grave, as testified by the Kosovo Declaration of Independence on February 17, 2008. The Declaration *inter alia* states that the new state is "[g]rateful that in 1999 the world intervened, thereby removing Belgrade's governance over Kosovo and placing Kosovo under United Nations interim administration."[4] Although this act of Kosovo may not change international relations as we have known them (as President Putin of Russia observed), it is certain to have a

1 Beitz, Charles (1991). "Sovereignty and Morality in International Affairs," in David Held (ed.), *Political Theory Today* (Stanford, CA: Stanford University Press), pp. 241, 236.

2 Weiss, Thomas G. (2000). "Researching Humanitarian Intervention: Some Lessons," *Journal of Peace Research* Vol. 38, No. 4, p. 422.

3 Smith, Michael J. (1998). "Humanitarian Intervention: An Overview of the Ethical Issues," *Ethics and International Affairs* Vol. 12, p. 68.

4 Kosovo Declaration of Independence; available at www.assembly-kosova.org/?krye=news&newsid=1635&lang=en.

critical impact on how the principle of sovereignty will be understood in the future.

The triad components of sovereignty, rights, and armed intervention are linked, as it happens, only in the case of Third World states. Therefore, this chapter argues that the sovereignty-as-anachronism thesis is deeply flawed from the perspective of Third World peoples and states. In this view, the promotion and protection of human rights hinge less on a critique of the doctrine of sovereignty and more on the elimination of neo-liberal and neo-imperial economic policies and political practices that are at the root of human-rights violations. This assertion, however, is not intended to be a defense of an absolute doctrine of sovereignty. Whereas the relational and relative nature of the doctrine of sovereignty may be recognized vis-à-vis a rapidly evolving international human-rights law, it does not necessitate support for the practice of unilateral armed humanitarian intervention (e.g., the North Atlantic Treaty Organization [NATO] intervention in Kosovo). There are alternative ways to prevent the gross violations of international human rights, including collective armed humanitarian intervention. This action can represent the legitimate exercise of power of the international community when it assumes a particular institutional embodiment and takes place in well-defined situations on which there is consensus within the international community.

In making these arguments, the chapter proceeds in the following way. The following section briefly explores the idea of legitimacy of international norms and enforcement measures, suggesting that these practices rest on a complex range of factors: procedural, substantive, and institutional. The third section examines the sovereignty-as-anachronism thesis and questions the presumed antinomy between the principle of sovereignty and the commitment of the international community to prevent the gross violations of human rights justifying unilateral armed humanitarian intervention. It contends that there are alternative and more effective ways of promoting and protecting human rights. The fourth section reviews two cases of unilateral armed humanitarian intervention since the end of the Cold War (i.e., Iraq and Kosovo) and argues that they flow from the impulse of domination rather than common humanity. This understanding, it proceeds, is confirmed by the ongoing war against Iraq and justified retrospectively on the grounds of restoring and promoting democracy and human rights. The critique gains further strength from the fact that the international community did not intervene when it was most required to do so (i.e., Rwanda). The fifth section describes two situations in which collective (i.e., authorized by the United Nations [UN]) armed humanitarian intervention may be seen as lawful and legitimate: to prevent genocide and when the international community is confronted with a combination of gross human-rights violations and the absence of an internal sociopolitical process capable of preventing or responding to them. However, even for such collective intervention under the auspices of the UN to be perceived as legitimate, it must meet a set of preconditions, both procedural and substantive. The sixth section offers some final reflections.

Legitimacy of Norms

The legitimacy of norms in international relations is usually associated with notions of procedural or substantive fairness; however, their meanings and content are contested. In regard to procedural fairness, the legitimacy of norms can be traced to either adherence to a positivist procedure or the outcome of deliberative democracy. Where substantive fairness is concerned, norms that lead to morally questionable consequences tend to lack legitimacy, which explains why the legitimacy of norms that are the subject of sustained resistance of social movements is seriously undermined.

The legitimacy of norms may be distinguished from the legitimacy of actions taken to enforce norms. The legitimacy of enforcement measures is a distinct moment that may rest on meeting a separate set of procedural and institutional preconditions. Thus, for example, where enforcement measures anticipate an institutional setting, the nature of the decision-making process is a factor in determining their legitimacy. The absence of deliberative democracy in the decision-making process is certain to undermine the legitimacy of enforcement actions. The selective enforcement of norms is another relevant factor. An example of how the neglect of diverse legitimacy criteria impacts the world of norms and enforcement action are the rules of international financial institutions (IFIs). The facts that IFI norms are prescribed through an undemocratic decision-making process, the sustained resistance to them by global social movements, and the selectivity displayed in regulating the monetary policies of member states undermine their legitimacy.

However, prima facie, the relationship between legality and legitimacy is an intimate one. Where the principle of nonuse of force is concerned, given its peremptory character, the relationship with legitimacy is internal and intrinsic.[5] Therefore, a heavy burden of proof must be discharged by a state

[5] It is worth recalling that the International Court of Justice had in the *Nicaragua* case declared Article 2, Paragraph 4, of the UN Charter as *jus cogens* and, in the more recent *Congo v. Uganda* case, it was described as "the cornerstone of the UN Charter" and "declaratory of customary international law." *Military and Paramilitary Activities in and Against Nicaragua (Nicaragua v. United States)*, 1986 ICJ Reports, paragraph 190; *Armed Activities on the Territory of the Congo (Democratic Republic of the Congo v. Uganda)*; available at

seeking to carve out an exception to the principle of non-use of force beyond the norm of self-defense or authorization under Chapter VII of the UN Charter. The same is the case with fundamental principles of international law, such as the principles of sovereign equality of states and nonintervention. Admittedly, there is no fixed essence to the fundamental international law principles. They evolve and are given meaning in changing historical contexts that may be transformed radically, often through developments elsewhere in the legal system. Thus, there may be competing values and principles at stake and no mathematical procedure is available to determine the validity and priority of one versus another. Sovereignty versus human rights is one such clash of norms. In short, there is no simple formula that can respond to questions of legitimacy of international norms and practices beyond respecting the idea of legality. In the final analysis, legitimacy is the outcome of a process of argumentation that involves appreciation of a range of factors, including the legality of actions, the meeting of fair substantive and procedural preconditions in the creation and enforcement of norms, and the availability of peaceful and democratic means of bringing about changes in the international legal system.

The complexities that inform the idea of legitimacy are unavoidable in a global order that still rests on the principle of sovereign equality of states. In these circumstances, it is always possible to contend that an action is illegal but legitimate because legal rules are not necessarily moral. However, under which conditions "illegal acts of reform" can be morally justified is contested,[6] for to accept the thesis that morality can trump law is to open the door to a range of national moralities aspiring to universality.[7] Classical realists such as Morgenthau precisely warned against a scenario of national moralities masquerading as universal morality.[8] Powerful states can use it to advance the "revolutionary claim" that "if the regime of international law fails, even the hegemonic imposition of a global liberal order is justified, even

www.icj-cij.org, paragraphs 148 and 162. See, generally, James Thuo Gathii (2007). "Armed Activities on the Territory of the Congo," *American Journal of International Law,* Vol. 101, pp. 142–149.

[6] Buchanan, Allen (2003). "Reforming the International Law of Humanitarian Intervention," in J. L. Holzgrefe & Robert O. Keohane (eds.), *Humanitarian Intervention: Ethical, Legal, and Political Dilemmas* (Cambridge: Cambridge University Press), pp. 130–175.

[7] Buchanan contends that these may be justified as a first approximation if they contribute toward "(a) bringing the system significantly closer to the ideal of the rule of law in its most fundamental elements, (b) rectifying the most serious substantive injustices supported by the system, or (c) ameliorating the defects in the system that impugn its legitimacy." Buchanan, op. cit., ibid.

[8] For a discussion, see Chimni, B. S. (1993). *International Law and World Order: A Critique of Contemporary Approaches* (New Delhi: Sage Publications), pp. 61–70.

by means that are hostile to international law itself."[9] The legitimacy in such cases, states also argue, can be conferred by the international system ex post rather than ex ante.[10] This thesis is said to have particular validity in the case of the UN because "its membership is based on formal sovereignty rather than a substantive definition of justice – in particular, it makes no practical demands on its members to be democratic or to respect the human rights of its citizens."[11]

In short, the principle of sovereignty, it is argued, can be trumped under certain circumstances. However, if this possibility is not to be abused, the circumstances under which it can be permitted must be agreed to by a preponderant majority of states. A new legality can be legitimate only if it is arrived at through, to quote the International Court of Justice (ICJ), "a very widespread and representative participation" of states in the international community,[12] for "it is precisely the core of democracy and human rights that forbids their unilateral realization at gunpoint."[13] Therefore, according to Habermas, "there is no sensible alternative to the ongoing development of international law into a cosmopolitan order that offers an equal and reciprocal hearing for the voices of all those affected."[14] This means that morality cannot trump international law unless there is, in this regard, an overwhelming consensus within the international community of states; in the normal course, international morality is coterminous with international law.[15]

What are the multiple voices saying in the current debate on unilateral armed humanitarian intervention? The sovereignty-as-anachronism debate is its key subject and therefore worthy of reflection.

Sovereignty as Anachronism: A Perspective

There are two overlapping arguments advanced in support of the sovereignty-as-anachronism thesis with implications for the idea of humanitarian

[9] Habermas, Jurgen (2005). "Interpreting the Fall of a Monument," in Max Pensky (ed.), *Globalizing Critical Theory* (Lanham, MD: Rowman & Littlefield Publishers), pp. 19–27.

[10] Fukuyama, Francis (2006). *America at the Crossroads: Democracy, Power, and the Neoconservative Legacy* (New Haven, CT: Yale Univerity Press), p. 96.

[11] Ibid., p. 158.

[12] North Sea Continental Shelf Cases (1969). *ICJ Reports*, p. 42. See, in this regard, Gathii, James Thuo (2005). "Assessing Claims of a New Doctrine of Preemptive War Under the Doctrine of Sources," *Osgoode Hall Law Journal*, Vol. 43, pp. 67–103.

[13] Ibid., p. 25.

[14] Ibid.

[15] Ibid.

intervention. First, there is the general contention that in the era of globalization, the growing interdependence of states has undermined the principle of sovereignty. However, the posited opposition between the concept of sovereignty and globalization is artificial; it merely facilitates the gratuitous critique of the concept of sovereignty and makes it easier for powerful states to justify "humanitarian intervention." The pathology of choice between sovereignty and globalization has as its firm basis in thinking in terms of fixed essences and in "either/or" language. Linear thinking fails to appreciate that in the real world, particularly in transitional states, opposites come to be linked as a part of a dynamic process of internal development – in this case, the development of global capitalism. This is because processes involve motion and development, of which contradiction is the motivating force; it is sustained through the struggle of opposites.[16] The opposites here – sovereignty and globalization – cannot be transcended without transforming the nature and character of contemporary global capitalism, for the uneven and unjust nature of the capitalist globalization process has meant that an important safeguard against it is precisely its opposite (i.e., sovereignty). Stated differently, the principle of sovereignty can be seen as helping overcome or transcending its own essence. After it helps establish a firm linkage between globalization and global justice, it would be rendered redundant and irrelevant.[17] Meanwhile, the emphasis should be on "the logic of the situation, the constant changeability of the situation, its primacy and the way in which it allows certain things to be possible and others not."[18]

Second – and this is the crucial argument to justify armed humanitarian intervention – is that sovereignty has been reconceptualized in the matrix of a rapidly developing international human-rights law. Thus, for example, Reisman wrote, "although the venerable term 'sovereignty' continues to be used in international legal practice, its referent in modern international law is

[16] This way of thinking represents dialectical thinking. As Jameson stated: "If at every moment in which we represent something to ourselves in a unified way we try to undo that and see the contradictions and multiplicities behind that particular experience, then we are thinking dialectically." Hardt, Michael & Weeks, Kethi (eds.) (2000). *The Jameson Reader* (Oxford: Blackwell), p. 160.

[17] The problem with formal logic is that it does not deal seriously with the concept of time. It is predominantly concerned with the scaffolding of a *static* world. Propositions, we are usually told, are either true or false but both true *and* false. In one and the same thing, one and the same property cannot be both present and lacking. All this is true enough, granting that the world does not change. As such, it is quite possible that one and the same thing has and has not one property (e.g., it first has it and then lacks it), and their truth-value varies with time. Von Wright, Georg Henrik (1983). *Philosophical Logic* (Oxford: Basil Blackwell), p. 92.

[18] Hardt & Weeks, see note 16, p. 159.

quite different. International law still protects sovereignty, but – not surprisingly – it is the people's sovereignty rather than the sovereign's sovereignty."[19] Likewise, former UN Secretary General, Kofi Annan, observed:

> States are now widely understood to be instruments at the service of their peoples, and not vice versa.... When we read the Charter today, we are more than ever conscious that its aim is to protect individual human beings, not to protect those who abuse them.[20]

If the Reisman–Annan view is correct, "humanitarian intervention" to protect the human rights of people is its natural corollary, almost in the same way as the principle of nonintervention accompanies the principle of sovereignty. The new vocabulary of sovereignty as responsibility encapsulates the essence of the Reisman–Annan approach.

Several arguments can be advanced to contest the Reisman–Annan approach inasmuch as it justifies armed humanitarian intervention. First, because the idea of armed humanitarian intervention is parasitic on human-rights law and discourse, a preliminary point worth making is that the idea of human rights is not an unmixed human good; the reality is far more complex. The dominance of neo-liberal ideology and policies in the current era means that human-rights discourse has come to entrench the private rights of individuals and corporations. Whereas the vocabulary of human rights is still powerful in embedding duties owed to ordinary people, it also helps in deepening, extending, and sustaining the structures of global corporate capitalism. To quote Evans, "in the current period, legitimate human rights can be defined only as that set of rights that requires government abstention from acts that violate the individual's freedom to innovate and to invest time, capital, and resources in processes of production and exchange."[21] The state and international institutions tend to focus on the rights of global capital when these clash with the rights of ordinary people. In summary, "far from offering protection to those unable to protect themselves, the once subversive idea of human rights is now used to lend legitimacy in the practices of powerful global economic actors."[22]

[19] Reisman, Michael W. (1990). "Sovereignty and Human Rights in Contemporary International Law," Editorial Comments, International Law After the Cold War, *American Journal of International Law*, Vol. 84, p. 866. See also Smith, op. cit., p. 76: "... a liberal ethics of world order subordinates the principle of state sovereignty to the recognition and respect of human rights."

[20] Annan, Kofi (1999). "Two Concepts of Sovereignty," *Economist*, September 18, p. 49.

[21] Evans, Tony (2000). "Citizenship and Human Rights in the Age of Globalization," *Alternatives*, Vol. 25, p. 416.

[22] Ibid., p. 415.

Second, an absence of dialectical thinking informs the debate on the root causes of human-rights violations. Linear thinking posits the sovereign state as a closed system (even as the idea of sovereignty is declared an anachronism); therefore, the external causes of human-rights violations are neglected. In reality, the tension between human rights and state sovereignty expresses the innermost contradiction of our age: a global system of production and a national system of governance and accountability.[23] Stated differently, the contradiction is between a transnational capitalist class that controls and appropriates the fruits of worldwide production and the majority of the peoples of the world who contribute their labors to it. Yet, the tendency is to represent the subject of sovereignty and human rights as simply a relationship between predator postcolonial states and their suffering populations. Erased from the picture is the role and complicity of global social forces and institutions in sustaining economic and political structures that lead to gross violations of human rights. This allows precisely those social forces that are complicit in human-rights violations to appear on the scene as saviors.[24] The idea here is not to posit a simplistic or unique relationship between external social forces and the violations of human rights. The postcolonial state, including a comprador state, possesses a sufficient degree of autonomy vis-à-vis global economic and political structures and, without doubt, is accountable for actions that lead to the violations of human rights of its peoples. However, at the same time, to neglect the role of imperialist policies and institutions is to participate in their oppression. There is, in other words, a certain disjunction in structures of transnational accountability that needs to be bridged for a humane resolution of the conflict between the ideas of sovereignty and human rights. To endorse the solution of meeting violence with greater violence in the name of human rights is to embrace a cynical world in which the victims are always subaltern peoples, first one set and then another.

Third, the dialectical perspective draws attention to colonial history that viewed European colonial expansion as justified by characterizing it as a civilizing mission. The basic idea of humanitarian intervention on behalf of an "international community" to "civilize" the space of intervention, in other words, is centuries old and historically has served the interests of imperial states in the international system.[25] It compels a closer scrutiny of both

[23] Chimni, B. S. (2004). "International Institutions Today: An Imperial Global State in the Making," *European Journal of International Law*, Vol. 15, No. 1, February, pp. 1–39.

[24] See the discussion on Rwanda, infra.

[25] Thus, a key theme of Richard Tuck's book, *The Rights of War and Peace*, is to trace from the sixteenth century, in the views of key European thinkers, "the balance . . . between the

the thesis that sovereignty is an anachronism and that armed humanitarian intervention takes place to promote and protect human rights, for "on most assessments, there have been no genuine cases."[26] It is important to appreciate that humanitarian intervention is a responsibility that can be exercised only by powerful states. The subaltern states in the international system are the eternal subjects of armed intervention and therefore need to be convinced that it does not represent the repetition of colonial logic and history.[27]

Fourth, although states are bound by international human-rights law obligations, the modes of enforcement are defined in the relevant human-rights treaties on the subject. As the ICJ pointed out in the *Nicaragua* case, "where human rights are protected by international conventions, that protection takes the form of such arrangements for monitoring or ensuring respect for human rights as are provided for in the conventions themselves."[28] Many treaty bodies and other legal processes have been created for this purpose. Although it is true that many states have become party to international human-rights conventions for instrumental reasons (e.g., improving their image in the international community), an incremental socialization process sees these norms internalized and gains a relative autonomy through "changing the self-understanding of the state, transforming social and political discourse, and the contribution of transnational human-rights advocacy networks."[29] While admittedly this is a slow process, it is more effective in the long run. In any case, armed external intervention cannot help sustain a violation- and violence-free environment for long; the observance of human rights cannot be ensured from the outside. Only a powerful internal social movement for the defense of human rights can sustain a culture for their promotion and protection.

priority of self-preservation *and the needs of a wider human society.*" Tuck, Richard (1999). *The Rights of War and Peace: Political Thought and International Order from Grotious to Kant* (Oxford: Oxford University Press), p. 36.

[26] Harris, D. J. (1998). *Cases and Materials on International Law*, fifth edition (London: Sweet and Maxwell), p. 918.

[27] The NATO bombing of the former Yugoslavia was an instance of the abuse of the so-called right of humanitarian intervention. Berman, therefore, aptly observed that after Kosovo, "it is no longer ethically possible – if it ever was – to talk about international human rights without consideration of the identity and means of its enforcers."Berman, Nathaniel (2000). "Imperial Rivalry and the Genealogy of Human Rights: The Nationality Decrees Case" *Proceedings of the 94th American Society of International Law,* April 5–8, p. 53.

[28] *International Court of Justice Reports, 1986*, paragraph 267.

[29] Risse, Thomas; Ropp, Stephen C.; & Sikkink, Kathryn (eds.) (1999). *The Power of Human Rights: International Norms and Domestic Change* (Cambridge: Cambridge University Press), p. 275.

Fifth, armed intervention may only result in sharpening the division between different sections and groups that have been living together for ages. In other words, "it seems best that people who have lived together in the past and will have to do so in the future should be allowed to work out their difficulties without imperial assistance, among themselves. The resolution won't be stable unless it is locally grounded; there is little chance that it will be consensual unless it is locally produced."[30] Furthermore, any attempt at unqualified endorsement of a norm of self-determination for minorities would open up many claims not conducive to the language of justice or multiculturalism.[31] The Kosovo Declaration of Independence testifies to this reality.

Finally, the legitimacy of "humanitarian intervention" in many ways is conjoined to the response of the international community by the "post-conflict" situation. As Annan stated, "When fighting stops, the international commitment to peace must be just as strong as was the commitment to war."[32] Intervening states, however, successfully disengage themselves from postconflict situations even as they affirm the right of humanitarian intervention.[33] It is even argued that because the postintervention situation is a complex social scenario, it is best that the intervening states do not get involved.[34] However, that argument represents to the subjects of intervention the worst of all worlds.

The repudiation of the sovereignty-as-anachronism thesis should not be seen as a defense of some form of absolute doctrine of sovereignty – a position that seriously clashes with contemporary international law.[35] Indeed, the absolute or Hegelian doctrine of state sovereignty historically has been associated with the right of a state to use force in international relations.[36]

[30] Walzer, Michael (1995). "The Politics of Rescue," *Social Research*, Vol. 62, No. 1, p. 55.

[31] Coicaud, Jean-Marc (2000). "Solidarity Versus Geostrategy: Kosovo and the Dilemmas of International Democratic Culture," in Albrecht Schnabel & Ramesh Thakur (eds.), *Kosovo and the Challenge of Humanitarian Intervention: Selective Indignation, Collective Action, and International Citizenship* (New York: United Nations University Press), p. 469.

[32] Annan, see note 20, p. 50.

[33] Chimni, B. S. (forthcoming). "Post-conflict Peace-Building and the Repatriation and Return of Refugees: Concepts, Practices, and Institutions."

[34] Reisman, W. Michael (2004). "Why Regime Change Is (Almost Always) a Bad Idea," *American Journal of International Law*, Vol. 98, pp. 516–525.

[35] Greenwood, Christopher (2000). "International Law and the NATO Intervention in Kosovo," *International and Comparative Law Quarterly*, Vol. 49, p. 929.

[36] Admittedly, Hegel's view of war was rather complex. However, even those scholars who seek to present a nuanced view of his thinking on war concede that there are passages in Hegel that are disturbing. Thus, for example, Dallmayr writes that "repeatedly Hegel speaks of the purging and invigorating effects of warfare, particularly in times when the moral fabric of a country has become ossified or stagnant, as was the case in the old German empire

In the world of international relations and law, the most decisive rejection of the absolute doctrine of sovereignty view was embodied in Article 2(4) of the UN Charter, which prohibits any state from using or threatening to use force against the political independence and territorial integrity of another state. There is consensus today that it is a peremptory norm of international law. In other words, it is states that insist on the legitimacy of unilateral armed humanitarian intervention in violation of Article 2(4) of the UN Charter that subscribe to the absolute doctrine of state sovereignty, not states that affirm the principle of sovereignty and nonintervention in accordance with the UN Charter and customary international law. Furthermore, it is not as if armed humanitarian intervention is not permissible in any circumstance. There are two key questions: (1) When are the violations of human rights of an order that the principles of sovereignty and nonintervention can be trumped? (2) This determination is to be arrived at through what process? These questions acquire importance because armed humanitarian intervention has not taken place when the situation cried out for it (e.g., Rwanda) and it has taken place without sufficient cause (e.g., Iraq and Kosovo) or has been used as a convenient argument to justify an illegal war (e.g., Iraq in 2003). The following section briefly reviews these cases.

The Cases of Iraq, Rwanda, and Kosovo

Northern Iraq: Safe Havens for Kurds or Pleasing Turkey and Securing Oil. The attempt to legitimize unilateral armed humanitarian intervention through the redefinition of the principle of sovereignty began in the post–Cold War period with the creation of safe havens in Iraq in 1991.[37] The aftermath of the Gulf War (1991) saw widespread civil conflict in Iraq. Shia

before Napolean." Dallmayr, Fred R., & Hegel, G. W. F. (1993). *Modernity and Politics*, (Newbury Park: Sage Publications), p. 157. Hegel, it may be recalled, wrote: "The nation as a state is mind in its substantive rationality and immediate actuality and is therefore the absolute power on earth. It follows that every state is sovereign and autonomous against its neighbors." Cited in Avineri, Shlomo (1992). "The Problem of War in Hegel's Thought," in Patrick Riley (ed.), *Essays on Political Philosophy* (Rochester, NY: University of Rochester Press), p. 244. This does not mean, of course, as Avineri points out, that Hegel glorified "concrete war" as opposed to exalting the "concept of war" or overlook the fact that he wished also to humanize war (ibid., pp. 246, 248). Be that as it may, Hegel certainly did not see any constraint imposed by *international law* on the use of force in international relations and subscribed, in our view, to an absolutist conception of sovereignty.

37 This section relies on B. S. Chimni (1995). "The Incarceration of Victims: Deconstructing Safety Zones," in Al-Nauimi, Najeeb & Richard Meese (eds.), *International Legal Issues Under the United Nations Decade of International Law* (Dordrecht: Martinus Nijhoff Publishers), pp. 73–92.

Muslims in the south and the Kurdish population in the north attempted to overthrow a weakened Saddam Hussein regime. By the first week of April 1991, both the Shi'ite revolt and the Kurdish uprising were put down with a strong hand by Saddam Hussein, leading to the massive outflow of refugees toward Turkey and Iran. In response, the UN Security Council (UNSC) adopted Resolution 688 on April 5, 1991, condemning "the repression of the Iraqi civilian population in many parts of Iraq" and asking Iraq to "immediately end" it.

The real concern of the United States and its allies was not the human rights of civilians in Iraq but rather the unwillingness of U.S. ally Turkey to accept Kurdish refugees. Western democracies had encouraged the Kurdish rebellion against the Iraqi regime, a move that invited expected repression from the brutal Saddam Hussein regime and eventually led to 700,000 Iraqi refugees fleeing to Iran and about half that number, mainly Kurd refugees, toward Turkey, which decided not to admit them. Turkey's attitude toward its Kurd minority is well known; historically, the Kurdish population in Turkey has enjoyed fewer rights than Iraqi Kurds. Turkey was fearful that Kurd refugees would fuel the separatist Kurdish movement within the country. Therefore, instead of admitting the refugees, Turkey sought to persuade its Western allies to provide humanitarian aid inside Iraq.[38] The situation at the Iraq–Turkey mountain border was grave.[39] A staff report issued by the U.S. Senate Subcommittee on Immigration and Refugee Affairs in May 1991 stated that "if the refugees had been permitted to cross the border – even by half a mile – to enter more hospitable Turkish valleys and facilities, some of the tragic loss of life could have been minimized during those desperate early days in April."[40] However, Turkey was adamant in not admitting the refugees, although it was obliged under international refugee law to provide temporary protection.[41]

[38] Wheeler, Nicholas (2000). *Saving Strangers: Humanitarian Intervention in International Society* (Oxford: Oxford University Press), p. 148.

[39] The U.S. Committee on Refugees (USCR) described the scene thus: "In early April 1991, the landscape on the sides of those mountains was one of chaos – mud, smoke, crowds, litter. Following days of walking under extremely harsh conditions, the refugees congregated in places exposed to the wind and cold with no sanitary facilities or fresh water other than the pounding, cold rain that froze at night. Most were concentrated in two areas, near Uludere and Cukurca. South of the town of Uludere, they huddled on the side of a steep mountain, nearly inaccessible to relief convoys because the dirt roads leading to it had been washed away in heavy rains. Any who ventured more than a hundred yards or so into Turkey were pushed back by Turkish soldiers, firing warning shots in the air." *World Refugee Survey, 1992*, p. 82.

[40] Ibid.

[41] Goodwin Gill, Guy S. (1986). "*Non-refoulement* and the New Asylum Seekers," *Virginia Journal of International Law*, Vol. 26, pp. 897–918; Perluss, Deborah, & Hartman, Joan F. (1986).

Instead, Turkish President Turgut Ozal proposed the idea of creating safety zones inside Iraq.[42] However, it was British Prime Minister John Major who first publicly aired the proposal, coming to the rescue of its ally rather than refugees.[43] U.S. President George H. W. Bush was initially reluctant to be drawn into what was perceived as a "Vietnam-style quagmire." It explains why although UNSC Resolution 688 "served to legitimize Turkey's decision to close its border,"[44] it did not contain a word about the creation of safe havens. Rather, it emphasized Article 2(7) of the UN Charter and reaffirmed "the commitment of all Member States to the sovereignty, territorial integrity and political independence of Iraq." In no way did the resolution permit military intervention on behalf of the Kurds.[45]

The immediate effects of denying asylum in Turkey to Kurdish refugees were widespread death and suffering.[46] However, instead of pressuring Turkey to provide asylum, on April 18, Iraq was compelled to conclude a Memorandum of Understanding with the UN Secretary General's Executive Delegate, Prince Saddrudin Aga Khan, allowing the UN to provide humanitarian assistance to displaced persons and returnees.[47] However, two days before the UN operations could begin, the United States, France, and Britain sent troops into northern Iraq to create a safe-haven zone for refugees. It was about 100 miles long and 25 miles deep and stretched along the western end of the Turkish–Iraqi border, including the city of Zakho.[48] Even those who characterize the intervention in northern Iraq as humanitarian accept the charge of Western selectivity when it did not create safe havens for Shiites and Marsh Arabs in southern Iraq.[49] There was apprehension that it "might lead to the break-up of Iraq, with Saudi Arabia particularly fearful of the emergence of an Iranian-backed Shiaite State in the south."[50] Besides, by creating safe havens in Iraq, the United States and allies also achieved other objectives,

"Temporary Refuge: Emergence of a Customary Norm," *Virginia Journal of International Law*, Vol. 26, pp. 551–626.

42 *Times* (London), April 21, 1991.

43 Turkey has only acceded to the 1951 UN Convention on Refugees, which carries a geographical limitation. It recognizes as refugees only those who have fled from Europe.

44 Suhrke, Astri (1993). "A Crisis Diminished: Refugees in the Developing World," *International Journal*, Vol. 48, No. 2, p. 235.

45 Wheeler, op. cit., p. 154.

46 Suhrke, Astri (1993). "Safeguarding the Right to Asylum," paper presented at the *Expert Group Meeting on Population Distribution and Migration*, Santacruz, Bolivia, January 18–22, unpublished, p. 22.

47 For the text of the Memorandum of Understanding, see *International Legal Materials*, Vol. 30, 1991, p. 860.

48 *World Refugee Survey, 1992*, p. 99.

49 Wheeler, op. cit., p. 169.

50 Ibid., p. 161.

including containing "a potential regional hegemon" and guaranteeing "free and secure access to oil reserves."[51] In summary, it is difficult to accept the claim that UNSC Resolution 688 marked the beginning of the redefinition of sovereignty to protect human rights. The fact that the no-fly zone coexisted with sanctions that killed many thousands of Iraqi children makes the claim even more unacceptable.

Rwanda: Looking the Other Way. In contrast to Iraq in 1991, powerful states did not intervene in Rwanda in 1994 when such action would have prevented genocide.[52] As is well known, despite early warnings, UN peacekeeping forces were reduced from 2,500 on April 1, 1994, to 270 by April 21, 1994, prior to the genocide in Rwanda[53]:

> Virtually everyone in Rwanda associated with the UN, the diplomatic community, or human-rights groups, knew about death lists, accelerating massacres, and threats to opposition politicians.... The UN military mission uncovered a high-level interahamwe informant, whose revelations led UN commander General Romeo Dallaire to send his famous fax of January 11, 1994, to the UN's headquarters in New York. In his fax, Dallaire reported that "Jean-Pierre [the interahamwe informer] has been ordered to register all Tutsi in Kigali. He suspects it is for their extermination. Example he gave was that in 20 minutes his personnel could kill up to 1,000 Tutsi.[54]

The Report of Eminent Persons Group, established by the Organization of African Unity to probe the genocide, continued:

> At the UN, the Security Council, led unremittingly by the United States, simply did not care enough about Rwanda to intervene appropriately. What makes the Security Council's betrayal of its responsibility even more intolerable is that the genocide was in no way inevitable. First, it could have been prevented entirely. Then, even once it was allowed to begin, the destruction could have been significantly mitigated. All that was required was a reasonable-sized international military force.... Nothing of the kind was ever authorized by the Security Council either before or during the genocide.[55]

[51] Schnabel, Albrecht, & Thakur, Ramesh. "Kosovo: The Changing Contours of World Politics, and the Challenge of World Order," in Schnabel & Thakur, see note 70, p. 2.

[52] In her book on the Rwandan genocide, Melvern concluded that the responsibility for the genocide squarely lay with a number of Western states. Melvern, Linda (2000). *A People Bertrayed: The Role of the West in Rwanda's Genocide* (London: Zed Books).

[53] Barnett, Michael (2000). *Eyewitness to a Genocide: The United Nations and Rwanda* (Ithaca, NY: Cornell University Press), p. 2.

[54] "OAU Report of the International Panel of Eminent Personalities Asked to Investigate the 1994 Genocide in Rwanda and the Surrounding Events" (2000); available at www.oau-oua.org/Document/ipep/ipep.htm, Executive Summary, paragraph 30.

[55] Ibid.

According to Barnett, the behavior of the United States in the period of genocide was "simply unconscionable"[56] and the behavior of other Western states was even more troubling. Barnett held France more responsible for what transpired in Rwanda. France and Belgium, according to him, "certainly knew more than they revealed at the time."[57] France, in particular, "was up to its neck in Rwanda, providing not only military assistance but also training to those who committed genocide."[58] Indeed, "France's behavior throughout the genocide was scandalous."[59] The multinational operation that it led into Rwanda on June 15 "had little to do with a desire to save Rwandan lives and more to do with scoring political points back home and protecting foreign policy interests in the region."[60] As Barnett pointedly noted, "At no time did France ever try and disarm the Rwandan army or the genocidaires as they fled into the area. At no time did it ever arrest a single suspected war criminal."[61] The attitude of the powerful states is best exemplified by the fact that they evacuated their own citizens, leaving behind Rwandan employees to face certain death.[62]

NATO Air Strikes Against the Former Yugoslavia: Morally Justified?[63] The NATO air strikes against the former Yugoslavia in 1999 raised a series of questions about the legitimacy of unilateral armed humanitarian intervention:

> Was the cause just: Were the human-rights abuses committed or threatened by the Belgrade authorities sufficiently serious to warrant outside involvement? Did those seeking secession manipulate external intervention to advance their political purposes? Were all peaceful means of resolving the conflict fully explored? Did the intervention receive appropriate authority? How could the bypassing and marginalization of the UN system by "a coalition of the willing," acting without Security Council approval, possibly be justified? Did the way in which the intervention was carried out in fact worsen the very human-rights situation it was trying to rectify? Or – against all this – was it the case that had NATO not intervened, Kosovo would have been at best the site of an ongoing, bloody, and destabilizing civil war, and at worst the

[56] Barnett, Michael (2000). See note 53, *Eyewitness to a Genocide: The United Nations and Rwanda* (Ithaca, NY: Cornell University Press), pp. x, 20.
[57] Ibid., p. 161.
[58] Ibid.
[59] Ibid., p. 171.
[60] Ibid., p. 147.
[61] Barnett, op. cit., p. 149.
[62] Ibid., p. 173.
[63] Some of the materials for the case analysis are taken from Chimni, B. S. (2001). "The International Law of Humanitarian Intervention," in *State Sovereignty in the Twenty-first Century: Concept, Relevance, and Limits* (New Delhi: Institute for Defense Studies and Analysis), pp. 103–132.

occasion for genocidal slaughter like that which occurred in Bosnia four years earlier?"[64]

The NATO bombing of the Federal Republic of Yugoslavia was justified by stating that whereas it was perhaps not in accordance with international law, it was morally justified[65]; that is, it was illegal but legitimate. The following reasons were advanced in support: (1) "the anti-interventionist regime has fallen out of sync with modern notions of justice"[66]; (2) in the absence of NATO air strikes, there would have been large outflows of refugees threatening the peace and security of the region; (3) NATO powers had exhausted all peaceful means to resolve the Kosovo problem[67]; (4) the selectivity of the NATO action was not unjustified because "prudence is not a bad guide to action, some degree of selectivity is inevitable, and it is better to uphold basic principles selectively than not at all"[68]; (5) the NATO action "was largely popular"[69]; and (6) NATO air strikes by and large conformed to international humanitarian law. In brief, it was contended that "Kosovo deserve(s) to be accounted one of the very few crises in recent history in which policy was 'norm driven' rather than 'interest driven' – solid national interests indeed being sacrificed to uphold a norm."[70]

However, critics believe that the air strikes were not morally justified.[71] First, the air strikes caused more harm than they set out to prevent. On the one hand, as Kaldor noted, "the NATO intervention did not save one Kosovo Albanian"[72]; on the other hand, the air war precipitated a sharp escalation of atrocities.[73]

64 *The Responsibility to Protect: Report of the International Commission on Intervention and State Sovereignty*, December 2001, paragraph 1.2; available at www.iciss.ca/report2-en.asp.

65 Cassesse, Antonio (1999). "Ex iniura ius oritur: Are We Moving Towards International Legitimation of Forcible Countermeasures in the World Community?"; available at www.ejil.org/journal/Vol.10/No.1/Com.html; Franck, Thomas M. (1999). "Break It, Don't Fake It," *Foreign Affairs*, July/August, pp. 116–118. See, however, Wheeler, op. cit., pp. 275ff.

66 Glennon, M. J. (1999). "The New Interventionism," *Foreign Affairs*, May/June, p. 2.

67 Blair, Tony (1999). "A New Generation Draws the Line," *Newsweek*, April 19.

68 Roberts, Adam (1996). *Humanitarian Action in War: Aid, Protection, and Impartiality in a Policy Vacuum*, Adelphi Paper 305, p. 20.

69 Glennon, op. cit., p. 2.

70 Bell, Coral. "Force, Diplomacy, and Norms," in Schnable & Thakur (eds.), *United Nations Peacekeeping Operations: Ad Hoc Missions*, pp. 456–57.

71 For a wholesale questioning of the facts and understanding of the war against Yugoslavia, see Herman, Edward S., & Peterson, David (2007). "The Dismantling of Yugoslavia: A Study in *In*humanitarian Intervention (and a Western Liberal-Left Intellectual and Moral Collapse)," *Analytical Monthly Review*, Vol. 5, No. 7 (October), pp. 1–58.

72 Kaldor, Mary (1999). "If War Knows No Bounds, We Need New Rules of Intervention," *Guardian Weekly*, July 14.

73 Wheeler, who defends NATO's action, notes: "... within weeks of the start of the bombing, thousands of Kosovar Albanians were killed, over half a million were driven from their

Second, NATO states did not exhaust the international law principle of peaceful settlement of disputes; political alternatives to the bombings were available but were deliberately excluded.[74] Thus, speaking of Rambouillet, Henry Kissinger observed that it "was not a negotiation – as is often claimed – but an ultimatum."[75] The Rambouillet documents called for "complete military occupation and political control of Kosovo by NATO, and effective NATO military occupation of the rest of Yugoslavia at NATO's will" and "it is hard to imagine that any country would consider such terms, except in the form of unconditional surrender."[76]

Third, NATO violated international humanitarian laws. The NATO bombing of civilian targets, the wanton destruction of civilian infrastructure, and the environmental disasters resulted in clear violations of international humanitarian laws.[77] Writing in the course of the NATO air strikes, former U.S. President Jimmy Carter noted that "the destruction of civilian life has now become senseless and excessively brutal: instead of focusing on Serbian military forces, missiles and bombs [were] concentrating on the destruction of bridges, railways, roads, electric power, and fuel and fresh water supplies. Serbian citizens report[ed] that they [were] living like cavemen, and their torment increase[d] daily."[78] Debray confirmed this scenario after his visit to the country.[79] Surely, the violations of international humanitarian law could not be justified in the name of "humanitarian intervention."[80]

homes to become refugees in neighbouring countries, and hundreds of thousands more found themselves internally displaced within Kosovo itself. The bombing almost certainly led the Serbs to intensify their campaign against the Kosovo Albanians," op. cit., p. 269. See also Hayden, op. cit.

74 Barutciski, M. (1999). "Western Diplomacy and the Kosovo Refugee Crisis," *Forced Migration*, No. 5, p. 8; Chomsky, op. cit.

75 Kissinger, Henry (1999). "New World Disorder," *Newsweek*, May 31, p. 22. See also Ali, Tariq (1999). "Springtime for NATO," *New Left Review*, March/April, 234, p. 65.

76 Chomsky, Noam (1999). "Judge the US by Deeds, Not Words," *New Statesman*, April 9, pp. 11–12; Chomsky, *New Generation Draws the Line: Kosovo, East Timor, and the Standards of the West*, op. cit., pp. 124–126. See also Falk, Richard (1999). "Kosovo, World Order, and the Future of International Law," *American Journal of International Law*, October; available at www.asil.org/Kosovo.htm#ed5.

77 Even those who defend NATO action admit that it raised "disturbing questions." Wheeler, op. cit., p. 271. Roberts, for instance, admits to "the possible environmental effects of certain NATO actions, including the release of chemicals resulting from certain air attacks, and the use of toxic materials (especially depleted uranium) in weapons and quantities of unexploded ordnance, which was a serious hazard after the war." Roberts, Adam (1999). "NATO's 'Humanitarian War' over Kosovo," *Survival*, Vol. 41, No. 3, p. 115.

78 Jimmy Carter (1999). "As a Peacemaker, America Is Blundering Badly," *International Herald Tribune*, May 28.

79 Regis, Debray (1999). "An Open Letter to President Chirac," *Guardian Weekly*, May 30.

80 Sandoz, Y. (1999). "Beware, the Geneva Conventions Are Under Fire," *International Herald Tribune*, July 14.

Fourth, the welfare of refugees leaving Kosovo was of little concern to NATO states, as evidenced by their attitude toward Kosovar Albanian refugees in the months prior to the bombing campaign. According to Human Rights Watch, in the first half of 1998 and "despite calls from UNHCR to halt deportations, Germany and Switzerland expelled more than a thousand rejected asylum seekers to Kosovo . . . under the terms of readmission agreements with the Federal Republic of Yugoslavia."[81] Scant attention was given to the fact that the NATO bombing affected "the second largest refugee caseload in Europe," approximately a half-million Serbian refugees from Croatia and Bosnia.[82] The harsh reality is that human-rights discourse was used to legitimize the use of force.

Fifth, there was little support for the NATO bombings in much of the Third World – despite the fact that Western media showed prejudice and oversimplification in their reporting of the NATO air strikes.[83] The developing countries formally "rejected the so-called right of humanitarian intervention, which has no basis in the UN Charter or in international law."[84]

There remains the question about the motives for NATO intervention. As Wheeler challenged, critics must adduce the evidence to support their contention that traditional motives of *realpolitik* explained Operation Allied Force.[85] The motives were perhaps the following: (1) the strategic location of Kosovo with regard to Europe and the Middle East[86]; (2) the urgent necessity to demonstrate the continuing relevance and effectiveness of NATO after the end of the Cold War[87]; (3) the intervention was used to send a message to the rest of the world that the United States (and its allies) would no longer be constrained by the UN system; and (4) "the stimulus for military production and sales" because NATO action would necessitate the replenishment of the stocks of Tomahawk cruise missiles and other weaponry used.[88] In short, NATO action in the former Yugoslavia was about global military and political dominance.

The War Against Iraq (2003). Turning to the war against Iraq, it was justified on three grounds: (1) Iraq possessed weapons of mass destruction, (2) the

[81] *Human Rights Watch Annual Report*, 1999.

[82] de Mello, Sergio (1999). "Briefing to the Security Council by Under-Secretary-General: The UN Inter-agency Needs Assessment Mission to the Federal Republic of Yugoslavia," available at www.reliefweb.int; UN Office for the Coordination of Humanitarian Affairs (OCHA), June 2.

[83] Said, Edward (1999). "The Blind Misleading the Blind," *New Statesman*, May 17, pp. 13–14.

[84] Cited by Roth, op. cit., p. 242, note 23.

[85] Wheeler, op. cit., p. 267.

[86] Chomsky, op. cit., p. 137.

[87] Chomsky, op. cit., pp. 126 ff.

[88] Ibid., p. 138.

Iraqi regime had links with Al Qaeda, and (3) the Iraqi people needed to be liberated from the brutal Saddam Hussein regime. At the end of the day, however, the Bush administration relied on the "human rights/democracy argument as its principal justification for the war."[89] However, the war against Iraq is difficult to classify as humanitarian intervention as the issue of human rights violations could have been addressed through peaceful means; there was no immediate crisis.[90] The war lacked complete legitimacy, compelling Habermas to conclude that, with Iraq, "the normative authority of the United States of America lies in ruins."[91] Falk added that "post hoc efforts at legalization should not be accorded much respect."[92] However, one is then entitled to ask how Habermas defended the Kosovo operation. Habermas believed that the humanitarian intervention in Kosovo had legitimacy because of "three circumstances":

> First, the intervention aimed the prevention of ethnic cleansing, which was known at the time of the intervention to be taking place. Second, it was tasked with fulfilling the provision of international law for emergency aid, addressed to all nations. And finally, we can refer to the undisputed democratic and rule-of-law character of all the members of the acting military coalition. *Today, the normative dissent has divided the West itself.*[93]

The first contention is contestable on the basis of available evidence. The second argument does not allow the violation of the principles of non-use of force and nonintervention into the internal affairs of states. Indeed, General Assembly Resolution 46/182 of 1991, entitled "Strengthening of the Coordination of Humanitarian Emergency Assistance of the United Nations," affirms to the contrary.[94] Finally, the legitimacy in the case of Kosovo is associated with the normative unity of Western democratic regimes. Historically, however, imperialism has been precisely the virtue of such regimes. The neocolonial exploitation of the formerly colonized societies makes it difficult to believe that Europe took advantage of "the chance to assume a reflexive

[89] Fukuyama, op. cit., p. 79. "Human protection became the only remaining justification for the US-led war after the failure to find any weapons of mass destruction in Iraq or to establish clear links to Al Qaeda." Macfarlane, S. Neil; Thielking, Carolin J.; & Weiss, Thomas G. (2004). "Review: The Responsibility to Protect: Is Anyone Interested in Humanitarian Intervention?," *Third World Quarterly*, Vol. 25, No. 5, p. 984.

[90] Macfarlane, Thielking, & Weiss, op. cit.

[91] Habermas, see note 9, p. 21.

[92] Falk, Richard A. (2003). "What Future for the UN Charter System of War Prevention?" *American Journal of International Law*, Vol. 97, No. 3. (July), p. 597.

[93] Ibid., p. 21. Emphasis added.

[94] UNGA Res. 46/182: Strengthening of the Coordination of Humanitarian Emergency Assistance of the United Nations 19, December 1991, adopted without a vote. It *inter alia* states in paragraph 3: "... humanitarian assistance should be provided with the consent of the affected country and in principle on the basis of an appeal by the affected country."

distance from themselves."[95] In brief, the justification of both the air strikes in the former Yugoslavia and the war against Iraq as representing cases of humanitarian intervention has greatly undermined the legitimacy of the idea of humanitarian intervention.

When Collective Humanitarian Intervention Is Permissible

The case studies of Iraq (1991 and 2003) and Kosovo (1999) reveal the problems with unilateral armed humanitarian intervention. Yet, one has to come to terms with the Annan query:

> Imagine for one moment that, in those dark days and hours leading up to the genocide, there had been a coalition of states ready and willing to act in defense of the Tutsi population, but the Council had refused or delayed giving the green light. Should such a coalition then have stood idly by while the horror unfolded?[96]

The fact is that if all the relevant information had been made available to the UNSC, it is difficult to believe that any permanent member would have vetoed or delayed authorization of the use of force to prevent genocide. The hypothetical question that Annan posed, therefore, is not helpful in determining the legitimacy of unilateral armed humanitarian intervention. Thus, the first permissible "humanitarian intervention" exception is the use of force authorized by the UNSC to prevent or stop genocide.

A second permissible exception may be carved out for covering "unique" situations such as that which prevailed in Somalia. UNSC Resolution 794 (1992) recognized "the *unique character* of the present situation in Somalia and mindful of its deteriorating, complex and extraordinary nature, requiring an immediate and exceptional response" (emphasis added).[97] The resolution anticipates that the facts and situation in an individual case would need to be carefully assessed before any action is recommended. Generally speaking, however, the uniqueness in legitimizing armed humanitarian intervention may be defined in terms of the temporary absence of internal social forces and a functional state to stop the gross violations of human rights. However,

[95] Habermas, Jurgen, & Derrida, Jacques (2005). "February 15; or, What Binds Europeans Together: A Plea for a Common Foreign Policy, Beginning in Core Europe," in Max Pensky (ed.), *Globalizing Critical Theory*, op. cit., p. 34.

[96] Annan, op. cit., p. 49.

[97] United Nations Security Council Resolution 794 (granting the Secretary-General Discretion in the Further Employment of Personnel of the United Nations Operation in Somails), S.C. res 794, 47 U.N. SCOR at 63, U.N. Doc. S/RES/794 (1992) can be accessed at http://www1.umn.edu/humanrts/peace/docs/scres794.html or http://www.javier-leon-diaz.com/humanitarianIssues/Resolution794.pdf

in the case of both exceptions, a number of preconditions would need to be met if collective armed humanitarian interventions are to be perceived as legitimate, particularly by Third World peoples.

First, the decision in favor of armed humanitarian intervention should not reflect only the views of the veto powers but also a wider consensus among members of the UNSC and, more generally, in the international community. It must not be forgotten that "the legitimacy of political authority depends to a large extent on perceptions and images."[98] The general image of the UNSC in the Third World is one of an organ in which power and not dialogue prevails and in which rules of discourse ethics are overcome by various threats and incentives. This image must be corrected to enhance the legitimacy of the actions authorized by it, which entails active consultation with key Third World states. In this respect, it will help to expand the membership of UNSC. The decisions of the UNSC also must be made more transparent. All available facts and interpretations of those facts should be considered to ensure that the UNSC will intervene in a situation when genocide is a real possibility or there is a genuinely unique situation. As the International Commission on Intervention and State Sovereignty noted: "Even where consensus has been reached on the types of situations which might warrant a military intervention, it will still be necessary in each case to determine whether events on the ground do in fact meet the criteria presented – actual or threatened large-scale loss of human life or ethnic cleansing. In many cases, competing 'facts' and versions of events will be produced – often for the specific purpose of leading or misleading external opinion. Obtaining fair and accurate information is difficult but essential."[99]

Second, unless there is an absolute imperative to act immediately, every attempt should be made to exhaust the principle of peaceful settlement of disputes. Adherence to the principle is important for several reasons: (1) it helps avoid the projection of violence as the solution to human-rights violations; (2) it recognizes that violence often exacerbates rather than contains the problem; and (3) the use of violence makes the return to normalcy in the postconflict situation difficult.

Third, the force used should not be excessive relative to the objectives to be achieved and should be in accord with international humanitarian laws (IHLs). Often, the mere presence or strengthening of peacekeeping forces would suffice to prevent genocide from unfolding. Where force is used, IHLs

[98] Klabbers, Jan (2001). "The Changing Image of International Organizations," in J.-M. Coicaud & V. Heiskanen (eds.), *The Legitimacy of International Organizations* (Tokyo: United Nations University Press), p. 224.

[99] "Responsibility to Protect," op. cit., paragraph 4.28.

must be scrupulously respected. Violation of IHLs substantially delegitimizes the claim of "humanitarian" intervention.

Conclusion

The legitimacy of armed humanitarian intervention has generated much debate in the past two decades. The debate will only become more heated in the wake of the Kosovo Declaration of Independence. From a subaltern and dialectical perspective, the recent unilateral armed humanitarian interventions lacked legitimacy. The principle of sovereignty is not an anachronism. The tension between sovereignty and human rights must be resolved without violating the peremptory principle of the nonuse of force because a "humanitarian war" is a contradiction in terms. War and its consequences – bombing and maiming people – can never be part of human rights and morality.[100]

Yet, it is difficult to assume an absolutist position and suggest that humanitarian intervention is not legitimate under any circumstances. What is certainly illegitimate is unilateral armed humanitarian intervention; historically, it has been abused, it is a right that only hegemonic states can exercise, it is selectively practiced, and it is likely to cause more harm than good. Conversely, subject to certain preconditions being met, collective armed humanitarian intervention under the auspices of the UN can be seen as a permissible response to prevent or stop genocide or gross violations of human rights. The fact that it is authorized by the UN goes a long way in ensuring that it takes place only when absolutely necessary, with the overwhelming consensus of the international community, and in compliance with other international-law obligations.

[100] Douzinas, Costas (2000). *The End of Human Rights: Critical Legal Thought at the Turn of the Century* (Oxford: Hart Publishing), p. 141.

PART IV: IN SEARCH OF NEW FORMS OF INTERNATIONAL LEGITIMACY: BETWEEN POWER AND PRINCIPLES

RALPH WILDE

11. Determining How the Legitimacy of Intervention Is Discussed: A Case Study of International Territorial Administration

In 1999, the United Nations (UN) embarked on an unusual task: taking over the administration of two territories, Kosovo and East Timor. Even though conceived as being temporary arrangements – the East Timor administration (i.e., the UN Transitional Administration in East Timor [UNTAET]) ended in 2002 and the Kosovo administration (i.e., the UN Interim Administration Mission in Kosovo [UNMIK]) is in the process of termination with Kosovo's Declaration of Independence in 2008 – like other shortlived but remarkably intrusive forms of intervention (e.g., so-called humanitarian intervention), the legitimacy of these missions implicates important political and practical questions.[1] How can the displacement of local people by foreign actors in the

[1] On the two missions, see Wilde, Ralph, *International Territorial Administration: How Trusteeship and the Civilizing Mission Never Went Away* (Oxford: Oxford University Press, 2008), [hereinafter "Wilde 2008"], pp. 1–12, 1–2n1, 16–18, 20, 22n64, 32–33, 34n95, 35, 42–43, 47, 54–56, 58, 60, 76, 85–86, 93, 95, 108–109, 138, 144–146, 148–150, 193–196, 199, 204n47, 206–207, 210, 212–213, 215–216, 220, 221–224, 226–231, 233–235, 238, 241–245, 250–252, 255, 257–259, 260n75, 261, 264–265, 270n120, 273–274, 275n140, 276–277, 290–291, 292n12, 293–296, 298n31, 301, 312n84, 344–353, 357–362, 382–384, 405, 413, 419–420, 424n541, 426, 427n553, 430, 433, 439, 440n9, 441n11, 442, 446–447, 449–450, 452n41, 455, 457 (on UNMIK); 2–5, 2n2, 6n16, 9–11, 16–17, 20, 26, 32, 34n95, 39, 42n116, 43, 47, 55, 60, 75, 82–83, 93, 95, 100, 172, 183–189, 198, 206–207, 213, 222, 223n130, 225–231, 234, 251n45, 252, 255, 257, 259–261, 265, 272–274, 275–757, 287, 290, 292n12, 294–295, 298n31, 344–348, 349n240, 351, 359–362, 376n341, 379–380, 382–384, 405–407, 413, 419–420, 424–426, 427n553, 430, 439, 433, 441n11, 443, 448, 450, 452; see also the source listed in ibid., in the List of Sources, Sections 5.1.2 (on UNMIK) and 5.1.3 (on UNAET), and the relevant sources in Section 5.1.1.

This chapter is a revised, updated version of an article published in the *European Journal of International Law* in 2004 and some of the ideas it contains are addressed in two short pieces published in the *ILSA Journal of International and Comparative Law* in 2003 and in Chapters 1 and 7 of the monograph cited in note 1. The reproduction herein of ideas from these earlier pieces is done with the kind permission of the editors of the two journals. Warm thanks are due to the other participants in the UNU workshop, to James Crawford for helpful comments on earlier drafts, and to Silvia Borelli for research assistance.

activity of territorial governance – an activity that echoes certain aspects of the colonial paradigm – be justified?[2] What are the objectives of international territorial administration (ITA) and are they politically sustainable as well as achievable?[3] To what extent are international organizations practically capable of carrying out the activity of territorial administration?[4] Are adequate mechanisms in place to ensure accountability?[5]

This chapter is not a substantive appraisal of such questions. Instead, it considers the prior issue of how the nature and purposes of the ITA projects have been represented in certain academic texts and the effects that these representations have had in setting the terms by which questions concerning the legitimacy of the projects have been defined and addressed. How commentators describe international intervention – why it happens, what it is trying to achieve – involves important political choices because these descriptions have an important role in determining how debates on the legitimacy of such interventions are conducted.

The potential connections between how intervention is described and which questions are then asked about it – and which are not – as far as its legitimacy is concerned are explored through the identification of four different "discursive strategies" within the texts discussed. Each strategy denotes a particular approach adopted in describing the ITA projects that risks telling a story about them that can lead to questions of legitimacy being approached in

[2] I discuss this in Wilde 2008, above note 1, Ch. 1, 8, & 9. See also the sources cited therein in the List of Sources, Section 5.2.4.

[3] I discuss this in Wilde, Ralph, "The Ambivalent Mandates of International Organizations in Bosnia-Herzegovina, Kosovo, and East Timor," in *Proceedings of the Joint Meeting of the Australian and New Zealand Society of International Law and the American Society of International Law*, 2000, p. 311; available at <http: //law.anu.edu.au/anzsil/>; Wilde, Ralph "From Danzig to East Timor and Beyond: The Role of International Territorial Administration," *AJIL*, Vol. 95, 2001, p. 583 [hereinafter "Wilde 2001a"]; and Wilde 2008, above note 1, *passim*.

[4] I discuss this in Wilde, Ralph, "The Complex Role of the Legal Adviser When International Organizations Administer Territory," *ASIL Proceedings*, Vol. 95, 2001, p. 51 [hereinafter "Wilde 2001b"]; and Wilde 2008, above note 1, Chapter 9. See also the sources cited in ibid., List of Sources, Section 5.2.1.

[5] I discuss this in Wilde 2001b, above note 4; Wilde, Ralph, "*Quis Custodiet Ipsos Custodes?*: Why and How UNHCR Governance of 'Development' Refugee Camps Should Be Subject to International Human Rights Law," *Yale Human Rights and Development Law Journal*, Vol. 1, 1998, p. 107; Wilde, Ralph, "Accountability and Administration in Bosnia, Kosovo, and East Timor," *ILSA Journal of International and Comparative Law*, Vol. 7, 2001, p. 455; Wilde, Ralph, "Understanding the International Territorial Administration Accountability Deficit: Trusteeship and the Legitimacy of International Organizations," *International Peacekeeping: The Yearbook of International Peace Operations*, Vol. 12, 2008, p. 93; Wilde 2008, above note 1, pp. 6–8, 22n64, 293n12, 426–428, 440–441, 532–535. See also the commentary ibid., List of Sources, Section 5.2.7.

a flawed fashion: that is, such questions are obscured, they are only partially captured, their significance is downgraded, and so on. This method of textual analysis owes much to "ideology critique" developed from certain ideas of Marx by social theorists including John Thompson, Terry Eagleton, and Slavoj Žižek and further explicated and applied in the context of international legal discourse by Susan Marks.[6]

The first discursive strategy situates ITA within a progressivist historical narrative, positioning the Kosovo and East Timor projects as the pinnacle of an evolutionary process, implying their legitimacy as the most advanced form of international intervention. The second approach unifies all the projects involving ITA through a simplified presentation of their purposes, using the "post-conflict" and "state-building" labels. In consequence, different (sometimes more politically contested) purposes that are also in play are ignored, and the legitimacy of such purposes is not considered. The third discursive strategy associates ITA with the concept of the "failed state," with the effect that the nature of the causes of that for which ITA is understood to be a remedy is distorted, rendering the case for legitimacy more easily made. Finally, the fourth discursive strategy presents ITA in a wholly or primarily technocratic manner, obscuring its political character and thereby failing to capture the full range of issues that must be considered when its legitimacy is appraised.

By identifying these four discursive strategies within the texts discussed and explaining their potentially negative consequences in terms of the quality of analysis concerning legitimacy engaged in, this chapter explores how important questions about the legitimacy of international intervention can end up not being asked, or only partially addressed, because of the way in which the story is told of why such intervention happens and what it is trying to achieve.

Historical Narratives: Exceptionalism and Progressivism

It has been common to describe the ITA projects in Kosovo and East Timor as unique because of the plenary administrative powers asserted, the

[6] See Thompson, John B., *Ideology and Modern Culture: Critical Social Theory in the Era of Mass Communication* (Stanford, CA: Stanford University Press, 1990); Eagleton, Terry, *Ideology: An Introduction* (London: Verso, 1991); Žižek, Slavoj (ed.), *Mapping Ideology* (London: Verso, 1994); Marks, Susan, *The Riddle of All Constitutions: International Law, Democracy, and the Critique of Ideology* (Oxford: Oxford University Press, 2000), in particular, Chapter 1; Marks, Susan, "Big Brother Is Bleeping Us – With the Message that Ideology Doesn't Matter," *European Journal of International Law*, Vol. 12, 2001, p. 109.

involvement of the UN in this activity, and the problems caused by the supposed lack of preexisting institutions. The UN "Brahimi Report" on peace operations placed two post–Cold War missions (i.e., UNMIK and UNTAET) in a class of their own as responding to "extreme" situations:

> United Nations operations were given executive law enforcement and administrative authority where local authority did not exist or was not able to function.[7]

Michael Matheson referred to "[t]he novel . . . undertakings in Kosovo and East Timor."[8] He also stated that in Kosovo, "the mission of the international civil presence . . . was unprecedented in scope and complexity" and that the task of UNTAET in East Timor was "of comparable scope and complexity."[9] Michèle Griffin and Bruce Jones stated that the missions

> . . . are more challenging than similar missions in Namibia (UNTAG), Cambodia (UNTAC) and Eastern Slavonia (UNTAES) because they involve the UN assuming vastly greater executive and legislative authority, in unstable environments completely lacking preexisting, functioning institutions, in the context of increasingly severe financial political and logistical constraints on UN capacity.[10]

They also stated that UNTAET and UNMIK took the UN into "uncharted territory . . . with mandates that are broader in scope and ambition than anything that went before."[11] For Hansjöerg Strohmeyer,

> [t]he scope of the challenges and responsibilities deriving from these mandates [UNMIK and UNTAET] was unprecedented in United Nations peacekeeping operations.[12]

As for working on the territory's legal and judicial system in particular, Strohmeyer stated that

> [n]owhere other than Kosovo and East Timor [where such a task was part of a UN mandate] . . . did this task require the establishment of a coherent judicial and legal system for an entire territory virtually from scratch.[13]

7 Panel on United Nations Peace Operations, Report to the United Nations Secretary-General, August 21, 2000, UN Doc. A/55/305–S/2000/809, reprinted in *ILM*, Vol. 39, 2000, p. 1432 [hereinafter "Brahimi Report"], paragraph 19.

8 Matheson, Michael J., United Nations Governance of Postconflict Societies, *AJIL*, Vol. 95, 2001, p. 76, at p. 83.

9 Matheson, above note 8, 79, & 81, respectively.

10 Griffin, Michèle, & Jones, Bruce, "Building Peace Through Transitional Authority: New Directions, Major Challenges," *International Peacekeeping*, Vol. 7, 2000, p. 75.

11 Ibid., p. 75.

12 Strohmeyer, Hansjörg,"Collapse and Reconstruction of a Judicial System: The United Nations Missions in Kosovo and East Timor," *AJIL*, Vol. 95, 2001, p. 46 [hereinafter "Strohmeyer"], at p. 46.

13 Strohmeyer, above note 12, p. 60.

Boris Kondoch remarked that

> [t]he scope of the responsibilities and the range of the mandate in these cases [UNMIK and UNTAET] were unprecedented in the history of UN peacekeeping missions.[14]

An extreme view held that the East Timor undertaking was unprecedented because nowhere else had UN administration been used to bring a new state into existence. Jarat Chopra, for example, proclaimed that

> . . . the UN is exercising sovereign authority within a fledgling nation for the first time in its history.[15]

John Sanderson identified "unprecedented boldness" in the scope of the mandate given to UNTAET, and stated that

> [t]he United Nations has not "occupied" a country before [UNTAET], depending on all previous occasions on some other body to perform the enforcement provisions while it goes about the business of helping to build new foundations for governance.[16]

The ITA projects in Kosovo and East Timor also often were portrayed as exceptional when they were discussed in terms of the taxonomies of "peacekeeping."[17] These taxonomies provide a framework for comparison

[14] Kondoch, Boris, "The United Nations Administration of East Timor," *Journal of Conflict and Security Law*, Vol. 6, 2001, p. 245 [hereinafter "Kondoch"], at p. 246.

[15] Chopra, Jarat, "The UN's Kingdom in East Timor," *Survival*, Vol. 42, 2000, p. 27 [hereinafter "Chopra 2000"], at 27. See also Traub, James, "Inventing East Timor," *Foreign Affairs*, Vol. 79, No. 4, 2000, p. 74, at p. 75 (the East Timor mission is exceptional because of the broad mandate and lack of preexisting institutions).

[16] John Sanderson, "The Cambodian Experience: A Success Story Still?," Ch. 9 in Ramesh Thakur & Albrecht Schnabel (eds.), *United Nations Peacekeeping Operations: Ad Hoc Missions, Permanent Engagement* (UN University Press, 2001), p. 155 [hereinafter "Sanderson"], at p. 159.

[17] For the representation of certain ITA projects as "peacekeeping" operations, see, for example, Durch, William J. (ed.), *The Evolution of UN Peacekeeping* (St Martin's Press, 1994) [hereinafter "Durch"]; Gray, C., *International Law and the Use of Force* (2nd ed., Oxford University Press, 2004), pp. 210–211 [hereinafter "Gray"]; Higgins, Rosalyn, *United Nations Peacekeeping, Vol. 2, Asia 1946–1967* (Oxford University Press, 1970); Higgins, Rosalyn, *United Nations Peacekeeping, Vol. 3, Africa 1946–1967* (Oxford University Press, 1980); James, Alan, *Peacekeeping in International Politics* (Palgrave Macmillan, 1990) [hereinafter "James"]; Kondoch, above note 14, p. 246; Morphet, Sally, "UN Peacekeeping and Election Monitoring," Ch. 7 in Adam Roberts & Benedict Kingsbury (eds.), *United Nations, Divided World: The UN's Roles in International Relations* (2nd ed., Clarendon Press, 1993); Ratner, Steven, *The New UN Peacekeeping: Building Peace in Lands of Conflict after the Cold War* (St. Martin's Press, 1995) [hereinafter "Ratner"]; United Nations, *The Blue Helmets: A Review of United Nations Peacekeeping* (3rd ed., United Nations Department of Public Information, 1996); White, Nigel, *Keeping the Peace: The United Nations and the Maintenance of International Peace and*

across (usually UN-conducted) peace operations by grading such operations *inter alia* according to their complexity.[18] Whether operations are "basic" or "complex," "simple" or "multifunctional" is usually determined according to size, scope of mandate, and presence or absence of a civilian component in addition to a military component. Granting partial and especially plenary administrative authority over territory to international organizations would seem to fall within the complex/multifunctional categories.

The dichotomy between simple and complex peace operations has usually been described in terms of "old" versus "new"[19] or "first generation" versus "second generation,"[20] suggesting that in general, changes in the complexity of peace missions have occurred in a linear fashion, with missions becoming progressively more complex. Such a suggestion is no accident – for many commentators, there was a "sea change" in the nature of peacekeeping from the late 1980s onward – a "turning point," in the words of Jarat Chopra.[21] Against the backdrop of the supposed post–Cold War internationalist revival and the emergence of "new" types of conflict that were both international and internal in character, there was a marked increase in complex UN peace operations, starting with UNTAG in Namibia in 1989.[22] Accordingly, there

Security (2nd ed., Manchester University Press, 1997); Zacarias, Agostinho, *The United Nations and International Peacekeeping* (Tauris Academic Studies, 1996). See the discussion in Wilde 2008, above note 1, Ch. 7, Section 7.4.

18 Another basis for classification is, of course, the relationship of the operation to the pursuit of peace: "peacekeeping" "peace building," etc. On this basis for classification and its relationship to international territorial administration, see, e.g., Wilde 2008, above note 1, Ch. 7, Section 7.4.

19 For example, Durch, above note 17, p. 9; Oliver Ramsbotham and Tom Woodhouse, *Encyclopedia of International Peacekeeping* (ABC-Clio Ltd., 1999); Ratner, above note 17.

20 For example, Thakur, Ramesh, & Schnabel, Albrecht, "Cascading Generations of Peacekeeping: Across the Mogadishu Line to Kosovo and Timor," Ch. 1 in Ramesh Thakur & Albrecht Schnabel (eds.), *United Nations Peacekeeping Operations: Ad Hoc Missions, Permanent Engagement* (UN University Press, 2001) [hereinafter "Thakur & Schnabel"]; Akashi, Yasusi, "The Politics of UN Peacekeeping from Cambodia to Yugoslavia," Ch. 8 in Ramesh Thakur & Albrecht Schnabel (eds.), *United Nations Peacekeeping Operations: Ad Hoc Missions, Permanent Engagement* (UN University Press, 2001); Chopra, Jarat, "Peace Maintenance: A Concept for Collective Political Authority," in "UN Peacekeeping: An Early Reckoning of the Second Generation," *ASIL Proc.*, Vol. 89, 1995, p. 280 [hereinafter "Chopra 1995"]; Michael Doyle, "Remarks," in "UN Peacekeeping: An Early Reckoning of the Second Generation," *ASIL Proc.*, Vol. 89, 1995, p. 275; Gray, above note 17, 210; Karns, Margaret P., & Mingst, Karen A., "Peacekeeping and the Changing Role of the United Nations: Four Dilemmas," Ch. 12 in Ramesh Thakur & Albrecht Schnabel (eds.), *United Nations Peacekeeping Operations: Ad Hoc Missions, Permanent Engagement* (UN University Press, 2001) [hereinafter "Karns & Mingst"], p. 230; Ramsbotham & Woodhouse (above), p. 93, 218–219; Ratner, above note 17; Kondoch, above note 14, p. 246.

21 Chopra 1995, above note 20, p. 280.

22 On the supposed change in the nature of conflict since 1988, see, for example, Kaldor, Mary, *New and Old Wars* (2nd ed., Polity Press, 2006) [hereinafter "Kaldor"]. On UN peace

was a paradigm shift from "first-generation" to "second-generation," from "old" to "new" peacekeeping.[23] After the creation of the Kosovo and East Timor administration projects, it was suggested that complexity reached such a level that a further "generation" of peacekeeping had been born. Christine Gray remarked that these two projects could be described as "third-generation" peacekeeping.[24] Boris Kondoch, citing W. Kühn, considered "peace enforcement" missions such as UNOSOM II in Somalia to be "third-generation" peacekeeping and UNTAET and UNMIK – because of their complexity – examples of "fourth-generation" peacekeeping.[25]

Thus, the language of generations and the old/new dichotomy has been deployed to present the history of international peace operations as a progressive evolution through successive generations of ever-increasing complexity. The exceptionalist portrayal of the complexity of the Kosovo and East Timor administration missions fits well into this historical narrative, taking the process one step further to a new generation of peace operations. Equally, the historical narrative supports the exceptionalist portrayal, by providing a basis – that is, the progressive increase in complexity over time – for the notion of historical distinctiveness. How do these mutually reinforcing presentations stand up to scrutiny? As I shall suggest, they are misleading in their own terms and unhelpful at a normative level.

First, the history of ITA suggests that describing the relative complexity of peace operations in order to denote a progressive increase in complexity over time as between individual missions is mistaken in its own terms. Elsewhere, I described this history in the following terms:

> [i]nternational organizations first exercised territorial administration in the Free City of Danzig, where the League of Nations enjoyed certain governmental prerogatives from 1920 to 1939. In addition, the League administered the German Saar Basin (the Saar) between 1920 and 1935, and the Colombian town and district of Leticia (Leticia) from 1933 to 1934. It also appointed the

operations since 1988, and the increase in them, see, for example, Durch, above note 17, pp. 9–12; Ramsbotham & Woodhouse, above note 20, pp. xiii–xix. Many scholars assert a causal relationship between the post-1988 upsurge in peacekeeping and the end of the Cold War. See, for example, Ratner, above note 17, pp. 14–16. For a critique of this thesis, see, for example, James, above note 17, pp. 362–366.

23 In a complementary development in academic discourse, Mary Kaldor describes a paradigmatic shift in the nature of armed conflict, from "old wars" to "new wars." Kaldor, above note 22.

24 Gray, above note 17, p. 210.

25 Kondoch, above note 14, p. 246. Most scholars consider "peace enforcement" missions as a special type of "second-generation" peacekeeping, rather than a separate "generation" of the peacekeeping paradigm. See, for example, the various remarks in "UN Peacekeeping: An Early Reckoning of the Second Generation," *ASIL Proc.*, Vol. 89, 1995, p. 275.

> president of the Upper Silesia Mixed Commission in 1922 and the chair of the Memel Harbor board in Lithuania in 1924. Immediately after the Second World War, Germany and Austria were administered by the Allies. With the creation of the United Nations, the new international organization was authorized in 1947 to exercise certain governmental powers in what would have become the Free Territory of Trieste, but the free territory plan was never realized.
>
> The United Nations first exercised territorial administration in the 1960s, asserting [through the United Nations Operation in the Congo (ONUC)] various administrative prerogatives in the Congo between 1960 and 1964, and administering West Irian for seven months between 1962 and 1963. In 1967, the UN Council for what was then South West Africa (later Namibia) was established to administer the territory, but South Africa prevented the council from taking up this role. Over twenty years later, in 1991 the United Nations was authorized to perform administrative functions in Western Sahara and Cambodia; although these functions were exercised in Cambodia from 1991 to 1992, they are yet to be fully performed in Western Sahara. From 1994 to 1996, a different institution – the EUAM [the European Union Administration in Mostar] – administered the city of Mostar in Bosnia and Herzegovina. Then, as part of the Dayton process, the territory of Eastern Slavonia, Baranja, and Western Sirmium (Eastern Slavonia) in Croatia was placed under UN administration from 1996 to 1998. In some of the aforementioned missions, and in others as well, the mandates of international organizations have called for the performance of two particular administrative functions: controlling or conducting some form of territory-wide popular consultation and/or "community building" through the creation of local institutions.[26]

Overlapping in time with the plenary administration missions in Kosovo and East Timor, and still in operation at the time of writing, the Office of the High Representative (OHR) has operated in Bosnia and Herzegovina since 1996, over time having asserted entitlements to perform acts of partial administration, such as imposing legislation and removing elected government officials.[27]

Whether one is focusing on plenary administration or partial administration, international organizations generally or the UN in particular, this history suggests that the complex international peace operations from 1988 onward are, in terms of their complexity, nothing new.[28]

[26] Wilde 2001a, above note 3, p. 586 (footnote omitted). For more information, see Wilde 2008, above note 1, Ch. 2, Section 2.2, and sources cited therein.

[27] On OHR, see Wilde 2008, above note 1, at 9n28, 15–16, 18, 28, 32n88, 35, 36, 42, 45, 48n6, 60, 64–69, 64–65n60, 66n66, 68n70, 70, 72, 75, 80–82, 91–94, 108, 135, 138–139, 141, 144, 149–150, 204n47, 208–211, 213–217, 219–220, 222–224, 227–238, 230n143, 231–232, 234, 244–246, 249–250, 255n57, 256, 259, 261, 265, 272–273, 276, 278, 282–296, 290–291, 293, 294, 301, 312, 346–350, 352, 353nn251–252, 359–360, 382–383, 404–405, 412, 426, 428, 430, 436, 446–447, 449, 451, 455.

[28] For a historical overview of international territorial administration projects, see, for example, Wilde 2001a, above note 3, and Wilde 2008, above note 1, Ch. 2.

The first complex peace operations involving plenary ITA were the Saar from 1920 to 1935 (in the League of Nations era) and West Irian from 1962 to 1963 (in the UN era); the first such missions involving partial administration were Danzig from 1920 to 1939 (in the League era) and the Congo from 1960 to 1964 (in the UN era).[29] Insofar as the Kosovo and East Timor missions involved plenary administration exercised by the UN, they are not unprecedented but follow on from the West Irian and Eastern Slavonia missions.[30] If the focus is broadened to international organizations generally, the precedents run back even further to the start of the League of Nations in 1920.

Some of the "generational" commentators focus on the "state-building" aspect of "post-conflict" peace operations: that exercising territorial prerogatives is one thing, but the use of such prerogatives for that purpose is a relatively new phenomenon. A similar approach has been adopted by many of the "exceptionalist" commentators, who emphasized not only the scope of the administrative prerogatives asserted in Kosovo and East Timor, but also the conditions in which these prerogatives were exercised – in particular, the perceived absence of preexisting institutions.

Regarding the "state-building" purpose, whereas ONUC in the 1960s is widely regarded as the first UN operation to engage in "peace enforcement,"[31] the equally pioneering "state-building" administrative activities of that same mission – exercising administration to enable the operation of certain government institutions, for example – are rarely acknowledged.[32] Yet, once the full scope of ONUC's operation is borne in mind, it becomes just as difficult to see a clear distinction between post- and pre-1989 operations on "state-building" grounds as it is on "enforcement" grounds.[33] Certainly, the next operations of these types did not take place until the post-1989 era (i.e.,

[29] On these missions, see, e.g., Wilde 2001a, above note 3; Wilde 2008, above note 1, at 11, 26, 42, 49, 49n13, 56, 60, 94, 108, 111–114, 128, 148, 150, 155, 193, 196–197, 199–202, 208, 210, 212, 216, 218–219, 225, 227, 229, 233, 241–248, 265, 269, 274–276, 343, 344n217, 365, 370–1, 376 (on the League administration of the Saar); 4, 13, 43, 50–51, 50–51n18, 60, 94, 153, 167–170, 188, 193, 195–196, 199, 205n57, 233, 242, 245, 266n98, 274, 278, 345, 380, 403–405, 437, 440 (on West Irian); 11, 26, 49, 49n12, 60, 94, 111, 114, 114n30, 116, 121–127, 128, 148–150, 213–214, 216, 227–228, 233–234, 244–245, 248, 274, 276n147, 287, 300, 343, 365, 370, 376 (on Danzig); 13, 16, 50, 50n17, 60, 94, 129–130, 131, 149, 189, 204–205, 228, 254, 255, 265n98, 272, 274, 276, 354n258, 356n265, 380, 382, 404, 405n467 (on the UN mission in the Congo (ONUC)).

[30] On Eastern Slavonia, see Wilde 2001a, above note 3, p. 589, and Wilde 2008, above note 1, at 56, 58, 58n37, 142n202, 243.

[31] E.g., Durch, above note 17, p. 8; Roy Lee, "United Nations Peacekeeping: Developments and Prospects", *Cornell Int'l L.J.*, Vol. 28, 1995, p. 619, at p. 624.

[32] A notable exception is Steven Ratner. See Ratner, above note 17, pp. 105–109.

[33] Like "state building," "peace enforcement" is often presented as a "new" phenomenon through the use of generational language, whether second or third.

Namibia in 1989 for "state-building" and UNOSOM II in 1991 for "peace enforcement"). The point is that the enterprise that lay behind these later operations was not unprecedented.

"State-building", then, is not an exclusively post-1989 phenomenon. However, a qualitative distinction perhaps can be made between UNMIK and UNTAET, on the one hand, and the "state-building" missions that came before them on the other. Arguably, the degree to which these two missions engaged in the reconstruction of infrastructure and governmental institutions was unprecedented – at least, if one discounts the Allied administration in Germany after World War II.[34]

A question remains, however, as to whether the scope of a "state-building" mandate should be the primary indicator – in addition to the breadth of the administrative prerogatives exercised – by which complexity and distinctiveness are measured. For example, what of plenary administration concerned with territorial disposition? Was the UN administration in Eastern Slavonia from 1995 to 1997, which necessitated the eventual transfer of administration of territory to authorities from whom local militias had hitherto sought independence, necessarily less complex than the two-and-a-half-year East Timor mission where – infrastructural problems notwithstanding – the eventual outcome for the territory was overwhelmingly supported by the population?[35] Similarly, what of administration missions aimed at facilitating a particularly controversial policy? Stepping back to the League of Nations era, can it really be said that the three-year-long mission in East Timor was more complex than the fifteen-year mission in the Saar? The League was involved in administering a territory, the title to which was bitterly contested between France and Germany, thereby enabling a key component of Germany's much-resented reparations program to proceed before organizing what was, in effect, a self-determination referendum and then implementing the result of that referendum.[36]

[34] Writing in 1999, before the Kosovo and East Timor projects, Ramsbotham & Woodhouse remarked that

> [t]he most extensive peace-building effort in history took place in Europe and Asia in the post–World War II era when the US and its allies assisted nations in those continents devastated by a decade of war.

Ramsbotham & Woodhouse, above note 20, xx. On the Allies in Germany, see Wilde 2001a, above note 3, p. 592, text accompanying note 47; Wilde 2008, above note 1, pp. 21, 23–25, 275n140, 309, 323, 328–329, 369–370, 428, and sources cited therein.

[35] On Eastern Slavonia, see above note 30.

[36] Wilde 2001a, above note 3, p. 589; Wilde 2008, above note 1, Ch. 6, in particular at pp. 196–197.

Neither *Agenda for Peace* nor *Agenda for Peace Supplement* nor the Brahimi Report seemed to show much interest in a progressivist presentation of the complexity of international peace operations, even though they were able, by virtue of their remit, to discount the League-era projects that so obviously undermine such a presentation. In *Agenda for Peace*, the terms "new" and "second-generation" peacekeeping were conspicuous by their absence.[37] Only one passing reference (in a table) was made to "classical" and "multifunctional" peacekeeping in *Agenda for Peace Supplement*[38]; similarly, the Brahimi Report made the odd reference to "new generation" or "newer generations" of peacekeeping without defining these terms or drawing any conclusions from their use.[39]

Nonetheless, the language of generations has come to play a central role in academic discourse on peace operations since the early 1990s. Therefore, on the one hand is a set of historical circumstances placing into question the notion that complex international peace operations are an exclusively late-twentieth-century phenomenon and, on the other hand, an established academic discourse predicated on this notion.

One of the few scholars writing in the "new" era to acknowledge the long-standing existence of complex international peace operations is Steven Ratner in his book, *The New UN Peacekeeping*.[40] However, as the title suggests, Ratner nonetheless adopted the language of generations and the new/old dichotomy in his study of such operations, perhaps because of the widespread currency such an approach has come to enjoy. One-quarter of his book concerns operations – the League of Nations projects and ONUC, for example – that take place before the "new" era, in some cases seventy years before.[41] Ratner must describe these projects as examples of the "new peacekeeping" and, in an effort to accommodate the obvious problem this raises with the new/old dichotomy, the presence of these projects in the "old" era has been explained in terms of "earlier efforts" at the "new" paradigm.[42] For example, the League administration in the Saar is "second-generation peacekeeping

[37] As are the terms "old" and "first-generation" peacekeeping. UN Secretary-General, *Agenda for Peace: Preventative Diplomacy, Peacemaking and Peacekeeping*, UN Doc A/47/277–S/24111, 17 June 1992, reproduced in *ILM*, Vol. 31, 1992, p. 956 [hereinafter "*Agenda for Peace*"].

[38] UN Secretary-General, *Supplement to Agenda for Peace: Position Paper of the Secretary General on the Occasion of the Fiftieth Anniversary of the United Nations*, UN Doc A/50/60 – S/1995/1, 3 Jan. 1995 [hereinafter "*Agenda for Peace Supplement*"], p. 5 ("Table. Some statistics on United Nations activities related to peace and security").

[39] Brahimi Report, above note 7, paras. 102, 128, 140.

[40] Ratner, above note 17.

[41] *Id.*, Part II.

[42] *Id.*, Ch. 4.

before its time."[43] When there are so many earlier efforts – stretching back over such a long period – of a supposedly new phenomenon, one should surely ask whether the dichotomies of new/old and first generation/second generation are helpful. Why insist that 1989 is the "time" of complex peace operations and not also 1919?

Clearly, some peace operations are more complex than others; moreover, some projects are associated with a "state-building" purpose, others are not. The point is that the complexity of international peace operations has waxed and waned since the start of the League of Nations. Similarly, the involvement of such operations in "state-building" has been present since at least the 1960s – and much earlier if one includes the Allies in post-war Germany. The "time" of complexity and civilian involvement in international peace operations has been the entire twentieth century.

To be sure, with the administration projects in Cambodia, Mostar, Eastern Slavonia, Bosnia and Herzegovina, Kosovo, East Timor, and UN-run refugee camps,[44] as well as the other complex peace missions without an administration component, the final decade of that century and the start of the twenty-first witnessed a marked upsurge in the use of peace operations that are or were both complex and engaged in a "state-building" enterprise. However, an upsurge in and intensification of an activity with a long-standing pedigree (with the possible exception of the ambitious scope of state building in Kosovo and East Timor) is not the same as the emergence of a new type of peace operation. The year 1989, then, marks a particular moment of renewal, not a qualitative (rather than quantitative) "turning point." Also, it is perhaps worth pointing out that the increase in peace operations since 1988 has covered both complex and relatively straightforward operations. Just as the "old" era contains several important examples of the

[43] *Id.*, 91. The League mandate in Danzig is "a variation on a theme" (*id.*, 94) and the various uses of international territorial administration in Leticia, Upper Silesia, and Memel are described as "forgotten forays here and there" (*id.*, 95). On these missions, see, for example, Wilde 2001a, above note 3, pp. 587–588 (Leticia), pp. 597–600 (Upper Silesia), p. 600 (Memel), and sources cited therein.

[44] On these administration missions, see Wilde 2001a, above note 3, pp. 584–585. On the United Nations Transitional Authority in Cambodia (UNTAC), see also Wilde 2008, above note 1, pp. 52n20, 57, 57n35, 131, 133, 149–150, 218–219, 227, 243–244, 258, 272–273, 276, 298n31, 345, 376n341, 383, 404; on the European Union Administration of Mostar (EUAM)), see *id.*, 56, 58, 58n36, 243, 258; on UNTAES in Eastern Slavonia, see the sources cited above note 30; on OHR in Bosnia Herzegovina, see the sources cited above in note 27; on the Kosovo and East Timor projects see the sources cited above in note 1; on "refugee" camps administration by the Office of the United Nations High Commissioner for Refugees (UNHCR), see *id.*, pp. 48, 60–62, 61–62nn49–51, 95, 108, 131, 204, 225, 227, 228, 229, 232, 254, 255, 256, 276, 380, 383, 400n445, 401n450, 430, 436.

"new" peacekeeping, so the "new" era is replete with "old"-style peacekeeping operations.[45]

Concerns of accurate historical description aside, the language of generations also manifests problems in terms of a potentially negative effect on the way issues of legitimacy are understood. Adopting a progressivist narrative to denote changes in complexity may be problematic because of the way it can serve as a legitimizing device. As "third"- or "fourth"-generation missions, the projects in East Timor and Kosovo are positioned as the culmination of a historical process. They represent progress in the development of peace operations from the "old" or "traditional" days. Not only does relative complexity mean newness, then, suggesting a break from the past; the language of generations, with its evolutionary connotations of progressive improvement, also has a normative import. By ascribing differences in complexity through the use of this language, therefore, peace operations are classified normatively simply according to the changes in their complexity. Thus, UNMIK and UNTAET, merely by virtue of their comparatively complex nature, are presented in terms that suggest relative legitimacy.

Of course, the adoption of relative complexity as the benchmark of legitimacy seems absurd. The point is not that scholars who use the language of generations necessarily wish to make such a suggestion but rather that the language used risks having this effect. Indeed, some commentators do seem to suggest that increased complexity somehow necessarily constitutes superior quality. John Sanderson, for example – although not using the generational language – focused exclusively on the degree of powers exercised by the East Timor mission and proclaimed this to be a "step forward of millennial proportions" in UN peace operations with the mission being of a "high-quality."[46]

The language of generations and old versus new peace operations (or peacekeeping) should perhaps be substituted with a taxonomy that does not

[45] Most scholars accept that in the "new" era, "old" and "new" peacekeeping coexist. Ratner, for example, states that "[t]oday we witness both the continuation of older first-generation missions as well as the establishment of new ones. Moreover, a given operation can evolve from one [first generation] to the other [second generation] over time..." Ratner, above note 17, at p. 17.

[46] Sanderson, above note 16, p. 159. A mirror image of this approach is adopted by Roger MacGinty and Gillian Robinson, who assert that smaller-scale missions "hold a greater possibility for success" than their larger counterparts. See MacGinty, Roger & Robinson, Gillian, "Peacekeeping and the Violence in Ethnic Conflict," Ch. 2 in Ramesh Thakur & Albrecht Schnabel (eds.), *United Nations Peacekeeping Operations: Ad Hoc Missions, Permanent Engagement* (UN University Press, 2001), 26.

connote a linear process of historical evolution – for example, "basic" versus "complex" or "multifunctional."

The exceptionalist portrayal of the Kosovo and East Timor projects may similarly be damaging on a normative level in that it hampers any attempt to identify commonalities, as well as differences, between these projects and the earlier administration projects. No doubt, these projects are unusual and each is in some respects unique. However, whether something is unique or ordinary is not self-evident; rather, one must choose a particular definition of the projects and then use this definition as the basis for comparison with previous operations. The question, then, is whether this definition and the conclusion of uniqueness it allows are politically sustainable when compared to possible alternative definitions and the conclusions to which they lead.

What marks the Kosovo and East Timor missions for most exceptionalist commentators is the scope of the "state-building" mandate with which they were associated. Whereas this can stand up to scrutiny, as suggested previously, the question to be asked is whether singling out the projects on this basis is helpful in the first place. The main problem is that in many other respects, the two projects do share commonalities with other projects. For example, the nature of the activity that was conducted – that is, the exercise of territorial prerogatives by an international organization – has taken place in various missions since the beginning of the League of Nations. Certainly, it has been put to many different uses, including "state-building"; at the same time, however, there are certain important issues of legitimacy that are raised simply by virtue of the activity itself, as suggested in the introduction to this chapter. Necessarily, these issues are not unique to the Kosovo and East Timor projects. Setting the two projects apart, therefore – although helpful insofar as one identifies a particular point of distinctiveness – necessarily shifts the focus away from the commonalities that operate in many other areas. As a result, valuable lessons that could be learned from previous projects, both political and practical in nature, are overlooked.

Unifying Narratives: Purposive Simplification and Essentialism

As well as emphasizing the nature of the activity being performed, representations of ITA projects also can suggest the purposes served by the activity. How these purposes are described, in turn, influences the manner in which the questions concerning legitimacy outlined in the introduction are framed and sometimes whether such questions are even asked in the first place. In this section, I identify two related purposes with which ITA projects are commonly associated – that is, addressing the consequences of armed conflict and so-called "state building" – and consider how these representations mediate the scope of legitimacy analysis.

I suggest that most commentary provided a false unity between the ITA projects in East Timor and Kosovo by simplifying the purposes they served both individually and collectively. Not only is this process misleading in terms of explaining the projects; on a normative level, it also risks partially obscuring the range of contested political issues at stake. By doing so, it downgrades the political significance of ITA generally, and individual projects in particular, potentially undermining calls for scrutiny and accountability.

Previously, I highlighted the positioning of ITA within the taxonomy of peace operations and the effect this had in the presentation of the Kosovo and/or East Timor project(s) as unique and groundbreaking in terms of the activity performed. A further consequence is that ITA is associated, in a particular manner, with the pursuit of peace. Many academic commentators have chosen to label ITA in terms that suggest it is essentially a "post-conflict" phenomenon, using the word "conflict" in the narrow sense of an armed conflict. Michael Matheson's article purporting to cover the administration of territory by the UN described this activity as "United Nations Governance of Postconflict Societies."[47]

Such presentations imply two things about ITA: (1) it is always used in the "post-conflict" context; and (2) it is necessarily concerned with addressing the consequences of conflict. In particular, the suggestion is that because of conflict, governance has broken down either partially or completely; therefore, administration by international actors is introduced to fill the gap and "reconstruct."

The first problem with the "post-conflict" label is that it is incorrect to state that ITA is always used after conflict. In West Irian, for example, UN

[47] Matheson also used the phrases "governance of societies affected by conflicts" and, on UNTAET in particular, "governance of a territory shattered by conflict." Matheson, above note 8, pp. 76 and 82 respectively. Although Matheson concerned himself with the administration of territory by the United Nations, he mentioned neither the UN administration in Eastern Slavonia, nor the UN conduct of popular consultations, nor the administrative activities of ONUC between 1960 and 1963. On these administrative activities, see the sources cited above in notes 30 (in relation to Eastern Slavonia) and 29 (in relation to ONUC). On consultations, see Wilde 2001a, above note 3, at p. 597 (consultations) and Wilde 2008, above note 1, at pp. 56–57, 57n33, 95, 153, 161, 163, 227, 243, 377. Matheson's article, together with an article by Hansjörg Strohmeyer discussing the Kosovo and East Timor projects, were included as part of a "Symposium on State Reconstruction after Conflict" in the *American Journal of International Law*, Vol. 95, 2001.

administration was used in 1962–1963 not because the territory was "war-torn" and thus required external administration but rather to ensure the smooth transfer of territorial control from the Netherlands to Indonesia.[48] The UN acted as a neutral "buffer" between control by the two states, avoiding the potential conflict that was feared had the transfer been made directly from one state to the other. Rather than "picking up the pieces" after the end of a conflict, here it was a device for preventing armed hostilities from breaking out in the first place.

Most ITA missions, however, have taken place after conflict. That said, it is unhelpful to assume that all or any of the purposes each has served can be understood in terms of responding to the consequences of conflict – an assumption arguably made if one labels the activity a "post-conflict" phenomenon.

When ONUC tried to fill the governmental vacuum in the Congo in the early 1960s, the perceived inability of local officials to perform governance was associated as much with the failure of the former colonial power (Belgium) to train them in governmental skills as it was with the armed conflict that ensued after independence was realized.[49] To be sure, ONUC was a "peacekeeping" operation; it had been created to address the conflict, and its military component pursued this objective vigorously, *inter alia* by attempting to prevent the secession of Katanga province (and so moving into what is now regarded as "peace enforcement").[50] However, the installation of ONUC to pursue these military objectives placed it in a position to exercise certain governmental functions for a broader set of reasons than merely the conflict. The fact that these functions were performed by the civilian component of a peacekeeping force perhaps led to the perception that they were to be explained wholly in terms of conflict. Indeed, many commentators mention these administrative activities only briefly, or ignore them altogether, focusing instead on ONUC's military role.[51]

Similarly, in Bosnia and Herzegovina, the role of the NATO-led military force in maintaining the cessation of armed hostilities received much more

[48] On the West Irian project, see the sources cited above note 29.

[49] Wilde 2001a, above note 3, p. 592, text accompanying note 50, and source cited therein; Wilde 2008, above note 1, Ch. 6, text accompanying note 53.

[50] Wilde 2001a, above note 3, source cited at p. 592n50; Wilde 2008, above note 1, Ch. 6, at p. 130.

[51] E.g., Derek Bowett, *United Nations Forces*, 1964, Ch. 6 on ONUC. Bowett takes the position that "[a] detailed description of the civilian relief operations in the Congo would be out of place in this present study of United Nations Forces," p. 248.

attention than the governmental activities of the OHR.[52] Even when OHR's activities are discussed, they are frequently represented as being exclusively concerned with the consequences of the 1992–1995 armed conflict in the country. Again, the presentation is that ITA is used in circumstances in which there are no functioning institutions and that these circumstances were brought about by the previous armed conflict.

Actually, the legislative activities of OHR operate alongside the lawmaking of domestic legislatures.[53] The reason given for OHR's performance of these activities has not been the absence of institutions run by local officials but, rather, that such institutions have sometimes failed to operate in a manner deemed suitable by OHR. Whereas this sometimes has been understood in terms of war-related practicalities, it has often been explained on the basis that the political agenda being pursued by the legislature ran counter to that promoted by OHR, or because members of the legislature were not deemed sufficiently rooted in the democratic tradition to perform their functions adequately. Again, whereas the latter reason (whatever its merits) may be explained in part because of the war, one must somehow discount altogether other factors (e.g., the consequences of decades of totalitarian rule) in order to suggest that conflict was its only cause. In removing government officials, OHR clearly has not attempted to fill a practical breakdown in governance; such actions actually created a governmental vacuum until the relevant position could be filled through appointment or election. Moreover, in most cases, dismissal has not been because of incompetence (which sometimes may be explained as a consequence of the conflict) but, rather, because of the policies espoused by the official in question, such as Serb nationalism in the case of Republika Srpksa President Nikola Poplasen (who was removed from office by OHR in 1999).[54]

In Bosnia and Herzegovina, an institution installed as part of a peace agreement has been engaged in promoting a liberal political and economic order. To suggest that this has been essentially a "post-conflict" agenda is to ignore the degree to which such activity also has been understood to be addressing the perceived problems arising from a centrally planned economy

[52] On OHR, see the sources cited above in note 27.

[53] On the domestic legislatures, see the Constitution of Bosnia and Herzegovina, Annex IV (with Annexes I and II) to the General Framework Agreement for Peace in Bosnia and Herzegovina, Paris, 14 Dec. 1995, approved by Bosnia and Herzegovina, Republika Srpska and Federation of Bosnia and Herzegovina, reprinted in *ILM*, Vol. 35, 1996, p. 117.

[54] See Office of the High Representative, Press Release, Removal from Office of Nikola Poplasen, Sarajevo, 5 March 1999, obtainable from www.ohr.int.

and a totalitarian system of governance – both of which, of course, predated the war.

In contrast to the Congo and Bosnia and Herzegovina, the presence of ITA in Kosovo and East Timor was rarely ignored in the discussion of those territories covering the UNTAET and UNMIK periods. At the same time, this activity again often has been explained wholly in terms of responding to the consequences of conflict. Ramesh Thakur and Albrecht Schnabel situated the Kosovo and East Timor missions within a class of missions "in countries affected by civil wars," where the "United Nations substitutes for collapsed local governments."[55] When UNTAET was described as a post-conflict mission (or that it is the administration of a "war-torn territory"), the implication was that the reason for the mission was that conflict – in particular, the post-referendum violence by pro-Indonesian militias – created a governmental vacuum and breakdown in infrastructure that had rendered governance by the East Timorese impossible. Michael Matheson stated that the Australian-led military force INTERFET, created to prevent the violence by the militias,

> . . . quickly restored order, but the violence had already destroyed a large number of homes and other buildings, caused the collapse of the civil administration and judicial systems, and damaged or destroyed much of the waterworks and other essential public services. As a result, the Security Council . . . decided to entrust the United Nations with the burden of governance of a territory shattered by conflict.[56]

What this typical presentation of UNTAET's creation ignores is that UN administration was actually envisaged before the violence, and the referendum, had taken place. In fact, it was provided for in the May Agreements that also established the terms of the referendum.[57] The original reason for UN administration had nothing to do with conflict; rather, it concerned the perceived inability of the East Timorese, in the short term, to govern themselves

[55] Thakur & Schnabel, above note 20. [56] Matheson, above note 8, p. 82.

[57] The relevant agreement states that, in the event that the East Timorese rejected the option of substantial autonomy within Indonesia in the popular consultation,

> . . . the Governments of Indonesia and Portugal and the Secretary-General shall agree on arrangements for a peaceful and orderly transfer of authority in East Timor [from Indonesia] to the United Nations. The Secretary-General shall, subject to the appropriate legislative mandate, initiate the procedure enabling East Timor to begin a process of transition towards independence.

Agreement between the Republic of Indonesia and the Portuguese Republic on the Question of East Timor, 5 May 1999, available at http://www.un.org/peace/etimor99/agreement/agreeFrame_Eng01.html [last accessed 15 June 2007], Art. 6.

once Indonesia had withdrawn. Of course, the violence that followed the referendum made governance by any actor, Timorese or international, extremely difficult. However, as an explanation for the very idea of UN administration – as opposed to the particular challenges that administration faced once it was introduced – it is incorrect.

A similar problem can be seen relative to the Kosovo mission. In describing the background to UNMIK, Matheson explained the "state of economic and social chaos" in Kosovo following the NATO bombing campaign, the military campaign by Serb forces against the Albanian population, and the withdrawal of all Serb and Yugoslav military and civilian officials.[58] He remarked that

> [c]learly, the international community had to establish a system of governance, at least for an interim period. Without such governance, the chaotic situation would present a continuing, acute threat of escalating violence and regional instability, as well as a serious humanitarian crisis.[59]

This suggests that UNMIK was conceived to respond to the preexisting situation of a governmental vacuum. Its purpose was essentially practical: "establishing a system of governance" where one did not exist.

Such a presentation fails to acknowledge that the withdrawal of Serb and Yugoslav officials that created the governmental vacuum was actually part of the same overall settlement – the "Peace Plan" agreed to by the then-Federal Republic of Yugoslavia (FRY) – that provided for UN administration.[60] The absence of the Serb and Yugoslav administrative authorities, therefore, cannot be considered separately from the presence of the UN administration mission; the purpose of the Serb and Yugoslav pullout was to make way for UNMIK. The UN was there not to fill a governmental vacuum but, rather, to replace an administration seemingly committed to the disenfranchisement of the Kosovar Albanians with another administration committed to the enfranchisement of that population. In other words, the reason for the UN administration was not to remedy a governmental breakdown but to engineer a fundamental change in government policy.

A similarly simplistic and misleading presentation of the purposes served by ITA missions can be seen when these missions are labeled

[58] Matheson, above note 8, p. 78. [59] *Id.*

[60] Agreement on the Principles (Peace Plan) to Move Towards a Resolution of the Kosovo Crisis Presented to the Leadership of the Federal Republic of Yugoslavia by the President of Finland, Martti Ahtisaari, representing the European Union, and Viktor Chernomyrdin, Special Representative of the President of the Russian Federation, June 3, 1999, UN Doc. S/1999/649, paras. 2 & 6 (on the withdrawal) and 3 & 5 (on the UN administrative presence).

collectively as "state-building," "nation-building," and "state-reconstruction" enterprises.[61] ITA is often associated with the "failed-states" paradigm, in that it has been sometimes used to respond to a problem – for example, the collapse of governmental infrastructure – that has come to be described in terms of state "failure." The notion of the failed state came to prominence within academic discourse through an article by Steven Ratner and David Helman, in which plenary territorial administration by the UN (labeled "United Nations conservatorship") was proposed as a mechanism for "saving" what were described as "failed states": entities in which government had collapsed.[62] The "failed states" paradigm has been criticized on a number of bases, from its essentialist use of language to the particularist basis for defining failure; the manner in which it sets up a dichotomous opposition within international relations between "successful" and "failed" states; and the way it condemns peoples for the deficiencies of their elites, from whom in practice they may be unable to escape.[63] I address the criticism concerning responsibility for governmental breakdown below.

For the present inquiry, the "failed states" paradigm is germane because for many commentators, state "failure" (i.e., governmental collapse) is presented as the sole context in which ITA is used, in general and/or in particular missions. Such missions are always concerned with promoting the existence of organized social and political institutions, especially governmental institutions, when these institutions are not functioning properly. As with the "post-conflict" label, this presentation is misleading in that some administration projects are aimed at entirely different objectives (e.g., West Irian).

Adopting the terms "postconflict" and "state-building" as labels to describe holistically the administration projects obscures the many other purposes that these missions can be created to serve, sometimes outside a

[61] On the representation of international territorial administration as a "state reconstruction" enterprise, see, for example, the inclusion of the articles by Matheson (describing some [but not all] of the UN projects) and Strohmeyer (discussing the Kosovo and East Timor projects) as part of a "Symposium on State Reconstruction after Conflict" in the *American Journal of International Law* (see Matheson, above note 8; Strohmeyer, above note 12). See also Wilde 2008, above note 1, Ch. 7, Section 7.3.3.

[62] Helman, Gerald B., & Ratner, Steven R., "Saving Failed States," *Foreign Policy*, Vol. 89, 1992, p. 3 [hereinafter "Helman & Ratner"]. The uncritical use of the term "failed state" is widespread; see the sources cited in Wilde 2008, above note 1, pp. 252–253n46.

[63] For some of these criticisms, see, e.g., Gordon, Ruth, "Saving Failed States: Sometimes a Neocolonialist Notion," *American University Journal of International Law and Policy*, Vol. 12, 1997, p. 903; Richardson, Henry J., "'Failed States,' Self-Determination, and Preventive Diplomacy: Colonialist Nostalgia and Democratic Expectations," *Temple International and Comparative Law Journal*, Vol. 10, 1996, p. 1 [hereinafter "Richardson"].

"post-conflict" situation and in the absence of any "state-building" objective. On a descriptive level, therefore, they are unhelpful – and, if we are seeking to understand why ITA takes place, they may be misleading.

For example, when Michael Matheson discussed the international approach taken with respect to Bosnia and Herzegovina at Dayton in 1995, he suggested that "governance was left to the Bosnian political entities."[64] The reason for this was presented as self-evident:

> [c]learly, the United Nations was reluctant to assume the functions of governing the territory of a sovereign state if indigenous institutions were available for the purpose.[65]

Having set up ITA as a policy institution used only when "indigenous institutions" break down after conflict, Matheson reinforced his thesis by invoking a situation that did not fit this scenario, implying a causal relationship between the presence of indigenous institutions and the absence of ITA. Quite apart from the nature of the causal relationship, which surely is not axiomatic, he seems to ignore what has happened in Bosnia and Herzegovina since Dayton. As previously mentioned, partial ITA (albeit by OHR rather than the UN) has ended up being exercised in that country, despite indigenous institutions being "available for the purpose."[66] Matheson's approach perhaps illustrates the problems that follow from assuming that ITA is only ever concerned with filling a governmental vacuum.

Considering the problems with the "post-conflict" and "state-building" labels on a descriptive level, we can see what is perhaps a more important problem on a normative level, in terms of how questions of legitimacy might be understood. The adoption of the labels for the projects collectively can operate as a legitimizing device, concealing other, relatively controversial policies with which the projects can sometimes be associated. Of course, the circumstances in which international organizations fill a supposed "vacuum" when governance has broken down do raise many political questions (e.g., Is there really a vacuum? Is consent obtained from local actors? How long should such missions last? How accountable are they?). However, if some of the other objectives outlined previously also are considered, ideas that are more politically contested are in play. For example, using ITA to effect a territorial transfer promotes a particular territorial outcome, thereby mediating the realization of self-determination claims. The transfer of West Irian to Indonesia treated the local population as if it

64 Matheson, above note 8, pp. 78.

65 *Id.*

66 Although Matheson mentions OHR in a footnote, its status as a counter-example to the thesis he puts forward in his main text is neither acknowledged nor addressed. *Id.*, note 19.

were not entitled to external self-determination, even though the agreement that provided for the transfer envisaged a post-transfer self-determination consultation.[67] Moreover, by enabling control by Indonesia, the UN administration made possible Indonesia's manipulation of the subsequent consultation, which was widely regarded as a sham.[68] Similarly, the use of ITA because local actors are deemed incapable of administration (as in East Timor) or incapable of "democratic" governance (as in Bosnia and Herzegovina and Kosovo) involves contested political decisions concerning the abilities of local actors and the standards adopted for governance. It is reminiscent of the civilizational standard associated with foreign-state administration under colonialism and the Mandate and Trusteeship systems, a standard that, of course, was criticized *inter alia* as a racist alibi for imperial conquest and exploitation.[69]

The purposes variously served by different ITA projects, therefore, often raise fundamental political issues that must be accounted for when the legitimacy of the projects is being appraised. Should West Irian have been handed over to Indonesia? By what standard were local actors deemed to be deficient in East Timor? Who should apply that standard? What ideas of democracy and multiethnic politics underlie the use of ITA to "promote" democracy in Bosnia and Herzegovina and Kosovo, and are these ideas supportable? To what extent does this use of ITA replicate certain aspects of the colonial paradigm?

The West Irian mission was criticized for selling out the people of the territory, some of whom have engaged in a struggle for self-determination ever since. OHR in Bosnia and Herzegovina has been criticized for seeking to promote democracy through dictatorial measures (e.g., the legally unreviewable removal of elected officials); UNTAET was criticized by the East Timorese for assuming that local people were incapable of governance; UNMIK in Kosovo was criticized for promoting the rights of the Kosovar Albanians in ways that disenfranchise the local Serbs. These and other important political questions are obscured by the presentation of all administration projects as concerned exclusively with governmental reconstruction after

[67] Wilde 2001a, above note 3, p. 588n27 and accompanying text and p. 591; Wilde 2008, above note 1, Ch. 6, at p. 168n67 and accompanying text and p. 169.

[68] Wilde 2001a, above note 3, p. 591n43.

[69] The parallels between international territorial administration and colonial trusteeship and the Mandate and Trusteeship systems, the meaning and significance of the standard of civilization, and the critiques that were made of colonial trusteeship, are discussed at length in Wilde 2008, above note 1, Ch. 8.

conflict. The "post-conflict" and "war-torn territories" labels legitimize the pursuit of entirely different and more controversial policy objectives by concealing these objectives and thereby preventing them from being scrutinized.

A further legitimizing feature of the "state reconstruction after conflict" label is that it presents the activity of ITA as essentially passive and reactive. Governmental institutions collapse and international administrators go in to rebuild. The reactive nature of this activity downgrades its political importance. When carrying out territorial administration, international organizations are not positive agents of change but rather merely reacting to events.

Therefore, relative to Kosovo, for example, Michael Matheson talked about how the "international community" "had to" create a system of governance in Kosovo because of the preexisting governmental breakdown. External events created an imperative to which the UN and Western states, as hitherto uninvolved bystanders, had to respond. This ignores the fact that the main feature of the "governmental breakdown" – that is, the withdrawal of the Serb and Yugoslav administrative presence – had been engineered by the West through the European Union (EU)– and Russian-brokered "Peace Plan," the terms of which were accepted by the then-FRY following the NATO bombing campaign of that country. At some level, governance did not break down in Kosovo – the West forced out one administration and replaced it with the UN. The degree to which the UN Secretariat and UN members generally – rather than particular members of the Security Council – had any control over this, of course, is another matter. The point is that UN administration was being used to actively displace one administration with another: it was part of the very process that created the governmental vacuum that it then went in to "fill."

A further problem arises when ITA missions are labeled "peace operations" or "peacekeeping missions," as often happens when their purposes are presented in the "post-conflict" manner discussed previously. In addition to the problems highlighted already, the use of these labels implies that ITA is an enterprise essentially concerned with the promotion of peace and the end of conflict. Considering the many different policies with which ITA missions are associated, one cannot escape the normative implication of this label that each policy – such as internal self-determination for the population of Kosovo during the UNMIK period – was pursued because it would lead to peace and an end to conflict and not also because it was of independent value. No doubt, one can debate whether the pursuit of peace is the fundamental objective of any political system; the problem with the peace-operation classification is that it implies that this debate is closed.

The peace-operation classification also operates as a further legitimating device: Who can argue with the general goal of preventing armed conflict? Considering the West Irian mission, for example, an operation having as its objective conflict prevention is fine on its own terms – arguably, the operation did prevent hostilities (although only between the Netherlands and Indonesia; the hostilities between local separatists and Indonesia continue to this day). At the same time, it effectively prevented the realization of self-determination on the part of the local population. Labeling that mission a "conflict-prevention" mission rather than, for example, a "denial of self-determination mission" legitimizes it by focusing on what it achieved (in terms of security), without highlighting the price that was paid for this achievement (in terms of self-determination).

Skewed Responsibility Narratives: Blame and the Failed-States Paradigm

Previously, I illustrated how the association of ITA projects with the "failed-state" concept was unfortunate because the institution is used not only in circumstances of governmental collapse. It was also suggested that the very idea of using the label "failed state" to denote governmental collapse is problematic. One such problem is that this label arguably denotes exclusive responsibility on the part of the state for the breakdown in governance. The state, its people, and its leaders alone have "failed."

Henry Richardson highlighted this feature of the "failed-state" concept and criticized it as simplistic.[70] Of course, state collapse often is due to indigenous factors, to a considerable degree, whether civil conflict or corrupt leadership. At the same time, clearly the involvement of foreign states, international financial institutions, and multinational corporations and the like can and does play a major role in mediating the state of local conditions, thereby affecting the viability of the economy and governmental infrastructure.

For example, should exclusive responsibility for the governmental breakdown in the Congo in the 1960s lie at the door of the Congolese people and their leaders? To make this assertion, one should somehow discount the role of Belgium, for example, which "failed" to prepare local people for government before independence and then intervened militarily in the country afterward

[70] Richardson, above note 63, *passim*.

to support certain factions during the civil war.[71] East Timor became a state in May 2002. Is it really appropriate to conceive responsibility for the problems in that state since then *solely* in terms of the local population? Clearly, one cannot look only at the behavior of local actors in seeking to appraise a particular national economy and political system. Regrettably, this is exactly what the "failed-state" concept encourages us to do.

The skewed notion of responsibility arguably suggested by the "failed-state" idea is not only misconceived; it also leads to policy prescriptions that, by themselves, may ignore the structural causes of the problems they seek to address. The "state-building" use of ITA is a case in point. Necessarily, this is concerned exclusively with the local causes of a collapse in infrastructure, seeking, for example, to improve local capacities for governance. Clearly, it has no remit with respect to, for example, the foreign states, international financial institutions, and multinational corporations that will play as important a role in shaping the future of the territory's economy as local people and their leaders. I am not suggesting that ITA should somehow be able to perform that second role; the point is that as a policy device, it is necessarily limited to addressing the local causes of whatever problem with which it is concerned. If we consider the remarkably intrusive nature of ITA, there is no comparable policy device that intervenes within other states, corporations, and international institutions to try to prevent – as ITA does on the national level – these bodies from making decisions that contribute to the factors that hamper a recovery from governmental collapse or precipitate such a collapse in the first place.

When Helman and Ratner discussed the "saving" of failed states, their prescription – that is, foreign administration – was limited to the indigenous governmental structure. They did not concern themselves with proposing other similarly intrusive mechanisms with respect to, for example, rich countries and multinational corporations. Necessarily, the proscription is reactive in that it is concerned with responding to state collapse when it has happened, thereby focusing exclusively on indigenous factors rather than seeking to prevent it in the first place, which would require a focus on both indigenous and exogenous factors. The result is a somewhat naïve and simplistic proposal that fits well with the narrow notion of responsibility of the "failed-state" paradigm. Therefore, when Margaret Karns and Karen Mingst stated that the "key question for the international community is what are the responsibilities of states, the United Nations (or regional IGOs), and other actors when states

[71] Wilde 2001a, above note 3, p. 592; Wilde 2008, above note 1, Ch. 7, p. 205.

fail," the responsibilities in question concern remedial measures of intervention "post-failure" in the territory concerned, not prophylactic measures concerning the behavior of these actors that might lead to state collapse in the first place.[72] Moreover, the "responsibilities" are conceived in terms suggestive of the charity of innocent bystanders (cf. the "saving" of failed states), not the liability of those who are partially complicit. The subtitle to Karns and Mingst's question about the "international community's responsibilities when states fail" is "[h]ow should choices be made as to where to direct scarce resources?"[73]

The asymmetrical conception of responsibility of the "failed-state" concept, then, is reflected in and supported by the regime of international policy institutions like ITA. One might venture that this asymmetry, of course, is no accident. One might ask who uses the language of "failed states" and what their interests are in doing so. The "failed-states" concept originated in Western scholarship and has been utilized in Western policy discourse. Examining this language may be helpful, therefore, in understanding Western ideas of a "failed" other and a "successful" self. Just as Edward Said studied "Orientalism" *inter alia* as a way of understanding how Western culture conceives itself through an alienated Oriental "other," the "failed-state" concept may be illuminating insofar as our understandings of those who use it are concerned.[74] As a basis for policy, however, it may be limited precisely because it reflects the interests of those who use it, and these interests may conflict with the interests of those relative to whom it is used. Indeed, exclusively locally based connotations of responsibility exculpate Western states and multinationals – and the international financial institutions they control – in terms of whatever actions these actors may have conducted that contributed to the so-called "failure" by the state concerned. Similarly, these actors do not face the prospect of intrusive policy institutions, like ITA, that seek to prevent whatever policies they may prosecute that led to state collapse.

We have, therefore, a suggestion of responsibility and an institution for addressing this responsibility that only takes in part of the picture. Can this not be supported, however, as the best that can be hoped for in an unequal world? Was Helman and Ratner's limited focus an attempt to address legitimate concerns about state collapse, while staying within the bounds of what was realistic in terms of the proscription put forward?

First, on pragmatic grounds, it may have little effect. The work done on the ground with local people may be undermined by the absence of comparative

[72] Karns & Mingst, above note 19, p. 218. [73] *Id.*, p. 220.

[74] Said, Edward, *Orientalism: Western Conceptions of the Orient* (Penguin Books, 1995 reissue with new afterword).

processes operating in those other arenas that are equally determinative of the policies concerned. Even if this were not the case, however, there is a second problem: the "failed-states" concept is not only about emphasizing a certain area of responsibility; it also can be seen as repudiating the notion that responsibility can reside elsewhere as well. The notion of the failed state, then, and its associated policy institutions like ITA may reflect and constitute not good first steps but rather the impediments that exist to broader notions of responsibility and mechanisms for implementing that responsibility.

The "failed-state" concept not only reflects our unequal world but also buttresses that inequality. When ITA is used in circumstances of state collapse, it may be serving merely to distract attention away from the structural, exogenous factors that both contributed to the collapse and will mediate the future economic development of the territory.

De-idealizing Narratives: The Technocratic Approach

> ... [T]here is a pressing issue in transitional civil administration that must be addressed, and that is the issue of "applicable law."[75]

Granting prerogatives involving territorial administration to international organizations, although (as suggested previously) not unique, is unusual. International organizations are not usually engaged in administering territorial units; therefore, when this activity takes place, a range of distinctive practical and political issues is raised. What is striking about some of the commentary on ITA is that it has presented the challenges raised by this unusual activity wholly or predominantly in practical terms. Technocratic matters – particularly relating to the ability and willingness of UN institutions to create, prosecute, and monitor territorial administration missions – are set out as the main or even only issues of consequence. This has a "de-idealizing" effect, in that it presents ITA as a phenomenon the legitimacy of which requires appraisal exclusively or overwhelmingly in practical terms and not, or much less, also according to political ideas. The legitimacy of individual projects, and ITA generally, then, is at best judged mainly or exclusively in terms of practical issues (e.g., is the UN up to the job). At worst, as an issue, it is set aside altogether from the set of questions commentators consider when they analyze ITA.

In a first for UN peace-operations reports, the Brahimi Report devoted a particular section to "transitional administrations," which from the missions it covered would seem to denote UN operations involving the exercise of

[75] Brahimi Report, above note 7, para. 79.

plenary administrative prerogatives.[76] In that section, the Brahimi Report was concerned exclusively with the capacity of the UN to engage in an activity that because of its scope involved "challenges and responsibilities that are unique among United Nations field operations."[77] Thus, it highlighted the "struggles of the United Nations to set up and manage" the operations in Kosovo and East Timor, given the ambitious nature of those two missions.[78] When the report then stated that "[b]eyond such challenges lies the larger question of whether the United Nations should be in this business at all," it went on to discuss the willingness and capacity of the Secretariat.[79] The "larger question," therefore, was presented solely in terms of whether the Secretariat wants to be given such difficult work.

Similarly, after describing some of the UN administration projects, Michael Matheson turned to what he described as the "policy" and the "legal" questions these projects raise. Under the "policy" heading, Matheson, who was writing during the operation of the Kosovo and East Timor projects, remarked that these projects

> ... raise serious policy questions about the practical capability of the United Nations to perform this role, the long-term political viability of relying on the United Nations to bear such burdens, and the availability of feasible alternatives to the United Nations for this purpose. Much will depend on whether the Organization is ultimately judged to have succeeded or failed in Kosovo or East Timor.[80]

Although the words "policy" and "political" were used, actually only practical issues were discussed. Like the Brahimi Report's "larger question," Matheson's "policy" concerns were essentially technocratic.

For the Brahimi Report, the only other concern highlighted was set out in the quotation extracted at the beginning of this section: the problem of deciding in Kosovo and East Timor what the applicable local law is and what it should be.[81] Typically, UN officials have no background in the national law of the territory concerned, and this law may be considered problematic anyway because of its association with the previous regime in the territory and/or its incompatibility with the relevant standards of international human rights law. This issue, and the related matter of getting the institutions of law and order up and running, was the main focus of Hansjoerg Strohmeyer's

[76] *Id.*, section H, from para. 76. Compare, for example, with *Agenda for Peace*, above note 37, and *Agenda for Peace Supplement*, above note 38.

[77] *Id.*, para. 77.

[78] *Id.*, para. 76.

[79] Ibid., para. 78.

[80] Matheson, see note 8, p. 83.

[81] Brahimi Report, above note 7, paras. 79–83.

discussion of the Kosovo and East Timor projects.[82] Both the Brahimi Report and Strohmeyer made proposals about how the "applicable law" issue might be addressed in future missions.[83]

Given the managerial approach adopted as the basis for appraisal, it is perhaps no surprise that when the choice between international organizations and states is discussed in terms of the identity of the administering actor, matters are sometimes considered on a purely practical level. The only question is who is best able to perform the task of territorial administration. When the Brahimi Report discussed the circumstances that led to the UN missions in Kosovo and East Timor, it mentioned the idea of "individual Member States taking over entire sectors of administration (sectoral responsibility)" as an alternative to the UN.[84] Deciding between the alternatives, however, was presented exclusively as a practical matter – state administration is, in principle, attractive over UN administration because of the expertise of state officials in the very business of government that is required in administration missions.[85] The reason sectoral responsibility was not considered in Kosovo and East Timor was similarly based on practicalities: it was proposed "too late in the process to iron out the details."[86] Again, this approach presents the choice – here, concerning the identity of the administering actor rather than foreign administration itself – as if it had no normative as well as practical implications.

In their proposal for "UN Conservatorship," Helman and Ratner nominated the UN in the role of the administering actor but did not explain their choice in this regard.[87] Equally, when at one point they suggested an alternative international organization, they made no comment as to the basis for choosing this actor over the UN:

> [i]n general, the United Nations would act as the administering authority, although a group of states might also perform that function, such as the European Community with respect to Bosnia.[88]

82 Strohmeyer, above note 12.

83 Brahimi Report, above note 7, paras. 82–83. Strohmeyer, above note 12, pp. 62–63.

84 Brahimi Report, above note 7, para. 129.

85 *Id.*

86 *Id.*

87 Matheson, above note 8, p. 83.

88 The Bosnia and Herzegovina suggestion was prescient: the member states of the EC, acting within the framework of the European Union, created the European Union Administration in Mostar (the EUAM), which administered the city between 1994 and 1996. See Wilde 2001a, above note 3, p. 590, and sources cited therein; Wilde 2008, above note 1, pp. 56, 58, 58n36, 243, 258.

This is one step farther from the Brahimi Report: the choice of administering actor is made without any explanation, practical or normative. Either, then, there is nothing in the choice or, more plausibly, whatever factor – normative or practical – leading to the choice of the UN is considered self-evident.

The practical issues highlighted in the technocratic approach are, no doubt, "large" and "pressing." Involving foreign actors in territorial administration is a remarkably ambitious enterprise on a practical level, and the choice of particular foreign actors – that is, international organizations or states – to perform this task may well be crucial to the effectiveness of the mission. At the same time, however, the large issues arising out of foreign territorial administration do not apply only to capacity and willingness; neither is the only pressing issue the matter of determining the applicable local law.

If one is asking, as the Brahimi Report did, whether the UN should be "in this business at all," one also should surely be concerned with the nature of "this business" on a political level and the normative character of the UN when compared with the alternatives of foreign states and other international organizations. One should address the political factors arising out of both the granting of the power of territorial government to a foreign actor and the choice of foreign actor to perform this role. For example, how does the idea of foreign administration replicate the colonial paradigm? Does the choice of foreign actor – between international organizations or states, between different international organizations – alter the answer to that question?[89] The exclusively or overwhelmingly technocratic approach adopted by the commentators discussed previously necessarily excludes such an analysis. Moreover, engaging in this analysis is not only worth doing in its own right; one also cannot fully appreciate the technical problems faced by the missions without addressing it first.

A related approach is to acknowledge and address certain normative questions raised by ITA, but to situate such a discussion within a broader focus of inquiry that is overwhelmingly technocratic. When Helman and Ratner discussed the merits of the idea of what they termed "UN conservatorship," they addressed the potential challenges of reconciling this idea with classical notions of state sovereignty, advocating consent by the territory concerned as a model to be adopted when such arrangements are constituted.[90] They then turned to five different "practical considerations," including cost and the need for a management facility within the UN Secretariat.[91] By addressing the issue of consent and not any other normative issue (e.g., accountability),

[89] See Wilde 2008, above note 1, Chs. 8 and 9.

[90] Helman & Ratner, above note 62, pp. 16–18. [91] *Id.*, pp. 18–20.

it is as if the other normative issues do not exist or are, at least, so lacking in importance as not to merit even a brief mention. Moreover, presenting this one normative issue in the context of five practical issues leaves the overall impression that the merits of the idea of ITA are to be assessed overwhelmingly in practical terms.

Normative questions are similarly avoided when they are labeled and discussed as practical and not also political in nature. Much of what Helman and Ratner addressed under the heading of "practical considerations" raised issues that are highly political. For example, the question of which UN organ should be assigned "overall responsibility for conservatorships, including the power to initiate and terminate them," was discussed in terms of practicability alone.[92] The General Assembly is "too large and unwieldy for effective oversight"; the Economic and Social Council (ECOSOC) is also "too large"; the Security Council, by comparison, "is the most efficient organ available."[93] Therefore, it is proposed that the Security Council pass a resolution establishing the conservatorship and then, because of its lack of experience in economic and social matters, establish a subgroup – not all of whose members need be on the Security Council – to oversee each conservatorship.[94] The only role for the General Assembly is to approve the budget.[95]

It is as if the only significance of the relative composition and remit among the Security Council, the ECOSOC, and the General Assembly is a practical one: composition goes only to efficiency, remit goes only to "experience." Of course, size often can have such a practical effect, and the history of the UN certainly would support a pessimistic conclusion in this regard. Equally, the remit of a particular organ undoubtedly affects the degree to which that organ is able to discharge responsibilities in a particular subject area. However, to suggest that such practical considerations should be the sole determinants of the choice of UN organ, as Helman and Ratner appeared to do, ignores the political differences between the different institutions that are both well known and significant to the particular issue of territorial administration.

For example, the Security Council's size makes it relatively streamlined but also comparatively unrepresentative when compared with the General Assembly. Given the colonial echoes of ITA, it may be that as far as UN authority is concerned, the General Assembly would prove politically more legitimate, "internationalizing" the phenomenon further by shifting the authoritative procedures into an arena in which all states are represented and on an equal

92 *Id.*, p. 18.
93 *Id.*
94 *Id.*, pp. 18–19.
95 *Id.*, p. 19.

basis.[96] This and other political factors surely need to be considered along with practical issues when discussing the relative merits of each UN organ.

Conclusion

Considering the legitimacy of ITA requires that far-reaching normative and practical questions be addressed. Regrettably, this activity sometimes can be represented in terms that obscure or downgrade the importance of these questions, thereby potentially degrading the quality of any resulting analysis on legitimacy. Such representations are realized through four different discursive strategies.

The first discursive strategy situates ITA within a progressivist historical narrative, positioning the Kosovo and East Timor projects as comprising the pinnacle of an evolutionary process. Misleading in its own terms, this presentation also may be damaging on a normative level in that it legitimates the recent projects on spurious grounds.

The second discursive strategy unifies all the administration projects through a simplified presentation of their purposes, using the "post-conflict" and "state-building" labels. Again, this is both misleading in its own terms and unhelpful normatively because it obscures the full range of purposes with which ITA has been associated, many of which are relatively controversial when compared to the "post-conflict" and "state-building" objectives.

The third discursive strategy associates ITA with a concept – the notion of the "failed state" – that arguably implies a skewed conception of responsibility. Apart from other problems, this legitimizes ITA by portraying the indigenous factors with which it is concerned as the exclusive cause of the problems it seeks to address. It is easier to justify the introduction of ITA with this narrow conception of responsibility than if the causes were presented in a more complex manner.

The fourth discursive strategy presents ITA in a wholly or primarily technocratic manner, obscuring and/or downgrading its political aspects and thereby potentially attenuating the range of issues considered in appraisals of the legitimacy of the activity in general and individual missions in particular.

Commentary on ITA not only reflects the political factors raised by the activity; by delineating the contours of the institution, it is also partially responsible for setting the terms by which it will be understood and its

[96] On the UN Trusteeship Council – its general function, its non-utilization in relation to East Timor, and the proposals for its abolition, see Wilde 2008, above note 1, pp. 98, 164n44, 165, 171, 277, 298n31, 337–338n194, 378, 382n366, 392–393, 418–419, 422, 424–427, 448, 450, and the sources cited therein.

legitimacy appraised. Representing ITA, therefore, is a political act, and the particular approach taken needs to be defended on a normative level. Such representations should be rooted in the desire to facilitate as broad a range of practical and political questions as possible.

Current and recent projects need to be situated within a historical context that highlights commonality without implying legitimacy through a progressivist narrative. At the same time, the projects should be disaggregated on a purposive level so that the full range of purposes with which they have been associated is appreciated. A narrow set of purposes, based on a misreading of the current and recent projects, should not be used to stand for ITA itself. When one such purpose – that is, state-building – is focused on, it should not be conceptualized in terms of state "failure"; in particular, responsibility for state collapse needs to be considered in a complex manner, taking in both indigenous and transnational actors. Finally (and it is perhaps surprising that this needs to be stated), granting international organizations administrative prerogatives over territory raises political as well as practical issues. The legitimacy of current, previous, and future ITA projects needs to be appraised on both normative and technocratic bases.[97]

[97] An attempt to engage in the kind of analysis set out in this paragraph is provided in Wilde 2008, above note 1.

JUN MATSUKUMA

12. The Legitimacy of Economic Sanctions: An Analysis of Humanitarian Exemptions of Sanctions Regimes and the Right to Minimum Sustenance

Thomas Franck pointed out that *legitimacy* is the generic label we have placed on factors that affect our willingness to comply voluntarily with commands,[1] and legitimacy is the standard by which the community measures a rule's capacity to obligate.[2]

With regard to the issue of the legitimacy of economic sanctions, there were long-standing discussions concerning the sanctions implemented against Iraq from 1990 to 2003. Reports by United Nations (UN) humanitarian agencies indicated that UN economic sanctions against Iraq had a negative impact on humanitarian conditions in that country despite the program of humanitarian exemptions.[3]

It has become customary to include certain exemptions in sanctions regimes. The most common exemptions are supplies intended for medical purposes; other common exemptions include food, educational equipment, publications, and news materials.[4] If the imposition of economic sanctions proved to be legal but the program of humanitarian exemptions relative to the economic sanctions was not working well, the Security Council was responsible for improving the program for the legitimacy of the sanctions regime, especially in light of evolving norms of human security. In this context, MacFarlane and Khong pointed out that the Security Council and other bodies within and around the UN moved both to make the protection of civilians and humanitarian assistance a potential reason for Chapter VII action

1 Franck, Thomas M. (1990). *The Power of Legitimacy Among Nations* (New York: Oxford University Press), p. 150.
2 Ibid., p. 206.
3 UNICEF survey of August 27, 1999, with updated statistics; available at www.unicef.org.
4 Lowenfeld, Andreas F. (2003). *International Economic Law* (Oxford: Oxford University Press), pp. 718–719.

against a state that was not fulfilling its responsibilities and to adjust the UN's own actions in order to consider their implications for civilians in target states.[5]

In 1996, Boutros Boutros-Ghali admitted that sanctions raised the ethical question of whether suffering inflicted on vulnerable groups in the targeted country is a legitimate means of exerting pressure on political leaders whose behavior is unlikely to be affected by the plight of their subjects.[6] In 2000, Kofi Annan pointed out that because economic sanctions have proved to be such a blunt and even counterproductive instrument, a number of governments and numerous civil-society organizations and think tanks around the world have explored ways to make sanctions "smarter" through better targeting.[7]

In this chapter, I discuss the legitimacy of economic sanctions by analyzing the humanitarian exemptions of sanctions and the right to minimum sustenance as a basic human need. I argue that it is an obligation of the UN to help the victims of the UN's economic sanctions rebuild their country because of the negative effect of the sanctions imposed on them.

In the first section, I analyze the legality of economic sanctions in light of the right to minimum sustenance. In particular, I examine the right to minimum sustenance in the International Covenants on Human Rights. In the second section, I examine the various aspects of the UN's sanctions against Iraq and the Oil-for-Food Program as an example of the humanitarian exemptions applied when imposing sanctions. In the third section, I present an argument that suggests that the concept of the right to minimum sustenance has a direct effect on the issue of the legitimacy of economic sanctions. I examine in particular the UN resolutions that prescribe the right to minimum sustenance in light of the legitimacy of sanctions. In the fourth section, I analyze the general issues surrounding the legitimacy of economic sanctions. In the concluding section, I emphasize that in order to strengthen the legitimacy of economic sanctions, they should be carefully targeted in support of clear objectives and monitored effectively.

5 MacFarlane, Neil S., & Khong, Yuen Foong (2006). *Human Security and the UN: A Critical History* (Indianapolis: Indiana University Press), p. 182.

6 United Nations (1995). "Report of the Secretary-General on the Work of the Organization. Supplement to an Agenda for Peace: Position Paper of the Secretary-General on the Occasion of the Fiftieth Anniversary of the United Nations," A/50/60-S/1995/1 (New York: General Assembly), paragraph 70.

7 Annan, Kofi (2000). "We the Peoples: The Role of the United Nations in the Twenty-first Century. Report of the Secretary-General," A/54/2000 (New York: General Assembly).

Legality of Economic Sanctions in Light of the Right to Minimum Sustenance

In recent years, there has been growing concern about the results of economic sanctions.[8] Cases such as Iraq have raised concerns about the effects of economic sanctions on impoverished people and question the continuing legality of these sanctions as a matter of general international law.[9] For example, in the Sanctions Committee, Cuba and Yemen wished to see a general exemption for foodstuffs, stating that they could never accept any definition that would allow the supply of foodstuffs only to avert famine because this would be in direct violation of the international human right to food.[10]

It is desirable to prove the existence of international customary law that illegalizes the use of food and medicine as embargo and sanctions measures in certain cases. In this section, I analyze the legality of economic sanctions in light of the right to minimum sustenance.

International legal scholars refer to the concept of the rights to food and health, in particular, as aspects of the right to minimum sustenance. Many academics have concluded that one should see the right to live as a minimum obligation of international community. Based on this concept, the Human Rights Program of the Harvard Law School held an interdisciplinary discussion on economic and social rights and the right to health.[11] Also, the General Assembly appointed a Special Rapporteur of the Commission on Human Rights on the right to food,[12] and the Economic and Social Council adopted the resolution on the right of everyone to the enjoyment of the highest attainable standard of physical and mental health.[13]

According to the concept of the right to food, Jean Ziegler, the Special Rapporteur of the Commission on Human Rights, developed it as follows:

> [A]s the Special Rapporteur has previously noted, the concept of the right to food is much stronger than the concept of food security. The right to food

[8] Weiss, Thomas G.; Cortright, David; Lopez, George A.; & Minear, Larry (1997). "Toward a Framework for Analysis," in Thomas G. Weiss, David Cortright, George A. Lopez, & Larry Minear (eds.), *Political Gain and Civilian Pain: Humanitarian Impacts of Economic Sanctions* (Lanham, MD: Rowman & Littlefield Pulishers, Inc.), pp. 35–53.

[9] Sands, P. J., & Klein, P. (2001). *Bowett's Law of International Institutions* (London: Sweet & Maxwell), p. 332.

[10] Gowlland-Debbas, Vera (1994). "Comments," in Harry H. G. Post (ed.), *International Economic Law and Armed Conflict* (Dordrecht: Nijhoff), pp. 163–173.

[11] Harvard Law School Human Rights Program (1995). *Economic and Social Rights and the Right to Health* (Boston: Harvard Law School Human Rights Program).

[12] United Nations (2002). A/RES/56/155 (New York: General Assembly), February 15; United Nations (2002). A/57/356 (New York: General Assembly).

[13] United Nations (2002). E/DEC/2002/259 (New York: ECOSOC).

> includes all the elements of food security – including availability, accessibility and utilization of food – but it also goes beyond the concept of food security because it emphasizes accountability. A rights-based approach focuses attention on the fact that making progress to reduce hunger is a legal obligation, not just a preference or choice.[14]

Considering the concept of the right to food, the right to minimum sustenance includes all the elements of human security – including availability, accessibility, and utilization of a basic human need. The right to minimum sustenance as a basic human need is more than freedom from hunger or a right for the mere survival of the people; it is also a right for the realization of the health and security of human beings.[15] In particular, it is important to clarify whether the concept of the right to minimum sustenance means that the Security Council must implement economic sanctions but must use humanitarian exemptions.

Reisman and Stevick suggested five principles that should guide the Security Council when imposing sanctions: (1) they should be based on lawful contingencies; (2) they should be necessary and proportionate; (3) they should maximize the distinction between combatants and noncombatants; (4) they should be periodically assessed; and (5) relief should be provided to injured third parties.[16]

According to the terms of Article 24(2) of the UN Charter, the Security Council shall act in accordance with the Purposes and Principles of the UN in discharging its duties. It might be argued that in taking enforcement action under Chapter VII, the Security Council is bound to not substantially undermine the promotion of respect for human rights.[17] It also has been argued that the Security Council, as an organ of the UN, must operate within the parameters of general international law, including international humanitarian law and the law of human rights. Human-rights specialists have argued that the law of human rights governs the use of sanctions. However, debates within the UN only infrequently refer to human rights. Roger Normand argued that the avoidable deaths in the Iraqi population, especially of children, violate the norms of international human-rights

[14] United Nations (2002). "The Right to Food: Note by the Secretary General," A/57/356 (New York: General Assembly).

[15] See, for the concept of the right to food, Alston, Philip, & Tomasevski, Katarina (1984). *The Right to Food* (Dordrecht: Nijhoff), p. 2.

[16] Reisman, W. M., & Stevick, D. L. (1998). "The Applicability of International Law Standards to United Nations Economic Sanctions Programmes," *European Journal of International Law* 9(1), pp. 86–141.

[17] Craven, Matthew (2002). "Humanitarianism and the Quest for Smarter Sanctions," *European Journal of International Law* 13(1), pp. 43–61.

law.[18] He argued that the UN's economic sanctions against Iraq violate the rights to health, life, and an adequate standard of living. We also can discuss these issues in light of the provisions of the International Covenants of Human Rights.

Before examining the issue of the right to minimum sustenance and its applicability to the issue of economic sanctions, it is necessary to analyze the provisions of the international human-rights covenant related to the right to minimum sustenance. According to Article 11, Paragraph 1, of the International Covenant on Economic, Social, and Cultural Rights (ICESCR), it is stipulated that "[t]he State Parties to the present Covenant recognize the right of everyone to an adequate standard of living for himself and his family, including adequate food, clothing and housing, and to the continuous improvement of living conditions."

Moreover, the second paragraph of the same article provides that "[t]he States Parties to the present Covenant, recognizing the fundamental right of everyone to be free from hunger, shall take, individually and through international co-operation, the measures, including specific programs, which are needed: (a) To improve methods of production, conservation and distribution of food by making full use of technical and scientific knowledge, by disseminating knowledge of the principles of nutrition and by developing or reforming agrarian systems in such a way as to achieve the most efficient development and utilization of natural resources; (b) Taking into account the problems of both food-importing and food-exporting countries to ensure an equitable distribution of world food supplies in relation to need." From this wording, it is clear that Article 11 serves as the central provision for the right to minimum sustenance.

According to Article 12, Paragraph 1, of the ICESCR, it is stipulated that "[t]he State Parties to the present Covenant recognize the right of everyone to the enjoyment of the highest attainable standard of physical and mental health." In the second paragraph of the same article, it further provides that

> [t]he steps to be taken by the States Parties to the present Covenant to achieve the full realization of this right shall include those necessary for:
>
> (a) The provision for the reduction of the stillbirth-rate and of infant mortality and for the healthy development of the child;

[18] Normand, Roger (1999). "A Human Rights Assessment of Sanctions: The Case of Iraq, 1990–1997," in Wilhelmus J. van Genugten (ed.), *United Nations Sanctions, Effectiveness and Effects, Especially in the Field of Human Rights: A Multidisciplinary Approach* (Antwerpen: Intersentia), pp. 19–33.

(b) The improvement of all aspects of environmental and industrial hygiene;
(c) The prevention, treatment and control of epidemic, endemic, occupational and other diseases;
(d) The creation of conditions which would assure to all medical service and medical attention in the event of sickness.

Brigit C. A. Toebes pointed out that the fact that a number of steps are mentioned in Paragraph 12(2) implies that the provision is more tangible than similar provisions that do not enumerate such steps.[19]

According to the International Covenant on Civil and Political Rights (ICCPR), Article 6 is concerned with the right to minimum sustenance; this is the provision of the right to life in international law. To be free from want is to be free from danger to one's life and to be able to live. Hence, this article must be realized with the positive participation of the states. In regard to the interpretation of this article, many states have strongly opposed a broad interpretation. The reason is that Article 6 was thought to be an article on civil rights and not on standards of living. In other words, for those who opposed a broad interpretation, the focus of this article was on protecting people from having their lives taken arbitrarily, not on protecting them from hunger, cold, or illness. However, the Human Rights Committee adopted the General Comment on this article, in which they criticized the previous narrow interpretation of Article 6 and stated that the Committee considers it desirable for states parties to take all possible measures to reduce infant mortality and to increase life expectancy, especially in adopting measures to eliminate malnutrition and epidemics.[20] Based on such an interpretation, states that do not take any measures to eradicate starvation will be violating Article 6 of the Covenant.

In summary, Article 11, Paragraph 2, and Article 12, Paragraph 2, of the ICESCR aim to realize, in particular, the right to minimum sustenance by having the states take positive measures – based on the interpretation that this right is part of common Article 1 as well as Article 11, Paragraph 1, and Article 12, Paragraph 1, of the ICESCR, and Article 6 of the ICCPR – and form the basic provisions related to the right to minimum sustenance.

There are two approaches that obligate states to realize the right to minimum sustenance under international law: the first aims to prove the existence

[19] Toebes, Brigit C. A. (1999). *The Right to Health as a Human Right in International Law* (Antwerpen: Intersentia), pp. 292–301.

[20] Human Rights Committee, General Comment 6, Article 6 (Sixteenth Session, 1982). "Compilation of General Comments and General Recommendations Adopted by Human Rights Treaty Bodies," UN Doc. HRI/GEN/1/Rev.1.

of international customary law regarding this right; the second aims to conclude a treaty that would stipulate this right under positive international law. Regarding the former, although repetitive state practice and *opinio juris* do exist to a certain degree, it is difficult to conclude at present that an international customary law exists that clarifies details of the obligations. Therefore, to consider the issue of states' obligations under international law today, one must turn to the latter approach. In this sense, Articles 11 and 12 of the ICESCR may be useful.

According to Article 11, the national obligation of the states is to take appropriate steps to ensure the realization of the right of everyone to an adequate standard of living for himself and his family, including adequate food, clothing, and housing, and to the continuous improvement of living conditions. Article 12 stipulates the steps to be taken by the states parties to achieve the full realization of the right of everyone to the enjoyment of the highest attainable standard of physical and mental health. Because the obligation to realize human rights relates to Article 2 of the Covenant, it is closely linked with the progressive-achievement principle of the first paragraph and the nondiscrimination principle of the second paragraph.

Paragraph 1 of Article 11 articulates the states to "take appropriate measures"; Paragraph 2 of Article 12 articulates "the steps to be taken by the States Parties." Whereas the second paragraph of Article 2 of the ICCPR stipulates clear and definite legislative measures that the states are obligated to take to realize human rights, the same article of the ICESCR does not provide as clear and definite a wording. Although it may be inferred from the Covenant that states are requested to take legislative and administrative measures, this is not an obligation that must be fulfilled immediately due to the wording "achieving progressively" in Article 2, Paragraph 2. The word *progressive* grants the states some time to implement their obligation, and the meaning of *progressive* is left unclear. If one extends the meaning of the wording, in the end, states may get away with taking no measures at all to realize the right to minimum sustenance.

Because it is necessary to take appropriate policy measures to progressively realize this right, the requests to states to legislate basic laws and to make policy declarations must not be neglected due to the word *progressive*. States must implement the Covenants in good faith, and they must establish comprehensive and consistent plans necessary for the progressive realization of the right to minimum sustenance. The details provided in Paragraph 2 of Article 11 and Paragraph 2 of Article 12 are examples of legislative and administrative measures that must be taken. Iraq ratified the ICESCR under the obligations of these provisions. In this context, the former government of Iraq had to implement the ICESCR with good faith.

In the present international society, in which the interdependence of states is becoming greater every day, the right to minimum sustenance cannot be attained solely by one state's national efforts. The ICESCR, reflecting the international character in the implementation of this right, stipulates the states' obligation to cooperate. For example, in Article 2, Paragraph 1, it is stated that "[e]ach State Party to the present Covenant undertakes to take steps individually, and through international assistance." Also in Article 11, Paragraph 1, it is stipulated that "the States Parties will take appropriate steps to ensure the realization of this right, recognizing to this effect the essential importance of international co-operation based on free consent." Moreover, in Paragraph 2, it obligates the states to "take, individually and through international co-operation, the measures, including specific programs, which are needed." However, during the process of realizing human beings' interests in the world community, there may be a conflict with state sovereignty or self-determination of the people because these may function contrary to the realization of everyone's right to minimum sustenance.

In Paragraph 2(b) of Article 11, it is stipulated that "taking into account the problems of both food-importing and food-exporting countries, to ensure an equitable distribution of world food supplies in relation to need." Could this be in conflict with Article 25, which states, "Nothing in the present Covenant shall be interpreted as impairing the inherent right of all peoples to enjoy and utilize fully and freely their natural wealth and resources"? Here, the relationship between the obligation of international cooperation and self-determination is similar to the relationship between the supranational world community and national sovereignty.

Regarding the scope of international obligations, the ICESCR, in its General Comment 12, proposed the following:

(a) Regarding the obligations of States parties;

> States parties should take steps to respect the enjoyment of the right to food in other countries, to protect that right, to facilitate access to food and to provide the necessary aid when required;
>
> States parties should refrain at all times from food embargoes or similar measures which endanger conditions for food production and access to food in other countries. Food should never be used as an instrument of political and economic pressure.

(b) Regarding the obligations of States and international organizations;

> States have a joint and individual responsibility to cooperate in providing disaster relief and humanitarian assistance in times of emergency, including assistance to refugees and internally displaced persons;
>
> Food aid should be provided in ways which do not adversely affect local producers and local markets.[21]

Regarding the scope of international obligations to protect the right to the highest attainable standard of health, the ICESCR, in its General Comment 14, proposed the following:

> (a) States parties have to respect the enjoyment of the right to health in other countries, and to prevent third parties from violating the right in other countries, if they are able to influence these third parties by way of legal or political means. Depending on the availability of resources, States should facilitate access to essential health facilities, goods and services in other countries, wherever possible and provide the necessary aid when required.
> (b) States parties have a joint responsibility to cooperate in providing disaster relief and humanitarian assistance in times of emergency, including assistance to refugees and internally displaced persons. Each State should contribute to this task to the maximum of its capacities.
> (c) States parties should refrain at all times from imposing embargoes or similar measures restricting the supply of another State with adequate medicines and medical equipment. Restrictions on such goods should never be used as an instrument of political and economic pressure.[22]

At present, these obligations do not exist as an international customary law. However, to secure the effectiveness of the right to minimum sustenance, institutionalization and legislation of these areas are urgently needed.

We also must analyze the legality of sanctions in light of international humanitarian law. According to the situation in Iraq, Security Council Resolution 1472 noted that under the provisions of Article 55 of the Fourth Geneva Convention, the Occupying Power has the duty to ensure food and medical supplies for the population and should bring in the necessary foodstuffs, medical stores, and other supplies if the resources of the occupied territory are inadequate. Moreover, this resolution requested all parties concerned to strictly abide by their obligations under international law, particularly the

[21] United Nations (1999). "The Right to Adequate Food," E/C.12/1999/5, General Comments, United Nations Committee on Economic, Social, and Cultural Rights (New York: Economic and Social Council), paragraph 12.

[22] United Nations (2000). "The Right to the Highest Attainable Standard of Health," E/C.12/2000/4, General Comments, United Nations Committee on Economic, Social, and Cultural Rights (New York: Economic and Social Council), paragraph 14.

Geneva Conventions and The Hague Regulations, including those relating to the essential civilian needs of the people of Iraq. Security Council Resolution 1483 called on all concerned to comply fully with their obligations under international law, including the Geneva Conventions and The Hague Regulations.

Even before the Iraq war, an argument was presented by some scholars stating that the UN sanctions against Iraq violated the principle of distinction and the principle of proportionality. In imposing comprehensive sanctions that caused the deaths of civilians, the advantages gained by sanctions were marginal; therefore, these sanctions violated the principle of proportionality. This argument was very controversial. Some critics said that the government of Iraq was to blame for not distributing humanitarian goods appropriately to their civilians. These critics stated that the main reason for the suffering of the Iraqi people was the fact that the government of Iraq is not cooperative. However, we must consider that the Security Council is at least responsible for taking effective measures to mitigate the impact of economic sanctions on innocent civilians. Regarding this issue, Marco Sassoli pointed out that UN economic sanctions have actually complied with the requirements of international humanitarian law.[23]

Under international humanitarian law, there are many treaty provisions that stipulate the right to minimum sustenance during armed conflict. One must note the fact that the right to minimum sustenance is not restricted to special situations, such as armed conflicts, but rather to all situations. The right to minimum sustenance provided in international humanitarian law is acknowledged by the world community as a norm applied in times of both peace and war, not just in times of armed conflict. Of course, international humanitarian law does not address matters such as the unequal distribution of humanitarian supplies, which is a political issue during times of peace. However, the right to minimum sustenance must be seen as a basic universal human right to be applied in times of both peace and war.

The Third and Fourth Geneva Conventions, and its First and Second Additional Protocols, include provisions concerning the rights to food and medical attention. These conventions and protocols contain the most notable provisions regarding the right to minimum sustenance during times of war. As is evident from these provisions, international law related to the right to minimum sustenance is surprisingly more established during times of war than peace. Many academics question the large gap in international

[23] Sassoli, Marco (2001). "Sanctions and International Humanitarian Law: Commentary," in V. Gowlland-Debbas (ed.), *United Nations Sanctions and International Law* (The Netherlands: Kluwer Law International), pp. 241–248.

law regarding the right to minimum sustenance in times of war and of peace.[24]

Those who see the right to minimum sustenance as a universal norm to be applied in times of both war and peace hold the view that the latter's international institutions are deficient compared with the former, and they stress the need for codification of international law protecting the right to minimum sustenance during times of peace.

UN Sanctions Against Iraq and the Oil-for-Food Program

Almost immediately after the 1990 Iraqi invasion of Kuwait, economic sanctions against Iraq were imposed. On August 6, 1990, the Security Council adopted Resolution 661, imposing a comprehensive ban on trade and financial transactions with Iraq. It also ordered that Iraqi assets be frozen worldwide.[25] Had the invasion of Kuwait not placed Iraq in a position to control the second-largest oil reserves in the world, it is unlikely that the world would have united in condemning Iraq.[26] In Resolution 666, the Security Council made explicit reference to humanitarian exemptions. In this resolution, the parties were reminded twice that they had to comply with international humanitarian law obligations.[27]

After the First Gulf War, the Security Council adopted Resolution 687 on April 3, 1991. In this resolution, the Security Council drew attention to the legal position of Iraq relative to chemical and biological weapons. It demanded that Iraq eliminate all its weapons of mass destruction (WMD). Resolution 687 was designed to reinforce Resolution 661 pending the meeting of various conditions, primarily the destruction of Iraqi WMD; it has often been referred to as the ceasefire resolution.[28] The sanctions remained in force,

[24] Ibid., p. 26.

[25] Hufbauer, Gary Clyde; Shott, Jeffrey J.; & Elliott, Kimberly Ann (1990). *Economic Sanctions Reconsidered: History and Current Policy*, Second Edition (Washington, DC: Institute for International Economics), pp. 283–298.

[26] Melby, Eric D. K. (1998). "Iraq," in Richard N. Haass (ed.), *Economic Sanctions and American Diplomacy* (New York: Council on Foreign Relations), pp. 107–128.

[27] Higgins, Rosalyn (1994). *Problems and Process: International Law and How We Use It* (Oxford: Clarendon Press), p. 183.

[28] Fassbender, Bardo (2002). "Uncertain Steps into a Post–Cold War World: The Role and Functioning of the UN Security Council After a Decade of Measures Against Iraq," *European Journal of International Law* 13(1): 273–303.

although those related to foodstuffs and supplies for essential civilian needs as well as financial payments were relaxed.[29]

In the early stages, there seemed to be a general view that the sanctions were deployed successfully against Iraq.[30] However, there is little doubt now that the economic sanctions against Iraq have not achieved their objectives and have negatively affected the civilian population of Iraq.[31] The economic sanctions against Iraq proved to be largely ineffective politically, partly because the domestic opposition in Iraq was weak and fragmented.[32] Some member states of the Security Council argued that the government of Iraq was responsible for the sanctions disaster. To clarify the main causes of this human tragedy, further scientific research is needed.[33] Whatever the causes, it is clear that the program of humanitarian exemptions did not adequately protect the people of Iraq from the effect of economic sanctions.

For example, in July 1993, the UN Food and Agriculture Organization (FAO) reported that a large and growing number of Iraqis had a lower food intake than the population in disaster-stricken African countries.[34] In September 1995, the World Food Program (WFP) reported that 70 percent of the population had little or no access to food and that Iraq had also suffered an increase in child mortality. A 1995 World Health Organization (WHO) report noted shortages of medicine, medical supplies, foodstuffs, and water purification and sanitation parts and equipment. At one point, Iraq had less than one tenth of the medicine needed.[35] The dismal picture of Iraqi social conditions was summarized in a November 1997 report to the

[29] Shrijver, Nico (1994). "The Use of Economic Sanctions by the UN Security Council: An International Law Perspective," in Harry H. G. Post (ed.), see note 10, pp. 123–161.

[30] "Case 90–1, US and UN *v.* Iraq (1990– : Invasion of Kuwait)," in Gary Clyde Hufbauer, Jeffrey J. Shott, & Kimberly Ann Elliott (eds.), *Economic Sanctions Reconsidered*, see note 24, pp. 283–298.

[31] Normand, Roger (1999). "A Human Rights Assessment of Sanctions: The Case of Iraq, 1990–1997," in W. J. M. van Genugren & G.A. de Groot (eds.), *United Nations Sanctions; Effectiveness and Effects, Especially in the Field of Human Rights: A Multidiciplinary Approach* (Antwerpen: Intersentia), pp. 19–33.

[32] Kaempfer, William H., & Lowenberg, Anton D. (2000). "A Public Choice Analysis of the Political Economy of International Sanctions," in Steve Chan & A. Cooper Drury (eds.), *Sanctions as Economic Statecraft: Theory and Practice* (Basingstoke: Macmillan), pp. 158–186.

[33] Garfield, Richard (2001). "Health and Well-Being in Iraq: Sanctions and the Impact of the Oil-for-Food Program," *Transnational Law and Contemporary Problems* 11(2): 277–298.

[34] Hoskins, Eric (1997). "The Humanitarian Impacts of Economic Sanctions and War in Iraq," in Thomas G. Weiss, David Cortright, George A. Lopez, & Larry Minear (eds.), see note 8, pp. 91–147.

[35] Reisman, W. M., and Stevick, D. L. (1998), see note 16.

Security Council by the Secretary-General.[36] He concluded that one third of children and one quarter of men and women under age twenty-six suffered from malnutrition.

In 1991, the Secretary-General brought a humanitarian crisis to the attention of the Security Council in the Ahtisaari Report.[37] In response, the Security Council tried to introduce a system of humanitarian exemptions to the economic sanctions.[38] However, the government of Iraq refused to accept the terms of Security Council Resolutions 706 and 712, which authorized the export of $1.6 billion of Iraqi petroleum during a six-month period. The government of Iraq insisted that this scheme violated the sovereignty of Iraq.

However, after long negotiations, in 1995, Security Council Resolution 986 introduced the Oil-for-Food Program, which was a plan for using Iraqi oil revenues to finance humanitarian relief. This provided for the sale of a predetermined maximum volume of Iraqi oil under UN supervision. Purchasers would pay directly into a UN-controlled escrow account that would be used to pay for UN-approved purchases of foodstuffs, medicine, and materials and supplies for essential civilian needs.[39] Resolution 986 made a concession to Iraqi concerns and gave the government of Iraq primary responsibility for the distribution of humanitarian goods, with the exception of the Kurdish areas in the north, where distribution was kept under direct UN control. The Oil-for-Food Program began in 1996 but it has proven ineffective in improving the humanitarian situation of the Iraqi population.

The first period of this program began in December 1996. In the initial stages, Iraq was permitted to sell $2 billion worth of oil every six months, with two thirds of that amount to be used to meet Iraq's humanitarian needs. Because of the complexity of the procedures regulated by the Memorandum of Understanding between the Secretariat of the UN and the government of Iraq, receipt of humanitarian supplies was delayed. The first oil was exported under the Oil-for-Food Program in December 1996 and the first shipment of supplies arrived in March 1997.

By the end of the first period of the program, only three hundred contracts had been approved among the six hundred contracts proposed. By the middle of April 1997, only 10 percent of the planned amount of food had been

[36] Cortright, David, & Lopez, George A. (2000). *The Sanctions Decade: Assessing UN Strategies in the 1990s* (London: Lynne Rienner Publishers), pp. 47–48.

[37] S/22366, March 20, 1991.

[38] Van Walsum, Peter (2004). "The Iraq Sanctions Committee," in David M. Malone (ed.), *The UN Security Council: From the Cold War to the Twenty-first Century* (Boulder, CO: Lynne Rienner Publishers, Inc.), pp. 181–183.

[39] Ibid., p. 182.

received; by July 1997, for medicine, it was only 1 percent. Iraq blamed the United States and the United Kingdom for suspending many contracts.[40] In February 1998, the Security Council adopted Resolution 1153 and extended the Oil-for-Food Program. Resolution 1153 approved Iraq to sell up to $5.25 billion of oil. The Security Council also approved Iraq to use the money financed by the Oil-for-Food Program to supply 40 percent of the electricity supplied before the First Gulf War.

In April 1998, a UN Children's Fund (UNICEF) report concluded that malnutrition was not a public-health problem in Iraq prior to the embargo but by 1997, it was estimated that about one million children under age five were malnourished.[41] In 1999, a Security Council panel (i.e., the Second Panel established pursuant to the note by the President of the Security Council of January 30, 1990) stated that the infant-mortality rates in Iraq were among the highest in the world, that low infant birth weights affected at least 23 percent of all births, and that chronic malnutrition affected every fourth child under five years of age.[42]

In addition, some Arab countries became concerned that the impact of economic sanctions was mainly on the average Iraqi, not on Saddam Hussein or his key supporters.[43] Whatever the effect of sanctions on the Iraqi economy, many critics argued that the economic devastation of the country would have little effect on Saddam Hussein's calculations and decisions.[44] It was expected that the hardships created by the sanctions would weaken the Iraqi regime and incite Iraqi citizens to rebel against their government, but there is no evidence that the sanctions had any such effect.[45]

In December 1999, Security Council Resolution 1284 endorsed the removal of a cap on oil sales by Iraq, but the resolution had a limited impact.[46] In December 2000, Security Council Resolution 1330 allowed for a cash

[40] Jabbar, Faleh A.; Shikara, Ahmad; & Sakai, Keiko (1998). *From Storm to Thunder: Unfinished Showdown Between Iraq and U.S., IDE Spot Survey, No. 11* (Tokyo: Institute of Developing Economies).

[41] UNICEF (1998). *Situation Analysis of Children and Women in Iraq, 1997* (New York: United Nations).

[42] United Nations (1999). "Report of the Second Panel Established Pursuant to the Note by the President of the Security Council of 30 January 1990 (S/1999/100), Concerning the Current Humanitarian Situation in Iraq," S/1999/346, Annex II (New York: Security Council), March 30.

[43] Melby, Eric D. K. (1998), see note 25.

[44] Selden, Zachary (1999). *Economic Sanctions as Instruments of American Foreign Policy* (Westport, CT: Praeger), p. 88.

[45] Hoskins, Eric (1997), see note 33.

[46] Alkadiri, Raad (2000). "Iraq: The Dilemma of Sanctions and Confrontation," in Rosemary Hollis (ed.), *Managing New Developments in the Gulf* (London: Royal Institute of International Affairs).

component, which has the potential to improve the effectiveness of the implementation of the program.

In May 2002, the Security Council adopted Resolution 1409, which adopted the revised Goods Review List (GRL) and the revised procedures related to the processing of applications to be financed from the UN escrow account. In this resolution, the Security Council authorized states to permit – subject to the procedures for application of the GRL – the sale or supply of any commodities or products. In addition, the Security Council decided to conduct regular, thorough reviews of the GRL and the procedures for its implementation and to consider any necessary adjustments. According to these revised procedures, it was required that each application for the sale of supplies of commodities or products to Iraq be forwarded to the Office of the Iraq Program (OIP) by the exporting states through permanent missions or by UN agencies and programs. Each application would be reviewed and registered by OIP within ten working days. After OIP registration, each application would be evaluated by technical experts from the UN Monitoring, Verification, and Inspection Commission (UNMOVIC) and the International Atomic Energy Agency (IAEA). In the absence of action by UNMOVIC and/or IAEA within the ten-working-day period, the application would be considered approved. If UNMOVIC and/or IAEA determined that the application contained any military-related commodities or products covered by the GRL, they would immediately inform the submitting mission or UN agency through the OIP. OIP would then forward the application containing the GRL items to the Iraq Sanctions Committee to evaluate whether the GRL items could be sold or supplied to Iraq.[47] In December 2002, the Security Council adopted Resolution 1447, which extended the Oil-for-Food program for a new period of 180 days.[48] However, David Rieff pointed out in 2003 that

> There may be indeed no way around [sanctions]. But in that case, we should be clear about what we are really saying, which is that there is no way around the ruined lives and the dead bodies strewn across the ruins of broken societies either. Ultimately, as hard as some officials like [U.S. Secretary of State] Albright tries to mitigate the worst effects of Iraq sanctions through oil-for-food and other reforms, opting for them meant choosing American security over Iraqi mass suffering.[49]

After the 2003 Iraq war began, the Security Council adopted Resolution 1472 on March 28, 2003, and called on the international community to

[47] United Nations (2002). S/RES/1409 (New York: Security Council).
[48] United Nations (2002). S/RES/1447 (New York: Security Council).
[49] Rief, David (2003). "Were Sanctions Right?," *New York Times Magazine*, July 27.

provide immediate humanitarian assistance to the people of Iraq. This resolution also authorized the Secretary-General and his representatives to establish alternative locations for the delivery, inspection, and authenticated confirmation of humanitarian supplies and equipment provided under the Oil-for-Food Program. The Security Council also decided to extend the Oil-for-Food Program until June 3, 2003, by adopting Resolution 1476 on April 24, 2003. After the war, the Security Council adopted Resolution 1483 on May 22, 2003, and decided to lift economic sanctions against Iraq. This resolution also requested that the Secretary-General continue, for a period of six months, the ongoing operations of the Oil-for-Food Program.

Other incidents also further eroded the legitimacy of economic sanctions. In October 2005, the Independent Inquiry Committee into the Oil-for-Food Program published a Report on Program Manipulation.[50] It concluded that there were illicit payments in the program.

Lakhdar Brahimi, Under-Secretary-General for the Secretary-General's Preventive Peacemaking Efforts, pointed out that Iraq is a painful case without substantial political gain.[51] Whereas the Oil-for-Food Program has met its priority objective of preventing mass starvation and the outbreak of epidemics, it has so far proven incapable of substantially improving the humanitarian situation in Iraq.[52] In the case of Iraq, food and health care became unaffordable for the poorer people after sanctions were imposed.[53] The grave humanitarian consequences of the sanctions regime undercut its legitimacy.[54]

The Right to Minimum Sustenance and Legitimacy of Economic Sanctions

Ian Hurd defines legitimacy as "an actor's normative belief that a rule or institution ought to be obeyed."[55] In this section, I argue that the evolving norm of the right to minimum sustenance has a direct effect on the issue

[50] In October 2005, the Independent Inquiry Committee into the United Nations Oil-for-Food Program published a report on programme manipulation.

[51] Brahimi, Lakhdar (1997). "Foreword," in Thomas G. Weiss, David Cortright, George A. Lopez, & Larry Minear, see note 8, pp. xi–xvi.

[52] Oette, Lutz (1999). "Die Entwicklung des Oil for Food-Programms und die gegenwärtige humanitäre Lage im Irak," *ZAÖRV* 59(3): 839–862.

[53] DeRose, Laurie; Messer, Ellen; & Millman, Sara (1998). *Who's Hungry? And How Do We Know? Food Shortage, Poverty, and Deprivation* (Tokyo: United Nations University Press), p. 173.

[54] Oudraat, Chantal de Jonge (2000). "Making Economic Sanctions Work," *Survival* 42(3): 105–127.

[55] Hurd, Ian (2007). *After Anarchy: Legitimacy and Power in the United Nations Security Council* (Princeton, NJ: Princeton University Press), p. 7.

of the legitimacy of economic sanctions. The continued maintenance of mandatory UN sanctions against Iraq had been controversial, partly due to the harm that the sanctions inflicted on the Iraqi people.[56] Concerns about the humanitarian consequences of sanctions played a major role in the debate about UN policy in Iraq and have eroded support for sanctions.[57]

Even if it is difficult to prove the existence of international customary law, we can claim that the measures causing grave human-rights violations undercut the legitimacy of any sanctions regime. For this purpose, it is useful to examine the resolutions and declarations adopted by the General Assembly and other international conferences,[58] as well as the practice of states in the activities of international organizations, to see whether they display the notion of legitimacy concerning prohibition of the use of food and medicine as a means of international sanctions. When we consider the legitimacy of economic sanctions, not the legality of them, it is important to analyze the General Assembly resolutions concerning the right to minimum sustenance as the will of the world community.

On November 27, 1996, the UN General Assembly adopted Resolution 51/22 on the elimination of coercive economic measures as a means of political and economic compulsion.[59] The intent of this resolution was to criticize the U.S. Helms–Burton Act. However, in a subsequent comment on this resolution, the former government of Iraq referred to the negative effect of sanctions on the most vulnerable members of their population and insisted that the first victims of such practices were the vulnerable sectors of the population, such as children, women, and the elderly.

UN General Assembly Resolution 56/155 stipulates that the General Assembly reaffirms the right of everyone to have access to safe and nutritious food, consistent with the right to adequate food and the fundamental right of everyone to be free from hunger in order to fully develop and maintain their physical and mental capacities.[60] In summary, the implementation of the right to minimum sustenance has an international character that can be acknowledged from this resolution.

[56] Reisman, W. M., & Stevick, D. L. (1998), see note 16, pp. 86–141.

[57] Cortright, David, & Lopez, George A. (2002). *Sanctions and the Search for Security: Challenges to UN Action* (London: Lynne Rienner Publishers), p. 27.

[58] United Nations (2002). A/RES/56/155 (New York: General Assembly), 15 February; Commission on Human Rights Resolution 2002/25, The World Food Summit (1996). "The Rome Declaration on World Food Security and the World Food Summit Plan of Action, Report of the World Food Summit" (WFS 96/REP), Part One, Appendix, ILO Recommendation No. 89, ILO Recommendation No. 135.

[59] United Nations (1996). A/RES/51/22 (New York: General Assembly), November 27.

[60] United Nations (2002). A/RES/56/155 (New York: General Assembly) February 15.

It is useful to examine the issue of the legitimacy of sanctions in light of the General Assembly resolutions regarding the right to minimum sustenance. According to Franck, whereas all primary and secondary rules of the global community are capable of generating a sense of obligation by virtue of their legitimacy, some are more legitimate and thus obligate more than others.[61]

To clarify the normative character of the General Assembly resolutions, it is important to examine the discussion of the so-called soft-law. New norms cannot be created as "hard law" overnight. In reality, these norms have to accumulate, for example, by adopting declarations and resolutions that have a less normative character. Therefore, the question of the legality of these resolutions has attracted the attention of many scholars. If the new rules articulated in the resolutions lead to the creation of international law in the future, although they might be an immature norm at the time of adoption, there may be some meaning attached that would enable them to be categorized as soft law.

However, whether they are legally binding is another issue. As mentioned previously, an international consensus does not exist providing legally binding force to such resolutions. In many cases, the very reason for the states to adopt resolutions rather than international treaties is that they do not wish to be legally bound. Moreover, regarding the matter of international state responsibility, it is difficult to think of "soft responsibilities of states" that are different from normal state responsibilities. What this concept of the "soft responsibilities of states" may actually mean is unclear as well.

The binding force of treaties is different from the nature of the General Assembly resolutions. Therefore, the normative force of the right to minimum sustenance is not discussed in this examination of the legally binding powers of the resolutions. Rather, the right to minimum sustenance forms the touchstone of legitimacy that specifies the universal will of the world community; however, the problem lies in the immaturity of the means by which this right is realized. According to Allen Buchanan, any legal system, whether domestic or international, can and should be criticized if it does not include rules and practices that provide adequate protection for human rights.[62] Thus, the General Assembly resolutions concerning the right to minimum sustenance are the expression of the universal will of human beings, and they illustrate the touchstone of legitimacy.

At the time of adoption, the Universal Declaration of Human Rights was viewed as a "common standard of achievement" for states and not binding

[61] Franck, Thomas M. (1990), see note 1, p. 207.

[62] Buchanan, Allen (2004). *Justice, Legitimacy, and Self-Determination* (Oxford: Oxford University Press), p. 119.

international law. However, based on the facts that it was drafted as an instrument that interpreted the UN Charter; that, in reality, states have generally complied with the UN Charter; and that many scholars and international and national courts have quoted the law, the Universal Declaration of Human Rights is viewed by some scholars as constituting a part of the binding norms of international law. The soft-law theory reflects such a viewpoint. However, there are those who strongly oppose this view because acknowledging normative value to the General Assembly resolutions fails to distinguish *lex lata* and *lex ferenda*.[63] For Myres McDougal, who theorized that effectiveness is one of the preconditions to customary law, the significance of the repetitive adoption of resolutions would be minimal.[64]

In short, this chapter does not take the approach of examining the right to minimum sustenance from the yet-to-be-refined "soft-law" perspective; rather, it maintains that the General Assembly resolutions express the normative belief of the world community. Moreover, the legitimacy of sanctions could be enhanced by fulfilling the requirements of these resolutions. If one sees the existence of the world community as the foundation of the General Assembly resolutions, it can be shown that the right to minimum sustenance is pursued by the world community and that the resolutions express the normative belief of the world community, which acknowledges the right to minimum sustenance for all. However, the opposing views might criticize that, in reality, each state has not taken effective measures to solve serious humanitarian problems and only by adopting repetitive resolutions regarding this right may not be interpreted as the normative belief of the world community.

Numerous resolutions have been adopted by the General Assembly related to the right to minimum sustenance; however, the most important instrument is the Universal Declaration of Human Rights, which was adopted to clearly define the provisions of Articles 55 and 56 of the UN Charter.

In Article 3, it is stated that "[e]veryone has the right to life, liberty, and the security of person." Also, in Article 22, it is provided that "[e]veryone, as a member of society, has the right to social security and is entitled to realization, through national effort and international co-operation and in accordance with the organization and resources of each State, the economic, social and cultural rights indispensable for his dignity and the free development of his personality."

63 Weil, Prosper (1983). "Towards Relative Normativity in International Law?," *American Journal of International Law* 77(3): 413–442.

64 McDougal, Myres S. (1987). *Studies in World Public Order* (Dordrecht, the Netherlands, Nijhoff), p. 12.

Article 25 is simple in the sense that it only provides the right as a "right to a standard of living adequate for the health and well-being of himself and of his family, including food, clothing, housing and medical care and social services." According to the broad wording of Article 25, it is apparent that the right to minimum sustenance as a basic human need is more than the freedom from hunger or a right for the mere survival of the people.

Also, in Article 28, it is stated that "[e]veryone is entitled to a social and international order in which the right and freedoms set forth in this Declaration can be fully realized." From this provision, one can see that the realization of those human rights stipulated in the Declaration is affected greatly by the national and international social structures and that such a perception underlies the Declaration.

Moreover, in Article 29, Paragraph 1, it is provided that "[e]veryone has duties to the community in which alone the free and full development of his personality is possible." This article is one of the rare provisions of the Declaration that stipulates obligations, particularly those of the individuals. It can be said from this article that the Universal Declaration, adopted without any opposition in 1948, clearly stipulates the right to minimum sustenance.

In addition to the Universal Declaration, it is useful to examine other General Assembly resolutions acknowledging the right to minimum sustenance. These resolutions are considered from the same viewpoint as the Universal Declaration; that is, they serve to illustrate the world community's normative belief, which acknowledges that the right to minimum sustenance and the legitimacy of sanctions could be enhanced by fulfilling the requirements of these resolutions.

Coicaud presents legitimacy as a process of justifying political power and obedience. If one views the activities of the international organizations that go beyond the sovereignties and boundaries of states to a certain degree to be a sign of the existence of a world community, then establishment of implementing mechanisms for guaranteeing legitimacy through international cooperation would not be an impossible task. Therefore, to address the issues of the legitimacy of economic sanctions, the activities of international organizations in the field of humanitarian assistance programs are examined.

Because humanitarian exemptions to economic sanctions are related closely to both economic and human-rights issues, numerous international organizations address humanitarian exemptions in the case of Iraq. The organizations that coped directly with this issue from the viewpoint of relief and development were the OIP, the UN Office for the Coordination of Humanitarian Affairs (OCHA), the FAO, the WHO, the WFP, the UN High Commissioner for Refugees (UNHCR), the UNICEF, and the UN Development

Program (UNDP). The UN organizations that were involved with this issue from a human-rights perspective included the Office of the High Commissioner for Human Rights (OHCHR) and the ICESCR. These activities of the various international organizations are of great importance as the sources of legitimacy that comprise a "right process."[65]

In the case of the three autonomous governorates in Northern Iraq under the sanctions regime, the UN agencies submitted to the Iraq Sanctions Committee, through the OIP, applications for approval to import goods and supplies and to procure and deliver them. They participated in the implementation of the Oil-for-Food Program in a wide range of sectors, such as food, health, and nutrition.[66]

The General Assembly resolutions and activities of international organizations clearly point out the normative belief of the world community concerning the right to minimum sustenance.[67] This suggests that the perception of the right to minimum sustenance exists in the world community and that the resolutions and activities are the expression of the normative belief of the states. The right to minimum sustenance is generally accepted as a universal value that transcends the cultural or religious differences of people.[68] In other words, the right to minimum sustenance reflects the universal will of human beings in the world community; however, the world community is immature in the sense that it currently lacks the measures to realize this right.

Toward Legitimated Economic Sanctions

To consider the legitimacy of sanctions, we must analyze the sources of legitimacy for the UN system. Here, we face a fundamental problem. We must find out who can determine the legitimacy of the Security Council resolutions that impose economic sanctions against Iraq and cause humanitarian problems.

Barry Carter argued that frequent ambiguity over the rationales and objectives of the use of sanctions has made it difficult to determine the starting

65 Franck, Thomas M. (1997). *Fairness in International Law and Institutions* (Oxford: Oxford University Press), p. 29.

66 Dupraz, Jean (2001). "UNICEF and the Sanctions Committee: Lessons Learned from Iraq," in V. Gowlland-Debbas, see note 22, pp. 155–163.

67 United Nations (2002). A/RES/56/155 (New York: General Assembly), February 15; United Nations (1978). A/RES/33/90 (New York: General Assembly); United Nations (1980). A/RES/35/135 (New York: General Assembly); United Nations (1984). A/RES/39/207 (New York: General Assembly).

68 "Universal Declaration on the Eradication of Hunger and Malnutrition," (1974). World Food Conference 16th Plenary Meeting, E/CONF.64/20, November 16.

point for measuring whether the use has been successful.[69] In contrast, Ignaz Seidl-Hohenveldern suggested that sanctions are always a desirable alternative to the use of military force, which gives them legitimacy.[70] Ian Clark pointed out that the practice of legitimacy describes the political negotiation among the members of international society as they seek out an accommodation between those seemingly absolute values and attempt to reconcile them with a working consensus to which all can feel bound.[71]

According to Franck, those institutions and rules perceived to have a high degree of legitimacy generate a correspondingly high sense of obligation on the part of the persons or states to which a command is addressed.[72] Ian Johnstone claimed that the legitimacy of the Security Council's decisions depends in part on the openness and participatory nature of the drafting process.[73] Conversely, Tetsuo Sato suggested that the more the Security Council steps into legally gray areas, the more legitimacy is required for its activities to be effective and acceptable.[74]

There is considerable literature but little conclusive evidence on whether sanctions are effective.[75] In practice, the UN has no significant intelligence-gathering capability of its own, and Security Council members have little data on which to judge whether sanctions are working or whether their failure warrants recourse to collective military measures under Article 42.[76] In the case of Iraq, however, there was considerable evidence that the sanctions prompted a human tragedy.

According to the terms of Article 1(1) of the UN Charter, one purpose of the UN is to bring about – by peaceful means and in conformity with the principles of justice and international law – adjustment or settlement of international disputes. Some scholars argue that the reference to justice and international law refers only to the basis of any peaceful settlement, not how

69 Carter, Barry E. (1988). *International Economic Sanctions* (Cambridge: Cambridge University Press), p. 13.

70 Seidl-Hohenveldern, Ignaz (1999). *International Economic Law*, 3rd Revised Edition (The Hague: Kluwer Law International), p. 160.

71 Clark, Ian (2005). *Legitimacy in International Society* (Oxford: Oxford University Press), pp. 29–30.

72 Franck, Thomas M. (1990), see note 1, p. 150.

73 Johnstone, Ian (1994). *Aftermath of the Gulf War: An Assessment of UN Action* (Boulder, CO: L. Rienner), p. 63.

74 Sato, Tetsuo (2001). "The Legitimacy of Security Council Activities Under Chapter VII of the UN Charter Since the End of the Cold War," in Jean-Marc Coicaud & Veijo Heiskanen (eds.), *The Legitimacy of International Organizations* (Tokyo: United Nations University Press), pp. 309–352.

75 Franck, Thomas M. (1995). *Fairness in International Law and Institutions* (Oxford: Clarendon Press), p. 290.

76 Ibid., pp. 291–292.

the Security Council conducts business. A proposal made in San Francisco to link the maintenance of international peace and security to international law was rejected because it might unduly hinder the work of the Security Council if it had to determine international legality before responding to a breach of the peace.[77] Hans Kelsen examined whether enforcement measures taken by the Security Council constitute sanctions in the legal sense or purely political measures. His conclusions lean toward considering the enforcement measures taken by the Council as discretionary political measures and not as sanctions.[78]

According to the system of humanitarian exemptions of economic sanctions, prohibitions of the use of food, medicine, and medical equipment as a means of sanctions are important. These points need further consideration in the future; however, to establish the system of humanitarian exemptions of sanctions, continuing efforts to clarify the obligations not to use food, medicine, and medical equipment as a means of sanctions are necessary.

In 1997, the UN ICESCR adopted General Comment No. 8, which examined the relationship between economic sanctions and respect for economic, social, and cultural rights. According to the General Comment, it is essential to distinguish between the basic objective of applying political and economic pressure on the governing elite of the country to persuade them to conform to international law, and the collateral infliction of suffering on the most vulnerable groups within the targeted country. The ICESCR concluded that two sets of obligations exist. The first set relates to the affected state; the imposition of sanctions does not in any way nullify or diminish the relevant obligations of that state party. The second set relates to the party or parties responsible for the imposition, maintenance, or implementation of the sanctions. The ICESCR stated that the rights enjoyed by the citizens of a state party were not extinguished by the adoption of a sanctions resolution in the Security Council. It is clear, however, that theory and practice diverge sharply in the situation of vulnerable groups in states such as Iraq. In later General Comments (i.e., Nos. 12 and 14), the ICESCR stated that states parties should refrain at all times from food embargoes and those that restrict the supply of another state with medicine and medical equipment, and that food and restrictions on medicine and medical

[77] Wolfrum, R. (1994). "Article 1," in B. Simma (ed.), *The Charter of the United Nations* (Oxford: Oxford University Press), pp. 49–56.

[78] Daoudi, M. S., & Dajani, M. S. (1983). *Economic Sanctions: Ideals and Experience* (London: Routledge & Kegan Paul), p. 75.

equipment should never be used as an instrument of political and economic pressure.[79]

In the Vienna Declaration and Programme of Action, states parties reaffirmed that food should not be used as a tool for political pressure.[80] In this context, the framework of humanitarian exemptions to economic sanctions should play an important role in guaranteeing the legitimacy of sanctioning regimes. However, in reality, by imposing sanctions, an appalling situation is created in targeted countries, whereby vulnerable populations are put in serious humanitarian situations. In the case of Iraq, economic sanctions imposed by the UN caused serious humanitarian problems. How can the notion of legitimacy function or play a role in coping with this kind of pathology of world community?

The population of a nation cannot be presumed to have consented to their leaders' actions, which comprise the basis for economic sanctions.[81] The measures of embargo on the export and import of food and medicine have been questioned in terms of whether they conform to the notion of legitimacy. Morally speaking, banning the import and export of food and medicine as a sanction is a method to be opposed. However, legally speaking (with the exception of the Geneva Conventions), it is not clear whether such measures are illegal. Some scholars assert that the exercise of economic sanctions with a view to destroying the world's food supply is against peremptory norms.[82]

In 2002, the UN adopted a resolution that stipulated that the General Assembly reiterate that food should not be used as an instrument of political or economic pressure. In this regard, it reaffirms the importance of international cooperation and solidarity, as well as the necessity of refraining from unilateral measures that are not in accordance with international law and the UN Charter and that endanger food security.[83] However, to prove that the prohibition of use of food and medicine as an instrument of political or economic pressure is international customary law, one must examine individual cases. At this time, it is difficult to conclude that the use of food and medicine as a means of placing international sanctions is generally prohibited.

[79] United Nations (1999). E/C.12/1999/5, United Nations Committee on Economic, Social, and Cultural Rights (New York: Economic and Social Council), paragraph 37.

[80] Vienna Declaration and Programme of Action, Part I, paragraph 31.

[81] Fausey, Joy K. (1999). "Does the United Nations' Use of Collective Sanctions to Protect Human Rights Violate Its Own Human Rights Standards?," *Connecticut Journal of International Law* 10, p. 193.

[82] Whiteman, (1977). "Jus Cogens in International Law, with a Projected List," *Georgia Journal of International and Comparative Law* 7: 609–626.

[83] United Nations (2002). A/RES/56/155 (New York: General Assembly), February 15.

Thus, considering this from the perspective that the realization of the aim of the Human Rights Covenants to avoid the gross human-rights violations is important, it is necessary to examine individual cases.

Although Article 11 of the ICESCR provides the obligation for international cooperation, because Article 4 allows limitations in cases where the "general welfare of the society" is to be promoted, Article 11 is subjected to such restrictions. However, when the deaths of many people cannot be avoided, using food and medicine as a means of sanctions constitutes a violation to Article 11 of the ICESCR.[84] There is a need to prove the existence of international customary law that illegalizes the use of food and medicine as embargo and sanctions measures in certain cases, in particular when there is fear of these measures causing grave human-rights violations.

In September 2000, the Office of the High Commissioner for Human Rights (OHCHR) prepared a paper on the human-rights impact of economic sanctions on Iraq for the meeting of the Executive Committee on Humanitarian Affairs. The OHCHR stated that the concerns expressed by the UN human-rights expert bodies and mechanisms, as well as by UN organs, agencies, and programs, suggested the need for urgent consideration of the human-rights dimension in assessing the impact of economic sanctions on the population of Iraq. The OHCHR also indicated that it is the obligation of the state concerned to take steps to the maximum of its available resources to provide the greatest possible protection for the economic, social, and cultural rights of each individual living within its jurisdiction. An embargo on goods such as foodstuffs and medical supplies could be regarded as inconsistent with the right to minimum sustenance, including the rights to food and health as expressed in the ICESCR. In a previous research project of the UN University on the issue of food as a human right, Phillip Alston noted that the duty not to use food as an international sanction is one of the duties of the state that could be derived from the obligation under international law.[85]

There exist situations in which the legality and the legitimacy of the states' actions may not be necessarily consistent. In other words, there is, on the one hand, the existence of the free actions of the sovereign states based on traditional international law and, on the other, the pursuit of the whole interest for a whole community that is developing based on the normative belief of world community. These two standpoints are in conflict.

[84] FAO Doc.C81/PV/5 (November 10, 1981), p. 7.

[85] Alston, Philip (1984). "International Law and the Right to Food," in A. Eide, W. B. Eide, S. Goonatilake, J. Gussow, & Omawale (eds.), *Food as a Human Right* (Tokyo: UN University Press), pp. 162–174.

More concretely, those actions of states that may be considered legal from the traditional perspective may be considered illegitimate from the interests of the world community and vice versa. In other words, international law is not developing in parallel with the transformation of the world community or – more precisely – with the changes in the values held by the world community. To cope with this reality, the fault lines of international legitimacy should be discussed. This is particularly important in the areas of international law that are in the process of being modified, particularly where fundamental changes in the actual basic condition of the world community can be observed and, due to these changes, the traditional rules are in need of amendment.

Identifying the fault lines of international legitimacy underlying the relations between economic sanctions and the right to minimum sustenance may not be easy. However, with the accumulation of resolutions that reflect the will of the world community regarding this matter and with the practice of states, the notion of legitimacy will undoubtedly be created in the future. In this context, we can conclude that for the legitimacy of sanctions, the sanctions regimes should be accompanied by systems that protect the right to minimum sustenance for people in the targeted countries.

Recently, the Security Council sought to make sanctions more targeted with greater humanitarian exemptions. Because the negative consequences of sanctions are regarded as collateral damage, the Security Council is trying to "smarten" and target the sanctions by making provisions for the alleviation of their side effects.[86] With regard to the negative humanitarian impact of the sanctions, some member states of the Security Council have raised the argument of targeted sanctions. The Security Council has endeavored to target sanctions by introducing humanitarian exemptions so as to alleviate their harmful effects. For example, Switzerland has adopted the idea of targeted sanctions and, in cooperation with the UN Secretariat, has organized international expert meetings in Interlaken and New York, which have come to be known as the "Interlaken Process."[87]

As I discussed in the previous section, in the case of Iraq, the Security Council initially exempted only supplies intended for medical purposes and certain basic foodstuffs. It later extended these exemptions to include supplies for essential civilian needs, including not only agricultural and educational

86 Craven, Matthew (2002), see note 17, pp. 43–61.

87 The Swiss Confederation in cooperation with the United Nations Secretariat and the Watson Institute for International Studies, Brown University (2001). *Targeted Financial Sanctions: A Manual for Design and Implementation: Contributions from the Interlaken Process* (Providence, RI: Thomas J. Watson Jr. Institute for International Studies).

supplies but also spare parts for the oil production infrastructure and water and sanitation supplies.

Practitioners agree that the better targeting of sanctions would increase their effectiveness while minimizing the negative humanitarian impact often experienced by large segments of civilian populations as a result of comprehensive sanctions regimes.[88] Recently in international society, significant attention has been given to the argument of smart sanctions,[89] which means more attention to the issue of the humanitarian impact of sanctions on civilians in the targeted countries.[90] The Security Council has tried to minimize the collateral damage of sanctions. However, in the case of Iraq, it has experienced difficulties, for various reasons, with the effective implementation of humanitarian exemptions.[91]

As examined herein, the right to minimum sustenance has been recognized in the world community. However, turning to the implementing measures of this right, it can be concluded that they are undeniably inefficient. It is possible to argue, then, that the system of humanitarian exemptions is necessary to guarantee the legitimacy of economic sanctions against targeted states.

Conclusions

When we consider the legitimacy of economic sanctions by analyzing the case of Iraq, we face certain fundamental questions. Can the alleged deaths of a great numbers of Iraqi civilians be justified to implement the mandate of the international community?[92] One of the lessons learned beyond Iraq is that the preferred solution would be for the Security Council to subject its sanctions regimes to a time limit.[93] The Security Council has followed this approach in the case of Sierra Leone, Liberia, Eritrea, and Ethiopia.[94]

88 Jeker, Rolf (1999). "Chairman's Report," Second Interlaken Seminar on Targeting United Nations Financial Sanction, Swiss Federal Office for Foreign Affairs; available at www.seco.admin.ch/imperial/md.

89 Cortright, David; Millar, Alistair; & Lopez, George A. (2001). "Smart Sanctions: Restructuring UN Policy in Iraq," A Report of the Fourth Freedom Forum and the Joam B. Kroc Institute for International Peace Studies, Notre Dame.

90 The Swiss Confederation in Cooperation with the United Nations Secretariat and the Watson Institute for International Studies, Brown University (2001), see note 86.

91 Alnasrawi, Abbas (2001). "Iraq: Economic Sanctions and Consequences, 1990–2000," *Third World Quarterly* 22(2): 205–218.

92 Cortright, David, & Lopez, George A. (eds.) (2000). *The Sanctions Decade: Assessing UN Strategies in the 1990s* (Boulder, CO: Lynne Rienner), pp. 46–47.

93 de Wet, Erika. *The Chapter VII Powers of the United Nations Security Council* (Oxford: Hart Publishing), (2004), pp. 250–255.

94 UN Security Council (2000). Security Council Resolution 1298 (Ethiopia and Eritrea); UN Security Council (2000). Security Council Resolution 1306 (Sierra Leone, Revolutionary United Front); UN Security Council (2001). Security Council Resolution 1343 (Liberia).

The World Summit Report pointed out that the world should call on the Security Council and the Secretary-General to ensure that fair and transparent procedures, in accordance with international law (particularly Security Council resolutions), exist for placing individuals and entities on sanctions lists and for removing them, as well as for granting humanitarian exemptions.[95]

Reisman and Stevick pointed out that much more refined economic sanctions programs should be designed.[96] They argue that the Security Council should redesignate the Oil-for-Food program as the "Civilian Economic Development Program."

At the same time, other questions should be discussed. What is the mandate of the international community? If we focus on the issues of peace and security, some states would argue that it is necessary for the UN to maintain sanctions. The difficult point is that, as John Dugard pointed out, the failure to hold out some prospect of judicial review to disenchanted states may prompt them to refuse to comply with Security Council measures.[97] However, if we focus on human-rights and humanitarian issues, we find that there are great numbers of victims suffering from economic sanctions. Marco Sassoli pointed out that as soon as international criminal justice functions effectively everywhere, the international community will abandon the archaic enforcement measure of economic sanctions, which inevitably are unjust and result in human suffering.[98]

When analyzing the issue of economic sanctions, we must consider fundamental questions. Nicolas Angelet argued that in view of the Security Council's failing procedural legitimacy and the problems concerning its composition, making reference to legal principles that are accepted by all UN members is the best means for the Council to foster the legitimacy of its decisions.[99] The UN's approach to the application of economic sanctions is contingent on the formulation of a number of principles, findings, and determinations by organs of the UN that provide the legitimate basis for UN action.[100]

The strategic goals of economic sanctions had been theoretically legitimated by the UN system, but there were certain doubts as to whether the Security Council effectively reflected world opinion. If it does not, we should consider reforming the Security Council to strengthen the legitimacy of the

[95] A/59/HLPM/CRP.1/Rev.2.

[96] Reisman, W. M., & Stevick, D. L. (1998), see note 16.

[97] Dugard, John (2001). "Judicial Review of Sanctions," in V. Gowlland-Debbas (ed.), see note 22, pp. 83–91.

[98] Kuhn, Michele (2001). "UN Sanctions and ICRC's Mandate," in V. Gowlland-Debbas (ed.), see note 22.

[99] Angelet, Nicolas (2001). "International Law Limits to the Security Council," in V. Gowlland-Debbas (ed.), see note 22, pp. 71–82.

[100] Zacklin, Ralph (1974). *The United Nations and Rhodesia* (New York: Prager), p. 45.

UN system. However, in the meantime, it is important to cope with the deficit of the UN system because the prime concerns are effectiveness and how the UN's objectives can best be achieved. In this context, MacFarlane and Khong pointed out that the second major effort by the Security Council to address protection concerned the humanitarian impact of sanctions; the humanitarian community had become increasingly vocal about the impact of general sanctions on the most vulnerable populations of targeted states.[101] We conclude that in the world community, there exists a perception based on the notion of legitimacy that it is the obligation of the UN to help victims of the UN's economic sanctions to rebuild their country because of the negative effect of the sanctions imposed on them. For example, on August 21, 2003, faced with the attack against the UN headquarters in Baghdad, the Secretary-General remarked to the UN staff: "The service of the UN is not simply a job. It is a calling, and those who have attacked us will not deflect us from it. We shall find a way to continue our work – that is, to continue helping the Iraqi people to rebuild their country and regain their sovereignty, under leaders of their own choosing."[102]

[101] MacFarlane Neil S., & Khong, Yuen Foong (2006), see note 5, pp. 181–182.
[102] Annan, Kofi (2003). *Secretary-General's Remarks to UN Staff* (New York: Secretary-General Office of the Spokesperson), August 21; available at www.un.org/apps/sg/sgstats.asp?nid=462.

HILARY CHARLESWORTH

Conclusion: The Legitimacies of International Law

In memory of Thomas Franck

International lawyers have been less interested in the concept of legitimacy than political scientists or international-relations scholars. Indeed, Thomas Franck lamented in 1987 that international lawyers positively avoided the topic.[1] The traditional approach was for lawyers to use the notions of legality and legitimacy more or less interchangeably; a legal context was assumed to confer automatically some type of legitimacy on the outcome of deliberations. It is striking that critiques of the substance of international law, such as those from the developing world or those drawing on critical and feminist theories, do not usually resort to the language of legitimacy to emphasize international law's inadequacies. Rather, they typically propose the creation of *more* law to remedy the deficiencies of the international legal system.

The North American Treaty Organization's (NATO's) bombing of Serbia and Kosovo in 1999 sparked an exploration of the differences between legality and legitimacy by international lawyers. The attack by NATO was certainly prima facie illegal: it was conducted without the endorsement of the United Nations (UN) Security Council[2] and it was not an obvious use of the right to self-defense recognized in the UN Charter.[3] Both scholars and politicians elaborated the idea of the *legitimacy* of the bombing – in the face of a humanitarian emergency caused by the Serbian government – to provide a contrast to

[1] Franck, Thomas (1987). "Why a Quest for Legitimacy?" 21 *UC Davis Law Review* 535. Franck's own work has been an exception in this regard: see Franck (1990). *The Power of Legitimacy Among Nations* (New York: Oxford University Press); Franck (2006). "The Power of Legitimacy and the Legitimacy of Power," 100 *American Journal of International Law* 88.

[2] UN Charter, Article 53.1. The Security Council later adopted Resolution 1244 (10 June 1999) in which it acknowledged the non-UN "international security presence" and resolved to coordinate closely with it.

[3] UN Charter, Article 51.

what they saw as the morally inadequate or unattractive *legal* response. Thus, as some of the contributors to this volume remind us, the Independent International Commission on Kosovo – sponsored by the Swedish government and including leading international jurists – argued that NATO's intervention was "legitimate but illegal."[4] The legitimacy of the attack derived from its status as a response to serious human-rights violations by Serbia. Bruno Simma expressed the sentiments of many international lawyers about Kosovo in arguing that "unfortunately, there do occur 'hard cases' in which terrible dilemmas must be faced and imperative political and moral considerations may appear to leave no choice but to act outside the law."[5] This type of argument resonated with the work of cosmopolitan scholars who argue for the legitimacy of moral exceptions to international legal strictures in cases of humanitarian emergency.

The invasion of Iraq in 2003 again encouraged international lawyers to invoke the language of legitimacy. One way that the question of legitimacy arose was as a synonym for international law; thus, many scholars argued that the Iraq invasion was illegal and that this fact alone rendered the invasion and occupation illegitimate.[6] Another use of the term *legitimacy* in the context of Iraq was as an antidote to illegality – for example, the argument that the only way that the illegality of the invasion could be expunged was to ensure that Iraq was rebuilt according to democratic principles.[7] Thus, the illegality of an event could be sidestepped if it generated a legitimate outcome. The Security Council implicitly endorsed this approach after the invasion.[8]

The uneasy relationship between law and legitimacy at the international level is well illustrated in the recent revival of interest in the once-marginal doctrine of humanitarian intervention. Scholars as well as politicians have pointed to the limitations of international law when faced with an oppressive regime because international law appears to prohibit nondefensive use of

4 *The Kosovo Report* (2000). (Oxford: Oxford University Press), pp. 288–289. The Commission criticized some aspects of the intervention, particularly its methods and the lack of anticipation of its consequences for civilians (pp. 288–289). For a discussion of the legality/legitimacy distinction in this context, see Wheeler, Nicholas (2000). "Reflections on the Legality and Legitimacy of NATO's Intervention in Kosovo," 4 *International Journal of Human Rights* 145.

5 Bruno, Simma (1999). "NATO, the UN, and the Use of Force: Legal Aspects," 10 *European Journal of International Law* 1, 22.

6 For example, Franck, Thomas (2003). "What Happens Now? The United Nations after Iraq," 97 *American Journal of International Law* 607.

7 For example, Slaughter, Anne-Marie (2003). "An American Vision of International Law?," *Proceedings of the Annual Meeting of the American Society of International Law 2003* 125, 127–128.

8 Security Council Resolution 1483.

force, even if inspired by humanitarian motives.[9] Thus, they have searched for alternative sources of legitimacy for foreign intervention. Just-war theories have been dusted off and reexamined as a method to circumvent the commitment to state consent in the international legal order. The Kosovo Commission, for example, concluded in 1999 that the use of force could be justified outside a purely defensive context if a number of conditions were met – for example, international humanitarian law must be adhered to and force should be a last resort. The Commission proposed that the legitimacy of humanitarian intervention, as far as possible, should be given legal expression – for example, by the suspension of the veto power of permanent members of the UN Security Council in the case of humanitarian emergencies or by the assertion of power by the UN General Assembly to authorize the use of force in such cases.[10]

The Kosovo Commission's concern to devise a legal basis for what were perceived as legitimate interventions was further developed in the report of the International Commission on Intervention and State Sovereignty (ICISS). The ICISS introduced the notion of a "Responsibility to Protect," thus deemphasizing the legitimacy of state sovereignty. If the international community has a responsibility to protect vulnerable people, this must override assertions of state sovereignty. The Kosovo Commission sought to shore up the legitimacy of the responsibility to protect doctrine through articulating a series of conditions for its use. For example, it was available only in cases of large-scale loss of life or "ethnic cleansing" and required the auspices of an international organization. The idea of a responsibility to protect was then taken up and developed in the report of the UN Secretary-General's High-Level Panel and it was included in the Secretary-General's 2005 report, *In Larger Freedom*; however, it appeared only in an attenuated form in the document generated by the 2005 World Summit.[11] Opposition to the idea lies in its potential manipulation by powerful states to pursue their own interests.

The development of the concept of a responsibility to protect during the past decade illustrates the tensions that exist between the international legal system – developed on the basis of state sovereignty and the primacy of state consent – and understandings of what is just in particular contexts. On one account, normative accounts of right action are difficult to square with traditional, positive international law. However, international law also endorses particular appeals to the opposing language of human rights/sovereignty,

[9] For example, Falk, Richard (2004). "Legality to Legitimacy: The Revival of the Just War Framework," 26 *Harvard International Review* 40.

[10] *The Kosovo Report* (2000). (Oxford: Oxford University Press), p. 291.

[11] UN Doc. A/Res/60/1, October 24, 2005, paragraph 138.

nonintervention/international justice, security/nonuse of unilateral force, and self-determination/territorial integrity, creating considerable space for oscillating and contradictory claims of legitimacy.

How should we understand the realm of legitimacy appealed to in international law and international relations? One strand of scholarship views legitimacy as essentially procedural. For example, Jean-Marc Coicaud's opening chapters present legitimacy as a process of justifying political power and obedience – the justification of "the disparity of power between those who lead and those who are led." This account thus requires that the governed recognize and consent to the right of governance by the governors. The same principle is taken to operate at both the national and international level; citizens constitute the governed nationally whereas on the international plane, states take on this character. The procedural account of legitimacy is basically sociological: it identifies the conditions under which a norm is accepted as legitimate. Consent of the governed (i.e., states) is central to this account.

Another approach to legitimacy is based on ideas of justice, focusing on the moral justification for a particular action. Thus, Allen Buchanan developed a normative theory of legitimacy.[12] For Buchanan, legitimacy is associated with an entity's moral basis for the exercise of political power – that is, a state or an international organization is legitimate if it is "morally justified in the attempt to make, apply, and enforce general rules within a jurisdiction."[13] Moral justification depends on whether an entity displays a minimum form of democracy and protects basic human rights. This account of legitimacy led Buchanan to scrutinize the idea of consent, so central to the international legal system. He argues that state consent "is of dubious moral significance in a system in which many states often do not represent all or even most of their citizens or take their basic interests seriously."[14] For Buchanan, "consent of the governed . . . is not necessary for the justified exercise of political power, whether within individual states or in the workings of international legal institutions."[15]

Ian Hurd offers yet another analysis of legitimacy, which presents it as a subjective phenomenon, "an actor's normative belief that a rule or institution ought to be obeyed."[16] Hurd's interest is the type of power that legitimacy confers in the context of the UN Security Council, and he makes the case

[12] Buchanan, Allen (2004). *Justice, Legitimacy, and Self-Determination: Moral Foundations for International Law* (Oxford: Oxford University Press), p. 235.

[13] Ibid., p. 187.

[14] Ibid., p. 234. See also ibid., p. 303.

[15] Ibid.

[16] Hurd, Ian (2007). *After Anarchy: Legitimacy and Power in the United Nations Security Council* (Princeton, NJ: Princeton University Press), p. 7.

that legitimacy is a potent currency. He has studied the way that legitimacy operated in particular episodes in the life of the Security Council, arguing that it is only incidentally connected to compliance with international legal rules.[17] Hurd emphasizes legitimacy as a matter of perception, of norm internalization, and he avoids any assessment of the moral value of what are taken to be legitimate actions or principles. Indeed, Hurd points out that activities that could be judged as appalling by some nevertheless can be accepted as legitimate by others.

The contributions to this book take various positions in the debate about the nature and functions of legitimacy: confirming, challenging, and contradicting procedural, normative, and subjective understandings of legitimacy. The common thread is their concern with fault lines within the concept of legitimacy – that is, weaknesses that lie beneath the surface, threatening to fracture the certainty of its foundations at any moment.

Ian Johnstone's chapter on deliberative legitimacy draws primarily on procedural accounts of legitimacy. Its focus is the nature of decision making in international institutions. Johnstone argues that rational deliberation can provide a level of legitimacy for decisions of international bodies where it might otherwise be in doubt because of the absence of the direct consent of member governments. This legitimacy is closely related to legality; Johnstone examines the Security Council's deliberations in the case of Kosovo in 1999 and Iraq in 2003 and explains how legal principles shaped the discussion – although there was considerable disagreement about the scope and extent of the principles. Johnstone shows that legal discourse is especially important to weaker members of the Security Council, although it also affects the actions of the permanent members. He links legitimacy of action to how closely it appears to comply with international law; thus, whereas the Kosovo intervention could be understood as part of the evolution of law, the Iraq invasion was too dramatic a break with legal principle to qualify for legitimacy.

In contrast, Nathaniel Berman proposes a situational and provisional account of legitimacy in his study of intervention. He argues that international law derives legitimacy from its capacity to reconcile apparently conflicting views on individual and collective identity and national and international political orders. Unlike Johnstone's optimism about deliberation as a route to a stable legitimacy, for Berman, legitimacy offers a temporary coherence – but its power lies in the ways that legitimacy is constantly reclaimed and reshaped. Although he eschews a fixed category of legitimacy, Berman seems to imagine a sphere of "real" and fixed *illegitimacy*; thus, he suggests that "we

[17] Ibid., pp. 44–45.

[should] continually goad power holders by comparing them to those in the past who are now viewed as unprincipled." This unstable or provisional form of legitimacy, he suggests, would "spur them on to avoid words and deeds deserving of the most ignominious illegitimacy."

Vasuki Nesiah's study of the developing relationship between humanitarianism and militarism is concerned with the way legitimacy is produced, and she points to the dangers of a normative concept of legitimacy. Nesiah links the 1884 Berlin Conference, at which European colonial powers settled their territorial claims in Africa, to the 2001 Bonn Conference that addressed the future of Afghanistan and to the reconstruction of Iraq after the 2003 invasion. She traces the human, legal, and political elements in the evolution of the doctrine of humanitarian intervention to the "Responsibility to Protect" and concludes that humanitarianism can be both in opposition and complementary to militarism. The U.S. invocation of the rights of women as a justification for the 2001 bombing of Afghanistan illustrates well this complex relationship. Nesiah therefore reminds us that legitimacy can be a volatile and manipulable concoction, although this does not lead her to embrace a purely procedural account of legitimacy. Her sympathies seem to rest implicitly with an alternative substantive conception of legitimacy, one that eschews colonial and patriarchal legacies.

Similarly but less ambivalently, B. S. Chimni identifies the motive of claimed humanitarian interventions in Kosovo and Iraq as the impulse of domination rather than the protection of human rights. He points out that intervention on humanitarian grounds can be practically conducted only by powerful states because subaltern states are not in a position to do so. He is concerned primarily with the perception of legitimacy by the Third World and argues that the legitimacy of developments in international law depends on "negotiations among all states in the international community." Chimni develops an account of legitimacy in the context of permissible humanitarian intervention that has both procedural and substantive elements. He concedes that action by the UN Security Council to prevent or stop genocide or in exceptional cases of state failure would be legitimate if it met certain conditions: intervention should be a last resort and uses of force should adhere to international humanitarian law; the decision to intervene must be made by a broader group than the permanent members of the Security Council; the workings of the Security Council must be more transparent and its decisions should perhaps be reviewable by the International Court of Justice; and prior cases of intervention should not form precedents for new interventions. Thus, for Chimni, unlike Buchanan, state sovereignty is an important factor in assessing legitimacy, but he constructs a more nuanced and porous account of sovereignty than that assumed by cosmopolitans.

In contrast to Nesiah and Chimni, Lorraine Elliott's chapter on cosmopolitan militaries and force endorses a substantive account of legitimacy based on cosmopolitan values. The rise of cosmopolitanism in international relations accords priority to supranational values (e.g., human rights) over claims based on national sovereignty. Elliott invokes the language of international responsibility to justify the use of force in cases of inhumanity, bolstered by legitimacy derived from superior forms of communication (i.e., dialogue and consent) rather than from brute power and force. Another element of practical legitimacy recognized by Elliott is normative consistency. Legitimacy also is derived from the cosmopolitan design and values of military forces. She links legitimacy squarely with moral acceptability and defines legality as "strict and formal accordance with international law." The two notions, however, are intertwined in Elliott's analysis: the legitimacy of cosmopolitan force rests to some extent on conformity with international law, and the force of international law relies in part on its legitimacy. For example, Elliott questions the legal weight of Security Council approval of uses of force (arguably determinative under the UN Charter) because of the illegitimacy of the Council's domination by its five permanent members. On this point, Elliott is in sharp disagreement with Johnstone, who argues that the Security Council's pattern of reasoned discourse generates legitimacy for the institution.

Although many contributors to this book focus on military intervention as the major context for discussions of legitimacy, several chapters venture into other fields. Peacekeeping operations and state-building are scrutinized in four chapters, from quite different perspectives. Nishkala Suntharalingam studies the legitimacy of regional peacekeeping operations compared with those of the UN and asks whether the capacity to use force is essential for legitimacy. She notes the "unique legitimacy" of the UN as an institution of universal membership and jurisdiction. In this sense, Suntharalingam associates institutional legitimacy with broad representation and effectiveness – thus, her approach is consistent with that of Coicaud's procedural analysis.

Ralph Wilde examines aspects of legitimacy in international territorial administration (ITA) and is critical of the failure of scholars to address the larger normative questions in this area. Wilde's conception of legitimacy fuses both substance and procedure: he is interested in the ethics, practicality, and accountability of the displacement of local people by international officials in territorial governance. He emphasizes the significance of language in manufacturing legitimacy by deemphasizing the political context of ITA. Thus, the popular terms *postconflict* and *state-building* can distract attention from the continuation of bitter conflicts or economic exploitation by international actors. So, too, the label "failed state" implies local responsibility for insecurity, discounting the involvement of external actors. Wilde points out that most discussion of international engagement in state-building tends to be highly technocratic, thereby avoiding issues of legitimacy.

Dianne Otto's chapter employs both procedural and substantive approaches to legitimacy in her study of Security Council Resolution 1325 (2000), which recognized the significance of women's roles on peacemaking and peacebuilding. Otto argues that Resolution 1325 can be understood as a response to challenges to the Security Council's legitimacy during the 1990s, and she draws on Hurd's analysis. In calling for the participation of women in all aspects of peacemaking processes, Resolution 1325 provided a form of procedural legitimacy in the sense that such participation offers symbolic validation of institutional decisions. However, the resolution did not advance new or transformative thinking with respect to the ideas of international peace and security, leaving them within a narrow, masculinist cast. In this sense, the resolution failed to contribute to the development of a normative legitimacy; indeed, Otto suggests, Resolution 1325 may provide even greater legitimacy for the unsatisfactory status quo.

The legitimacy of economic sanctions is analyzed by Jun Matsukuma, using a case study of the Iraq sanctions. He distinguishes legitimacy from legality and argues that the Security Council must take responsibility for enhancing the legitimacy of sanctions regimes that cause widespread suffering, even if they are strictly within the letter of the law. At the same time, Matsukuma suggests that Security Council resolutions, although formally binding under the UN Charter, could be considered unlawful if they were inconsistent with "objective" rules of international law. In this sense, the concepts of legality and legitimacy overlap; their core substance for Matsukuma seems to be the protection of basic human rights; and in the context of sanctions, the critical right he identifies is that to food or minimum sustenance.

This book illustrates some of the fault lines of international legitimacy. The term *legitimacy* can be used in a great range of ways, from procedural to substantive, but there are weaknesses and ambiguities under its surface that make it inherently unstable. For example, the lack of precision of the use of the concept in international law and politics allows it to be invoked in contradictory ways. Moreover, concepts of legitimacy may change radically depending on whether the audience is national, regional, or global. This does not mean that legitimacy has little value on the international plane but rather that its contingency and fragility should be recognized. The contributions to this book both capture some of the complexity and richness of the concept and suggest an agenda for further debate and research, including questions such as whether it is possible to separate procedural and substantive accounts of legitimacy; whether and how legitimacy can be created through performance; and the relationship of legitimacy to illegitimacy.

Another issue raised by the contributions to this book is whether legitimacy is at the margins or the heart of international law. Does law define the totality or a subset of the category of legitimate actions on the international plane? Is it possible to act legally but illegitimately? Illegally but legitimately? One approach is typified by Stephen Wheatley's analysis of the political transition in Iraq.[18] He argues that legitimacy rests on consistency with the constitutional framework of the UN Charter and principles of international law, in accordance with the practice of the UN Security Council in like cases and adherence to a principle of "public reason." In a similar vein, Franck has argued that the pursuit of legitimacy is critical for international law because legitimacy is directly connected to compliance. If law is regarded as legitimate, the behavior of states will conform to the law; indeed, legitimacy keeps "the bumblebee of international law aloft"[19] and lack of legitimacy would "propel the descent into anarchy or social chaos."[20]

I argue that we should understand the relationship of international law and legitimacy in a less instrumental way. As Hurd points out, legitimacy rests on the internalization of norms; however, this is a process quite distinct from compliance.[21] International law may be one contributor to legitimacy, but it is not the only or the most important element. Indeed, in some circumstances, breaches of international law may increase the legitimacy of an action for some of the players involved, a type of legitimacy through defiance.[22] This may be because an actor thinks that it has more to gain from breaching international law than from complying with it in a particular case, or because an actor has a history of skepticism toward international law. For example, some scholars were able to claim that the invasion of Iraq in 2003 was legitimate even if, strictly, it was a breach of international law rules, by emphasizing the repressive regime that was overthrown and the outdated nature of

18 Wheatley, Stephen (2006). "The Security Council, Democratic Legitimacy, and Regime Change in Iraq," 17 *European Journal of International Law* 531. For another account of the legitimacy of international law, see Kumm, Mattias (2004). "The Legitimacy of International Law: A Constitutionalist Framework of Analysis," 15 *European Journal of International Law* 907.

19 Franck, Thomas (2006). "The Power of Legitimacy and the Legitimacy of Power," 100 *American Journal of International Law* 88, 92.

20 Ibid., pp. 91–92.

21 Hurd, p. 44.

22 Berman, Nathaniel, this volume.

international law rules with respect to the use of force.[23] Coalition politicians and their advisers also took up these tactics, portraying themselves as the vanguard of a more human-rights–responsive international community.[24]

It may be useful for international lawyers to consider legitimacy not as a source of legal compliance or as a moral benchmark but rather as a process by which institutional or social inequalities can be justified.[25] On this analysis, legitimacy is a mechanism that deflects attention from disparities in political or economic power, generating stability.[26] Legitimation is a way of gaining power, but the gains can be fragile because of successful rival struggles for legitimacy. Whereas legitimacy incidentally may affect compliance with international law in certain circumstances, such an approach raises questions about how international law is made and whose interests are embedded in it. It draws attention to the mechanics of the decision making by international legal institutions and the techniques and rituals used to encourage the internalization of norms by various groups of actors. It explains why the principles and institutions of international law are constantly under challenge from actors pursuing different dispensations of political and economic power. Understanding legitimacy as a process of construction to gain support for particular substantive results, rather than as an outcome in itself, allows us to judge the quality and the politics of the results and to be alert to the inequalities that they obscure.

[23] For example, Glennon, Michael (2003). "Why the Security Council Failed," 83(3) *Foreign Affairs*.

[24] E.g., Australian Prime Minister John Howard, Speech at the National Press Club, Canberra, March 14, 2003.

[25] Hurd, Ian (2008). "Security Council Expansion and Institutional Legitimacy: Five Hypotheses in Search of a Test," 14 *Global Governance 199*.

[26] Ibid.

Index

Lightning Source UK Ltd.
Milton Keynes UK
UKHW02f1953010718
325045UK00022B/335/P

9 781107 404557